THE OFFICIAL GUIDE FOR GMAT REVIEW

Prepared for the
Graduate Management Admission Council
by Educational Testing Service

Inquiries concerning this publication should be directed to GMAT Program Direction Office,
Educational Testing Service, CN 6101, Princeton, New Jersey 08541-6101.

USA: 0-446-38435-6
CAN: 0-446-38436-4

In association with Warner Books, Inc., a Warner Communications Company

Contents

Graduate Management Admission Council

The Graduate Management Admission Council (GMAC) is an organization of graduate business and management schools sharing a common interest in professional management education. The Council provides information to schools and prospective students to help both make reasoned choices in the admission process. It also provides a forum for the exchange of information through research, educational programs, and other services among the broad constituency of individuals and institutions concerned with management education.

The Council has three basic service objectives:

1. to enhance the management education admission process by:

   - developing and administering appropriate assessment instruments;

   - developing other services and materials related to the selection process;

   - informing schools and students about the appropriate use of such instruments and materials;

   - providing opportunities for the exchange of information between students.

2. to broaden knowledge about management education by:

   - conducting education research;

   - disseminating information about relevant research;

   - encouraging the development and exchange of information by professionals in the field.

3. to promote the highest standards of professional practice in the administration of management education programs and related activities by:

   - developing appropriate standards of practice;

   - offering educational programs and publications to provide essential knowledge, skills, and values;

   - providing other opportunities for professional development.

The Council currently contracts with Educational Testing Service (ETS) for development of GMAT test material, administration of the GMAT test, and preparation and distribution of GMAT score reports. The Council also determines policies and procedures for research and development of the GMAT; for publication of materials for students, guidance counselors, and admissions officers; and for nontesting services offered to management schools and applicants.

Member Schools

Atlanta University
Graduate School of Business Administration

Babson College
Graduate Program

Boston College
Graduate School of Management

Boston University
School of Management

Bowling Green State University
College of Business Administration

Brigham Young University
Graduate School of Management

Carnegie-Mellon University
Graduate School of Industrial Administration

College of William and Mary
School of Business Administration

Columbia University
Graduate School of Business

Cornell University
Samuel Curtis Johnson
Graduate School of Management

Dartmouth College
Amos Tuck School of Business Administration

Duke University
Fuqua School of Business

East Carolina University
School of Business

Emory University
School of Business Administration

Florida State University
College of Business

Georgia Institute of Technology
College of Management

Georgia State University
College of Business Administration

Hofstra University
School of Business

Indiana University (Bloomington)
Graduate School of Business

Kent State University
Graduate School of Management

Marquette University
College of Business Administration

Massachusetts Institute of Technology
Sloan School of Management

Michigan State University
Graduate School of Business Administration

New York University
Graduate School of Business Administration

Northeastern University
Graduate School of Business

Northwestern University
J. L. Kellogg Graduate School of Management

Ohio State University
College of Administrative Science

Pennsylvania State University
College of Business Administration

Purdue University
Krannert Graduate School of Management

Rutgers University
Graduate School of Management

San Francisco State University
School of Business

Seton Hall University
W. Paul Stillman School of Business

Southern Methodist University
Edwin L. Cox School of Business

Stanford University
Graduate School of Business

State University of New York at Buffalo
School of Management

Syracuse University
School of Management

Texas A&M University
College of Business Administration

Texas Christian University
M. J. Neeley School of Business

Tulane University
A.B. Freeman School of Business

University of Alabama
Graduate School of Business

University of Arizona
College of Business and Public Administration

University of California, Berkeley
Graduate School of Business Administration

University of California, Los Angeles
Graduate School of Management

University of Chicago
Graduate School of Business

University of Cincinnati
College of Business Administration

University of Connecticut (Storrs)
School of Business Administration

University of Denver
Graduate School of Business and Public Management

University of Georgia
Graduate School of Business Administration

University of Hawaii
College of Business Administration

University of Illinois at Chicago
College of Business Administration

University of Kansas
College of Business

University of Maryland
College of Business and Management

University of Michigan
Graduate School of Business Administration

University of Minnesota
School of Management

University of Missouri, Columbia
College of Business and Public Administration

University of Missouri—St. Louis
School of Business Administration

University of North Carolina at Chapel Hill
Graduate School of Business Administration

University of Notre Dame
College of Business Administration

University of Oklahoma
College of Business Administration

University of Pennsylvania
Wharton Graduate Division

University of Pittsburgh
Graduate School of Business

University of Rhode Island
College of Business Administration

University of Rochester
Graduate School of Management

University of South Carolina
College of Business Administration

University of South Florida
College of Business Administration

University of Southern California
Graduate School of Business Administration

University of Tennessee
College of Business Administration

University of Texas at Austin
Graduate School of Business

University of Tulsa
College of Business Administration

University of Utah
Graduate School of Business

University of Virginia
Colgate Darden Graduate School of Business Administration

University of Washington
Graduate School of Business Administration

University of Wisconsin—Milwaukee
School of Business Administration

Vanderbilt University
Owen Graduate School of Management

Virginia Polytechnic Institute and State University
College of Business

Washington State University
College of Business and Economics

Washington University (St. Louis)
Graduate School of Business Administration

Introduction

The Official Guide for GMAT Review has been designed and written by the staff of Educational Testing Service, which prepares the Graduate Management Admission Test used by many graduate schools of business and management as one criterion in considering applications for admission to their graduate programs. This book is intended to be a general guide to the kinds of verbal and mathematical questions likely to appear in the GMAT. All questions used to illustrate the various types of questions are taken from three actual editions of the GMAT administered after June 1982.*

The GMAT is not a test of knowledge in specific subjects—for example, it does not test knowledge specifically or uniquely acquired in accounting or economics courses. Rather, it is a test of certain skills and abilities that have been found to contribute to success in graduate programs in business and management. For this reason, it is useful to familiarize yourself with the general types of questions likely to be found in editions of the GMAT and the reasoning skills and problem-solving strategies that these types of questions demand. This book illustrates various types of questions that appear in the GMAT and explains in detail some of the most effective strategies for mastering these questions.

The most efficient and productive way to use this book is to read first through Chapter 1. Each type of question is briefly described, the directions are given, one or two examples are presented, and the skills each question type measures are outlined. You should pay particular attention to the directions for each question type. This is especially important for the Data Sufficiency and Analysis of Situations questions, which have lengthy and complex directions.

Chapters 3-7 provide detailed illustrations and explanations of individual question types. After you read Chapter 1, you will find the most advantageous way to use the book is to choose a chapter on a particular question type, read carefully the introductory material, and then do the sample test in that chapter. As you take the sample test, follow the directions and time specifications given. When you complete a sample test, use the answer key that follows it to check your responses. Then review the sample test carefully, spending as much time as is necessary to familiarize yourself with the range of questions or problems presented in the sample test.

You may find it useful to read through all of Chapter 2, Math Review, before working through Chapters 3, Problem Solving, and 4, Data Sufficiency, or you may wish to use Chapter 2 as a reference, noting the suggested sections at the end of each explanation in Chapters 3 and 4 as you go along. However, since Chapter 2 is intended to provide you with a comprehensive review of the basic mathematical concepts used in the quantitative sections of the GMAT, you may find it valuable to read through the chapter as a whole.

The introductory material, sample tests, and answer keys to the sample tests in Chapter 5, Reading Comprehension, Chapter 6, Analysis of Situations, and Chapter 7, Sentence Correction, should be approached in the way suggested above. The explanatory materials for Reading Comprehension and Analysis of Situations have been written as thorough explanations of the reasoning and problem-solving challenges each question type presents. Demonstrating strategies for successfully meeting these challenges, regardless of the particular content of the questions or problems that appear in a specific edition of the GMAT, is the objective of these explanations. Consequently, flipping from a particular question to a particular explanation will be counterproductive. In Chapter 6, Analysis of Situations, each possible answer to every question on the sample test is explained. This comprehensive approach to explaining Analysis of Situations questions has been designed to give you as complete an understanding as possible of this question type.

After you complete the review and practice built in to each chapter you should turn to Chapter 8, which includes three complete GMAT tests. It will be most helpful in preparing yourself to take the GMAT if you regard the tests in Chapter 8 as facsimiles of the test you will take for scoring. Time yourself on each section, and follow the directions exactly as given.

Following each test reprinted in Chapter 8 is an answer key, information about scoring and score interpretation, and an explanation for every question on that test. Guidelines for the use of GMAT scores are also given.

In every explanation of a question in the *Guide*, the general level of difficulty for each question is given to provide you with a guide to how difficult past test-takers have found these questions when they appeared on a nationally administered GMAT.

---

*The material in *The Official Guide for GMAT Review* is intended to familiarize you with the types of questions found on the GMAT. Although the questions on the sample tests in Chapters 3-7 represent the general nature of the questions on the test, it is possible that a type of question not illustrated by and explained in the *Guide* may appear on the GMAT. It is also possible that material illustrated by and explained in the *Guide* may not appear on the test.

1 Description of the Graduate Management Admission Test

The Graduate Management Admission Test is designed to help graduate schools assess the qualifications of applicants for advanced study in business and management. The test can be used by both schools and students in evaluating verbal and mathematical skills as well as general knowledge and preparation for graduate study. Note, however, that GMAT scores should be considered as only one of several indicators of ability.

Format

The current GMAT consists entirely of multiple-choice questions, which are divided among eight separately timed sections; the total testing time is about four hours. Each question offers five choices from which the examinee is to select the best answer.

Every form of the test contains two sections of trial questions that are needed for pretesting and equating purposes. These questions, however, are not identified, and you should do your best on all questions. The answers to trial questions are not counted in your test score.

Both the Graduate Management Admission Council and Educational Testing Service are aware of the limits of the multiple-choice format, particularly in measuring an applicant's ability to formulate general concepts or to develop detailed supportive or opposing arguments. However, in a national testing program designed for a wide variety of people with different backgrounds, the use of a large number of short, multiple-choice questions has proved to be an effective and reliable way of providing a fair and valid evaluation.

Content

It is important to recognize that the GMAT evaluates skills and abilities that develop over relatively long periods of time. Although the sections are basically verbal or mathematical, the complete test provides one method of measuring overall ability. The GMAT does not test specific knowledge obtained in college course work, and it does not seek to measure achievements in any specific areas of study.

The Graduate Management Admission Council recognizes that questions arise concerning techniques for taking standardized examinations such as the GMAT, and it is hoped that the descriptions, sample tests, and explanations given here, along with the full-length sample tests, will give you a practical familiarity with both the concepts and techniques required by GMAT questions.

The material on the following pages provides a general description and brief discussion of the objectives and techniques for each question type and applies to editions of the GMAT appearing in June 1982 and thereafter.

Following this general description of the GMAT are a math review designed to help you review basic mathematical skills useful in the Problem Solving and Data Sufficiency sections of the GMAT and five chapters, one for each question type, that present sample tests with answer keys and detailed explanations of the specific question type and of all questions and answers from the sample tests. (The sample tests are made up of questions that have appeared in the actual GMAT.) Methods of determining the best answer to a particular kind of question as well as explanations of the different kinds of questions appearing in any one section are also presented in these chapters. The general level of difficulty for each question is given to provide you with a guide to how past candidates have performed. Chapter 8 contains three full-length GMAT tests. These are followed by answer keys, explanations for each question, and scoring information, which explains how GMAT scores are calculated and how they are interpreted.

Problem Solving Questions

This section of the GMAT is designed to test (1) basic mathematical skills, (2) understanding of elementary mathematical concepts, and (3) the ability to reason quantitatively and to solve quantitative problems. Approximately half the problems in the test are in a mathematical setting; the remainder are based on "real life" situations.

WHAT IS MEASURED

Problem Solving questions test your ability to understand verbal descriptions of situations and to solve problems using arithmetic, elementary algebra, or commonly known concepts of geometry.

The directions for Problem Solving questions read as follows:

Directions: In this section solve each problem, using any available space on the page for scratchwork. Then indicate the best of the answer choices given.

Numbers: All numbers used are real numbers.

Figures: Figures that accompany problems in this test are intended to provide information useful in solving the problems. They are drawn as accurately as possible EXCEPT when it is stated in a specific problem that its figure is not drawn to scale. All figures lie in a plane unless otherwise indicated.

Data Sufficiency Questions

Each of the problems in the Data Sufficiency section of the GMAT consists of a question, often accompanied by some initial information, and two statements, labeled (1) and (2), containing additional information. You must decide whether sufficient information to answer the question is given by either (1) or (2) individually or—if not—by both combined.

These are the directions that you will find for the Data Sufficiency section of the GMAT. Read them carefully.

Directions: Each of the data sufficiency problems below consists of a question and two statements, labeled (1) and (2), in which certain data are given. You have to decide whether the data given in the statements are *sufficient* for answering the question. Using the data given in the statements *plus* your knowledge of mathematics and everyday facts (such as the number of days in July or the meaning of *counterclockwise*), you are to blacken space

A if statement (1) ALONE is sufficient, but statement (2) alone is not sufficient to answer the question asked;

B if statement (2) ALONE is sufficient, but statement (1) alone is not sufficient to answer the question asked;

C if BOTH statements (1) and (2) TOGETHER are sufficient to answer the question asked, but NEITHER statement ALONE is sufficient;

D if EACH statement ALONE is sufficient to answer the question asked;

E if statements (1) and (2) TOGETHER are NOT sufficient to answer the question asked, and additional data specific to the problem are needed.

Numbers: All numbers used are real numbers.

Figures: A figure in a data sufficiency problem will conform to the information given in the question, but will not necessarily conform to the additional information given in statements (1) and (2).

You may assume that lines shown as straight are straight and that angle measures are greater than zero.

You may assume that the position of points, angles, regions, etc., exist in the order shown.

All figures lie in a plane unless otherwise indicated.

Example:

In $\triangle PQR$, what is the value of x?

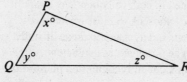

(1) $PQ = PR$
(2) $y = 40$

Explanation: According to statement (1), $PQ = PR$; therefore, $\triangle PQR$ is isosceles and $y = z$. Since $x + y + z = 180$, $x + 2y = 180$. Since statement (1) does not give a value for *y,* you cannot answer the question using statement (1) by itself. According to statement (2), $y = 40$; therefore, $x + z = 140$. Since statement (2) does not give a value for *z,* you cannot answer the question using statement (2) by itself. Using both statements together you can find *y* and *z;* therefore, you can find *x,* and the answer to the problem is C.

WHAT IS MEASURED

Data Sufficiency questions are designed to measure your ability to analyze a quantitative problem, to recognize which information is relevant, and to determine at what point there is sufficient information to solve the problem.

Reading Comprehension Questions

The Reading Comprehension section is made up of several reading passages about which you will be asked interpretive, applicative, and inferential questions. The passages are approximately 500 words long, and they discuss topics from the social sciences, the physical and biological sciences, and the humanities. Because each section includes at least one passage from each of the three areas you will probably be generally familiar with some of the material; however, neither the passages nor the questions assume detailed knowledge of the topics discussed.

WHAT IS MEASURED

Reading Comprehension questions measure your ability to understand, analyze, and apply information and concepts presented in written form. All questions are to be answered on the basis of what is stated or implied in the reading material, and no specific knowledge of the material is required. Reading Comprehension, therefore, evaluates your ability to

* understand words and statements in the reading passages (Questions of this type are not vocabulary questions. These questions test your understanding of and ability to use specialized terms as well as your understanding of the English language. You may also find that questions of this type ask about the overall meaning of a passage);

* understand the logical relationships between significant points and concepts in the reading passages (For example, such questions may ask you to determine the strong and weak points of an argument or to evaluate the importance of arguments and ideas in a passage);

* draw inferences from facts and statements in the reading passages (The inference questions will ask you to consider factual statements or information and, on the basis of that information, reach a general conclusion);

* understand and follow the development of quantitative concepts as they are presented in verbal material (This may involve the interpretation of numerical data or the use of simple arithmetic to reach conclusions about material in a passage).

The directions for Reading Comprehension questions read as follows:

Directions: Each passage in this group is followed by questions based on its content. After reading a passage, choose the best answer to each question and blacken the corresponding space on the answer sheet. Answer all questions following a passage on the basis of what is *stated* or *implied* in that passage.

Analysis of Situations Questions

The Analysis of Situations section of the GMAT asks you to classify on the basis of relative importance the considerations that make up a management or business situation. Each section contains at least one passage describing a decision-making process that is occasioned by the need to solve a problem. The passage discusses the nature of the problem, gives the considerations related to the situation, and suggests possible solutions to the problem.

In each passage a decision must be made: which of the possible alternatives will best solve the problem? Generally, no decision is reached in the passage, but the possible alternatives are fully examined, and the considerations that affect the outcome are evaluated from different points of view. Given this information, you must classify a number of considerations as objectives, factors, assumptions, or unimportant issues. You must also decide how important each of the factors is in making the decision. If a factor is of primary importance, it is a major factor. If a factor is only of secondary importance, it is a minor factor. If an aspect of the decision-making situation is insignificant as a factor, it is an unimportant issue.

WHAT IS MEASURED

The Analysis of Situations section is one measure of your ability to analyze and evaluate the major aspects of a business or management situation. It tests your perception of the financial, material, and legal aspects of a problem in terms of their importance with respect to each other and with respect to making a decision.

This section does not presuppose either practical or academic knowledge of specific business terms and practices. Although many of the passages are based on business or management situations, the problems can be solved using only common sense and logical reasoning.

The directions for Analysis of Situations questions read as follows:

Directions: Each passage in this section is followed by numbered considerations that require classification, as illustrated by the following example:

John Atkins, the owner of a service station in Leeway, wanted to open a station in Eastown. A computer company had plans to set up operations in Eastown, and Atkins, foreseeing an increase in traffic near the plant, was eager to acquire land in Eastown so that he could expand his business to serve commuting workers. Ideally, Atkins wanted a piece of land large enough to permit him to build a tire store as part of the new station; he also wanted to keep the cost of purchasing the land as well as the cost of clearing it for construction as low as possible. Atkins identified three possible properties; one on Moore Road, another on Route 5, and a third on Snow Lane. The purchase prices of the properties were $42,000, $36,000, and $34,000, respectively. The properties required different expenditures for clearing. In the case of the Snow Lane site, a diner would have to be demolished and pavement removed, Atkins knew that his decision required deliberation.

The following numbered considerations are related to the passage above. Evaluate each consideration separately in terms of the passage and on the answer sheet blacken space

A if the consideration is an *Objective* in making the decision; that is, one of the outcomes, results, or goals that the decision-maker seeks;

B if the consideration is a *Major Factor* in making the decision; that is, a consideration, explicitly mentioned in the passage, that is basic to reaching the decision;

C if the consideration is a *Minor Factor* in making the decision; that is, a consideration that is of secondary importance to reaching the decision and that bears on a Major Factor;

D if the consideration is an *Assumption* in making the decision; that is, a relevant supposition or projection made by the decision-maker before reaching the decision;

E If the consideration is an *Unimportant Issue* in making the decision; that is, a consideration that is insignificant or not immediately relevant to reaching the decision.

SAMPLE QUESTIONS

1. Increase in traffic near the new computer plant

   Ⓐ Ⓑ Ⓒ ● Ⓔ

2. Acquisition of a sufficiently large piece of land

   ● Ⓑ Ⓒ Ⓓ Ⓔ

3. Cost of clearing a piece of land

   Ⓐ ● Ⓒ Ⓓ Ⓔ

4. Cost of demolishing the diner on the Snow Lane site

   Ⓐ Ⓑ ● Ⓓ Ⓔ

5. Cost of starting up the new computer plan

   Ⓐ Ⓑ Ⓒ Ⓓ ●

The best classification for number 1 is (D), an *Assumption,* since Atkins supposes that automobile traffic will increase near the new computer plant. The best classification for number 2 is (A), an *Objective,* since one of Atkins' goals is to obtain a piece of land large enough to permit him to include a tire store as part of his new station. (B), a *Major Factor,* is the best classification for number 3. The cost of clearing a property is a basic consideration to Atkins since he wants to prepare a property for construction at the lowest possible cost. The best classification for number 4 is (C), a *Minor Factor.* The cost of demolishing the diner on the Snow Lane site contributes to the total cost of clearing that site. That is, the cost of demolition is a secondary consideration that bears on a major factor. Finally, the best classification for number 5 is (E), an *Unimportant Issue,* since there is no logical connection between the cost of starting up the computer plant and Atkins' decision about which property to choose.

Sentence Correction Questions

Sentence Correction questions ask you which of the five choices best expresses an idea or relationship. The questions will require you to be familiar with the stylistic conventions and grammatical rules of standard written English and to demonstrate your ability to improve incorrect or ineffective expressions.

WHAT IS MEASURED

Sentence Correction questions test two broad aspects of language proficiency:

1. *Correct expression.* A correct sentence is grammatically and structurally sound. It conforms to all the rules of standard written English (for example: noun-verb agreement, noun-pronoun agreement, pronoun consistency, pronoun case, and verb tense sequence). Further, a correct sentence will not have dangling, misplaced, or improperly formed modifiers, will not have unidiomatic or inconsistent expressions, and will not have faults in parallel construction.

2. *Effective expression.* An effective sentence expresses an idea or relationship clearly and concisely as well as gramatically. This does not mean that the choice with the fewest and simplest words is necessarily the best answer. It means that there are no superfluous words or needlessly complicated expressions in the best choice.

   In addition, an effective sentence uses proper diction. (Diction refers to the standard dictionary meaning of words and the appro-meaning of words and the appropriateness of words in context.) In evaluating the diction of a sentence, you must be able to recognize whether the words are well chosen, accurate, and suitable for the context.

The directions for Sentence Correction questions read as follows:

Directions: In each of the following sentences, some part of the sentence or the entire sentence is underlined. Beneath each sentence you will find five ways of phrasing the underlined part. The first of these repeats the original; the other four are different. If you think the original is better than any of the alternatives, choose answer A; otherwise choose one of the others. Select the best version and blacken the corresponding space on your answer sheet.

This is a test of correctness and effectiveness of expression. In choosing answers, follow the requirements of standard written English; that is, pay attention to grammar, choice of words, and sentence construction. Choose the answer that expresses most effectively what is presented in the original sentence; this answer should be clear and exact, without awkwardness, ambiguity, or redundancy.

Examples:
A thunderclap is a complex acoustic signal <u>as a result of</u> rapid expansion of heated air in the path of a lightning flash.

(A) as a result of
(B) caused as a result of
(C) resulting because of the
(D) resulting from the
(E) that results because there is

In choice A, *is a . . . . signal as a result of* is incorrect. It is the thunderclap that results from the expansion; its being a signal is irrelevant. In choice B, it is superfluous to use both *caused* and *result,* and it is also superfluous to use both *result* and *because* in choices C and E. In choice C, *because of* is not the correct preposition to use after *resulting; from* is correct and is used in the best answer, D.

<u>Ever since the Civil War, the status of women was</u> a live social issue in this country.

(A) Ever since the Civil War, the status of women was
(B) Since the Civil War, women's status was
(C) Ever since the Civil War, the status of women has been
(D) Even at the time of the Civil War, the status of women has been
(E) From the times of the Civil War, the status of women has been

In choice A, the verb following *women* should be *has been,* not *was,* because *ever since* denotes a period of time continuing from the past into the present. For the same reason, *was* is inappropriately used with *since* in choice B. In choice D, *even at* changes the meaning of the original sentence substantially and does not fit with *has been; was* is correct with *even at.* In choice E, *times* is incorrect; the standard phrase is *from the time of.* C is the best answer.

General Test-Taking Suggestions

1. Although the GMAT stresses accuracy more than speed, it is important to use the allotted time wisely. You will be able to do so if you are familiar with the mechanics of the test and the kinds of materials, questions, and directions in the test. Therefore, become familiar with the formats and requirements of each section of the test.

2. After you become generally familiar with all question types, use the individual chapters on each question type in this book (Chapters 3-7), which include sample tests and detailed explanations, to prepare yourself for the actual GMAT tests in Chapter 8. When taking the tests, try to follow all the requirements specified in the directions and keep within the time limits. While these tests are useful for familiarization, they cannot be used to predict your performance on the actual test.

3. Read all test directions carefully. Since many answer sheets give indications that the examinees do not follow directions, this suggestion is particularly important. The directions explain exactly what each section requires in order to answer each question type. If you read hastily, you may miss important instructions and seriously jeopardize your scores.

4. Answer as many questions as possible, but avoid random guessing. Your GMAT scores will be based on the number of questions you answer correctly minus a fraction of the number you answer incorrectly. Therefore, it is unlikely that mere guessing will improve your scores significantly, and it does take time. However, if you have some knowledge of a question and can eliminate at least one of the answer choices as wrong, your chance of getting the best answer is improved, and it will be to your advantage to answer the question. If you know nothing at all about a particular question, it is probably better to skip it. The number of omitted questions will not be subtracted.

5. Take a watch to the examination and be sure to note the time limits for each section. Since each question has the same weight, it is not wise to spend too much time on one question if that causes you to neglect other questions.

6. Make every effort to pace yourself. Work steadily and as rapidly as possible without being careless.

7. A wise practice is to answer the questions you are sure of first. Then, if time permits, go back and attempt the more difficult questions.

8. Read each question carefully and thoroughly. Before answering a question, determine exactly what is being asked. Never skim a question or the possible answers. Skimming may cause you to miss important information or nuances in the question.

9. Do not become upset if you cannot answer a question. A person can do very well without answering every question or finishing every section. No one is expected to get a perfect score.

10. When you take the test, you will mark your answers on a separate answer sheet. As you go through the test, be sure that the number of each answer on the answer sheet matches the corresponding question number in the test book. Your answer sheet may contain space for more answers or questions than there are in the test book. Do not be concerned, but be careful. Indicate each of your answers with a dark mark that completely fills the response position on the answer sheet. Light or partial marks may not be properly read by the scoring machine. Indicate only one response to each question, and erase all unintended marks completely.

GMAT: Test Specifications

All editions of the GMAT are constructed to measure the same skills and meet the same specifications. Thus, each section of the test is constructed according to the same specifications for every edition of the GMAT. These specifications include definite requirements for the number of questions, the points tested by each question, the kinds of questions, and the difficulty of each question.

Because the various editions of the test inevitably differ somewhat in difficulty, they are made equivalent to each other by statistical methods.

This equating process makes it possible to assure that all reported scores of a given value denote approximately the same level of ability regardless of the edition being used or of the particular group taking the test at a given time.

Test Development Process

Educational Testing Service professional staff responsible for developing the verbal measures of the GMAT have backgrounds and advanced degrees in the humanities or in measurement. Those responsible for the quantitative portion have advanced degrees in mathematics or related fields.

Standardized procedures have been developed to guide the test-generation process, to assure high-quality test material, to avoid idiosyncratic questions, and to encourage development of test material that is widely appropriate.

An important part of the development of test material is the review process. Each question, as well as any stimulus material on which questions are based, must be reviewed by several independent critics. In appropriate cases, questions are also reviewed by experts outside ETS who can bring fresh perspectives to bear on the questions in terms of actual content or in terms of test sensitivity to minority and women's concerns.

After the questions have been reviewed and revised as appropriate, they are assembled into clusters suitable for trial during actual administrations of the GMAT. In this manner, new questions are tried out under standard testing conditions, by representative samples of GMAT examinees. Questions being tried out do not affect examinees' scores but are themselves evaluated: they are analyzed statistically for usefulness and weaknesses. The questions that perform satisfactorily become part of a pool of questions from which future editions of the GMAT can be assembled; those that do not are rewritten to correct the flaws and tried out again— or discarded.

In preparing those sections of the GMAT that will contribute to the scoring process, the test assembler uses only questions that have been successfully tried out. The test assembler considers not only each question's characteristics but also the relationship of the question to the entire group of questions with respect to the test specification discussed above. When the test has been assembled, it is reviewed by a second test specialist and by the test development coordinator for the GMAT. After satisfactory resolution of any points raised in these reviews, the test goes to a test editor. The test editor's review is likely to result in further suggestions for change, and the test assembler must decide how these suggested changes will be handled. If a suggested change yields an editorial improvement, without jeopardizing content integrity, the change is adopted; otherwise, new wording is sought that will meet the dual concerns of content integrity and editorial style. The review process is continued at each stage of test assembly and copy preparation, down to careful scrutiny of the final proof immediately prior to printing.

All reviewers except the editor and proofreader must attempt to answer each question without the help of the answer key. Thus, each reviewer "takes the test," uninfluenced by knowledge of what the question writer or test assembler believed each answer should be. The answer key is certified as official only after at least three reviewers have agreed independently on the correct answer for each question.

The extensive, careful procedure described here has been developed over the years to assure that every question in any new edition of the GMAT is appropriate and useful and that the combination of questions that make up the new edition is satisfactory. Nevertheless, the appraisal is not complete until after the new edition has been administered during a national test administration and subjected to a rigorous process of item analysis to see whether each question yields the expected results. This further appraisal sometimes reveals that a question is not satisfactory after all; it may prove to be ambiguous, or require information beyond the scope of the test, or be otherwise unsuitable. Answers to such questions are not used in computing scores.

2 Math Review

Although this chapter provides a review of some of the mathematical concepts of arithmetic, algebra, and geometry, it is not intended to be a textbook. You should use this chapter to familiarize yourself with the kinds of topics that are tested in the GMAT. You may wish to consult an arithmetic, algebra, or geometry book for a more detailed discussion of some of the topics.

The topics that are covered in Section A, arithmetic, include:

1. Properties of integers
2. Fractions
3. Decimals
4. Real numbers
5. Positive and negative numbers
6. Ratio and proportion
7. Percents
8. Equivalent forms of a number
9. Powers and roots of numbers
10. Mean
11. Median
12. Mode

The content of Section B, algebra, does not extend beyond what is covered in a first-year high school course. The topics included are:

1. Simplifying algebraic expressions
2. Equations
3. Solving linear equations with one unknown
4. Solving two linear equations with two unknowns
5. Solving factorable quadratic equations
6. Exponents
7. Absolute value
8. Inequalities

Section C, geometry, is limited primarily to measurement and intuitive geometry or spatial visualization. Extensive knowledge of theorems and the ability to construct proofs, skills that are usually developed in a formal geometry course, are not tested. The topics included in this section are:

1. Lines
2. Intersecting lines and angles
3. Perpendicular lines
4. Parallel lines
5. Polygons (convex)
6. Triangles
7. Quadrilaterals
8. Circles
9. Solids
10. Rectangular solids
11. Cylinders
12. Pyramids
13. Coordinate geometry

Section D, word problems, presents examples of and solutions to the following types of word problems:

1. Rate
2. Work
3. Mixture
4. Interest
5. Discount
6. Profit
7. Sets
8. Geometry
9. Measurement
10. Data interpretation

A. Arithmetic

1. INTEGERS

An *integer* is any number in the set. $\{\ldots, -3, -2, -1, 0, 1, 2, 3, \ldots\}$. If x and y are integers and $x \neq 0$, x is a *divisor (factor)* of y provided that $y = xn$ for some integer n. In this case y is also said to be *divisible* by x or to be a *multiple* of x. For example, 7 is a divisor or factor of 28 since $28 = 7 \cdot 4$, but 6 is not a divisor of 28 since there is no integer n such that $28 = 6n$.

Any integer that is divisible by 2 is an *even integer;* the set of even intergers is $\{\ldots -4, -2, 0, 2, 4, 6, 8, \ldots\}$. Integers that are not divisible by 2 are *odd integers;* $\{\ldots -3, -1, 1, 3, 5, \ldots\}$ is the set of odd integers.

If at least one factor of a product of integers is even, then the product is even; otherwise the product is odd. If two integers are both even or both odd, then their sum and their difference are even. Otherwise, their sum and their difference are odd.

A *prime* number is an integer that has exactly two different positive divisors, 1 and itself. For example, 2, 3, 5, 7, 11, and 13 are prime numbers, but 15 is not, since 15 has four different positive divisors, 1, 3, 5, and 15. The number 1 is not a prime number, since it has only one positive divisor.

The numbers -2, -1, 0, 1, 2, 3, 4, 5 are *consecutive integers*. Consecutive integers can be represented by n, n + 1, n + 2, n + 3, . . ., where n is an integer. The numbers 0, 2, 4, 6, 8 are *consecutive even integers,* and 1, 3, 5, 7, 9 are *consecutive odd integers*. Consecutive even integers can be represented by 2n, 2n + 2, 2n + 4, . . ., and consecutive odd integers can be represented by 2n + 1, 2n + 3, 2n + 5, . . ., where n is an integer.

Properties of the integer 1. If n is any number, then $1 \cdot n = n$, and for any number $n \neq 0$, $n \cdot \frac{1}{n} = 1$. The number 1 can be expressed in many ways, e.g., $\frac{n}{n} = 1$ for any number $n \neq 0$. Multiplying or dividing an expression by 1, in any form, does not change the value of that expression.

Properties of the integer zero. The integer zero is neither positive nor negative. If n is any number, then $n + 0 = n$ and $n \cdot 0 = 0$. Division by zero is not defined.

2. FRACTIONS

In a fraction $\frac{n}{d}$, n is the *numerator* and d is the *denominator*. The denominator of a fraction can never be zero, because division by zero is not defined.

Two fractions are said to be *equivalent* if they represent the same number. For example, $\frac{4}{8}$, $\frac{3}{6}$, and $\frac{1}{2}$ are equivalent since all three represent the number $\frac{1}{2}$.

Addition and subtraction of fractions. To add or subtract two fractions with the same denominator, simply perform the required operation with the numerators, leaving the denominators the same. For example, $\frac{3}{5} + \frac{4}{5} = \frac{3+4}{5} = \frac{7}{5}$, and $\frac{5}{7} - \frac{2}{7} = \frac{5-2}{7} = \frac{3}{7}$. If two fractions do not have the same denominator, express them as equivalent fractions with the same denominator. For example, to add $\frac{3}{5}$ and $\frac{4}{7}$, multiply the numerator and denominator of the first fraction by 7 and the numerator and denominator of the second fraction by 5, obtaining $\frac{21}{35}$ and $\frac{20}{35}$, respectively;

$$\frac{21}{35} + \frac{20}{35} = \frac{41}{35}.$$

Also,

$$\frac{2}{3} + \frac{1}{6} = \frac{2}{3} \cdot \frac{2}{2} + \frac{1}{6} = \frac{4}{6} + \frac{1}{6} = \frac{5}{6}$$

Multiplication and division of fractions. To multiply two fractions, simply multiply the two numerators and multiply the two denominators. For example, $\frac{2}{3} \times \frac{4}{7} = \frac{2 \times 4}{3 \times 7} = \frac{8}{21}$.

To divide by a fraction, invert the divisor (i.e., find its *reciprocal*) and multiply. For example, $\frac{2}{3} \div \frac{4}{7} = \frac{2}{3} \times \frac{7}{4} = \frac{14}{12} = \frac{7}{6}$.

In the problem above, the reciprocal of $\frac{4}{7}$ is $\frac{7}{4}$. In general, the reciprocal of a fraction $\frac{n}{d}$ is $\frac{d}{n}$, where n and d are not zero.

Mixed numbers. A number that consists of a whole number and a fraction, e.g., $7\frac{2}{3}$, is a mixed number. $7\frac{2}{3}$ means $7 + \frac{2}{3}$.

To change a mixed number into a fraction, multiply the whole number by the denominator of the fraction and add this number to the numerator of the fraction; then put the result over the denominator of the fraction. For example.

$$7\frac{2}{3} = \frac{(3 \times 7) + 2}{3} = \frac{23}{3}.$$

3. DECIMALS

In the decimal system, the position of the period or *decimal point* determines the place value of the digits. For example, the digits in the number 7,654.321 have the following place values:

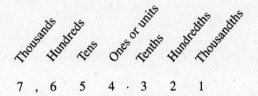

$$7 \quad , \quad 6 \quad 5 \quad 4 \quad \cdot \quad 3 \quad 2 \quad 1$$

Some examples of decimals follow.

$$0.321 = \frac{3}{10} + \frac{2}{100} + \frac{1}{1,000} = \frac{321}{1,000}$$

$$0.0321 = \frac{0}{10} + \frac{3}{100} + \frac{2}{1,000} + \frac{1}{10,000} = \frac{321}{10,000}$$

$$1.56 = 1 + \frac{5}{10} + \frac{6}{100} = \frac{156}{100}$$

Sometimes decimals are expressed as the product of a number with only one digit to the left of the decimal point and a power of 10. For example, 231 may be written as 2.31×10^2 and 0.0231 may be written as 2.31×10^{-2}. The exponent on the 10 indicates the number of places that the decimal point is to be moved in the number that is to be multiplied by a power of 10 in order to obtain the product. The decimal point is moved to the right if the exponent is positive and to the left if the exponent is negative. For example, 20.13×10^3 is equal to 20,130 and 1.91×10^{-4} is equal to 0.000191.

Addition and subtraction of decimals. To add or subtract two decimals, the decimal points of both numbers should be lined up. If one of the numbers has fewer digits to the right of the decimal point than the other, zeros may be inserted to the right of the last digit. For example, to add 17.6512 and 653.27, set up the numbers in a column and add:

$$\begin{array}{r} 17.6512 \\ + 653.2700 \\ \hline 670.9212 \end{array}$$

Likewise, 653.27 minus 17.6512 =

$$\begin{array}{r} 653.2700 \\ - 17.6512 \\ \hline 635.6188 \end{array}$$

Multiplication of decimals. To multiply decimals, multiply the numbers as if they were whole numbers and then insert the decimal point in the product so that the number of digits to the right of the decimal point is equal to the sum of the numbers of digits to the right of the decimal points in the numbers being multiplied. For example:

$$
\begin{array}{r}
2.09 \quad \text{(2 digits to the right)} \\
\times \ 1.3 \quad \text{(1 digit to the right)} \\
\hline
627 \\
209 \quad\ \\
\hline
2.717 \quad \text{(2 + 1 = 3 digits to the right)}
\end{array}
$$

Division of decimals. To divide a number (the dividend) by a decimal (the divisor), move the decimal point of the divisor to the right until the divisor is a whole number. Then move the decimal point of the dividend the same number of places to the right, and divide as you would by a whole number. The decimal point in the quotient will be directly above the decimal point in the new dividend. For example, to divide 698.12 by 12.4:

$$12.4\ \overline{)698.12}$$

will be replaced by

$$124\ \overline{)6981.2}$$

and the division would proceed as follows:

$$
\begin{array}{r}
56.3 \\
124\ \overline{)6981.2} \\
\underline{620\quad\ } \\
781\quad \\
\underline{744\quad} \\
372 \\
\underline{372}
\end{array}
$$

4. REAL NUMBERS

All *real* numbers correspond to points on the number line and all points on the number line correspond to real numbers. All real numbers except zero are either positive or negative.

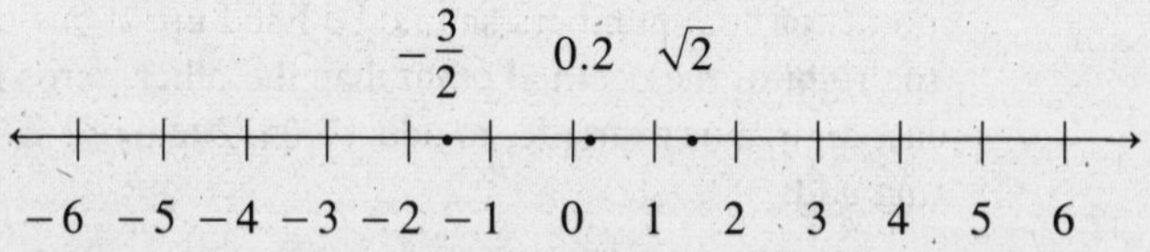

On a number line, numbers corresponding to points to the left of zero are negative and numbers corresponding to points to the right of zero are positive. For any two numbers on the number line, the number to the left is less than the number to the right; for example,

$-4 < -3, \frac{1}{2} < \frac{3}{4}$, and $0.05 < 0.12$.

To say that the number n is between 1 and 4 on the number line means that $n > 1$ and $n < 4$; i.e., $1 < n < 4$.

The distance between a number and zero on the number line is called the *absolute value* (magnitude) of the number. Thus 3 and -3 have the same absolute value, 3, since they are both three units from zero. The absolute value of 3 is denoted $|3|$. Examples of absolute values of numbers are

$$|-5| = |5| = 5, \left|-\frac{7}{2}\right| = \frac{7}{2}, \text{ and } |0| = 0.$$

Note that the absolute value of any nonzero number is positive.

5. POSITIVE AND NEGATIVE NUMBERS

Addition and subtraction. To add two numbers that have the same sign, add the absolute values of the numbers and insert the common sign. For example:

$$(-7) + (-9) = -16$$

because

$$(-7) + (-9) = -(|-7| + |-9|) = -(7 + 9) = -16.$$

To add two numbers with different signs, find the positive difference between their absolute values and insert the sign of the number with the greater absolute value. For example,

$$(-13) + 19 = 6$$

because

$$(-13) + 19 = +(|19| - |-13|) = +(19 - 13) = 6.$$

Similarly,

$$-16 + 8 = -8$$

because

$$-16 + 8 = -(|-16| - |8|) = -(16 - 8) = -8.$$

To subtract one number from another, express the difference as a sum and add as indicated above. That is, $a - b = a + (-b)$. For example:

$$(-7) - (5) = -7 + (-5) = -12$$
$$6 - (-4) = 6 + [-(-4] = 6 + 4 = 10$$
$$-54 - (-23) = -54 + [-(-23)] = -54 + 23$$
$$= -(54 - 23) = -31$$

(Note that for any number n, $-(-n) = n$.)

Multiplication and division. To multiply or divide two numbers with the same sign, multiply or divide their absolute values; thus, the product and quotient are positive. For example:

$$(-13)(-3) = (13)(3) = 39$$
$$(-14) \div (-2) = 14 \div 2 = 7$$

To multiply or divide two numbers with different signs, multiply or divide their absolute values and insert a negative sign; thus, the product and quotient are negative. For example:

$$(13)(-3) = -(13)(3) = -39$$
$$(-14) \div 2 = -(14 \div 2) = -7$$

Some properties of real numbers that are used frequently follow. If x, y, and z are real numbers, then

(1) $x + y = y + x$ and $xy = yx$.

For example, $8 + 3 = 3 + 8 = 11$, and $17 \cdot 5 = 5 \cdot 17 = 85$.

(2) $(x + y) + z = x + (y + z)$ and $(x \cdot y)z = x(y \cdot z)$.

For example, $(7 + 5) + 2 = 7 + (5 + 2) = 14$, and $(5 \cdot \sqrt{3})(\sqrt{3}) = 5(\sqrt{3} \cdot \sqrt{3}) = 5 \cdot 3 = 15$.

(3) $x(y + z) = xy + xz$.

For example, $718(36) + 718(64) = 718(36 + 64) = 718(100) = 71,800$.

6. RATIO AND PROPORTION

The *ratio* of the number a to the number b (b $\neq$ 0) is $\frac{a}{b}$.

A ratio may be expressed or represented in several ways. For example, the ratio of the number 2 to the number 3 can be written 2 to 3, 2:3, and $\frac{2}{3}$. The order of the terms of a ratio is important. For example, the ratio of the number of months with exactly 30 days to the number with exactly 31 days is $\frac{4}{7}$, not $\frac{7}{4}$.

A *proportion* is a statement that two ratios are equal; for example, $\frac{2}{3} = \frac{8}{12}$ is a proportion. One way to solve a proportion involving an unknown is to cross multiply, obtaining a new equality. For example, to solve for n in the proportion $\frac{2}{3} = \frac{n}{12}$, cross multiply, obtaining $24 = 3n$; then divide both sides by 3, to get $n = 8$.

7. PERCENTS

Percent means per hundred or number out of 100. A percent can be represented as a fraction with a denominator of 100, or as a decimal. For example,

$37\% = \frac{37}{100} = 0.37$.

To find a certain percent of a number, multiply the number by the percent expressed as a decimal or fraction. For example:

$$20\% \text{ of } 90 = 0.20 \times 90 = 18$$

or

$$20\% \text{ of } 90 = \frac{20}{100} \times 90 = \frac{1}{5} \times 90 = 18.$$

Percents greater than 100. Percents greater than 100 are represented by numbers greater than 1. For example:

$$300\% = \frac{300}{100} = 3$$

$$250\% \text{ of } 80 = 2.5 \times 80 = 200$$

Percents less than 1. The percent 0.5% means $\frac{1}{2}$ of 1 percent. For example, 0.5% of 12 is equal to $0.005 \times 12 = 0.06$.

Percent change. Often a problem will ask for the percent increase or decrease from one quantity to another quantity. For example, "If the price of an item increases from $24 to $30, what is the percent increase in price?" To find the percent increase, first find the amount of the increase; then divide this increase by the original amount, and express this quotient as a percent. In the example above, the percent increase would be found in the following way: the amount of the increase is $(30 - 24) = 6$.

Therefore, the percent increase is $\frac{6}{24} = 0.25 = 25\%$.

Likewise, to find the percent decrease (e.g., the price of an item is reduced from $30 to $24), first find the amount of the decrease; then divide this decrease by the original amount, and express this quotient as a percent. In the example above, the amount of decrease is $(30 - 24) = 6$. Therefore, the percent decrease is

$\frac{6}{30} = 0.20 = 20\%$.

Note that the percent increase from 24 to 30 is not the same as the percent decrease from 30 to 24.

In the following example, the increase is greater than 100 percent: If the cost of a certain house in 1983 is 300 percent of its cost in 1970, by what percent did the cost increase?

If n is the cost in 1970, then the percent increase is equal to $\frac{3n - n}{n} = \frac{2n}{n} = 2$, or 200 percent.

8. EQUIVALENT FORMS OF A NUMBER

In solving a particular problem, it may be helpful to convert the given form of a number to a more convenient form.

To convert a fraction to a decimal, divide the numerator by the denominator, e.g., $\frac{3}{4} = 0.75$.

$$
\begin{array}{r}
0.75 \\
4 \overline{)3.00} \\
\underline{28} \\
20 \\
\underline{20}
\end{array}
$$

To convert a number to a percent, multiply by 100. For example, $0.75 = (0.75 \times 100)\% = 75\%$.

The decimal 0.625 means $\frac{625}{1,000}$ (see page 17). This fraction may be simplified by dividing the numerator and denominator by common factors. For example:

$\frac{625}{1,000} = \frac{5 \cdot \cancel{5} \cdot \cancel{5} \cdot \cancel{5}}{2 \cdot 2 \cdot 2 \cdot \cancel{5} \cdot \cancel{5} \cdot \cancel{5}} = \frac{5}{8}$

To convert a percent to a decimal, divide by 100; e.g.:

$$24\% = \frac{24}{100} = 0.24$$

In the following examples, it is helpful to convert from one form of a number to another form.

Of the following, which is LEAST?

(A) 35%　(B) $\frac{9}{20}$　(C) 0.42　(D) $\frac{(0.9)(4)}{10}$　(E) $\frac{3}{13}$

These numbers can be compared more easily if they are all converted to decimals:

$$35\% = 0.35$$

$$\frac{9}{20} = 0.45$$

$$0.42 = 0.42$$

$$\frac{(0.9)(4)}{10} = 0.36$$

$$\frac{3}{13} = 0.23 \text{ (to 2 decimal places)}$$

Thus, $\frac{3}{13}$ is the least of the numbers.

9. POWERS AND ROOTS OF NUMBERS

When a number k is to be used n times as a factor in a product, it can be expressed as k^n, which means the nth power of k. For example, $2^2 = 2 \times 2 = 4$ and $2^3 = 2 \times 2 \times 2 = 8$ are powers of 2.

Squaring a number that is greater than 1, or raising it to a higher power, results in a larger number; squaring a number between 0 and 1 results in a smaller number. For example.

$$3^2 = 9 \qquad\qquad (9 > 3)$$

$$\left(\frac{1}{3}\right)^2 = \frac{1}{9} \qquad\qquad \left(\frac{1}{9} < \frac{1}{3}\right)$$

$$(0.1)^2 = 0.01 \qquad\qquad (0.01 < 0.1)$$

A *square root* of a non-negative number n is a number that when squared is equal to n. Every positive number n has two square roots, one positive and the other negative, but $\sqrt{n}$ denotes the positive number whose square is n. For example, $\sqrt{9}$ denotes 3. The two square roots of 9 are $\sqrt{9} = 3$ and $-\sqrt{9} = -3$.

10. MEAN

The *average (arithmetic mean)* of n values is equal to the sum of the n values divided by n. For example, the average (arithmetic mean) of 9, 6, 5, and 12 is $\frac{9 + 6 + 5 + 12}{4} = 8$.

11. MEDIAN

When an odd number of values are ordered from least to greatest or from greatest to least, the value in the middle is the *median;* i.e., there are equal numbers of values above and below the median. For example, the median of 4, 7, 3, 10, and 8 is 7, since, when ordered from least to greatest (3,4,7,8,10), 7 is the middle value. When there is an even number of values, the median is the average of the two middle values. For example, the median of 5,3,2,10,7, and 8 is $\frac{5 + 7}{2} = 6$.

12. MODE

The *mode* of a list of values is the value that occurs most frequently. For example, the mode of 1, 3, 6, 4, 3, and 5 is 3. A list of values may have more than one mode. For example, the list of values 1,2,3,3,3,5,7,10,10,10,20 has two modes, 3 and 10.

B. Algebra

In algebra, a letter such as x or n is used to represent an unknown quantity. For example, suppose Pam has 5 more pencils than Fred. If you let f represent the number of pencils that Fred has, then the number of pencils that Pam has is f + 5.

A combination of letters and mathematical operations, such as $f + 5$, $\dfrac{3x^3}{2x - 5}$, and $19x^2 + 6x + 3$, is called an *algebraic expression*.

In the expression $9x - 6$, $9x$ and -6 are *terms* of the expression; 9 is called the *coefficient* of x.

1. SIMPLIFYING ALGEBRAIC EXPRESSIONS

Often when working with algebraic expressions, it is necessary to simplify them by factoring or combining *like* terms. For example, the expression $6x + 5x$ is equivalent to $(6 + 5)x$ or $11x$. In the expression $9x - 3y$, 3 is a factor common to both terms: $9x - 3y = 3(3x - y)$. In the expression $5x^2 + 6y$, there are no like terms and no common factors.

If there are common factors in the numerator and denominator of an expression, they can be divided out, provided that they are not equal to zero.

For example, if $x \neq 3$, $\dfrac{3xy - 9y}{x - 3}$ is equal to $\dfrac{3y(x - 3)}{x - 3}$; since $\dfrac{x - 3}{x - 3}$ is equal to 1, $\dfrac{3y(x - 3)}{x - 3} = 3y \cdot 1 = 3y$.

To multiply two algebraic expressions, each term of one expression is multiplied by each term of the other expression. For example:

$$(3x - 4)(9y + x) \text{ is equal to } 3x(9y + x) - 4(9y + x) =$$
$$(3x)(9y) + (3x)(x) + (-4)(9y) + (-4)(x) =$$
$$27xy + 3x^2 - 36y - 4x$$

An algebraic expression can be evaluated by substituting values of the unknowns in the expression. For example, if $x = 3$ and $y = -2$, $3xy - x^2 + y$ can be evaluated as

$$3(3)(-2) - (3)^2 + (-2) = -18 - 9 - 2 = -29.$$

2. EQUATIONS

A statement that two algebraic expressions are equal is an *equation*. Some examples of equations are

$$5x - 2 = 9$$

and

$$3x + 1 = y - 2.$$

Two equations having the same solution(s) are *equivalent*. For example,

$$2 + x = 3$$

and

$$4 + 2x = 6$$

are equivalent equations, as are

$$3x - y = 6$$

and

$$6x = 2y + 12.$$

3. SOLVING LINEAR EQUATIONS WITH ONE UNKNOWN

To solve a linear equation (i.e., to find the value of the unknown that satisfies the equation) you need to isolate the unknown on one side of the equation. This can be done by performing the same mathematical operations on both sides of the equation.

Remember that if the same number is added to or subtracted from both sides of the equation, this does not change the equality; likewise, multiplying or dividing both sides by the same nonzero number does not change the equality. For example, to solve the equation $\frac{5x - 6}{3} = 4$ for x, you can isolate x using the following steps:

$$\frac{5x - 6}{3} = 4$$

$$5x - 6 = 12 \quad \text{(multiplying by 3)}$$

$$5x = 12 + 6 = 18 \quad \text{(adding 6)}$$

$$x = \frac{18}{5} \quad \text{(dividing by 5)}$$

The solution, $\frac{18}{5}$, can be checked by substituting it in the original equation for x to determine whether it satisfies that equation. For example:

$$\frac{5\left(\frac{18}{5}\right) - 6}{3} = \frac{18 - 6}{3} = \frac{12}{3} = 4$$

Therefore, the value of x obtained above is the solution.

4. SOLVING TWO LINEAR EQUATIONS WITH TWO UNKNOWNS

If you have two linear equations that are not equivalent, you can find any values for the two unknowns that satisfy both equations. One way to solve for the two unknowns is to express one of the unknowns in terms of the other using one of the equations, and then substitute it into the remaining equation to obtain an equation with one unknown. This equation can be solved and the value substituted in one of the equations to find the value of the other unknown. For example, the following two equations can be solved for x and y.

$$(1) \quad 3x + 2y = 11$$
$$(2) \quad x - y = 2$$

In equation (2), $x = 2 + y$. Substitute $2 + y$ in equation (1) for x:

$$3(2 + y) + 2y = 11$$
$$6 + 3y + 2y = 11$$
$$6 + 5y = 11$$
$$5y = 5$$
$$y = 1$$

If $y = 1$, then $x = 2 + 1 = 3$.

Another way to solve for x and y is to solve the two equations simultaneously. The purpose is to eliminate one of the unknowns. This can be done by making the coefficients of one of the unknowns the same (disregarding the sign) in both equations and either adding the equations or subtracting one equation from the other. For example, to solve the equations below simultaneously

$$(1) \quad 6x + 5y = 29$$
$$(2) \quad 4x - 3y = -6$$

multiply equation (1) by 3 and equation (2) by 5 to get

$$18x + 15y = 87$$
$$20x - 15y = -30$$

By adding the two equations you can eliminate y and get $38x = 57$ or $x = \frac{3}{2}$. Then substitute $\frac{3}{2}$ for x in one of the equations to find $y = 4$. These answers can be checked by substituting both values into both of the original equations.

5. SOLVING FACTORABLE QUADRATIC EQUATIONS

An equation that can be put in the standard form

$$ax^2 + bx + c = 0,$$

where a, b, and c are real numbers and $a \neq 0$, is a *quadratic* equation. For example,

$$x^2 + 6x + 5 = 0,$$

$$x^2 - 2x = 0,$$

and

$$x^2 - 4 = 5$$

are quadratic equations. Some quadratic equations can be solved by factoring. For example:

(1) $x^2 + 6x + 5 = 0$

$(x + 5)(x + 1) = 0$

$x + 5 = 0$ or $x + 1 = 0$

$x = -5$ or $x = -1$

(2) $x^2 - 2x = 0$

$x(x - 2) = 0$

$x = 0$ or $x = 2$

(3) $3x^2 - 3 = 8x$

$3x^2 - 8x - 3 = 0$

$(3x + 1)(x - 3) = 0$

$3x + 1 = 0$ or $x - 3 = 0$

$x = \frac{1}{3}$ or $x = 3$

In general, first put the quadratic equation into the standard form $ax^2 + bx + c = 0$, then factor the left-hand side of the equation, i.e., find two linear expressions whose product is the given quadratic expression. Since the product of the factors is equal to zero, at least one of the factors must be equal to zero. The values found by setting the factors equal to zero are called the *roots* of the equation. These roots can be checked by substituting them into the original equation to determine whether they satisfy the equation.

A quadratic equation has at most two real roots and may have just one or even no real root. For example, the equation $x^2 - 6x + 9 = 0$ can be expressed as $(x - 3)^2 = 0$ or $(x - 3)(x - 3) = 0$; thus the only root is 3.

The equation $x^2 + 1 = 0$ has no real root. Since the square of any real number is greater than or equal to zero, $x^2 + 1$ must be greater than zero.

An expression in the form $a^2 - b^2$ is equal to

$$(a - b)(a + b).$$

For example, if

$$9x^2 - 25 = 0,$$

then

$$(3x - 5)(3x + 5) = 0;$$

$$3x - 5 = 0 \text{ or } 3x + 5 = 0$$

$$x = \frac{5}{3} \text{ or } x = -\frac{5}{3}.$$

Therefore, the roots are $\frac{5}{3}$ and $-\frac{5}{3}$.

6. EXPONENTS

A positive integer exponent on a number indicates the number of times that number is to be a factor in the product. For example, x^5 means $x \cdot x \cdot x \cdot x \cdot x$; i.e., x is a factor in the product 5 times.

Some rules about exponents are:

Let r, s, x, and y be positive integers.

(1) $(x^r)(x^s) = x^{(r+s)}$; for example $2^2 \cdot 2^3 = 2^{(2+3)} = 2^5 = 32$.

(2) $(x^r)(y^r) = (xy)^r$; for example, $3^3 \cdot 4^3 = 12^3 = 1{,}728$.

(3) $\left(\dfrac{x}{y}\right)^r = \dfrac{x^r}{y^r}$; for example, $\left(\dfrac{2}{3}\right)^3 = \dfrac{2^3}{3^3} = \dfrac{8}{27}$.

(4) $\dfrac{x^r}{y^s} = x^{r-s}$; for example, $\dfrac{4^5}{4^2} = 4^{5-2} = 4^3 = 64$.

(5) $(x^r)^s = x^{rs} = (x^s)^r$; for example, $(x^3)^4 = x^{12} = (x^4)^3$.

(6) $x^{\frac{r}{s}} = \left(x^{\frac{1}{s}}\right)^r = \left(x^r\right)^{\frac{1}{s}} = \sqrt[s]{x^r}$ for example, $x^{\frac{1}{2}} = \sqrt{x}$ and $9^{\frac{1}{2}} = \sqrt{9} = 3$.

(7) $x^{-r} = \dfrac{1}{x^r}$; for example, $3^{-2} = \dfrac{1}{3^2} = \dfrac{1}{9}$.

(8) $x^0 = 1$; for example $6^0 = 1$; 0^0 is undefined.

The rules above also apply when r, s, x and y are not integers. Furthermore, the rules also apply when the numbers are negative, except for (5) and (6), which hold in some cases but not others.

7. ABSOLUTE VALUE

The absolute value of x, denoted $|x|$, is defined to be x if $x \geq 0$ and $-x$ if $x < 0$. Note that $\sqrt{x^2}$ denotes the non-negative square root of x^2, that is $\sqrt{x^2} = |x|$.

8. INEQUALITIES

An *inequality* is a statement that uses one of the following symbols:

$\neq$ not equal to

$>$ greater than

$\geq$ greater than or equal to

$<$ less than

$\leq$ less than or equal to

Some examples of inequalities are $5x - 3 < 9$, $6x \geq y$, and $\dfrac{1}{2} < \dfrac{3}{4}$. Solving an inequality is similar to solving an equation; the unknown is isolated on one side of the inequality. Like an equation, the same number can be added to or subtracted from both sides of the inequality or both sides of an inequality can be multiplied or divided by a positive number without changing the truth of the inequality. However, multiplying or dividing an inequality by a negative number reverses the order of the inequality. For example, $6 > 2$, but $(-1)(6) < (-1)(2)$.

To solve the inequality $3x - 2 > 5$ for x, isolate x by using the following steps:

$$3x - 2 > 5$$
$$3x \;\;\; > 7 \text{ (adding 2 to both sides)}$$
$$x > \frac{7}{3} \text{ (dividing both sides by 3)}$$

To solve the inequality $\frac{5x - 1}{-2} < 3$ for x, isolate x by using the following steps:

$$\frac{5x - 1}{-2} < 3$$

$$5x - 1 > -6 \text{ (multiplying both sides by } -2)$$

$$5x > -5 \text{ (adding 1 to both sides)}$$

$$x > -1 \text{ (dividing both sides by 5)}$$

C. Geometry

1. LINES

In geometry, the word "line" refers to a straight line.

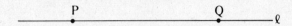

The line above can be referred to as line PQ or line ℓ. The part of the line from P to Q is called a *line segment*. P and Q are the *endpoints* of the segment. The notation PQ is used to denote both the segment and the length of the segment. The intention of the notation can be determined from the context.

2. INTERSECTING LINES AND ANGLES

If two lines intersect, the opposite angles are verticle angles and have the same measure. In the figure

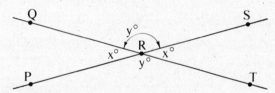

∠PRQ and ∠SRT are vertical angles and ∠QRS and ∠PRT are vertical angles.

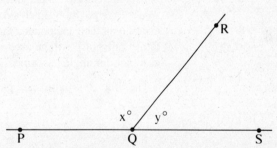

In the figure above, PQS is a straight line, or straight angle, and x + y = 180. ∠PQR and ∠RQS are adjacent angles since they share a common side.

An angle that has a measure of 90° is a *right* angle.

Two angles whose measures sum to 90° are *complementary* angles, and two angles whose measures sum to 180° are *supplementary* angles.

3. PERPENDICULAR LINES

If two lines intersect at right angles, the lines are *perpendicular*. For example:

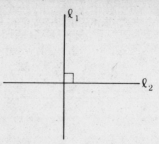

ℓ_1 and ℓ_2 are perpendicular, denoted by $\ell_1 \perp \ell_2$. A right angle symbol in an angle of intersection indicates that the lines are perpendicular.

4. PARALLEL LINES

If two lines that are in the same plane do not intersect, the two lines are *parallel*. In the figure

lines ℓ_1 and ℓ_2 are parallel, denoted by $\ell_1 \parallel \ell_2$. If two parallel lines are intersected by a third line, as shown below, the angle measures are related in the following ways, where $x + y = 180$.

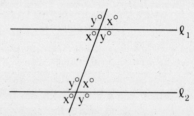

5. POLYGONS (CONVEX)

A *polygon* is a closed plane figure formed by three or more line segments, called the *sides* of the polygon. Each side intersects exactly two other sides at their endpoints and only at their endpoints. The points of intersection of the sides are *vertices*. The term "polygon" will be used to mean a convex polygon, i.e., a polygon in which each interior angle has a measure of less than 180°.

The following figures are polygons:

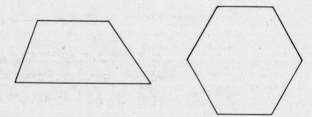

The following figures are not polygons:

-28-

A polygon with three sides is a *triangle;* with four sides, a *quadrilateral;* with five sides, a *pentagon;* and with six sides, a *hexagon.*

The sum of the angle measures of a triangle is 180°. In general, the sum of the angle measures of a polygon with n sides is equal to (n − 2)180°. For example, a pentagon has (5 − 2)180 = (3)180 = 540 degrees.

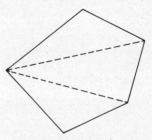

Note that a pentagon can be partitioned into three triangles and therefore the sum of the angle measures can be found by adding the sum of the angle measures of three triangles.

The *perimeter* of a polygon is the sum of the lengths of its sides.

The commonly used phrase ''area of a polygon (or any other plane figure)'' will be used to mean the area of the region enclosed by that figure.

6. TRIANGLES

An *equilateral* triangle has all sides of equal length. All angles of an equilateral triangle have equal measure. An *isosceles* triangle has at least two sides of the same length. If two sides of a triangle have the same length, then the two angles opposite those sides have the same measure. Conversely, if two angles of a triangle have the same measure, then the sides opposite those angles have the same length. In isosceles triangle PQR,

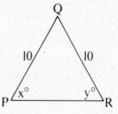

x = y since PQ = QR.

A triangle that has a right angle is a *right* triangle. In a right triangle, the side opposite the right angle is the *hypotenuse,* and the other two sides are the *legs.* An important theorem concerning right triangles is the *Pythagorean theorem,* which states: In a right triangle, the square of the length of the hypotenuse is equal to the sum of the squares of the lengths of the legs.

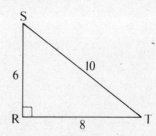

In right $\triangle RST$, $(RS)^2 + (RT)^2 = (ST)^2$. For example, if $RS = 6$ and $RT = 8$, then $ST = 10$, since $6^2 + 8^2 = 36 + 64 = 100 = (ST)^2$ and $ST = \sqrt{100}$. Any triangle in which the lengths of the sides are in the ratio 3:4:5 is a right triangle. In general, if a, b, and c are the lengths of the sides of a triangle and $a^2 + b^2 = c^2$, then the triangle is a right triangle.

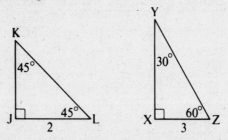

In 45°-45°-90° triangles, the lengths of the sides are in the ratio $1:1:\sqrt{2}$. For example, in $\triangle JKL$, if $JL = 2$, then $JK = 2$, and $KL = 2\sqrt{2}$. In 30°-60°-90° triangles, the lengths of the sides are in the ratio $1:\sqrt{3}:2$. For example, in $\triangle XYZ$, if $XZ = 3$, then $XY = 3\sqrt{3}$, and $YZ = 6$.

Area. The area of a triangle is equal to:
$$\frac{\text{(the length of the altitude)} \times \text{(the length of the base)}}{2}$$

The *altitude* of a triangle is the segment drawn from a vertex perpendicular to the side opposite that vertex. Relative to that vertex and altitude, the opposite side is called the *base*.

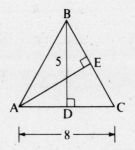

In $\triangle ABC$, BD is the altitude to base AC and AE is the altitude to base BC. The area of $\triangle ABC$ is equal to

$$\frac{BD \times AC}{2} = \frac{5 \times 8}{2} = 20.$$

The area is also equal to $\frac{AE \times BC}{2}$. If $\triangle ABC$ above is isosceles and $AB = BC$, then altitude BD bisects the base; i.e., $AD = DC = 4$. Similarly, any altitude of an equilateral triangle bisects the side to which it is drawn.

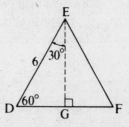

In equilateral triangle DEF, if $DE = 6$, then $DG = 3$, and $EG = 3\sqrt{3}$. The area of $\triangle DEF$ is equal to $\frac{3\sqrt{3} \times 6}{2} = 9\sqrt{3}$.

7. QUADRILATERALS

A polygon with four sides is a *quadrilateral.* A quadrilateral in which both pairs of opposite sides are parallel is a *parallelogram.* The opposite sides of a parallelogram also have equal length.

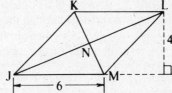

In parallelogram JKLM, JK ∥ LM and JK = LM; KL ∥ JM and KL = JM.

The diagonals of a parallelogram bisect each other (i.e., KN = NM and JN = NL).

The area of a parallelogram is equal to

(the length of the altitude) × (the length of the base).

The area of JKLM is equal to 4 × 6 = 24.

A parallelogram with right angles is a *rectangle,* and a rectangle with all sides of equal length is a *square.*

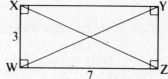

The perimeter of WXYZ = 2(3) + 2(7) = 20 and the area of WXYZ is equal to 3 × 7 = 21. The diagonals of a rectangle are equal; therefore WY = XZ = $\sqrt{9 + 49}$ = $\sqrt{58}$.

Note that a quadrilateral can have two right angles and not be a rectangle. For example, the figures

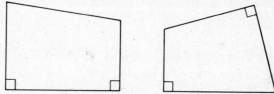

are not rectangles. But, if a quadrilateral has at least three right angles, then it must be a rectangle.

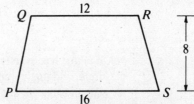

A quadrilateral with two sides that are parallel, as shown above, is a *trapezoid.* The area of trapezoid PQRS may be calculated as follows:

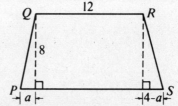

$$\text{Area} = 12 \times 8 + \frac{1}{2}(8a) + \frac{1}{2}(8)(4 - a) = 96 + 16 = 112$$

The area of the trapezoid is also equal to

$$\frac{1}{2}(\text{sum of bases})(\text{height}) = \frac{1}{2}(QR + PS)(8) = \frac{1}{2}(28 \times 8) = 112.$$

8. CIRCLES

A *circle* is a set of points in a plane that are all located the same distance from a fixed point (the *center* of the circle).

A *chord* of a circle is a line segment that has its endpoints on the circle. A chord that passes through the center of the circle is a *diameter* of the circle. A *radius* of a circle is a segment from the center of the circle to a point on the circle. The words "diameter" and "radius" are also used to refer to the lengths of these segments.

The *circumference* of a circle is the distance around the circle. If r is the radius of the circle, then the circumference is equal to $2\pi r$, where π is approximately $\frac{22}{7}$ or 3.14. The area of a circle of radius r is equal to πr^2.

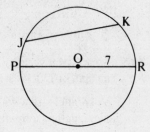

In the circle above, O is the center of the circle and JK and PR are chords. PR is a diameter and OR is a radius. If OR = 7, then the circumference of the circle is $2\pi(7) = 14\pi$ and the area of the circle is $\pi(7)^2 = 49\pi$.

The number of degrees of arc in a circle (or the number of degrees in a complete revolution) is 360.

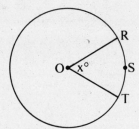

In the circle with center O above, the length of arc RST is $\frac{x}{360}$ of the circumference of the circle; e.g., if x = 60, arc RST has length $\frac{1}{6}$ of the circumference of the circle.

A line that has exactly one point in common with the circle is said to be *tangent* to the circle, and that common point is called the *point of tangency*. A radius or diameter with an endpoint at the point of tangency is perpendicular to the tangent line, and, conversely, a line that is perpendicular to a diameter at one of its endpoints is tangent to the circle at that endpoint.

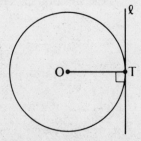

The line ℓ above is tangent to the circle and radius OT is perpendicular to ℓ.

Two different circles that have the same center, as shown below, are *concentric* circles.

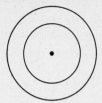

If each vertex of a polygon lies on a circle, then the polygon is *inscribed* in the circle and the circle is *circumscribed* about the polygon. If each side of a polygon is tangent to a circle, then the polygon is *circumscribed* about the circle and the circle is *inscribed* in the polygon.

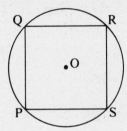 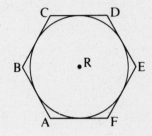

Quadrilateral PQRS is inscribed in circle O and hexagon ABCDEF is circumscribed about circle R.

If a triangle is inscribed in a circle so that one of its sides is a diameter of the circle, then the triangle is a right triangle.

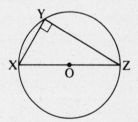

In the circle above, XZ is a diameter and the measure of $\angle XYZ = 90°$.

9. SOLIDS

The following are examples of three-dimensional figures called *solids:*

Rectangular   Cylinder   Pyramid   Sphere   Cone
Solid

10. RECTANGULAR SOLIDS

The *rectangular solid* shown above is formed by six rectangular surfaces. Each rectangular surface is a *face.* Each solid or dotted line segment is an *edge,* and each point at which the edges meet is a *vertex.* A rectangular solid has six faces, twelve edges, and eight vertices. Opposite faces are parallel rectangles that have the same dimensions. A rectangular solid in which all edges are of equal length in a *cube.*

The *surface area* of a rectangular solid is equal to the sum of the areas of all the faces. The *volume* is equal to

$$(\text{length}) \times (\text{width}) \times (\text{height});$$
in other words, $(\text{area of base}) \times (\text{height})$.

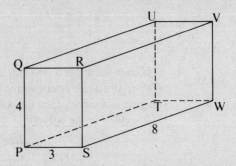

In the rectangular solid above, the dimensions are 3, 4, and 8. The surface area is equal to $2(3 \times 4) + 2(3 \times 8) + 2(4 \times 8) = 136$. The volume is equal to $3 \times 4 \times 8 = 96$.

11. CYLINDERS

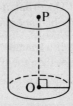

The figure above is a right circular *cylinder*. The two bases are circles of the same size with centers O and P, respectively, and altitude (height) OP is perpendicular to the bases. The surface area of a right circular cylinder with a base of radius r and height h is equal to $2(\pi r^2) + 2\pi rh$ (the sum of the areas of the two bases plus the area of the curved surface).

The volume of a cylinder is equal to $\pi r^2 h$, i.e.:

$$(\text{area of base}) \times (\text{height}).$$

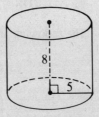

In the cylinder above, the surface area is equal to

$$2(25\pi) + 2\pi(5)(8) = 130\pi,$$

and the volume is equal to

$$25\pi(8) = 200\pi.$$

12. PYRAMIDS

Another solid with plane surfaces as faces is a *pyramid*. One of the faces (called the base) can be a polygon with any number of edges; the remaining faces are triangles. The figures below are pyramids. The shaded faces are the bases.

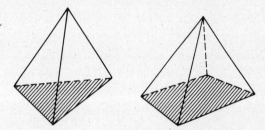

In the pyramid below, PQRS is a square, and the four triangles are the same size. V, the lower endpoint of altitude TV, is the center of the square.

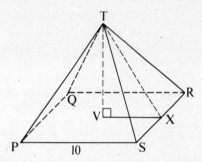

If altitude TV = 12 and VX = $\frac{1}{2}$ PS = 5, then, by the Pythagorean theorem,

TX = $\sqrt{5^2 + 12^2}$ = 13. Since TX = 13, and SX = $\frac{1}{2}$ RS = 5, therefore

TS = $\sqrt{13^2 + 5^2}$ = $\sqrt{194}$.

13. COORDINATE GEOMETRY

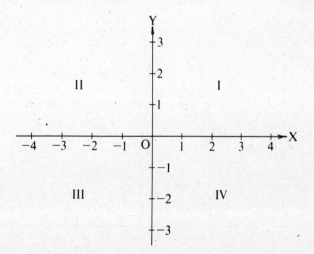

The figure above shows the (rectangular) *coordinate plane*. The horizontal line is called the *x-axis* and the perpendicular vertical line is called the *y-axis*. The point at which these two axes intersect, designated O, is called the *origin*. The axes divide the plane into four quadrants, I, II, III, and IV, as shown.

Each point in the plane has an *x-coordinate* and a *y-coordinate*. A point is identified by an ordered pair (x,y) of numbers in which the x-coordinate is the first number and the y-coordinate is the second number.

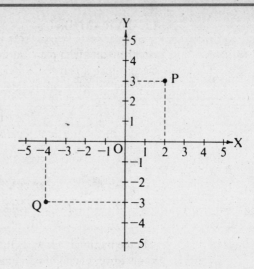

In the graph above, the (x,y) coordinates of point P are (2,3) since P is 2 units to the right of the y-axis (i.e., x = 2) and 3 units above the x-axis (i.e., y = 3). Similarly, the (x,y) coordinates of point Q are (−4, −3). The origin O has coordinates (0,0).

One way to find the distance between two points in the coordinate plane is to use the Pythagorean theorem.

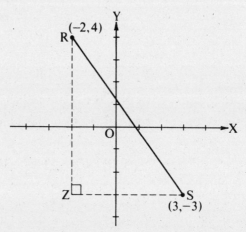

To find the distance between points R and S using the Pythagorean theorem, draw in the triangle as shown. Note that Z has (x,y) coordinates (−2, −3), RZ = 7, and ZS = 5. Therefore, the distance between R and S is equal to:

$$\sqrt{7^2 + 5^2} = \sqrt{74}.$$

D. Word Problems

Many of the principles discussed in this chapter are used to solve word problems. The following discussion of word problems illustrates some of the techniques and concepts used in solving such problems.

1. RATE PROBLEMS

The distance that an object travels is equal to the product of the average speed at which it travels and the amount of time it takes to travel that distance; i.e.,

$$\text{Rate} \times \text{Time} = \text{Distance}$$

Example 1: If a car travels at an average speed of 70 kilometers per hour for 4 hours, how many kilometers does it travel?

Solution: Since rate × time = distance, simply multiply 70 km/hour × 4 hours. Thus, the car travels 280 kilometers in 4 hours.

To determine the average rate at which an object travels, divide the total distance traveled by the total amount of time.

Example 2: On a 400-mile trip car X traveled half the distance at 40 miles per hour and the other half at 50 miles per hour. What was the average speed of car X?

Solution: First it is necessary to determine the amount of traveling time. During the first 200 miles the car traveled at 40 mph; therefore, it took $\frac{200}{40} = 5$ hours to travel the first 200 miles. During the second 200 miles the car traveled at 50 mph; therefore, it took $\frac{200}{50} = 4$ hours to travel the second 200 miles. Thus, the average speed of car X was $\frac{400}{9} = 44\frac{4}{9}$ mph. Note that the average speed is *not* $\frac{40 + 50}{2} = 45$.

Some of the problems can be solved by using ratios.

Example 3: If 5 shirts cost $44, then, at this rate, what is the cost of 8 shirts?

Solution: If c is the cost of the 8 shirts, then $\frac{5}{44} = \frac{8}{c}$. Cross multiplication results in the equation

$$5c = 8 \times 44 = 352$$
$$c = \frac{352}{5} = 70.40$$

The 8 shirts cost $70.40.

2. WORK PROBLEMS

In a work problem, the rates at which certain persons or machines work alone are usually given, and it is necessary to compute the rate at which they work together (or vice versa).

The basic formula for solving work problems is: $\frac{1}{r} + \frac{1}{s} = \frac{1}{h}$, where r and s are, for example, the number of hours it takes Rae and Sam, respectively, to complete a job when working alone and h is the number of hours it takes Rae and Sam to do the job when working together. The reasoning is that in 1 hour Rae does $\frac{1}{r}$ of the job, Sam does $\frac{1}{s}$ of the job, and Rae and Sam together do $\frac{1}{h}$ of the job.

Example 1: If machine X can produce 1,000 bolts in 4 hours and machine Y can produce 1,000 bolts in 5 hours, in how many hours can machines X and Y, working together at these constant rates, produce 1,000 bolts?

Solution: $\quad \frac{1}{4} + \frac{1}{5} = \frac{1}{h}$

$$\frac{5}{10} + \frac{4}{20} = \frac{1}{h}$$

$$\frac{9}{20} = \frac{1}{h}$$

$$9h = 20$$

$$h = \frac{20}{9} = 2\frac{2}{9} \text{ hours}$$

Working together, machines X and Y can produce 1,000 bolts in $2\frac{2}{9}$ hours.

Example 2: If Art and Rita can do a job in 4 hours when working together at their respective rates and Art can do the job alone in 6 hours, in how many hours can Rita do the job alone?

Solution: $\frac{1}{6} + \frac{1}{R} = \frac{1}{4}$

$$\frac{R + 6}{6R} = \frac{1}{4}$$

$$4R + 24 = 6R$$

$$24 = 2R$$

$$12 = R$$

Working alone, Rita can do the job in 12 hours.

3. MIXTURE PROBLEMS

In mixture problems, substances with different characteristics are combined, and it is necessary to determine the characteristics of the resulting mixture.

Example 1: If 6 pounds of nuts that cost $1.20 per pound are mixed with 2 pounds of nuts that cost $1.60 per pound, what is the cost per pound of the mixture?

Solution: The total value of the 8 pounds of nuts is

$$6(\$1.20) + 2(\$1.60) = \$10.40.$$

The price per pound is $\frac{\$10.40}{8} = \$1.30$.

Example 2: How many liters of a solution that is 15 percent salt must be added to 5 liters of a solution that is 8 percent salt so that the resulting solution is 10 percent salt?

Solution: Let n represent the number of liters of the 15% solution. The amount of salt in the 15% solution [0.15n] plus the amount of salt in the 8% solution [(0.08)(5)] must be equal to the amount of salt in the 10% mixture [0.10 (n + 5)]. Therefore,

$$0.15n + 0.08(5) = 0.10 (n + 5)$$
$$15n + 40 = 10n + 50$$
$$5n = 10$$
$$n = 2 \text{ liters}$$

Two liters of the 15% salt solution must be added to the 8% solution to obtain the 10% solution.

4. INTEREST PROBLEMS

Interest can be computed in two basic ways. With simple annual interest, the interest is computed on the principal only. If interest is compounded, then interest is computed on the principal as well as on any interest already earned.

Example 1: If $8,000 is invested at 6 percent simple annual interest, how much interest is earned after 3 months?

Solution: Since the annual interest rate is 6%, the interest for 1 year is

$(0.06) (8,000) = \$480$. The interest earned in 3 months is $\frac{3}{12}(480) = \$120$.

Example 2: If $10,000 is invested at 10 percent annual interest, compounded semian-nually, what is the balance after 1 year?

Solution: The balance after the first 6 months would be
10,000 + (10,000)(0.05) = 10,500. The balance after one year would be
10,500 + (10,500)(0.05) = $11,025.

5. DISCOUNT

If a price is discounted by n percent, then the price becomes (100 − n) percent of the original price.

Example 1: A certain customer paid $24 for a dress. If that price represented a 25 percent discount on the original price of the dress, what was the original price of the dress?

Solution: If p is the original price of the dress, then 0.75p is the discounted price and 0.75p = $24 or p = $32. The original price of the dress was $32.

Example 2: The price of an item is discounted by 20 percent and then this reduced price is discounted by an additional 30 percent. These two discounts are equal to an overall discount of what percent?

Solution: If p is the original price of the item, then 0.8p is the price after the first dis-count. The price after the second discount is (0.7)(0.8)p = 0.56p. This represents an overall discount of 44 percent (100 − 56).

6. PROFIT

Profit is equal to revenues minus expenses, i.e., selling price minus cost.

Example 1: A certain appliance costs a merchant $30. At what price should the mer-chant sell the appliance in order to make a gross profit of 50 percent of the cost of the appliance?

Solution: If s is the selling price of the appliance, then s − 30 = (0.5)(30) or s = $45. The merchant should sell the appliance for $45.

7. SETS

If S is the set of numbers 1, 2, 3, and 4, you can write S = {1,2,3,4}. Sets can also be represented by Venn diagrams. That is, the relationship among the members of sets can be represented by circles.

Example 1: Each of 25 people is enrolled in history, mathematics, or both. If 20 are enrolled in history and 18 are enrolled in mathematics, how many are enrolled in both history and mathematics?

Solution: The 25 people can be divided into three sets: those who study history only, those who study mathematics only, and those who study history and mathematics. Thus a diagram may be drawn as follows where n is the number of people enrolled in both courses, 20-n is the number enrolled in history only, and 18-n is the num-ber enrolled in mathematics only.

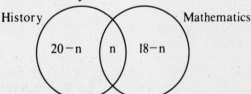

Since there is a total of 25 people, (20 − n) + n + (18 − n) = 25, or n = 13. Thirteen people are enrolled in both history and mathematics. Note that 20 + 18 − 13 = 25.

Example 2: In a certain production lot, 40 percent of the toys are red and the remaining toys are green. Half of the toys are small and half are large. If 10 percent of the toys are red and small, and 40 toys are green and large, how many of the toys are red and large?

Solution: For this kind of problem, it is helpful to organize the information in a table:

	red	green	
small	10%		50%
large			50%
	40%	60%	100%

The numbers in the table are the percents given. The following percents can be computed on the basis of what is given:

	red	green	
small	10%	40%	50%
large	30%	20%	50%
	40%	60%	100%

Since 20% of the number of toys (n) are green and large, $0.20n = 40$ (40 toys are green and large), or $n = 200$. Therefore, 30% of the 200 toys, or $(0.3)(200) = 60$, are red and large.

8. GEOMETRY PROBLEMS

The following is an example of a word problem involving geometry.

Example 1:

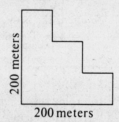

200 meters

200 meters

The figure above shows a piece of land. If all angles shown are right angles, what is the perimeter of the piece of land?

Solution: For reference, label the figure as

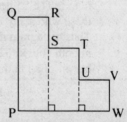

If all the angles are right angles, then QR + ST + UV = PW, and RS + TU + VW = PQ. Hence, the perimeter of the land is $2PW + 2PQ = 2 \times 200 + 2 \times 200 = 800$ meters.

9. MEASUREMENT PROBLEMS

Some questions on the GMAT involve metric units of measure, whereas others involve English units of measure. However, except for units of time, if a question requires conversion from one unit of measure to another, the relationship between those units will be given.

Example 1: A train travels at a constant rate of 25 meters per second. How many kilometers does it travel in 5 minutes? (1 kilometer = 1,000 meters)

Solution: In 1 minute the train travels $(25)\cdot(60) = 1,500$ meters, so in 5 minutes it travels 7,500 meters. Since 1 kilometer = 1,000 meters, 7,500 meters equals $\frac{7,500}{1,000}$ or 7.5 kilometers.

10. DATA INTERPRETATION

Occasionally a question or set of questions will be based on data provided in a table or graph. Some examples of tables and graphs are given below.

Example 1:

UNITED STATES POPULATION—BY AGE GROUP
(in thousands)

Age	Population
17 years and under	63,376
18-44 years	86,738
45-64 years	43,845
65 years and over	24,054

How many people are 44 years old or younger?

Solution: The figures in the table are given in thousands. The answer in thousands can be obtained by adding 63,376 thousand and 86,738 thousand. The result is 150,114 thousand, which is 150,114,000.

Example 2:

AVERAGE TEMPERATURE AND PRECIPITATION IN CITY X

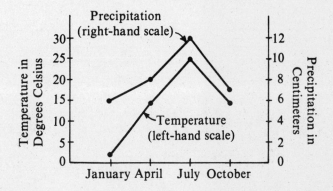

What is the average temperature and precipitation in city X during April?

Solution: Note that the scale on the left applies to the temperature line graph and the one on the right applies to the precipitation line graph.

Reading the graph, during April the average temperature is approximately 14° Celsius and the average precipitation is 8 centimeters.

Example 3:

DISTRIBUTION OF AL'S WEEKLY NET SALARY

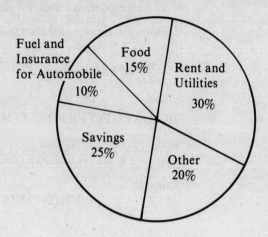

Weekly Net Salary = $350

To how many of the categories listed was at least $80 of Al's weekly net salary allocated?

Solution: In the circle graph the relative sizes of the sectors are proportional to their corresponding values and the sum of the percents given is 100%. $\frac{80}{350}$ is approximately 23%, so at least $80 was allocated to each of 2 categories—Rent and Utilities, and Savings—since their allocations are each greater than 23%.

3 Problem Solving

In these questions you are to solve each problem and select the best of the five answer choices given. The mathematics required to answer the questions does not extend beyond that assumed to be common to the mathematics background of all examinees.

The following pages include test-taking strategies, a sample test (with an answer key), and detailed explanations of every problem on the sample test. These explanations present possible problem-solving strategies for the problems. At the end of each explanation is a reference to the particular section(s) of Chapter 2, Math Review, that you may find helpful in reviewing the mathematical concepts on which the problem is based.

Test-Taking Strategies for Problem Solving

1. Pacing yourself is very important. Take a watch with you and consult it from time to time. Work as carefully as possible, but do not spend valuable time checking answers or pondering over problems that you find difficult. Make a check mark in your test book next to the troublesome problems or those problems you feel you should double-check. When you have completed the section, go back and spend the remaining time on those difficult problems. Remember, each question has the same weight.

2. Space is available in the test book for scratchwork. Working a problem out in writing may help you avoid errors in solving the problem. If diagrams or figures are not presented, it may help if you draw your own.

3. Read each question carefully to determine what information is given and what is being asked. For word problems, take one step at a time, reading each sentence carefully and translating the information into equations.

4. Before attempting to answer a question, scan the answer choices; otherwise you may waste time putting answers in a form that is not given (for example, putting an answer in the form $\frac{\sqrt{2}}{2}$ when the options are given in the form $\frac{1}{\sqrt{2}}$

or finding the answer in decimal form, such as 0.25,

when the choices are given in fractional form, such as $\frac{1}{4}$).

5. For questions that require approximations, scan the options to get some idea of the required closeness of approximation; otherwise, you may waste time on long computations where a short mental process would serve as well (for example, taking 48 percent of a number instead of half the number).

6. If you cannot solve a problem but you can eliminate some of the options as being unlikely, you should guess. If the options are equally plausible, you should not guess. Remember, a percentage of the wrong answers will be subtracted from the number of right answers to compensate for guessing, but the number of omitted questions will not be substracted.

When you take the sample test, use the answer spaces on page 45 to mark your answers.

Answer Spaces for Problem Solving Sample Test

-45-

1 Ⓐ Ⓑ Ⓒ Ⓓ Ⓔ	6 Ⓐ Ⓑ Ⓒ Ⓓ Ⓔ	11 Ⓐ Ⓑ Ⓒ Ⓓ Ⓔ	16 Ⓐ Ⓑ Ⓒ Ⓓ Ⓔ	21 Ⓐ Ⓑ Ⓒ Ⓓ Ⓔ
2 Ⓐ Ⓑ Ⓒ Ⓓ Ⓔ	7 Ⓐ Ⓑ Ⓒ Ⓓ Ⓔ	12 Ⓐ Ⓑ Ⓒ Ⓓ Ⓔ	17 Ⓐ Ⓑ Ⓒ Ⓓ Ⓔ	22 Ⓐ Ⓑ Ⓒ Ⓓ Ⓔ
3 Ⓐ Ⓑ Ⓒ Ⓓ Ⓔ	8 Ⓐ Ⓑ Ⓒ Ⓓ Ⓔ	13 Ⓐ Ⓑ Ⓒ Ⓓ Ⓔ	18 Ⓐ Ⓑ Ⓒ Ⓓ Ⓔ	23 Ⓐ Ⓑ Ⓒ Ⓓ Ⓔ
4 Ⓐ Ⓑ Ⓒ Ⓓ Ⓔ	9 Ⓐ Ⓑ Ⓒ Ⓓ Ⓔ	14 Ⓐ Ⓑ Ⓒ Ⓓ Ⓔ	19 Ⓐ Ⓑ Ⓒ Ⓓ Ⓔ	24 Ⓐ Ⓑ Ⓒ Ⓓ Ⓔ
5 Ⓐ Ⓑ Ⓒ Ⓓ Ⓔ	10 Ⓐ Ⓑ Ⓒ Ⓓ Ⓔ	15 Ⓐ Ⓑ Ⓒ Ⓓ Ⓔ	20 Ⓐ Ⓑ Ⓒ Ⓓ Ⓔ	25 Ⓐ Ⓑ Ⓒ Ⓓ Ⓔ

5
15
25

$4x + 30 = 42$

$4x = 12 \quad \rightarrow x = 3$

$\frac{1}{4} \times 80 \%$

20

PROBLEM SOLVING SAMPLE TEST

25 Questions

Directions: In this section solve each problem, using any available space on the page for scratchwork. Then indicate the best of the answer choices given.

Numbers: All numbers used are real numbers.

Figures: Figures that accompany problems in this test are intended to provide information useful in solving the problems. They are drawn as accurately as possible EXCEPT when it is stated in a specific problem that its figure is not drawn to scale. All figures lie in a plane unless otherwise indicated.

1. A certain type of concrete mixture is to be made of cement, sand, and gravel in a ratio $1:3:5$ by weight. What is the greatest number of kilograms of this mixture that can be made with 5 kilograms of cement?

   (A) $13\frac{1}{3}$ (B) 15   (C) 25   (D) 40   (E) 45

2. On the line segment RS above are 5 equally spaced dark segments, each with length 6. If x is the distance between dark segments and the length of RS is 42, then $x =$

   (A) 2   (B) 3   (C) 6   (D) 12   (E) 30

3. Audrey went shopping with D dollars. She spent 20 per cent of her money on a blouse and 25 per cent of what was left on a pair of shoes. What per cent of the original D dollars did she spend?

   (A) 25%   (B) 40%   (C) 45%
   (D) 47%   (E) 50%

```
     7 3 4
     5 ■ 8
  +  9 ■ 2
  ---------
   2,2 ■ 4
```

4. In the addition problem above, the number ■ must be

   (A) 5   (B) 6   (C) 7   (D) 8   (E) 9

5. If $x < 0$, which of the following is NOT necessarily true?

   (A) $x^2 + x^3 < 0$ (B) $x^5 < x^2$ (C) $x^2 > 0$

   (D) $\frac{1}{x} < 0$ (E) $\frac{1}{x^2} > 0$

GO ON TO THE NEXT PAGE.

6. There are 4 card-processing machines in an office. The fastest of these machines processes x cards in 7 hours and the slowest processes x cards in 8 hours. Which of the following could NOT be the average time per machine for each of the 4 machines to process x cards?

(A) 7.2   (B) 7.3   (C) 7.5   (D) 7.6   (E) 7.7

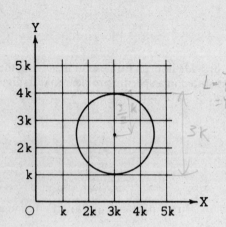

7. If the area of the circle above is 64π, what is the value of k ?

(A) 2   (B) $\frac{8}{3}$ (C) 4   (D) $\frac{16}{3}$ (E) 12

8. If $P = \frac{S}{1 + nr}$ and P, S, n, and r are positive numbers, then in terms of P, S, and r what does n equal?

(A) $\frac{S - P}{Pr}$ (B) $\frac{S}{rP} - 1$ (C) $\frac{S - P}{r}$

(D) $\frac{S}{P} - r$ (E) $\frac{Pr}{S} - 1$

9. Both the length and width of a certain rectangle are even numbers, and the length is three times the width. Each of the following could be the perimeter of such a rectangle EXCEPT

(A) 32   (B) 64   (C) 120   (D) 160   (E) 192

10. A, B, and C each drove 100-mile legs of a 300-mile course at speeds of 40, 50, and 60 miles per hour, respectively. What fraction of the total time did A drive?

(A) $\frac{15}{74}$ (B) $\frac{4}{15}$ (C) $\frac{15}{37}$ (D) $\frac{3}{5}$ (E) $\frac{5}{4}$

11. An even number x divided by 7 gives some quotient plus a remainder of 6. Which of the following, when added to x, gives a sum which must be divisible by 14 ?

(A) 1   (B) 3   (C) 7   (D) 8   (E) 13

12. If x is a real number such that $\frac{4}{3}x^4 = \frac{27}{4}$, then x is

(A) $\frac{9}{4}$ (B) $\frac{3}{2}$ (C) $\frac{9}{4}$ or $-\frac{9}{4}$

(D) $\sqrt{3}$ or $-\sqrt{3}$ (E) $\frac{3}{2}$ or $-\frac{3}{2}$

13. If x is the product of three consecutive positive integers, which of the following must be true?

   I. x is an integer multiple of 3.
   II. x is an integer multiple of 4.
   III. x is an integer multiple of 6.

(A) I only   (B) II only   (C) I and II only
(D) I and III only   (E) I, II, and III

GO ON TO THE NEXT PAGE.

14. In a student body the ratio of men to women was 1 to 4. After 140 additional men were admitted, the ratio of men to women became 2 to 3. How large was the student body after the additional men were admitted?

(A) 700   (B) 560   (C) 280   (D) 252   (E) 224

15. The number of diagonals of a polygon of n sides is given by the formula $d = \frac{1}{2}n(n - 3)$. If a polygon has twice as many diagonals as sides, how many sides does it have?

(A) 3   (B) 5   (C) 6   (D) 7   (E) 8

16. If a taxi driver charges x cents for the first quarter-mile of a trip and $\frac{x}{5}$ cents for each additional quarter-mile, what is the charge, in cents, for a trip whose distance in miles is the whole number y ?

(A) $\frac{x + xy}{125}$

(B) $\frac{4x + 4xy}{5}$

(C) $\frac{4x + xy}{500}$

(D) $\frac{4x + xy}{5}$

(E) $\frac{xy}{25}$

17. In order to give his customers a 25 per cent discount on the price and still net a 25 per cent profit on the cost of an item, at what price should a merchant mark an item if it cost him $16.80 ?

(A) $21.00   (B) $21.90   (C) $25.20
(D) $26.25   (E) $28.00

18. Of the following, which best approximates $\frac{(0.1667)(0.8333)(0.3333)}{(0.2222)(0.6667)(0.1250)}$?

(A) 2.00   (B) 2.40   (C) 2.43
(D) 2.50   (E) 3.43

19. When an object is dropped, the number of feet N that it falls is given by the formula $N = \frac{1}{2}gt^2$, where t is the time in seconds since it was dropped and g is 32.2. If it takes 5 seconds for the object to reach the ground, how many feet does it fall during the last 2 seconds?

(A) 64.4   (B) 96.6   (C) 161.0
(D) 257.6   (E) 402.5

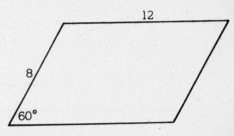

20. In the figure above, the area of the parallelogram is

(A) 40   (B) $24\sqrt{3}$ (C) 72
(D) $48\sqrt{3}$ (E) 96

GO ON TO THE NEXT PAGE.

21. A man drove his automobile d_1 kilometers at the rate of r_1 kilometers per hour and an additional d_2 kilometers at the rate of r_2 kilometers per hour. In terms of d_1, d_2, r_1, and r_2, what was his average speed, in kilometers per hour, for the entire trip?

(A) $\dfrac{d_1 + d_2}{\dfrac{d_1}{r_1} + \dfrac{d_2}{r_2}}$

(B) $\dfrac{d_1 + d_2}{r_1 + r_2}$

(C) $\dfrac{\dfrac{d_1 + d_2}{r_1 + r_2}}{d_1 + d_2}$

(D) $\dfrac{\dfrac{d_1}{r_1} + \dfrac{d_2}{r_2}}{d_1 + d_2}$

(E) It cannot be determined from the information given.

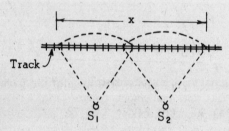

22. In the figure above, two searchlights S_1 and S_2 are located 10,000 feet apart; each covers an area of radius 10,000 feet, and each is located 8,000 feet from the railroad track. To the nearest 1,000 feet, what is the total length x of track spanned by the searchlights?

(A) 24,000   (B) 22,000   (C) 20,000

(D) 16,000   (E) 12,000

23. A boy walking along a road at 3 kilometers per hour is overtaken by a truck traveling at 40 kilometers per hour. If the truck breaks down 1 kilometer beyond where it passes the boy, how many minutes after the breakdown does the boy reach the truck?

(A) $21\frac{1}{2}$ (B) 20   (C) $18\frac{34}{37}$

(D) $18\frac{26}{43}$ (E) $18\frac{1}{2}$

24. In the figure above, the square region is divided into four nonoverlapping triangular regions. If the area of the square region is 4, what is the sum of the perimeters of the four triangular regions?

(A) 8
(B) $8 + 4\sqrt{2}$
(C) 16
(D) $8 + 8\sqrt{2}$
(E) $16\sqrt{2}$

25. How many three-digit numerals begin with a digit that represents a prime number and end with a digit that represents a prime number?

(A) 16   (B) 80   (C) 160   (D) 180   (E) 240

END OF SAMPLE TEST

Answer Key for Sample Test

PROBLEM SOLVING

1.	E	14.	B
2.	B	15.	D
3.	B	16.	B
4.	B	17.	E
5.	A	18.	D
6.	A	19.	D
7.	D	20.	D
8.	A	21.	A
9.	C	22.	B
10.	C	23.	E
11.	D	24.	D
12.	E	25.	C
13.	D		

Explanatory Material: Problem Solving

The following discussion is intended to familarize you with the most efficient and effective approaches to the kinds of problems common to Problem Solving. The questions on the sample test in this chapter are generally representative of the kinds of problems you will encounter in this section of the GMAT. Remember that it is the problem-solving strategy that is important, not the specific details of a particular problem. Note that each explanation is followed by a reference to the particular section of Chapter 2, Math Review, that explains the mathematical principles on which the question is based.

1. A certain type of concrete mixture is to be made of cement, sand, and gravel in a ratio 1:3:5 by weight. What is the greatest number of kilograms of this mixture that can be made with 5 kilograms of cement?

    (A) $13\frac{1}{3}$
    (B) 15
    (C) 25
    (D) 40
    (E) 45

In the concrete mixture, 3 times as much sand as cement, or 15 kilograms of sand, is needed and 5 times as much gravel as cement, or 25 kilograms of gravel, is needed. The total weight of the mixture with 5 kilograms of cement would be $5 + 15 + 25 = 45$ kilograms. Thus, the best answer is E. This is an easy question. (See Chapter 2, Math Review, Section A.6.)

R ●—6—■—x—●—6—■—x—●—6—■—x—●—6—■—x—●—6—● S

2. On the line segment RS above are 5 equally spaced dark segments, each with length 6. If x is the distance between dark segments and the length of RS is 42, then x =

    (A) 2
    (B) 3
    (C) 6
    (D) 12
    (E) 30

The length of RS is equal to 42, which is equal to $5(6) + 4x$. Thus, $4x = 12$ and x is 3. The best answer is B. This is a very easy question. (See Chapter 2, Math Review, Section B.3.)

3. Audrey went shopping with D dollars. She spent 20 percent of her money on a blouse and 25 percent of what was left on a pair of shoes. What percent of the original D dollars did she spend?

    (A) 25%
    (B) 40%
    (C) 45%
    (D) 47%
    (E) 50%

Audrey spent 0.2D on the blouse and $0.25(1-0.2)D = 0.2D$ on the shoes. The total amount that she spent was 0.4D or 40% of the original D dollars. Thus, the best answer is B. This is an easy question. (See Chapter 2, Math Review, Section A.7 and Section B, introduction.)

$$\begin{array}{r} 7\,3\,4 \\ 5\,\square\,8 \\ +\ 9\,\square\,2 \\ \hline 2{,}2\,\square\,4 \end{array}$$

4. In the addition problem above, the number □ must be

    (A) 5
    (B) 6
    (C) 7
    (D) 8
    (E) 9

Note that a 1 is carried from the units' column to the tens' column and a 1 is also carried from the tens' column to the hundreds' column. Therefore, $4 + \square + \square = 10 + \square$ or $\square = 6$. Thus, the best answer is B. This is an easy question. (See Chapter 2, Math Review, Section A.3.)

5. If x < 0, which of the following is NOT necessarily true?

(A) $x^2 + x^3 < 0$

(B) $x^5 < x^2$

(C) $x^2 > 0$

(D) $\dfrac{1}{x} < 0$

(E) $\dfrac{1}{x^2} > 0$

In this question, the answer must be found by examining the choices. If x < 0, then x raised to an even integer power is positive and x raised to an odd integer power is negative. In A, then, $x^2 > 0$ and $x^3 < 0$; however, if $x = -\dfrac{1}{2}$,

$$x^2 + x^3 = \dfrac{1}{4} - \dfrac{1}{8} > 0.$$

Thus, A is not necessarily true, and the best answer is A. It can be shown as follows that the others must be true, but once you find a correct choice, you do not need to spend time verifying the others. Since $x^5 < 0$ and $x^2 > 0$, $x^5 < x^2$; thus B and C are true. $\dfrac{1}{x}$ is negative since x is negative, and $\dfrac{1}{x^2}$ is positive since x^2 is positive; thus D and E must also be true. This is a moderately difficult question. (See Chapter 2, Math Review, Section A.5, Section A.9, and Section B.6.)

6. There are 4 card-processing machines in an office. The fastest of these machines processes x cards in 7 hours and the slowest processes x cards in 8 hours. Which of the following could NOT be the average time per machine for each of the 4 machines to process x cards?

(A) 7.2

(B) 7.3

(C) 7.5

(D) 7.6

(E) 7.7

The total amount of time for the 4 machines to process x cards each is greater than or equal to $7 + 8 + 2(7) = 29$ (the time it would take if the other 2 machines were as fast as the fastest) and less than or equal to $7 + 8 + 2(8) = 31$ (the time it would take if the other 2 were as slow as the slowest). Therefore, the average time per machine is between $\dfrac{29}{4} = 7.25$ and $\dfrac{31}{4} = 7.75$, inclusive. Since 7.2 is less than 7.25, the average time could not be 7.2; thus, the best answer is A. This is a moderately difficult question. (See Chapter 2, Math Review, Section A.10.)

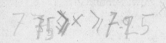

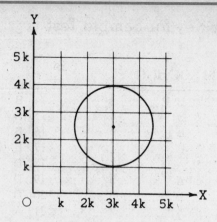

7. If the area of the circle above is 64π, what is the value of k?

(A) 2

(B) $\dfrac{8}{3}$

(C) 4

(D) $\dfrac{16}{3}$

(E) 12

Since the diameter of the circle is $4k - k = 3k$, the radius in terms of k is $\dfrac{3}{2}k$; therefore, the area of the circle is

$$\pi\left(\dfrac{3}{2}k\right)^2 = 64\pi.$$

Solving for k, you get

$$\dfrac{9}{4}k^2 = 64$$

$$k^2 = \dfrac{256}{9}$$

$$k = \dfrac{16}{3}$$

and the best answer is D. This is a moderately difficult question. (See Chapter 2, Math Review, Section C.8.)

8. If $P = \dfrac{S}{1 + nr}$ and P, S, n, and r are positive numbers, then in terms of P, S, and r what does n equal?

(A) $\dfrac{S - P}{Pr}$

(B) $\dfrac{S}{rP} - 1$

(C) $\dfrac{S - P}{r}$

(D) $\dfrac{S}{P} - r$

(E) $\dfrac{Pr}{S} - 1$

To find the value of n in terms of P, S, and r, it is necessary to get n by itself on one side of the equation. The following algebraic manipulations can be done:

$$P(1 + nr) = S \quad \text{(multiplying both sides by } 1 + nr)$$
$$1 + nr = \frac{S}{P} \quad \text{(dividing by P)}$$
$$nr = \frac{S}{P} - 1 = \frac{S - P}{P} \quad \text{(subtracting 1 and getting a common denominator)}$$
$$n = \frac{S - P}{Pr} \quad \text{(dividing by r)}$$

Therefore, the best answer is A. This is a moderately difficult question. (See Chapter 2, Math Review, Section B.3.)

9. Both the length and width of a certain rectangle are even numbers, and the length is three times the width. Each of the following could be the perimeter of such a rectangle EXCEPT

(A) 32
(B) 64
(C) 120
(D) 160
(E) 192

If w is the width of the rectangle and 3w is its length, then the perimeter is 8w. Since w is even, the perimeter divided by 8 must be an even number. Dividing each of the given perimeters by 8, you get an even number for all except C, $\frac{120}{8} = 15$. Thus, the best answer is C. This is a moderately difficult question. (See Chapter 2, Math Review, Section C.7.)

10. A, B, and C each drove 100-mile legs of a 300-mile course at speeds of 40, 50, and 60 miles per hour, respectively. What fraction of the total time did A drive?

(A) $\frac{15}{74}$
(B) $\frac{4}{15}$
(C) $\frac{15}{37}$
(D) $\frac{3}{5}$
(E) $\frac{5}{4}$

The amount of time that A, B, and C each drove is $\frac{100}{40} = \frac{5}{2}$ hours, $\frac{100}{50} = 2$ hours, and $\frac{100}{60} = \frac{5}{3}$ hours, respectively. A drove $\dfrac{\frac{5}{2}}{\frac{5}{2} + 2 + \frac{5}{3}}$ of the total time.

$$\frac{\frac{5}{2}}{\frac{5}{2} + 2 + \frac{5}{3}} = \frac{\frac{5}{2}}{\frac{15 + 12 + 10}{6}} = \frac{5 \cdot 6}{2(37)} = \frac{15}{37}$$

Thus, the best answer is C. This is a moderately difficult question. (See Chapter 2, Math Review, Section D.1.)

11. An even number x divided by 7 gives some quotient plus a remainder of 6. Which of the following, when added to x, gives a sum which must be divisible by 14?

(A) 1
(B) 3
(C) 7
(D) 8
(E) 13

The number x can be expressed by $x = 7q + 6$, where q is an integer. If the sum of x and another number is to be divisible by 14, then the sum must be even and the number added to x must also be even. The only even number given in the choices is 8. It can be shown as follows that $x + 8$ is divisible by 7.
$$x + 8 = 7q + 6 + 8$$
$$= 7q + 14$$
$$= 7(q + 2)$$

Thus, if $x + 8$ is divisible by 2 and by 7, it is also divisible by 14 and the best answer is D. This is a moderately difficult question. (See Chapter 2, Math Review, Section A.1 and Section B.2.)

12. If x is a real number such that $\frac{4}{3}x^4 = \frac{27}{4}$, then x is

(A) $\frac{9}{4}$
(B) $\frac{3}{2}$
(C) $\frac{9}{4}$ or $-\frac{9}{4}$
(D) $\sqrt{3}$ or $-\sqrt{3}$
(E) $\frac{3}{2}$ or $-\frac{3}{2}$

If $\frac{4}{3}x^4 = \frac{27}{4}$, then $x^4 = \frac{27}{4} \cdot \frac{3}{4} = \frac{81}{16}$. To find the value of x, it is necessary to take the fourth root of $\frac{81}{16}$. This is the number that when raised to the fourth power is equal to $\frac{81}{16}$. Since $\frac{81}{16} = \left(\frac{3}{2}\right)\left(\frac{3}{2}\right)\left(\frac{3}{2}\right)\left(\frac{3}{2}\right) = \left(-\frac{3}{2}\right)\left(-\frac{3}{2}\right)\left(-\frac{3}{2}\right)\left(-\frac{3}{2}\right)$, the fourth roots of $\frac{81}{16}$ are $\frac{3}{2}$ and $-\frac{3}{2}$. Thus, the best answer is E.

13. If x is the product of three consecutive positive integers, which of the following must be true?

I. x is an integer multiple of 3.
II. x is an integer multiple of 4.
III. x is an integer multiple of 6.

(A) I only
(B) II only
(C) I and II only
(D) I and III only
(E) I, II, and III

For any three consecutive positive integers, one of the integers must be divisible by 3 and at least one of the integers must be divisible by 2 (e.g., 1, 2, 3; 9, 10, 11). Therefore, x must be a multiple of 3 and a multiple of 6. If two of the integers are even, then x must be a multiple of 4; however, if two of the integers are odd, x is not necessarily a multiple of 4. Therefore, the best answer is D. This is a moderately difficult question. (See Chapter 2, Math Review, Section A.1.)

14. In a student body the ratio of men to women was 1 to 4. After 140 additional men were admitted, the ratio of men to women became 2 to 3. How large was the student body after the additional men were admitted?

   (A) 700
   (B) 560
   (C) 280
   (D) 252
   (E) 224

Let m equal the original number of men; then 4m is the number of women. After 140 additional men are admitted, the ratio is 2:3, i.e., $\frac{m + 140}{4m} = \frac{2}{3}$. Cross multiplication results in the equation

$$3m + 420 = 8m$$
$$5m = 420$$
$$m = 84$$

The total number of students after the additional men were admitted is m + 140 + 4m = 84 + 140 + 4(84) = 560, and the best answer is B. This is a difficult question. (See Chapter 2, Math Review, Section A.6 and Section B.3.)

15. The number of diagonals of a polygon of n sides is given by the formula d = $\frac{1}{2}$n(n − 3). If a polygon has twice as many diagonals as sides, how many sides does it have?

   (A) 3
   (B) 5
   (C) 6
   (D) 7
   (E) 8

You want d to equal 2n or

$$\frac{1}{2}n(n - 3) = 2n$$
$$n^2 - 3n = 4n$$
$$n^2 = 7n$$
$$n = 7 \text{ since } n \neq 0.$$

Thus, the best answer is D. This is a difficult question. (See Chapter 2, Math Review, Section B.2 and Section C.5.)

16. If a taxi driver charges x cents for the first quarter-mile of a trip and $\frac{x}{5}$ cents for each additional quarter-mile, what is the charge, in cents, for a trip whose distance in miles is the whole number y?

   (A) $\frac{x + xy}{125}$

   (B) $\frac{4x + 4xy}{5}$

   (C) $\frac{4x + xy}{500}$

   (D) $\frac{4x + xy}{5}$

   (E) $\frac{xy}{25}$

The total number of quarter-miles in the trip is 4y. The charge for the first quarter-mile is x, and the charge for the remaining (4y − 1) quarter-miles is $(4y - 1)\frac{x}{5}$. The total charge for the trip is

$$x + \frac{4xy - x}{5} = \frac{5x + 4xy - x}{5} = \frac{4x + 4xy}{5}.$$

The best answer is B. This is a difficult question. (See Chapter 2, Math Review, Section B.2 and Section D.1.)

17. In order to give his customers a 25 percent discount on the price and still net a 25 percent profit on the cost of an item, at what price should a merchant mark an item if it cost him $16.80?

   (A) $21.00
   (B) $21.90
   (C) $25.20
   (D) $26.25
   (E) $28.00

Remember that profit = selling price − cost. Here the profit, which is 25 percent of the cost, is equal to 0.25($16.80) = $4.20. The selling price after the 25 percent discount must be $16.80 + $4.20 = $21.00. Therefore, the price before the discount is $\frac{\$21}{0.75}$ = $28 (the price with the 25 percent discount is equal to 75 percent of the price before the discount) and the best answer is E. This is a difficult question. (See Chapter 2, Math Review, Section A.7 and Section D.6.)

18. Of the following, which best approximates $\frac{(0.1667)(0.8333)(0.3333)}{(0.2222)(0.6667)(0.1250)}$?

   (A) 2.00
   (B) 2.40
   (C) 2.43
   (D) 2.50
   (E) 3.43

One way to approach this question is to recognize that the decimals in the expression are approximations of fractions. For example, 0.3333 is approximately $\frac{1}{3}$, and 0.1667, which is half of 0.3333, is approximately $\frac{1}{6}$. Thus the expression is approximately equal to $\dfrac{\left(\frac{1}{6}\right)\left(\frac{5}{6}\right)\left(\frac{1}{3}\right)}{\left(\frac{2}{9}\right)\left(\frac{2}{3}\right)\left(\frac{1}{8}\right)}$.

This fractional expression can be written as

$$\left(\frac{1}{6}\right)\left(\frac{5}{6}\right)\left(\frac{1}{3}\right)\left(\frac{9}{2}\right)\left(\frac{3}{2}\right)\left(\frac{8}{1}\right).$$

(Dividing by a fraction is the same as multiplying by its reciprocal.) It is not necessary to multiply all numbers in this expression. Common factors in the numerator and denominator can be canceled:

$$\left(\frac{1}{6}\right)\left(\frac{5}{6}\right)\left(\frac{1}{3}\right)\left(\frac{9}{2}\right)\left(\frac{3}{2}\right)\left(\frac{8}{1}\right) = \frac{5}{2} = 2.5$$

Thus 2.50 best approximates the expression, and the best answer is D. This is a difficult question. (See Chapter 2, Math Review, Section A.2 and Section A.3.)

19. When an object is dropped, the number of feet N that it falls is given by the formula $N = \frac{1}{2}gt^2$, where t is the time in seconds since it was dropped and g is 32.2. If it takes 5 seconds for the object to reach the ground, how many feet does it fall during the last 2 seconds.

(A) 64.4
(B) 96.6
(C) 161.0
(D) 257.6
(E) 402.5

If it takes 5 seconds for the object to reach the ground, then by substituting 5 into the formula, you can find that it is dropped from a distance of $\frac{1}{2}(32.2)25 = 402.5$ feet above the ground. Similarly, in the first 3 seconds the object falls $\frac{1}{2}(32.2)9 = 144.9$ feet. Therefore, in the last 2 seconds the object falls $402.5 - 144.9 = 257.6$ feet, and the best answer is D. This is a difficult question. (See Chapter 2, Math Review, Section B.2.)

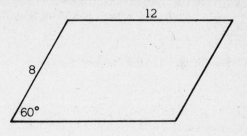

20. In the figure above, the area of the parallelogram is

(A) 40
(B) $24\sqrt{3}$
(C) 72
(D) $48\sqrt{3}$
(E) 96

The area of a parallelogram is equal to altitude × base. It is helpful to draw in an altitude:

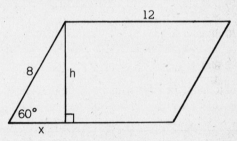

Since the triangle formed is a 30° - 60° - 90° triangle, x = 4 and h = $4\sqrt{3}$. Thus the area of the parallelogram is $(4\sqrt{3})(12) = 48\sqrt{3}$, and the best answer is D. This is a difficult question. (See Chapter 2, Math Review, Section C.6 and Section C.7.)

21. A man drove his automobile d_1 kilometers at the rate of r_1 kilometers per hour and an additional d_2 kilometers at the rate of r_2 kilometers per hour. In terms of d_1, d_2, r_1, and r_2, what was his average speed, in kilometers per hour, for the entire trip?

(A) $\dfrac{d_1 + d_2}{\dfrac{d_1}{r_1} + \dfrac{d_2}{r_2}}$

(B) $\dfrac{d_1 + d_2}{r_1 + r_2}$

(C) $\dfrac{\dfrac{d_1 + d_2}{r_1 + r_2}}{d_1 + d_2}$

(D) $\dfrac{\dfrac{d_1}{r_1} + \dfrac{d_2}{r_2}}{d_1 + d_2}$

(E) It cannot be determined from the information given.

The average speed for the entire trip is equal to the total distance driven divided by the total time. The total distance driven is $d_1 + d_2$. Since rate × time = distance, time = $\dfrac{\text{distance}}{\text{rate}}$ and the total time is equal to $\dfrac{d_1}{r_1} + \dfrac{d_2}{r_2}$. Therefore, the average speed is $\dfrac{d_1 + d_2}{\dfrac{d_1}{r_1} + \dfrac{d_2}{r_2}}$ and the best answer is A. This is a difficult

question. (See Chapter 2, Math Review, Section D.1.)

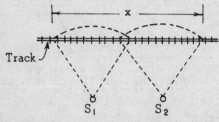

22. In the figure above, two searchlights S_1 and S_2 are located 10,000 feet apart; each covers an area of radius 10,000 feet, and each is located 8,000 feet from the railroad track. To the nearest 1,000 feet, what is the total length x of track spanned by the searchlights?

    (A) 24,000
    (B) 22,000
    (C) 20,000
    (D) 16,000
    (E) 12,000

It is helpful to label the known distances on the figure.

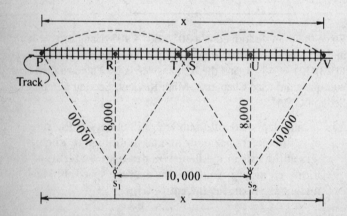

Using the Pythagorean theorem, you find that

$$(PR)^2 + (8,000)^2 = (10,000)^2$$

and get PR = RS = TU = UV = 6,000. Therefore, x is equal to PR + 10,000 + UV = 22,000, and the best answer is B. This is a difficult question. (See Chapter 2, Math Review, Section C.6.)

23. A boy walking along a road at 3 kilometers per hour is overtaken by a truck traveling at 40 kilometers per hour. If the truck breaks down 1 kilometer beyond where it passes the boy, how many <u>minutes</u> after the breakdown does the boy reach the truck?

    (A) $21\frac{1}{2}$

    (B) 20

    (C) $18\frac{34}{37}$

    (D) $18\frac{26}{43}$

    (E) $18\frac{1}{2}$

The amount of time that it takes the boy to walk 1 kilometer is equal to $\dfrac{1 \text{ km}}{3 \text{ km/h}} = \dfrac{1}{3}$ hour or 20 minutes. The truck breaks down in $\dfrac{1 \text{ km}}{40 \text{ km/h}} = \dfrac{1}{40}$ hour or $1\frac{1}{2}$ minutes after it passes the boy. Therefore, the amount of time that elapses between the moment the truck breaks down and the moment the boy reaches the truck is $20 - 1\frac{1}{2} = 18\frac{1}{2}$ minutes, and the best answer is E.

This is a difficult question. (See Chapter 2, Math Review, Section D.1.)

24. In the figure above, the square region is divided into four nonoverlapping triangular regions. If the area of the square region is 4, what is the sum of the perimeters of the four triangular regions?

    (A) 8
    (B) $8 + 4\sqrt{2}$
    (C) 16
    (D) $8 + 8\sqrt{2}$
    (E) $16\sqrt{2}$

If the area of the square region is 4, then each side of the square has length 2, and each diagonal has length $2\sqrt{2}$. The lengths of the sides of each triangle are 2, $\sqrt{2}$, and $\sqrt{2}$, and the perimeter of each triangle is $2 + \sqrt{2} + \sqrt{2}$. Therefore, the sum of the four perimeters is equal to $4(2 + 2\sqrt{2}) = 8 + 8\sqrt{2}$, and the best answer is D. This is a difficult question. (See Chapter 2, Math Review, Section C.6 and Section C.7.)

25. How many three-digit numerals begin with a digit
    that represents a prime number and end with a digit
    that represents a prime number?

    (A) 16
    (B) 80
    (C) 160
    (D) 180
    (E) 240

The prime numbers that are digits are 2,3,5, and 7. There are
10 three-digit numerals that begin with 2 and end with 2
(202, 212, 222, . . ., 292) or a total of 40 that begin with 2
and end in a prime digit. There are also 40 such numerals beginning with each of the digits 3,5, and 7. Thus, the total
number of three-digit numerals that begin and end with a
digit that represents a prime number is 4(40) = 160 and the
best answer is C. This is a very difficult question. (See Chapter 2, Math Review, Section A.1.)

4 Data Sufficiency

In this section of the GMAT, you are to classify each problem according to the five fixed answer choices, rather than find a solution to the problem. Each problem consists of a question and two statements. You are to decide whether the information in each statement alone is sufficient to answer the question or, if neither is, whether the information in the two statements together is sufficient.

The following pages include test-taking strategies, a sample test (with an answer key), and detailed explanations of every problem from the sample test. These explanations present possible problem-solving strategies for the examples. At the end of each explanation is a reference to the particular section(s) of Chapter 2, Math Review, that you may find helpful in reviewing the mathematical concepts on which the the problem is based.

Test-Taking Strategies for Data Sufficiency

1. Do not waste valuable time solving a problem; you are only to determine whether sufficient information is given to solve the problem. After you have considered statement (1), make a check mark next to (1) if you can determine the answer and a cross mark if you cannot. Be sure to disregard all the information learned from statement (1) while considering statement (2). This is very difficult to do and often results in erroneously choosing answer C when the answer should be B or choosing B when the answer should C. Suppose statement (2) alone is sufficient. Then a check mark next to (1) indicates that D is the correct answer; a cross mark next to (1) indicates that B is correct. Suppose statement (2) alone is not sufficient. A check mark next to (1) indicates that A is the correct answer; a cross mark next to (1) indicates that you must now consider whether the two statements taken together give sufficient information; if they do, the answer is C; if not, the answer is E.

2. If you determine that the information in statement (1) is sufficient to answer the question, the answer is necessarily either A or D. If you are not sure about statement (1) but you know that statement (2) alone is sufficient, the answer is necessarily either B or D. If neither statement taken alone is sufficient, the answer is either C or E. Thus, if you have doubts about certain portions of the information given but are relatively sure about other portions, you can logically eliminate two or three options and more than double your chances of guessing correctly.

3. Remember that when you are determining whether there is sufficient information to answer a question of the form, "What is the value of y?" the information given must be sufficient to find one and only one value for y. Being able to determine minimum or maximum values or an answer of the form $y = x + 2$ is not sufficient, because such answers constitute a range of values rather than "the value of y."

4. When geometric figures are involved, be very careful not to make unwarranted assumptions based on the figures. A triangle may appear to be isosceles, but can you detect the difference in the lengths of segments 1.8 inches long and 1.85 inches long? Furthermore, the figures are not necessarily drawn to scale; they are generalized figures showing little more than intersecting line segments and the betweenness of points, angles, and regions.

When you take the sample test, use the answer spaces on page 61 to mark your answers.

Answer Spaces for Data Sufficiency Sample Test

1 ⒶⒷⒸⒹⒺ	6 ⒶⒷⒸⒹⒺ	11 ⒶⒷⒸⒹⒺ	16 ⒶⒷⒸⒹⒺ	21 ⒶⒷⒸⒹⒺ
2 ⒶⒷⒸⒹⒺ	7 ⒶⒷⒸⒹⒺ	12 ⒶⒷⒸⒹⒺ	17 ⒶⒷⒸⒹⒺ	22 ⒶⒷⒸⒹⒺ
3 ⒶⒷⒸⒹⒺ	8 ⒶⒷⒸⒹⒺ	13 ⒶⒷⒸⒹⒺ	18 ⒶⒷⒸⒹⒺ	23 ⒶⒷⒸⒹⒺ
4 ⒶⒷⒸⒹⒺ	9 ⒶⒷⒸⒹⒺ	14 ⒶⒷⒸⒹⒺ	19 ⒶⒷⒸⒹⒺ	24 ⒶⒷⒸⒹⒺ
5 ⒶⒷⒸⒹⒺ	10 ⒶⒷⒸⒹⒺ	15 ⒶⒷⒸⒹⒺ	20 ⒶⒷⒸⒹⒺ	25 ⒶⒷⒸⒹⒺ

DATA SUFFICIENCY SAMPLE TEST
25 Questions

Directions: Each of the data sufficiency problems below consists of a question and two statements, labeled (1) and (2), in which certain data are given. You have to decide whether the data given in the statements are sufficient for answering the question. Using the data given in the statements plus your knowledge of mathematics and everyday facts (such as the number of days in July or the meaning of counterclockwise), you are to blacken space

- A if statement (1) ALONE is sufficient, but statement (2) alone is not sufficient to answer the question asked;
- B if statement (2) ALONE is sufficient, but statement (1) alone is not sufficient to answer the question asked;
- C if BOTH statements (1) and (2) TOGETHER are sufficient to answer the question asked, but NEITHER statement ALONE is sufficient;
- D if EACH statement ALONE is sufficient to answer the question asked;
- E if statements (1) and (2) TOGETHER are NOT sufficient to answer the question asked, and additional data specific to the problem are needed.

Numbers: All numbers used are real numbers.

Figures: A figure in a data sufficiency problem will conform to the information given in the question, but will not necessarily conform to the additional information given in statements (1) and (2).

You may assume that lines shown as straight are straight and that angle measures are greater than zero.

You may assume that the position of points, angles, regions, etc., exist in the order shown.

All figures lie in a plane unless otherwise indicated.

Example:

In $\triangle PQR$, what is the value of x?

(1) $PQ = PR$

(2) $y = 40$

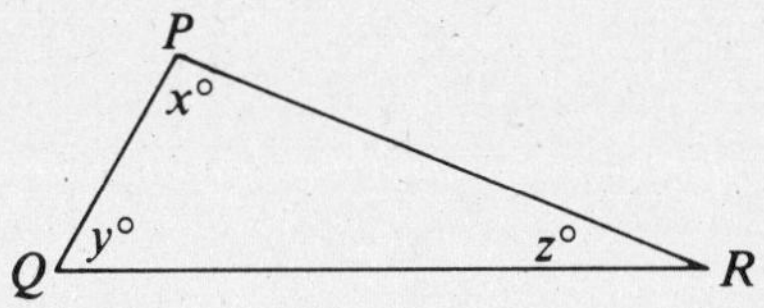

Explanation: According to statement (1), $PQ = PR$; therefore, $\triangle PQR$ is isosceles and $y = z$. Since $x + y + z = 180$, $x + 2y = 180$. Since statement (1) does not give a value for y, you cannot answer the question using statement (1) by itself. According to statement (2), $y = 40$; therefore, $x + z = 140$. Since statement (2) does not give a value for z, you cannot answer the question using statement (2) by itself. Using both statements together, you can find y and z; therefore, you can find x, and the answer to the problem is C.

GO ON TO THE NEXT PAGE.

A Statement (1) ALONE is sufficient, but statement (2) alone is not sufficient.
B Statement (2) ALONE is sufficient, but statement (1) alone is not sufficient.
C BOTH statements TOGETHER are sufficient, but NEITHER statement ALONE is sufficient.
D EACH statement ALONE is sufficient.
E Statements (1) and (2) TOGETHER are NOT sufficient.

1. What is the 1st term in sequence S ?

   (1) The 3rd term in S is 2.

   (2) The 2nd term in S is twice the 1st, and the 3rd term is three times the 2nd.

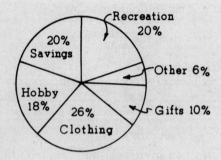

2. The chart above shows how Jeff spent his earnings for one year. How much did Jeff spend for clothing?

   (1) He spent $18 during the year on tennis balls.

   (2) He spent $190 during the year on recreation.

3. Is $x > y$?

   (1) $0 < x < 0.75$
   (2) $0.25 < y < 1.0$

4. Car X and car Y ran a 500-kilometer race. What was the average speed of car X ?

   (1) Car X completed the race in 6 hours and 40 minutes.

   (2) Car Y, at an average speed of 100 kilometers per hour, completed the race 1 hour and 40 minutes before car X crossed the finish line.

5. In a refinery, the capacity of oil tank A is 70 per cent of the capacity of oil tank B. How many more gallons of oil are in tank A than in tank B ?

   (1) Tank A is 90 per cent full; tank B is 50 per cent full.

   (2) When full, tank A contains 50,000 gallons of oil.

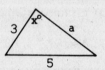

6. What is the area of the triangle above?

   (1) $a^2 + 9 = 25$
   (2) $x = 90$

GO ON TO THE NEXT PAGE.

7. What is the remainder when the positive integer x is divided by 2 ?

    (1) x is an odd integer.

    (2) x is a multiple of 3.

8. Is $x > y$?

    (1) $x^2 > y^2$

    (2) $x - y > 0$

9. If the ratio of men to women employed by Company S in 1975 was $\frac{1}{2}$, what is the ratio of men to women employed by Company S in 1976 ?

    (1) Company S employed 20 more women in 1976 than in 1975.

    (2) Company S employed 20 more men in 1976 than in 1975.

10. Exactly how many bonds does Bob have?

    (1) Of Bob's bonds, exactly 21 are worth at least $5,000 each.

    (2) Of Bob's bonds, exactly 65 per cent are worth less than $5,000 each.

11. What is the volume of rectangular box R ?

    (1) The total surface area of R is 12 square meters.

    (2) The height of R is 50 centimeters.

12. What is the value of the two-digit number x ?

    (1) The sum of the two digits is 4.

    (2) The difference between the two digits is 2.

13. A rectangle is defined to be "silver" if and only if the ratio of its length to its width is 2 to 1. If rectangle S is silver, is rectangle R silver?

    (1) R has the same area as S.

    (2) The ratio of one side of R to one side of S is 2 to 1.

14. Is $xy < 0$?

    (1) $x^2y^3 < 0$

    (2) $xy^2 > 0$

GO ON TO THE NEXT PAGE.

-65-

A Statement (1) ALONE is sufficient, but statement (2) alone is not sufficient.
B Statement (2) ALONE is sufficient, but statement (1) alone is not sufficient.
C BOTH statements TOGETHER are sufficient, but NEITHER statement ALONE is sufficient.
D EACH statement ALONE is sufficient.
E Statements (1) and (2) TOGETHER are NOT sufficient.

15. If x is an integer, is $\frac{x}{2}$ an <u>even</u> integer?

(1) x is a multiple of 2.
(2) x is a multiple of 4.

16. What is the value of x − y ?

(1) x − y = y − x
(2) x − y = x² − y²

17. If x = y², what is the value of y − x ?

(1) x = 4
(2) x + y = 2

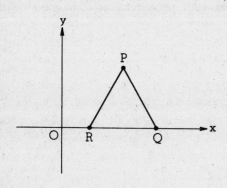

18. In the figure above, R and Q are points on the x-axis. What is the area of equilateral △PQR ?

(1) The coordinates of point P are (6, 2√3).
(2) The coordinates of point Q are (8, 0).

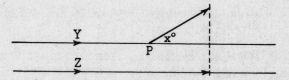

19. Cars Y and Z travel side by side at the same rate of speed along parallel roads as shown above. When car Y reaches point P, it forks to the left at angle x°, changes speed, and continues to stay even with car Z as shown by the dotted line. The speed of car Y beyond point P is what per cent of the speed of car Z ?

(1) The speed of car Z is 50 miles per hour
(2) x = 45

20. If each of the 20 bolts of fabric on a shelf is either 100 percent cotton, 100 percent wool, or a mixture of cotton and wool, how many bolts are cotton and wool mixtures?

(1) Of the 20 bolts, 18 contain some wool and 14 contain some cotton.
(2) Of the 20 bolts, 6 are 100 percent wool.

21. If xy ≠ 0, what is the value of $\frac{x^4y^2 - (xy)^2}{x^3y^2}$?

(1) x = 2
(2) y = 8

GO ON TO THE NEXT PAGE.

A Statement (1) ALONE is sufficient, but statement (2) alone is not sufficient.
B Statement (2) ALONE is sufficient, but statement (1) alone is not sufficient.
C BOTH statements TOGETHER are sufficient, but NEITHER statement ALONE is sufficient.
D EACH statement ALONE is sufficient.
E Statements (1) and (2) TOGETHER are NOT sufficient.

22. Are there exactly 3 distinct symbols used to create the code words in language Q ?

   (1) The set of all code words in language Q is the set of all possible distinct horizontal arrangements of one or more symbols, with no repetition.

   (2) There are exactly 15 code words in language Q.

23. If x, y, and z are the lengths of the three sides of a triangle, is y > 4 ?

   (1) z = x + 4

   (2) x = 3 and z = 7

24. How many minutes long is time period X ?

   (1) Time period X is 3 hours long.

   (2) Time period X starts at 11 p.m. and ends at 2 a.m.

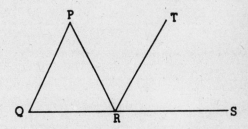

25. In the figure above, QRS is a straight line and line TR bisects ∠PRS. Is it true that lines TR and PQ are parallel?

   (1) PQ = PR

   (2) QR = PR

END OF SAMPLE TEST

Answer Key for Sample Test

DATA SUFFICIENCY

1.	C	14.	C
2.	B	15.	B
3.	E	16.	A
4.	D	17.	C
5.	C	18.	A
6.	D	19.	B
7.	A	20.	A
8.	B	21.	A
9.	E	22.	C
10.	C	23.	D
11.	E	24.	A
12.	E	25.	B
13.	E		

Explanatory Material: Data Sufficiency

The following discussion of Data Sufficiency is intended to familarize you with the most efficient and effective approaches to the kinds of problems common to Data Sufficiency. The problems on the sample test in this chapter are generally representative of the kinds of questions you will encounter in this section of the GMAT. Remember that it is the problem-solving strategy that is important, not the specific details of a particular question.

1. **What is the 1st term in sequence S ?**

    (1) **The 3rd term in S is 2.**
    (2) **The 2nd term in S is twice the 1st, and the 3rd term is three times the 2nd.**

It is clear that (1) offers no help in determining the first term in S. Thus, the answer is B, C, or E. Although (2) gives the relationships among the first three terms in S, it is not sufficient to answer the question asked, and the answer must be C or E. From (1) and (2) together it can be determined that the 2nd term is $\frac{1}{3}$ the 3rd term $\left(\frac{1}{3}(2) = \frac{2}{3}\right)$ and the 1st term is $\frac{1}{2}$ the 2nd term $\left(\frac{1}{2}\left(\frac{2}{3}\right) = \frac{1}{3}\right)$. Therefore, the best answer is C.

This is an easy question. (See Chapter 2, Math Review, Section B.2.)

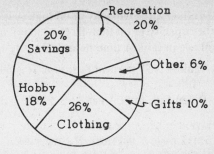

2. **The chart above shows how Jeff spent his earnings for one year. How much did Jeff spend for clothing?**

    (1) **He spent $18 during the year on tennis balls.**
    (2) **He spent $190 during the year on recreation.**

From (1) you know that Jeff spent at least $18 on "recreation" expenses. Since you do not know what additional expenses are included in that 20 percent recreation expense, (1) alone is not sufficient to answer the question. Thus, the answer must be B, C, or E. From (2), you know that $190 is equal to 20 percent of Jeff's earnings. You can compute Jeff's earnings and the amount spent on clothing. Therefore, the best answer is B. This is an easy question. (See Chapter 2, Math Review, Section A.7.)

3. **Is x > y?**

    (1) **0 < x < 0.75**
    (2) **0.25 < y < 1.0**

Clearly neither (1) nor (2) alone is sufficient to determine whether x > y; thus, the answer must be C or E. Statements (1) and (2) together are also not sufficient to answer the question. For example, if x = 0.6 and y = 0.5, x > y; but, if x = 0.6 and y = 0.9, x < y. Both these examples are consistent with (1) and (2); therefore, the best answer is E. This is an easy question. (See Chapter 2, Math Review, Section B.8.)

4. **Car X and car Y ran a 500-kilometer race. What was the average speed of car X?**

    (1) **Car X completed the race in 6 hours and 40 minutes.**
    (2) **Car Y, at an average speed of 100 kilometers per hour, completed the race 1 hour and 40 minutes before car X crossed the finish line.**

Statement (1) is sufficient because from statement (1) the average speed of car X can be determined by dividing 500 kilometers by $6\frac{2}{3}$ hours; thus, the answer is A or D.

Statement (2) implies that car Y took 5 hours to complete the race and car X took $6\frac{2}{3}$ hours. Therefore, (2) alone is also sufficient to determine the average speed of car X, and the best answer is D. This is an easy question. (See Chapter 2, Math Review, Section D.1.)

5. In a refinery, the capacity of oil tank A is 70 percent of the capacity of oil tank B. How many more gallons of oil are in tank A than in tank B?

   (1) Tank A is 90 percent full; tank B is 50 percent full.
   (2) When full, tank A contains 50,000 gallons of oil.

Since you do not know the number of gallons in either tank A or tank B, (1) alone is not sufficient; the answer must be B, C, or E. From (2) alone, you can determine the capacities of tanks A and B, but you do not know whether the tanks are full, so the answer must be C or E. Using (1) and (2) together, you can determine the number of gallons in A and B; therefore, the best answer is C. This is a moderately difficult question. (See Chapter 2, Math Review, Section A.7.)

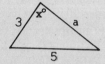

6. What is the area of the triangle above?

   (1) $a^2 + 9 = 25$
   (2) $x = 90$

Statement (1) implies that $a = 4$. Thus, the figure shows a 3-4-5 triangle, and so $x = 90$. Therefore, the area of the triangle is $\frac{(3)(4)}{2}$, and the answer is A or D. Statement (2) indicates that the triangle is a right triangle. Therefore, since $a = 4$, the area is $\frac{(3)(4)}{2}$, and the best answer is D. This is a moderately difficult question. (See Chapter 2, Math Review, Section C.6.)

7. What is the remainder when the positive integer x is divided by 2?

   (1) x is an odd integer.
   (2) x is a multiple of 3.

Statement (1) is sufficient because from (1) you know that the remainder is 1; whenever an odd integer is divided by 2, the remainder is 1. Thus, the answer is A or D. The question cannot be answered from (2) alone because x could be odd (e.g., 3) or could be even (e.g., 6). Therefore, the best answer is A. This is a moderately difficult question. (See Chapter 2, Math Review, Section A. 1.)

8. Is $x > y$?

   (1) $x^2 > y^2$
   (2) $x - y > 0$

Statement (1) is insufficient to determine whether $x > y$ because (1) implies nothing about the signs of x and y. For example, if $x = 3$ and $y = 2$, $x > y$, but if $x = -3$ and $y = 2$, $x < y$. Thus, the answer is B, C, or E. By adding y to both sides of (2), you get $x > y$; therefore, the best answer is B. This is a moderately difficult question. (See Chapter 2, Math Review, Section A.9 and Section B.8)

9. If the ratio of men to women employed by Company S in 1975 was $\frac{1}{2}$, what is the ratio of men to women employed by Company S in 1976?

   (1) Company S employed 20 more women in 1976 than in 1975.
   (2) Company S employed 20 more men in 1976 than in 1975.

Clearly, neither (1) nor (2) alone is sufficient to determine the ratio for 1976 since neither gives any information about the actual numbers of men or women employed in either 1975 or 1976. Thus, the answer must be C or E. If n is the number of men employed in 1975, then from (1) and (2) together the ratio of men to women employed in 1976 is $\frac{n + 20}{2n + 20}$. Since you do not know the value of n, you cannot determine the ratio for 1976, and the best answer is E. This is a moderately difficult question. (See Chapter 2, Math Review, Section A.6.)

10. Exactly how many bonds does Bob have?

    (1) Of Bob's bonds, exactly 21 are worth at least $5,000 each.
    (2) Of Bob's bonds, exactly 65 percent are worth less than $5,000 each.

Statement (1) tells you the number of bonds that Bob has that are worth at least $5,000, but you do not know how many of Bob's bonds are worth less than $5,000 each; the answer must be B, C, or E. Statement (2) alone is also not sufficient, because it only gives the percent of Bob's bonds that are worth less than $5,000 each. However, (2) does tell you that 35 percent of Bob's bonds are worth at least $5,000 each. From (1) and (2) together you know that 35 percent of Bob's bonds is equal to 21, and the best answer is C. This is a moderately difficult question. (See Chapter 2, Math Review, Section A.7.)

11. What is the volume of rectangular box R?

    (1) The total surface area of R is 12 square meters.
    (2) The height of R is 50 centimeters.

For this problem it may be helpful to draw a diagram:

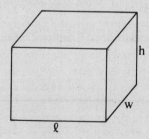

From (1) you know that $2 (\ell w + wh + \ell h) = 12$, but since you do not know, ℓ, w, or h, (1) is not sufficient to determine the volume of the box ($\ell \times w \times h$), and the answer must be B, C, or E. Since (2) gives just one dimension of the box, it is also not sufficient to determine the volume, and the answer must be C or E. From (1) and (2) together you know that

$$\ell w + \frac{w}{2} + \frac{\ell}{2} = 6,$$

because 50 centimeters = $\frac{1}{2}$ meter, but you still need to know either the length or the width of the box to determine its volume. The best answer is E. This is a moderately difficult question. (See Chapter 2, Math Review, Section C.10.)

12. **What is the value of the two-digit number x?**

   (1) **The sum of the two digits is 4.**
   (2) **The difference between the two digits is 2.**

Statement (1) implies that x is 13, 22, 31, or 40; thus (1) alone is insufficient, and the answer must be B, C, or E. Statement (2) implies that x could have any one of a number of values, including 13, 24, 31, 42, ... From (1) and (2) together there are still two possibilities for x, 13 and 31; therefore, the best answer is E. This is a moderately difficult question. (See Chapter 2, Math Review, Section A.1.)

13. **A rectangle is defined to be "silver" if and only if the ratio of its length to its width is 2 to 1. If rectangle S is silver, is rectangle R silver?**

   (1) **R has the same area as S.**
   (2) **The ratio of one side of R to one side of S is 2 to 1.**

Statement (1) alone is not sufficient to answer the question because R could have the same dimensions as S (e.g., 4 × 2) and be silver, or R could have different dimensions (e.g., 8 × 1) and not be silver. Thus, the answer is B, C, or E. Statement (2) alone does not tell anything about the relationship between the other sides of R and S, and so it is not sufficient; the answer must be C or E. The logic applied to (1) can also be applied to the information given in (2); thus (1) and (2) together are not sufficient, and the best answer is E. This is a moderately difficult question. (See Chapter 2, Math Review, Section C.7.)

14. **Is xy<0?**

   (1) $x^2y^3 < 0$
   (2) $xy^2 > 0$

Statement (1) implies that $x \neq 0$ and $y \neq 0$ since the product is not equal to zero. x^2 must be greater than zero because the square of any nonzero number is positive. A positive number times a negative number equals a negative number; thus $y^3 < 0$ since $x^2y^3 < 0$. Likewise, if $y^3 < 0$, $y < 0$. However, (1) is not sufficient to determine whether $xy < 0$ because you do not know whether $x > 0$ or $x < 0$; thus, the answer is B, C, or E. Similarly, from (2) alone you know that $x > 0$ since $xy^2 > 0$ and $y^2 > 0$, but you do not know whether $y > 0$ or $y < 0$. Combining the information from (1) and (2) you know $y < 0$ and $x > 0$, and so $xy < 0$; the best answer is C. This is a difficult question. (See Chapter 2, Math Review, Section A.5.)

15. **If x is an integer, is $\frac{x}{2}$ an <u>even</u> integer?**

   (1) **x is a multiple of 2.**
   (2) **x is a multiple of 4.**

Statement (1) implies that x is an even integer, but not that $\frac{x}{2}$ is necessarily even. For example, if x = 8, $\frac{x}{2}$ is even, but if x = 6, $\frac{x}{2}$ is odd; in both cases (1) is satisfied. Thus, the answer is B, C, or E. Statement (2) implies that $x = 2 \cdot 2 \cdot n$, where n is an integer. Hence, $\frac{x}{2} = 2n$ and 2n is even. Therefore, the best answer is B. This is a difficult question. (See Chapter 2, Math Review, Section A.1.)

16. **What is the value of x − y?**

   (1) $x - y = y - x$
   (2) $x - y = x^2 - y^2$

From (1) you know that $2x = 2y$ or $x = y$, and $x - y = 0$; thus, the answer is A or D. Statement (2) can be expressed as $x - y = (x - y)(x + y)$, which implies that $x - y = 0$ or $x + y = 1$; however, this is not sufficient to determine the value of x − y. For example, if $x = y = \frac{1}{2}$, $x - y = 0$, but if x = 2 and y = −1, $x - y = 3$. Therefore, the best answer is A. This is a difficult question. (See Chapter 2, Math Review, Section B.1 and Section B.4.)

17. **If $x = y^2$, what is the value of y − x?**

   (1) **x = 4**
   (2) **x + y = 2**

From (1) you find that y = 2 or y = −2, but which of these values y has cannot be determined. Therefore, (1) alone is not sufficient to answer the question asked, and the answer is B, C, or E. Substituting y^2 for x in (2), you find that y = 1 or y = −2; therefore, (2) alone is not sufficient, and the answer is C or E. Using (1) and (2) together, you find that x = 4, y = −2, and $y - x = -2 - 4 = -(2 + 4) = -6$. Therefore, the best answer is C. This is a difficult question. (See Chapter 2, Math Review, Section B.5.)

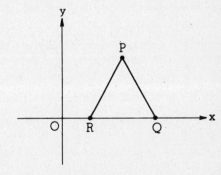

18. **In the figure above, R and Q are points on the x-axis. What is the area of equilateral △PQR?**

   (1) **The coordinates of point P are $(6, 2\sqrt{3})$.**
   (2) **The coordinates of point Q are (8, 0).**

Statement (1) gives the height of triangle PQR, and, since ΔPQR is equilateral, its other dimensions can be determined:

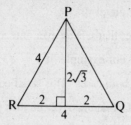

Thus, the area of ΔPQR is $\frac{(2\sqrt{3})(4)}{2}$, and the answer is A or D. Since (2) does not give any information about the coordinates of either of the other points, the length of RQ cannot be determined, and (2) is insufficient. Therefore, the best answer is A. This is a difficult question. (See Chapter 2, Math Review, Section C.6 and Section C.13.)

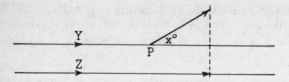

19. Cars Y and Z travel side by side at the same rate of speed along parallel roads as shown above. When car Y reaches point P, it forks to the left at angle x°, changes speed, and continues to stay even with car Z as shown by the dotted line. The speed of car Y beyond point P is what percent of the speed of car Z?

(1) The speed of car Z is 50 miles per hour.

(2) x = 45

This is a rate/distance problem; it is helpful to keep in mind that rate × time = distance (i.e., symbolically r × t = d). In this case the times for Y and Z are equal, and so you have the equation $\frac{d_y}{r_y} = \frac{d_z}{r_z}$. Since (1) does not give any information about the distances traveled, it is not sufficient, and the answer must be B, C, or E. Since the angles of the triangle formed are 45°, 45°, and 90° and d_y is the hypotenuse of the triangle, (2) implies that $d_y = \sqrt{2}\, d_z$. Therefore $\frac{\sqrt{2}\, d_z}{r_y} = \frac{d_z}{r_z}$. From this information it can be determined that $r_y = \sqrt{2}\, r_z$, and therefore the speed of car Y beyond point P is $100\sqrt{2}$ percent of the speed of car Z. Thus, the best answer is B. This is a difficult question. (See Chapter 2, Math Review, Section A.7, Section C.6, and Section D.1.)

20. If each of the 20 bolts of fabric on a shelf is either 100 percent cotton, 100 percent wool, or a mixture of cotton and wool, how many bolts are cotton and wool mixtures?

(1) Of the 20 bolts, 18 contain some wool and 14 contain some cotton.

(2) Of the 20 bolts, 6 are 100 percent wool.

One way to solve this problem is to draw a circle diagram.

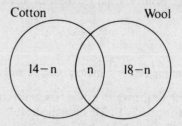

From (1), if n is the number of bolts that are cotton and wool mixtures, then $(14 - n) + n + (18 - n) = 20$, and $n = 12$. Therefore, (1) is sufficient to answer the question, and the answer must be A or D. From (2),

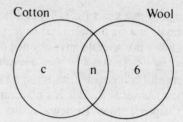

if c is the number of bolts that are 100 percent cotton, then $c + n + 6 = 20$. Since the number of bolts that are 100 percent cotton cannot be determined, the question cannot be answered from (2) alone. Therefore, the best answer is A. This is a difficult question. (See Chapter 2, Math Review, Section D.7.)

21. If $xy \neq 0$, what is the value of $\frac{x^4y^2 - (xy)^2}{x^3y^2}$?

(1) x = 2

(2) y = 8

It is helpful to simplify the expression in the question:

$$\frac{x^4y^2 - (xy)^2}{x^3y^2} = \frac{y^2(x^4 - x^2)}{x^3y^2} = \frac{x^4 - x^2}{x^3}$$

$$= \frac{x^2(x^2 - 1)}{x^2(x)} = \frac{x^2 - 1}{x}$$

Since statement (1) gives the value of x, the value of the expression can be determined, and the answer is A or D. Statement (2) alone is insufficient to answer the question asked because the value of x is not given and is not deducible. Hence, the value of the expression cannot be determined from (2), and the best answer is A. This is a difficult question. (See Chapter 2, Math Review, Section B.1.)

22. Are there exactly 3 distinct symbols used to create the code words in language Q?

(1) The set of all code words in language Q is the set of all possible distinct horizontal arrangements of one or more symbols, with no repetition.

(2) There are exactly 15 code words in language Q.

Statement (1) tells you what code words are, but it does not say anything about the number of symbols. For example, if there is only one symbol, a, there is just 1 code word; but if there are 2 symbols, a and b, there are 4 code words, a, b, ab, and ba. Thus (1) is not sufficient, and the answer must be B, C, or E. Statement (2) alone is insufficient since it does not specify what code words are; therefore, the answer must be C or E. From (1) and (2) and the examples given above, you know that there must be more than 2 symbols if there are to be 15 code words. If there are 3 symbols, a, b, and c, then the code words are a, b, c, ab, ba, ac, ca, bc, cb, abc, acb, bac, bca, cab, and cba; i.e., there are 15 code words. Clearly, if there were 4 or more symbols, there would be more than 15 code words. Thus, the best answer is C. This is a difficult question. (See Chapter 2, Math Review, Section D.7.)

23. **If x, y, and z are the lengths of the three sides of a triangle, is y > 4?**

    (1) $z = x + 4$
    (2) $x = 3$ and $z = 7$

The sum of the lengths of any two sides of a triangle is always greater than the length of the third side; therefore, $x + y > z$. Statement (1) implies $x + y > x + 4$, and $y > 4$. Therefore, the answer must be A or D. Statement (2) implies $3 + y > 7$ and $y > 4$. Thus, the best answer is D. This is a very difficult question. (See Chapter 2, Math Review, Section B.8 and Section C.6.)

24. **How many minutes long is time period X?**

    (1) Time period X is 3 hours long.

    (2) Time period X starts at 11 p.m. and ends at 2 a.m.

Statement (1) is sufficient because from (1) you can determine that time period X is 180 minutes long; thus, the answer must be A or D. Statement (2) alone is not sufficient to answer the question because you do not know whether the two times given are for consecutive days. This is a question that depends not on calculation but on your analysis of the assumptions made or not made by the statement. Therefore, the best answer is A. This is a very difficult question.

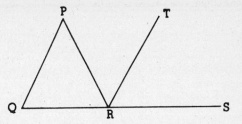

25. **In the figure above, QRS is a straight line and line TR bisects ∠PRS. Is it true that lines TR and PQ are parallel?**

    (1) **PQ = PR**
    (2) **QR = PR**

Let the angles of the figure have the following measures:

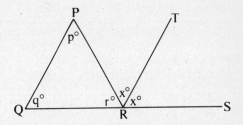

Since QRS is a straight line, $r + 2x = 180$. For PQ∥TR, x must equal p. From (1) you know that $q = r$, but there is no way to determine whether $p = x$. So the answer must be B, C, or E. From (2) you know that $q = p$ and that $r + 2p = 180 = r + 2x$ and thus $p = x$. Therefore, PQ∥TR, and the best answer is B. This is a very difficult question. (See Chapter 2, Math Review, Section C.4 and Section C.5.)

5 Reading Comprehension

There are six kinds of Reading Comprehension questions, each of which tests a different reading skill. The following pages include descriptions of the various question types, test-taking strategies, a sample test (with an answer key), and detailed explanations of every question on the sample test. The explanations further illustrate the ways in which Reading Comprehension questions evaluate basic reading skills.

Reading Comprehension questions include:

1. **Questions that ask about the main idea of a passage**
   Each Reading Comprehension passage in the GMAT is a unified whole—that is, the individual sentences and paragraphs support and develop one main idea or central point. Sometimes you will be told the central point in the passage itself, and sometimes it will be necessary for you to determine the central point from the overall organization or development of the passage. You may be asked in this kind of question to recognize a correct restatement, or paraphrase, of the main idea of a passage; to identify the author's primary purpose, or objective, in writing the passage; or to assign a title that summarizes briefly and pointedly the main idea developed in the passage.

2. **Questions that ask about the supporting ideas presented in a passage**
   These questions measure your ability to comprehend the supporting ideas in a passage and to differentiate those supporting ideas from the main idea. The questions also measure your ability to differentiate ideas that are *explicitly stated* in a passage from ideas that are *implied* by the author but are not explicitly stated. You may be asked about facts cited in a passage, or about the specific content of arguments presented by the author in support of his or her views, or about descriptive details used to support or elaborate on the main idea. Whereas questions about the main idea ask you to determine the meaning of a passage *as a whole,* questions about supporting ideas ask you to determine the meanings of individual sentences and paragraphs that *contribute* to the meaning of the passage as a whole. One way to think about these questions is to see them as questions asking for the main point of *one small part* of the passage.

3. **Questions that ask for inferences based on information presented in a passage**
   These questions ask about ideas that are not explicitly stated in a passage but are *strongly implied* by the author. Unlike questions about supporting details, which ask about information that is directly stated in a passage, inference questions ask about ideas or meanings that must be inferred from information that is directly stated. Authors can make their points in indirect ways, suggesting ideas without actually stating them. These questions measure your ability to infer an author's intended meaning in parts of a passage where the meaning is only suggested. The questions do not ask about meanings or implications that are remote from the passage but about meanings that are developed indirectly or implications specifically suggested by the author. To answer these questions, you may have to carry statements made by the author one step beyond their literal meanings, or recognize the *opposite* of a statement made by the author, or identify the intended meaning of a word used figuratively in a passage. If a passage explicitly states an effect, for example, you may be asked to infer its cause. If the author compares two phenomena, you may be asked to infer the basis for the comparison. You may be asked to infer the characteristics of an old policy from an explicit description of a new one. When you read a passage, therefore, you should concentrate not only on the explicit meaning of the author's words, but also on the more subtle meaning implied by those words.

4. **Questions that ask how information given in a passage can be applied to a context outside the passage itself**
These questions measure your ability to discern the relationships between situations or ideas presented by the author and other situations or ideas that might parallel those in the passage. In this kind of question, you may be asked to identify a hypothetical situation that is comparable to a situation presented in the passage, or to select an example that is similar to an example provided in the passage, or to apply ideas given in the passage to a situation not mentioned by the author, or to recognize ideas that the author would probably agree or disagree with on the basis of statements made in the passage. Unlike inference questions, these questions use ideas or situations *not* taken from the passage. Ideas and situations given in a question are *like* those given in the passage, and they parallel ideas and situations given in the passage. Therefore, to answer the question, you must do more than recall what you read. You must recognize the essential attributes of ideas and situations presented in the passage when they appear in different words and in an entirely new context.

5. **Questions that ask about the logical structure of a passage**
These questions ask you to analyze and evaluate the organization and the logic of a passage. They may ask how a passage is constructed: for instance, does it define, does it compare or contrast, does it present a new idea, does it refute an idea. They may also ask how the author persuades readers to accept his or her assertions, or about the reason behind the author's use of any particular supporting detail. You may also be asked to identify assumptions that the author is making, to assess the strengths and weaknesses of the author's arguments, or to recognize appropriate counterarguments. These questions measure your ability not only to comprehend a passage but to evaluate it critically. However, it is important for you to realize that these questions do not rely on any kind of formal logic, nor do they require that you be familiar with specific terms of logic or argumentation. You can answer these questions using only the information in the passage and careful reasoning.

6. **Questions that ask about the style and tone of a passage**
These questions ask about the language of a passage and about the ideas in a passage that may be expressed through its language. You may be asked to deduce the author's attitude toward an idea, a fact, or a situation from the words that he or she uses to describe it. You may also be asked to select a word that accurately describes the tone of a passage—for instance, "critical," "questioning," "objective," or "enthusiastic." To answer this type of question, you will have to consider the language of the passage as a whole: it takes more than one pointed critical word to make the tone of an entire passage "critical." Sometimes, these questions ask what audience the passage was probably intended for or what type of publication it probably appeared in. Style and tone questions may apply to one small part of the passage or to the passage as a whole. To answer them, you must ask yourself what meanings are contained in the words of a passage beyond their literal meanings. Were such words selected because of their emotional content, or because of their suggestiveness, or because a particular audience would expect to hear them? Remember, these questions measure your ability to discern meaning expressed by the author through his or her choice of words.

Test-Taking Strategies for Reading Comprehension

1. You should not expect to be completely familiar with any of the material presented in Reading Comprehension passages. You may find some passages easier to understand than others, but all passages are designed to present a challenge. If you have some familiarity with the material being presented in a passage, do not let this knowledge influence your choice of answers to the questions. Answer all questions on the basis of what is *stated or implied* in the passage itself.

2. Since the questions require specific and detailed understanding of the material in a passage, analyze each passage carefully the first time you read it. There are approximately 1,500 words of text in the entire Reading Comprehension section. This means that, even if you read at the relatively slow rate of 250 words per minute, you will be able to read the passages in about 6 minutes and will have about 24 minutes left for answering the questions. You should, of course, be sure to allow sufficient time to work on each passage and its questions. There are other ways of approaching Reading Comprehension passages: some test-takers prefer to skim the passages the first time through or even to read the questions before reading the passages. You should choose the method most suitable for you.

3. Underlining parts of a passage may be helpful to you. Focus on key words and phrases and try to follow exactly the development of separate ideas. In the margins, note where each important idea, argument, or set of related facts begins. Make every effort to avoid losing the sense of what is being discussed. If you become lost, you will have to go back over the material, and that wastes time. Keep the following in mind:

   - Note how each fact relates to an idea or an argument.
   - Note where the passage moves from one idea to the next.
   - Separate main ideas from supporting ideas.
   - Determine what conclusions are reached and why.

4. Read the questions carefully, making certain that you understand what is being asked. An answer choice may be incorrect, even though it accurately restates information given in the passage, if it does not answer the question. If you need to, refer back to the passage for clarification.

5. Read all the choices carefully. Never assume that you have selected the best answer without first reading all the choices.

6. Select the choice that best answers the question in terms of the information given in the passage. Do not rely on outside knowledge of the material for answering the questions.

7. Remember that understanding, not speed, is the critical factor in reading comprehension.

When you take the sample test, use the answer spaces on page 79 to mark your answers.

Answer Spaces for Reading Comprehension Sample Test

1 Ⓐ Ⓑ Ⓒ Ⓓ Ⓔ   6 Ⓐ Ⓑ Ⓒ Ⓓ Ⓔ   11 Ⓐ Ⓑ Ⓒ Ⓓ Ⓔ   16 Ⓐ Ⓑ Ⓒ Ⓓ Ⓔ   21 Ⓐ Ⓑ Ⓒ Ⓓ Ⓔ

2 Ⓐ Ⓑ Ⓒ Ⓓ Ⓔ   7 Ⓐ Ⓑ Ⓒ Ⓓ Ⓔ   12 Ⓐ Ⓑ Ⓒ Ⓓ Ⓔ   17 Ⓐ Ⓑ Ⓒ Ⓓ Ⓔ   22 Ⓐ Ⓑ Ⓒ Ⓓ Ⓔ

3 Ⓐ Ⓑ Ⓒ Ⓓ Ⓔ   8 Ⓐ Ⓑ Ⓒ Ⓓ Ⓔ   13 Ⓐ Ⓑ Ⓒ Ⓓ Ⓔ   18 Ⓐ Ⓑ Ⓒ Ⓓ Ⓔ   23 Ⓐ Ⓑ Ⓒ Ⓓ Ⓔ

4 Ⓐ Ⓑ Ⓒ Ⓓ Ⓔ   9 Ⓐ Ⓑ Ⓒ Ⓓ Ⓔ   14 Ⓐ Ⓑ Ⓒ Ⓓ Ⓔ   19 Ⓐ Ⓑ Ⓒ Ⓓ Ⓔ   24 Ⓐ Ⓑ Ⓒ Ⓓ Ⓔ

5 Ⓐ Ⓑ Ⓒ Ⓓ Ⓔ   10 Ⓐ Ⓑ Ⓒ Ⓓ Ⓔ   15 Ⓐ Ⓑ Ⓒ Ⓓ Ⓔ   20 Ⓐ Ⓑ Ⓒ Ⓓ Ⓔ   25 Ⓐ Ⓑ Ⓒ Ⓓ Ⓔ

READING COMPREHENSION SAMPLE TEST

25 Questions

Directions: Each passage in this group is followed by questions based on its content. After reading a passage, choose the best answer to each question and blacken the corresponding space on the answer sheet. Answer all questions following a passage on the basis of what is stated or implied in that passage.

Most economists in the United States seem captivated by the spell of the free market. Consequently, nothing seems good or normal that does not accord with the requirements of the free market.
(5) A price that is determined by the seller or, for that matter, established by anyone other than the aggregate of consumers seems pernicious. Accordingly, it requires a major act of will to think of price-fixing (the determination of prices by the
(10) seller) as both "normal" and having a valuable economic function. In fact, price-fixing is normal in all industrialized societies because the industrial system itself provides, as an effortless consequence of its own development, the price-fixing
(15) that it requires. Modern industrial planning requires and rewards great size. Hence, a comparatively small number of large firms will be competing for the same group of consumers. That each large firm will act with consideration of
(20) its own needs and thus avoid selling its products for more than its competitors charge is commonly recognized by advocates of free-market economic theories. But each large firm will also act with full consideration of the needs that it has in
(25) common with the other large firms competing for the same customers. Each large firm will thus avoid significant price-cutting, because price-cutting would be prejudicial to the common interest in a stable demand for products. Most economists
(30) do not see price-fixing when it occurs because they expect it to be brought about by a number of explicit agreements among large firms; it is not.
Moreover, those economists who argue that allowing the free market to operate without inter-
(35) ference is the most efficient method of establishing prices have not considered the economies of non-socialist countries other than the United States. These economies employ intentional price-fixing, usually in an overt fashion. Formal price-fixing
(40) by cartel and informal price-fixing by agreements covering the members of an industry are commonplace. Were there something peculiarly efficient about the free market and inefficient about price-fixing, the countries that have avoided the first
(45) and used the second would have suffered drastically in their economic development. There is no indication that they have.
Socialist industry also works within a framework of controlled prices. In the early 1970's,
(50) the Soviet Union began to give firms and industries some of the flexibility in adjusting prices that a

more informal evolution has accorded the capitalist system. Economists in the United States have hailed the change as a return to the free market.
(55) But Soviet firms are no more subject to prices established by a free market over which they exercise little influence than are capitalist firms; rather, Soviet firms have been given the power to fix prices.

1. The primary purpose of the passage is to
   (A) refute the theory that the free market plays a useful role in the development of industrialized societies
   (B) suggest methods by which economists and members of the government of the United States can recognize and combat price-fixing by large firms
   (C) show that in industrialized societies price-fixing and the operation of the free market are not only compatible but also mutually beneficial
   (D) explain the various ways in which industrialized societies can fix prices in order to stabilize the free market
   (E) argue that price-fixing, in one form or another, is an inevitable part of and benefit to the economy of any industrialized society

2. The passage provides information that would answer which of the following questions about price-fixing?
   I. What are some of the ways in which prices can be fixed?
   II. For what products is price-fixing likely to be more profitable than the operation of the free market?
   III. Is price-fixing more common in socialist industrialized societies or in nonsocialist industrialized societies?

   (A) I only
   (B) III only
   (C) I and II only
   (D) II and III only
   (E) I, II, and III

GO ON TO THE NEXT PAGE.

3. The author's attitude toward "Most economists in the United States" (line 1) can best be described as

    (A) spiteful and envious
    (B) scornful and denunciatory
    (C) critical and condescending
    (D) ambivalent but deferential
    (E) uncertain but interested

4. It can be inferred from the author's argument that a price fixed by the seller "seems pernicious" (line 7) because

    (A) people do not have confidence in large firms
    (B) people do not expect the government to regulate prices
    (C) most economists believe that consumers as a group should determine prices
    (D) most economists associate fixed prices with communist and socialist economies
    (E) most economists believe that no one group should determine prices

5. The suggestion in the passage that price-fixing in industrialized societies is normal arises from the author's statement that price-fixing is

    (A) a profitable result of economic development
    (B) an inevitable result of the industrial system
    (C) the result of a number of carefully organized decisions
    (D) a phenomenon common to industrialized and nonindustrialized societies
    (E) a phenomenon best achieved cooperatively by government and industry

6. According to the author, price-fixing in nonsocialist countries is often

    (A) accidental but productive
    (B) illegal but useful
    (C) legal and innovative
    (D) traditional and rigid
    (E) intentional and widespread

7. According to the author, what is the result of the Soviet Union's change in economic policy in the 1970's?

    (A) Soviet firms show greater profit.
    (B) Soviet firms have less control over the free market.
    (C) Soviet firms are able to adjust to technological advances.
    (D) Soviet firms have some authority to fix prices.
    (E) Soviet firms are more responsive to the free market.

8. With which of the following statements regarding the behavior of large firms in industrialized societies would the author be most likely to agree?

    (A) The directors of large firms will continue to anticipate the demand for products.
    (B) The directors of large firms are less interested in achieving a predictable level of profit than in achieving a large profit.
    (C) The directors of large firms will strive to reduce the costs of their products.
    (D) Many directors of large firms believe that the government should establish the prices that will be charged for products.
    (E) Many directors of large firms believe that the price charged for products is likely to increase annually.

9. In the passage, the author is primarily concerned with

    (A) predicting the consequences of a practice
    (B) criticizing a point of view
    (C) calling attention to recent discoveries
    (D) proposing a topic for research
    (E) summarizing conflicting opinions

GO ON TO THE NEXT PAGE.

The discoveries of the white dwarf, the neutron star, and the black hole, coming well after the discovery of the red giant, are among the most exciting developments in decades because they
(5) may well present physicists with their greatest challenge since the failure of classical mechanics. In the life cycle of a star, after all of the hydrogen and helium fuel has been burned, the delicate balance between the outward nuclear radiation pres-
(10) sure and the stable gravitational force becomes disturbed and slow contraction begins. As compression increases, a very dense plasma forms. If the initial star had a mass of less than 1.4 solar masses (1.4 times the mass of our sun), the pro-
(15) cess ceases at a density of 1,000 tons per cubic inch, and the star becomes a white dwarf. However, if the star was originally more massive, the white dwarf plasma cannot resist the gravitational pressures, and, in a rapid collapse, all nuclei of
(20) the star are converted to a gas of free neutrons. Gravitational attraction compresses this neutron gas rapidly until a density of 10^9 tons per cubic inch is reached; at this point the strong nuclear force resists further contraction. If the mass of
(25) the star was between 1.4 and a few solar masses, the process stops here, and we have a neutron star.

But if the original star was more massive than a few solar masses, even the strong nuclear forces
(30) cannot resist the gravitational crunch. The neutrons are forced into one another to form heavier hadrons—and these in turn coalesce to form heavier entities, of which we as yet know nothing. At this point, a complete collapse of
(35) the stellar mass occurs; existing theories predict a collapse to infinite density and infinitely small dimensions. Well before this, however, the surface gravitational force would become so strong that no signal could ever leave the star—
(40) any photon emitted would fall back under gravitational attraction—and the star would become a black hole in space.

This gravitational collapse poses a fundamental challenge to physics. When the most widely
(45) accepted theories predict such improbable things as infinite density and infinitely small dimensions, it simply means that we are missing some vital insight. This last happened in physics in the 1930's, when we faced a fundamental paradox
(50) concerning atomic structure. At that time, it was recognized that electrons moved in stable orbits about nuclei in atoms. However, it was also recognized that if a charge is accelerated, as it must be to remain in orbit, it radiates energy;
(55) so, theoretically, the electron would be expected eventually to spiral into the nucleus and destroy the atom. Studies centered around this paradox led to the development of quantum mechanics. It may well be that an equivalent advance awaits us in
(60) investigating the theoretical problems presented by the phenomenon of gravitational collapse.

10. The primary purpose of the passage is to

(A) offer new explanations for the collapse of stars
(B) explain the origins of black holes, neutron stars, and white dwarfs
(C) compare the structure of atoms with the structure of the solar system
(D) explain how the collapse of stars challenges accepted theories of physics
(E) describe the imbalance between radiation pressure and gravitational force

11. According to the passage, in the final stages of its development our own sun is likely to take the form of a

(A) white dwarf
(B) neutron star
(C) red giant
(D) gas of free neutrons
(E) black hole

12. According to the passage, an imbalance arises between nuclear radiation pressure and gravitational force in stars because

(A) the density of a star increases as it ages
(B) radiation pressure increases as a star increases in mass
(C) radiation pressure decreases when a star's fuel has been consumed
(D) the collapse of a star increases its gravitational force
(E) a dense plasma decreases the star's gravitational force

GO ON TO THE NEXT PAGE.

13. The author asserts that the discoveries of the white dwarf, the neutron star, and the black hole are significant because these discoveries

   (A) demonstrate the probability of infinite density and infinitely small dimensions
   (B) pose the most comprehensive and fundamental problem faced by physicists in decades
   (C) clarify the paradox suggested by the collapse of electrons into atomic nuclei
   (D) establish the relationship between mass and gravitational pressure
   (E) assist in establishing the age of the universe by tracing the life histories of stars

14. The passage contains information that answers which of the following questions?

   I. What is the density limit of the gravitational collapse of neutron stars?
   II. At what point in its life cycle does a star begin to contract?
   III. What resists the gravitational collapse of a star?

   (A) I only
   (B) III only
   (C) I and II only
   (D) II and III only
   (E) I, II, and III

15. The author introduces the discussion of the paradox concerning atomic structure (lines 48-58) in order to

   (A) show why it was necessary to develop quantum mechanics
   (B) compare the structure of an atom with the structure of a star
   (C) demonstrate by analogy that a vital insight in astrophysics is missing
   (D) illustrate the contention that improbable things do happen in astrophysics
   (E) argue that atoms can collapse if their electrons do not remain in orbit

16. According to the passage, paradoxes are useful in scientific investigation because they

   (A) point to the likelihood of impending discoveries
   (B) assist scientists in making comparisons with other branches of knowledge
   (C) disprove theories that have been called into question
   (D) call attention to inadequacies of existing theory
   (E) suggest new hypotheses that can be tested by observation

GO ON TO THE NEXT PAGE.

At the time Jane Austen's novels were published—between 1811 and 1818—English literature was not part of any academic curriculum. In addition, fiction was under strenuous attack.
(5) Certain religious and political groups felt novels had the power to make so-called immoral characters so interesting that young readers would identify with them; these groups also considered novels to be of little practical use. Even Cole-
(10) ridge, certainly no literary reactionary, spoke for many when he asserted that "novel-reading occasions the destruction of the mind's powers."

These attitudes toward novels help explain why Austen received little attention from early nine-
(15) teenth-century literary critics. (In any case, a novelist published anonymously, as Austen was, would not be likely to receive much critical attention.) The literary response that was accorded her, however, was often as incisive as twentieth-
(20) century criticism. In his attack in 1816 on novelistic portrayals "outside of ordinary experience," for example, Scott made an insightful remark about the merits of Austen's fiction. Her novels, wrote Scott, "present to the reader an accurate and exact
(25) picture of ordinary everyday people and places, reminiscent of seventeenth-century Flemish painting." Scott did not use the word "realism," but he undoubtedly used a standard of realistic probability in judging novels. The critic Whately
(30) did not use the word realism either, but he expressed agreement with Scott's evaluation, and went on to suggest the possibilities for moral instruction in what we have called Austen's realistic method. Her characters, wrote Whately,
(35) are persuasive agents for moral truth since they are ordinary persons "so clearly evoked that we feel an interest in their fate as if it were our own." Moral instruction, explained Whately, is more likely to be effective when conveyed through recog-
(40) nizably human and interesting characters than when imparted by a sermonizing narrator. Whately especially praised Austen's ability to create characters who "mingle goodness and villainy, weakness and virtue, as in life they are always
(45) mingled." Whately concluded his remarks by comparing Austen's art of characterization to Dickens', stating his preference for Austen's.

Yet the response of nineteenth-century literary critics to Austen was not always so laudatory, and
(50) often anticipated the reservations of twentieth-century critics. An example of such a response was Lewes' complaint in 1859 that Austen's range of subjects and characters was too narrow. Praising her verisimilitude, Lewes added that nonethe-
(55) less her focus was too often upon only the unlofty and the commonplace. (Twentieth-century Marxists, on the other hand, were to complain about what they saw as her exclusive emphasis on a lofty upper-middle class.) In any case, having been
(60) rescued by some literary critics from neglect and indeed gradually lionized by them, Austen steadily reached, by the mid-nineteenth century, the enviable pinnacle of being considered controversial.

17. The primary purpose of the passage is to

(A) demonstrate the nineteenth-century preference for realistic novels rather than romantic ones
(B) explain why Jane Austen's novels were not included in any academic curriculum in the early nineteenth century
(C) urge a reassessment of Jane Austen's novels by twentieth-century literary critics
(D) describe some of the responses of nineteenth-century critics to Jane Austen's novels as well as to fiction in general
(E) argue that realistic character portrayal is the novelist's most difficult task as well as the aspect of a novel most likely to elicit critical response

18. The passage supplies information for answering which of the following questions?

(A) Was Whately aware of Scott's remarks about Jane Austen's novels?
(B) Who is an example of a twentieth-century Marxist critic?
(C) Who is an example of a twentieth-century critic who admired Jane Austen's novels?
(D) What is the author's judgment of Dickens?
(E) Did Jane Austen express her opinion of those nineteenth-century critics who admired her novels?

19. The author mentions that English literature "was not part of any academic curriculum" (line 3) in the early nineteenth century in order to

(A) emphasize the need for Jane Austen to create ordinary, everyday characters in her novels
(B) give support to those religious and political groups that had attacked fiction
(C) give one reason why Jane Austen's novels received little critical attention in the early nineteenth century
(D) suggest the superiority of an informal and unsystematized approach to the study of literature
(E) contrast nineteenth-century attitudes toward English literature with those toward classical literature

GO ON TO THE NEXT PAGE.

20. The passage supplies information to suggest that the religious and political groups mentioned in lines 5-9 and Whately might have agreed that a novel

(A) has little practical use
(B) has the ability to influence the moral values of its readers
(C) is of most interest to readers when representing ordinary human characters
(D) should not be read by young readers
(E) needs the sermonizing of a narrator in order to impart moral truths

21. The author quotes Coleridge (lines 11-12) in order to

(A) refute the literary opinions of certain religious and political groups
(B) make a case for the inferiority of novels to poetry
(C) give an example of a writer who was not a literary reactionary
(D) illustrate the early nineteenth-century belief that fiction was especially appealing to young readers
(E) indicate how widespread was the attack on novels in the early nineteenth century

22. The passage suggests that twentieth-century Marxists would have admired Jane Austen's novels more if the novels, as the Marxists understood them, had

(A) described the values of upper-middle class society
(B) avoided moral instruction and sermonizing
(C) depicted ordinary society in a more flattering light
(D) portrayed characters from more than one class of society
(E) anticipated some of the controversial social problems of the twentieth century

23. It can be inferred from the passage that Whately found Dickens' characters to be

(A) especially interesting to young readers
(B) ordinary persons in recognizably human situations
(C) less liable than Jane Austen's characters to have a realistic mixture of moral qualities
(D) more often villainous and weak than virtuous and good
(E) less susceptible than Jane Austen's characters to the moral judgments of a sermonizing narrator

24. According to the passage, the lack of critical attention paid to Jane Austen can be explained by all of the following nineteenth-century attitudes toward the novel EXCEPT the

(A) assurance felt by many people that novels weakened the mind
(B) certainty shared by many political commentators that the range of novels was too narrow
(C) lack of interest shown by some critics in novels that were published anonymously
(D) fear exhibited by some religious and political groups that novels had the power to portray immoral characters attractively
(E) belief held by some religious and political groups that novels had no practical value

25. The author would most likely agree that which of the following is the best measure of a writer's literary success?

(A) Inclusion of the writer's work in an academic curriculum
(B) Publication of the writer's work in the writer's own name
(C) Existence of debate among critics about the writer's work
(D) Praise of the writer's work by religious and political groups
(E) Ability of the writer's work to appeal to ordinary people

END OF SAMPLE TEST

Answer Key for Sample Test

READING COMPREHENSION

1. E	14. E
2. A	15. C
3. C	16. D
4. C	17. D
5. B	18. A
6. E	19. C
7. D	20. B
8. A	21. E
9. B	22. D
10. D	23. C
11. A	24. B
12. C	25. C
13. B	

Explanatory Material: Reading Comprehension

The following discussion of Reading Comprehension is intended to familarize you with the most efficient and effective approaches to the kinds of problems common to Reading Comprehension. The particular questions on the sample test in this chapter are generally representative of the kinds of questions you will encounter in this section of the GMAT. Remember that it is the problem-solving strategy that is important, not the specific details of a particular question.

1. **The primary purpose of the passage is to**

   (A) refute the theory that the free market plays a useful role in the development of industrialized societies
   (B) suggest methods by which economists and members of the government of the United States can recognize and combat price-fixing by large firms
   (C) show that in industrialized societies price-fixing and the operation of the free market are not only compatible but also mutually beneficial
   (D) explain the various ways in which industrialized societies can fix prices in order to stabilize the free market
   (E) argue that price-fixing, in one form or another, is an inevitable part of and benefit to the economy of any industrialized society

The best answer is E. The author contends in lines 7-15 that price-fixing is normal and beneficial in industrialized societies. The author proceeds to support this assertion with descriptions of various forms of price-fixing in various kinds of industrialized societies (lines 23-29, 36-42, and 48-59). Moreover, in lines 42-47, in the context of a discussion of nonsocialist countries other than the United States, the author indirectly restates the argument in favor of price-fixing. This is a question of medium difficulty.

2. **The passage provides information that would answer which of the following questions about price-fixing?**

   I. What are some of the ways in which prices can be fixed?
   II. For what products is price-fixing likely to be more profitable than the operation of the free market?
   III. Is price-fixing more common in socialist industrialized societies or in nonsocialist industrialized societies?

   (A) I only
   (B) III only
   (C) I and II only
   (D) II and III only
   (E) I, II, and III

This question asks whether one or more of the questions identified by Roman numerals can be answered on the basis of the information given in the passage. In questions of this kind, each part identified by a Roman numeral must be considered individually. Question I can be answered by information in lines 26-27, 31-32, 38-42, and 50-53 of the passage, which mention some different ways of fixing prices. Questions II and III cannot be answered from information provided by the passage. The best answer, therefore, is A (I only). This is a very difficult question.

3. **The author's attitude toward "Most economists in the United States" (line 1) can best be described as**

   (A) spiteful and envious
   (B) scornful and denunciatory
   (C) critical and condescending
   (D) ambivalent but deferential
   (E) uncertain but interested

The best answer is C. Determining the author's attitude toward a topic requires locating all references to the topic in the passage and considering both the literal meanings and the connotations of the words used concerning the topic. Thus, the author refers to "most economists" or "economists in the United States" or "those economists" in lines 1-2, 29-32, 33-37, and 53-54. The author describes them as "captivated by the spell of the free market," as failing to see price-fixing when it occurs, as failing to consider the economies of nonsocialist countries other than the United States, and as mistakenly "hailing" price-fixing in the Soviet Union as a return to the free market. The choice that best describes these references is "critical and condescending." This is a question of medium difficulty.

4. It can be inferred from the author's argument that a price fixed by the seller ''seems pernicious'' (line 7) because

   (A) people do not have confidence in large firms
   (B) people do not expect the government to regulate prices
   (C) most economists believe that consumers as a group should determine prices
   (D) most economists associate fixed prices with communist and socialist economies
   (E) most economists believe that no one group should determine prices

The best answer is C. Lines 1-7 allow one to infer that it is to ''Most economists'' (line 1) that a price fixed by the seller ''seems pernicious,'' and that these economists consider price-fixing pernicious because they believe that only the ''aggregate of consumers'' (line 7) should establish prices. This is a relatively easy question.

5. The suggestion in the passage that price-fixing in industrialized societies is normal arises from the author's statement that price-fixing is

   (A) a profitable result of economic development
   (B) an inevitable result of the industrial system
   (C) the result of a number of carefully organized decisions
   (D) a phenomenon common to industrialized and nonindustrialized societies
   (E) a phenomenon best achieved cooperatively by government and industry

The best answer is B, based on lines 11-15, which state that price-fixing is normal in all industrialized societies because the industrial system provides price-fixing ''as an effortless consequence of its own development.'' This is a relatively easy question.

6. According to the author, price-fixing in nonsocialistic countries is often

   (A) accidental but productive
   (B) illegal but useful
   (C) legal and innovative
   (D) traditional and rigid
   (E) intentional and widespread

The best answer is E, based on lines 38 (''intentional price-fixing'') and 41-42 (''commonplace''). This is a question of medium difficulty.

7. According to the author, what is the result of the Soviet Union's change in economic policy in the 1970's?

   (A) Soviet firms show greater profit.
   (B) Soviet firms have less control over the free market.
   (C) Soviet firms are able to adjust to technological advances.
   (D) Soviet firms have some authority to fix prices.
   (E) Soviet firms are more responsive to the free market.

The best answer is D. In lines 49-53, the author states that, in the early 1970's, the Soviet Union gave firms some ''flexibility in adjusting prices.'' In lines 58-59, the author states that what these firms have in fact been given is ''the power to fix prices.'' Thus, the result of the Soviet Union's change in economic policy in the 1970's is choice D, ''Soviet firms have some authority to fix prices.'' This is a very easy question.

8. With which of the following statements regarding the behavior of large firms in industrialized societies would the author be most likely to agree?

   (A) The directors of large firms will continue to anticipate the demand for products.
   (B) The directors of large firms are less interested in achieving a predictable level of profit than in achieving a large profit.
   (C) The directors of large firms will strive to reduce the costs of their products.
   (D) Many directors of large firms believe that the government should establish the prices that will be charged for products.
   (E) Many directors of large firms believe that the price charged for products is likely to increase annually.

The best answer is A. The author discusses the behavior of large firms in industrialized societies in lines 15-29. In lines 26-29, the author refers to the firms' ''common interest in a stable demand for products.'' It can be inferred from these references that the author believes that the directors of large firms currently anticipate the demand for products. Since the author describes price-fixing as an ongoing phenomenon (lines 11-29), it can be inferrred that the author would be likely to agree that the large firms' directors will also continue to anticipate the demand for products. This is a relatively difficult question.

9. In the passage, the author is primarily concerned with

   (A) predicting the consequences of a practice
   (B) criticizing a point of view
   (C) calling attention to recent discoveries
   (D) proposing a topic for research
   (E) summarizing conflicting opinions

The best answer is B. Throughout the passage, the author criticizes the point of view of ''most economists in the United States''—those who believe that the free market is best and that price-fixing is pernicious. Thus, the first paragraph argues that price-fixing is normal and valuable in all industrialized countries. The second paragraph argues that the experience of nonsocialist countries other than the United States provides no support for the point of view of these economists. The third paragraph argues that these economists are wrong in thinking that the Soviet Union has moved toward a free market. Thus, it can be inferred that the author's primary concern is to criticize this point of view. This is a relatively easy question.

10. The primary purpose of the passage is to

(A) offer new explanations for the collapse of stars
(B) explain the origins of black holes, neutron stars, and white dwarfs
(C) compare the structure of atoms with the structure of the solar system
(D) explain how the collapse of stars challenges accepted theories of physics
(E) describe the imbalance between radiation pressure and gravitational force

The best answer is D. The central idea of the passage is that the final possible stage in the gravitational collapse of a star, a black hole, produces a state of affairs in which "widely accepted theories predict . . . improbable things" (lines 44-45). This situation, the author points out, "may well present physicists with their greatest challenge" since the failure of classical physics (lines 5-6) and "poses a fundamental challenge to physics" (lines 43-44). The idea of challenge is reinforced by the analogy drawn between this situation in physics and the atomic structure paradox of the 1930's. Thus the whole purpose of the passage is to explain the process of gravitational collapse and to suggest how this challenges accepted theories in physics. This is a relatively easy question.

11. According to the passage, in the final stages of its development our own sun is likely to take the form of a

(A) white dwarf
(B) neutron star
(C) red giant
(D) gas of free neutrons
(E) black hole

The best answer is A because lines 12-16 indicate that all stars with a mass less than 1.4 times the mass of our sun will collapse into white dwarfs. As our sun fits this condition, it must eventually collapse into a white dwarf. This is a question of medium difficulty.

12. According to the passage, an imbalance arises between nuclear radiation pressure and gravitational force in stars because

(A) the density of a star increases as it ages
(B) radiation pressure increases as a star increases in mass
(C) radiation pressure decreases when a star's fuel has been consumed
(D) the collapse of a star increases its gravitational force
(E) a dense plasma decreases the star's gravitational force

The best answer is C because lines 7-11 indicate that a disturbance in the balance between outward nuclear radiation and stable inward gravitational force occurs "after all of the hydrogen and helium fuel has been burned." Since "slow contraction begins" after the fuel is consumed, and since the gravitational force is stable, the imbalance must be caused by a lessening in the outward radiation pressure. This is a relatively difficult question.

13. The author asserts that the discoveries of the white dwarf, the neutron star, and the black hole are significant because these discoveries

(A) demonstrate the probability of infinite density and infinitely small dimensions
(B) pose the most comprehensive and fundamental problem faced by physicists in decades
(C) clarify the paradox suggested by the collapse of electrons into atomic nuclei
(D) establish the relationship between mass and gravitational pressure
(E) assist in establishing the age of the universe by tracing the life histories of stars

The best answer is B. Lines 1-6 state that the discoveries of the white dwarf, the neutron star, and the black hole are among the most exciting developments in recent physics and "may well present physicists with their greatest challenge since the failure of classical mechanics." This "challenge" is explained in the rest of the passage, where it is described as "fundamental" (line 43), as being of a magnitude that was last seen in physics "in the 1930's" (lines 48-49), and as conceivably leading to an advance the equivalent of the development of quantum mechanics (lines 57-61). Thus the author considers the discoveries significant because they pose problems of a magnitude that physics has not seen since the 1930's. This is a relatively easy question.

14. The passage contains information that answers which of the following questions?

I. What is the density limit of the gravitational collapse of neutron stars?
II. At what point in its life cycle does a star begin to contract?
III. What resists the gravitational collapse of a star?

(A) I only
(B) III only
(C) I and II only
(D) II and III only
(E) I, II, and III

The best answer is E. Question I is answered in lines 21-23, where it is stated that in the case of neutron stars, gravitational compression continues until a density of 10^9 tons per cubic inch is reached. Question II is answered in lines 7-11, where it is stated that stars begin to contract after all hydrogen and helium fuel has been burned. Question III has three answers, depending on what stage a star is in. First, outward nuclear radiation resists gravitational collapse (lines 8-10); next the white dwarf plasma resists gravitational collapse (lines 18-19); and finally the strong nuclear force resists gravitational collapse (lines 21-24). Thus all three questions are answered in the passage and E is the correct choice. This is a relatively difficult question.

15. The author introduces the discussion of the paradox concerning atomic structure (lines 48-58) in order to

  (A) show why it was necessary to develop quantum mechanics
  (B) compare the structure of an atom with the structure of a star
  (C) demonstrate by analogy that a vital insight in astrophysics is missing
  (D) illustrate the contention that improbable things do happen in astrophysics
  (E) argue that atoms can collapse if their electrons do not remain in orbit

The best answer is C. In lines 44-48 the author introduces the discussion of the atomic structure paradox by noting that when improbable things happen it means that physicists "are missing some vital insight." The author then states that "This last happened in physics in the 1930's, when we faced a fundamental paradox concerning atomic structure" (lines 48-50). The author closes the discussion by suggesting "that an equivalent advance awaits us" (line 59) in astrophysics. Together these imply that the author sees an analogy between the atomic structure paradox and the gravitational collapse problem in astrophysics, and anticipates that the second will be solved in the same way as the first, by a new vital insight. This is a question of medium difficulty.

16. According to the passage, paradoxes are useful in scientific investigation because they

  (A) point to the likelihood of impending discoveries
  (B) assist scientists in making comparisons with other branches of knowledge
  (C) disprove theories that have been called into question
  (D) call attention to inadequacies of existing theory
  (E) suggest new hypotheses that can be tested by observation

The best answer is D. Two paradoxes are described in the passage, the atomic structure problem of the 1930's and the gravitational collapse problem, and both are depicted as calling attention to problems in existing scientific theories. In lines 57-58 the author notes that work in atomic structure physics focused on the inconsistencies of the existing theories, and in lines 44-48 that the discoveries of such paradoxical phenomena as infinite density and infinitely small dimensions tell physicists that "some vital insight" is missing within existing theory. Thus in both cases the paradoxes serve to point out problems with existing theories and to draw the attention of physicists toward solving them. This is a relatively difficult question.

17. The primary purpose of the passage is to

  (A) demonstrate the nineteenth-century preference for realistic novels rather than romantic ones
  (B) explain why Jane Austen's novels were not included in any academic curriculum in the early nineteenth century
  (C) urge a reassessment of Jane Austen's novels by twentieth-century literary critics
  (D) describe some of the responses of nineteenth-century critics to Jane Austen's novels as well as to fiction in general
  (E) argue that realistic character portrayal is the novelist's most difficult task as well as the aspect of a novel most likely to elicit critical response

The best answer is D. When asked to identify the primary purpose of a passage, you must select the answer choice that states what the passage, as a whole, achieves. Choice D correctly identifies the passage as descriptive and goes on to accurately state the broad categories of things described. The passage does not contrast realistic and romantic novels, as choice A suggests. Austen's absence from academic curricula is mentioned only to support a larger point; thus, choice B is incorrect. Choice C is incorrect because the passage judges twentieth-century assessments satisfactory, leaving no reason to urge reassessment. Nothing is mentioned about the relative difficulty of realistic character portrayal or its tendency to attract more criticism than other aspects of novels; thus choice E can be eliminated. This is a relatively easy question.

18. The passage supplies information for answering which of the following questions?

  (A) Was Whately aware of Scott's remarks about Jane Austen's novels?
  (B) Who is an example of a twentieth-century Marxist critic?
  (C) Who is an example of a twentieth-century critic who admired Jane Austen's novels?
  (D) What is the author's judgment of Dickens?
  (E) Did Jane Austen express her opinion of those nineteenth-century critics who admired her novels?

The best answer is A. In order to answer this question, you should work through each of the choices, checking whether or not the passage supplies enough information to answer the question posed in the choice. Lines 30-31 tell us that Whately "expressed agreement with Scott's evaluation" of Austen's fictions; in order to agree, Whately must have been aware of Scott's remarks. Thus, an answer to the question posed in choice A is provided. Although the passage mentions Marxists, none is specifically named, thus choice B can be eliminated. The same reasoning eliminates choice C. Choice D can be eliminated because, while Whately's opinion *is* mentioned, the author's own is not. Choice E can be eliminated, because the passage nowhere indicates that Austen was even aware of criticism of her work. This is a question of medium difficulty.

19. The author mentions that English literature "was not part of any academic curriculum" (line 3) in the early nineteenth century in order to

(A) emphasize the need for Jane Austen to create ordinary, everyday characters in her novels
(B) give support to those religious and political groups that had attacked fiction
(C) give one reason why Jane Austen's novels received little critical attention in the early nineteenth century
(D) suggest the superiority of an informal and unsystematized approach to the study of literature
(E) contrast nineteenth-century attitudes toward English literature with those toward classical literature

The best answer is C. This question asks you to identify a reason for the author's selection of a particular supporting detail in the passage. You can approach this question by first rereading the part of the passage cited. Then, determine the reason for the author's selection and pick the answer choice that most nearly states what you consider the reason. Lines 13-15 are a straightforward indication of the author's reason for mentioning the absence of English literature in academic curricula: it is one indication of "attitudes . . . [that] help explain" why Austen was neglected by critics around the time her fiction was published. Choice C is very nearly a restatement of that idea. This is a relatively easy question.

20. The passage supplies information to suggest that the religious and political groups mentioned in lines 5-9 and Whately might have agreed that a novel

(A) has little practical use
(B) has the ability to influence the moral values of its readers
(C) is of most interest to readers when representing ordinary human characters
(D) should not be read by young readers
(E) needs the sermonizing of a narrator in order to impart moral truths

The best answer is B. This question requires you to start with a proposition *not* stated in the passage, i.e., that Whately and the groups mentioned share an opinion. The answer choices present possible opinions. Using the information given in the passage, you must determine which of the possible opinions could have been held in common. The passage indicates that the religious and political groups feared that readers would identify with immoral characters. It suggests that Whately thought that novels could be vehicles of moral instruction. Although they disagree about the value of such influence, they agree that novels can influence moral behavior. The other choices contain opinions that one or the other, but not both, holds (choices A, C, D), or an opinion that can not be attributed to either (choice E). This is a relatively easy question.

21. The author quotes Coleridge (lines 11-12) in order to

(A) refute the literary opinions of certain religious and political groups
(B) make a case for the inferiority of novels to poetry
(C) give an example of a writer who was not a literary reactionary
(D) illustrate the early nineteenth-century belief that fiction was especially appealing to young readers
(E) indicate how widespread was the attack on novels in the early nineteenth century

The best answer is E. This question asks you to identify a reason for the author's choice of a particular quotation in the passage. You can approach the question by first determining the reason and then selecting the answer choice that most nearly states what you consider that reason. The reference to Coleridge appears in a paragraph devoted to outlining the extent of opposition to novel-reading at the time of the publication of Austen's fiction. The phrase "Even Coleridge, certainly no literary reactionary . . ." (lines 9-10) suggests that Coleridge might be expected to differ, but the quotation demonstrates that Coleridge, too, was suspicious of novels. It illustrates the point that fiction was under strenuous, and widespread, attack. Choice E is very nearly a restatement of that idea. This is a relatively easy question.

22. The passage suggests that twentieth-century Marxists would have admired Jane Austen's novels more if the novels, as the Marxists understood them, had

(A) described the values of upper-middle class society
(B) avoided moral instruction and sermonizing
(C) depicted ordinary society in a more flattering light
(D) portrayed characters from more than one class of society
(E) anticipated some of the controversial social problems of the twentieth century

The best answer is D. The question requires you to determine a quality that Marxists find admirable in fiction, but that is missing from Austen's fiction. You should first look for the specific reference to Marxists. Lines 56-59 indicate that Marxists criticize Austen's fiction for its exclusive focus on the upper-middle class. This suggests that a Marxist criterion for judging novels involves the degree to which a novel represents a variety of social classes. If Austen's novels had portrayed characters from more than one class of society, as choice D states, it can be inferred that Marxists would value them more highly. Choice A is incorrect, because it states precisely what the Marxists object to. There is no information to support any of the remaining choices. This is a question of medium difficulty.

23. It can be inferred from the passage that Whately found Dickens' characters to be

(A) especially interesting to young readers
(B) ordinary persons in recognizably human situations
(C) less liable than Jane Austen's characters to have a realistic mixture of moral qualities
(D) more often villainous and weak than virtuous and good
(E) less susceptible than Jane Austen's characters to the moral judgments of a sermonizing narrator

The best answer is C. This question requires you to infer Whately's opinion of Dickens' characters. It is important to note that Dickens' method of characterization is mentioned only in contrast to Austen's. Lines 41-45 indicate that Whately particularly admired in Austen's characters a mingling of ''goodness and villainy, weakness and virtue, as in life they are always mingled.'' The passage then indicates that Whately preferred Austen's ''art of characterization'' to that of Dickens. Such a preference implies a significant difference between the two writers, suggesting that Dickens' method lacks a central characteristic of Austen's, that is, portrayal of characters with realistically mixed virtues and flaws. Choice C is very nearly a restatement of that idea. This is a relatively difficult question.

24. According to the passage, the lack of critical attention paid to Jane Austen can be explained by all of the following nineteenth-century attitudes toward the novel EXCEPT the

(A) assurance felt by many people that novels weakened the mind
(B) certainty shared by many political commentators the range of novels was too narrow
(C) lack of interest shown by some critics in novels that were published anonymously
(D) fear exhibited by some religious and political groups that novels had the power to portray immoral characters attractively
(E) belief held by some religious and political groups that novels had no practical value

The best answer is B. This question requires you to evaluate each of the answer choices and to judge which is not mentioned in the passage as an explanation for the critical neglect Austen suffered in the nineteenth century. Each of the answer choices could conceivably serve as an explanation, so it is important that you carefully consider what the passage actually mentions. The explanations offered in the first paragraph of the passage are those stated in choices A, D, and E. Lines 16-18 indicate that books published annonymously were unlikely to be reviewed; thus, choice C is also one of the explanations cited in the passage. The passage does not suggest that concerns about the narrow range of Austen's novels resulted in critical neglect; in fact, the contrary is suggested (lines 51-56). Thus B is the best choice. This is a question of medium difficulty.

25. The author would most likely agree that which of the following is the best measure of a writer's literary success?

(A) Inclusion of the writer's work in an academic curriculum
(B) Publication of the writer's work in the writer's own name
(C) Existence of debate among critics about the writer's work
(D) Praise of the writer's work by religious and political groups
(E) Ability of the writer's work to appeal to ordinary people

The best answer is C. This question requires you to determine, on the basis of ideas presented in the passage, what the author might think of an idea not presented in the passage, in this case, what constitutes the best measure of literary success. Although choices A, D, and E are plausible measures of a writer's success, nothing in the passage suggests that the author considers any of them ''best,'' while choice B is not clearly a criterion for judgment. Lines 61-63, however, indicate that Austen has reached the ''enviable pinnacle of being considered controversial,'' that is, the highest point one can reach. Thus, from the author's point of view, the best measure of an author's success is, as paraphrased in choice C, the existence of debate about the author. This is a question of medium difficulty.

6 Analysis of Situations

In an Analysis of Situations passage you must classify on the basis of relative importance the considerations that make up a management or business situation. Therefore, you should keep in mind six basic elements of the situations presented in the passages you will read. These six elements are the decision-maker, the choices, the objectives, the factors (major and minor), the assumptions, and unimportant issues. Each of the six elements is explained below.

The decision-maker is the person or group of persons in the business or management situation who must make the best choice for solving the problem.

The choices are the alternatives available to the decision-maker for solving the problem. Each alternative will have both advantages and disadvantages; the decision-maker wishes to pick the alternative that will best solve the problem.

The objectives are the goals the decision-maker is trying to achieve. Put another way, the objectives are the conditions that will exist after the problem has been solved, that is, after the decision has been made and the choice implemented. For example a decision-maker might need a suitable location for a factory. The decision-maker's problem is needing a new factory location. One of the decision-maker's objectives is ''a suitable location for the factory.'' The acquisition of such a location is an objective because it is an important condition that will exist after the decision-maker has chosen from among the alternative locations and implemented that choice. In short, acquiring the location solves the problem.

It must be emphasized, however, that even though Analysis of Situations passages are generally developed in terms of one important decision to be made, the decision-maker may have several important objectives. Analysis of Situations passages frequently have more than one objective. These objectives can be either concrete or abstract. In relocating a factory, the decision-maker may wish to be nearer the market and may also wish to make a social contribution to the community at large. Other objectives may include, but are not limited to, such things as improved equipment, expanded production, compliance with laws, achievement of a good business reputation, or customer good will. You should keep in mind that although objectives are usually stated early in a passage, they may appear in any part of the passage.

The factors are the financial, material, or time considerations that make up the business situation and that will influence, in varying degrees, the choice of an alternative. Factors can include a wide variety of concrete and abstract considerations. Factors may include, but are not limited to, such things as cost, available space, production schedules, compliance with laws, business reputation, or customer good will. There are two types of factors, major and minor.

- Major factors are those aspects of the business situation that have direct and significant influence on the decision concerning which alternative to choose in order to solve a problem. Major factors are decisive in determining whether or not an objective can be reached. For example, the cost of equipment may be decisive in determining whether an objective of not significantly increasing a budget can be achieved. This kind of relationship to an objective gives a factor major importance.

  Major factors may sometimes, but not always, be divided into smaller elements. For example, the final cost of a piece of equipment will include maintenance costs, shipping costs, and finance costs. Thus, depending on the passage, the total cost of a piece of equipment might be a major factor whereas shipping cost for the equipment would not. Major factors are always stated explicitly in the passage.

- Minor factors are those aspects of the business situation that bear on and influence major factors. Minor factors may be more specific than major factors, and may frequently contribute to major factors. As stated above, if a decision-maker's objective is to avoid significantly increasing a budget, the cost of a piece of equipment may be a major factor. The shipping cost of the equipment, or the distance to be shipped, depending on the situation, may be a minor factor. These minor factors bear directly on the major factor of cost of equipment.

A consideration that is to be classified as a minor factor may take the form either of a secondary consideration that is relevant to only one of the choices or of a secondary consideration that is relevant to more than one of the choices. For example, either "the shipping costs of bulldozer X" or "the shipping costs of all the bulldozers under consideration" can be, again depending on the decision to be made, minor factors.

It is especially important to realize that whether an aspect of the business situation is a factor or an objective depends on the specific details of the situation as stated and developed in the passage. For example, in one situation "compliance with laws" may be a factor. There may be, however, situations in which "compliance with laws" can be an objective. Since this is so, you must always evaluate each passage independently.

The assumptions are the relevant suppositions and projections made by the decision-maker *before* he or she evaluates the factors. These suppositions and projections are relevant in that they establish a framework within which the decision-maker works, and they are accepted by the decision-maker as true without explanation. For example, if a seller assumes that the market for a product will increase, he or she then evaluates the factors involved in each of the alternatives and makes a decision accordingly. Assumptions often take the form of projections about future events. Sometimes the assumptions are suppositions about the quality of an entity. Assumptions may either be stated explicitly in a passage or remain unstated, yet logically inferrable.

You should keep in mind that, although assumptions are made before the factors are weighed, these assumptions do not necessarily precede, chronologically, the discussion or evaluation of factors that occurs in a passage. It is true that often a decision-maker will first set out his or her assumptions and then begin preliminary evaluation and discussion of the factors. On the other hand, sometimes suppositions are raised, as in real life, in the course of a discussion or an evaluation. These suppositions are, however, brought up before any final evaluation of factors is made—before, in other words, a decision is reached. Thus, an assumption may be made "before the factors are weighed" in a strictly chronological sense as the Analysis of Situations passage develops, or an assumption may be made "before the factors are weighed" in the sense that the assumption precedes a final decision.

Unimportant issues are elements of the business situation that do not influence the choice of the best solution, do not bear on or influence a major factor in any appreciable way, and do not appear as part of the decision-maker's relevant assumptions about the business situation.

The numbered considerations that follow an Analysis of Situations passage are intended to determine how well you can classify the elements of the business situation into (A) objectives, (B) major factors, (C) minor factors, (D) assumptions, and (E) unimportant issues.

The following pages include test-taking strategies, a sample test, and detailed explanations of each consideration from the sample test. These explanations further illustrate the way the elements explained above work in Analysis of Situations passages, by explaining every possible classification of each consideration, not just the correct classification. The case studies appearing in the sample test are not designed to present examples of either good or poor administrative practices.

Test-Taking Strategies for Analysis of Situations

1. Become thoroughly familiar with the definitions of each element of Analysis of Situations passages as discussed above and as given in the directions for the Analysis of Situations section in the test itself.

2. Read the passages carefully. They will usually be about 850 words long. Since this material establishes complex relationships among the elements of the business situation, it may be wise to analyze the passage closely the first time through.

3. While reading a passage, try to identify the basic elements.

   a. The decision-maker and some of the objectives will usually be clearly stated early in the passage.

   b. A survey of the available choices will usually appear toward the beginning of the passage. Recognizing and isolating the choices will help you establish clearly the decision to be made.

   c. The greater part of the remainder of the passage will be a detailed discussion of the choices available to the decision-maker and the factors and conditions involved in each choice. Read this material carefully.

   Note the arguments for and against each proposed solution, and note the factors that seem to determine the course of the discussion. Remember that the factors should be weighed with an awareness that the decision-maker is working toward the best possible choice.

4. Read carefully each of the numbered considerations that follow a passage. Determine as precisely as possible the exact nature of the fact or concept involved in the consideration. Is it something that the decision-maker wants? Is it something that will influence making the best choice? How significant is the consideration in determining the best choice?

5. Keeping the entire business situation clearly and completely in mind, try to determine where the consideration fits into the process of making the best choice.

6. Select the answer that most nearly describes your evaluation of the consideration.

   When you take the sample test, use the answer spaces on page 97 to mark your answers.

Answer Spaces for Analysis of Situations Sample Test

1 Ⓐ Ⓑ Ⓒ Ⓓ Ⓔ   10 Ⓐ Ⓑ Ⓒ Ⓓ Ⓔ   19 Ⓐ Ⓑ Ⓒ Ⓓ Ⓔ   28 Ⓐ Ⓑ Ⓒ Ⓓ Ⓔ

2 Ⓐ Ⓑ Ⓒ Ⓓ Ⓔ   11 Ⓐ Ⓑ Ⓒ Ⓓ Ⓔ   20 Ⓐ Ⓑ Ⓒ Ⓓ Ⓔ   29 Ⓐ Ⓑ Ⓒ Ⓓ Ⓔ

3 Ⓐ Ⓑ Ⓒ Ⓓ Ⓔ   12 Ⓐ Ⓑ Ⓒ Ⓓ Ⓔ   21 Ⓐ Ⓑ Ⓒ Ⓓ Ⓔ   30 Ⓐ Ⓑ Ⓒ Ⓓ Ⓔ

4 Ⓐ Ⓑ Ⓒ Ⓓ Ⓔ   13 Ⓐ Ⓑ Ⓒ Ⓓ Ⓔ   22 Ⓐ Ⓑ Ⓒ Ⓓ Ⓔ   31 Ⓐ Ⓑ Ⓒ Ⓓ Ⓔ

5 Ⓐ Ⓑ Ⓒ Ⓓ Ⓔ   14 Ⓐ Ⓑ Ⓒ Ⓓ Ⓔ   23 Ⓐ Ⓑ Ⓒ Ⓓ Ⓔ   32 Ⓐ Ⓑ Ⓒ Ⓓ Ⓔ

6 Ⓐ Ⓑ Ⓒ Ⓓ Ⓔ   15 Ⓐ Ⓑ Ⓒ Ⓓ Ⓔ   24 Ⓐ Ⓑ Ⓒ Ⓓ Ⓔ   33 Ⓐ Ⓑ Ⓒ Ⓓ Ⓔ

7 Ⓐ Ⓑ Ⓒ Ⓓ Ⓔ   16 Ⓐ Ⓑ Ⓒ Ⓓ Ⓔ   25 Ⓐ Ⓑ Ⓒ Ⓓ Ⓔ   34 Ⓐ Ⓑ Ⓒ Ⓓ Ⓔ

8 Ⓐ Ⓑ Ⓒ Ⓓ Ⓔ   17 Ⓐ Ⓑ Ⓒ Ⓓ Ⓔ   26 Ⓐ Ⓑ Ⓒ Ⓓ Ⓔ   35 Ⓐ Ⓑ Ⓒ Ⓓ Ⓔ

9 Ⓐ Ⓑ Ⓒ Ⓓ Ⓔ   18 Ⓐ Ⓑ Ⓒ Ⓓ Ⓔ   27 Ⓐ Ⓑ Ⓒ Ⓓ Ⓔ

ANALYSIS OF SITUATIONS SAMPLE TEST

35 Questions

Directions: Each passage in this section is followed by numbered considerations that require classification, as illustrated by the following example:

> John Atkins, the owner of a service station in Leeway, wanted to open a station in Eastown. A computer company had plans to set up operations in Eastown, and Atkins, foreseeing an increase in traffic near the plant, was eager to acquire land in Eastown so that he could expand his business to serve commuting workers. Ideally, Atkins wanted a piece of land large enough to permit him to build a tire store as part of the new station; he also wanted to keep the cost of purchasing the land as well as the cost of clearing it for construction as low as possible. Atkins identified three possible properties: one on Moore Road, another on Route 5, and a third on Snow Lane. The purchase prices of the properties were $42,000, $36,000, and $34,000, respectively. The properties required different expenditures for clearing. In the case of the Snow Lane site, a diner would have to be demolished and pavement removed. Atkins knew that his decision required deliberation.

The following numbered considerations are related to the passage above. Evaluate each consideration separately in terms of the passage and on the answer sheet blacken space

A if the consideration is an Objective in making the decision; that is, one of the outcomes, results, or goals that the decision-maker seeks;

B if the consideration is a Major Factor in making the decision; that is, a consideration, explicitly mentioned in the passage, that is basic to reaching the decision;

C if the consideration is a Minor Factor in making the decision; that is, a consideration that is of secondary importance to reaching the decision and that bears on a Major Factor;

D if the consideration is an Assumption in making the decision; that is, a relevant supposition or projection made by the decision-maker before reaching the decision;

E if the consideration is an Unimportant Issue in making the decision; that is, a consideration that is insignificant or not immediately relevant to reaching the decision.

1. Increase in traffic near the new computer plant   Ⓐ Ⓑ Ⓒ ● Ⓔ

2. Acquisition of a sufficiently large piece of land   ● Ⓑ Ⓒ Ⓓ Ⓔ

3. Cost of clearing a piece of land   Ⓐ ● Ⓒ Ⓓ Ⓔ

4. Cost of demolishing the diner on the Snow Lane site   Ⓐ Ⓑ ● Ⓓ Ⓔ

5. Cost of starting up the new computer plant   Ⓐ Ⓑ Ⓒ Ⓓ ●

GO ON TO THE NEXT PAGE.

The best classification for number 1 is (D), an Assumption, since Atkins supposes that automobile traffic will increase near the new computer plant. The best classification for number 2 is (A), an Objective, since one of Atkins' goals is to obtain a piece of land large enough to permit him to include a tire store as part of his new station. (B), a Major Factor, is the best classification for number 3. The cost of clearing a property is a basic consideration to Atkins since he wants to prepare a property for construction at the lowest possible cost. The best classification for number 4 is (C), a Minor Factor. The cost of demolishing the diner on the Snow Lane site contributes to the total cost of clearing that site. That is, the cost of demolition is a secondary consideration that bears on a major factor. Finally, the best classification for number 5 is (E), an Unimportant Issue, since there is no logical connection between the cost of starting up the computer plant and Atkins' decision about which property to choose.

NOW READ THE PASSAGES AND CLASSIFY THE CONSIDERATIONS FOLLOWING THEM.

GO ON TO THE NEXT PAGE.

For fifteen years Rose and Paul Chung have owned and operated a convenience grocery store. They rely for the bulk of their trade on local shoppers who buy a few items, and local workers who buy coffee and sandwiches to take out.

The building in which the store is located has recently changed hands, and the new owner has informed the Chungs that when their lease expires, on August 15, they must move out. Since their business advantage results from the store's convenient location, combined with the long hours the store is open, they know that their present customers will not follow them to another location unless it is an equally convenient one right in the same town.

They confer with a real estate agent, stressing their need for a building in a convenient location, and emphasizing that they do not want a store that will require extensive remodeling. They are particularly concerned that the floor in any store they rent will support their heavy freezer and refrigerator cases without expensive structural modifications. The rent for their present store is only $300 per month; as long as the volume of their business remains at the present level, they will not be able to pay more than $100 over that. They do not require extensive parking facilities, but they do need a few parking spaces, because they feel that people will not stop at a convenience store unless they can park easily. Moreover, the Chungs stress that they want any store building they rent to have as much floor space as their present store, and at least a limited amount of storage space in the back of the store.

There are three stores that will be available for rent in town within the next few months. One, on School Street, the street next to the Chungs' present location, is as conveniently located as their present store, but has space to park only two cars in front of the store. The rent for the School Street store is only $350 per month, but the floor space is somewhat less than they have now, and there is virtually no storage space. In addition, the floor would need to have some extra beams installed to support the refrigerator and freezer cases. The School Street store will be empty on August 1, so the Chungs could move without closing down for more than a day or two. The Chungs are convinced that the business should be closed for the fewest possible number of days, since, they believe, the customers of a convenience store often shop there out of habit, and too long a delay in reopening could cause the permanent loss of some customers.

Another store, on Lanning Street, is six blocks from the center of town, not so centrally located as the School Street store. The Lanning Street store has slightly less floor space than the Chungs' present store, but has a great deal of storage space, and the floor is strong enough to hold all the cases. The rent of the store is $450, more than the Chungs want to pay, but the store has a parking lot for six cars, which the Chungs feel will bring in enough new customers and new trade to justify the higher rent. This store will be vacant and available on August 15, so even if the Chungs could move the fixtures and equipment in directly from the old store, there would be a delay of up to a week before they could reopen for business.

A third store, on Prospect Street, is several blocks from the Chungs' present store, but is still in the center of town, and would be just as convenient for the customers as the present store. The floor space is about the same as the present store, and there is more storage space. The rent of the Prospect Street store is $300, the same amount the Chungs now pay, but the floor of the store would not support the cases without new beams and joists, a fairly expensive remodeling job. There is room to park two or three cars next to the store, and since the street is not a busy one, customers could park on the street in front of the store. The Prospect Street store, however, would not be available for the Chungs to move into until September 1, although the work of strengthening the floor would be done before that date if they chose this location. The September 1 date presents difficulties, however, because the Chungs not only would have to close their business for three weeks, but also would have the extra expense of storing the fixtures and the nonperishable stock for two or three weeks.

After collecting all this information from the real estate agent, the Chungs went home to evaluate the three locations, in order to decide which of the available stores will offer the greatest advantages and the fewest drawbacks.

GO ON TO THE NEXT PAGE.

Directions: The following numbered considerations are related to the passage above. You may refer back to the passage and to the directions at the beginning of this section. Evaluate each consideration separately in terms of the passage and on the answer sheet blacken space

A if the consideration is an Objective in making the decision; that is, one of the outcomes, results, or goals that the decision-maker seeks;

B if the consideration is a Major Factor in making the decision; that is, a consideration, explicitly mentioned in the passage, that is basic to reaching the decision;

C if the consideration is a Minor Factor in making the decision; that is, a consideration that is of secondary importance to reaching the decision and that bears on a Major Factor;

D if the consideration is an Assumption in making the decision; that is, a relevant supposition or projection made by the decision-maker before reaching the decision;

E if the consideration is an Unimportant Issue in making the decision; that is, a consideration that is insignificant or not immediately relevant to reaching the decision.

1. Minimizing the number of days the business will be closed for the move

2. Detrimental effect of closing the business for an extended period of time

3. Amount of traffic on Lanning Street

4. Date the Chungs can open their business in a new location

5. Amount of storage space in the present store

6. Number of hours the new store would be open

7. Anticipation of losses in perishable stock during the move

8. Convenience of the location of each of the three stores

9. Date the Chungs could begin to move into the School Street store

10. Cost of transporting the fixtures and stock to a new location

11. Finding a new location with enough floor space

12. Relation between adequate convenient parking and the success of a convenience store

13. Amount of traffic on Prospect Street

14. Selection of a new store that will not need extensive renovation

15. Need for keeping the business in the same town

16. Strength of the floor structure in the three available locations

17. Amount of floor and storage space in each of the available stores

18. A store with a rent of no more than $400 a month

GO ON TO THE NEXT PAGE.

The Croftside Hospital's Benefit Committee must make a change in the operation of its major fund-raising event, an annual antiques fair, known locally as The Fair. It has become difficult to recruit enough volunteers to manage all the aspects of the organization of The Fair, and because the competition from similar events has increased, the ticket sales have begun to decline. The committee has decided to engage a professional manager; the secretary of the committee has written to three professional managers:

Dear _____:

The Croftside Hospital Benefit Committee plans to engage a professional manager for our Antiques Fair, which is held the last week of March. Since The Fair's traditional character is one of the features responsible for its success, we want to continue to have it on the same date and to retain as many of our present exhibitors as possible. The Fair features 45 exhibitors, each paying a $75 fee; ticket sales have been 2,000 on the average (at $3 each). The committee wants to continue to operate the lunch counter.

Please send information about your fee for managing The Fair, the number of tickets you expect would be sold, and the shortest contract you would accept. How much responsibility would your staff take for the organization of The Fair, including the preparation and dismantling of the exhibit space? In addition, we need to know the size of your advertising budget.

Sincerely,

James P. Harvey
Secretary

The secretary received the following replies:

SPINNING WHEEL PROMOTIONS

Dear Mr. Harvey:

Spinning Wheel Promotions' terms are as follows: SWP receives the exhibitor's participation fees, while the sponsor receives the fees from ticket sales. SWP would insist that you raise the fee to $100 and expand to 60 exhibitors. SWP could recommend a number of new exhibitors who would be suitable; you will have no trouble filling the additional spaces. A fair under SWP management can expect ticket sales of 2,500 to 2,800, making your proceeds nearly the same as they are now. SWP's schedule would necessitate a mid-April date for The Fair. Our company would allocate $1,000 for advertising in trade magazines; local advertising is the sponsor's responsibility. We would take complete responsibility for the organization of The Fair, except for the preparation and cleaning up of the exhibit space. We have no interest in managing the food service, but must have some control over the quality of exhibitors. Since we use a three-year contract, we could allow your present exhibitors to return the first year, but their subsequent participation would depend on the quality of their exhibits.

Sincerely,

Jane Zellerman
Spinning Wheel Promotions

GO ON TO THE NEXT PAGE.

TURNER ANTIQUES FAIRS, INC.

Dear Mr. Harvey:

Our schedule would allow us to manage the Croftside Antiques Fair in the last week of March, which we would be happy to do if your committee makes some changes in the scope of The Fair. We would require that you expand to seventy-five exhibitors and raise the fee to $100. We also would specify a ticket price of $3.50. You could expect ticket sales of 3,000 to 3,500.

FEES: Manager receives fifty percent of exhibitor fees and fifty percent of ticket sales.

ADVERTISING: Manager pays for all advertising. Estimated budget: $2,500.

CONTRACT: Five years.

EXHIBITORS: Manager screens and approves all exhibitors.

PREPARATION: Manager does all advance preparation and supervises setting up and cleaning of exhibit space; sponsoring organization provides personnel to set up and clean.

FOOD SERVICE: Manager must approve menu; food service is the responsibility of the sponsor. Manager receives a commission amounting to twenty percent of the dollar volume of the sales.

Under our terms, you should increase your net proceeds from The Fair.

Marcia Turner
Turner Antiques Fairs, Inc.

RIVERSIDE PROMOTIONS

Dear Mr. Harvey:

We would be happy to manage the Croftside Antiques Fair the last week in March. We receive the exhibitor' fees, while you as the sponsoring organization receive the admission fees. We would spend $500 for advertising in trade magazines and would expect you to spend an equivalent amount on local advertising. We use a one-year contract and would be happy to allow the committee to select the exhibitors. Should you want to replace any of your present exhibitors, we have a roster of over 100 potential exhibitors and would be pleased to make recommendations.

Riverside Promotions takes complete charge of the management of The Fair, including advance organization, setting up and cleaning up the exhibit space. We also include the management of the food service at The Fair, and part of our arrangement is that we will be the sole purveyor of refreshments at The Fair.

Riverside Promotions specializes in small, local events such as your fair; we are sure that our management would be satisfactory to your committee.

Sincerely,

Bill Oberhaus
Riverside Promotions

After receiving these replies, Mr. Harvey decided to call a meeting of the Benefit Committee to discuss the three proposals.

GO ON TO THE NEXT PAGE.

Directions: The following numbered considerations are related to the passage above. You may refer back to the passage and to the directions at the beginning of this section. Evaluate each consideration separately in terms of the passage and on the answer sheet blacken space

A if the consideration is an Objective in making the decision; that is, one of the outcomes, results, or goals that the decision-maker seeks;

B if the consideration is a Major Factor in making the decision; that is, a consideration, explicitly mentioned in the passage, that is basic to reaching the decision;

C if the consideration is a Minor Factor in making the decision; that is, a consideration that is of secondary importance to reaching the decision and that bears on a Major Factor;

D if the consideration is an Assumption in making the decision; that is, a relevant supposition or projection made by the decision-maker before reaching the decision;

E if the consideration is an Unimportant Issue in making the decision; that is, a consideration that is insignificant or not immediately relevant to reaching the decision.

19. Number of tickets each manager expects to sell

20. Spinning Wheel Promotions' standards of quality for exhibitors

21. The various managers' willingness to retain the present exhibitors

22. Size of the space presently allocated to each exhibitor in The Fair

23. Retaining many of the present exhibitors in The Fair

24. Continuing to operate the lunch counter at The Fair

25. Disadvantageousness of a change in the date of The Fair

26. The percentage of the exhibitor fees Turner Antiques Fairs, Inc. retains

27. Length of time The Fair has been in operation

28. Value of continuing The Fair as a major fund-raising event

29. Continued availability of volunteers for the lunch counter at The Fair

30. The various managers' stipulations about the operation of the lunch counter

31. Dates of the other antiques fairs in the area

32. Amount Riverside Promotions expects the committee to spend for local advertising

33. Turner Antiques Fairs' twenty percent commission on lunch counter sales

34. Size of the fee each manager will charge

35. Number of people each of the three managers employs

END OF SAMPLE TEST

Answer Key for Sample Test

ANALYSIS OF SITUATIONS

1. A		19. B	
2. D		20. C	
3. E		21. B	
4. B		22. E	
5. E		23. A	
6. E		24. A	
7. E		25. D	
8. B		26. C	
9. C		27. E	
10. E		28. D	
11. A		29. D	
12. D		30. B	
13. C		31. E	
14. A		32. C	
15. D		33. C	
16. B		34. B	
17. B		35. E	
18. A			

Explanatory Material: Analysis of Situations

The following discussion is intended to familiarize you with the most efficient and effective approaches to the kinds of problems common to Analysis of Situations. The particular examples on the sample test in this chapter are generally representative of the kinds of considerations you will encounter in this section of the GMAT. Remember that it is the problem-solving strategy that is important, not the specific details of a particular explanation.

Each consideration is followed by five explanations, one for each of the possible classifications. These explanations are designed to illustrate strategies for arriving at the correct classification.

1. **Minimizing the number of days the business will be closed for the move**

   (A) The correct classification for this consideration is A, an objective, because the fourth paragraph of the passage states that "the Chungs are convinced that the business should be closed for the fewest possible number of days." In other words, one of the Chungs' objectives is to keep to a minimum the number of days their business will be closed. This classification is of medium difficulty.

   (B) B is not the correct classification because "Minimizing the number of days the business will be closed for the move" is not a basic consideration that will be weighed by the Chungs during their evaluation of each location. That is, minimizing the number of days is not a fundamental consideration that would be applied to each location to determine which one is most suitable. The Chungs will evaluate a location in terms of the number of days their business would be closed if they moved to that location, but keeping to a minimum the number of closed days is an objective for the Chungs, not a factor in their decision. See (A) for an explanation of why the correct classification is A, an objective. This classification is of medium difficulty.

   (C) C is not the correct classification because "Minimizing the number of days the business will be closed for the move" is not a consideration that bears on or contributes to a major factor. That is, minimizing the number of days is not a consideration the Chungs will weigh in the course of evaluating the basic considerations that will determine which location is most suitable. It is true that the Chungs will evaluate a location in terms of how long their business would be closed if they moved to that location; it is also true that, in the course of this evaluation, the Chungs will weigh any factor that bears on how long their business would be closed. But keeping to a minimum the number of closed days is not such a factor; it is, rather, an objective of the Chungs. See (A) for an explanation of why the correct classification is A, an objective. This classification is of medium difficulty.

   (D) D is not the correct classification because "Minimizing the number of days the business will be closed for the move" is not a consideration that the Chungs assume. Minimizing the number of days does not provide, as assumptions sometimes do, a framework that leads to the establishment of an objective. Rather, "Minimizing the number of days the business will be closed for the move" is itself an objective for the Chungs. See (A) for an explanation of why the correct classification is A, an objective. This classification is of medium difficulty.

   (E) E is not the correct classification because "Minimizing the number of days the business will be closed for the move" is a consideration that is relevant to the decision. Minimizing the number of days is relevant because it is an objective the Chungs want to achieve and thus is fundamental in guiding the decision-making process. See (A) for an explanation of why the correct classification is A, an objective. This classification is of medium difficulty.

2. **Detrimental effect of closing the business for an extended period of time**

   (A) A is not the correct classification because the "Detrimental effect of closing the business for an extended period of time" is not an objective that the Chungs wish to achieve. That is, in making a decision about which location to choose, the Chungs do not seek the negative consequences of closing their business for a long period of time. The Chungs do have as an objective not keeping their business closed for an extended period of time, but that such a long-term closing would be detrimental to their business is an assumption or supposition they make, not an objective they seek to achieve. See (D) for an explanation of why the correct classification is D, an assumption. This classification is of medium difficulty.

(B) B is not the correct classification because the "Detrimental effect of closing the business for an extended period of time" is not a basic consideration that will be weighed by the Chungs during their evaluation of each location. That is, this detrimental effect is not a fundamental consideration that would be applied to each location to determine which one is most suitable. The Chungs will evaluate a location in terms of the number of days their business would be closed if they moved to that location, but that it would be detrimental to the business to be closed for very many days is an assumption or supposition the Chungs make, not a factor in picking a location. See (D) for an explanation of why the correct classification is D, an assumption. This classification is of medium difficulty.

(C) C is not the correct classification because the "Detrimental effect of closing the business for an extended period of time" is not a consideration that bears on or contributes to a major factor. That is, this detrimental effect is not a consideration that the Chungs will weigh in the course of evaluating the basic considerations that will determine which location is most suitable. It is true that the Chungs will evaluate a location in terms of how long their business would be closed if they moved to that location; it is also true that, in the course of this evaluation, the Chungs will weigh any factor that bears on how long their business would be closed. But the detrimental effect of closing the business for an extended period of time is not such a factor; it is, rather, an assumption the Chungs make. See (D) for an explanation of why the correct classification is D, an assumption. This classification is of medium difficulty.

(D) The correct classification for this consideration is D, an assumption. The passage's fourth paragraph tells you that the Chungs believe that "too long a delay in reopening could cause the permanent loss of some customers." In other words, the Chungs believe, or suppose, or project that there will be a detrimental effect on their business if it closes for an extended period of time. Note that this assumption provides a framework for the decision, a framework for the establishment of an objective: the Chungs' assuming that there will be a detrimental effect leads them to set an objective of opening the business quickly. This classification is of medium difficulty.

(E) E is not the correct classification because the "Detrimental effect of closing the business for an extended period of time" is a consideration that is relevant to the decision. This effect is relevant to the decision because it is assumed by the Chungs before they evaluate the prospective locations and come to a decision. More specifically, it is relevant in that it provides the framework for the establishment of an objective: because the Chungs assume there will be such a detrimental effect, they set an objective of opening the business quickly. See (D) for an explanation of why the correct classification is D, an assumption. This classification is of medium difficulty.

3. **Amount of traffic on Lanning Street**

(A) A is not the correct classification because the Chungs do not have as an objective the "Amount of traffic on Lanning Street." That is, this amount is not something the Chungs seek to achieve. The Chungs do have as an objective obtaining a store in a location with adequate easy parking, but the amount of traffic at the Lanning Street location is an irrelevant consideration in their decision about which location to choose, not an objective they seek to achieve. See (E) for an explanation of why the correct classification is E, an unimportant issue. This classification is relatively difficult.

(B) B is not the correct classification because the "Amount of traffic on Lanning Street" is not a basic consideration that will be weighed by the Chungs during their evaluation of each location. That is, the amount is not of fundamental importance in the choice of a location. Indeed, the amount is an irrelevant consideration in the Chungs' decision. See (E) for an explanation of why the correct classification is E, an unimportant issue. This classification is relatively difficult.

(C) C is not the correct classification because the "Amount of traffic on Lanning Street" is not a consideration that bears on or contributes to a major factor. That is, the amount is not a consideration the Chungs will weigh in the course of evaluating the basic considerations that will determine which location is most suitable. It is true that the Chungs will evaluate a location in terms of how much easy parking it allows; it is also true that, in the course of evaluating the parking at a location, the Chungs will weigh any factor that bears on or contributes to how much convenient parking is available. But the amount of traffic on Lanning Street is not such a factor; it is, rather, an irrelevant consideration for the Chungs. See (E) for an explanation of why the correct classification is E, an unimportant issue. This classification is relatively difficult.

(D) D is not the correct classification because the "Amount of traffic on Lanning Street" is not a consideration that the Chungs assume. That is, the amount is not a supposition or projection that the Chungs make about their situation. The "Amount of traffic on Lanning Street" does not provide, as assumptions sometimes do, a framework that leads to the establishment of an objective. See (E) for an explanation of why the correct classification is E, an unimportant issue. This classification is relatively difficult.

(E) The correct classification for this consideration is E, an unimportant issue, because the "Amount of traffic on Lanning Street" is irrelevant to the decision. That is, the Chungs do not seek this amount as an objective, project it as an assumption, or use it to evaluate the alternatives. It is true that the amount of traffic on Lanning Street might at first appear to bear on the amount of convenient parking available at that location. Further thought, however, indicates otherwise. There is no indication that additional convenient parking would be available because of the amount of traffic on Lanning Street. More importantly, even if the traffic patterns produced additional parking, the Chungs would not need to take this parking into account since the Lanning location already has a lot with six parking spaces, more parking than any other location. Indeed, the fifth paragraph of the passage makes it clear that six spaces are adequate for the Chungs in the sense that the lot will bring in enough new customers. The amount of traffic is, therefore, irrelevant to the decision since it would not make Lanning Street more or less attractive to the Chungs. This classification is relatively difficult.

4. **Date the Chungs can open their business in a new location**

(A) A is not the correct classification because the Chungs do not have as an objective the date they can open in a new location. That is, the Chungs do not seek to achieve this date. The Chungs do have as an objective opening their business as soon as possible, but the date they can open in a new location is a major factor in picking a location, not an objective they seek to achieve. See (B) for an explanation of why the correct classification is B, a major factor. This classification is relatively easy.

(B) The correct classification for this consideration is B, a major factor. This can be determined from the fourth paragraph of the passage, where you are told that the Chungs want their business to be closed the fewest number of days possible, or, put another way, to be open as soon as possible. Given this objective, it is logical that the "Date the Chungs can open their business in a new location" will be a major factor because this date is basic in determining how well a lo-

cation will meet the objective of having the business open quickly. This classification is relatively easy.

(C) C is not the correct classification because the "Date the Chungs can open their business in a new location" is not a consideration that bears on or contributes to a major factor. That is, this date is not a consideration to which the Chungs will give only secondary weight in the course of evaluating the basic considerations that will determine which location is most suitable. It is true that the Chungs wish to move to a location that will permit them to open their business as soon as possible; it is also true that the Chungs will give secondary importance to any factor that bears on when their business will be able to open if they move to a particular location. But the actual date when the Chungs can open their business is not itself a secondary factor; it is, rather, a major factor. See (B) for an explanation of why the correct classification is B, a major factor. This classification is relatively easy.

(D) D is not the correct classification because the "Date the Chungs can open their business in a new location" is not a consideration that the Chungs assume. That is, this date is not a consideration that the Chungs only suppose, but is an existing, confirmable fact that they will know when they make their decision, and is basic to that decision. See (B) for an explanation of why the correct classification is B, a major factor. (Note also that the date the Chungs can open their business does not provide, as assumptions sometimes do, a framework that leads to the establishment of an objective.) This classification is relatively easy.

(E) E is not the correct classification because the "Date the Chungs can open their business in a new location" is a consideration that is relevant to the decision. The date by which the Chungs can open at a prospective location is relevant because it is crucial in permitting the Chungs to determine which location will allow them to open their business as soon as possible. See (B) for an explanation of why the correct classification is B, a major factor. This classification is relatively easy.

5. **Amount of storage space in the present store**

(A) A is not the correct classification because the Chungs do not have as an objective the amount of storage space in their present store. That is, the Chungs do not seek this amount of space. The Chungs do have as an objective a store with the same amount of floor space as their present store. However, a new store with an amount of space equal to the amount in the present store is not the same concept as the amount of space in the present store. In addition, floor space is not the same as storage space. Thus, the amount of storage space in the present store is not an objective, but is rather an unimportant issue. See (E) for an explanation of why the correct classification is E, an unimportant issue. This classification is of medium difficulty.

(B) B is not the correct classification because the "Amount of storage space in the present store" is not a basic consideration that will be weighed by the Chungs during their evaluation of the prospective locations. That is, this amount is not a fundamental consideration that will be applied to each location to determine which one is most suitable. The Chungs will evaluate a location in terms of the amount of floor and storage space it contains, but the amount of storage space in the present store is not a factor in their decision. See (E) for an explanation of why the correct classification is E, an unimportant issue. This classification is of medium difficulty.

(C) C is not the correct classification because the "Amount of storage space in the present store" is not a consideration that bears on or contributes to a major factor. That is, this amount is not a consideration the Chungs will weigh in the course of evaluating the basic considerations that will determine which location is most suitable. It is true that the Chungs will evaluate a location in terms of how much floor and storage space it contains; it is also true that, in the course of evaluating the floor and storage space of a location, the Chungs will weigh any factor that bears on or contributes to how much floor and storage space is available. But the amount of storage space in the present store is not such a factor; it is, rather, an irrelevant consideration for the Chungs. See (E) for an explanation of why the correct classification is E, an unimportant issue. This classification is of medium difficulty.

(D) D is not the correct classification because the "Amount of storage space in the present store" is not a consideration that the Chungs assume. That is, this amount is not a supposition or projection that the Chungs make about their situation. The "Amount of storage space in the present store" does not provide, as assumptions sometimes do, a framework that leads to the establishment of an objective. See (E) for an explanation of why the correct classification is E, an unimportant issue. This classification is of medium difficulty.

(E) The correct classification for this consideration is E, an unimportant issue, because the "Amount of storage space in the present store" is irrelevant to the decision. That is, the Chungs do not seek this amount as an objective or project it as an assumption, nor will they use it to evaluate the three locations. Note that while the third paragraph of the passage indicates that the Chungs want "at least a limited amount of storage space" and seek the same amount of "floor space

as their present store," there is no indication that the amount of storage space in their present store has any bearing on their decision. This classification is of medium difficulty.

6. **Number of hours the new store would be open**

(A) A is not the correct classification because the Chungs do not have as an objective the "Number of hours the new store would be open." That is, the Chungs do not seek this number. The Chungs presumably wish to be open a certain number of hours (this is never explicitly stated in the passage). However, wanting to be open a certain number of hours is not the same concept as the number of hours the new store would be open. Rather than being an objective of the Chungs, the number of hours the new store would be open is irrelevant to the decision. See (E) for an explanation of why the correct classification is E, an unimportant issue. This classification is very easy.

(B) B is not the correct classification because the "Number of hours the new store would be open" is not a basic consideration that will be weighed by the Chungs during their evaluation of the prospective locations. That is, this number is not a fundamental consideration that will be applied to each location to determine which one is most suitable. Rather, this number is irrelevant to the Chungs' decision. See (E) for an explanation of why the correct classification is E, an unimportant issue. This classification is very easy.

(C) C is not the correct classification because the "Number of hours the new store would be open" is not a consideration that bears on or contributes to a major factor. That is, this number is not a consideration the Chungs will weigh in the course of evaluating the basic considerations that will determine which location is most suitable. Rather, this number is irrelevant to the decision about which location to choose. See (E) for an explanation of why the correct classification is E, an unimportant issue. This classification is very easy.

(D) D is not the correct classification because the "Number of hours the new store would be open" is not a consideration that the Chungs assume. That is, this number is not a relevant supposition the Chungs make about their situation. This number does not provide, as assumptions sometimes do, a framework that leads to the establishment of an objective. See (E) for an explanation of why the correct classification is E, an unimportant issue. This classification is very easy.

(E) The correct classification for this consideration is E, an unimportant issue, because the "Number of hours the new store would be open" is irrelevant to the decision. That is, the Chungs do not seek this number as an objective or suppose it as a relevant assumption, nor will they use it to evaluate the three locations. This number does not make any of the prospective store locations more or less attractive to the Chungs. In addition, there is no indication in the passage that there would be any constraints on the number of hours the new store would be open regardless of which location is chosen. In short, the "Number of hours the new store would be open" is not logically related to choosing a new location. This classification is very easy.

7. **Anticipation of losses in perishable stock during the move**

   (A) A is not the correct classification because there is no indication that the Chungs, in making their move to a new location, seek the anticipation of losses in perishable stock. That is, the Chungs do not have the "Anticipation of losses in perishable stock during the move" as an objective. Rather, the anticipation of losses in perishable stock is an unimportant issue. See (E) for an explanation of why the correct classification is E, an unimportant issue. This classification is relatively difficult.

   (B) B is not the correct classification because "Anticipation of losses in perishable stock during the move" is not a basic consideration that will be weighed by the Chungs during their evaluation of the prospective locations. That is, the anticipation of losses is not a fundamental consideration that will be applied to each location to determine which one is most suitable. See (E) for an explanation of why the correct classification is E, an unimportant issue. This classification is relatively difficult.

   (C) C is not the correct classification because the "Anticipation of losses in perishable stock during the move" is not a consideration that bears on or contributes to a major factor. That is, anticipation of losses in perishable stock is not a consideration the Chungs will weigh in the course of evaluating the basic considerations that will determine which location is most suitable. See (E) for an explanation of why the correct classification is E, an unimportant issue. This classification is relatively difficult.

   (D) D is not the correct classification because "Anticipation of losses in perishable stock during the move" is not a consideration that the Chungs assume. "Anticipation of losses in perishable stock during the move" does not provide, as assumptions sometimes do, a framework that leads to the establishment of an objective. See (E) for an explanation of why the correct

classification is E, an unimportant issue. This classification is relatively difficult.

   (E) The correct classification for this consideration is E, an unimportant issue, because "Anticipation of losses in perishable stock during the move" is irrelevant to the decision. That is, "Anticipation of losses in perishable stock during the move" is not an objective of the Chungs, or a factor that they will use in evaluating the three prospective locations, or a supposition or projection that they make. Anticipation of losses in perishable stock is, in the context of this passage, not logically related to choosing a new location. Anticipation of losses is, in short, not relevant to the Chungs' decision. This classification is relatively difficult.

8. **Convenience of the location of each of the three stores**

   (A) A is not the correct classification because the "Convenience of the location of each of the three stores" is not an objective of the Chungs. That is, in picking a new store location, the Chungs do not seek the convenience of each store's location. The Chungs do seek a convenient store location, but the convenience of the location of each of the three stores is not the same concept as a convenient store location. The convenience of the location of each of the three stores is not an objective of the Chungs but a major factor in their decision. See (B) for an explanation of why the correct classification is B, a major factor. This classification is relatively easy.

   (B) The correct classification for this consideration is B, a major factor. This can be determined from the third paragraph of the passage, where you are told that the Chungs have a "need for a building in a convenient location." Given this objective of a convenient store location, it is logical that the "Convenience of the location of each of the three stores" will be a major factor because it is basic in determining how well a location will satisfy the objective of a convenient store location. This classification is relatively easy.

   (C) C is not the correct classification because the "Convenience of the location of each of the three stores" is not a consideration that bears on or contributes to a major factor. That is, this convenience is not a consideration to which the Chungs will give only secondary weight in the course of evaluating the basic considerations that will determine which location is most suitable. It is true that the Chungs want a convenient store location; it is also true that the Chungs will give secondary importance to any factor that bears on the convenience of a store's location. But the convenience of each of the store locations is not itself a secondary factor; rather, it is a major factor. See (B) for an explanation of why the correct classification is B, a major factor. This classification is relatively easy.

(D) D is not the correct classification because the "Convenience of the location of each of the three stores" is not a consideration that the Chungs assume. That is, this convenience is not something the Chungs only suppose or project, but is an existing, confirmable fact that they will have on hand when they make a decision and is basic to that decision. See (B) for an explanation of why the correct classification is B, a major factor. (Note also that convenience of the location of each of the three stores does not provide, as assumptions sometimes do, a framework that leads to the establishment of an objective). This classification is relatively easy.

(E) E is not the correct classification because the "Convenience of the location of each of the three stores" is a consideration that is relevant to the decision. This convenience is relevant because it is crucial in permitting the Chungs to determine which location will be the most convenient. See (B) for an explanation of why the correct classification is B, a major factor. This classification is relatively easy.

9. **Date the Chungs could begin to move into the School Street store**

(A) A is not the correct classification because the Chungs do not have as an objective the date they could begin to move into the School Street store. That is, achieving this date is not something the Chungs seek. The Chungs do have as an objective opening their business as soon as possible, but the date they could move into the School Street store is a minor factor in their evaluation of the School Street location, not an objective they seek to achieve. See (C) for an explanation of why the correct classification is C, a minor factor. This classification is relatively difficult.

(B) B is not the correct classification because the "Date the Chungs could begin to move into the School Street store" is not a basic consideration that will be weighed by the Chungs during their evaluation of each location. That is, the date is not of fundamental importance in the choice of a location. It is true that the Chungs will consider the date when they are evaluating the suitability of the School Street location, but the date is of a secondary rather than a basic importance. See (C) for an explanation of why the correct classification is C, a minor factor. This classification is relatively difficult.

(C) The correct classification for this consideration is C, a minor factor. The passage indicates that the Chungs want their store to be open in a new location as soon as possible. It follows that the date the Chungs can open their business in a new location, including the School Street location, is a major factor. The "Date the Chungs could begin to move into the School Street store" is a minor factor because it

bears on and contributes to this major factor. Note that this major factor is influenced by other considerations—e.g., the amount of time needed to prepare the store for opening—besides the move-in date. Because the move-in date only contributes to, is only one influence on, the opening date, this consideration is a minor factor. This classification is relatively difficult.

(D) D is not the correct classification because the "Date the Chungs could begin to move into the School Street store" is not a consideration the Chungs assume. That is, this date is not a supposition or projection that they make about their situation, but is a confirmable fact that they will know when they make their decision, and is of secondary importance to that decision. See (C) for an explanation of why the correct classification is C, a minor factor. (Note also that the date they can move into the School Street store does not establish, as assumptions sometimes do, a framework that leads to the establishment of an objective). This classification is relatively difficult.

(E) E is not the correct classification because the "Date the Chungs could begin to move into the School Street store" is a consideration that is relevant to the decision. This date is relevant because it is a minor factor that bears on a major factor. See (C) for an explanation of why the correct classification is C, a minor factor. This classification is relatively difficult.

10. **Cost of transporting the fixtures and stock to a new location**

(A) A is not the correct classification because there is no indication that the Chungs, in moving to a new location, seek the cost of transporting the fixtures and stock to a new location. That is, the Chungs do not have this cost as an objective. Rather, such a cost is irrelevant to their decision. See (E) for an explanation of why the correct classification is E, an unimportant issue. This classification is relatively difficult.

(B) B is not the correct classification because the "Cost of transporting the fixtures and stock to a new location" is not a basic consideration that will be weighed by the Chungs during their evaluation of the prospective locations. Rather, this cost is irrelevant for the Chungs since it will not help them decide which location is most suitable. See (E) for an explanation of why the correct classification is E, an unimportant issue. This classification is relatively difficult.

(C) C is not the correct classification because the "Cost of transporting the fixtures and stock to a new location" is not a consideration that bears on or contributes to a major factor. That is, this cost is not a consideration that the Chungs will weigh in the course of evaluating the basic considerations that will determine which location is most suitable. It might be argued that this transportation cost is a minor factor because it bears on the overall cost of getting started at a location. However, this overall cost is not explicitly mentioned in the passage as a basic consideration for the Chungs and therefore is not a major factor of which the transportation cost is a part. In addition, the transportation cost is irrelevant to the decision at hand—picking a location. See (E) for an explanation of why the correct classification is E, an unimportant issue. This classification is relatively difficult.

(D) D is not the correct classification because the "Cost of transporting the fixtures and stock to a new location" is not a consideration that the Chungs assume. That is, this cost is not a supposition or projection they make about their situation, but a confirmable, though irrelevant, fact they will know when they make their decision. Nor does the transportation cost provide, as assumptions sometimes do, a framework that leads to the establishment of an objective. See (E) for an explanation of why the correct classification is E, an unimportant issue. This classification is relatively difficult.

(E) The correct classification for this consideration is E, an unimportant issue, because the "Cost of transporting the fixtures and stock to a new location" is irrelevant to the decision. That is, this cost is neither an objective of the Chungs, nor a factor that they will use in evaluating the three prospective locations, nor a supposition or projection that they make. Note that while it might be argued that the Chungs would consider this cost to be a factor in their decision, there is no indication whatever in the passage that the Chungs are concerned with transportation cost. And, indeed, even if the Chungs were so concerned, the transportation cost would still be irrelevant to their decision. The reason the cost would still be irrelevant is that it would be effectively equal for the locations being considered—all are very close to the present store—and thus would not be a factor that would help the Chungs differentiate among the alternatives. This classification is relatively difficult.

11. Finding a new location with enough floor space

(A) The correct classification for this consideration is A, an objective, because the third paragraph of the passage tells you that the Chungs want a store with "as much floor space as their present store." In other words, one of the Chungs' goals is finding a new store location that has enough floor space, i.e., as much as the current store has. This classification is relatively easy.

(B) B is not the correct classification because "Finding a new location with enough floor space" is not a basic consideration that will be weighed by the Chungs during their evaluation of each location. That is, finding a new location with enough floor space is not a fundamental consideration that will be applied to each location to determine which one is most suitable. The Chungs will evaluate a location in terms of how much floor space it contains, but finding a new location with enough floor space is an objective for the Chungs, not a factor in their decision. See (A) for an explanation of why the correct classification is A, an objective. This classification is relatively easy.

(C) C is not the correct classification because "Finding a new location with enough floor space" is not a consideration that bears on or contributes to a major factor. That is, finding a location with adequate floor space is not a consideration the Chungs will weigh in the course of evaluating the basic considerations that will determine which location is most suitable. It is true that the Chungs will evaluate a location in terms of how much floor and storage space it contains; it is also true that, in the course of evaluating the floor and storage space they would have if they moved to a location, the Chungs will weigh any factor that bears on how much floor and storage space would be available. But finding a new location with enough floor space is not such a factor; it is, rather, an objective of the Chungs. See (A) for an explanation of why the correct classification is A, an objective. This classification is relatively easy.

(D) D is not the correct classification because "Finding a new location with enough floor space" is not a consideration that the Chungs assume about their situation. Finding such a new location does not provide, as assumptions sometimes do, a framework that leads to the establishment of an objective. Rather, "Finding a new location with enough floor space" is itself an objective for the Chungs. See (A) for an explanation of why the correct classification is A, an objective. This classification is relatively easy.

(E) E is not the correct classification because "Finding a new location with enough floor space" is a consideration that is relevant to the decision. Finding such a new location is relevant because it is an objective the Chungs want to achieve and thus is fundamental in guiding the decision-making process. See (A) for an explanation of why the correct classification is A, an objective. This classification is relatively easy.

12. **Relation between adequate convenient parking and the success of a convenience store**

(A) A is not the correct classification because the "Relation between adequate convenient parking and the success of a convenience store" is not an objective that the Chungs wish to achieve. That is, the Chungs do not seek this relation. The Chungs do seek a new store in a location that has adequate convenient parking, but that there is a relationship between such parking and the success of a convenience store is an assumption or supposition they make, not an objective they wish to achieve. See (D) for an explanation of why the correct classification is D, an assumption. This classification is of medium difficulty.

(B) B is not the correct classification because the "Relation between adequate convenient parking and the success of a convenience store" is not a basic consideration that will be weighed by the Chungs during their evaluation of each location. That is, this relation is not a fundamental consideration that will be applied to each location to determine which is most suitable. The amount of convenient parking available at each location is such a consideration, a major factor, but the relationship between adequate convenient parking and the success of a convenience store is an assumption, not a major factor. See (D) for an explanation of why the correct classification is D, an assumption. This classification is of medium difficulty.

(C) C is not the correct classification because the "Relation between adequate convenient parking and the success of a convenience store" is not a consideration that bears on or contributes to a major factor. That is, this relation is not a consideration the Chungs will weigh in the course of evaluating the basic considerations that will determine which location is most suitable. Rather, this relation is an assumption or supposition that the Chungs make. See (D) for an explanation of why the correct classification is D, an assumption. This classification is of medium difficulty.

(D) The correct classification for this consideration is D, an assumption. The third paragraph of the passage states that the Chungs feel that "people will not stop at a convenience store unless they can park easily." In other words, the Chungs believe that a causal relationship exists between adequate convenient parking at a convenience store and people's willingness to stop at that store. And since people's willingness to stop is very likely to translate into economic success for a store, it follows that the Chungs assume or suppose a causal relation between adequate convenient parking and the success of a convenience store. Their assuming this relation sets a framework for the decision, a framework for the establishment

of an objective: because the Chungs assume such a relation exists, and since they obviously want their convenience store to be successful, they set as a goal the acquisition of a location that has enough easy parking. This classification is of medium difficulty.

(E) E is not the correct classification because the "Relation between adequate convenient parking and the success of a convenience store" is relevant to the decision. This relation is relevant to the decision because it is assumed by the Chungs before they evaluate the prospective locations and come to a decision. More specifically, this relation is relevant in that it provides the framework for the establishment of an objective. See (D) for an explanation of why the correct classification is D, an assumption. This classification is of medium difficulty.

13. **Amount of traffic on Prospect Street**

(A) A is not the correct classification because the Chungs do not have as an objective the "Amount of traffic on Prospect Street." That is, this amount is not something the Chungs seek to achieve. The Chungs do have as an objective obtaining a store in a location with adequate easy parking, but the amount of traffic at the Prospect Street location is a minor factor in their evaluation of that location, not an objective they seek to achieve. See (C) for an explanation of why the correct classification is C, a minor factor. This classification is of medium difficulty.

(B) B is not the correct classification because the "Amount of traffic on Prospect Street" is not a basic consideration that will be weighed by the Chungs during their evaluation of each location. That is, this amount is not of fundamental importance in the choice of a location. It is true that the Chungs will consider this amount when they are evaluating the suitability of the Prospect Street location, but the amount is of secondary rather than basic importance. See (C) for an explanation of why the correct classification is C, a minor factor. This classification is of medium difficulty.

(C) The correct classification for this consideration is C, a minor factor. The passage indicates that the Chungs want a location where customers can park easily. It follows that the amount of easy parking available at a location, including the Prospect Street location, is a major factor. The "Amount of traffic on Prospect Street" is a minor factor because it bears on, or influences, this major factor. This influence is made explicit in the sixth paragraph of the passage, where you are told that "since the street is not a busy one, customers could park on the street in front of the store." Note that the overall amount of easy parking at Prospect Street is influenced by both the available room next to the store and the lack of busy traffic on the street, which in turn permits on-street parking. Because the amount of traffic only contributes to, is only one influence on, the amount of easy parking, this consideration is a minor factor. This classification is of medium difficulty.

(D) D is not the correct classification because the "Amount of traffic on Prospect Street" is not a consideration that the Chungs assume. That is, this amount is not a supposition or projection they make about their situation, but a confirmable fact that they will know when they make their decision, and of secondary importance to that decision. See (C) for an explanation of why the correct classification is C, a minor factor. (Note also that this amount does not provide, as assumptions sometimes do, a framework that leads to the establishment of an objective.) This classification is of medium difficulty.

(E) E is not the correct classification because the "Amount of traffic on Prospect Street" is a consideration that is relevant to the decision. This amount is relevant because it is a minor factor that bears on a major factor. See (C) for an explanation of why the correct classification is C, a minor factor. This classification is of medium difficulty.

14. **Selection of a new store that will not need extensive renovation**

(A) The correct classification for this consideration is A, an objective, because the third paragraph of the passage tells you that the Chungs "do not want a store that will require extensive remodeling," specifically, extensive remodeling of the floor structure. In other words, one of the Chungs' objectives is the selection of a store that requires little renovation. This classification is relatively easy.

(B) B is not the correct classification because "Selection of a new store that will not need extensive renovation" is not a basic consideration that will be weighed by the Chungs during their evaluation of each location. That is, selecting a store that needs little renovation is not a fundamental consideration that will be applied to each store location to determine which one is most suitable. The Chungs will evaluate a store location in terms of how much renovation it will need, specifically how much renovation of the floor structure, but selecting a store that needs little renovation is an objective for the Chungs, not a factor in their decision. See (A) for an explanation of why the correct classification is A, an objective. This classification is relatively easy.

(C) C is not the correct classification because "Selection of a new store that will not need extensive renovation" is not a consideration that bears on or contributes to a major factor. That is, selecting a new store that does not require extensive remodeling is not a consideration the Chungs will weigh in the course of evaluating the basic considerations that will determine which location is most suitable. It is true that the Chungs will evaluate a store location in terms of how much renovation—specifically, floor structure renovation—that location will require; it is also true that, in the course of this evaluation, the Chungs will weigh any factor that bears on how much floor structure renovation is required. But selecting a new store that will not need much renovation is not such a factor; it is, rather, an objective of the Chungs. See (A) for an explanation of why the correct classification is A, an objective. This classification is relatively easy.

(D) D is not the correct classification because "Selection of a new store that will not need extensive renovation" is not a consideration that the Chungs assume about their situation. Selecting a new store that will not need extensive remodeling does not provide, as assumptions sometimes do, a framework that leads to the establishment of an objective. Rather, the selection of a new store that does not require extensive renovation is itself an objective for the Chungs. See (A) for an explanation of why the correct classification is A, an objective. This classification is relatively easy.

(E) E is not the correct classification because "Selection of a new store that will not need extensive renovation" is a consideration that is relevant to the decision. Selection of such a new store is relevant because it is an objective the Chungs want to achieve and thus is fundamental in guiding the decision-making process. See (A) for an explanation of why the correct classification is A, an objective. This classification is relatively easy.

15. **Need for keeping the business in the same town**

(A) A is not the correct classification because the "Need for keeping the business in the same town" is not an objective the Chungs wish to achieve. That is, the Chungs do not seek this need. The Chungs do have as an objective keeping the business in the same town, but that there is a need for keeping the business in the same town is an assumption or supposition they make, not an objective they seek to achieve. See (D) for an explanation of why the correct classification is D, an assumption. This classification is difficult.

(B) B is not the correct classification because the "Need for keeping the business in the same town" is not a basic consideration that will be weighed by the Chungs during their evaluation of each location. That is, this need is not a fundamental consideration that will be applied to each location to determine which is most suitable; it is, rather, an assumption or supposition the Chungs make. See (D) for an explanation of why the correct classification is D, an assumption. This classification is difficult.

(C) C is not the correct classification because the "Need for keeping the business in the same town" is not a consideration that bears on or contributes to a major factor. That is, this need is not a consideration the Chungs will weigh in the course of evaluating the basic considerations that will determine which location is most suitable. Rather, this need is an assumption or supposition that the Chungs make. See (D) for an explanation of why the correct classification is D, an assumption. This classification is difficult.

(D) The correct classification for this consideration is D, an assumption. The second paragraph of the passage states that the Chungs "know that their present customers will not follow them to another location unless it is . . . right in the same town." Given this information and making the common-sense inference that the Chungs want to retain their customers, one can logically infer that the Chungs assume or project that they have a need—i.e., to retain their customers—for keeping their business in the same town. This need sets a framework for the decision, a framework for the establishment of an objective: because the Chungs suppose they have a need for keeping their business in the same town, they set as an objective obtaining a new location in the same town. Put another way, the Chungs' assumption that this need exists causes them to consider only local locations. This classification is difficult.

(E) E is not the correct classification because the "Need for keeping the business in the same town" is relevant to the decision. This need is relevant to the decision because it is assumed by the Chungs before they evaluate the prospective locations and come to a decision. More specifically, it is relevant in that it provides the framework for the establishment of an objective. See (D) for an explanation of why the correct classification is D, an assumption. This classification is difficult.

16. **Strength of the floor structure in the three available locations**

(A) A is not the correct classification because the Chungs do not have as an objective the "Strength of the floor structure in the three available locations." That is, the Chungs do not seek this strength. The Chungs do want a store with a strong floor, but the strength of the floor structure is a major factor in the choice of a new location, not an objective the Chungs seek. See (B) for an explanation of why the correct classification is B, a major factor. This classification is very easy.

(B) The correct classification for this consideration is B, a major factor. This can be determined from the passage's third paragraph, where you are told that the Chungs are "concerned that the floor in any store they rent will support their heavy freezer and refrigerator cases." The Chungs, in short, want a store with a strong enough floor. Given this objective, it is logical that the "Strength of the floor structure in the three available locations" will be a major factor because it is basic in determining how well a location will satisfy the objective of having a strong floor. This classification is very easy.

(C) C is not the correct classification because the "Strength of the floor structure in the three available locations" is not a consideration that bears on or contributes to a major factor. That is, this strength is not a consideration to which the Chungs will give only secondary weight in the course of evaluating the basic considerations that will determine which location is most suitable. It is true that the Chungs wish to move to a location with a strong floor; it is also true that the Chungs will give secondary importance to any factor that bears on the strength of the floor structure in the available locations. But the strength of the floor structure is not itself a secondary factor; it is, rather, a major factor. See (B) for an explanation of why the correct classification is B, a major factor. This classification is very easy.

(D) D is not the correct classification because the "Strength of the floor structure in the three available locations" is not a consideration that the Chungs assume. That is, the strength of the respective floors is not something the Chungs only suppose or project, but is an existing, confirmable fact that they will have on hand when they make a decision and is basic to that decision. See (B) for an explanation of why the correct classification is B, a major factor. (Note also that the strength of the floor structure does not provide, as assumptions sometimes do, a framework that leads to the establishment of an objective). This classification is very easy.

(E) E is not the correct classification because the "Strength of the floor structure in the three available locations" is a consideration that is relevant to the decision. The strength of the respective floors is relevant because it is crucial in permitting the Chungs to determine which location will provide them with the best floor for their heavy cases. See (B) for an explanation of why the correct classification is B, a major factor. This classification is very easy.

17. **Amount of floor and storage space in each of the available stores**

(A) A is not the correct classification because the Chungs do not have as an objective the "Amount of floor and storage space in each of the available stores." That is, the Chungs do not seek this amount. In the third paragraph of the passage, you are told that the Chungs want a store with "as much floor space as their present store, and at least a limited amount of storage space," but the amount of floor and storage space in each of the available stores is a major factor in the choice of a new location, not an objective the Chungs seek to achieve. See (B) for an explanation of why the correct classification is B, a major factor. This classification is very easy.

(B) The correct classification for this consideration is B, a major factor. This can be determined from the third paragraph of the passage, where you are told that the Chungs, in moving to a new location, want "as much floor space as their present store, and at least a limited amount of storage space." Given this objective, it is logical that the "Amount of floor and storage space in each of the available stores" will be a major factor because it is basic in determining how well a location will satisfy the objective of a store with as much floor space as the present store and at least a limited amount of storage space. This classification is very easy.

(C) C is not the correct classification because the "Amount of floor and storage space in each of the available stores" is not a consideration that bears on or contributes to a major factor. That is, this amount is not a consideration to which the Chungs will give only secondary weight in the course of evaluating the basic considerations that will determine which location is most suitable. It is true that the Chungs want a new store with a particular amount of floor and storage space; it is also true that the Chungs will give secondary importance to any factors that bear on the amount of floor and storage space in the available stores. But the amount of floor and storage space available is not itself a secondary factor; it is, rather, a major factor. See (B) for an explanation of why the correct classification is B, a major factor. This classification is very easy.

(D) D is not the correct classification because the "Amount of floor and storage space in each of the available stores" is not a consideration that the Chungs assume. That is, this amount is not something the Chungs only suppose or project, but is an existing, confirmable fact that they will have on hand when they make a decision and that will be basic to that decision. See (B) for an explanation of why the correct classification is B, a major factor. (Note also that the amount of floor and storage

space does not provide, as assumptions sometimes do, a framework that leads to the establishment of an objective.) This classification is very easy.

(E) E is not the correct classification because the "Amount of floor and storage space in each of the available stores" is a consideration that is relevant to the decision. This amount is relevant because it is crucial in permitting the Chungs to determine which location will provide them with the most advantageous amount of floor and storage space. See (B) for an explanation of why the correct classification is B, a major factor. This classification is very easy.

18. **A store with a rent of no more than $400 a month**

(A) The correct classification for this consideration is A, an objective, because the third paragraph of the passage tells you that the Chungs "will not be able to pay more than $100 over" their current rent of $300. In other words, one of the Chungs' objectives is to have a store in a new location in which the rent does not exceed $400. This classification is relatively difficult.

(B) B is not the correct classification because "A store with a rent of no more than $400 a month" is not a basic consideration that will be weighed by the Chungs during their evaluation of each prospective store location; that is, it is not a fundamental consideration that will be applied to each location to determine which one is most suitable. The Chungs will evaluate a location in terms of its rental charge, but having a store with a rent of no more than $400 a month is an objective the Chungs wish to achieve after they have evaluated the three locations and picked one of them, rather than a factor in their decision. See (A) for an explanation of why the correct classification is A, an objective. This classification is relatively difficult.

(C) C is not the correct classification because "A store with a rent of no more than $400 a month" is not a consideration that bears on or contributes to a major factor. That is, a store with a rent of no more than $400 is not a consideration the Chungs will weigh in the course of evaluating the basic considerations that will determine the most suitable location. It is true that the Chungs will evaluate a location in terms of how much rent they will have to pay if they move to that location; it is also true that, in the course of evaluating the rental charge at a specific location, the Chungs will weigh any factor that bears on that rental charge. But obtaining a store with a rent of no more than $400 is not such a factor; it is, rather, an objective of the Chungs. See (A) for an explanation of why the correct classification is A, an objective. This classification is relatively difficult.

(D) D is not the correct classification because "A store with a rent of no more than $400 a month" is not a consideration that the Chungs assume about their situation. "A store with a rent of no more than $400 a month" does not provide, as assumptions sometimes do, a framework that leads to the establishment of an objective. Rather, "A store with rent of no more than $400 a month" is itself an objective for the Chungs. See (A) for an explanation of why the correct classification is A, an objective. This classification is relatively difficult.

(E) E is not the correct classification because "A store with a rent of no more than $400 a month" is relevant to the decision. A store with such a rent is relevant because it is an objective that the Chungs want to achieve in choosing a location, and thus is fundamental in guiding the decision-making process. See (A) for an explanation of why the correct classification is A, an objective. This classification is relatively difficult.

19. **Number of tickets each manager expects to sell**

(A) A is not the correct classification because the committee does not have as an objective the "Number of tickets each manager expects to sell." That is, in picking a manager, the committee does not seek this number. See (B) for an explanation of why the correct classification is B, a major factor. This classification is of medium difficulty.

(B) The correct classification for this consideration is B, a major factor. Harvey's letter requests information from the prospective managers concerning "the number of tickets [they] expect would be sold." This explicit request indicates that the number of tickets each manager expects to sell is a consideration that the committee will weigh carefully and will be of fundamental importance in the decision concerning which manager to choose. This classification is of medium difficulty.

(C) C is not the correct classification because the "Number of tickets each manager expects to sell" is not a consideration to which the committee will attach only secondary weight in the course of evaluating the basic considerations that will determine which manager is most suitable. See (B) for an explanation of why the correct classification is B, a major factor. This classification is of medium difficulty.

(D) D is not the correct classification because the "Number of tickets each manager expects to sell" is not a consideration that the committee assumes. That is, the number of tickets each expects to sell is not a consideration that the committee supposes or projects. It is true that it could be argued that, from the point of view of a manager, the number he or

she expects to sell is a projection. However, it must be kept in mind that, for the decision-maker, the point of view from which all considerations are to be evaluated, this number is a fact. That is, the committee accepts as a fact that, for example, 3,000 to 3,500 is the number of tickets Turner Antiques Fairs projects it will sell. More importantly, the number of tickets each manager expects to sell functions as a factor in the committee's decision since this number makes a manager more or less attractive to the committee. See (B) for an explanation of why the correct classification is B, a major factor. This classification is of medium difficulty.

(E) E is not the correct classification because the "Number of tickets each manager expects to sell" is relevant to the decision. This number is relevant because it is explicitly requested by a member of the committee. This explicit request indicates that the number of tickets each manager expects to sell will be weighed heavily by the committee in evaluating a manager's appropriateness. See (B) for an explanation of why the correct classification is B, a major factor. This classification is of medium difficulty.

20. **Spinning Wheel Promotions' standards of quality for exhibitors**

(A) A is not the correct classification because the committee does not have as an objective "Spinning Wheel Promotions' standards of quality for exhibitors." That is, these standards are not something the committee wishes to achieve. Rather than an objective, these standards are a minor factor in the committee's decision. See (C) for an explanation of why the correct classification is C, a minor factor. This classification is relatively difficult.

(B) B is not the correct classification because "Spinning Wheel Promotions' standards of quality for exhibitors" is not a basic consideration that the committee will weigh in the course of its evaluation of each manager. That is, these standards are not of fundamental importance in the choice of a manager. While the committee will consider these standards when it evaluates the suitability of Spinning Wheel Promotions as a manager, these standards will be of secondary rather than basic importance. See (C) for an explanation of why the correct classification is C, a minor factor. This classification is relatively difficult.

(C) The correct classification for this consideration is C, a minor factor. Harvey's letter indicates that the committee wants to retain as many of The Fair's present exhibitors as possible. It follows that the willingness of each of the managers, including Spinning Wheel Promotions, to retain the present exhibitors, is a major factor. "Spinning Wheel Promotions' standards of quality for exhibitors" is a minor factor because it bears on, helps influence, this major factor. Note that Spinning Wheel Promotions' willingness to retain the present exhibitors is made up of both its unequivocal willingness to allow present exhibitors to return the first year of its contract, and its contingent willingness to allow these exhibitors to return in the next two years, depending on the quality, as determined by Spinning Wheel's standards, of their exhibits. Because the standards of quality only contribute to Spinning Wheel's overall willingness, indeed only contribute to part of that willingness, these standards are a minor factor. This classification is relatively difficult.

(D) D is not the correct classification because "Spinning Wheel Promotions' standards of quality for exhibitors" is not a consideration the committee assumes. That is, these standards are not a supposition or projection the committee makes about its situation, but are factors the committee will weigh when it makes its decision, factors that are of secondary importance to that decision. See (C) for an explanation of why the correct classification is C, a minor factor. (Note also, that these standards do not establish, as assumptions sometimes do, a framework that leads to the establishment of an objective.) This classification is relatively difficult.

(E) E is not the correct classification because "Spinning Wheel Promotions' standards of quality for exhibitors" is a consideration that is relevant to the decision. These standards are relevant because they are a minor factor that bears on a major factor. See (C) for an explanation of why the correct classification is C, a minor factor. This classification is relatively difficult.

21. **The various managers' willingness to retain the present exhibitors**

(A) A is not the correct classification because the committee does not have as an objective "The various managers' willingness to retain the present exhibitors." That is, in picking a manager, the committee does not seek the willingness of the various managers to retain the present exhibitors. The committee does have as an objective retaining many of the present exhibitors, but the willingness of the various managers to retain present exhibitors is a major factor in picking a manager, not an objective. See (B) for an explanation of why the correct classification is B, a major factor. This classification is of medium difficulty.

(B) The correct classification for this consideration is B, a major factor. This can be determined from the first paragraph of Harvey's letter, where you are told that the committee wants to retain as many of the present exhibitors as possible. Given the objective, it is logical that "The various managers' willingness to re-

tain the present exhibitors" will be a major factor because this willingness is basic in permitting the committee to determine to what extent it will meet its objective. This classification is of medium difficulty.

(C) C is not the correct classification because "The various managers' willingness to retain the present exhibitors" is not a consideration that bears on or contributes to a major factor. That is, this willingness is not a consideration to which the committee will give only secondary weight in the course of evaluating the basic considerations that will determine which manager is most suitable. It is true that the committee wishes to retain many of the present exhibitors; it is also true that the committee will give secondary importance to any factor that bears on the willingness of a particular manager to retain the present exhibitors. But the willingness of the various managers is not itself a secondary factor; it is a major factor. See (B) for an explanation of why the correct classification is B, a major factor. This classification is of medium difficulty.

(D) D is not the correct classification because "The various managers' willingness to retain the present exhibitors" is not a consideration that the committee assumes. That is, this willingness is not a consideration that the committee only supposes, but is an existing, confirmable fact that the committee will have when it makes its decision and is basic to that decision. See (B) for an explanation of why the correct classification is B, a major factor. (Note also, that this willingness does not provide, as assumptions sometimes do, a framework that leads to the establishment of an objective.) This classification is of medium difficulty.

(E) E is not the correct classification because "The various managers' willingness to retain the present exhibitors" is a consideration that is relevant to the decision. This willingness is relevant because it is crucial in permitting the committee to determine to what extent it will meet its objective of retaining many of the present exhibitors. See (B) for an explanation of why the correct classification is B, a major factor. This is a classification of medium difficulty.

22. **Size of the space presently allocated to each exhibitor in The Fair**

(A) A is not the correct classification because the committee does not wish, in picking a manager, to obtain the "Size of the space presently allocated to each exhibitor in The Fair." That is, this size is not one of the committee's objectives. The committee does have as an objective the retention of many of The Fair's present exhibitors, but the particular size of the space allocated to present exhibitors is irrelevant to the decision. See (E) for an explanation of why the correct classification is E, an unimportant issue. This classification is very easy.

(B) B is not the correct classification because the "Size of the space presently allocated to each exhibitor in The Fair" is not a basic consideration that will be weighed by the committee during its evaluation of each prospective manager. That is, this size is not a fundamental consideration that will be applied to each prospective manager to determine which one is most suitable. See (E) for an explanation of why the correct classification is E, an unimportant issue. This classification is very easy.

(C) C is not the correct classification because the "Size of the space presently allocated to each exhibitor in The Fair" is not a consideration that bears on or contributes to a major factor. That is, the size of the space that each exhibitor currently has is not a consideration the committee will weigh in the course of evaluating the basic considerations that will determine which manager is most suitable. See (E) for an explanation of why the correct classification is E, an unimportant issue. This classification is very easy.

(D) D is not the correct classification because the "Size of the space presently allocated to each exhibitor in The Fair" is not a consideration that the committee assumes. That is, the size of the space that each exhibitor currently has is not a relevant supposition or projection the committee makes about its situation. The "Size of the space presently allocated to each exhibitor in The Fair" does not provide, as assumptions sometimes do, a framework that leads to the establishment of an objective. See (E) for an explanation of why the correct classification is E, an unimportant issue. This classification is very easy.

(E) The correct classification for this consideration is E, an unimportant issue, because the "Size of the space presently allocated to each exhibitor in The Fair" is irrelevant to the decision. That is, the committee does not seek this size as an objective or project it as an assumption. Nor will the committee use this size to evaluate each manager. In short, there is no logical connection between the size of the space each exhibitor currently has and the decision about which manager to choose. This classification is very easy.

23. **Retaining many of the present exhibitors in The Fair**

(A) The correct classification for this consideration is A, an objective, because the first paragraph of Harvey's letter tells you explicitly that the committee wants "to retain as many of [its] present exhibitors as possible." In other words, one of the goals the committee seeks to achieve is retaining a large number of the current exhibitors in The Fair. This classification is of medium difficulty.

(B) B is not the correct classification because "Retaining many of the present exhibitors in The Fair" is not a basic consideration that will be weighed by the committee during its evaluation of each prospective manager. That is, "Retaining many of the present exhibitors in The Fair" is not a fundamental consideration that will be applied to each manager to determine which one is most suitable. The committee will evaluate a manager in terms of the manager's willingness to retain present exhibitors, but retaining many present exhibitors is an objective for the committee, not a factor in its decision. See (A) for an explanation of why the correct classification is A, an objective. This classification is of medium difficulty.

(C) C is not the correct classification because "Retaining many of the present exhibitors in The Fair" is not a consideration that bears on or contributes to a major factor. That is, "Retaining many of the present exhibitors in The Fair" is not a consideration that the committee will weigh in the course of evaluating the basic considerations that will determine which manager is most suitable. It is true that the committee will evaluate a manager in terms of the manager's willingness to retain present exhibitors; it is also true that, in the course of evaluating each manager's willingness, the committee will weigh any factors that bear on this willingness. However, retaining many present exhibitors is not such a factor, but is rather an objective of the committee. See (A) for an explanation of why the correct classification is A, an objective. This classification is of medium difficulty.

(D) D is not the correct classification because "Retaining many of the present exhibitors in The Fair" is not a consideration that the committee assumes. That is, this consideration is not a supposition or projection the committee makes about its situation. "Retaining many of the present exhibitors in The Fair" does not provide, as assumptions sometimes do, a general framework that leads to the establishment of an objective. Rather, retaining many of the present exhibitors is itself an objective for the committee. See (A) for an explanation of why the correct classification is A, an objective. This classification is of medium difficulty.

(E) E is not the correct classification because "Retaining many of the present exhibitors in The Fair" is relevant to the decision. "Retaining many of the present exhibitors in The Fair" is relevant to the decision because it is an objective that the committee wishes to achieve and thus is fundamental in guiding the decision-making process. See (A) for an explanation of why the correct classification is A, an objective. This classification is of medium difficulty.

24. Continuing to operate the lunch counter at The Fair

(A) The correct classification for this consideration is A, an objective, because the first paragraph of Harvey's letter tells you explicitly that the "committee wants to continue to operate the lunch counter." In other words, one of the goals the committee seeks to achieve is the continued operation of The Fair's lunch counter. This classification is relatively difficult.

(B) B is not the correct classification because "Continuing to operate the lunch counter at The Fair" is not a basic consideration that will be weighed by the committee during its evaluation of each prospective manager. That is, continuing to operate the lunch counter is not a fundamental consideration that will be applied to each prospective manager to determine which one is most suitable. The committee will evaluate a manager in terms of the manager's stipulations about the operation of the lunch counter, but continuing to operate the lunch counter is an objective for the committee, not a factor in its decision. See (A) for an explanation of why the correct classification is A, an objective. This classification is relatively difficult.

(C) C is not the correct classification because "Continuing to operate the lunch counter at The Fair" is not a consideration that bears on or contributes to a major factor. That is, continuing to operate the lunch counter is not a consideration that the committee will weigh in the course of evaluating the basic considerations that will determine which manager is most suitable. It is true that the committee will evaluate a manager in terms of the manager's stipulations about the operation of the lunch counter; it is also true that, in the course of evaluating each manager's stipulations, the committee will weigh any factors that bear on, or make up a part of, these stipulations. But continuing to operate the lunch counter is not such a factor; it is, rather, an objective of the committee. See (A) for an explanation of why the correct classification is A, an objective. This classification is relatively difficult.

(D) D is not the correct classification because "Continuing to operate the lunch counter at The Fair" is not a consideration that the committee assumes. That is, continuing to operate the lunch counter is not a supposition or projection that the committee makes about its situation. Continuing to operate the lunch counter does not provide, as assumptions sometimes do, a general framework that leads to the establishment of an objective. Rather, continuing to operate the lunch counter is itself an objective for the committee. See (A) for an explanation of why the correct classification is A, an objective. This classification is relatively difficult.

(E) E is not the correct classification because "Continuing to operate the lunch counter at The Fair" is a consideration that is relevant to the decision. Continuing to operate the lunch counter is relevant to the decision because it is an objective that the committee wishes to achieve and thus is fundamental in guiding the decision-making process. See (A) for an explanation of why the correct classification is A, an objective. This classification is relatively difficult.

25. Disadvantageousness of a change in the date of The Fair

(A) A is not the correct classification because the "Disadvantageousness of a change in the date of The Fair" is not an objective that the committee wishes to achieve. That is, in making a decision about which manager to choose, the committee does not hope to obtain either a new date for The Fair or the disadvantageous consequences that would attend setting a new date. Rather than an objective of the committee, the disadvantageousness of a change in The Fair's date is an assumption the committee makes. See (D) for an explanation of why the correct classification is D, and assumption. This classification is very difficult.

(B) B is not the correct classification because the "Disadvantageousness of a change in the date of The Fair" is not a basic consideration that will be weighed by the committee during the evaluation of each manager. That is, this disadvantageousness is not a fundamental consideration that will be applied to each manager to determine which one is most suitable. The committee will evaluate a manager in terms of whether or not the manager proposes to change the present date of The Fair, but that it would be disadvantageous to change the date is an assumption or a supposition the committee makes, not a factor in picking a manager. See (D) for an explanation of why the correct classification is D, an assumption. This classification is very difficult.

(C) C is not the correct classification because the "Disadvantageousness of a change in the date of The Fair" is not a consideration that bears on a major factor. That is, this disadvantageousness is not a consideration the committee will weigh in the course of evaluating the basic considerations that will determine which manager is most suitable. It is true that the committee will evaluate a manager in terms of whether or not the manager proposes to change the present date of The Fair; it is also true that, in the course of evaluating whether or not a manager proposes to change the date, the committee will weigh any factor that bears on the manager's position concerning the date. But that it would be disadvantageous to change the traditional date is not such a factor; it is, rather, an assumption of the committee.

See (D) for an explanation of why the correct classification is D, an assumption. This classification is very difficult.

(D) The correct classification for this consideration is D, an assumption. Harvey states that The Fair's success depends partly on its traditional character. Having The Fair on the same date contributes to this character. Thus, it is logical to infer that the committee assumes it would be disadvantageous to change the traditional date, since The Fair's success would be jeopardized. (The committee obviously wants a successful Fair). Note that this assumption provides a framework for the decision: because the committee assumes a new date would be disadvantageous, it wishes to retain The Fair's traditional date. In short, this unstated assumption provides the framework for the establishment of an objective, the retention of the traditional date. This classification is very difficult.

(E) E is not the correct classification because the "Disadvantageousness of a change in the date of The Fair" is a consideration that is relevant to the decision. The disadvantageousness of a change in the date is relevant to the decision because it is an assumption the committee makes before it evaluates the prospective managers and comes to a decision. More specifically, it is relevant in that it provides the framework for the establishment of an objective. See (D) for an explanation of why the correct classification is D, an assumption. This classification is very difficult.

26. **The percentage of the exhibitor fees Turner Antiques Fairs, Inc. retains**

(A) A is not the correct classification because the committee does not have as an objective "The percentage of the exhibitor fees Turner Antiques Fairs, Inc. retains." That is, obtaining this percentage is not something the committee wishes. Rather than an objective, this percentage is a minor factor in the committee's decision. See (C) for an explanation of why the correct classification is C, a minor factor. This classification is relatively difficult.

(B) B is not the correct classification because "The percentage of the exhibitor fees Turner Antiques Fairs, Inc. retains" is not a basic consideration that the committee will weigh in the course of its evaluation of each manager. That is, this percentage is not of fundamental importance in the choice of a manager. While the committee will consider this percentage when it evaluates the suitability of Turner as a manager, this percentage will be of secondary rather than basic importance. See (C) for an explanation of why the correct classification is C, a minor factor. This classification is relatively difficult.

(C) The correct classification for this consideration is C, a minor factor. Harvey's letter indicates that the management fee charged by a company is a consideration basic to the committee's choice of a manager, in other words, a major factor. The percentage of exhibitor fees retained by Turner Antiques is a minor factor because it bears on, is part of, Turner's total management fee. Note that Turner's total fee is made up of both a percentage of exhibitor fees and a percentage of ticket sales. Because the percentage of exhibitor fees only contributes to, is only a part of, the overall management fee, this percentage is a minor factor. This classification is relatively difficult.

(D) D is not the correct classification because "The percentage of the exhibitor fees Turner Antiques Fairs, Inc. retains" is not a consideration the committee assumes. That is, this percentage is not a supposition or projection that the committee makes about its situation, but is a confirmable fact that the committee will have on hand when it makes its decision, and is of secondary importance to that decision. See (C) for an explanation of why the correct classification is C, a minor factor. (Note also that this percentage does not establish, as assumptions sometimes do, a framework that leads to the establishment of an objective.) This classification is relatively difficult.

(E) E is not the correct classification because "The percentage of the exhibitor fees Turner Antiques Fairs, Inc. retains" is a consideration that is relevant to the decision. This percentage is relevant because it is a minor factor that bears on a major factor. See (C) for an explanation of why the correct classification is C, a minor factor. This classification is relatively difficult.

27. **Length of time The Fair has been in operation**

(A) A is not the correct classification because the committee does not wish, in picking a manager, to obtain or have the "Length of time The Fair has been in operation." That is, the "Length of time The Fair has been in operation" is not one of the committee's objectives or goals. See (E) for an explanation of why the correct classification is E, an unimportant issue. This classification is very easy.

(B) B is not the correct classification because the "Length of time The Fair has been in operation" is not a basic consideration that will be weighed by the committee during its evaluation of each prospective manager. That is, this period of time is not a fundamental consideration that will be applied to each prospective manager to determine which one is most suitable. See (E) for an explanation of why the correct classification is E, an unimportant issue. This classification is very easy.

(C) C is not the correct classification because the "Length of time The Fair has been in operation" is not a consideration that bears on or contributes to a major factor. That is, this time period is not a consideration that the committee will weigh in the course of evaluating the basic considerations that will determine which manager is most suitable. See (E) for an explanation of why the correct classification is E, an unimportant issue. This classification is very easy.

(D) D is not the correct classification because the "Length of time The Fair has been in operation" is not a consideration that the committee assumes. That is, this period of time is not a relevant supposition or projection that the committee makes about its situation. The "Length of time The Fair has been in operation" does not provide, as assumptions sometimes do, a framework that leads to the establishment of an objective. See (E) for an explanation of why the correct classification is E, an unimportant issue. This classification is very easy.

(E) The correct classification for this consideration is E, an unimportant issue, because the "Length of time The Fair has been in operation" is irrelevant to the decision. That is, the committee does not seek this period of time as an objective or project it as a relevant assumption. Nor will the committee use this time period as a means of evaluating each manager. While The Fair is an annual event and most likely has been in existence for more than a few years, the actual length of its existence is a fact that is extraneous to, has no logical connection with, the choice of a new manager. This classification is very easy.

28. **Value of continuing The Fair as a major fund-raising event**

(A) A is not the correct classification because the "Value of continuing The Fair as a major fund-raising event" is not an objective that the committee wishes to achieve. That is, the committee does not seek this value. The committee does have as an objective continuing The Fair as a major fund-raising event. But that there is a value attached to continuing The Fair as a major fund-raising event is an assumption the committee makes, not an objective it seeks to achieve. See (D) for an explanation of why the correct classification is D, an assumption. This classification is relatively difficult.

(B) B is not the correct classification because the "Value of continuing The Fair as a major fund-raising event" is not a basic consideration that will be weighed by the committee during its evaluation of each manager. That is, this value is not a fundamental consideration that will be applied to each manager to determine which one is most suitable; it is, rather, an assumption or supposition the committee

makes. See (D) for an explanation of why the correct classification is D, an assumption. This classification is relatively difficult.

(C) C is not the correct classification because the "Value of continuing The Fair as a major fund-raising event" is not a consideration that bears on or contributes to a major factor. That is, this value is not a consideration that the committee will weigh in the course of evaluating the basic considerations that will determine which manager is most suitable. Rather, this value is an assumption or supposition that the committee makes. See (D) for an explanation of why the correct classification is D, an assumption. This classification is relatively difficult.

(D) The correct classification for this consideration is D, an assumption. The first paragraph of the passage indicates that The Fair is a major fund-raising event for the committee but that ticket sales have begun to decline. That the committee assumes that a value attaches to continuing The Fair as a major fund-raising event is inferable from the fact that the committee is making plans to find a new manager to help ensure the success of the future money-making operations of The Fair. In other words, the fact that the committee is seeking to find a professional who will successfully run The Fair, that is, turn around declining ticket sales, indicates that the committee believes there is value in continuing The Fair as a major fund-raising event. Put another way, the committee would not be making plans to find a manager who will improve The Fair's financial picture, that is, allow The Fair to continue to be a good fund-raiser, if it did not believe or assume that there was value in having The Fair continue to be a major fund-raiser. This classification is relatively difficult.

(E) E is not the correct classification because the "Value of continuing The Fair as a major fund-raising event" is a consideration that is relevant to the decision. This value is relevant to the decision because it is assumed by the committee before it evaluates the prospective managers and comes to a decision. See (D) for an explanation of why the correct classification is D, an assumption. This classification is relatively difficult.

29. **Continued availability of volunteers for the lunch counter at The Fair**

(A) A is not the correct classification because the "Continued availability of volunteers for the lunch counter at The Fair" is not an objective the committee wishes to achieve. That is, the committee does not seek this availability. The committee does have as an objective continuing to operate the lunch counter, but that there will be a continued availability of volunteers to handle the workings of the committee-operated lunch counter is an assumption the committee makes, not an objective it seeks to achieve. See (D) for an explanation of why the correct classification is D, an assumption. This classification is relatively difficult.

(B) B is not the correct classification because the "Continued availability of volunteers for the lunch counter at The Fair" is not a basic consideration that will be weighed by the committee during its evaluation of each manager. That is, this continued availability is not a fundamental consideration that will be applied to each manager to determine which one is most suitable. It is true that the committee will evaluate a prospective manager in terms of the manager's stipulations about the operation of the lunch counter, but that there will be a continued availability of volunteers to work at the lunch counter is an assumption the committee makes, not a factor in its decision. See (D) for an explanation of why the correct classification is D, an assumption. This classification is relatively difficult.

(C) C is not the correct classification because the "Continued availability of volunteers for the lunch counter at The Fair" is not a consideration that bears on or contributes to a major factor. That is, this availability is not a consideration that the committee will weigh in the course of evaluating the basic considerations that will determine which manager is most suitable. Rather, this availability is an assumption or supposition the committee makes. See (D) for an explanation of why the correct classification is D, an assumption. This classification is relatively difficult.

(D) The correct classification for this consideration is D, an assumption. The first paragraph of the passage indicates that the committee has, in the past, recruited volunteers to handle all the aspects of the Fair's organization, including, by implication, the running of the lunch counter. However, because there are insufficient volunteers to continue to handle all aspects of The Fair's organization, the committee has now decided to turn over the management of The Fair to a professional manager. Significantly, though, one aspect of The Fair's management that the committee does not wish to turn over to a manager is the operation of the lunch counter. Given all these facts, it is logical to conclude that the committee assumes or believes that there will continue to be an availability of volunteers to handle the details of running the lunch counter. Put another way, the committee would not exempt the lunch counter from the control of a professional manager unless it assumed a continued availability of volunteers to handle the counter's operation. This classification is relatively difficult.

(E) E is not the correct classification because the "Continued availability of volunteers for the lunch counter at The Fair" is a consideration that is relevant to the decision. This availability is relevant to the decision because it is assumed by the committee before it evaluates each prospective manager and comes to a decision. See (D) for an explanation of why the correct classification is D, an assumption. This classification is relatively difficult.

30. **The various managers' stipulations about the operation of the lunch counter**

(A) A is not the correct classification because the committee does not have as an objective "The various managers' stipulations about the operation of the lunch counter." That is, the committee does not seek these stipulations. The committee does have as an objective continuing to operate the lunch counter, but each manager's terms regarding the operation of the lunch counter is a major factor in picking a manager, not an objective the committee seeks. See (B) for an explanation of why the correct classification is B, a major factor. This classification is of medium difficulty.

(B) The correct classification for this consideration is B, a major factor. This can be determined from the first paragraph of Harvey's letter, where you are told that the committee "wants to continue to operate the lunch counter." Given this objective, it is logical that "The various managers' stipulations about the operation of the lunch counter" will be a major factor because these stipulations are basic in determining to what extent the committee will meet its goal of continuing to operate the lunch counter. This classification is of medium difficulty.

(C) C is not the correct classification because "The various managers' stipulations about the operation of the lunch counter" is not a consideration that bears on or contributes to a major factor. That is, the stipulations are not a consideration to which the committee will give only secondary weight in the course of evaluating the basic considerations that will determine which manager is most suitable. It is true that the committee wants to continue to operate the lunch counter; it is also true that the committee will give secondary importance to any factor that bears on a manager's terms about the operation of the lunch counter. But the managers' terms are not themselves a secondary factor; they are, rather, a major factor. See (B) for an explanation of why the correct classification is B, a major factor. This classification is of medium difficulty.

(D) D is not the correct classification because "The various managers' stipulations about the operation of the lunch counter" is not a consideration that the committee assumes. That is, these stipulations are not a consideration that the committee only supposes, but are existing, confirmable facts that it will have when it makes its decision, and are basic to that decision. See (B) for an explanation of why the correct classification is B, a major factor. (Note also that the stipulations do not provide, as assumptions sometimes do, a framework that leads to the establishment of an objective.) This classification is of medium difficulty.

(E) E is not the correct classification because "The various managers' stipulations about the operation of the lunch counter" is a consideration that is relevant to the decision. These stipulations are relevant because they are crucial in permitting the committee to determine to what extent it will meet its objective of operating the lunch counter. See (B) for an explanation of why the correct classification is B, a major factor. This classification is of medium difficulty.

31. **Dates of the other antiques fairs in the area**

(A) A is not the correct classification because the committee does not wish, in picking a manager, to obtain or have the dates of other fairs in the area. That is, the "Dates of other antiques fairs in the area" is not one of the committee's objectives. The committee does have as an objective the retention of The Fair's traditional date, but the dates of other fairs are irrelevant to the decision at hand. See (E) for an explanation of why the correct classification is E, an unimportant issue. This classification is relatively difficult.

(B) B is not the correct classification because the "Dates of the other antiques fairs in the area" is not a basic consideration that will be weighed by the committee during its evaluation of each prospective manager. That is, when other fairs are held is not a fundamental consideration that will be applied to each prospective manager to determine which one is most suitable. See (E) for an explanation of why the correct classification is E, an unimportant issue. This classification is relatively difficult.

(C) C is not the correct classification because the "Dates of the other antiques fairs in the area" is not a consideration that bears on or contributes to a major factor. That is, when other fairs are held is not a consideration that the committee will weigh in the course of evaluating the basic considerations that will determine which manager is most suitable. See (E) for an explanation of why the correct classification is E, an unimportant issue. This classification is relatively difficult.

(D) D is not the correct classification because the "Dates of the other antiques fairs in the area" is not a consideration that the committee assumes. That is, it is not a relevant supposition or projection that the committee makes about its situation. The "Dates of other antiques fairs in the area" does not provide, as assumptions sometimes do, a framework that leads to the establishment of an objective. See (E) for an explanation of why the correct classification is E, an unimportant issue. This classification is relatively difficult.

(E) The correct classification for this consideration is E, an unimportant issue, because the "Dates of the other antique fairs in the area" is irrelevant to the decision. That is, the committee does not seek these dates as an objective or project them as an assumption. Nor will the committee use these dates to evaluate each manager. The passage does indicate that there are rival fairs, but there is no logical connection between the dates of these fairs and the decision about which manager to choose. This classification is relatively difficult.

32. **Amount Riverside Promotions expects the committee to spend for local advertising**

(A) A is not the correct classification because the committee does not have as an objective "Amount Riverside Promotions expects the committee to spend for local advertising." That is, the committee does not wish to achieve this amount. Rather, this amount is a minor factor in the committee's evaluation of Riverside Promotions. See (C) for an explanation of why the correct classification is C, a minor factor. This classification is of medium difficulty.

(B) B is not the correct classification because the "Amount Riverside Promotions expects the committee to spend for local advertising" is not a basic consideration that will be weighed by the committee during its evaluation of each manager. That is, this amount is not of fundamental importance in the choice of a manager. It is true that the committee will consider this amount when it is evaluating the suitability of Riverside Promotions, but the amount is of secondary rather than basic importance. See (C) for an explanation of why the correct classification is C, a minor factor. This classification is of medium difficulty.

(C) The correct classification for this consideration is C, a minor factor. The second paragraph of Harvey's letter indicates that the committee wants to know the size of each manager's advertising budget. This explicit request indicates that each manager's advertising budget, including Riverside Promotions' budget, will be a major factor in the choice of a manager. The "Amount Riverside Promotions expects the committee to spend for local advertising" is a minor

-125-

factor because it bears on, is part of, Riverside's overall advertising budget. Note that this budget is made up of both the $500 that Riverside would spend for magazine advertisements and the $500 that the committee must spend on local advertising. Because this latter amount only contributes to the overall advertising budget, the amount is a minor factor. This classification is of medium difficulty.

(D) D is not the correct classification because the "Amount Riverside Promotions expects the committee to spend on local advertising" is not a consideration that the committee assumes. That is, this amount is not a supposition or projection that the committee makes about its situation, but a confirmable fact that the committee will know when it makes its decision, and of secondary importance to that decision. See (C) for an explanation of why the correct classification is C, a minor factor. (Note also that this amount does not establish, as assumptions sometimes do, a framework that leads to the establishment of an objective). This classification is of medium difficulty.

(E) E is not the correct classification because the "Amount Riverside Promotions expects the committee to spend for local advertising" is relevant to the decision. This amount is relevant because it is a minor factor that bears on a major factor. See (C) for an explanation of why the correct classification is C, a minor factor. This classification is of medium difficulty.

33. **Turner Antiques Fairs' twenty percent commission on lunch counter sales**

(A) A is not the correct classification because the committee does not have as an objective "Turner Antiques Fairs' twenty percent commission on lunch counter sales." That is, the committee does not wish to achieve this commission. Rather, this commission is a minor factor in the committee's evaluation of Turner Antiques Fairs. See (C) for an explanation of why the correct classification is C, a minor factor. This classification is relatively difficult.

(B) B is not the correct classification because "Turner Antiques Fairs' twenty percent commission on lunch counter sales" is not a basic consideration that will be weighed by the committee during its evaluation of each manager. That is, this commission is not of fundamental importance in the choice of a manager. It is true that the committee will consider this commission when it is evaluating the suitability of Turner as a manager, but the commission is of secondary rather than basic importance. See (C) for an explanation of why the correct classification is C, a minor factor. This classification is relatively difficult.

(C) The correct classification for this consideration is C, a minor factor. The first paragraph of Harvey's letter indicates that the committee wants to continue to operate the lunch counter. Given this objective, it is logical that the various managers' stipulations about the operation of the lunch counter, including those of Turner Antiques Fairs, would be a major factor. "Turner Antiques Fairs' twenty percent commission on lunch counter sales" is a minor factor because it bears on, is one of, Turner's stipulations. Note that these stipulations also include requirements concerning the approval of the lunch counter menu and the responsibility for food service. Because the commission is only one of several stipulations, it is a minor factor. This classification is relatively difficult.

(D) D is not the correct classification because "Turner Antiques Fairs' twenty percent commission on lunch counter sales" is not a consideration that the committee assumes. That is, this commission is not a supposition or projection that the committee makes about its situation, but a confirmable fact that the committee will know when it makes its decision, and of secondary importance to that decision. See (C) for an explanation of why the correct classification is C, a minor factor. (Note also that this commission does not establish, as assumptions sometimes do, a framework that leads to the establishment of an objective.) This classification is relatively difficult.

(E) E is not the correct classification because "Turner Antiques Fairs' twenty percent commission on lunch counter sales" is relevant to the decision. This commission is relevant because it is a minor factor that bears on a major factor. See (C) for an explanation of why the correct classification is C, a minor factor. This classification is relatively difficult.

34. **Size of the fee each manager will charge**

(A) A is not the correct classification because the committee does not have as an objective in making its decision the size of each manager's fee. That is, in picking a manager, the committee does not seek the "Size of the fee each manager will charge." See (B) for an explanation of why the correct classification is B, a major factor. This classification is very easy.

(B) The correct classification for this consideration is B, a major factor. Harvey's letter requests information from the prospective managers concerning their "fee for managing The Fair." This explicit request indicates that the size of the fee that a manager will charge is a consideration that the committee will weigh carefully and that will be of fundamental importance in the decision concerning which manager to choose. This classification is very easy.

(C) C is not the correct classification because the ''Size of the fee each manager will charge'' is not a consideration that bears on or contributes to a major factor. That is, each manager's fee is not a consideration to which the committee will attach only secondary weight in the course of evaluating the basic considerations that will determine which manager is most suitable. It is true that the committee will give secondary importance to any factor that bears on the size of a manager's fee, but that fee is not itself a secondary factor. Rather, the fee is a major factor. See (B) for an explanation of why the correct classification is B, a major factor. This classification is very easy.

(D) D is not the correct classification because the size of each manager's fee is not a consideration that the committee assumes. That is, the size of each manager's fee is not a consideration that the committee only supposes, but is an existing, confirmable fact that the committee will have on hand when it makes its decision, and is basic to that decision. See (B) for an explanation of why the correct classification is B, a major factor. (Note also that the size of each manager's fee does not provide, as assumptions sometimes do, a framework that leads to the establishment of an objective.) This classification is very easy.

(E) E is not the correct classification because the ''Size of the fee each manager will charge'' is a consideration that is relevant to the decision. The size of each manager's fee is relevant because it is information that is explicitly requested by a member of the committee. This explicit request indicates that a manager's fee will be weighed heavily by the committee in making its decision. See (B) for an explanation of why the correct classification is B, a major factor. This classification is very easy.

35. **Number of people each of the three managers employs**

(A) A is not the correct classification because the committee does not wish, in picking a manager, to obtain or have the ''Number of people each of the three managers employs.'' That is, this number is not one of the committee's objectives. See (E) for an explanation of why the correct classification is E, an unimportant issue. This classification is relatively easy.

(B) B is not the correct classification because the ''Number of people each of the three managers employs'' is not a basic consideration that will be weighed by the committee during its evaluation of each prospective manager. That is, this number is not a fundamental consideration that will be applied to each manager to determine which one is most suitable. See (E) for an explanation of why the correct classification is E, an unimportant issue. This classification is relatively easy.

(C) C is not the correct classification because the ''Number of people each of the three managers employs'' is not a consideration that bears on or contributes to a major factor. That is, this number is not a consideration that the committee will weigh in the course of evaluating the basic considerations that will determine which manager is most suitable. See (E) for an explanation of why the correct classification is E, an unimportant issue. This classification is relatively easy.

(D) D is not the correct classification because the ''Number of people each of the three managers employs'' is not a consideration that the committee assumes. That is, this number is not a relevant supposition or projection that the committee makes about its situation. The ''Number of people each of the three mangers employs'' does not provide, as assumptions sometimes do, a framework that leads to the establishment of an objective. See (E) for an explanation of why the correct classification is E, an unimportant issue. This classification is relatively easy.

(E) The correct classification for this consideration is E, an unimportant issue, because the ''Number of people each of the three managers employs'' is irrelevant to the decision. That is, the committee does not seek this number as an objective or project it as an assumption. Nor will the committee use the number to evaluate each manager. It is true that the committee is interested in how much responsibility each manager's staff would take for the organization of The Fair, and it might appear that the number of people each manager employs would have an effect on how much responsibility each manager's staff would take for the organization of The Fair. However, there is no necessary logical connection between the size of a staff in and of itself and how much responsibility a manager is willing to take. A manager with a small, but efficient, staff might be willing to take more responsibility for The Fair's management than would a manager with a large, but inefficient, staff. In short, the ''Number of people each of the three managers employs'' is an unimportant issue in the decision. This classification is relatively easy.

7 Sentence Correction

A sample Sentence Correction test begins on page 133; answers to the questions follow the test. After the answers are explanations for all of the questions. These explanations address types of grammatical and syntactical problems you are likely to encounter in the Sentence Correction section of the GMAT.

Study Suggestions

1. One way to gain familiarity with the basic conventions of standard written English is to read material that reflects standard usage. Suitable material will usually be found in good magazines and nonfiction books, editorials in outstanding newspapers, and the collections of essays used by many college and university writing courses.

2. A general review of basic rules of grammar and practice with writing exercises are also ways of studying for the Sentence Correction section. If you have papers that have been carefully evaluated for grammatical errors, it may be helpful to review the comments and corrections.

Test-Taking Strategies for Sentence Correction

1. Read the entire sentence carefully. Try to understand the specific idea or relationship that the sentence should express.

2. Since the part of the sentence that *may* be incorrect is underlined, concentrate on evaluating the underlined part for errors and possible corrections before reading the answer choices.

3. Read each answer choice carefully. Choice A always repeats the underlined portion of the original sentence. Choose A if you think that the sentence is best as it stands, but only after examining all of the other choices.

4. Try to determine how well each choice corrects whatever you consider wrong with the original sentence.

5. Make sure that you evaluate the sentence and the choices in terms of general clarity, grammatical and idiomatic usage, economy and precision of language, and appropriateness of diction.

6. Read the whole sentence, substituting the choice that you prefer for the underlined part. A choice may be wrong because it does not fit grammatically or structurally with the rest of the sentence. Remember that some sentences will require no corrections. The answer to such sentences should be A.

When you take the sample test, use the answer spaces on page 131 to mark your answers.

Answer Spaces for Sentence Correction Sample Test

1 Ⓐ Ⓑ Ⓒ Ⓓ Ⓔ	6 Ⓐ Ⓑ Ⓒ Ⓓ Ⓔ	11 Ⓐ Ⓑ Ⓒ Ⓓ Ⓔ	16 Ⓐ Ⓑ Ⓒ Ⓓ Ⓔ	21 Ⓐ Ⓑ Ⓒ Ⓓ Ⓔ
2 Ⓐ Ⓑ Ⓒ Ⓓ Ⓔ	7 Ⓐ Ⓑ Ⓒ Ⓓ Ⓔ	12 Ⓐ Ⓑ Ⓒ Ⓓ Ⓔ	17 Ⓐ Ⓑ Ⓒ Ⓓ Ⓔ	22 Ⓐ Ⓑ Ⓒ Ⓓ Ⓔ
3 Ⓐ Ⓑ Ⓒ Ⓓ Ⓔ	8 Ⓐ Ⓑ Ⓒ Ⓓ Ⓔ	13 Ⓐ Ⓑ Ⓒ Ⓓ Ⓔ	18 Ⓐ Ⓑ Ⓒ Ⓓ Ⓔ	23 Ⓐ Ⓑ Ⓒ Ⓓ Ⓔ
4 Ⓐ Ⓑ Ⓒ Ⓓ Ⓔ	9 Ⓐ Ⓑ Ⓒ Ⓓ Ⓔ	14 Ⓐ Ⓑ Ⓒ Ⓓ Ⓔ	19 Ⓐ Ⓑ Ⓒ Ⓓ Ⓔ	24 Ⓐ Ⓑ Ⓒ Ⓓ Ⓔ
5 Ⓐ Ⓑ Ⓒ Ⓓ Ⓔ	10 Ⓐ Ⓑ Ⓒ Ⓓ Ⓔ	15 Ⓐ Ⓑ Ⓒ Ⓓ Ⓔ	20 Ⓐ Ⓑ Ⓒ Ⓓ Ⓔ	25 Ⓐ Ⓑ Ⓒ Ⓓ Ⓔ

SENTENCE CORRECTION SAMPLE TEST

25 Questions

Directions: In each of the following sentences, some part of the sentence or the entire sentence is underlined. Beneath each sentence you will find five ways of phrasing the underlined part. The first of these repeats the original; the other four are different. If you think the original is better than any of the alternatives, choose answer A; otherwise choose one of the others. Select the best version and blacken the corresponding space on your answer sheet.

This is a test of correctness and effectiveness of expression. In choosing answers, follow the requirements of standard written English; that is, pay attention to grammar, choice of words, and sentence construction. Choose the answer that expresses most effectively what is presented in the original sentence; this answer should be clear and exact, without awkwardness, ambiguity, or redundancy.

1. After the Civil War Harriet Tubman, herself an escaped slave, continued her efforts in behalf of former slaves, helping to educate freedmen, supporting children, and she was assisting impoverished old people.

   (A) she was assisting impoverished old people
   (B) impoverished old people were assisted
   (C) to assist impoverished old people
   (D) assisting impoverished old people
   (E) also in assisting impoverished old people

2. The percentage of the labor force that is unemployed has dropped sharply this month, even though it may be only temporarily.

   (A) even though it may be only temporarily
   (B) but it may be temporary only
   (C) but the drop may be only temporary
   (D) even though the drop may only be temporary
   (E) but such a drop may only be a temporary one

3. As more and more subjects take the Rorschach test, the body of information tying styles of response with specific problems or tendencies grow, and the predictive power of the test increases.

   (A) with specific problems or tendencies grow, and the predictive power of the test increases
   (B) with specific problems or tendencies grow, and the predictive powers increase in the test
   (C) to specific problems or tendencies grow, and the predictive power of the test increases
   (D) to specific problems or tendencies grows, and the predictive power of the test increases
   (E) and specific problems and tendencies grow, increasing the predictive power of the test

4. Unlike the Second World War, when long voyages home aboard troopships gave soldiers a chance to talk out their experiences and begin to absorb them, Vietnam returnees often came home by jet, singly or in small groups.

   (A) Second World War, when long voyages home aboard troopships gave soldiers
   (B) soldier coming home after the Second World War on long voyages aboard troopships who had
   (C) soldiers of the Second World War, whose long voyage home aboard a troopship gave him
   (D) troopships on long voyages home after the Second World War which gave the soldier
   (E) soldiers of the Second World War, whose long voyages home aboard troopships gave them

5. Contestants in many sports prepare for competition by eating pasta as part of a "carbohydrate-loading" regimen that is supposed to provide quick energy.

   (A) prepare for competition by eating pasta as
   (B) prepare for competition and eat pasta, which is
   (C) prepare for competition by eating pasta because this is
   (D) eat pasta to prepare for competing, which is
   (E) eat pasta to prepare for competing as

GO ON TO THE NEXT PAGE.

6. In August 1883, Krakatoa erupted and sent clouds of dust, ash, and sulphate to a height of 50 miles, blotted out the sun for more than two days within a 50-mile radius and for nearly a day at an observation post 130 miles away.

   (A) blotted out the sun for more than two days within
   (B) blotting out the sun for more than two days within
   (C) the sun being blotted out for more than two days in
   (D) having blotted out the sun for more than two days in
   (E) for more than two days blotting out the sun within

7. Added to the increase in hourly wages requested last July, the railroad employees are now seeking an expanded program of retirement benefits.

   (A) Added to the increase in hourly wages requested last July, the railroad employees are now seeking an expanded program of retirement benefits.
   (B) Added to the increase in hourly wages which had been requested last July, the employees of the railroad are now seeking an expanded program of retirement benefits.
   (C) The railroad employees are now seeking an expanded program of retirement benefits added to the increase in hourly wages that were requested last July.
   (D) In addition to the increase in hourly wages that were requested last July, the railroad employees are now seeking an expanded program of retirement benefits.
   (E) In addition to the increase in hourly wages requested last July, the employees of the railroad are now seeking an expanded program of retirement benefits.

8. Child prodigies are marked not so much by their skills but instead by the fact that these skills are fully developed at a very early age.

   (A) but instead
   (B) rather than
   (C) than
   (D) as
   (E) so much as

9. The department defines a private passenger vehicle as one registered to an individual with a gross weight of less than 8,000 pounds.

   (A) as one registered to an individual with a gross weight of less than 8,000 pounds
   (B) to be one that is registered to an individual with a gross weight of less than 8,000 pounds
   (C) as one that is registered to an individual and that has a gross weight of less than 8,000 pounds
   (D) to have a gross weight less than 8,000 pounds and being registered to an individual
   (E) as having a gross weight of less than 8,000 pounds and registered to an individual

10. Urban officials want the census to be as accurate and complete as possible for the reason that the amount of low-income people in a given area affect the distribution of about fifty billion dollars a year in federal funds.

   (A) for the reason that the amount of low-income people in a given area affect
   (B) for the reason because the amount of low-income people in a given area effects
   (C) in that the amount of low-income people in given areas effect
   (D) because the number of low-income people in a given area affects
   (E) because the numbers of low-income people in given areas effects

GO ON TO THE NEXT PAGE.

11. After the Arab conquest of Egypt in A. D. 640, Arabic <u>became the dominant language of the Egyptians, replacing older languages</u> and writing systems.

(A) became the dominant language of the Egyptians, replacing older languages
(B) became the dominant language of the Egyptians, replacing language systems that were older
(C) becomes the dominant language of the Egyptians and it replaced older languages
(D) becomes the dominant language of the Egyptians and it replaced languages that were older
(E) becomes the dominant language of the Egyptians, having replaced languages that were older

12. The use of gravity waves, which do not interact with matter <u>in the way electromagnetic waves do, hopefully will enable</u> astronomers to study the actual formation of black holes and neutron stars.

(A) in the way electromagnetic waves do, hopefully will enable
(B) in the way electromagnetic waves do, will, it is hoped, enable
(C) like electromagnetic waves, hopefully will enable
(D) like electromagnetic waves, would enable, hopefully
(E) such as electromagnetic waves do, will, it is hoped, enable

13. <u>If a single strain of plant is used for a given crop over a wide area, a practice fostered by modern seed-marketing methods, it</u> increases the likelihood that the impact of a single crop disease or pest will be disastrous.

(A) If a single strain of plant is used for a given crop over a wide area, a practice fostered by modern seed-marketing methods, it
(B) If a single strain of plant is used for a given crop over a wide area, as is fostered by modern seed-marketing methods, it
(C) A practice fostered by modern seed-marketing methods, a single strain of plant used for a given crop over a wide area
(D) A single strain of plant used for a given crop over a wide area, a practice fostered by modern seed-marketing methods,
(E) The use of a single strain of plant for a given crop over a wide area, a practice fostered by modern seed-marketing methods,

14. A majority of the international journalists surveyed view nuclear power stations as unsafe at present but <u>that they will, or could,</u> be made sufficiently safe in the future.

(A) that they will, or could,
(B) that they would, or could,
(C) they will be or could
(D) think that they will be or could
(E) think the power stations would or could

15. A controversial figure throughout most of his public life, the Black leader Marcus Garvey advocated <u>that some Blacks return to Africa, the land that, to him, symbolized the possibility of freedom.</u>

(A) that some Blacks return to Africa, the land that, to him, symbolized the possibility of freedom
(B) that some Blacks return to the African land symbolizing the possibility of freedom to him
(C) that some Blacks return to Africa which was the land which symbolized the possibility of freedom to him
(D) some Black's returning to Africa which was the land that to him symbolized the possibility of freedom
(E) some Black's return to the land symbolizing the possibility of freedom to him, Africa

GO ON TO THE NEXT PAGE.

16. The fear of rabies is well founded; <u>few people are known to recover from the disease after the appearance of the clinical symptoms.</u>

    (A) few people are known to recover from the disease after the appearance of the clinical symptoms
    (B) few people are known to have recovered from the disease once the clinical symptoms have appeared
    (C) there are few known people who have recovered from the disease once the clinical symptoms have appeared
    (D) after the clinical symptoms appear, there are few known people who have recovered from the disease
    (E) recovery from the disease is known for only a few people after the clinical symptoms appear

17. The growth of the railroads led to the abolition of local times, <u>which was determined by when the sun reached the observer's meridian and differing</u> from city to city, and to the establishment of regional times.

    (A) which was determined by when the sun reached the observer's meridian and differing
    (B) which was determined by when the sun reached the observer's meridian and which differed
    (C) which were determined by when the sun reached the observer's meridian and differing
    (D) determined by when the sun reached the observer's meridian and differed
    (E) determined by when the sun reached the observer's meridian and differing

18. <u>Although partially destroyed, the archaeologists were able to infer</u> from what remained of the inscription that the priest Zonainos was buried in the crypt.

    (A) Although partially destroyed, the archaeologists were able to infer
    (B) Although partially destroyed, the archaeologists had inferred
    (C) Although it had been partially destroyed, the archaeologists were able to infer
    (D) Partially destroyed though it had been, the archaeologists had been able to infer
    (E) Destroyed partially, the archaeologists were able to infer

19. <u>For all his professed disdain of such activities,</u> Auden was an inveterate literary gossip.

    (A) For all his professed disdain of such activities,
    (B) Having always professed disdain for such activities,
    (C) All such activities were, he professed, disdained, and
    (D) Professing that all such activities were disdained,
    (E) In spite of professions of disdaining all such activities,

20. The earnings of women are <u>well below that of men in spite of educational differences that are diminishing</u> between the sexes.

    (A) well below that of men in spite of educational differences that are diminishing
    (B) much below that of men's despite educational differences diminishing
    (C) much below men in spite of diminishing educational differences
    (D) well below those of men in spite of diminishing educational differences
    (E) below men's despite their educational differences that are diminishing

GO ON TO THE NEXT PAGE.

21. Acid rain and snow result from the chemical reactions between industrial emissions of sulfur dioxide and nitrogen oxides with atmospheric water vapor to produce highly corrosive sulfuric and nitric acids.

(A) with atmospheric water vapor to produce highly corrosive sulfuric and nitric acids
(B) with atmospheric water vapor producing highly corrosive sulfuric and nitric acids
(C) and atmospheric water vapor which has produced highly corrosive sulfuric and nitric acids
(D) and atmospheric water vapor which have produced sulfuric and nitric acids which are highly corrosive
(E) and atmospheric water vapor to produce highly corrosive sulfuric and nitric acids

22. It is characteristic of the Metropolitan Museum of Art, as of virtually every great American museum, the taste of local collectors has played at least as large a part in the formation of their collections as has the judgments of the art historian.

(A) of virtually every great American museum, the taste of local collectors has played at least as large a part in the formation of their collections as has
(B) of virtually every great American museum, that the taste of local collectors has played at least as large a part in the formation of their collections as has
(C) it is of virtually every great American museum, that the taste of local collectors has played at least as large a part in the formation of its collections as have
(D) it is of virtually every great American museum, that the taste of local collectors have played at least as large a part in the formation of its collections as have
(E) it is of virtually every great American museum, the taste of local collectors has played at least as large a part in the formation of its collections as has

23. There has been a 30- to 40-fold increase in the incidence of malaria caused by increasing mosquito resistance against pesticides.

(A) increase in the incidence of malaria caused by increasing mosquito resistance against
(B) increase in the incidence of malaria because of increasing resistance of mosquitoes to
(C) increasing malaria incidence because of increasing resistance of mosquitoes to
(D) incidence of malaria increase caused by increasing mosquito resistance against
(E) incidence of malaria increase because of increased mosquito resistance to

24. Aging is a property of all animals that reach a fixed size at maturity, and the variations in life spans among different species are far greater as that among individuals from the same species: a fruit fly is ancient at 40 days, a mouse at 3 years, a horse at 30, a man at 100, and some tortoises at 150.

(A) among different species are far greater as that among individuals from
(B) among different species are far greater than that among individuals from
(C) among different species are far greater than those among individuals of
(D) between different species are far more than that between individuals of
(E) between different species are greater by far than is that between individuals from

25. The herbicide Oryzalin was still being produced in 1979, three years after the wives of workers producing the chemical in Rensselaer, New York, were found to have borne children with heart defects or miscarriages, and none of their pregnancies was normal.

(A) to have borne children with heart defects or miscarriages, and none of their pregnancies was
(B) to have had children born with heart defects or miscarriages, and none of the pregnancies was
(C) either to have had children with heart defects or miscarriages, without any of their pregnancies being
(D) either to have had miscarriages or to have borne children with heart defects; none of the pregnancies was
(E) either to have had miscarriages or children born with heart defects, without any of their pregnancies being

END OF SAMPLE TEST

Answer Key for Sample Test

SENTENCE CORRECTION

1. D	14. D
2. C	15. A
3. D	16. B
4. E	17. E
5. A	18. C
6. B	19. A
7. E	20. D
8. D	21. E
9. C	22. C
10. D	23. B
11. A	24. C
12. B	25. D
13. E	

Explanatory Material: Sentence Correction

The following discussion of Sentence Correction is intended to familiarize you with the most efficient and effective approaches to Sentence Correction. The particular questions on the sample test in this chapter are generally representative of the kinds of questions you will encounter in this section of the GMAT. Remember that it is the problem-solving strategy that is important, not the specific details of a particular question.

1. After the Civil War Harriet Tubman, herself an escaped slave, continued her efforts in behalf of former slaves, helping to educate freedmen, supporting children, and she was assisting impoverished old people.

   (A) she was assisting impoverished old people
   (B) impoverished old people were assisted
   (C) to assist impoverished old people
   (D) assisting impoverished old people
   (E) also in assisting impoverished old people

The corrected sentence must conclude with a verb phrase that is parallel with the two preceding verb phrases, *helping to educate freedmen* and *supporting children*; in other words, the final phrase should begin with another present participle, or "-ing" verb form. Choice A breaks the parallel by adding *she was* and thus making another independent clause. Choice B, also an independent clause, employs a passive verb (*were assisted*) instead of a present participle, and C uses an infinitive (*to assist*) instead of a present participle. In E, *in* produces a prepositional rather than a participial phrase. Choice D, the best answer, supplies the parallel verb form. This is an easy question.

2. The percentage of the labor force that is unemployed has dropped sharply this month, <u>even though it may be only temporarily.</u>

   (A) even though it may be only temporarily
   (B) but it may be temporary only
   (C) but the drop may be only temporary
   (D) even though the drop may only be temporary
   (E) but such a drop may only be a temporary one

In choices A and B, the pronoun *it* has no noun referent and must be replaced by a noun such as *drop*. That noun should be modified by an adjective (*temporary*), not an adverb (*temporarily*). In choices A and D, *even though* misstates the relationship between ideas by suggesting that unemployment dropped sharply despite the possibility that the drop is temporary; *but* suggests nothing more than a contrast between a recent drop and possible future reversal. In choices B, D, and E, *only* is separated from the adjective it modifies; in the correct answer *only* should (or must) immediately precede *temporary*. The phrase *such a drop* in E wrongly implies that this drop is but one example of a whole class of similar events being discussed. C is correct for this difficult question.

3. As more and more subjects take the Rorschach test, the body of information tying styles of response <u>with specific problems or tendencies grow, and the predictive power of the test increases.</u>

   (A) with specific problems or tendencies grow, and the predictive power of the test increases
   (B) with specific problems or tendencies grow, and the predictive powers increase in the test
   (C) to specific problems or tendencies grow, and the predictive power of the test increases
   (D) to specific problems or tendencies grows, and the predictive power of the test increases
   (E) and specific problems and tendencies grow, increasing the predictive power of the test

The grammatical subject of this sentence is *body,* and so the correct verb form is *grows*; hence choices A, B, C, and E are incorrect because they use *grow*. Also, the best answer will start with *to* because the correct form of expression is *tying X to Y.* The wording of B illogically suggests that predictive powers are growing within the test, not that the predictive power of the test increases. D is the best choice for this question of average difficulty.

4. Unlike the <u>Second World War, when long voyages home aboard troopships gave soldiers</u> a chance to talk out their experiences and begin to absorb them, Vietnam returnees often came home by jet, singly or in small groups.

(A) Second World War, when long voyages home aboard troopships gave soldiers

(B) soldier coming home after the Second Word War on long voyages aboard troopships who had

(C) soldiers of the Second World War, whose long voyage home aboard a troopship gave him

(D) troopships on long voyages home after the Second World War which gave the soldier

(E) soldiers of the Second World War, whose long voyages home aboard troopships gave them

The sentence with choice A wrongly compares *Vietnam returnees* with *the Second World War*. In choice B, the singular *soldier* does not agree in number with the plural *returnees*; also, B is awkward because the pronoun *who* is so far from its noun referent, *soldier,* that it seems to modify *troopships,* the nearest noun. Choice C correctly compares *soldiers* with *returnees,* but the singular *him* does not agree with the plural *soldiers.* In choice D, *returnees* are compared with *troopships, which* illogically refers to *the Second World War,* and *soldier* is singular rather than plural. Choice E is the best answer: the comparison is logical, the nouns and pronouns agree in number, and the pronoun references are clear. The question is moderately easy.

5. Contestants in many sports <u>prepare for competition by eating pasta as</u> part of a "carbohydrate-loading" regimen that is supposed to provide quick energy.

(A) prepare for competition by eating pasta as

(B) prepare for competition and eat pasta, which is

(C) prepare for competition by eating pasta because this is

(D) eat pasta to prepare for competing, which is

(E) eat pasta to prepare for competing as

Choice A is correct. In choice B, *which* is ambiguous: it is not clear whether *which* refers only to *pasta,* the nearest noun, or to the whole preceding clause. Moreover, *and* incorrectly suggests that contestants eat pasta in addition to preparing for competition, not that they eat pasta as a means of preparation. Choice C wrongly states that contestants eat pasta not to become prepared but simply because pasta is part of a regimen. Also, *this* may refer either to *pasta* or to *eating pasta.* In D, *which* is ambiguous, and *for competition* would be more idiomatic. Choice E says that those who eat pasta are competing not as athletes but as *part of a "carbohydrate-loading" regimen.* This question is of middle difficulty.

6. In August 1883, Krakatoa erupted and sent clouds of dust, ash, and sulphate to a height of 50 miles, <u>blotted out the sun for more than two days within</u> a 50-mile radius and for nearly a day at an observation post 130 miles away.

(A) blotted out the sun for more than two days within

(B) blotting out the sun for more than two days within

(C) the sun being blotted out for more than two days in

(D) having blotted out the sun for more than two days in

(E) for more than two days blotting out the sun within

In choice A, *blotted* is incorrect; the present participial *blotting . . .* is needed to described an event that is simultaneous with the action of the main clause. Choice B presents the correctly formed modifier. The passive construction of choice C does not indicate that Krakatoa was responsible for blotting out the sun; also, *within* would be preferable to *in* here. The verb form as well as the preposition can be faulted in D; *having blotted* states that Krakatoa had blotted out the sun before it erupted. Choice E produces a sentence that is ungrammatical and lacks parallelism: *blotting out the sun* must precede *for more . . .* and *for nearly . . .* if it is to be modified by both phrases. This is an easy question.

7. <u>Added to the increase in hourly wages requested last July, the railroad employees are now seeking an expanded program of retirement benefits.</u>

(A) Added to the increase in hourly wages requested last July, the railroad employees are now seeking an expanded program of retirement benefits.

(B) Added to the increase in hourly wages which had been requested last July, the employees of the railroad are now seeking an expanded program of retirement benefits.

(C) The railroad employees are now seeking an expanded program of retirement benefits added to the increase in hourly wages that were requested last July.

(D) In addition to the increase in hourly wages that were requested last July, the railroad employees are now seeking an expanded program of retirement benefits.

(E) In addition to the increase in hourly wages requested last July, the employees of the railroad are now seeking an expanded program of retirement benefits.

Choice A presents a dangling modifier. The phrase beginning the sentence can fit nowhere in the sentence and make logical sense. Coming first, it modifies *employees,* the nearest free noun in the main clause; i.e., choice A says that the employees were added to the increase in hourly wages. Choice B also begins with a dangling modifier; moreover, the simple past tense *requested* is needed to place an action before the present action *are . . . seeking.* In choice C, *were* does not agree in number with the subject of the clause, *increase,* and it is not clear whether *added to the increase* is supposed to modify *program* or *benefits.* Choice D also lacks agreement (*increase . . . were*). Choice E is best for this question of medium difficulty.

8. Child prodigies are marked not so much by their skills <u>but instead</u> by the fact that these skills are fully developed at a very early age.

   (A) but instead
   (B) rather than
   (C) than
   (D) as
   (E) so much as

The idiomatic form for this kind of statement is *not so much by X as by Y.* Hence, D is correct. Each of the other options produces an unidiomatic statement. This question is of middle difficulty.

9. The department defines a private passenger vehicle <u>as one registered to an individual with a gross weight of less than 8,000 pounds.</u>

   (A) as one registered to an individual with a gross weight of less than 8,000 pounds
   (B) to be one that is registered to an individual with a gross weight of less than 8,000 pounds
   (C) as one that is registered to an individual and that has a gross weight of less than 8,000 pounds
   (D) to have a gross weight less than 8,000 pounds and being registered to an individual
   (E) as having a gross weight of less than 8,000 pounds and registered to an individual

Choices A and B say that the *individual,* not the *vehicle,* has a gross weight of less than 8,000 pounds, and *defines . . . to be* in B is incorrect. Choice C, the best answer, produces the correct phrase (*defines . . . as*) and clarifies the statement with a parallel construction (*one that is . . . and that has . . .*). In choice D, *defines . . . to have* is faulty, *of* is missing between *weight* and *less,* and *being* is not parallel with *to have.* In choice E, the verb forms *having* and *registered* are not parallel. The question is a little more difficult than the average.

10. Urban officials want the census to be as accurate and complete as possible <u>for the reason that the amount of low-income people in a given area affect</u> the distribution of about fifty billion dollars a year in federal funds.

    (A) for the reason that the amount of low-income people in a given area affect
    (B) for the reason because the amount of low-income people in a given area effects
    (C) in that the amount of low-income people in given areas effect
    (D) because the number of low-income people in a given area affects
    (E) because the numbers of low-income people in given areas effects

The best answer will start with *because.* The initial phrase of A is wordy, that of B is unidiomatic, and that of C does not precisely establish causal relationship. Also, *amount* is incorrect; *number* refers to a group of countable members, whereas *amount* is for undifferentiated masses such as *sand* or *water.* There is no subject-verb agreement in A (*amount . . . affect*), C (*amount . . . effect*), or E (*numbers . . . effects*); moreover, the proper verb here is *affects,* not *effects.* In E, *numbers* and *areas* should be singular, not only to agree with the verb but also to refer precisely to the sum total of low-income people in each region where the census is conducted. Choice D is correct for this moderately easy question.

11. After the Arab conquest of Egypt in A.D. 640, Arabic <u>became the dominant language of the Egyptians, replacing older languages</u> and writing systems.

    (A) became the dominant language of the Egyptians, replacing older languages
    (B) became the dominant language of the Egyptians, replacing languages that were older
    (C) becomes the dominant language of the Egyptians and it replaced older languages
    (D) becomes the dominant language of the Egyptians and it replaced languages that were older
    (E) becomes the dominant language of the Egyptians, having replaced languages that were older

In choice A, the best answer, *older* is placed so that it modifies both *languages* and *writing systems.* Choice B is incorrect because the wording suggests that Arabic replaced all writing systems, not just older ones. The present tense *becomes* in choice C is inconsistent with *replaced.* Also, *and* implies that two separate events are being discussed: that Arabic became the dominant language and then that it replaced older languages. Choice D combines the erroneous wording of choice B, the tense problem of choice C, and the imprecise use of *and.* Choice E includes wording and tense mistakes, and, contrary to the sense of the sentence, *having replaced* states that Arabic replaced older languages before the Arab conquest of Egypt. This is an easy question.

12. The use of gravity waves, which do not interact with matter in the way electromagnetic waves do, hopefully will enable astronomers to study the actual formation of black holes and neutron stars.

   (A) in the way electromagnetic waves do, hopefully will enable
   (B) in the way electromagnetic waves do, will, it is hoped, enable
   (C) like electromagnetic waves, hopefully will enable
   (D) like electromagnetic waves, would enable, hopefully
   (E) such as electromagnetic waves do, will, it is hoped, enable

Choices A, C, and D use *hopefully* to mean "it is hoped" rather than "in a hopeful manner"; such usage still meets with strong and widespread opposition from editors, lexicographers, and authors of usage handbooks. In addition, because they misuse *like*, choices C and D are potentially ambiguous. As a comparative preposition, "like" relates noun to noun, not verb to verb; i.e., C and D seem to say that gravity waves do not interact with matter that is like electromagnetic waves. Choice E is incorrect because *such as*, like *like*, connects *matter* and *waves*, not *interact* and *do*. Choice B is the best answer for this difficult question.

13. If a single strain of plant is used for a given crop over a wide area, a practice fostered by modern seed-marketing methods, it increases the likelihood that the impact of a single crop disease or pest will be disastrous.

   (A) If a single strain of plant is used for a given crop over a wide area, a practice fostered by modern seed-marketing methods, it
   (B) If a single strain of plant is used for a given crop over a wide area, as is fostered by modern seed-marketing methods, it
   (C) A practice fostered by modern seed-marketing methods, a single strain of plant used for a given crop over a wide area
   (D) A single strain of plant used for a given crop over a wide area, a practice fostered by modern seed-marketing methods,
   (E) The use of a single strain of plant for a given crop over a wide area, a practice fostered by modern seed-marketing methods,

Choice A is faulty because the pronoun *it* and the appositive *a practice* each lack a noun referent. Nor are there logical referents in choice B for *as is* and *it*. Choice C entails a false appositive: the sentence now says that the *single strain of plant* is itself a practice fostered by modern seed-marketing methods, not that the *use* of a single strain is such a practice. Choice D reverses the order of the constructions, but the appositive remains illogical. Choice E is correct: *use* is the proper subject for the verb *increases* and a logical governing noun for the appositive *practice*. This question is of middle difficulty.

14. A majority of the international journalists surveyed view nuclear power stations as unsafe at present but that they will, or could, be made sufficiently safe in the future.

   (A) that they will, or could,
   (B) that they would, or could,
   (C) they will be or could
   (D) think that they will be or could
   (E) think the power stations would or could

The corrected sentence must have a compound main verb *view . . . but (verb)*; that is, the best answer above must begin with a verb that can be linked with *view* to complete the construction. Consequently, choices A, B, and C are incorrect. In choice E, *would* is faulty because it suggests without warrant that the stations would be made safe if some unnamed conditions were met. Choice D is best: *that*, although not essential, is preferable here; *they* is better than the needless repetition of *power stations* in choice E; and the verb tenses are correct. The question is more difficult than the average.

15. A controversial figure throughout most of his public life, the Black leader Marcus Garvey advocated that some Blacks return to Africa, the land that, to him, symbolized the possibility of freedom.

   (A) that some Blacks return to Africa, the land that, to him, symbolized the possibility of freedom
   (B) that some Blacks return to the African land symbolizing the possibility of freedom to him
   (C) that some Blacks return to Africa which was the land which symbolized the possibility of freedom to him
   (D) some Black's returning to Africa which was the land that to him symbolized the possibility of freedom
   (E) some Black's return to the land symbolizing the possibility of freedom to him, Africa

Choice A is correct. In choice B, the phrase *the African land symbolizing the possibility of freedom to him* suggests without reason that only one of the various African lands symbolized the possibility of freedom to Garvey. The double use of *which* to create needless clauses within clauses makes C very wordy and awkward. The *which* clause is awkward in D also, and the singular possessive *Black's* is erroneous. *Black's* is again wrong in E, and the noun *Africa* is clumsily placed as an appositive coming after the lengthy phrase that describes it. This question is of middle difficulty.

16. The fear of rabies is well founded; <u>few people are known to recover from the disease after the appearance of the clinical symptoms.</u>

   (A) few people are known to recover from the disease after the appearance of the clinical symptoms
   (B) few people are known to have recovered from the disease once the clinical symptoms have appeared
   (C) there are few known people who have recovered from the disease once the clinical symptoms have appeared
   (D) after the clinical symptoms appear, there are few known people who have recovered from the disease
   (E) recovery from the disease is known for only a few people after the clinical symptoms appear

Choice A does not clarify the timing of events but rather suggests that a few people continue to recover indefinitely. In B, the best choice, *have recovered* and *have appeared* indicate that the action of recovery is completed rather than ongoing. In choice C, the impersonal construction (*there are*) is needlessly wordy; moreover, the placement of *known* wrongly implies that the issue is whether the people rather than the instances of recovery are known. Choice D further confuses matters by placing the *after* phrase well before *recovered,* the verb it modifies. Choice E is indirect and unidiomatic. The question is of average difficulty.

17. The growth of the railroads led to the abolition of local times, <u>which was determined by when the sun reached the observer's meridian and differing</u> from city to city, and to the establishment of regional times.

   (A) which was determined by when the sun reached the observer's meridian and differing
   (B) which was determined by when the sun reached the observer's meridian and which differed
   (C) which were determined by when the sun reached the observer's meridian and differing
   (D) determined by when the sun reached the observer's meridian and differed
   (E) determined by when the sun reached the observer's meridian and differing

In choice A, *was* is incorrect; the verb must be *were* to agree with *times.* Also, *which* becomes the subject of a compound verb that lacks parallelism: *was determined . . . and differing.* In choice B, *was* is again incorrect, and the use of two *which* clauses is awkward. In choice C, *which were determined . . . and differing* is another faulty compound verb. Choice D presents a false compound: *determined* is an adjective modifying *local times* and *differed* is the simple past tense of *to differ.* Because they serve different grammatical functions, these words cannot be treated as parallel elements joined by *and.* Choice E is best: without *which, determined* and *differing* function not as verb elements but as parallel modifiers of *local times.* This question is very difficult.

18. <u>Although partially destroyed, the archaeologists were able to infer</u> from what remained of the inscription that the priest Zonainos was buried in the crypt.

   (A) Although partially destroyed, the archaeologists were able to infer
   (B) Although partially destroyed, the archaeologists had inferred
   (C) Although it had been partially destroyed, the archaeologists were able to infer
   (D) Partially destroyed though it had been, the archaeologists had been able to infer
   (E) Destroyed partially, the archaeologists were able to infer

In choice A, the phrase *Although partially destroyed* modifies *archaeologists,* the nearest noun and the subject of the sentence; in other words, choice A says that the archaeologists were partially destroyed. They fare no better in choice B, where the change in verb form alone cannot save them. Choice C is correct: *partially destroyed* describes *it,* which refers to *the inscription.* The opening phrase of choice D is needlessly wordy and awkward, and *had been able to infer* fails to indicate that the archaeologists made their inference after the inscription had been partially destroyed. In choice E, *were able to infer* establishes the sequence of events, but the archaeologists are now *destroyed partially.* This is a question of middle difficulty.

19. <u>For all his professed disdain of such activities,</u> Auden was an inveterate literary gossip.

   (A) For all his professed disdain of such activities,
   (B) Having always professed disdain for such activities,
   (C) All such activities were, he professed, disdained, and
   (D) Professing that all such activities were disdained,
   (E) In spite of professions of disdaining all such activities,

Choice A is correct and idiomatically phrased. Choice B fails to express the sense that Auden indulged in literary gossip despite professing disdain for it. Choices C, D, and E do not establish precisely that Auden was the one professing disdain for literary gossip. The *and* in C makes the disembodied professions of disdain and the indulgence in gossip seem like wholly separate matters, and E is especially awkward. The question is of middle difficulty.

20. In many job areas, the earnings of women are <u>well below that of men in spite of educational differences that are diminishing</u> between the sexes.

   (A) well below that of men in spite of educational differences that are diminishing
   (B) much below that of men's despite educational differences diminishing
   (C) much below men in spite of diminishing educational differences
   (D) well below those of men in spite of diminishing educational differences
   (E) below men's despite their educational differences that are diminishing

In choice A, the pronoun *that* does not agree in number with its noun, *earnings*; the phrasing is wordy and does not convey the sense that diminishing the educational differences between the sexes would be expected to narrow the gap in earnings. In choice B, *that* and the possessive *men's* are faulty, and *much below* is less idiomatic than *well below*; furthermore, the sentence with B is awkward. Choice C illogically compares *the earnings of women* to *men* rather than to *the earnings of men*. In choice E, *their* seems to refer to *earnings, men's* is not parallel with *of women,* and the phrasing is unclear. Choice D is best for this fairly easy question.

21. Acid rain and snow result from the chemical reactions between industrial emissions of sulfur dioxide and nitrogen oxides <u>with atmospheric water vapor to produce highly corrosive sulfuric and nitric acids.</u>

   (A) with atmospheric water vapor to produce highly corrosive sulfuric and nitric acids
   (B) with atmospheric water vapor producing highly corrosive sulfuric and nitric acids
   (C) and atmospheric water vapor which has produced highly corrosive sulfuric and nitric acids
   (D) and atmospheric water vapor which have produced sulfuric and nitric acids which are highly corrosive
   (E) and atmospheric water vapor to produce highly corrosive sulfuric and nitric acids

Choices A and B are faulty because the idiomatic form of expression is *between X and Y,* not *between X with Y.* Also, in choice B *producing . . .* modifies the nearest noun, *water vapor,* rather than *chemical reactions* and thereby seems to say that the water vapor alone produced the corrosive acids. Choices C and D are clumsy, and both misuse *which*: in C *which has . . .* illogically modifies *water vapor,* and in D it is unclear whether *which have* modifies *reactions* or *sulfur dioxide, nitrogen oxides,* and *water vapor* taken together. E is the best choice for this very difficult question.

22. It is characteristic of the Metropolitan Museum of Art, as <u>of virtually every great American museum, the taste of local collectors has played at least as large a part in the formation of their collections as has</u> the judgments of the art historian.

   (A) of virtually every great American museum, the taste of local collectors has played at least as large a part in the formation of their collections as has
   (B) of virtually every great American museum, that the taste of local collectors has played at least as large a part in the formation of their collections as has
   (C) it is of virtually every great American museum, that the taste of local collectors has played at least as large a part in the formation of its collections as have
   (D) it is of virtually every great American museum, that the taste of local collectors have played at least as large a part in the formation of its collections as have
   (E) it is of virtually every great American museum, the taste of local collectors has played at least as large a part in the formation of its collections as has

In the corrected sentence, *It is characteristic of* should be paralleled by *as it is of,* and this parallel construction should be completed by *that* before *the taste. . . .* Choice A lacks these elements as well as noun-pronoun agreement (*Museum . . . their*) and noun-verb agreement (*judgments . . . has*). Choice B rectifies only the missing *that.* Lack of agreement (*taste . . . have*) makes choice D wrong. Choice E needs *that* before *the taste* and *as have* in place of *as has.* C is the best answer. The question is a little more difficult than the average.

23. There has been a 30- to 40-fold increase in the incidence of malaria caused by increasing mosquito resistance against pesticides.

(A) increase in the incidence of malaria caused by increasing mosquito resistance against
(B) increase in the incidence of malaria because of increasing resistance of mosquitoes to
(C) increasing malaria incidence because of increasing resistance of mosquitoes to
(D) incidence of malaria increase caused by increasing mosquito resistance against
(E) incidence of malaria increase because of increased mosquito resistance to

Choice A can be faulted because it is not at first clear whether *caused by* modifies *increase* or *malaria*. Also, the proper expression here and in choice D is not *resistance against* but *resistance to*. Choices C, D, and E are wrong because the completed sentence must read *30- to 40-fold increase*. In these choices, *30- to 40-fold* illogically modifies *incidence*; furthermore, *incidence of . . . increase* in D and E is illogical. Choice B is best. The question is a little easier than the average.

24. Aging is a property of all animals that reach a fixed size at maturity, and the variations in life spans among different species are far greater as that among individuals from the same species: a fruit fly is ancient at 40 days, a mouse at 3 years, a horse at 30, a man at 100, and some tortoises at 150.

(A) among different species are far greater as that among individuals from
(B) among different species are far greater than that among individuals from
(C) among different species are far greater than those among individuals of
(D) between different species are far more than that between individuals of
(E) between different species are greater by far than is that between individuals from

Choice A is incorrect on several grounds: *greater as* should be *greater than*, *that* should be *those* to agree in number with its referent, *variations*, and *from* should be *of*. Choice B amends only the first error. Choice C is the best answer. In D, *between* is faulty because many more than two species are being considered, *more* illogically refers to the quantity rather than the size of variations in life span, and *that* does not agree with *variations*. Besides including *between, that,* and *from,* choice E is needlessly wordy and lacks agreement in verb number. This question is moderately easy.

25. The herbicide Oryzalin was still being produced in 1979, three years after the wives of workers producing the chemical in Rensselaer, New York, were found to have borne children with heart defects or miscarriages, and none of their pregnancies was normal.

(A) to have borne children with heart defects or miscarriages, and none of their pregnancies was
(B) to have had children born with heart defects or miscarriages, and none of the pregnancies was
(C) either to have had children with heart defects or miscarriages, without any of their pregnancies being
(D) either to have had miscarriages or to have borne children with heart defects; none of the pregnancies was
(E) either to have had miscarriages or children born with heart defects, without any of their pregnancies being

Choices A and B are incorrect because *with* governs both *heart defects* and *miscarriages*; in other words, choice A says that the children and not the women suffered the miscarriages. For the sentence to make sense, *miscarriages* must be the object of a verb that has *wives* as its subject. Also, *their* in choices A, C, and E is ambiguous because it is far from its referent, *wives*. Choices C and E lack parallel construction: a verb form like the one after *either* should appear after *or*. Choice D is the best answer for this difficult question.

8 Three Authentic Graduate Management Admission Tests

The tests that follow are Graduate Management Admission Tests that have been slightly modified. An actual test book contains eight sections, two of which consist of trial questions that are not counted in the scoring. Those trial questions have been omitted from these tests. Also, the total testing time for any one of these tests is three hours; the actual test takes four hours.

Taking these tests will help you become acquainted with testing procedures and requirements and thereby approach the real test with more assurance. Therefore, you should try to take these tests under conditions similiar to those in an actual test administration, observing the time limitations, and thinking about each question seriously.

The facsimiles of the response portion of a GMAT answer sheet on pages 149, 221, and 289 may be used to mark your answers to the tests. After you have taken the tests, compare your answers with the correct ones on pages 191, 261, and 329 and determine your scores using the information that follows the answer keys.

Answer Sheet: Form A

SECTION 1	SECTION 2	SECTION 3	SECTION 4	SECTION 5	SECTION 6
1 Ⓐ Ⓑ Ⓒ Ⓓ Ⓔ	1 Ⓐ Ⓑ Ⓒ Ⓓ Ⓔ	1 Ⓐ Ⓑ Ⓒ Ⓓ Ⓔ	1 Ⓐ Ⓑ Ⓒ Ⓓ Ⓔ	1 Ⓐ Ⓑ Ⓒ Ⓓ Ⓔ	1 Ⓐ Ⓑ Ⓒ Ⓓ Ⓔ
2 Ⓐ Ⓑ Ⓒ Ⓓ Ⓔ	2 Ⓐ Ⓑ Ⓒ Ⓓ Ⓔ	2 Ⓐ Ⓑ Ⓒ Ⓓ Ⓔ	2 Ⓐ Ⓑ Ⓒ Ⓓ Ⓔ	2 Ⓐ Ⓑ Ⓒ Ⓓ Ⓔ	2 Ⓐ Ⓑ Ⓒ Ⓓ Ⓔ
3 Ⓐ Ⓑ Ⓒ Ⓓ Ⓔ	3 Ⓐ Ⓑ Ⓒ Ⓓ Ⓔ	3 Ⓐ Ⓑ Ⓒ Ⓓ Ⓔ	3 Ⓐ Ⓑ Ⓒ Ⓓ Ⓔ	3 Ⓐ Ⓑ Ⓒ Ⓓ Ⓔ	3 Ⓐ Ⓑ Ⓒ Ⓓ Ⓔ
4 Ⓐ Ⓑ Ⓒ Ⓓ Ⓔ	4 Ⓐ Ⓑ Ⓒ Ⓓ Ⓔ	4 Ⓐ Ⓑ Ⓒ Ⓓ Ⓔ	4 Ⓐ Ⓑ Ⓒ Ⓓ Ⓔ	4 Ⓐ Ⓑ Ⓒ Ⓓ Ⓔ	4 Ⓐ Ⓑ Ⓒ Ⓓ Ⓔ
5 Ⓐ Ⓑ Ⓒ Ⓓ Ⓔ	5 Ⓐ Ⓑ Ⓒ Ⓓ Ⓔ	5 Ⓐ Ⓑ Ⓒ Ⓓ Ⓔ	5 Ⓐ Ⓑ Ⓒ Ⓓ Ⓔ	5 Ⓐ Ⓑ Ⓒ Ⓓ Ⓔ	5 Ⓐ Ⓑ Ⓒ Ⓓ Ⓔ
6 Ⓐ Ⓑ Ⓒ Ⓓ Ⓔ	6 Ⓐ Ⓑ Ⓒ Ⓓ Ⓔ	6 Ⓐ Ⓑ Ⓒ Ⓓ Ⓔ	6 Ⓐ Ⓑ Ⓒ Ⓓ Ⓔ	6 Ⓐ Ⓑ Ⓒ Ⓓ Ⓔ	6 Ⓐ Ⓑ Ⓒ Ⓓ Ⓔ
7 Ⓐ Ⓑ Ⓒ Ⓓ Ⓔ	7 Ⓐ Ⓑ Ⓒ Ⓓ Ⓔ	7 Ⓐ Ⓑ Ⓒ Ⓓ Ⓔ	7 Ⓐ Ⓑ Ⓒ Ⓓ Ⓔ	7 Ⓐ Ⓑ Ⓒ Ⓓ Ⓔ	7 Ⓐ Ⓑ Ⓒ Ⓓ Ⓔ
8 Ⓐ Ⓑ Ⓒ Ⓓ Ⓔ	8 Ⓐ Ⓑ Ⓒ Ⓓ Ⓔ	8 Ⓐ Ⓑ Ⓒ Ⓓ Ⓔ	8 Ⓐ Ⓑ Ⓒ Ⓓ Ⓔ	8 Ⓐ Ⓑ Ⓒ Ⓓ Ⓔ	8 Ⓐ Ⓑ Ⓒ Ⓓ Ⓔ
9 Ⓐ Ⓑ Ⓒ Ⓓ Ⓔ	9 Ⓐ Ⓑ Ⓒ Ⓓ Ⓔ	9 Ⓐ Ⓑ Ⓒ Ⓓ Ⓔ	9 Ⓐ Ⓑ Ⓒ Ⓓ Ⓔ	9 Ⓐ Ⓑ Ⓒ Ⓓ Ⓔ	9 Ⓐ Ⓑ Ⓒ Ⓓ Ⓔ
10 Ⓐ Ⓑ Ⓒ Ⓓ Ⓔ	10 Ⓐ Ⓑ Ⓒ Ⓓ Ⓔ	10 Ⓐ Ⓑ Ⓒ Ⓓ Ⓔ	10 Ⓐ Ⓑ Ⓒ Ⓓ Ⓔ	10 Ⓐ Ⓑ Ⓒ Ⓓ Ⓔ	10 Ⓐ Ⓑ Ⓒ Ⓓ Ⓔ
11 Ⓐ Ⓑ Ⓒ Ⓓ Ⓔ	11 Ⓐ Ⓑ Ⓒ Ⓓ Ⓔ	11 Ⓐ Ⓑ Ⓒ Ⓓ Ⓔ	11 Ⓐ Ⓑ Ⓒ Ⓓ Ⓔ	11 Ⓐ Ⓑ Ⓒ Ⓓ Ⓔ	11 Ⓐ Ⓑ Ⓒ Ⓓ Ⓔ
12 Ⓐ Ⓑ Ⓒ Ⓓ Ⓔ	12 Ⓐ Ⓑ Ⓒ Ⓓ Ⓔ	12 Ⓐ Ⓑ Ⓒ Ⓓ Ⓔ	12 Ⓐ Ⓑ Ⓒ Ⓓ Ⓔ	12 Ⓐ Ⓑ Ⓒ Ⓓ Ⓔ	12 Ⓐ Ⓑ Ⓒ Ⓓ Ⓔ
13 Ⓐ Ⓑ Ⓒ Ⓓ Ⓔ	13 Ⓐ Ⓑ Ⓒ Ⓓ Ⓔ	13 Ⓐ Ⓑ Ⓒ Ⓓ Ⓔ	13 Ⓐ Ⓑ Ⓒ Ⓓ Ⓔ	13 Ⓐ Ⓑ Ⓒ Ⓓ Ⓔ	13 Ⓐ Ⓑ Ⓒ Ⓓ Ⓔ
14 Ⓐ Ⓑ Ⓒ Ⓓ Ⓔ	14 Ⓐ Ⓑ Ⓒ Ⓓ Ⓔ	14 Ⓐ Ⓑ Ⓒ Ⓓ Ⓔ	14 Ⓐ Ⓑ Ⓒ Ⓓ Ⓔ	14 Ⓐ Ⓑ Ⓒ Ⓓ Ⓔ	14 Ⓐ Ⓑ Ⓒ Ⓓ Ⓔ
15 Ⓐ Ⓑ Ⓒ Ⓓ Ⓔ	15 Ⓐ Ⓑ Ⓒ Ⓓ Ⓔ	15 Ⓐ Ⓑ Ⓒ Ⓓ Ⓔ	15 Ⓐ Ⓑ Ⓒ Ⓓ Ⓔ	15 Ⓐ Ⓑ Ⓒ Ⓓ Ⓔ	15 Ⓐ Ⓑ Ⓒ Ⓓ Ⓔ
16 Ⓐ Ⓑ Ⓒ Ⓓ Ⓔ	16 Ⓐ Ⓑ Ⓒ Ⓓ Ⓔ	16 Ⓐ Ⓑ Ⓒ Ⓓ Ⓔ	16 Ⓐ Ⓑ Ⓒ Ⓓ Ⓔ	16 Ⓐ Ⓑ Ⓒ Ⓓ Ⓔ	16 Ⓐ Ⓑ Ⓒ Ⓓ Ⓔ
17 Ⓐ Ⓑ Ⓒ Ⓓ Ⓔ	17 Ⓐ Ⓑ Ⓒ Ⓓ Ⓔ	17 Ⓐ Ⓑ Ⓒ Ⓓ Ⓔ	17 Ⓐ Ⓑ Ⓒ Ⓓ Ⓔ	17 Ⓐ Ⓑ Ⓒ Ⓓ Ⓔ	17 Ⓐ Ⓑ Ⓒ Ⓓ Ⓔ
18 Ⓐ Ⓑ Ⓒ Ⓓ Ⓔ	18 Ⓐ Ⓑ Ⓒ Ⓓ Ⓔ	18 Ⓐ Ⓑ Ⓒ Ⓓ Ⓔ	18 Ⓐ Ⓑ Ⓒ Ⓓ Ⓔ	18 Ⓐ Ⓑ Ⓒ Ⓓ Ⓔ	18 Ⓐ Ⓑ Ⓒ Ⓓ Ⓔ
19 Ⓐ Ⓑ Ⓒ Ⓓ Ⓔ	19 Ⓐ Ⓑ Ⓒ Ⓓ Ⓔ	19 Ⓐ Ⓑ Ⓒ Ⓓ Ⓔ	19 Ⓐ Ⓑ Ⓒ Ⓓ Ⓔ	19 Ⓐ Ⓑ Ⓒ Ⓓ Ⓔ	19 Ⓐ Ⓑ Ⓒ Ⓓ Ⓔ
20 Ⓐ Ⓑ Ⓒ Ⓓ Ⓔ	20 Ⓐ Ⓑ Ⓒ Ⓓ Ⓔ	20 Ⓐ Ⓑ Ⓒ Ⓓ Ⓔ	20 Ⓐ Ⓑ Ⓒ Ⓓ Ⓔ	20 Ⓐ Ⓑ Ⓒ Ⓓ Ⓔ	20 Ⓐ Ⓑ Ⓒ Ⓓ Ⓔ
21 Ⓐ Ⓑ Ⓒ Ⓓ Ⓔ	21 Ⓐ Ⓑ Ⓒ Ⓓ Ⓔ	21 Ⓐ Ⓑ Ⓒ Ⓓ Ⓔ	21 Ⓐ Ⓑ Ⓒ Ⓓ Ⓔ	21 Ⓐ Ⓑ Ⓒ Ⓓ Ⓔ	21 Ⓐ Ⓑ Ⓒ Ⓓ Ⓔ
22 Ⓐ Ⓑ Ⓒ Ⓓ Ⓔ	22 Ⓐ Ⓑ Ⓒ Ⓓ Ⓔ	22 Ⓐ Ⓑ Ⓒ Ⓓ Ⓔ	22 Ⓐ Ⓑ Ⓒ Ⓓ Ⓔ	22 Ⓐ Ⓑ Ⓒ Ⓓ Ⓔ	22 Ⓐ Ⓑ Ⓒ Ⓓ Ⓔ
23 Ⓐ Ⓑ Ⓒ Ⓓ Ⓔ	23 Ⓐ Ⓑ Ⓒ Ⓓ Ⓔ	23 Ⓐ Ⓑ Ⓒ Ⓓ Ⓔ	23 Ⓐ Ⓑ Ⓒ Ⓓ Ⓔ	23 Ⓐ Ⓑ Ⓒ Ⓓ Ⓔ	23 Ⓐ Ⓑ Ⓒ Ⓓ Ⓔ
24 Ⓐ Ⓑ Ⓒ Ⓓ Ⓔ	24 Ⓐ Ⓑ Ⓒ Ⓓ Ⓔ	24 Ⓐ Ⓑ Ⓒ Ⓓ Ⓔ	24 Ⓐ Ⓑ Ⓒ Ⓓ Ⓔ	24 Ⓐ Ⓑ Ⓒ Ⓓ Ⓔ	24 Ⓐ Ⓑ Ⓒ Ⓓ Ⓔ
25 Ⓐ Ⓑ Ⓒ Ⓓ Ⓔ	25 Ⓐ Ⓑ Ⓒ Ⓓ Ⓔ	25 Ⓐ Ⓑ Ⓒ Ⓓ Ⓔ	25 Ⓐ Ⓑ Ⓒ Ⓓ Ⓔ	25 Ⓐ Ⓑ Ⓒ Ⓓ Ⓔ	25 Ⓐ Ⓑ Ⓒ Ⓓ Ⓔ
26 Ⓐ Ⓑ Ⓒ Ⓓ Ⓔ	26 Ⓐ Ⓑ Ⓒ Ⓓ Ⓔ	26 Ⓐ Ⓑ Ⓒ Ⓓ Ⓔ	26 Ⓐ Ⓑ Ⓒ Ⓓ Ⓔ	26 Ⓐ Ⓑ Ⓒ Ⓓ Ⓔ	26 Ⓐ Ⓑ Ⓒ Ⓓ Ⓔ
27 Ⓐ Ⓑ Ⓒ Ⓓ Ⓔ	27 Ⓐ Ⓑ Ⓒ Ⓓ Ⓔ	27 Ⓐ Ⓑ Ⓒ Ⓓ Ⓔ	27 Ⓐ Ⓑ Ⓒ Ⓓ Ⓔ	27 Ⓐ Ⓑ Ⓒ Ⓓ Ⓔ	27 Ⓐ Ⓑ Ⓒ Ⓓ Ⓔ
28 Ⓐ Ⓑ Ⓒ Ⓓ Ⓔ	28 Ⓐ Ⓑ Ⓒ Ⓓ Ⓔ	28 Ⓐ Ⓑ Ⓒ Ⓓ Ⓔ	28 Ⓐ Ⓑ Ⓒ Ⓓ Ⓔ	28 Ⓐ Ⓑ Ⓒ Ⓓ Ⓔ	28 Ⓐ Ⓑ Ⓒ Ⓓ Ⓔ
29 Ⓐ Ⓑ Ⓒ Ⓓ Ⓔ	29 Ⓐ Ⓑ Ⓒ Ⓓ Ⓔ	29 Ⓐ Ⓑ Ⓒ Ⓓ Ⓔ	29 Ⓐ Ⓑ Ⓒ Ⓓ Ⓔ	29 Ⓐ Ⓑ Ⓒ Ⓓ Ⓔ	29 Ⓐ Ⓑ Ⓒ Ⓓ Ⓔ
30 Ⓐ Ⓑ Ⓒ Ⓓ Ⓔ	30 Ⓐ Ⓑ Ⓒ Ⓓ Ⓔ	30 Ⓐ Ⓑ Ⓒ Ⓓ Ⓔ	30 Ⓐ Ⓑ Ⓒ Ⓓ Ⓔ	30 Ⓐ Ⓑ Ⓒ Ⓓ Ⓔ	30 Ⓐ Ⓑ Ⓒ Ⓓ Ⓔ
31 Ⓐ Ⓑ Ⓒ Ⓓ Ⓔ	31 Ⓐ Ⓑ Ⓒ Ⓓ Ⓔ	31 Ⓐ Ⓑ Ⓒ Ⓓ Ⓔ	31 Ⓐ Ⓑ Ⓒ Ⓓ Ⓔ	31 Ⓐ Ⓑ Ⓒ Ⓓ Ⓔ	31 Ⓐ Ⓑ Ⓒ Ⓓ Ⓔ
32 Ⓐ Ⓑ Ⓒ Ⓓ Ⓔ	32 Ⓐ Ⓑ Ⓒ Ⓓ Ⓔ	32 Ⓐ Ⓑ Ⓒ Ⓓ Ⓔ	32 Ⓐ Ⓑ Ⓒ Ⓓ Ⓔ	32 Ⓐ Ⓑ Ⓒ Ⓓ Ⓔ	32 Ⓐ Ⓑ Ⓒ Ⓓ Ⓔ
33 Ⓐ Ⓑ Ⓒ Ⓓ Ⓔ	33 Ⓐ Ⓑ Ⓒ Ⓓ Ⓔ	33 Ⓐ Ⓑ Ⓒ Ⓓ Ⓔ	33 Ⓐ Ⓑ Ⓒ Ⓓ Ⓔ	33 Ⓐ Ⓑ Ⓒ Ⓓ Ⓔ	33 Ⓐ Ⓑ Ⓒ Ⓓ Ⓔ
34 Ⓐ Ⓑ Ⓒ Ⓓ Ⓔ	34 Ⓐ Ⓑ Ⓒ Ⓓ Ⓔ	34 Ⓐ Ⓑ Ⓒ Ⓓ Ⓔ	34 Ⓐ Ⓑ Ⓒ Ⓓ Ⓔ	34 Ⓐ Ⓑ Ⓒ Ⓓ Ⓔ	34 Ⓐ Ⓑ Ⓒ Ⓓ Ⓔ
35 Ⓐ Ⓑ Ⓒ Ⓓ Ⓔ	35 Ⓐ Ⓑ Ⓒ Ⓓ Ⓔ	35 Ⓐ Ⓑ Ⓒ Ⓓ Ⓔ	35 Ⓐ Ⓑ Ⓒ Ⓓ Ⓔ	35 Ⓐ Ⓑ Ⓒ Ⓓ Ⓔ	35 Ⓐ Ⓑ Ⓒ Ⓓ Ⓔ

Print your full name here:_____
(last)   (first)   (middle)

Graduate Management
Admission Test

SECTION I

Time—30 minutes

25 Questions

Directions: Each of the data sufficiency problems below consists of a question and two statements, labeled (1) and (2), in which certain data are given. You have to decide whether the data given in the statements are sufficient for answering the question. Using the data given in the statements plus your knowledge of mathematics and everyday facts (such as the number of days in July or the meaning of counterclockwise), you are to blacken space

A   if statement (1) ALONE is sufficient, but statement (2) alone is not sufficient to answer the question asked;

B   if statement (2) ALONE is sufficient, but statement (1) alone is not sufficient to answer the question asked;

C   if BOTH statements (1) and (2) TOGETHER are sufficient to answer the question asked, but NEITHER statement ALONE is sufficient;

D   if EACH statement ALONE is sufficient to answer the question asked;

E   if statements (1) and (2) TOGETHER are NOT sufficient to answer the question asked, and additional data specific to the problem are needed.

Numbers: All numbers used are real numbers.

Figures: A figure in a data sufficiency problem will conform to the information given in the question, but will not necessarily conform to the additional information given in statements (1) and (2).

You may assume that lines shown as straight are straight and that angle measures are greater than zero.

You may assume that the position of points, angles, regions, etc., exist in the order shown.

All figures lie in a plane unless otherwise indicated.

Example:

In $\triangle PQR$, what is the value of x?

(1) $PQ = PR$

(2) $y = 40$

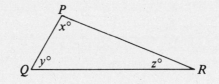

Explanation: According to statement (1), $PQ = PR$; therefore, $\triangle PQR$ is isosceles and $y = z$. Since $x + y + z = 180$, $x + 2y = 180$. Since statement (1) does not give a value for y, you cannot answer the question using statement (1) by itself. According to statement (2), $y = 40$; therefore, $x + z = 140$. Since statement (2) does not give a value for z, you cannot answer the question using statement (2) by itself. Using both statements together, you can find y and z; therefore, you can find x, and the answer to the problem is C.

1. What is the value of x?

(1) $5x - 3 = 7$

(2) $\frac{x}{10} = \frac{1}{5}$

2. How many students are enrolled in the Groveville Public Schools?

(1) There are 30 students per classroom in the Groveville Public Schools.

(2) The student-teacher ratio is 20 to 1 in the Groveville Public Schools.

GO ON TO THE NEXT PAGE.

A Statement (1) ALONE is sufficient, but statement (2) alone is not sufficient.
B Statement (2) ALONE is sufficient, but statement (1) alone is not sufficient.
C BOTH statements TOGETHER are sufficient, but NEITHER statement ALONE is sufficient.
D EACH statement ALONE is sufficient.
E Statements (1) and (2) TOGETHER are NOT sufficient.

3. P is a particle on the circle shown above. What is the length of the path traveled by P in one complete revolution around the circle?

(1) The diameter of the circle is 1.5 meters.

(2) The particle P moves in a clockwise direction at 0.5 meter per second.

4. If the price of potatoes is $0.20 per pound, what is the maximum number of potatoes that can be bought for $1.00 ?

(1) The price of a bag of potatoes is $2.80.

(2) There are 15 to 18 potatoes in every 5 pounds.

5. A sewing store buys fabric X by the bolt at the wholesale price. If each bolt contains 50 meters of fabric X, what is the wholesale price of a bolt of fabric X ?

(1) The store sells fabric X for $6.25 per meter.

(2) The store sells fabric X at 25 percent above the wholesale price.

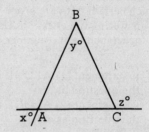

6. In $\triangle ABC$ above, if $AB = BC$, what is the value of y ?

(1) x = 50

(2) z = 130

7. In a sequence of numbers in which each term is 2 more than the preceding term, what is the fourth term?

(1) The last term is 90.

(2) The first term is 2.

GO ON TO THE NEXT PAGE.

A Statement (1) ALONE is sufficient, but statement (2) alone is not sufficient.
B Statement (2) ALONE is sufficient, but statement (1) alone is not sufficient.
C BOTH statements TOGETHER are sufficient, but NEITHER statement ALONE is sufficient.
D EACH statement ALONE is sufficient.
E Statements (1) and (2) TOGETHER are NOT sufficient.

8. How much nitrogen is needed in the mixture used by a lawn maintenance company to fertilize the grass on a certain portion of a golf course?

(1) The portion of the golf course to be fertilized is 30 meters by 50 meters.

(2) The amount of fertilizer needed is 40 kilograms, and the fertilizer must be composed of nitrogen, phosphorus, and potash in the proportions 5: 7: 4, respectively.

9. A certain alloy contains only lead, copper, and tin. How many pounds of tin are contained in 56 pounds of the alloy?

(1) By weight the alloy is $\frac{3}{7}$ lead and $\frac{5}{14}$ copper.

(2) By weight the alloy contains 6 parts lead and 5 parts copper.

10. If n is a positive integer, are n and 1 the only positive divisors of n ?

(1) n is less than 14.

(2) If n is doubled, the result is less than 27.

11. What is the perimeter of △PQR ?

(1) The measures of ∠PQR, ∠QRP, and ∠RPQ are x°, 2x°, and 3x°, respectively.

(2) The altitude of △PQR from Q to PR is 4.

12. Two accountants, Rhodes and Smith, went to a business meeting together. Rhodes drove to the meeting and Smith drove back from the meeting. If Rhodes and Smith each drove 140 kilometers, what was the average speed, in kilometers per hour, at which Rhodes drove?

(1) The average speed at which Smith drove was 70 kilometers per hour.

(2) Rhodes drove for exactly 2 hours.

13. If ϕ is an operation, is the value of b ϕ c greater than 10 ?

(1) $x \phi y = x^2 + y^2$ for all x and y.

(2) b = 3 and c = 2

14. What percent of the employees of Company X are technicians?

(1) Exactly 40 percent of the men and 55 percent of the women employed by Company X are technicians.

(2) At Company X, the ratio of the number of technicians to the number of nontechnicians is 9 to 11.

GO ON TO THE NEXT PAGE.

A Statement (1) ALONE is sufficient, but statement (2) alone is not sufficient.
B Statement (2) ALONE is sufficient, but statement (1) alone is not sufficient.
C BOTH statements TOGETHER are sufficient, but NEITHER statement ALONE is sufficient.
D EACH statement ALONE is sufficient.
E Statements (1) and (2) TOGETHER are NOT sufficient.

15. If tank X contains only gasoline, how many kiloliters of gasoline are in tank X ?

(1) If $\frac{1}{2}$ of the gasoline in tank X were pumped out, the tank would be filled to $\frac{1}{3}$ of its capacity.

(2) If 0.75 kiloliter of gasoline were pumped into tank X, it would be filled to capacity.

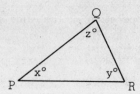

16. In $\triangle PQR$ above, is PQ > PR ?

(1) x = y

(2) y = z

17. Is the positive integer x an even number?

(1) If x is divided by 3, the remainder is 2.

(2) If x is divided by 5, the remainder is 2.

18. Land for a pasture is enclosed in the shape of a 6-sided figure; all sides are the same length and all angles have the same measure. What is the area of the enclosed land?

(1) Each side is 8 meters long.

(2) The distance from the center of the land to the midpoint of one of the sides is $4\sqrt{3}$ meters.

19. In a retail store, the average (arithmetic mean) sale for month M was d dollars. Was the average (arithmetic mean) sale for month J at least 20 percent higher than that for month M ?

(1) For month M, total revenue from sales was $3,500.

(2) For month J, total revenue from sales was $6,000.

20. In a certain store, item X sells for 10 percent less than item Y. What is the ratio of the store's revenue from the sales of item X to that from the sales of item Y ?

(1) The store sells 20 percent more units of item Y than of item X.

(2) The store's revenue from the sales of item X is $6,000 and from the sales of item Y is $8,000.

GO ON TO THE NEXT PAGE.

A Statement (1) ALONE is sufficient, but statement (2) alone is not sufficient.
B Statement (2) ALONE is sufficient, but statement (1) alone is not sufficient.
C BOTH statements TOGETHER are sufficient, but NEITHER statement ALONE is sufficient.
D EACH statement ALONE is sufficient.
E Statements (1) and (2) TOGETHER are NOT sufficient.

21. During a 3-year period, the profits of Company X changed by what percent from the second year to the third year?

    (1) The increase in profits of Company X from the first year to the second year was the same as the increase from the first year to the third year.

    (2) For Company X, the profits for the first year were $13,800 and the profits for the third year were $15,900.

22. A pyramidal-shaped box to protect a plant is constructed with 4 lateral faces and an open bottom. What is the lateral area of the box?

    (1) The base of the pyramid is a polygon with all sides of equal length, and the perimeter of the base is 1 meter.

    (2) The lateral faces are isosceles triangles that have the same size and shape.

23. What is the value of $x^2 - y^2$?

    (1) $x + y = 2x$
    (2) $x + y = 0$

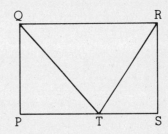

24. In rectangular region PQRS above, T is a point on side PS. If PS = 4, what is the area of region PQRS ?

    (1) $\triangle QTR$ is equilateral.
    (2) Segments PT and TS have equal length.

25. Does x = 2 ?

    (1) x is a number such that $x^2 - 3x + 2 = 0$.
    (2) x is a number such that $x^2 - x - 2 = 0$.

S T O P

IF YOU FINISH BEFORE TIME IS CALLED, YOU MAY CHECK YOUR WORK ON THIS SECTION ONLY. DO NOT WORK ON ANY OTHER SECTION IN THE TEST.

SECTION II

Time—30 minutes

35 Questions

Directions: Each passage in this section is followed by numbered considerations that require classification, as illustrated by the following example:

> John Atkins, the owner of a service station in Leeway, wanted to open a station in Eastown. A computer company had plans to set up operations in Eastown, and Atkins, foreseeing an increase in traffic near the plant, was eager to acquire land in Eastown so that he could expand his business to serve commuting workers. Ideally, Atkins wanted a piece of land large enough to permit him to build a tire store as part of the new station; he also wanted to keep the cost of purchasing the land as well as the cost of clearing it for construction as low as possible. Atkins identified three possible properties: one on Moore Road, another on Route 5, and a third on Snow Lane. The purchase prices of the properties were $42,000, $36,000, and $34,000, respectively. The properties required different expenditures for clearing. In the case of the Snow Lane site, a diner would have to be demolished and pavement removed. Atkins knew that his decision required deliberation.

The following numbered considerations are related to the passage above. Evaluate each consideration separately in terms of the passage and on the answer sheet blacken space

A if the consideration is an <u>Objective</u> in making the decision; that is, one of the outcomes, results, or goals that the decision-maker seeks;

B if the consideration is a <u>Major Factor</u> in making the decision; that is, a consideration, explicitly mentioned in the passage, that is basic to reaching the decision;

C if the consideration is a <u>Minor Factor</u> in making the decision; that is, a consideration that is of secondary importance to reaching the decision and that bears on a Major Factor;

D if the consideration is an <u>Assumption</u> in making the decision; that is, a relevant supposition or projection made by the decision-maker before reaching the decision;

E if the consideration is an <u>Unimportant Issue</u> in making the decision; that is, a consideration that is insignificant or not immediately relevant to reaching the decision.

1. Increase in traffic near the new computer plant   Ⓐ Ⓑ Ⓒ ● Ⓔ

2. Acquisition of a sufficiently large piece of land   ● Ⓑ Ⓒ Ⓓ Ⓔ

3. Cost of clearing a piece of land   Ⓐ ● Ⓒ Ⓓ Ⓔ

4. Cost of demolishing the diner on the Snow Lane site   Ⓐ Ⓑ ● Ⓓ Ⓔ

5. Cost of starting up the new computer plant   Ⓐ Ⓑ Ⓒ Ⓓ ●

GO ON TO THE NEXT PAGE.

The best classification for number 1 is (D), an <u>Assumption</u>, since Atkins supposes that automobile traffic will increase near the new computer plant. The best classification for number 2 is (A), an <u>Objective</u>, since one of Atkins' goals is to obtain a piece of land large enough to permit him to include a tire store as part of his new station. (B), a <u>Major Factor</u>, is the best classification for number 3. The cost of clearing a property is a basic consideration to Atkins since he wants to prepare a property for construction at the lowest possible cost. The best classification for number 4 is (C), a <u>Minor Factor</u>. The cost of demolishing the diner on the Snow Lane site contributes to the total cost of clearing that site. That is, the cost of demolition is a secondary consideration that bears on a major factor. Finally, the best classification for number 5 is (E), an <u>Unimportant Issue</u>, since there is no logical connection between the cost of starting up the computer plant and Atkins' decision about which property to choose.

NOW READ THE PASSAGES AND CLASSIFY THE CONSIDERATIONS FOLLOWING THEM.

GO ON TO THE NEXT PAGE.

Supersonics, Incorporated, of Cambridge, Massachusetts, is a medium-sized company that manufactures high-priced stereo loudspeakers with unusually good frequency response. Supersonics wishes to increase its sales; it recently learned from a market survey that it can accomplish this best by developing and successfully marketing a new product. Supersonics therefore commissioned a task force to propose new products and to recommend one of them for development.

The task force's report read, in part:

Introduction

The task force included representatives from the research, marketing, finance, and production staffs. We limited our discussion to stereo equipment because we consider development of products in other areas of consumer electronics to be beyond Supersonics' present competence. We also attempted to work within the constraints that the finance staff members outlined—minimizing costs, not expanding staff, and keeping the need for new capital relatively low.

The marketing staff members suggested that we avoid developing products such as a line of inexpensive, poorer-quality loudspeakers that would damage our reputation for high quality. We believe that Supersonics' current customer population is composed mainly of "audiophiles"—devotees of high-fidelity sound—who are willing to pay for high quality and who are typically aged 18-35 (though an increasing proportion are older than 35). The marketing staff members advised us to work toward retaining these customers while also attempting to attract new buyers.

* * * * * *

Criteria

We agreed that the following criteria should weigh heavily in selecting a new product: the ease with which technical problems can be overcome in developing the desired product, the cost of the research needed to develop the product, the time required to complete the research, the availability at Supersonics of research staff with the expertise necessary to conduct the research, the capital investment required to manufacture the new product, and the marketability of the new product over the next ten years.

* * * * * *

Alternatives

We considered many ideas, rejecting those (such as developing a line of AM-FM radios) that rated lowest on the selection criteria. We ultimately focused on three alternatives:

1. Develop a method for further refining the frequency response in our current loudspeakers and market the improved loudspeakers in place of our current line.
2. Develop the technology to produce high-quality automobile stereo loudspeakers and add them as a new product line.
3. Develop a "sound enhancer"—a device that will create for listeners the illusion of being in the concert hall—and market it as an innovative stereo component.

* * * * * *

GO ON TO THE NEXT PAGE.

Summary of Advantages and Disadvantages of
Alternatives

1. Develop an improved loudspeaker: Although our
researchers encountered only minor technical
problems in the original research for our current loudspeakers, they face somewhat greater
technical obstacles in developing a method to
further refine our loudspeakers' frequency response. Nevertheless, technical success is
probable within a year. Because our researchers
have special expertise in frequency response, no
new research staff will be needed. Research
expenses will be low because Supersonics already
owns all the equipment needed to conduct tests of
frequency response. The capital investment
required to manufacture the improved speakers
will also be minimal because Supersonics' existing production facilities can be used with only
minor modifications. However, market success
is by no means assured, since market surveys
indicate that the market for high-priced, high-
quality loudspeakers will not grow substantially
over the next decade and since research studies
show that it is difficult even for audiophiles to
detect refinements in the frequency response of
loudspeakers.

2. Develop the technology to produce high-quality
automobile stereo loudspeakers: Technical
success is virtually certain, and the research
can be done quickly, with no new hiring. However, the research will require purchase of
some new laboratory equipment, and a moderate
amount of capital will be needed to set up a new
assembly line. Market success is probable but
not certain; there is a large potential market
with good growth prospects, consisting mainly
of audiophiles who do not yet own automobile
stereo systems, but an effective advertising
campaign will be necessary to persuade them to
purchase automobile stereos.

3. Develop a sound enhancer: Technical success is
uncertain because Supersonics' researchers are
inexperienced in the field of psychoacoustics and
because it is difficult to simulate concert hall
acoustics. New research equipment, new researchers with expertise in psychoacoustics, and
several years of research will be needed. Capital
investment required for eventual production will
be high. However, the payoff in market success
could well be large. Claims made by loudspeaker
manufacturers in their advertising have created
in audiophiles an enormous unfulfilled demand for
"the concert hall illusion." If our sound en-
hancers produce this illusion, many audiophiles
will buy them. Moreover, potential market
growth is great because the sound enhancer
might eventually become a standard part of conventional stereo systems and thus obtain many
new nonaudiophile customers for Supersonics.

GO ON TO THE NEXT PAGE

Directions: The following numbered considerations are related to the passage above. You may refer back to the passage and to the directions at the beginning of this section. Evaluate each consideration separately in terms of the passage and on the answer sheet blacken space

A if the consideration is an <u>Objective</u> in making the decision; that is, one of the outcomes, results, or goals that the decision-maker seeks;

B if the consideration is a <u>Major Factor</u> in making the decision; that is, a consideration, explicitly mentioned in the passage, that is basic to reaching the decision;

C if the consideration is a <u>Minor Factor</u> in making the decision; that is, a consideration that is of secondary importance to reaching the decision and that bears on a Major Factor;

D if the consideration is an <u>Assumption</u> in making the decision; that is, a relevant supposition or projection made by the decision-maker before reaching the decision;

E if the consideration is an <u>Unimportant Issue</u> in making the decision; that is, a consideration that is insignificant or not immediately relevant to reaching the decision.

1. Probability of Supersonics achieving technical success in developing a line of AM-FM radios

2. Supersonics' ownership of the equipment needed to conduct tests of frequency response

3. Advertising campaign needed to persuade audiophiles to purchase automobile stereo systems

4. Cost of the research needed to develop a new product

5. A relatively low requirement for new capital

6. Supersonics' lack of expertise in the development of products other than stereo equipment

7. Seriousness of the technical problems that Supersonics' researchers encountered in conducting the original research for Supersonics' current loudspeakers

8. Staff currently available at Supersonics who have expertise in conducting research on an improved loudspeaker, an automobile stereo loudspeaker, or a sound enhancer

9. Development of a new stereo product that can be marketed successfully

10. Increase in the proportion of Supersonics' customers who are older than 35

11. Merit of an attempt to attract new customers

12. Marketability of the alternatives

13. Difficulty for most people of detecting refinements in the frequency response of loudspeakers

14. Continued business with Supersonics' current customers

15. Preponderance of audiophiles among Supersonics' current customers

16. Difficulty of simulating concert hall acoustics

17. Inclusion of representatives from the research, marketing, finance, and production staffs on the task force

GO ON TO THE NEXT PAGE.

In 1978 a new wing was added to Kingwood Hospital, and the directors of the hospital decided that it was time to reevaluate the hospital's supply system. In order to determine what type of supply system would best suit the needs of Kingwood Hospital, the directors retained Cynthia Veragetti, an expert in such matters, as a consultant.

After Veragetti arrived at Kingwood, she first surveyed all hospital personnel directly involved in patient care because she believed that a suitable supply system would be one that the majority of the hospital's personnel favored. Veragetti also believed that the number of patients entering Kingwood Hospital would increase over the next several years because she expected the population of the area to increase. She therefore wanted a supply system that would be able to accommodate the increase. As she continued to study the hospital, Veragetti determined that any supply system that she would select would have to provide nurses with quick access to all essential medicines and equipment; at the same time, she realized that a supply system would have to be set up so that only authorized personnel would have access to potentially dangerous medicines. Veragetti had also determined that Kingwood Hospital needed a supply system that would facilitate the inventory of supplies, enable administrators to track the distribution of medicine and equipment throughout the hospital, and minimize the distance that any nurse or orderly would have to travel to obtain supplies during a shift. Moreover, because Veragetti felt that supply emergencies would probably occur, she wanted a supply system that would allow hospital personnel to transfer equipment from one section of the hospital to another more quickly than they could under the present arrangement.

Discussions with the directors of Kingwood Hospital led Veragetti to believe that the cost of building the new wing would probably make the directors reluctant to spend much money on more construction or other new expenses. For that reason, Veragetti wanted to recommend a supply system that would not require extensive remodeling or the addition of new personnel.

Among the supply systems that Veragetti was considering were the central, floor, and station systems. The central supply system, which was the one most similar to the system Kingwood Hospital currently used, was attractive because it would facilitate inventory procedures and seemed to provide a secure place in which to store medicines. Veragetti, however, noted that the rooms that would be used for storage in such a system had windows at street level, and she assumed that this would compromise security. A more important drawback was that a central supply system would require nurses and orderlies to walk a great distance; Veragetti, however, thought that an unused elevator, which adjoined one of the proposed storerooms, could be remodeled and used, thus decreasing the distance that personnel on other floors would have to travel.

The floor supply system would of course greatly reduce the distance traveled by personnel and would also allow equipment on one floor to be easily transferred to another. Because each floor abutted a central administrative area, Veragetti felt that restricting access to potentially dangerous medicines would not pose a problem. Veragetti thought that the room needed for storing supplies could be found within the administrative areas because she knew that additional, more comfortable office space was available for administrators on the ground floor. Since the central administrative areas did not have enough electrical outlets to accommodate the appliances necessary in a supply area, some remodeling would be needed.

The station supply system (there were several nursing stations on each floor of Kingwood Hospital) would reduce the distance that personnel would travel even more than would the floor supply system. Not all medicines and equipment could be stored at each station, but Veragetti thought that it would be necessary only to store particular medicines and equipment at each station, since all of the patients under the supervision of a station generally have the same types of ailments. Thus Veragetti supposed that the medicines most often needed would be the medicines nearest at hand. Potentially dangerous medicines, however, would be least secure if Kingwood Hospital used a station supply system since, she gathered, the storage areas would have to border the hallways. Because different medicines would be stored at different stations, a station supply system would not facilitate the distribution of supplies among floors if an emergency occurred.

Although the nurses and orderlies preferred the station supply system, administrative personnel favored the central supply system. All three systems would be able to utilize available facilities, yet all three would require some remodeling. Veragetti thought that the floor and station systems would be able to accommodate an increased number of patients; the central supply system, on the other hand, would be the one least likely to require additional personnel. Veragetti decided to consider these and other alternatives further before making her recommendation.

GO ON TO THE NEXT PAGE.

<u>Directions:</u> The following numbered considerations are related to the passage above. You may refer back to the passage and to the directions at the beginning of this section. Evaluate each consideration separately in terms of the passage and on the answer sheet blacken space

    A if the consideration is an <u>Objective</u> in making the decision; that is, one of the outcomes, results, or goals that the decision-maker seeks;

    B if the consideration is a <u>Major Factor</u> in making the decision; that is, a consideration, explicitly mentioned in the passage, that is basic to reaching the decision;

    C if the consideration is a <u>Minor Factor</u> in making the decision; that is, a consideration that is of secondary importance to reaching the decision and that bears on a Major Factor;

    D if the consideration is an <u>Assumption</u> in making the decision; that is, a relevant supposition or projection made by the decision-maker before reaching the decision;

    E if the consideration is an <u>Unimportant Issue</u> in making the decision; that is, a consideration that is insignificant or not immediately relevant to reaching the decision.

18. Efficient use of personnel time

19. Remodeling needed for a new supply system

20. Amount of difficulty encountered by hospital personnel in transferring essential medicines and equipment from one section of the hospital to another under any of the new supply systems

21. Value of a supply system that is favored by hospital personnel who are directly involved in patient care

22. Use of hallways by people other than personnel who are authorized to have access to supplies

23. Determining the types of medication needed by patients at Kingwood Hospital

24. A supply system that does not require extensive remodeling within Kingwood Hospital

25. Type of supply system favored by the majority of the hospital's personnel

26. Length of time needed to build the new wing

27. Quick access to essential medicines and equipment

28. Length of shift worked by nurses and orderlies under each of the alternatives

29. Restricted access to potentially dangerous medicines

30. Future population increase in area around Kingwood Hospital

31. Disinclination of directors to budget much money for remodeling as a result of expenses incurred when the new wing was built

32. Availability of office space on the ground floor

33. Number of additional hospital personnel likely to be required by a new supply system

34. Anticipated size of Kingwood Hospital's budget for medicines

35. Unsatisfactoriness of a storage area in which access to supplies cannot be carefully controlled

S T O P

IF YOU FINISH BEFORE TIME IS CALLED, YOU MAY CHECK YOUR WORK ON THIS SECTION ONLY.
DO NOT WORK ON ANY OTHER SECTION IN THE TEST.

SECTION III

Time—30 minutes

20 Questions

Directions: In this section solve each problem, using any available space on the page for scratchwork. Then indicate the best of the answer choices given.

Numbers: All numbers used are real numbers.

Figures: Figures that accompany problems in this test are intended to provide information useful in solving the problems. They are drawn as accurately as possible EXCEPT when it is stated in a specific problem that its figure is not drawn to scale. All figures lie in a plane unless otherwise indicated.

1. A national travel survey in 1977 found that Americans took 382.6 million trips within the United States. California was the destination of 38 million trips. Approximately what percent of the trips had California as the destination?

   (A) 0.01%   (B) 0.1%   (C) 1%

   (D) 3.8%   (E) 10%

2. How many of the integers between 25 and 45 are even?

   (A) 21   (B) 20   (C) 11   (D) 10   (E) 9

3. If taxi fares were $1.00 for the first $\frac{1}{5}$ mile and $0.20 for each $\frac{1}{5}$ mile thereafter, then the taxi fare for a 3-mile ride was

   (A) $1.56
   (B) $2.40
   (C) $3.00
   (D) $3.80
   (E) $4.20

4. A computer routine was developed to generate two numbers, (x, y), the first being a random number between 0 and 100 inclusive, and the second being less than or equal to the square root of the first. Each of the following pairs satisfies this routine EXCEPT

   (A) (99, 10)
   (B) (85, 9)
   (C) (50, 7)
   (D) (1, 1)
   (E) (1, 0)

GO ON TO THE NEXT PAGE

-166-

5. A warehouse had a square floor with area 10,000 square meters. A rectangular addition was built along one entire side of the warehouse that increased the floor area by one-half as much as the original floor area. How many meters did the addition extend beyond the original building?

(A) 10   (B) 20   (C) 50   (D) 200   (E) 500

6. A digital wristwatch was set accurately at 8:30 a.m. and then lost 2 seconds every 5 minutes. What time was indicated on the watch at 6:30 p.m. of the same day if the watch operated continuously until that time?

(A) 5:56
(B) 5:58
(C) 6:00
(D) 6:23
(E) 6:26

7. If x and y are integers and $xy = 5$, then $(x + y)^2 =$

(A) 13   (B) 16   (C) 25   (D) 26   (E) 36

GO ON TO THE NEXT PAGE.

Questions 8-9 refer to the following graphs.

REVENUE FOR STORE X DURING WEEK 1

Distribution of Total Revenue

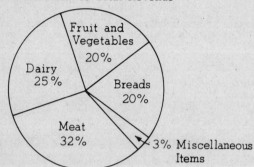

Amount of Revenue from Dairy Products

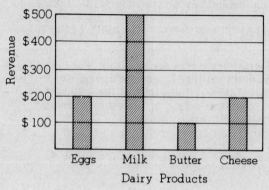

8. During week 1, revenue from eggs provided what percent of the total revenue for Store X ?

(A) 4%
(B) 5%
(C) 8%
(D) 20%
(E) 25%

9. If the revenue from the sale of apples was equal to the revenue from the sale of miscellaneous items, what percent of the revenue from the sale of fruit and vegetables was accounted for by apples?

(A) 60%
(B) 15%
(C) 12%
(D) 6%
(E) 3%

GO ON TO THE NEXT PAGE.

10. The (x, y) pair $(-1, 1)$ satisfies which of the following equations?

    I. $2x^3 - y^2 = -3$
    II. $2x^2 - y^3 = 1$
    III. $x^2 - 2y^3 = -1$

    (A) I only
    (B) I and II only
    (C) I and III only
    (D) II and III only
    (E) I, II, and III

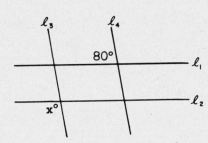

Note: Figure not drawn to scale.

11. If $\ell_1 \parallel \ell_2$ in the figure above, what is the value of x?

    (A) 80
    (B) 90
    (C) 100
    (D) 120
    (E) It cannot be determined from the information given.

12. A 5-liter jug contains 4 liters of a saltwater solution that is 15 percent salt. If 1.5 liters of the solution spills out of the jug, and the jug is then filled to capacity with water, approximately what percent of the resulting solution in the jug is salt?

    (A) $7\frac{1}{2}\%$

    (B) $9\frac{3}{8}\%$

    (C) $10\frac{1}{2}\%$

    (D) 12%

    (E) 15%

13. The average (arithmetic mean) of 3 different positive integers is 100 and the largest of these 3 integers is 120. What is the least possible value of the smallest of these 3 integers?

    (A) 1   (B) 10   (C) 61   (D) 71   (E) 80

GO ON TO THE NEXT PAGE.

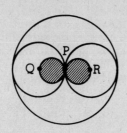

14. In the figure above, the five circles have points in common as shown. P is the center of the largest circle, Q and R are centers of the medium-sized circles, and Q, P, and R are points on a straight line. What fraction of the largest circular region is shaded?

(A) $\frac{1}{16}$ (B) $\frac{1}{8}$ (C) $\frac{3}{16}$ (D) $\frac{1}{4}$ (E) $\frac{1}{2}$

15. If $xyz \neq 0$ and x percent of y percent of z is t, then z =

(A) $\frac{100t}{xy}$

(B) $\frac{1,000t}{xy}$

(C) $\frac{10,000t}{xy}$

(D) $\frac{xy}{10,000t}$

(E) $\frac{10,000xy}{t}$

16. A plane traveled k miles in the first 96 minutes of flight time. If it completed the remaining 300 miles of the trip in t minutes, what was its average speed, in miles per hour, for the entire trip?

(A) $\frac{60(k+300)}{96+t}$

(B) $\frac{kt+96(300)}{96t}$

(C) $\frac{k+300}{60(96+t)}$

(D) $\frac{5k}{8} + \frac{60(300)}{t}$

(E) $\frac{5k}{8} + 5t$

GO ON TO THE NEXT PAGE

17. A merchant sells an item at a 20 percent discount, but still makes a gross profit of 20 percent of the cost. What percent of the cost would the gross profit on the item have been if it had been sold without the discount?

(A) 20%
(B) 40%
(C) 50%
(D) 60%
(E) 75%

18. A milliner bought a job lot of hats, $\frac{1}{4}$ of which were brown. The milliner sold $\frac{2}{3}$ of the hats including $\frac{4}{5}$ of the brown hats. What fraction of the unsold hats were brown?

(A) $\frac{1}{60}$ (B) $\frac{2}{15}$ (C) $\frac{3}{20}$ (D) $\frac{3}{5}$ (E) $\frac{3}{4}$

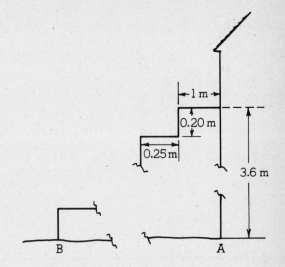

Note: Figure not drawn to scale.

19. Each step of a staircase is 0.25 meter wide and 0.20 meter high, as shown in the figure above. All angles shown in the figure are right angles. If the height of the staircase is 3.6 meters and the landing at the top of the staircase is 1 meter wide, how long, in meters, is AB?

(A) 3.0
(B) 4.25
(C) 4.5
(D) 5.25
(E) 5.5

20. How many integers n greater than 10 and less than 100 are there such that, if the digits of n are reversed, the resulting integer is n + 9?

(A) 5 (B) 6 (C) 7 (D) 8 (E) 9

S T O P

IF YOU FINISH BEFORE TIME IS CALLED, YOU MAY CHECK YOUR WORK ON THIS SECTION ONLY.
DO NOT WORK ON ANY OTHER SECTION IN THE TEST.

SECTION IV

Time—30 minutes

25 Questions

Directions: In each of the following sentences, some part of the sentence or the entire sentence is underlined. Beneath each sentence you will find five ways of phrasing the underlined part. The first of these repeats the original; the other four are different. If you think the original is better than any of the alternatives, choose answer A; otherwise choose one of the others. Select the best version and blacken the corresponding space on your answer sheet.

This is a test of correctness and effectiveness of expression. In choosing answers, follow the requirements of standard written English; that is, pay attention to grammar, choice of words, and sentence construction. Choose the answer that expresses most effectively what is presented in the original sentence; this answer should be clear and exact, without awkwardness, ambiguity, or redundancy.

1. Never before in the history of music have musical superstars been able to command so extraordinary fees of the kind they do today.

   (A) so extraordinary fees of the kind they do today
   (B) so extraordinary fees as they are today
   (C) such extraordinary fees as they do today
   (D) such extraordinary fees of the kind today's have
   (E) so extraordinary a fee of the kind they can today

2. As it becomes more frequent to have spouses who both work outside the home, companies are beginning to help in finding new employment for the spouses of transferred employees.

   (A) it becomes more frequent to have spouses who both work outside the home
   (B) it becomes more frequent to have couples both working outside the home
   (C) it becomes more common that both husband and wife should be working outside the home
   (D) it becomes more common for both husband and wife to work outside the home
   (E) couples in which both of the spouses working outside the home become more common

3. Like the one reputed to live in Loch Ness, also an inland lake connected to the ocean by a river, inhabitants of the area around Lake Champlain claim sightings of a long and narrow "sea monster."

   (A) Like the one reputed to live in Loch Ness, also an inland lake connected to the ocean by a river, inhabitants of the area around Lake Champlain claim sightings of a long and narrow "sea monster."
   (B) Inhabitants of the area around Lake Champlain claim sightings of a long and narrow "sea monster" similar to the one reputed to live in Loch Ness, which, like Lake Champlain, is an inland lake connected to the ocean by a river.
   (C) Inhabitants of the area around Lake Champlain claim sightings of a long and narrow "sea monster" similar to Loch Ness's, which, like Lake Champlain, is an inland lake connected to the ocean by a river.
   (D) Like Loch Ness's reputed monster, inhabitants of the area around Lake Champlain, also an inland lake connected to the ocean by a river, claim sightings of a long and narrow "sea monster."
   (E) Similar to that reputed to live in Loch Ness, inhabitants of the area around Lake Champlain, also an inland lake connected to the ocean by a river, claim sightings of a long and narrow "sea monster."

GO ON TO THE NEXT PAGE.

-173-

4. <u>Since 1965 there are four times as many Black college students enrolled</u>, and the one million Black people in college today represent 11 percent of all college students.

(A) Since 1965 there are four times as many Black college students enrolled
(B) The enrollment of Black college students was only one-fourth in 1965
(C) The enrollment of Black college students has increased four times from 1965 on
(D) Quadrupling since 1965, there are now four times as many Black college students enrolled
(E) The enrollment of Black college students has quadrupled since 1965

5. A common disability in test pilots is hearing impairment, <u>a consequence of sitting too close to large jet engines for long periods of time.</u>

(A) a consequence of sitting too close to large jet engines for long periods of time
(B) a consequence from sitting for long periods of time too near to large jet engines
(C) a consequence which resulted from sitting too close to large jet engines for long periods of time
(D) damaged from sitting too near to large jet engines for long periods of time
(E) damaged because they sat too close to large jet engines for long periods of time

6. Europe's travel industry is suffering as a result of a sluggish economy, a stretch of bad weather, <u>as well as the chilling effects of terrorist activity that is persistent</u>.

(A) as well as the chilling effects of terrorist activity that is persistent
(B) and the chilling effect of terrorist activity that is persistent
(C) but persistent terrorist activity has had a chilling effect too
(D) and the chilling effects of persistent terrorist activity
(E) as well as the chilling effects of terrorist activity that persists

7. Opening with tributes to jazz-age divas like Bessie Smith and closing with Koko Taylor's electrified gravel-and-thunder songs, <u>the program will trace</u> the blues' vigorous matriarchal line over more than 50 years.

(A) the program will trace
(B) the program shall trace
(C) there will be a program tracing
(D) it is a program that traces
(E) it will be a program tracing

8. In 1929 relatively small declines in the market ruined many <u>speculators having bought on margin; they had to sell, and</u> their selling pushed other investors to the brink.

(A) speculators having bought on margin; they had to sell, and
(B) speculators who had bought on margin; having had to sell,
(C) speculators who had bought on margin; they had to sell, and
(D) speculators, those who had bought on margin; these speculators had to sell, and
(E) speculators, who, having bought on margin and having to sell,

9. The mistakes children make in learning to speak tell linguists more about <u>how they learn language</u> than the correct forms they use.

(A) how they learn language than
(B) how one learns language than
(C) how children learn language than do
(D) learning language than
(E) their language learning than do

10. Building large new hospitals in the bistate area would constitute a wasteful use of resources, <u>on the basis of avoidance of duplicated facilities alone.</u>

(A) on the basis of avoidance of duplicated facilities alone
(B) on the grounds of avoiding duplicated facilities alone
(C) solely in that duplicated facilities should be avoided
(D) while the duplication of facilities should be avoided
(E) if only because the duplication of facilities should be avoided

GO ON TO THE NEXT PAGE.

11. Freedman's survey showed that people living in small towns and rural areas consider themselves <u>no happier than do people living</u> in big cities.

(A) no happier than do people living
(B) not any happier than do people living
(C) not any happier than do people who live
(D) no happier than are people who are living
(E) not as happy as are people who live

12. <u>It may someday be worthwhile to try to recover uranium from seawater,</u> but at present this process is prohibitively expensive.

(A) It may someday be worthwhile to try to recover uranium from seawater
(B) Someday, it may be worthwhile to try and recover uranium from seawater
(C) Trying to recover uranium out of seawater may someday be worthwhile
(D) To try for the recovery of uranium out of seawater may someday be worthwhile
(E) Recovering uranium from seawater may be worthwhile to try to do someday

13. The underlying physical principles that control the midair gyrations of divers and gymnasts are the same <u>as the body orientation controlling</u> astronauts in a weightless environment.

(A) as the body orientation controlling
(B) as the body orientation which controls
(C) as those controlling the body orientation of
(D) ones to control the body orientation of
(E) ones used in controlling the body orientation of

14. The spraying of pesticides can be carefully planned, but accidents, <u>weather conditions that could not be foreseen, and pilot errors often cause much larger deposits of spray than they had</u> anticipated.

(A) weather conditions that could not be foreseen, and pilot errors often cause much larger deposits of spray than they had
(B) weather conditions that cannot be foreseen, and pilot errors often cause much larger deposits of spray than
(C) unforeseeable weather conditions, and pilot errors are the cause of much larger deposits of spray than they had
(D) weather conditions that are not foreseeable, and pilot errors often cause much larger deposits of spray than
(E) unforeseeable weather conditions, and pilot errors often cause much larger deposits of spray than they had

15. <u>To read of</u> Abigail Adams' lengthy separation from her family, her difficult travels, and her constant battles with illness is to feel intensely how harsh life was even for the so-called aristocracy of Revolutionary times.

(A) To read of
(B) Reading about
(C) Having read about
(D) Once one reads of
(E) To have read of

16. <u>A star will compress itself into a white dwarf, a neutron star, or a black hole after it passes through a red giant stage, depending on mass.</u>

(A) A star will compress itself into a white dwarf, a neutron star, or a black hole after it passes through a red giant stage, depending on mass.
(B) After passing through a red giant stage, depending on its mass, a star will compress itself into a white dwarf, a neutron star, or a black hole.
(C) After passing through a red giant stage, a star's mass will determine if it compresses itself into a white dwarf, a neutron star, or a black hole.
(D) Mass determines whether a star, after passing through the red giant stage, will compress itself into a white dwarf, a neutron star, or a black hole.
(E) The mass of a star, after passing through the red giant stage, will determine whether it compresses itself into a white dwarf, a neutron star, or a black hole.

GO ON TO THE NEXT PAGE.

17. In the main, incidents of breakdowns in nuclear reactors have not resulted from lapses of high technology but commonplace inadequacies in plumbing and wiring.

   (A) not resulted from lapses of high technology but
   (B) resulted not from lapses of high technology but from
   (C) resulted from lapses not of high technology but
   (D) resulted from lapses not of high technology but have stemmed from
   (E) resulted not from lapses of high technology but have stemmed from

18. Seeming to be the only organization fighting for the rights of poor people in the South, Hosea Hudson, a laborer in Alabama, joined the Communist party in 1931.

   (A) Seeming to be
   (B) As
   (C) In that they seemed
   (D) Since it seemed
   (E) Because it seemed to be

19. Although many art patrons can readily differentiate a good debenture from an undesirable one, they are much less expert in distinguishing good paintings and poor ones, authentic art and fakes.

   (A) much less expert in distinguishing good paintings and poor ones, authentic art and
   (B) far less expert in distinguishing good paintings from poor ones, authentic art from
   (C) much less expert when it comes to distinguishing good paintings and poor ones, authentic art from
   (D) far less expert in distinguishing good paintings and poor ones, authentic art and
   (E) far less the expert when it comes to distinguishing between good painting, poor ones, authentic art, and

20. Rules banning cancer-causing substances from food apply to new food additives and not to natural constituents of food because their use as additives is entirely avoidable.

   (A) their use as additives is
   (B) as additives, their use is
   (C) the use of such additives is
   (D) the use of such additives are
   (E) the use of them as additives is

21. The average weekly wage nearly doubled in the 1970's, rising from $114 to $220, yet the average worker ended the decade with a decrease in what their pay may buy.

   (A) with a decrease in what their pay may buy
   (B) with what was a decrease in what they were able to buy
   (C) having decreased that which they could buy
   (D) decreasing in purchasing power
   (E) with a decrease in purchasing power

22. Since chromosome damage may be caused by viral infections, medical x-rays, and exposure to sunlight, it is important that the chromosomes of a population to be tested for chemically induced damage be compared with those of a control population.

   (A) to be tested for chemically induced damage be compared with
   (B) being tested for damage induced chemically are compared with
   (C) being tested for chemically induced damage should be compared to
   (D) being tested for chemically induced damage are to be compared to
   (E) that is to be tested for chemically induced damage are to be comparable with

23. The suspect in the burglary was advised of his right to remain silent, told he could not leave, and was interrogated in a detention room.

   (A) of his right to remain silent, told he could not leave, and was
   (B) of his right to remain silent, told he could not leave, and
   (C) of his right to remain silent and that he could not leave and
   (D) that he had a right to remain silent, could not leave, and was
   (E) that he had a right to remain silent, that he could not leave, and was

GO ON TO THE NEXT PAGE.

24. The United States petroleum industry's cost to meet environmental regulations is projected at ten percent of the price per barrel of refined petroleum by the end of the decade.

(A) The United States petroleum industry's cost to meet environmental regulations is projected at ten percent of the price per barrel of refined petroleum by the end of the decade.

(B) The United States petroleum industry's cost by the end of the decade to meet environmental regulations is estimated at ten percent of the price per barrel of refined petroleum.

(C) By the end of the decade, the United States petroleum industry's cost of meeting environmental regulations is projected at ten percent of the price per barrel of refined petroleum.

(D) To meet environmental regulations, the cost to the United States petroleum industry is estimated at ten percent of the price per barrel of refined petroleum by the end of the decade.

(E) It is estimated that by the end of the decade the cost to the United States petroleum industry of meeting environmental regulations will be ten percent of the price per barrel of refined petroleum.

25. The relationship between corpulence and disease remain controversial, although statistics clearly associate a reduced life expectancy with chronic obesity.

(A) remain controversial, although statistics clearly associate a reduced life expectancy with

(B) remain controversial, although statistics clearly associates a reduced life expectancy with

(C) remain controversial, although statistics clearly associates reduced life expectancy to

(D) remains controversial, although statistics clearly associate a reduced life expectancy with

(E) remains controversial, although statistics clearly associates reduced life expectancy to

S T O P

IF YOU FINISH BEFORE TIME IS CALLED, YOU MAY CHECK YOUR WORK ON THIS SECTION ONLY.
DO NOT WORK ON ANY OTHER SECTION IN THE TEST.

SECTION V

Time—30 minutes

25 Questions

Directions: Each passage in this group is followed by questions based on content. After reading a passage, choose the best answer to each question and blacken the corresponding space on the answer sheet. Answer all questions following a passage on the basis of what is stated or implied in that passage.

(This passage was written in 1978.)

Recent years have brought minority-owned businesses in the United States unprecedented opportunities—as well as new and significant risks. Civil rights activists have long argued that one of
(5) the principal reasons why Blacks, Hispanics, and other minority groups have difficulty establishing themselves in business is that they lack access to the sizable orders and subcontracts that are generated by large companies. Now Congress, in appar-
(10) ent agreement, has required by law that businesses awarded federal contracts of more than $500,000 do their best to find minority subcontractors and record their efforts to do so on forms filed with the government. Indeed, some federal and local agen-
(15) cies have gone so far as to set specific percentage goals for apportioning parts of public works contracts to minority enterprises.

Corporate response appears to have been substantial. According to figures collected in 1977,
(20) the total of corporate contracts with minority businesses rose from $77 million in 1972 to $1.1 billion in 1977. The projected total of corporate contracts with minority businesses for the early 1980's is estimated to be over $3 billion per year with no
(25) letup anticipated in the next decade.

Promising as it is for minority businesses, this increased patronage poses dangers for them, too. First, minority firms risk expanding too fast and overextending themselves financially, since most
(30) are small concerns and, unlike large businesses, they often need to make substantial investments in new plants, staff, equipment, and the like in order to perform work subcontracted to them. If, thereafter, their subcontracts are for some reason
(35) reduced, such firms can face potentially crippling fixed expenses. The world of corporate purchasing can be frustrating for small entrepreneurs who get requests for elaborate formal estimates and bids. Both consume valuable time and resources, and a
(40) small company's efforts must soon result in orders, or both the morale and the financial health of the business will suffer.

A second risk is that White-owned companies may seek to cash in on the increasing apportion-
(45) ments through formation of joint ventures with minority-owned concerns. Of course, in many instances there are legitimate reasons for joint ventures; clearly, White and minority enterprises can team up to acquire business that neither could
(50) acquire alone. But civil rights groups and minority business owners have complained to Congress about minorities being set up as "fronts" with White back-

ing, rather than being accepted as full partners in legitimate joint ventures.
(55) Third, a minority enterprise that secures the business of one large corporate customer often runs the danger of becoming—and remaining—dependent. Even in the best of circumstances, fierce competition from larger, more established companies
(60) makes it difficult for small concerns to broaden their customer bases; when such firms have nearly guaranteed orders from a single corporate benefactor, they may truly have to struggle against complacency arising from their current success.

1. The primary purpose of the passage is to

(A) present a commonplace idea and its inaccuracies
(B) describe a situation and its potential drawbacks
(C) propose a temporary solution to a problem
(D) analyze a frequent source of disagreement
(E) explore the implications of a finding

2. The passage supplies information that would answer which of the following questions?

(A) What federal agencies have set percentage goals for the use of minority-owned businesses in public works contracts?
(B) To which government agencies must businesses awarded federal contracts report their efforts to find minority subcontractors?
(C) How widespread is the use of minority-owned concerns as "fronts" by White backers seeking to obtain subcontracts?
(D) How many more minority-owned businesses were there in 1977 than in 1972?
(E) What is one set of conditions under which a small business might find itself financially overextended?

GO ON TO THE NEXT PAGE.

3. According to the passage, civil rights activists maintain that one disadvantage under which minority-owned businesses have traditionally had to labor is that they have

(A) been especially vulnerable to governmental mismanagement of the economy
(B) been denied bank loans at rates comparable to those afforded larger competitors
(C) not had sufficient opportunity to secure business created by large corporations
(D) not been able to advertise in those media that reach large numbers of potential customers
(E) not had adequate representation in the centers of government power

4. The passage suggests that the failure of a large business to have its bids for subcontracts result quickly in orders might cause it to

(A) experience frustration but not serious financial harm
(B) face potentially crippling fixed expenses
(C) have to record its efforts on forms filed with the government
(D) increase its spending with minority subcontractors
(E) revise its procedure for making bids for federal contracts and subcontracts

5. The author implies that a minority-owned concern that does the greater part of its business with one large corporate customer should

(A) avoid competition with larger, more established concerns by not expanding
(B) concentrate on securing even more business from that corporation
(C) try to expand its customer base to avoid becoming dependent on the corporation
(D) pass on some of the work to be done for the corporation to other minority-owned concerns
(E) use its influence with the corporation to promote subcontracting with other minority concerns

6. It can be inferred from the passage that, compared with the requirements of law, the percentage goals set by "some federal and local agencies" (lines 14-15) are

(A) more popular with large corporations
(B) more specific
(C) less controversial
(D) less expensive to enforce
(E) easier to comply with

7. Which of the following, if true, would most weaken the author's assertion that, in the 1970's, corporate response to federal requirements (lines 18-19) was substantial?

(A) Corporate contracts with minority-owned businesses totaled $2 billion in 1979.
(B) Between 1970 and 1972, corporate contracts with minority-owned businesses declined by 25 percent.
(C) The figures collected in 1977 underrepresented the extent of corporate contracts with minority-owned businesses.
(D) The estimate of corporate spending with minority-owned businesses in 1980 is approximately $10 million too high.
(E) The $1.1 billion represented the same percentage of total corporate spending in 1977 as did $77 million in 1972.

8. The passage most likely appeared in

(A) a business magazine
(B) an encyclopedia of Black history to 1945
(C) a dictionary of financial terms
(D) a yearbook of business statistics
(E) an accounting textbook

9. The author would most likely agree with which of the following statements about corporate response to working with minority subcontractors?

(A) Annoyed by the proliferation of "front" organizations, corporations are likely to reduce their efforts to work with minority-owned subcontractors in the near future.
(B) Although corporations showed considerable interest in working with minority businesses in the 1970's, their aversion to government paperwork made them reluctant to pursue many government contracts.
(C) The significant response of corporations in the 1970's is likely to be sustained and conceivably be increased throughout the 1980's.
(D) Although corporations are eager to cooperate with minority-owned businesses, a shortage of capital in the 1970's made substantial response impossible.
(E) The enormous corporate response has all but eliminated the dangers of overexpansion that used to plague small minority-owned businesses.

GO ON TO THE NEXT PAGE.

In strongly territorial birds such as the indigo bunting, song is the main mechanism for securing, defining, and defending an adequate breeding area. When population density is high, only the strongest males can retain a suitable area. The weakest males do not breed or are forced to nest on poor or marginal territories.

During the breeding season, the male indigo bunting sings in his territory; each song lasts two or three seconds with a very short pause between songs. Melodic and rhythmic characteristics are produced by rapid changes in sound frequency and some regularity of silent periods between sounds. These modulated sounds form recognizable units, called figures, each of which is reproduced again and again with remarkable consistency. Despite the large frequency range of these sounds and the rapid frequency changes that the bird makes, the number of figures is very limited. Further, although we found some unique figures in different geographical populations, more than 90 percent of all the figures of birds from different regions are alike. Indigo bunting figures are extremely stable on a geographic basis. In our studies of isolated buntings we found that male indigo buntings are capable of singing many more types of figures than they usually do. Thus, it would seem that they copy their figures from other buntings they hear singing.

Realizing that the ability to distinguish the songs of one species from those of another could be an important factor in the evolution of the figures, we tested species recognition of a song. When we played a tape recording of a lazuli bunting or a painted bunting, male indigo buntings did not respond, even when a dummy of a male indigo bunting was placed near the tape recorder. Playing an indigo bunting song, however, usually brought an immediate response, making it clear that a male indigo bunting can readily distinguish songs of its own species from those of other species.

The role of the song figures in intraspecies recognition was then examined. We created experimental songs composed of new figures by playing a normal song backwards, which changed the detailed forms of the figures without altering frequency ranges or gross temporal features. Since the male indigos gave almost a full response to the backward song, we concluded that a wide range of figure shapes can evoke positive responses. It seems likely, therefore, that a specific configuration is not essential for intraspecies recognition, but it is clear that song figures must conform to a particular frequency range, must be within narrow limits of duration, and must be spaced at particular intervals.

There is evidence that new figures may arise within a population through a slow process of change and selection. This variety is probably a valuable adaptation for survival: if every bird sang only a few types of figures, in dense woods or underbrush a female might have difficulty recognizing her mate's song, and a male might not be able to distinguish a neighbor from a stranger. Our studies led us to conclude that there must be a balance between song stability and conservatism, which lead to clear-cut species recognition, and song variation, which leads to individual recognition.

10. The primary purpose of the passage is to

(A) raise new issues
(B) explain an enigma
(C) refute misconceptions
(D) reconcile differing theories
(E) analyze a phenomenon

11. According to the passage, which of the following is true about the number and general nature of figures sung by the indigo bunting?

(A) They are established at birth.
(B) They evolve slowly as the bird learns.
(C) They are learned from other indigo buntings.
(D) They develop after the bird has been forced onto marginal breeding areas.
(E) They gradually develop through contact with prospective mates.

12. It can be inferred that the investigation that determined the similarity among more than 90 percent of all the figures produced by birds living in different regions was undertaken to answer which of the following questions?

   I. How much variation, if any, is there in the figure types produced by indigo buntings in different locales?
  II. Do local populations of indigo buntings develop their own dialects of figure types?
 III. Do figure similarities among indigo buntings decline with increasing geographic separation?

(A) II only
(B) III only
(C) I and II only
(D) II and III only
(E) I, II, and III

GO ON TO THE NEXT PAGE.

13. It can be inferred from the passage that the existence of only a limited number of indigo bunting figures serves primarily to

(A) ensure species survival by increasing competition among the fittest males for the females
(B) increase population density by eliminating ambiguity in the figures to which the females must respond
(C) maintain the integrity of the species by restricting the degree of figure variation and change
(D) enhance species recognition by decreasing the number of figure patterns to which the bird must respond
(E) avoid confusion between species by clearly demarcating the figure patterns of each species

14. It can be inferred that a dummy of a male indigo bunting was placed near the tape recorder that played the songs of different species in order to try to

(A) simulate the conditions in nature
(B) rule out visual cues as a factor in species recognition
(C) supply an additional clue to species recognition for the indigo bunting
(D) provide data on the habits of bunting species other than the indigo bunting
(E) confound the indigo buntings in the experiment

15. According to the passage, the authors played a normal indigo bunting song backwards in order to determine which of the following?

(A) What are the limits of the frequency range that will provide recognition by the indigo bunting?
(B) What is the time duration necessary for recognition by the indigo bunting?
(C) How specific must a figure shape be for it to be recognized by the indigo bunting?
(D) How does variation in the pacing of song figures affect the indigo bunting's recognition of the figures?
(E) Is the indigo bunting responding to cues other than those in the song figures?

16. According to the passage, the indigo buntings' songs function in which of the following ways?

  I. To delineate a breeding area
  II. To defend a breeding area
  III. To identify the birds to their mates

(A) I only
(B) II only
(C) I and III only
(D) II and III only
(E) I, II, and III

GO ON TO THE NEXT PAGE.

Despite their many differences of temperament and of literary perspective, Emerson, Thoreau, Hawthorne, Melville, and Whitman share certain beliefs. Common to all these writers is their
(5) humanistic perspective. Its basic premises are that humans are the spiritual center of the universe and that in them alone is the clue to nature, history, and ultimately the cosmos itself. Without denying outright the existence either of a deity or of brute
(10) matter, this perspective nevertheless rejects them as exclusive principles of interpretation and prefers to explain humans and the world in terms of humanity itself. This preference is expressed most clearly in the Transcendentalist principle
(15) that the structure of the universe literally duplicates the structure of the individual self; therefore, all knowledge begins with self-knowledge.

This common perspective is almost always universalized. Its emphasis is not upon the
(20) individual as a particular European or American, but upon the human as universal, freed from the accidents of time, space, birth, and talent. Thus, for Emerson, the "American Scholar" turns out to be simply "Man Thinking"; while, for Whitman,
(25) the "Song of Myself" merges imperceptibly into a song of all the "children of Adam," where "every atom belonging to me as good belongs to you."

Also common to all five writers is the belief that individual virtue and happiness depend upon
(30) self-realization, which, in turn, depends upon the harmonious reconciliation of two universal psychological tendencies: first, the self-asserting impulse of the individual to withdraw, to remain unique and separate, and to be responsible only to
(35) himself or herself, and second, the self-transcending impulse of the individual to embrace the whole world in the experience of a single moment and to know and become one with that world. These conflicting impulses can be seen in the
(40) democratic ethic. Democracy advocates individualism, the preservation of the individual's freedom and self-expression. But the democratic self is torn between the duty to self, which is implied by the concept of liberty, and the duty to society,
(45) which is implied by the concepts of equality and fraternity.

A third assumption common to the five writers is that intuition and imagination offer a surer road to truth than does abstract logic or scientific
(50) method. It is illustrated by their emphasis upon introspection—their belief that the clue to external nature is to be found in the inner world of individual psychology—and by their interpretation of experience as, in essence, symbolic. Both these stresses
(55) presume an organic relationship between the self and the cosmos of which only intuition and imagination can properly take account. These writers' faith in the imagination and in themselves as practitioners of imagination led them to conceive
(60) of the writer as a seer and enabled them to achieve supreme confidence in their own moral and metaphysical insights.

17. The author's discussion of Emerson, Thoreau, Hawthorne, Melville, and Whitman is primarily concerned with explaining

(A) some of their beliefs about the difficulties involved in self-realization
(B) some of their beliefs concerning the world and the place that humanity occupies in the universal order
(C) some of their beliefs concerning the relationship between humanism and democracy
(D) the way some of their beliefs are shaped by differences in temperament and literary outlook
(E) the effects of some of their beliefs on their writings

18. According to the passage, the humanistic perspective of the five writers presupposes which of the following?

    I. The structure of the universe can be discovered through self-knowledge.
    II. The world can be explained in terms of humanity.
    III. The spiritual and the material worlds are incompatible.

(A) I only
(B) II only
(C) I and II only
(D) II and III only
(E) I, II, and III

19. The author quotes Whitman primarily in order to

(A) show that the poet does not agree with Emerson
(B) indicate the way the poet uses the humanist ideal to praise himself
(C) suggest that the poet adapts the basic premises of humanism to his own individual outlook on the world
(D) illustrate a way the poet expresses the relationship of the individual to the humanistic universe
(E) demonstrate that the poet is concerned with the well-being of all humans

GO ON TO THE NEXT PAGE.

20. According to the passage, the five writers object to the scientific method primarily because they think it

   (A) is not the best way to obtain an understanding of the relationship between the individual and the cosmos

   (B) is so specialized that it leads to an understanding of separate parts of the universe but not of the relationships among those parts

   (C) cannot provide an adequate explanation of intuition and imagination

   (D) misleads people into believing they have an understanding of truth, when they do not

   (E) prevents people from recognizing the symbolic nature of experience

21. Which of the following statements would be compatible with the beliefs of the five writers as described in the passage?

   I. Democracy works as a form of government because every individual is unique.

   II. Nature alone exists, and each person is nothing more than a shadow of that substance which is the world.

   III. The human mind is capable of discovering the meaning of life and understanding the order in the universe.

   (A) I only

   (B) III only

   (C) I and II only

   (D) I and III only

   (E) I, II, and III

22. It can be inferred that intuition is important to the five writers primarily because it provides them with

   (A) information useful for understanding abstract logic and scientific method

   (B) the discipline needed in the search for truth

   (C) inspiration for their best writing

   (D) clues to the interpretation of symbolic experience

   (E) the means of resolving conflicts between the self and the world

23. The author discusses "the democratic ethic" (lines 39-46) in order to

   (A) explain the relationship between external experience and inner imagination

   (B) support the notion that the self contains two conflicting and irreconcilable factions

   (C) illustrate the relationship between the self's desire to be individual and its desire to merge with all other selves

   (D) elaborate on the concept that the self constantly desires to realize its potential

   (E) give an example of the idea that, in order to be happy, the self must reconcile its desires with external reality

24. It can be inferred that the idea of "an organic relationship between the self and the cosmos" (lines 55-56) is necessary to the thinking of the five writers because such a relationship

   (A) enables them to assert the importance of the democratic ethic

   (B) justifies their concept of the freedom of the individual

   (C) sustains their faith in the existence of a deity

   (D) is the foundation of their humanistic view of existence

   (E) is the basis for their claim that the writer is a seer

25. The passage is most relevant to which of the following areas of study?

   (A) Aesthetics and logic

   (B) History and literature

   (C) Theology and sociology

   (D) Anthropology and political science

   (E) Linguistics and art

S T O P

IF YOU FINISH BEFORE TIME IS CALLED, YOU MAY CHECK YOUR WORK ON THIS SECTION ONLY.
DO NOT WORK ON ANY OTHER SECTION IN THE TEST.

SECTION VI

Time—30 minutes

20 Questions

Directions: In this section solve each problem, using any available space on the page for scratchwork. Then indicate the best of the answer choices given.

Numbers: All numbers used are real numbers.

Figures: Figures that accompany problems in this test are intended to provide information useful in solving the problems. They are drawn as accurately as possible EXCEPT when it is stated in a specific problem that its figure is not drawn to scale. All figures lie in a plane unless otherwise indicated.

1. An investor purchased x shares of stock at a certain price. If the stock then increased in price $0.25 per share and the total increase for the x shares was $12.50, how many shares of stock had been purchased?

   (A) 25   (B) 50   (C) 75   (D) 100   (E) 125

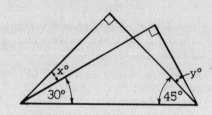

2. If $x > 0$ and $x^2 = 161$, what is the best whole number approximation of x ?

   (A) 13   (B) 18   (C) 41   (D) 80   (E) 2,560

3. In the figure above, what is the value of 2x − y ?

   (A) 0   (B) 15   (C) 30   (D) 45   (E) 60

GO ON TO THE NEXT PAGE.

4. $\dfrac{\dfrac{1}{2}\left(\dfrac{\dfrac{3}{4}}{\dfrac{2}{3}}\right)}{\dfrac{2}{9}} =$

(A) $\dfrac{81}{32}$ (B) $\dfrac{9}{4}$ (C) $\dfrac{9}{8}$ (D) $\dfrac{1}{8}$ (E) $\dfrac{1}{18}$

5. At a special sale, 5 tickets can be purchased for the price of 3 tickets. If 5 tickets are purchased at this sale, the amount saved will be what percent of the original price of the 5 tickets?

(A)   20%

(B) $33\dfrac{1}{3}\%$

(C)   40%

(D)   60%

(E) $66\dfrac{2}{3}\%$

6. Which of the following is equal to $\dfrac{3}{8}$ of 1.28 ?

(A) $\dfrac{24}{5}$

(B) $\dfrac{12}{25}$

(C) $\dfrac{13}{50}$

(D) $\dfrac{6}{25}$

(E) $\dfrac{4}{25}$

GO ON TO THE NEXT PAGE.

7. Working independently, Tina can do a certain job in 12 hours. Working independently, Ann can do the same job in 9 hours. If Tina works independently at the job for 8 hours and then Ann works independently, how many hours will it take Ann to complete the remainder of the job?

(A) $\frac{2}{3}$ (B) $\frac{3}{4}$ (C) 1 (D) 2 (E) 3

8. A factory normally produces x units per working day. In a month with 22 working days, no units are produced in the first y working days because of a strike. How many units must be produced per day on each of the rest of the working days of the month in order to have an average of x units per working day for the entire month?

(A) 11x

(B) 22x

(C) $\frac{22x}{y}$

(D) $\frac{22x}{22-y}$

(E) $\frac{22x}{22xy-y}$

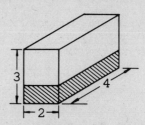

9. An enclosed rectangular tank with dimensions 2 meters by 3 meters by 4 meters is filled with water to a depth of 1 meter as shown by the shaded region in the figure above. If the tank is turned so that it rests on one of its smallest faces, the depth, in meters, of the water will be

(A) $\frac{2}{3}$ (B) 1 (C) $\frac{4}{3}$ (D) $\frac{5}{3}$ (E) 2

GO ON TO THE NEXT PAGE

Week	Number of Tickets Sold
1	1,000,000
2	1,000,000
3	750,000
4	250,000

10. A person bought a ticket to a ball game for $15 and later sold the ticket for $60. What was the percent increase in the price of the ticket?

(A)   25%

(B) 33 $\frac{1}{3}$ %

(C)   75%

(D)   300%

(E)   400%

11. A decorator bought a bolt of defective cloth that he judged to be $\frac{3}{4}$ usable, in which case the cost would be $0.80 per usable yard. If it was later found that only $\frac{2}{3}$ of the bolt could be used, what was the actual cost per usable yard?

(A) $0.60
(B) $0.90
(C) $1.00
(D) $1.20
(E) $1.70

12. The table above shows the number of tickets sold during each of the first 4 weeks after a movie was released. The producer of the movie received 10 percent of the revenue from every ticket sold with a guaranteed minimum of $200,000 per week for the first 4 weeks. If tickets sold for $4 each, how much did the producer receive for the first 4 weeks?

(A) $800,000
(B) $900,000
(C) $1,000,000
(D) $1,200,000
(E) $1,300,000

13. If x, y, and z are single-digit integers and $100(x) + 1,000(y) + 10(z) = N$, what is the units' digit of the number N ?

(A) 0   (B) 1   (C) x   (D) y   (E) z

GO ON TO THE NEXT PAGE.

14. Three stacks containing equal numbers of chips are to be made from 9 red chips, 7 blue chips, and 5 green chips. If all of these chips are used and each stack contains at least 1 chip of each color, what is the maximum number of red chips in any one stack?

(A) 7
(B) 6
(C) 5
(D) 4
(E) 3

15. Three automobiles travel distances that are in the ratios of $1:2:3$. If the ratios of the traveling times over these distances for these automobiles are $3:2:1$ in the same respective order, what are the ratios of their respective average speeds?

(A) $1:1:1$
(B) $1:2:3$
(C) $1:3:9$
(D) $3:2:1$
(E) $3:4:3$

16. Over the last three years a scientist had an average (arithmetic mean) yearly income of $45,000. The scientist earned $1\frac{1}{2}$ times as much the second year as the first year and $2\frac{1}{2}$ times as much the third year as the first year. What was the scientist's income the second year?

(A) $9,000
(B) $13,500
(C) $27,000
(D) $40,500
(E) $45,000

17. How many two-digit whole numbers yield a remainder of 1 when divided by 10 and also yield a remainder of 1 when divided by 6?

(A) None   (B) One   (C) Two
(D) Three   (E) Four

GO ON TO THE NEXT PAGE.

18. If $x \neq 3$ and $\dfrac{x^2 - 9}{2y} = \dfrac{x - 3}{4}$, then, in terms of y, $x =$

(A) $\dfrac{y - 6}{2}$

(B) $\dfrac{y - 3}{2}$

(C) $y - 3$

(D) $y - 6$

(E) $\dfrac{y + 6}{2}$

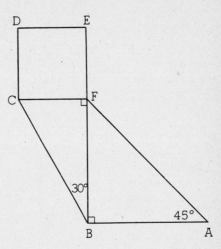

20. In the figure above, square CDEF has area 4. What is the area of $\triangle ABF$?

(A) $2\sqrt{2}$ (B) $2\sqrt{3}$ (C) 4   (D) $3\sqrt{3}$ (E) 6

19. The figure above shows the shape of a sign to be placed in front of a flower store. The sign has a semicircle on each side of the square. If the sign is 3 centimeters thick and if each side of the square is 50 centimeters long, what is the volume, in cubic centimeters, of the sign?

(A) $1,250\pi + 2,500$
(B) $3,750\pi$
(C) $3,750\pi + 7,500$
(D) $5,000\pi + 7,500$
(E) $11,250\pi$

S T O P

IF YOU FINISH BEFORE TIME IS CALLED, YOU MAY CHECK YOUR WORK ON THIS SECTION ONLY.
DO NOT WORK ON ANY OTHER SECTION IN THE TEST.

Answer Key
And Explanatory Material

ANSWER KEY: FORM A

#	SECTION 1	SECTION 2	SECTION 3	SECTION 4	SECTION 5	SECTION 6
1	D	E	D	C	B	C
2	E	C	C	D	C	A
3	A	C	C	B	C	B
4	C	C	A	A	A	A
5	C	A	C	A	C	C
6	D	D	D	C	B	A
7	B	B	A	A	E	E
8	A	A	A	C	A	C
9	A	A	B	D	A	B
10	E	E	D	E	C	E
11	B	C	B	A	C	B
12	B	B	A	A	C	E
13	C	B	C	B	D	A
14	B	A	B	B	B	B
15	C	C	C	C	D	C
16	B	C	A	E	C	C
17	E	E	C	B	B	E
18	D	A	C	E	C	A
19	E	B	D	A	C	C
20	D	B	D	C	A	E
21	A	C	B	E	B	A
22	E	C	E	A	C	A
23	E	C	E	B	B	A
24	A	A	D	E	D	A
25	C	C	D	C	A	A
26	A	E	B	A	A	A
27	A	A	A	A	A	A
28	A	A	A	A	A	A
29	A	A	A	A	A	A
30	A	D	D	A	A	A
31	A	D	A	A	A	A
32	A	C	A	A	A	A
33	A	B	A	A	A	A
34	A	E	A	A	A	A
35	A	D	A	A	A	A

Explanatory Material:
Data Sufficiency

1. What is the value of x?

(1) $5x - 3 = 7$

(2) $\frac{x}{10} = \frac{1}{5}$

Statement (1) implies that $x = 2$. Thus, the answer is A or D. Since statement (2) also implies that $x = 2$, the best answer is D. This is a very easy question.

2. How many students are enrolled in the Groveville Public Schools?

(1) There are 30 students per classroom in the Groveville Public Schools.

(2) The student-teacher ratio is 20 to 1 in the Groveville Public Schools.

Statement (1) alone is insufficient to answer the question asked since you do not know the number of classrooms. Thus, the answer must be B, C, or E. Statement (2) alone also is insufficient because you do not know the number of teachers. Clearly (1) and (2) together are insufficient, so the best answer is E. This is an easy question.

P

3. P is a particle on the circle shown above. What is the length of the path traveled by P in one complete revolution around the circle?

(1) The diameter of the circle is 1.5 meters.

(2) The particle P moves in a clockwise direction at 0.5 meter per second.

Since the circumference of a circle is π times the diameter, statement (1) alone is sufficient. Thus, the answer must be A or D. Statement (2) alone is not sufficient because no information is given concerning the amount of time particle P takes to make one complete revolution. Therefore, the best answer is A. This is an easy question.

4. If the price of potatoes is $0.20 per pound, what is the maximum number of potatoes that can be bought for $1.00?

(1) The price of a bag of potatoes is $2.80.

(2) There are 15 to 18 potatoes in every 5 pounds.

Clearly statement (1) alone is not sufficient to answer the question. Thus, the answer must be B, C, or E. Statement (2) alone is sufficient because 5 pounds of potatoes can be bought for $1.00 and the maximum number of potatoes in 5 pounds is 18. Therefore, B is the best answer. This is an easy question.

5. A sewing store buys fabric X by the bolt at the wholesale price. If each bolt contains 50 meters of fabric X, what is the wholesale price of a bolt of fabric X?

(1) The store sells fabric X for $6.25 per meter.

(2) The store sells fabric X at 25 percent above the wholesale price.

Neither statement (1) alone nor statement (2) alone is sufficient to answer the question; thus, the answer must be C or E. From (1) and (2) together you know that $6.25 equals 1.25 times the wholesale price, or that the wholesale price is $5.00 per meter. Thus, the best answer is C. This is an easy question.

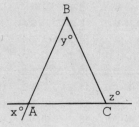

6. In △ABC above, if AB = BC, what is the value of y?

(1) $x = 50$

(2) $z = 130$

From statement (1) you know that the measure of ∠BAC is 50°, since vertical angles have the same measure. Since AB = BC, the measure of ∠BCA is also 50°. Therefore, $y = 180 - (50 + 50)$ or $y = 80$. Thus, the answer is A or D. From statement (2) you know that the measure of ∠BCA is 50° because ∠BCA is a supplement of the angle labeled z°; again you can determine that $y = 80$. Therefore, the best answer is D. This is an easy question.

7. In a sequence of numbers in which each term is 2 more than the preceding term, what is the fourth term?

(1) The last term is 90.

(2) The first term is 2.

Statement (1) alone is not sufficient because you do not know the first term of the sequence nor the number of terms. For example, the sequence 80, 82, 84, 86, 88, 90 and the sequence 82, 84, 86, 88, 90 are both consistent with (1) and the information given in the question; however, the fourth term is different in each of these cases. Thus, the answer must be B, C, or E. From (2) you know that the first four terms are 2, 4, 6, and 8. Therefore, the best answer is B. This is an easy question.

8. How much nitrogen is needed in the mixture used by a lawn maintenance company to fertilize the grass on a certain portion of a golf course?

    (1) The portion of the golf course to be fertilized is 30 meters by 50 meters.

    (2) The amount of fertilizer needed is 40 kilograms, and the fertilizer must be composed of nitrogen, phosphorus, and potash in the proportions 5:7:4, respectively.

Statement (1) alone is clearly insufficient to answer the question since it provides no information about the amount of nitrogen needed. Thus, the answer must be B, C, or E. Statement (2) alone is sufficient: Since the ratios of the three ingredients in the fertilizer are 5:7:4, the amount of nitrogen is 5/16 of 40, or 12.5 kilograms. Therefore, the best answer is B. This is an easy question.

9. A certain alloy contains only lead, copper, and tin. How many pounds of tin are contained in 56 pounds of the alloy?

    (1) By weight the alloy is $\frac{3}{7}$ lead and $\frac{5}{14}$ copper.

    (2) By weight the alloy contains 6 parts lead and 5 parts copper.

From statement (1) you know that the alloy is $\frac{3}{14}$ tin by weight so that $\frac{3}{14} \cdot 56$ or 12 pounds of the alloy is tin. Thus, the answer is A or D. Since statement (2) does not tell you how many parts tin are in the alloy, you cannot answer the question from (2) alone. Therefore, the best answer is A. This is a moderately difficult question.

10. If n is a positive integer, are n and 1 the only positive divisors of n?

    (1) n is less than 14.

    (2) If n is doubled, the result is less than 27.

From statement (1) you do not know whether or not n is a prime number, and thus whether n and 1 are the only positive divisors of n. For example, 1 and 5 are the only positive divisors of 5, but 2 and 3 as well as 1 and 6 are positive divisors of 6. Thus, the answer must be B, C, or E. Since statement (2) is no more restrictive than (1), the best answer is E. This is an easy question.

11. What is the perimeter of $\triangle PQR$?

    (1) The measures of $\angle PQR$, $\angle QRP$, and $\angle RPQ$ are $x°$, $2x°$, and $3x°$, respectively.

    (2) The altitude of $\triangle PQR$ from Q to PR is 4.

For this problem, drawing a figure may be helpful:

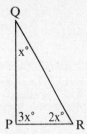

From statement (1) you know that $x = 30$, $2x = 60$, and $3x = 90$, since $6x = 180$; however, you do not know the length of any side, and therefore (1) alone is not sufficient. Thus, the answer must be B, C, or E. Since the perimeter cannot be found given only the length of an altitude, statement (2) alone is insufficient, and the answer must be C or E. From (1) and (2) together, since $\triangle PQR$ is a 30-60-90 right triangle, the

altitude from Q to PR is PQ, so $PQ = 4$; therefore, $PR = \frac{4\sqrt{3}}{3}$, $RQ = \frac{8\sqrt{3}}{3}$, and the best answer is C. This is a moderately difficult question.

12. Two accountants, Rhodes and Smith, went to a business meeting together. Rhodes drove to the meeting and Smith drove back from the meeting. If Rhodes and Smith each drove 140 kilometers, what was the average speed, in kilometers per hours, at which Rhodes drove?

    (1) The average speed at which Smith drove was 70 kilometers per hour.

    (2) Rhodes drove for exactly 2 hours.

Statement (1) alone is clearly insufficient to answer the question because no relationship between the driving speeds of Rhodes and Smith is given. Thus, the answer must be B, C, or E. From statement (2) you know that Rhodes' average driving speed was 140/2 or 70 kilometers per hour. Therefore, the best answer is B. This is an easy question.

13. If ϕ is an operation, is the value of $b \phi c$ greater than 10?

    (1) $x \phi y = x^2 + y^2$ for all x and y.

    (2) $b = 3$ and $c = 2$

Statement (1) alone is not sufficient to answer the question because you do not know the value of b and c; statement (2) alone is not sufficient because you do not know what operation ϕ represents. Thus, the answer must be C or E. From (1) and (2) together you know that $3\phi2 = 3^2 + 2^2 = 13$; therefore, the best answer is C. This is a moderately difficult question.

14. What percent of the employees of Company X are technicians?

    (1) Exactly 40 percent of the men and 55 percent of the women employed by Company X are technicians.

    (2) At Company X, the ratio of the number of technicians to the number of nontechnicians is 9 to 11.

If the number of men employed at Company X is m and the number women is w, then from (1) the ratio of the number of technicians to the total number of employees is $\frac{0.40m + 0.55w}{m + w}$. Since you do not know any relationship between m and w, (1) alone is insufficient. For example, if m = w, then 47.5 percent of the employees are technicians; but if w = 2m, then 50 percent of the employees are technicians. Thus, the answer is B, C, or E. Statement (2) implies that $\frac{9}{20}$, or 45 percent, of the employees are technicians. Therefore, the best answer is B. This is a moderately difficult question.

15. If tank X contains only gasoline, how many kiloliters of gasoline are in tank X?

    (1) If $\frac{1}{2}$ of the gasoline in tank X were pumped out, the tank would be filled to $\frac{1}{3}$ of its capacity.

    (2) If 0.75 kiloliter of gasoline were pumped into tank X, it would be filled to capacity.

From statement (1) you know that the amount of gasoline in the tank is $\frac{2}{3}$ of the tank's capacity, but you do not know the tank's capacity, and so (1) alone is insufficient. Thus, the answer is B, C, or E. From statement (2) you know only that the amount of gasoline in the tank is 0.75 kiloliters less than the tank's capacity, and so (2) alone is insufficient. Therefore, the answer is C or E. If the capacity of the tank is x kiloliters, then (1) and (2) together imply that $x - 0.75 = \frac{2}{3}x$, or x = 2.25 kiloliters. Thus, there are 1.5 kiloliters of gasoline in the tank and the best answer is C. This is a moderately difficult question.

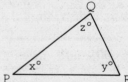

16. In △PQR above is PQ > RP?

    (1) x = y

    (2) y = z

Statement (1) implies that PQ = QR; however, the base PR may or may not equal PQ, and so (1) alone is not sufficient. Thus, the answer must be B, C, or E. Statement (2) implies that PQ = PR, or that PQ is not greater than PR. Therefore, the best answer is B. This is a difficult question.

17. Is the positive integer x an even number?

    (1) If x is divided by 3, the remainder is 2.

    (2) If x is divided by 5, the remainder is 2.

Statement (1) implies that x = 3u + 2, where u is an integer. If u is even, then x is even; but, if u is odd, then x is odd, so (1) alone is not sufficient. Thus, the answer must be B, C, or E. Similarly, statement (2) alone is not sufficient, and the answer must be C or E. From (1) and (2) together you know only that x = 15q + 2, so all that can be concluded is that x and q are both even or both odd. Therefore, the best answer is E. This is a difficult question.

18. Land for a pasture is enclosed in the shape of a 6-sided figure; all sides are the same length and all angles have the same measure. What is the area of the enclosed land?

    (1) Each side is 8 meters long.
    (2) The distance from the center of the land to the midpoint of one of the sides is $4\sqrt{3}$ meters.

For this problem, drawing a figure may be helpful:

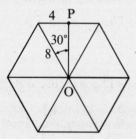

Since six sides have the same length and the six interior angles have the same measure, each of the six triangles shown above is equilateral; therefore, the area of the enclosed land is 6 times the area of any of these triangular regions. From (1) you can determine that the altitude OP shown in the figure has length $4\sqrt{3}$ m and that the area of the enclosed land is $(4\sqrt{3})(4)(6)m^2$, or $9\sqrt{3}$ m². Therefore, the answer must be A or D. Similarly, from (2) you can determine that the length of each side is 8 m, and thus that the total area is $96\sqrt{3}$ m². Thus, the best answer is D. This is a difficult question.

19. In a retail store, the average (arithmetic mean) sale for month M was d dollars. Was the average (arithmetic mean) sale for month J at least 20 percent higher than that for month M?

    (1) For month M, total revenue from sales was $3,500.

    (2) For month J, total revenue from sales was $6,000.

Note that to find the average sale for a month, you need to know the number of sales for the month as well as the total revenue from these sales. Since statements (1) and (2) give only the total revenue from sales for each of the two months, the best answer is E. This is a difficult question.

20. In a certain store, item X sells for 10 percent less than item Y. What is the ratio of the store's revenue from the sales of item X to that from the sales of item Y?

   (1) The store sells 20 percent more units of item Y than of item X.

   (2) The store's revenue from the sales of item X is $6,000 and from the sales of item Y is $8,000.

If the price that item Y sells for is y dollars, then the price that item X sells for is 9y dollars. If the store sells n units of item X, then from (1) you know that it sells 1.2n units of item Y. Thus, the ratio of the revenue from the sales of item X to the revenue from the sales of item Y is $\frac{(0.9y)n}{(1.2n)y}$ or $\frac{3}{4}$.

Thus, the answer must be A or D. Statement (2) alone is sufficient because $\frac{\$6,000}{\$8,000} = \frac{3}{4}$; therefore, the best answer is D. This is a difficult question.

21. During a 3-year period, the profits of Company X changed by what percent from the second year to the third year?

   (1) The increase in profits of Company X from the first year to the second year was the same as the increase from the first year to the third year.

   (2) For Company X, the profits for the first year were $13,800 and the profits for the third year were $15,900.

From statement (1) you know that the profits for the third year amounted to the same as those for the second year, so there was no percent change in profits from the second year to the third year. Thus, the answer must be A or D. Obviously (2) is insufficient, giving no information concerning profits for the second year. Therefore, the best answer is A. This is a difficult question.

22. A pyramidal-shaped box to protect a plant is constructed with 4 lateral faces and an open bottom. What is the lateral area of the box?

   (1) The base of the pyramid is a polygon with all sides of equal length, and the perimeter of the base is 1 meter.

   (2) The lateral faces are isosceles triangles that have the same size and shape.

Statement (1) alone is not sufficient since neither the exact shape of the pyramid nor its height is known. Statement (2) gives additional information about the shape of the pyramid but not enough to determine the shape, and since (2) also does not give any additional numerical data, the answer must be C or E. From (1) and (2) together you still do not know the exact shape of the pyramid nor, more importantly, its height. Therefore, the best answer is E. This is a difficult question.

23. What is the value of $x^2 - y^2$?

   (1) x + y = 2x

   (2) x + y = 0

Note that $x^2 - y^2 = (x + y)(x - y)$ will have a value of 0 if either x + y = 0 or x - y = 0. Since statement (1) implies that x - y = 0, statement (1) alone is sufficient to determine that the value of $x^2 - y^2$ is 0. Thus, the answer must be A or D. Since (2) also implies that $x^2 - y^2 = 0$, the best answer is D. This is a difficult question.

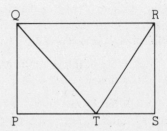

24. In rectangular region PQRS above, T is a point on side PS. If PS = 4, what is the area of region PQRS?

   (1) △QTR is equilateral.

   (2) Segments PT and TS have equal length.

Note that the area of region PQRS is twice the area of △QTR; QP equals the length of the altitude from point T to side QR, and thus the area of △QTR is (½)QP·QR. From statement (1) alone you can determine the area of △QTR and thus the area of region PQRS. Since the altitude from T to side QR is opposite ∠TQR = 60°, it has length $2\sqrt{3}$, and the area of △QTR is $4\sqrt{3}$. Thus, the answer is A or D. Since statement (2) does not imply the length of PQ, the best answer is A. This is a difficult question.

25. Does x = 2?

   (1) x is a number such that $x^2 - 3x + 2 = 0$.

   (2) x is a number such that $x^2 - x - 2 = 0$.

Since $x^2 - 3x + 2 = (x - 2)(x - 1)$, statement (1) implies that x = 2 or x = 1. Since you do not know which of these two values x is equal to, the answer must be B, C, or E. Since $x^2 - x - 2 = (x - 2)(x + 1)$, statement (2) implies that x = -1 or x = 2, so statement (2) alone also is not sufficient, and the answer must be C or E. Together (1) and (2) imply that x = 2; therefore, the best answer is C. This is a difficult question.

Explanatory Material: Analysis of Situations

1. Probability of Supersonics achieving technical success in developing a line of AM-FM radios

The correct classification for this consideration is E, an unimportant issue, because the "Probability of Supersonics achieving technical success in developing a line of AM-FM radios" is irrelevant to the decision. That is, since the task force specifically rejected developing a line of AM-FM radios as a means of increasing sales, the probability of achieving success in this area has no bearing on the task force's decision concerning which of the remaining alternatives to choose. This classification is of medium difficulty.

2. Supersonics' ownership of the equipment needed to conduct tests of frequency response

The correct classification for this consideration is C, a minor factor. The paragraph headed *Criteria* indicates that the cost of the research needed to develop the new product will be an important consideration in choosing an alternative. Since already owning some of the necessary equipment will help reduce the research costs required for the development of an improved loudspeaker, this ownership of necessary equipment is a minor factor that serves to reduce the total research cost required, which is a major factor. This classification is relatively difficult.

3. Advertising campaign needed to persuade audiophiles to purchase automobile stereo systems

The correct classification for this consideration is C, a minor factor. The passage indicates that marketability of an alternative, including the automobile loudspeaker alternative, will be an important criterion. It is reasonable to believe that the marketability will be influenced, especially over a ten-year period, by demographics, popular trends, and other changes. Thus, the need for an effective advertising campaign to capture and maintain the market for high-quality automobile stereo loudspeakers is a factor that contributes to overall marketability. Therefore, this consideration is a minor factor. This classification is relatively difficult.

4. Cost of the research needed to develop a new product

The correct classification for this consideration is B, a major factor. The paragraph on *Criteria* indicates that the cost of research needed to develop a new product will be an important consideration in choosing an alternative. Although minimizing costs is a broad objective, the paragraph on *Criteria* indicates that specific cost areas will be evaluated separately. Thus, the total cost of research would be a major factor. This classification is easy.

5. A relatively low requirement for new capital

The correct classification for this consideration is A, an objective, because the *Introduction* to the task force's report indicates that the task force was guided by the desire to keep "the need for new capital relatively low." Thus, if the task

force was guided by a relatively low requirement for new capital, such a requirement will also be an objective in making the final decision. This classification is very difficult.

6. Supersonics' lack of expertise in the development of products other than stereo equipment

The correct classification for this consideration is D, an assumption. The *Introduction* to the task force's report tells you that the task force limited its discussion to stereo equipment "because we consider development of products in other areas of consumer electronics to be beyond Supersonics' present competence." In other words, Supersonics projects or assumes that it cannot competently develop products other than stereo equipment and this assumption provides a framework for the decision-making process in that it (the assumption) causes the task force to limit the choice of alternatives to stereo equipment. This classification is very difficult.

7. Seriousness of the technical problems that Supersonics' researchers encountered in conducting the original research for Supersonics' current loudspeakers

The correct classification for this consideration is E, an unimportant issue. Supersonics is faced with making a decision about a future product and there is, at best, only a very remote relationship between the company's past technical problems and the decision concerning which new product to select for development. This classification is relatively difficult.

8. Staff currently available at Supersonics who have expertise in conducting research on an improved loudspeaker, an automobile stereo loudspeaker, or a sound enhancer

The correct classification for this consideration is B, a major factor. In the *Introduction* to the task force's report, you are told that the company wishes to avoid expanding the staff. Given this goal, the staff currently available for research on the possible alternatives will be a major factor; the existing staff will be basic in determining which alternative can be developed without additional staff. This idea is further reinforced in the *Criteria* section of the report, where you are told that "the availability at Supersonics of research staff with the expertise necessary to conduct the research" is one of the criteria that will weigh heavily in the final decision. This classification is of medium difficulty.

9. Development of a new stereo product that can be marketed successfully

The correct classification for this consideration is A, an objective, because the opening paragraph tells you that the company wishes to increase its sales and that the market survey indicates this can best be done by developing and successfully marketing a new product. Therefore, one of the goals of the company is to develop a successful new product. This classification is easy.

10. Increase in the proportion of Supersonics' customers who are older than 35

The correct classification for this consideration is E, an unimportant issue, because the increase in customers older than 35 is irrelevant to the decision. Although this population is mentioned in the *Introduction* of the task force's report, an increase in the proportion is neither an objective of the company nor a consideration in evaluating the alternatives. While it is true that the task force seems to project or assume that the proportion will increase, this increase is not used in any way to establish a general framework for the decision, and thus is irrelevant to the decision. This classification is difficult.

11. Merit of an attempt to attract new customers

The correct classification for this consideration is D, an assumption. The *Introduction* to the task force's report indicates that attempting to attract new customers is an objective of the task force. Given this objective, it is logical to conclude that the task force must assume or believe that there is some merit in making this attempt. The merit in the attempt would be that sales might increase. This classification is very difficult.

12. Marketability of the alternatives

The correct classification for this consideration is B, a major factor. The *Criteria* section of the task force's report tells you that "the marketability of the new product over the next ten years" is a criterion that will weigh heavily in selecting the new product. In other words, the marketability of the alternatives is a consideration that is basic in determining the decision. This classification is of medium difficulty.

13. Difficulty for most people of detecting refinements in the frequency response of loudspeakers

The correct classification for this consideration is C, a minor factor. The *Criteria* section of the task force's report tells you that marketability will weigh heavily in selecting the new product, and the discussion of the improved-loudspeaker alternative indicates that a number of factors will influence the marketability of this alternative. One of the factors influencing marketability is that even audiophiles have difficulty in detecting refinements in the frequency response of loudspeakers. Therefore, since marketability is a major factor and since the difficulty of detecting refinements in frequency response will contribute to, that is, detract from, marketability, this consideration is a minor factor. This classification is relatively difficult.

14. Continued business with Supersonics' current customers

The correct classification for this consideration is A, an objective, because in the *Introduction* of the task force's report the marketing staff advises the task force "to work toward retaining these [the current] customers." In other words, one of the goals for Supersonics is continued business with its current customers. This classification is relatively difficult.

15. Preponderance of audiophiles among Supersonics' current customers

The correct classification for this consideration is D, an assumption. The *Introduction* to the task force's report states this assumption explicitly: "We believe that Supersonics' current customer population is composed mainly of 'audiophiles'." In other words, the task force, in setting its goals, assumes or believes that a preponderance of the company's current customers are audiophiles. This assumption sets a framework for the establishment of a goal in that, having assumed this preponderance, the task force sets a goal of choosing a new stereo product that is of high quality and thus appealing to audiophiles. This classification is difficult.

16. Difficulty of simulating concert hall acoustics

The correct classification for this consideration is C, a minor factor. You are told in the *Criteria* section of the task force's report that the cost of research and the time required for research are important considerations in making the decision. The discussion of the sound enhancer tells you that "it is difficult to simulate concert hall acoustics". This difficulty will have a contributing effect on the cost of and the time required for research on the sound enhancer. Since this technical problem contributes to the major considerations of time and cost, it is a minor factor. This classification is relatively difficult.

17. Inclusion of representatives from the research, marketing, finance, and production staffs on the task force

The correct classification for this consideration is E, an unimportant issue. The composition of the task force is not an objective of the decision, a factor in evaluating the alternatives, or an assumption that sets a framework for the decision. This classification is relatively difficult.

18. Efficient use of personnel time

The correct classification for this consideration is A, an objective. The second paragraph of the passage tells you that Veragetti wants a system that will "provide nurses with quick access to all essential medicines and equipment," and that will "minimize the distance that any nurse or orderly would have to travel to obtain supplies. . . ." These outcomes will increase the efficiency with which supplies are handled at Kingwood Hospital. One of Veragetti's objectives, therefore, is to select a system that will permit all members of the hospital staff to waste little or no time when handling supplies or, in other words, to use their work time efficiently. This classification is difficult.

19. Remodeling needed for a new supply system

The correct classification for this consideration is B, a major factor. The third paragraph of the passage tells you explicitly that Veragetti wants to select a system that "would not require extensive remodeling. . . ." Given this goal, the amount of remodeling associated with each proposed alternative will be basic to choosing among them, will be, in other words, a major factor. This classification is relatively difficult.

20. **Amount of difficulty encountered by hospital personnel in transferring essential medicines and equipment from one section of the hospital to another under any of the new supply systems**

The correct classification for this consideration is B, a major factor. The second paragraph of the passage states that the new system must provide nurses with quick access to medicines and equipment, and it should also allow hospital personnel to transfer equipment quickly from one section of the hospital to another. If installing a system that generally facilitates equipment and supply transfer or facilitates access to medicines is a goal, then the system that presents the least difficulty best meets the goal. The degree of difficulty that staff members would encounter in transferring or obtaining equipment and medicines under each of the proposed systems is thus a major factor. This factor must be weighed in order to determine how well any alternative meets the objective of allowing hospital personnel to transfer supplies and equipment "more quickly." This classification is of medium difficulty.

21. **Value of a supply system that is favored by hospital personnel who are directly involved in patient care**

The correct classification for this consideration is D, an assumption. In the second paragraph of the passage, you are told that Veragetti "believed that a suitable supply system would be the one that the majority of the hospital's personnel favored." In other words, Veragetti projects or assumes that there is in fact an actual value in having a system favored by hospital personnel who are directly involved in patient care. This classification is very difficult.

22. **Use of hallways by people other than personnel who are authorized to have access to supplies**

The correct classification for this consideration is C, a minor factor. As the passage states, one of Veragetti's goals for the new supply system is to limit access to potentially dangerous medicines to authorized personnel (see paragraph two). The security of the proposed supply systems is thus a major factor. One possible threat to security would be the accessibility of any storage areas located near hallways. Use of those hallways by patients, visitors, maintenance personnel, and others not authorized to administer medication would compromise security, as would street-level windows in the storage areas, use of glass-fronted cabinets to store medications, and inadequate locks. Since use of the hallways by people without authorized access to potentially dangerous medications is one of several contributory factors to decreased security, this consideration is a minor factor. This classification is relatively difficult.

23. **Determining the types of medication needed by patients at Kingwood Hospital**

The correct classification for this consideration is E, an unimportant issue, because it is irrelevant to the decision being made. The types of medication needed by patients at Kingwood Hospital will be what they are no matter which supply system is chosen, so Veragetti does not seek to determine those types of medication as one of her goals, project them as one of her assumptions, or consider them when weighing alternatives. This classification is relatively difficult.

24. **A supply system that does not require extensive remodeling within Kingwood Hospital**

The correct classification for this consideration is A, an objective, because the passage tells you specifically that Veragetti wants to recommend a system that "would not require extensive remodeling. . . ." She bases this goal on her supposition or projection that the hospital's directors will be unwilling to defray the cost of a major remodeling job. This classification is relatively difficult.

25. **Type of supply system favored by the majority of the hospital's personnel**

The correct classification for this consideration is B, a major factor. In the opening paragraph of the passage, you are told that Veragetti has been retained "to determine what type of supply system would best suit the needs of Kingwood Hospital." In the second paragraph, the passage states that Veragetti "believed that a suitable supply system would be one that the majority of the hospital's personnel favored." On the basis of that belief, Veragetti surveys all hospital personnel directly involved in patient care to learn their preferences. She then uses the information obtained from that survey to help evaluate the three alternatives she is considering. Because the preferences of staff members are treated by Veragetti as basic to her decision, and because they bear directly on her goal of selecting a system that the majority of the staff will favor, this consideration is a major factor. This classification is difficult.

26. **Length of time needed to build the new wing**

The correct classification for this consideration is E, an unimportant issue, because it has no bearing on the decision Veragetti is making now. The new wing has already been completed, so its construction time is a fact, not a supposition, a projection, or a prospective result of any decision concerning a new supply system. Veragetti does not consider the length of time needed to build the new wing when evaluating possible new supply systems. This classification is easy.

27. **Quick access to essential medicines and equipment**

The correct classification for this consideration is A, an objective, because the passage explicitly identifies "quick access" for nurses to the medicines and equipment they need as a desired outcome of the decision. In addition, you are told in the second paragraph that Veragetti desires to minimize travel distance for both nurses and orderlies as well as transfer time between sections. Both of these considerations would result in quicker access to essential medicines and equipment not only for nurses but also for other hospital personnel. In other words, one of the results Veragetti is seeking by her decision is to make supplies immediately available to staff members who need them. This classification is relatively difficult.

28. **Length of shift worked by nurses and orderlies under each of the alternatives**

The correct classification for this consideration is E, an unimportant issue. The length of the shifts worked by nurses and orderlies at Kingwood Hospital is not relevant to Veragetti's decision. Veragetti does not identify shift length as one of her goals, nor does she make projections or suppositions about shift length before developing a set of factors that she will consider. She does not include shift length among the variables to be weighed in making her decision. Because the passage does not state or imply a relationship between shift length and the type of supply system chosen, this consideration is an unimportant issue. This classification is easy.

29. **Restricted access to potentially dangerous medicines**

The correct classification for this consideration is A, an objective. The second paragraph of the passage states explicitly that "a supply system would have to be set up so that only authorized personnel would have access to potentially dangerous medicines." In other words, Veragetti seeks to restrict access to potentially dangerous medicines to those staff members authorized to handle such medicines. Because restricting access to potentially dangerous medicines is one of the outcomes Veragetti hopes to achieve by her decision, it is an objective. This classification is difficult.

30. **Future population increase in area around Kingwood Hospital**

The correct classification for this consideration is D, an assumption, because you are told in the second paragraph that Veragetti "expected the population of the area to increase." Anticipating such an increase, and projecting it as part of her early planning for the decision, helps to establish the context in which the choice of a suitable supply system will be made. That is, Veragetti's supposition that a population increase will occur leads her to set a goal of choosing "a supply system that would be able to accommodate the increase." This classification is of medium difficulty.

31. **Disinclination of directors to budget much money for remodeling as a result of expenses incurred when the new wing was built**

The correct classification for this consideration is D, an assumption. In the third paragraph of the passage, you are told that conversations with the hospital's directors "led Veragetti to believe that the cost of building the new wing would probably make the directors reluctant to spend much money on more construction or other new expenses." This belief, or supposition, on Veragetti's part helps to create a framework for the decision she must make. On the basis of that supposition, she formulates two goals—a supply system that will require little or no remodeling and one that will not require hiring additional staff. This classification is relatively difficult.

32. **Availability of office space on the ground floor**

The correct classification for this consideration is C, a minor factor. One of Veragetti's goals is to minimize remodeling costs. Therefore, it is logical that the amount of remodeling that would be required under each of the alternatives is a major factor in her decision. One secondary consideration that bears on the amount of remodeling necessary is the availability of alternative space for displaced staff members if existing offices are converted to storage areas. The fact that such space already exists and would not have to be built is thus a minor factor in the decision, bearing on the total remodeling cost. This classification is of medium difficulty.

33. **Number of additional hospital personnel likely to be required by a new supply system**

The correct classification for this consideration is B, a major factor. You are told in the third paragraph that Veragetti has as one of her goals "a supply system that would not require . . . the addition of new personnel." Since one of her goals is to avoid hiring new staff, the number of new staff that would probably be required for a new supply system is a major consideration that must be taken into account when evaluating each of the alternative systems. This classification is relatively difficult.

34. **Anticipated size of Kingwood Hospital's budget for medicines**

The correct classification for this consideration is E, an unimportant issue, because the size of Kingwood Hospital's budget for medicines has no direct or indirect bearing on the decision Veragetti must make. She does not project the size of the budget for medicines as an assumption, nor does she apply it to the alternatives as one of the relevant variables. She is anxious to avoid budget increases for staff salaries and new construction, both of which bear directly on the cost of funding a new supply system, but there is no evidence in the passage that a relationship exists between the factors relevant to choosing a new supply system and the budget for part of the supplies inventory. This classification is of medium difficulty.

35. Unsatisfactoriness of a storage area in which access to supplies cannot be carefully controlled

The correct classification for this consideration is D, an assumption. In the second paragraph you are told that Veragetti "realized that a supply system would have to be set up so that only authorized personnel would have access to potentially dangerous medicines." To put it another way, she presupposes that a system accessible to unauthorized personnel would be unsatisfactory. Using that supposition as a basis, she formulates the goal of a system that provides a secure area for potentially dangerous medicines, and she then considers the potential security of each of the proposed systems. This classification is very difficult.

Explanatory Material: Problem Solving I

1. A national travel survey in 1977 found that Americans took 382.6 million trips within the United States. California was the destination of 38 million trips. Approximately what percent of the trips had California as the destination?

(A) 0.01%   (B) 0.1%   (C) 1%
(D) 3.8%   (E) 10%

By rounding 382.6 to 380, it can readily be seen that 38 million is approximately 1/10 or 10 percent of 382.6 million. Thus, the best answer is E. This is an easy question.

2. How many of the integers between 25 and 45 are even?

(A) 21   (B) 20   (C) 11   (D) 10   (E) 9

The even integers between 25 and 45 are 2(13), 2(14), . . ., 2(22). Thus, there are as many even integers between 25 and 45 as there are consecutive integers between 12 and 23. It may be faster to jot them down and count, or to think: 22 integers minus the first 12 integers is 10 integers. Thus, the best answer is D. This is an easy question.

3. If taxi fares were \$1.00 for the first $\frac{1}{5}$ mile and \$0.20 for each $\frac{1}{5}$ mile thereafter, then the taxi fare for a 3-mile ride was

(A) \$1.56
(B) \$2.40
(C) \$3.00
(D) \$3.80
(E) \$4.20

The 3-mile trip can be thought of as fifteen $\frac{1}{5}$-mile segments.

Then the fare would be \$1.00 for the first segment plus \$0.20(14) for the remaining fourteen segments of the trip, or \$1.00 + \$2.80 = \$3.80. Thus, the best answer is D. This is an easy question.

4. A computer routine was developed to generate two numbers, (x, y), the first being a random number between 0 and 100 inclusive, and the second being less than or equal to the square root of the first. Each of the following pairs satisfies this routine EXCEPT

(A) (99, 10)
(B) (85, 9)
(C) (50, 7)
(D) (1, 1)
(E) (1, 0)

On examination of each of the choices, it is noted that $10 > \sqrt{99}$, $9 < \sqrt{85}$, $7 < \sqrt{50}$, $1 = \sqrt{1}$, and $0 < \sqrt{1}$. A is the only option containing a second number that is NOT less than or equal to the square root of the first number. Thus, the best answer is A. This is an easy question.

5. A warehouse had a square floor with area 10,000 square meters. A rectangular addition was built along one entire side of the warehouse that increased the floor area by one-half as much as the original floor area. How many meters did the addition extend beyond the original building?

(A) 10   (B) 20   (C) 50   (D) 200   (E) 500

Since the floor was square, the sides of the floor were $\sqrt{10,000}$ or 100 meters. Since the rectangular addition was made on one entire side of the square, its width can be found by using the area formula $A = lw$: $\frac{10,000}{2} = 100w$ and $w = 50$. Thus, the best answer is C. This is an easy question.

6. A digital wristwatch was set accurately at 8:30 a.m., and then lost 2 seconds every 5 minutes. What time was indicated on the watch at 6:30 p.m. of the same day if the watch operated continuously until that time?

(A) 5:56
(B) 5:58
(C) 6:00
(D) 6:23
(E) 6:26

If the watch lost 2 seconds every 5 minutes, it lost $2\left(\frac{60 \text{ min}}{5 \text{ min}}\right)$ or 24 seconds every hours. From 8:30 a.m. until 6:30 p.m., a total of 10 hours elapsed and the watch lost a total of (24 sec/hr)(10 hrs) or 240 seconds. Therefore, the watch lost $\frac{240 \text{ sec}}{60 \text{ sec/min}}$ or 4 minutes in all. At 6:30 p.m., the watch showed 6:26. Thus, the best answer is E. This is an easy question.

7. If x and y are integers and xy = 5, then $(x + y)^2 =$

(A) 13 (B) 16 (C) 25 (D) 26 (E) 36

Since x and y are integers and the product xy equals 5, a positive prime number, x and y must be either −1 and −5 or 1 and 5. Regardless of which pair of values x and y have, $(x + y)^2 = 36$. Thus, the best answer is E. This is a moderately difficult question.

Questions 8-9 refer to the following graphs.

REVENUE FOR STORE X DURING WEEK 1

Distribution of Total Revenue

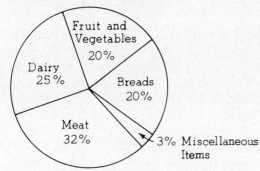

Amount of Revenue from Dairy Products

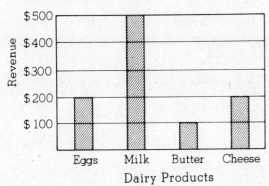

8. During week 1, revenue from eggs provided what percent of the total revenue for Store X?

(A) 4%
(B) 5%
(C) 8%
(D) 20%
(E) 25%

From the bar graph, it can be determined that total revenue from dairy products was $200 + $500 + $100 + $200 = $1,000, and the revenue from eggs was $\frac{200}{1,000}$ or $\frac{1}{5}$ of the total for dairy products. The circle graph shows that 25 percent of the store's revenue was from dairy products. Therefore, revenue from eggs provided $\frac{1}{5}$ of 25 percent or 5 percent of the total revenues for store X. Thus, the best answer is B. This is a moderately difficult question.

9. If the revenue from the sale of apples was equal to the revenue from the sale of miscellaneous items, what percent of the revenue from the sale of fruit and vegetables was accounted for by apples?

(A) 60%
(B) 15%
(C) 12%
(D) 6%
(E) 3%

Let t represent the total revenue. The circle graph shows that revenue from the sale of miscellaneous items (or apples) was 0.03t and revenue from fruits and vegetables was 0.20t. Therefore, revenue from the sale of apples as a percent of revenues from the sale of fruits and vegetables was $\frac{0.03t}{0.20t} = \frac{3}{20} = 15\%$. Thus, the best answer is B. This is a moderately difficult question.

10. The (x, y) pair (−1, 1) satisfies which of the following equations?

 I. $2x^3 - y^2 = -3$
 II. $2x^2 - y^3 = 1$
 III. $x^2 - 2y^3 = -1$

(A) I only
(B) I and II only
(C) I and III only
(D) II and III only
(E) I, II, and III

By substituting −1 for x and 1 for y in each of the equations, it can be verified that (−1,1) satisfies all three equations:

 I. $2(-1)^3 - 1^2 = -2 - 1 = -3$
 II. $2(-1)^2 - (1)^3 = 2 - 1 = 1$
 III. $(-1)^2 - 2(1)^3 = 1 - 2 = -1$

Thus, the best answer is E. This is a moderately difficult question.

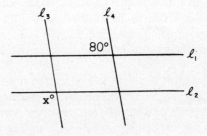

Note: Figure not drawn to scale.

11. If $\ell_1 \parallel \ell_2$ in the figure above, what is the value of x?

(A) 80
(B) 90
(C) 100
(D) 120
(E) It cannot be determined from the information given.

-201-

Since the problem states that ℓ_1 is parallel to ℓ_2 and the figure shows that ℓ_4 intersects these parallel lines at an 80-degree angle, all of the angles associated with lines ℓ_1, ℓ_2, and ℓ_4 measure either 80 degrees or 100 degrees. However, since no information is given about the slope of line ℓ_3, the value of x could be any number between 0 and 180. Thus, the best answer is E. This is a moderately difficult question.

12. A 5-liter jug contains 4 liters of a saltwater solution that is 15 percent salt. If 1.5 liters of the solution spills out of the jug, and the jug is then filled to capacity with water, approximately what percent of the resulting solution in the jug is salt?

(A) $7\frac{1}{2}\%$

(B) $9\frac{3}{8}\%$

(C) $10\frac{1}{2}\%$

(D) 12%

(E) 15%

At the outset the jug contains 4 liters of the solution, but 1.5 liters are spilled, leaving only 2.5 liters. If 15 percent of the solution is salt, the jug contains 0.15(2.5) = 0.375 liters of salt. When water is added to fill the jug to capacity, the jug will contain 5 liters of a weaker solution. Since no salt was added, there is still 0.375 liters of salt in the weaker solution.

Therefore, the resulting solution contains $\frac{0.375}{5}$ = 7.5% salt.

Thus, the best answer is A. This is a moderately difficult question.

13. The average (arithmetic mean) of 3 different positive integers is 100 and the largest of these 3 integers is 120. What is the least possible value of the smallest of these 3 integers?

(A) 1 (B) 10 (C) 61 (D) 71 (E) 80

If the average of three integers is 100, then the sum of the three integers is 3(100) or 300. If the largest of the three is 120, then the sum of the other two must be 300 − 120 = 180. Suppose that x is the smaller of the two integers and y is the larger. Now x will assume its least value when y assumes its greatest value since x + y = 180. Since 120 is the greatest of the three integers, y can assume a maximum value of 119, and the least possible value of x is 180 − 119 = 61. Thus, the best answer is C. This is a moderately difficult question.

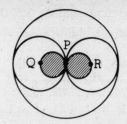

14. In the figure above, the five circles have points in common as shown. P is the center of the largest circle, Q and R are centers of the medium-sized circles, and Q, P, and R are points on a straight line. What fraction of the largest circular region is shaded?

(A) $\frac{1}{16}$ (B) $\frac{1}{8}$ (C) $\frac{3}{16}$ (D) $\frac{1}{4}$ (E) $\frac{1}{2}$

Since points Q, P, and R are points on a line and P is the center of the largest circle, Q, P, and R lie on the diameter of the largest circle and also on the diameters of the four smaller circles. Thus, it becomes obvious that the diameter of the largest circle is 4 times the diameter of one of the smallest circles; similarly the radius of the largest circle is 4 times the radius of the smallest circle. Therefore, if the radius of the smallest circle is r, the radius of the largest circle is 4r and the ratio of the area of the shaded region to the area of the largest circle is

$$\frac{2(\pi r^2)}{\pi (4r)^2} = \frac{2\pi r^2}{16\pi r^2} = \frac{1}{8}.$$

Thus, the best answer is B. This is a moderately difficult question.

15. If xyz ≠ 0 and x percent of y percent of z is t, then z =

(A) $\frac{100t}{xy}$

(B) $\frac{1,000t}{xy}$

(C) $\frac{10,000t}{xy}$

(D) $\frac{xy}{10,000t}$

(E) $\frac{10,000xy}{t}$

x percent of y percent of z is equivalent to $\left(\frac{x}{100}\right)\left(\frac{y}{100}\right) z$, which is equal to t. If $\frac{xyz}{10,000}$ = t, then xyz = 10,000t and z = $\frac{10,000t}{xy}$. Thus, the best answer is C. This is a difficult question.

16. A plane traveled k miles in the first 96 minutes of flight time. If it completed the remaining 300 miles of the trip in t minutes, what was its average speed, in miles per hour, for the entire trip?

(A) $\dfrac{60(k + 300)}{96 + t}$

(B) $\dfrac{kt + 96(300)}{96t}$

(C) $\dfrac{k + 300}{60(96 + t)}$

(D) $\dfrac{5k}{8} + \dfrac{60(300)}{t}$

(E) $\dfrac{5k}{8} + 5t$

The average speed, in miles per hour, for the entire trip is equal to the total distance in miles (k + 300) divided by the total time in hours, $\left(\dfrac{96 + t}{60}\right)$ or $\dfrac{k + 300}{\frac{96 + t}{60}}$. The division can be simplified by multiplying both the numerator and denominator by 60 and obtaining $\dfrac{60(k + 300)}{96 + t}$. Thus, the best answer is A. This is a difficult question.

17. A merchant sells an item at a 20 percent discount, but still makes a gross profit of 20 percent of the cost. What percent of the cost would the gross profit on the item have been if it had been sold without the discount?

(A) 20%
(B) 40%
(C) 50%
(D) 60%
(E) 75%

Let x represent the price before the 20 percent discount and let c represent the cost. Then the merchant sold the item for 0.8x, which was equal to 120% of the cost c. Algebraically, the relationship is 0.8x = 1.2c and x = 1.5c = cost plus 50% profit. Thus, had the item been sold at the original price, the gross profit would have been 50 percent of the cost. Thus, the best answer is C. This is a difficult question.

18. A milliner bought a job lot of hats, $\frac{1}{4}$ of which were brown. The milliner sold $\frac{2}{3}$ of the hats including $\frac{4}{5}$ of the brown hats. What fraction of the unsold hats were brown?

(A) $\frac{1}{60}$ (B) $\frac{2}{15}$ (C) $\frac{3}{20}$ (D) $\frac{3}{5}$ (E) $\frac{3}{4}$

Let t be the total number of hats in the lot. Then, from the information in the problem, the following table of values can be assembled:

Hats sold: $\frac{2t}{3}$	Brown hats: $\frac{1}{4}t$
Hats unsold: $\left(t - \dfrac{2t}{3}\right) = \dfrac{t}{3}$	Brown hats sold: $\dfrac{4}{5}\left(\dfrac{t}{4}\right) = \dfrac{t}{5}$
	Brown hats unsold: $\dfrac{1}{5}\left(\dfrac{t}{4}\right) = \dfrac{t}{20}$

To find the fraction of the unsold hats that were brown, it is necessary to take the ratio of brown hats unsold $\left(\dfrac{t}{20}\right)$ to total unsold hats $\left(\dfrac{t}{3}\right)$. The ratio $\dfrac{t}{20} : \dfrac{t}{3} = \dfrac{3}{20}$. Thus, the best answer is C. This is a difficult question.

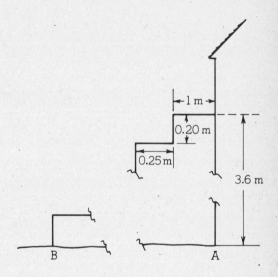

Note: Figure not drawn to scale.

19. Each step of a staircase is 0.25 meter wide and 0.20 meter high, as shown in the figure above. All angles shown in the figure are right angles. If the height of the staircase is 3.6 meters and the landing at the top of the staircase is 1 meter wide, how long, in meters, is AB?

(A) 3.0
(B) 4.25
(C) 4.5
(D) 5.25
(E) 5.5

The sum of the widths of the steps, including the landing, is equal to the length of AB. This can be seen by projecting the width of each step onto segment AB. Therefore, to find the length of AB, it is sufficient to find the number of steps, each 0.25 meters wide, and then to add on the 1-meter width of the landing at the top. Since the rise (total height) up to the last step before the landing is 3.6 − 0.20 or 3.4 meters, you can find the number of steps by dividing this total height by the height of each step. Thus, $3.4 \div 0.20 = 17$ steps, and length AB is $17(0.25) + 1 = 5.25$ meters. Thus, the best answer is D. This is a difficult question.

20. How many integers n greater than 10 and less than 100 are there such that, if the digits of n are reversed, the resulting integer is n + 9?

(A) 5 (B) 6 (C) 7 (D) 8 (E) 9

To solve a problem that involves the digits of a number, it is convenient to let t represent the tens' digit and u represent the units' digit. Since n is between 10 and 100, n is a two-digit number that has the value $10t + u$ and $n + 9$ can be represented by the expression $(10t + u) + 9$. If the digits of n are reversed, the value of the resulting integer will be $10u + t$. According to the problem, $10u + t = n + 9$ or $10u + t = (10t + u) + 9$, which simplifies to $u = t + 1$. In other words, n must be a two-digit number in which the units' digit is one more than the tens' digit. The eight numbers that have this property are 12, 23, 34, 45, 56, 67, 78, and 89. Thus, the best answer is D. This is a difficult question.

Explanatory Material: Sentence Correction

1. Never before in the history of music have musical superstars been able to command so extraordinary fees of the kind they do today.

(A) so extraordinary fees of the kind they do today
(B) so extraordinary fees as they are today
(C) such extraordinary fees as they do today
(D) such extraordinary fees of the kind today's have
(E) so extraordinary a fee of the kind they can today

The correct form of expression will include the phrase *such extraordinary fees as*. In A, B, and E, *so* in place of *such* produces the ungrammatical phrase *so. . .fees* where *such. . .fees* is required. Also, *do* is needed to complete the verb *command: are* in B and *have* in D produce the ungrammatical verb forms *are command* and *have command*. Finally *as*, not *of the kind*, correctly completes the construction begun by *such*. C is the answer to this easy question.

2. As it becomes more frequent to have spouses who both work outside the home, companies are beginning to help in finding new employment for the spouses of transferred employees.

(A) it becomes more frequent to have spouses who both work outside the home
(B) it becomes more frequent to have couples both working outside the home
(C) it becomes more common that both husband and wife should be working outside the home
(D) it becomes more common for both husband and wife to work outside the home
(E) couples in which both of the spouses working outside the home become more common

The phrasing of A and B is imprecise: *frequent* describes an event that recurs often; *common* is needed here to describe a general condition. Also, it is not clear who is *to have* the spouses. In B, *couples* creates an additional problem; the intended meaning is that both *spouses* (two people) work outside the home, not that both *couples* (four people) do. C is wordy and potentially ambiguous in that *should be working* could be read as *ought to work*. E, wordy and garbled, does not clearly indicate what it is that is becoming common—*couples, spouses,* or households in which both husband and wife work outside the home. D is correct for this fairly easy question.

3. Like the one reputed to live in Loch Ness, also an inland lake connected to the ocean by a river, inhabitants of the area around Lake Champlain claim sightings of a long and narrow "sea monster."

(A) Like the one reputed to live in Loch Ness, also an inland lake connected to the ocean by a river, inhabitants of the area around Lake Champlain claim sightings of a long and narrow "sea monster."
(B) Inhabitants of the area around Lake Champlain claim sightings of a long and narrow "sea monster" similar to the one reputed to live in Loch Ness, which, like Lake Champlain, is an inland lake connected to the ocean by a river.
(C) Inhabitants of the area around Lake Champlain claim sightings of a long and narrow "sea monster" similar to Loch Ness's, which, like Lake Champlain, is an inland lake connected to the ocean by a river.
(D) Like Loch Ness's reputed monster, inhabitants of the area around Lake Champlain, also an inland lake connected to the ocean by a river, claim sightings of a long and narrow "sea monster."
(E) Similar to that reputed to live in Loch Ness, inhabitants of the area around Lake Champlain, also an inland lake connected to the ocean by a river, claim sightings of a long and narrow "sea monster."

Choices A, D, and E illogically compare the monster reputed to live in Loch Ness to the inhabitants of the area around Lake Champlain, not to the monster that some local inhabitants claim to have sighted. Furthermore, in E the phrase *Similar to that reputed to live in Loch Ness* is needlessly wordy and indirect. C is faulty because the pronoun *which* would refer to *Loch Ness,* not to the *"sea monster" similar to Loch Ness's.* B, the best choice, uses *which* correctly and makes a logical comparison. The question is a little easier than middle difficulty.

4. Since 1965 there are four times as many Black college students enrolled, and the one million Black people in college today represent 11 percent of all college students.

   (A) Since 1965 there are four times as many Black college students enrolled
   (B) The enrollment of Black college students was only one-fourth in 1965
   (C) The enrollment of Black college students has increased four times from 1965 on
   (D) Quadrupling since 1965, there are now four times as many Black college students enrolled
   (E) The enrollment of Black college students has quadrupled since 1965

The comparison in A is incomplete: the reader may be left wondering, *four times as many* as what? B, also incomplete, would have to say something like "one-fourth of the present enrollment" to make clear sense. Taken out of context, the meaning of C is uncertain: C could be read as saying that *the enrollment of Black college students has increased* fourfold or that it has increased four different times. D presents a dangling modifier because there is no noun in the main clause that *Quadrupling since 1965* can modify: Black college students have not quadrupled since 1965; their enrollment has. E states the idea clearly and correctly. The question is moderately easy.

5. A common disability in test pilots is hearing impairment, a consequence of sitting too close to large jet engines for long periods of time.

   (A) a consequence of sitting too close to large jet engines for long periods of time
   (B) a consequence from sitting for long periods of time too near to large jet engines
   (C) a consequence which resulted from sitting too close to large jet engines for long periods of time
   (D) damaged from sitting too near to large jet engines for long periods of time
   (E) damaged because they sat too close to large jet engines for long periods of time

Choice A is correct. Choice B is faulty because *a consequence from* is unidiomatic and because the modifying phrases are awkwardly placed. In C, *a consequence which resulted* is redundant in that *consequence* expresses the idea of *result,* and *from* is again wrong. D and E both present dan-

gling modifiers in that nothing named in the main clause can be said to be *damaged;* i.e., the pilots' *hearing* has been damaged, but their *hearing impairment* has not. The question is of middle difficulty.

6. Europe's travel industry is suffering as a result of a sluggish economy, a stretch of bad weather, as well as the chilling effects of terrorist activity that is persistent.

   (A) as well as the chilling effects of terrorist activity that is persistent
   (B) and the chilling effect of terrorist activity that is persistent
   (C) but persistent terrorist activity has had a chilling effect too
   (D) and the chilling effects of persistent terrorist activity
   (E) as well as the chilling effects of terrorist activity that persists

The best answer for this question will begin with *and* because the phrase *the chilling effects* is the last of three parallel elements in a list, which should follow the form "X, Y, and Z." A and E are incorrect because *as well as* cannot replace *and* in such a list. Moreover, these answer choices are wordy and suggest without warrant that there is terrorist activity that does *not* affect Europe's travel industry because it is not persistent. B amends only the first fault. C is incorrect because *and,* not *but,* should precede the last element in an inclusive series; in this case, *but* introduces an independent clause that deviates from the structure of parallel noun phrases. D is correct for this easy question.

7. Opening with tributes to jazz-age divas like Bessie Smith and closing with Koko Taylor's electrified gravel-and-thunder songs, the program will trace the blues' vigorous matriarchal line over more than 50 years.

   (A) the program will trace
   (B) the program shall trace
   (C) there will be a program tracing
   (D) it is a program that traces
   (E) it will be a program tracing

Choice A is best because *will* is appropriate for simple future tense. In B, *shall* implies intent or determination on the part of the *program.* In addition to being needlessly wordy, C, D, and E create problems in modification because the verb phrase *Opening . . .* seems to describe *there* or *it* rather than *program;* for the modification to be clear and logical, *program* must be the first noun and grammatical subject of the main clause. The question is a little easier than middle difficulty.

8. In 1929 relatively small declines in the market ruined many speculators having bought on margin; they had to sell, and their selling pushed other investors to the brink.

   (A) speculators having bought on margin; they had to sell, and
   (B) speculators who had bought on margin; having had to sell,
   (C) speculators who had bought on margin; they had to sell, and
   (D) speculators, those who had bought on margin; these speculators had to sell, and
   (E) speculators, who, having bought on margin and having to sell,

Choice A can be faulted because *having bought on margin* does not precisely establish a sequence of events; *who had bought on margin* is needed to indicate that the speculators made their purchases before there were declines in the market and before they were forced to sell. B supplies the needed phrasing but introduces another problem: the phrase *having had to sell* dangles for lack of an appropriate noun to modify, and the sentence illogically states that *their selling,* not the *speculators,* had to sell. Choice C is correct. D is needlessly wordy, awkward, and repetitious. E is ungrammatical because *who* is presented as the subject of a clause with no completing verb. The question is of middle difficulty.

9. The mistakes children make in learning to speak tell linguists more about how they learn language than the correct forms they use.

   (A) how they learn language than
   (B) how one learns language than
   (C) how children learn language than do
   (D) learning language than
   (E) their language learning than do

In choice A, the pronoun reference is awkward and potentially ambiguous because a plural noun, *linguists,* comes between *they* and its noun referent, *children.* In addition, *do* is needed after *than* in A, B, and D to prevent the misreading that mistakes tell linguists more about how children learn language than about correct forms. B also entails a shift in voice and number between *one* and *they.* In E, the grammar of the sentence does not clearly specify wither *their language learning* refers to the accomplishments of children or linguists. C is the best choice; the question is a little more difficult than the average.

10. Building large new hospitals in the bistate area would constitute a wasteful use of resources, on the basis of avoidance of duplicated facilities alone.

   (A) on the basis of avoidance of duplicated facilities alone
   (B) on the grounds of avoiding duplicated facilities alone
   (C) solely in that duplicated facilities should be avoided
   (D) while the duplication of facilities should be avoided
   (E) if only because the duplication of facilities should be avoided

Choices A and B are unclear and imprecise: *on the basis of avoidance. . .* and *on the grounds of avoiding. . .* do not present reasons that support the statement in the main clause, and *alone* seems illogically to modify *duplicated facilities.* Also, *duplicated facilities* in A, B, and C identifies the problem with the facilities that have been duplicated, not with the act of duplicating facilities; for example, C apparently advises people to avoid facilities that have been duplicated. In D, *while* establishes no logical relation between the main clause and the rest of the sentence. E is best: *if only because* introduces a reason for the preceding statement, and the remainder of the answer choice is logically worded. The question is difficult.

11. Freedman's survey showed that people living in small towns and rural areas consider themselves no happier than do people living in big cities.

   (A) no happier than do people living
   (B) not any happier than do people living
   (C) not any happier than do people who live
   (D) no happier than are people who are living
   (E) not as happy as are people who live

Choice A is correct. In B, C, and E, the phrases beginning with *not* in place of *no* are wordy and unidiomatic. In D and E, the use of *are* presents a verb substitution problem: *are* cannot take the place of the verb *consider,* as *do* can in A, because *consider* is something that people *do,* not something that they *are.* D and E thus fail to compare the attitudes of the two groups of people, referring instead only to how those in small towns and rural areas consider themselves. E also distorts the intended meaning by saying that people living in small towns and rural areas consider themselves less happy than people living in big cities. The question is of middle difficulty.

12. It may someday be worthwhile to try to recover uranium from seawater, but at present this process is prohibitively expensive.

   (A) It may someday be worthwhile to try to recover uranium from seawater
   (B) Someday, it may be worthwhile to try and recover uranium from seawater
   (C) Trying to recover uranium out of seawater may someday be worthwhile
   (D) To try for the recovery of uranium out of seawater may someday be worthwhile
   (E) Recovering uranium from seawater may be worthwhile to try to do someday

Choice A is best. In choice B, *Someday* is misplaced. Coming first and set off with a comma, it refers loosely to the whole clause; the placement of *someday* in A allows the word to modify the verb precisely. Also, *try to* in A is preferable to *try and* in B. Although *try and* is acceptable in informal contexts, many editors and usage handbooks prefer *try to* in formal writing. In C, *recover. . .out of* is unidiomatic. D is needlessly wordy and contains *recovery . . . out of*. E awkwardly inverts logical word order by placing *to try to do* well after *recovering*. This is a difficult question.

13. The underlying physical principles that control the midair gyrations of divers and gymnasts are the same as the body orientation controlling astronauts in a weightless environment.

   (A) as the body orientation controlling
   (B) as the body orientation which controls
   (C) as those controlling the body orientation of
   (D) ones to control the body orientation of
   (E) ones used in controlling the body orientation of

Choice A illogically identifies the *physical principles* of line 1 as *body orientations*, not as principles; moreover, the original sentence confusedly states that body orientation controls the astronauts, not that physical principles control their body orientation. B changes *controlling* to *which controls*, but the logical problems remain. C correctly uses the plural pronoun *those* to identify principles as principles. By substituting *to control* for *that control* (line 1), D violates parallel construction. E, wordy and imprecise, seems to imply that some external agency is using physical principles to control the body orientation of astronauts. The question is of average difficulty.

14. The spraying of pesticides can be carefully planned, but accidents, weather conditions that could not be foreseen, and pilot errors often cause much larger deposits of spray than they had anticipated.

   (A) weather conditions that could not be foreseen, and pilot errors often cause much larger deposits of spray than they had
   (B) weather conditions that cannot be foreseen, and pilot errors often cause much larger deposits of spray than
   (C) unforeseeable weather conditions, and pilot errors are the cause of much larger deposits of spray than they had
   (D) weather conditions that are not foreseeable, and pilot errors often cause much larger deposits of spray than
   (E) unforeseeable weather conditions, and pilot errors often cause much larger deposits of spray than they had

Choices A, C, and E are faulty because the pronoun *they* has no logical noun to which it can refer; also *could not be foreseen* in A seems to describe specific weather conditions in the past, not ones that are still unforeseeable and so continue to affect spraying. B corrects both problems. C contains the unattached *they* and inflates *cause* to *are the cause of;* moreover, by changing *cause* from a verb to a noun, C states that all three factors acting together constitute the one and only cause of excessive deposits. The initial phrase of D is less compact and idiomatic than that of B. This question is difficult.

15. To read of Abigail Adams' lengthy separation from her family, her difficult travels, and her constant battles with illness is to feel intensely how harsh life was even for the so-called aristocracy of Revolutionary times.

   (A) To read of
   (B) Reading about
   (C) Having read about
   (D) Once one reads of
   (E) To have read of

Choice A is correct because the sentence must begin with a verb form that completes the construction *To. . .is to feel.* Each of the other choices breaks the parallelism in some way, and B and C substitute *about* for *of*, the preferred preposition here. E begins with *To*, but *have read* creates a disjunction of tenses by placing the action of reading in the past while *to feel* is still in the present. The question is of middle difficulty.

16. A star will compress itself into a white dwarf, a neutron star, or a black hole after it passes through a red giant stage, depending on mass.

    (A) A star will compress itself into a white dwarf, a neutron star, or a black hole after it passes through a red giant stage, depending on mass.
    (B) After passing through a red giant stage, depending on its mass, a star will compress itself into a white dwarf, a neutron star, or a black hole.
    (C) After passing through a red giant stage, a star's mass will determine if it compresses itself into a white dwarf, a neutron star, or a black hole.
    (D) Mass determines whether a star, after passing through the red giant stage, will compress itself into a white dwarf, a neutron star, or a black hole.
    (E) The mass of a star, after passing through the red giant stage, will determine whether it compresses itself into a white dwarf, a neutron star, or a black hole.

Choice A is ambiguous because the grammatical function of *depending on mass* is uncertain: the phrase could modify either the whole preceding statement or only the words *after it passes through a red giant stage*. In the latter case, choice A states in effect that a star depends on its mass as it passes through this phase, not that the fate of the star depends on the star's mass. Choice B suffers from the same ambiguity. Choices C and E illogically maintain that the star's mass, not the star itself, passes through the red giant stage to assume another form. Choice D is the correct answer for this difficult question.

17. In the main, incidents of breakdowns in nuclear reactors have <u>not resulted from lapses of high technology but</u> commonplace inadequacies in plumbing and wiring.

    (A) not resulted from lapses of high technology but
    (B) resulted not from lapses of high technology but from
    (C) resulted from lapses not of high technology but
    (D) resulted from lapses not of high technology but have stemmed from
    (E) resulted not from lapses of high technology but have stemmed from

Parallelism requires that in a *not. . .but. . .* construction, the words after *not* and *but* have the same grammatical form and function. Choice A breaks the parallel because *not resulted. . .but commonplace* erroneously links a verb and an adjective. Choice B is correct. The wording in C creates a false parallel between *lapses . . . of high technology* and *lapses . . . of commonplace inadequacies* because *lapses* precedes and governs both elements in the *not. . .but. . .* construction. D and E lack grammatical parallelism and would be needlessly wordy even if *not* had been appropriately placed before *resulted*. This question is of middle difficulty.

18. <u>Seeming to be</u> the only organization fighting for the rights of poor people in the South, Hosea Hudson, a laborer in Alabama, joined the Communist party in 1931.

    (A) Seeming to be
    (B) As
    (C) In that they seemed
    (D) Since it seemed
    (E) Because it seemed to be

Choices A and B wrongly identify Hosea Hudson, not the Communist party, as the organization under discussion. In choice C, the plural pronoun *they* does not agree in number with the singular noun *party. In that* in C and *Since* in D are less direct and idiomatic than *Because* in this context, and *to be* is needed to complete the predicate begun by *seemed*. E is the correct answer for this question of middle difficulty.

19. Although many art patrons can readily differentiate a good debenture from an undesirable one, they are <u>much less expert in distinguishing good paintings and poor ones, authentic art and</u> fakes.

    (A) much less expert in distinguishing good paintings and poor ones, authentic art and
    (B) far less expert in distinguishing good paintings from poor ones, authentic art from
    (C) much less expert when it comes to distinguishing good paintings and poor ones, authentic art from
    (D) far less expert in distinguishing good paintings and poor ones, authentic art and
    (E) far less the expert when it comes to distinguishing between good painting, poor ones, authentic art, and

The best answer will follow the idiomatic form *distinguishing X from Y*. The substitution of *and* for *from* makes choices A, C, D, and E faulty. Moreover, *far* is a better modifier of *less expert* than *much* is in A and C, *when it comes to distinguishing* is wordy in C and E, and E fails to acknowledge that two distinctions are being considered—one between good and poor paintings, another between authentic art and fakes. B is the correct answer for this question of middle difficulty.

20. Rules banning cancer-causing substances from food apply to new food additives and not to natural constituents of food because <u>their use as additives is</u> entirely avoidable.

    (A) their use as additives is
    (B) as additives, their use is
    (C) the use of such additives is
    (D) the use of such additives are
    (E) the use of them as additives is

Choices A, B, and E are incorrect because the pronouns *their* and *them* could refer to any of several plural nouns. B and E are also awkwardly constructed. In choice D, the plural verb *are* does not agree in number with the singular noun *use*. Choice C is correct for this question of middle difficulty.

21. The average weekly wage nearly doubled in the 1970's, rising from $114 to $220, yet the average worker ended the decade with a decrease in what their pay may buy.

 (A) with a decrease in what their pay may buy
 (B) with what was a decrease in what they were able to buy
 (C) having decreased that which they could buy
 (D) decreasing in purchasing power
 (E) with a decrease in purchasing power

Choices A, B, and C incorrectly use a plural pronoun, *their* or *they,* to refer to a singular noun, *worker.* Moreover, A and B are wordy and awkwardly constructed, and C wrongly asserts that the *average worker* decreased the amount or value of what could be bought. D misrepresents the intended meaning by saying that at the end of the decade, the *average worker*—not the money—was *decreasing in purchasing power.* E is the correct answer for this easy question.

22. Since chromosome damage may be caused by viral infections, medical x-rays, and exposure to sunlight, it is important that the chromosomes of a population to be tested for chemically induced damage be compared with those of a control population.

 (A) to be tested for chemically induced damage be compared with
 (B) being tested for damage induced chemically are compared with
 (C) being tested for chemically induced damage should be compared to
 (D) being tested for chemically induced damage are to be compared to
 (E) that is to be tested for chemically induced damage are to be comparable with

Choice A is best because the infinitive *to be tested* and the subjunctive *be compared* are correct for describing a hypothetical course of action. Also, *compared with* rather than *compared to* is preferred when a comparison is intended, as here with *chromosomes,* to reveal differences among things of the same order. Choice B lacks the infinitive and subjunctive forms, and *damage induced chemically* is more awkward than the comparable phrase in A. C and D have *being* instead of *to be* and *to* instead of *with;* also *should* and *are to* do not belong in the subjunctive. E is wordy, *are to* again intrudes, and *comparable* changes the meaning of the statement. This question is difficult.

23. The suspect in the burglary was advised of his right to remain silent, told he could not leave, and was interrogated in a detention room.

 (A) of his right to remain silent, told he could not leave, and was
 (B) of his right to remain silent, told he could not leave, and
 (C) of his right to remain silent and that he could not leave and
 (D) that he had a right to remain silent, could not leave, and was
 (E) that he had a right to remain silent, that he could not leave, and was

The best answer will exhibit parallelism. Choice B correctly forms a parallel structure: *was advised. . ., told. . ., and interrogated. . . .* Because all three verbs are governed by the *was* in line 1, the *was* after *and* in choice A is not merely unnecessary but actually wrong because it disrupts the parallel. Choice C is wordy and ungrammatical: the syntax forces *was advised* rather than *was* to govern all three elements, a construction that becomes impossible with *was advised. . .interrogated.* A similar misconstruction in D produces the misstatement that the suspect *was advised that he. . .was interrogated.* E forms a list of nonparallel elements; placing *and* after *silent* and dropping the commas would make E grammatical but no less wordy. This question is very difficult.

24. The United States petroleum industry's cost to meet environmental regulations is projected at ten percent of the price per barrel of refined petroleum by the end of the decade.

 (A) The United States petroleum industry's cost to meet environmental regulations is projected at ten percent of the price per barrel of refined petroleum by the end of the decade.
 (B) The United States petroleum industry's cost by the end of the decade to meet environmental regulations is estimated at ten percent of the price per barrel of refined petroleum.
 (C) By the end of the decade, the United States petroleum industry's cost of meeting environmental regulations is projected at ten percent of the price per barrel of refined petroleum.
 (D) To meet environmental regulations, the cost to the United States petroleum industry is estimated at ten percent of the price per barrel of refined petroleum by the end of the decade.
 (E) It is estimated that by the end of the decade the cost to the United States petroleum industry of meeting environmental regulations will be ten percent of the price per barrel of refined petroleum.

Choices A, B, C, and D are awkward and confusing. In A, for example, the issue is not the *industry's cost* but the cost to the industry; also, *to meet* should be *of meeting* here, *projected at* is unidiomatic, and *by the end of the decade* is placed so that its meaning is unclear. B and C suffer from many of the same problems. The wording of D implies that *cost. . .is estimated* in order *to meet environmental regulations.* E alone makes a logical statement and varies verb tense to indicate that the issue is present estimates of future costs. The question is moderately difficult.

25. The relationship between corpulence and disease <u>remain controversial, although statistics clearly associate a reduced life expectancy with</u> chronic obesity.

   (A) remain controversial, although statistics clearly associate a reduced life expectancy with
   (B) remain controversial, although statistics clearly associates a reduced life expectancy with
   (C) remain controversial, although statistics clearly associates reduced life expectancy to
   (D) remains controversial, although statistics clearly associate a reduced life expectancy with
   (E) remains controversial, although statistics clearly associates reduced life expectancy to

Choice A is incorrect because *remain* should be *remains;* the subject of the verb is *relationship,* not *corpulence and disease,* which are hardly controversial. Choices B and C are similarly flawed, and *associates* in B, C, and E should be *associate* to agree with the intended number of *statistics.* Finally, *associate(s). . .to* is unidiomatic in C and E. This is a moderately easy question.

Explanatory Material:
Reading Comprehension

1. The primary purpose of the passage is to

   (A) present a commonplace idea and its inaccuracies
   (B) describe a situation and its potential drawbacks
   (C) propose a temporary solution to a problem
   (D) analyze a frequent source of disagreement
   (E) explore the implications of a finding

The best answer is B. The author begins by describing in the first two paragraphs the new opportunities for minority-owned businesses in the United States engendered by changes in federal law. The author then goes on in the last three paragraphs to point out three specific risks for minority-owned businesses posed by the new federal laws. Thus a situation is described and the drawbacks that it might entail are suggested. This is a very easy question.

2. The passage supplies information that would answer which of the following questions?

   (A) What federal agencies have set percentage goals for the use of minority-owned businesses in public works contracts?
   (B) To which government agencies must businesses awarded federal contracts report their efforts to find minority subcontractors?
   (C) How widespread is the use of minority-owned concerns as "fronts" by White backers seeking to obtain subcontracts?
   (D) How many more minority-owned businesses were there in 1977 than in 1972?
   (E) What is one set of conditions under which a small business might find itself financially overextended?

The best answer is E. Choices A and B can be eliminated because the passage mentions only "some federal and local agencies" (lines 14-15), not any specific ones. C and D can be eliminated because no specific data are provided about minority-owned firms except in the area of the value of their corporate contracts. Only E is clearly answered by the passage; the author describes in lines 33-36 the possibility of a reduction in subcontracts leaving a small business that had just expanded (lines 28-33) financially overextended. This is a question of medium difficulty.

3. According to the passage, civil rights activists maintain that one disadvantage under which minority-owned businesses have traditionally had to labor is that they have

   (A) been especially vulnerable to governmental mismanagement of the economy
   (B) been denied bank loans at rates comparable to those afforded larger competitors
   (C) not had sufficient opportunity to secure business created by large corporations
   (D) not been able to advertise in those media that reach large numbers of potential customers
   (E) not had adequate representation in the centers of government power

The best answer is C because lines 4-9 state that civil rights activists have long argued that a problem for members of minority groups who are attempting to establish businesses has been that minority groups "lack access to the sizable orders and subcontracts that are generated by large companies." This is a very easy question.

4. The passage suggests that the failure of a large business to have its bids for subcontracts result quickly in orders might cause it to

   (A) experience frustration but not serious financial harm
   (B) face potentially crippling fixed expenses
   (C) have to record its efforts on forms filed with the government
   (D) increase its spending with minority subcontractors
   (E) revise its procedure for making bids for federal contracts and subcontracts

The best answer is A. In lines 28-36 the author points out that small businesses might have to make substantial new investments to meet the demands of a large subcontract, and that small businesses could thus "face potentially crippling fixed expenses." Large businesses, the author suggests in line 30, would not have to make such investments, and therefore would not face serious financial consequences. In lines 39-42 the author notes that if a company is small, it must get orders quickly, or "the financial health of the business will suffer." Thus, although any firm would suffer if it did not receive orders for subcontracts quickly, only small firms facing large fixed expenses would experience serious financial harm. Large firms do not face or can handle these expenses. This is a very difficult question.

5. The author implies that a minority-owned concern that does the greater part of its business with one large corporate customer should

   (A) avoid competition with larger, more established concerns by not expanding
   (B) concentrate on securing even more business from that corporation
   (C) try to expand its customer base to avoid becoming dependent on the corporation
   (D) pass on some of the work to be done for the corporation to other minority-owned concerns
   (E) use its influence with the corporation to promote subcontracting with other minority concerns

The best answer is C. The passage states in lines 55-57 that becoming dependent on one large corporate customer constitutes a "danger" for a minority enterprise. It is then noted in lines 58-64 that it is "difficult for small concerns to broaden their customer bases" even at the best of times, but that it is important that they "struggle against complacency." Thus, the author implies that a minority firm should attempt to escape the danger of dependency on a single corporate customer, and that in order to do so such a firm must try to expand its customer base. This is a very easy question.

6. It can be inferred from the passage that, compared with the requirements of law, the percentage goals set by "some federal and local agencies" (lines 14-15) are

   (A) more popular with large corporations
   (B) more specific
   (C) less controversial
   (D) less expensive to enforce
   (E) easier to comply with

The best answer is B. Lines 9-14 state that the law mandates that businesses simply "do their best" to use minority subcontractors and report their efforts to the federal government. In contrast, the author notes in lines 14-17 that some federal and local agencies have gone much further, "so far as to set specific percentage goals." Thus, it can be inferred that the author considers the percentage goals of the federal and local agencies to be more specific than the more general requirements of federal law. This is a relatively easy question.

7. Which of the following, if true, would most weaken the author's assertion that, in the 1970's, corporate response to federal requirements (lines 18-19) was substantial?

   (A) Corporate contracts with minority-owned businesses totaled $2 billion in 1979.
   (B) Between 1970 and 1972, corporate contracts with minority-owned businesses declined by 25 percent.
   (C) The figures collected in 1977 underrepresented the extent of corporate contracts with minority-owned businesses.
   (D) The estimate of corporate spending with minority-owned businesses in 1980 is approximately $10 million too high.
   (E) The $1.1 billion represented the same percentage of total corporate spending in 1977 as did $77 million in 1972.

The best answer is E. The author's assertion that, in the 1970's, the corporate response to federal requirements was substantial rests on the fact that "corporate contracts with minority businesses rose from $77 million in 1972 to $1.1 billion in 1977" (lines 20-22). The author's claim that such a rise indicates a substantial corporate response to federal requirements would be weakened if other factors were at work. Such a condition is presented only in choice E, where it is stated that the percentage of corporate spending remained constant; this implies that the increased dollar amount allocated to minority businesses was due simply to general economic growth, and that minority businesses proportionally gained nothing during those years. This is a question of medium difficulty.

8. The passage most likely appeared in

    (A) a business magazine
    (B) an encyclopedia of Black history to 1945
    (C) a dictionary of financial terms
    (D) a yearbook of business statistics
    (E) an accounting textbook

The best answer is A. The passage presents general information about a business topic in a manner accessible to the interested reading public. The language is not technical, the statistics are few, and yet the focus is resolutely on a contemporary business phenomenon. This style suggests a publication oriented toward presenting general news and analysis of the business world to the interested public. Of the five choices only A does this. B focuses on the wrong time period, C on a task—definition of financial terms—not performed by the passage, and D and E on information not present to any significant degree in the passage. This is a very easy question.

9. The author would most likely agree with which of the following statements about corporate response to working with minority subcontractors?

    (A) Annoyed by the proliferation of "front" organizations, corporations are likely to reduce their efforts to work with minority-owned subcontractors in the near future.
    (B) Although corporations showed considerable interest in working with minority businesses in the 1970's, their aversion to government paperwork made them reluctant to pursue many government contracts.
    (C) The significant response of corporations in the 1970's is likely to be sustained and conceivably be increased throughout the 1980's.
    (D) Although corporations are eager to cooperate with minority-owned businesses, a shortage of capital in the 1970's made substantial response impossible.
    (E) The enormous corporate response has all but eliminated the dangers of overexpansion that used to plague small minority-owned businesses.

The best answer is C, because the author states in lines 22-25 that "no letup [is] anticipated" in the projected total of corporate contracts with minority businesses throughout the next decade. There is no support in the passage for any of the other choices. This is a relatively easy question.

10. The primary purpose of the passage is to

    (A) raise new issues
    (B) explain an enigma
    (C) refute misconceptions
    (D) reconcile differing theories
    (E) analyze a phenomenon

The best answer is E. When asked to identify the primary purpose of a passage, you should select the answer choice that states what the passage as a whole achieves. The passage is primarily a discussion of a natural phenomenon, the song of the male indigo bunting. This discussion focuses on the components, form, and function of the song. Such a discussion can correctly be called an analysis, and E presents such a choice. There is no evidence in the passage that suggests that the issues presented are new (choice A), or that any of the matters discussed are enigmas or misconceptions (choices B and C). The discussion is not primarily a presentation of theory but of empirical evidence and observed phenomena; thus, choice D is not correct. This is a relatively easy question.

11. According to the passage, which of the following is true about the number and general nature of figures sung by the indigo bunting?

    (A) They are established at birth.
    (B) They evolve slowly as the bird learns.
    (C) They are learned from other indigo buntings.
    (D) They develop after the bird has been forced onto marginal breeding areas.
    (E) They gradually develop through contact with prospective mates.

The best answer is C. To answer this question, you should examine each of the choices to determine which makes an accurate statement, based on evidence in the passage, about the number and general nature of the figures sung by the indigo bunting. In the second paragraph, the author concludes that male indigo buntings in a natural environment copy figures from other buntings, a fact that explains why the number and general nature of figures remain limited. Thus, choice C is true and is the intended answer. The other choices are plausible statements, but they are not asserted in the passage. This is a relatively easy question.

12. It can be inferred that the investigation that determined the similarity among more than 90 percent of all the figures produced by birds living in different regions was undertaken to answer which of the following questions?

    I.   How much variation, if any, is there in the figure types produced by indigo buntings in different locales?
    II. Do local populations of indigo buntings develop their own dialects of figure types?
    III. Do figure similarities among indigo buntings decline with increasing geographic separation?

    (A) II only
    (B) III only
    (C) I and II only
    (D) II and III only
    (E) I, II, and III

The best answer is E. The format of this question requires you to evaluate each of the questions designated with Roman numerals separately and carefully. In this question, you must infer from the passage what information the investigation discussed in the second paragraph was designed to obtain. According to the passage, the investigation yielded information that permitted researchers to draw conclusions about variation in figure types, about unique figures among birds, and about the effects of increasing geographic separation. The second paragraph describes some of the strategies used by the investigators to obtain precisely this information. I, II, and III are all questions that the investigators set out to explore, and E is the correct answer. This is a question of medium difficulty.

13. It can be inferred from the passage that the existence of only a limited number of indigo bunting figures serves primarily to

(A) ensure species survival by increasing competition among the fittest males for the females
(B) increase population density by eliminating ambiguity in the figures to which the females must respond
(C) maintain the integrity of the species by restricting the degree of figure variation and change
(D) enhance species recognition by decreasing the number of figure patterns to which the bird must respond
(E) avoid confusion between species by clearly demarcating the figure patterns of each species

The best answer is D. This question requires you to determine why the number of indigo bunting figures is as limited as it is. In order to make this determination, it is necessary to consider several facts presented in the passage and their relationship to each other. The third paragraph indicates that the songs serve as a means of recognition for members of the same species. The fourth paragraph discusses the strict limitations on the ways in which figures are produced. The last paragraph indicates that "song stability and conservatism," that is, limits to the numbers of figures and variations, are essential for clear-cut species recognition. Choice D is a statement of that idea. This is a relatively difficult question.

14. It can be inferred that a dummy of a male indigo bunting was placed near the tape recorder that played the songs of different species in order to try to

(A) simulate the conditions in nature
(B) rule out visual cues as a factor in species recognition
(C) supply an additional clue to species recognition for the indigo bunting
(D) provide data on the habits of bunting species other than the indigo bunting
(E) confound the indigo buntings in the experiment

The best answer is B. This question requires you to determine the reason for the researcher's use of a dummy male indigo bunting. The passage indicates that the sight of the dummy was not enough to cause subject male indigo buntings to react to songs of lazuli and painted buntings. This result

suggests that the indigo bunting identifies others of the species on the basis of song rather than sight. The fact that the researchers performed an additional check in which an indigo bunting song, did, in fact, provoke responses from the subject indigos further rules out visual clues. This is a relatively difficult question.

15. According to the passage, the authors played a normal indigo bunting song backwards in order to determine which of the following?

(A) What are the limits of the frequency range that will provide recognition by the indigo bunting?
(B) What is the time duration necessary for recognition by the indigo bunting?
(C) How specific must a figure shape be for it to be recognized by the indigo bunting?
(D) How does variation in the pacing of song figures affect the indigo bunting's recognition of the figures?
(E) Is the indigo bunting responding to cues other than those in the song figures?

The best answer is C. The fourth paragraph states that the researchers played songs backwards, a technique that changed the forms of the figures without changing frequency ranges or gross temporal features. Since figure shape, therefore, is the only element to be altered, the results of the experiment would give information about the role of figure shape in species recognition. Choice C is the only choice that addresses the question of figure shapes, and, in fact, the fourth paragraph indicates that the experiment was designed to determine what changes in detail would fail to elicit responses from the subject buntings. This is a question of medium difficulty.

16. According to the passage, the indigo buntings' songs function in which of the following ways?

I. To delineate a breeding area
II. To defend a breeding area
III. To identify the birds to their mates

(A) I only
(B) II only
(C) I and III only
(D) II and III only
(E) I, II, and III

The best answer is E. The format of this question requires you to evaluate each of the phrases designated with Roman numerals separately and carefully. The question requires you to look up information explicitly stated in the passage. The first sentence in the first paragraph states that in birds such as the indigo bunting, "song is the main mechanism for securing, defining, and defending an adequate breeding area." I and II are restatements of parts of this idea. The last paragraph indicates that songs serve the function of identification within the species and that females can differentiate the songs of their mates from those of other males, thus indicating that III is also correct; therefore, E (I, II, and III) is the best choice. This is a question of medium difficulty.

17. The author's discussion of Emerson, Thoreau, Hawthorne, Melville, and Whitman is primarily concerned with explaining

    (A) some of their beliefs about the difficulties involved in self-realization
    (B) some of their beliefs concerning the world and the place that humanity occupies in the universal order
    (C) some of their beliefs concerning the relationship between humanism and democracy
    (D) the way some of their beliefs are shaped by differences in temperament and literary outlook
    (E) the effects of some of their beliefs on their writings

The best answer is B. This question asks you to identify the choice that best states the primary concern, or central topic, of the author's discussion. Thus, the best answer must be comprehensive enough to include all aspects of the author's discussion. Choice A mentions one aspect of the author's discussion, which appears in the third paragraph along with the topic mentioned in choice C. Neither of these choices includes the matters under discussion in paragraphs one, two, and four. Choices D and E mention topics not discussed in the passage. Choice B presents a broad topic that includes the matters discussed in all four paragraphs of the passage. This is a question of medium difficulty.

18. According to the passage, the humanistic perspective of the five writers presupposes which of the following?

    I. The structure of the universe can be discovered through self-knowledge.
    II. The world can be explained in terms of humanity.
    III. The spiritual and the material worlds are incompatible.

    (A) I only
    (B) II only
    (C) I and III only
    (D) II and III only
    (E) I, II, and III

The best answer is C. This question asks you to evaluate the three statements designated with Roman numerals in terms of "the humanistic perspective of the five writers." Paragraph one discusses the "humanistic perspective" (line 5) and explains its "basic premises" (lines 5-8). After looking back at paragraph one, you can decide whether or not the "humanistic perspective" presupposes statements I, II, and/or III. The last sentence of paragraph one says that ". . . all knowledge begins with self-knowledge"; thus, statement I is a presupposition of the "humanistic perspective." Lines 5-13 explain in

some detail the point briefly stated in statement II. The point made in statement III is neither stated nor implied in the passage. This is a question of medium difficulty.

19. The author quotes Whitman primarily in order to

    (A) show that the poet does not agree with Emerson
    (B) indicate the way the poet uses the humanist ideal to praise himself
    (C) suggest that the poet adapts the basic premises of humanism to his own individual outlook on the world
    (D) illustrate a way the poet expresses the relationship of the individual to the humanistic universe
    (E) demonstrate that the poet is concerned with the well-being of all humans

The best answer is D. This question asks you to identify the function of a quotation in the author's discussion. First, locate the quotation from Whitman in lines 24-27. The first two sentences of the paragraph make the point that the five writers under discussion emphasize not the individual, but the "human as universal" (line 21). The author of the passage then says, "Thus, for Emerson . . . while, for Whitman" (lines 22-24). The use of the word "Thus" indicates that the author is giving a specific instance or example of the point. The only choice that states a purpose for the quotation compatible with the author's point in this paragraph is D. This is a question of medium difficulty.

20. According to the passage, the five writers object to the scientific method primarily because they think it

    (A) is not the best way to obtain an understanding of the relationship between the individual and the cosmos
    (B) is so specialized that it leads to an understanding of separate parts of the universe but not of the relationships among those parts
    (C) cannot provide an adequate explanation of intuition and imagination
    (D) misleads people into believing they have an understanding of truth, when they do not
    (E) prevents people from recognizing the symbolic nature of experience

The best answer is A. The author of the passage, in the first sentence of the fourth paragraph, says that the five writers assumed "that intuition and imagination offer a surer road to truth" than the scientific method, and that they presumed "an organic relationship between the self and the cosmos of which only intuition and imagination can properly take account" (lines 55-57). Choice A restates this point by saying that the scientific method "is not the best way to obtain an understanding of the relationship between the individual and the cosmos." Choices B, C, D, and E mention plausible possible objections to the use of the scientific method, but none of these are mentioned in the passage. This is a relatively difficult question.

21. Which of the following statements would be compatible with the beliefs of the five writers as described in the passage?

  I. Democracy works as a form of government because every individual is unique.
  II. Nature alone exists, and each person is nothing more than a shadow of that substance which is the world.
  III. The human mind is capable of discovering the meaning of life and understanding the order in the universe.

  (A) I only
  (B) III only
  (C) I and II only
  (D) I and III only
  (E) I, II, and III

The best answer is B. This question asks you to evaluate statements I, II, and III and decide whether each of the three statements is compatible with the beliefs of the authors as they are presented in the passage. Statement I concerns democracy, which is discussed in the passage in lines 39-46. It is clear from these lines that I is not compatible with the authors' beliefs as they are presented in the passage. Statement II begins "Nature alone exists. . ."; this part of the statement directly contradicts the discussion of the humanistic perspective in the first paragraph of the passage. Statement III summarizes the basic points made about the humanistic perspective in the first paragraph. This is a relatively difficult question.

22. It can be inferred that intuition is important to the five writers primarily because it provides them with

  (A) information useful for understanding abstract logic and scientific method
  (B) the discipline needed in the search for truth
  (C) inspiration for their best writing
  (D) clues to the interpretation of symbolic experience
  (E) the means of resolving conflicts between the self and the world

The best answer is D. In the fourth paragraph of the passage, the author says that the five writers assume that intuition and imagination "offer a surer road to truth" (lines 48-49). The author of the passage then gives two illustrations of this assumption, one of which is the writers' emphasis on "interpretation of experience as, in essence, symbolic." Choice A can be eliminated because the fourth paragraph states that intuition and imagination are alternatives to logic and scientific method. The material in choices B and C is not implied in the fourth paragraph. Choice E suggests, correctly, that intuition and imagination connect the self to the world, but the resolution of conflicts between the self and world mentioned in E is not discussed in the passage. This is a very difficult question.

23. The author discusses "the democratic ethic" (lines 39-46) in order to

  (A) explain the relationship between external experience and inner imagination
  (B) support the notion that the self contains two conflicting and irreconcilable factions
  (C) illustrate the relationship between the self's desire to be individual and its desire to merge with all other selves
  (D) elaborate on the concept that the self constantly desires to realize its potential
  (E) give an example of the idea that, in order to be happy, the self must reconcile its desires with external reality

The best answer is C. First, reread the lines cited in the question. They appear at the end of the third paragraph, which begins with a statement of the five writers' belief in the necessity for "harmonious reconciliation of two universal psychological tendencies. . ." (lines 31-32), tendencies of withdrawal, on the one hand, and outreach, on the other (lines 32-38). The next sentence introduces the "democratic ethic" as an illustration of such reconciliation. Thus, choice C is the only choice that expresses the connection between the first part of the paragraph and the example of the democratic ethic. This is a question of medium difficulty.

24. It can be inferred that the idea of "an organic relationship between the self and the cosmos" (lines 55-56) is necessary to the thinking of the five writers because such a relationship

  (A) enables them to assert the importance of the democratic ethic
  (B) justifies their concept of the freedom of the individual
  (C) sustains their faith in the existence of a deity
  (D) is the foundation of their humanistic view of existence
  (E) is the basis for their claim that the writer is a seer

The best answer is D. This question asks you to connect the quoted phrase to "the thinking of the five writers." Choice A is inadequate because nothing in the passage suggests that the five writers asserted the importance of the democratic ethic. Choice B mentions the concept of the freedom of the individual, which is certainly implicit in the five writers' beliefs, but the relationship cited in the quoted phrase cannot be said to justify their concept. Choice C makes a statement unsupported by the passage. Choice E is related to the quoted phrase, in that the writers' faith in the imagination, which is the mental pathway to understanding the relationship cited in the quoted phrase, led them to see the writer as a seer. The necessary connection between the quoted phrase and the writers' beliefs, however, comes from their shared humanistic perspective, explained in detail in the first and fourth paragraphs, a perspective that is grounded in the idea contained in the quoted phrase. This is a relatively difficult question.

25. The passage is most relevant to which of the following areas of study?

(A) Aesthetics and logic
(B) History and literature
(C) Theology and sociology
(D) Anthropology and political science
(E) Linguistics and art

The best answer is B. Choices A and E mention areas of study not relevant to the subject of the passage, the common beliefs of five writers. Choices C and D each mention one area, theology and political science, respectively, that could be seen as connected to the discussion presented in the passage. However, the principal concerns of sociology and anthropology are not connected with the subject of the passage. The central concerns of the passage, presenting the ideas and beliefs of significant thinkers, are the principal concerns of the fields of history and literature. This is a very difficult question.

Explanatory Material: Problem Solving II

1. An investor purchased x shares of stock at a certain price. If the stock then increased in price $0.25 per share and the total increase for the x shares was $12.50, how many shares of stock had been purchased?

(A) 25 (B) 50 (C) 75 (D) 100 (E) 125

If each of the x shares of stock increased by $0.25, and the total increase was $12.50, then $0.25x = 12.50$ and $x = 12.50/0.25 = 50$. Thus, the best answer is B. This is a very easy question.

2. If $x > 0$ and $x^2 = 161$, what is the best whole number approximation of x?

(A) 13 (B) 18 (C) 41 (D) 80 (E) 2,560

Since $x^2 = 161$ and x is positive, $x = \sqrt{161}$. Since $12^2 = 144$ and $13^2 = 169$, $12 < \sqrt{161} < 13$. Therefore, 13 is the best whole number approximation of x among the options given, and the best answer is A. This is a very easy question.

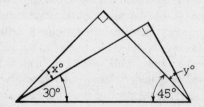

3. In the figure above, what is the value of $2x - y$?

(A) 0 (B) 15 (C) 30 (D) 45 (E) 60

In both right triangles, the sum of the measures of the two acute angles must equal 90°. Therefore, $x + 30 + 45 = 90$, $x = 15$; and $y + 45 + 30 = 90$, $y = 15$. Thus, $2x - y = 2(15) - 15 = 15$, and the best answer is B. This is an easy question.

4. $\dfrac{\frac{1}{2}\left(\frac{\frac{3}{4}}{\frac{2}{3}}\right)}{\frac{2}{9}} =$

(A) $\dfrac{81}{32}$ (B) $\dfrac{9}{4}$ (C) $\dfrac{9}{8}$ (D) $\dfrac{1}{8}$ (E) $\dfrac{1}{18}$

To simplify, $\dfrac{\frac{1}{2}\left(\frac{\frac{3}{4}}{\frac{2}{3}}\right)}{\frac{2}{9}} = \dfrac{\frac{1}{2}\left(\frac{3}{4} \cdot \frac{3}{2}\right)}{\frac{2}{9}} = \dfrac{\frac{9}{16}}{\frac{2}{9}} = \dfrac{9}{16} \cdot \dfrac{9}{2} = \dfrac{81}{32}.$

Thus, the best answer is A. This is an easy question.

5. At a special sale, 5 tickets can be purchased for the price of 3 tickets. If 5 tickets are purchased at this sale, the amount saved will be what percent of the original price of the 5 tickets?

(A) 20%
(B) $33\frac{1}{3}\%$
(C) 40%
(D) 60%
(E) $66\frac{2}{3}\%$

If 5 tickets at sale price s cost the same as 3 tickets at the regular price p, then $5s = 3p$ and $s = \frac{3}{5}p$. Since the sale price is $\frac{3}{5}$ or 60 percent of the original price, $\frac{2}{5}$ or 40 percent is saved. Thus, the best answer is C. This is an easy question.

6. Which of the following is equal to $\frac{3}{8}$ of 1.28?

(A) $\dfrac{24}{5}$
(B) $\dfrac{12}{25}$
(C) $\dfrac{13}{50}$
(D) $\dfrac{6}{25}$
(E) $\dfrac{4}{25}$

$\frac{3}{8}$ of $1.28 = \left(\frac{3}{8}\right)\left(\frac{\overset{32}{\cancel{128}}}{\underset{25}{\cancel{100}}}\right) = \left(\frac{3}{\cancel{8}}\right)\left(\frac{\overset{4}{\cancel{32}}}{25}\right) = \dfrac{12}{25}.$

Thus, the best answer is B. This is an easy question.

7. Working independently, Tina can do a certain job in 12 hours. Working independently, Ann can do the same job in 9 hours. If Tina works independently at the job for 8 hours and then Ann works independently, how many hours will it take Ann to complete the remainder of the job?

   (A) $\frac{2}{3}$ (B) $\frac{3}{4}$ (C) 1 (D) 2 (E) 3

Since Tina can do the job in 12 hours, in 8 hours she can do 8/12, or 2/3, of the job. This leaves 1/3 of the job for Ann to complete. Since Ann can do the job in 9 hours, she can do 1/3 of the job in 3 hours. Thus, the best answer is E. This is an easy question.

8. A factory normally produces x units per working day. In a month with 22 working days, no units are produced in the first y working days because of a strike. How many units must be produced per day on each of the rest of the working days of the month in order to have an average of x units per working day for the entire month?

   (A) 11x

   (B) 22x

   (C) $\frac{22x}{y}$

   (D) $\frac{22x}{22-y}$

   (E) $\frac{22x}{22xy-y}$

To have an average of x units per day for the 22 days, a total of 22x units must be produced in the shorter period, 22 − y days. The number to be produced per day =

$$\frac{\text{total production}}{\text{number of production days}} = \frac{22x}{22-y}.$$ Thus, the best answer is D. This is a moderately difficult question.

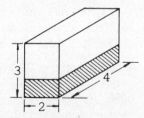

9. An enclosed rectangular tank with dimensions 2 meters by 3 meters by 4 meters is filled with water to a depth of 1 meter as shown by the shaded region in the figure above. If the tank is turned so that it rests on one of its smallest faces, the depth, in meters, of the water will be

   (A) $\frac{2}{3}$ (B) 1 (C) $\frac{4}{3}$ (D) $\frac{5}{3}$ (E) 2

The total volume of water in the tank is 2·4·1 = 8 cubic meters. If the tank were placed on one of its 2-meter by 3-meter faces, the total volume of water could be expressed as 2·3·d = 6d cubic meters, where d is the depth of the water.

Since the volume of the water is the same regardless of the face on which the tank rests,

6d = 8, or d = $\frac{4}{3}$ meters. Thus, the best answer is C. This is a moderately difficult question.

10. A person bought a ticket to a ball game for $15 and later sold the ticket for $60. What was the percent increase in the price of the ticket?

    (A) 25%

    (B) $33\frac{1}{3}$%

    (C) 75%

    (D) 300%

    (E) 400%

The increase in the price was $60 − $15 = $45. Therefore, the percent increase was $\frac{\$45}{\$15}$ = 3 = 300%. Thus, the best answer is D. This is a moderately difficult question.

11. A decorator bought a bolt of defective cloth that he judged to be $\frac{3}{4}$ usable, in which case the cost would be $0.80 per usable yard. If it was later found that only $\frac{2}{3}$ of the bolt could be used, what was the actual cost per usable yard?

    (A) $0.60
    (B) $0.90
    (C) $1.00
    (D) $1.20
    (E) $1.70

Of the N original yards of cloth, $\frac{3N}{4}$ were judged to be usable. Therefore, the total cost for the usable yards can be represented by $0.80\left(\frac{3N}{4}\right)$. If, in fact, only 2/3 of N are usable, and c is the cost per usable yard, the total cost for the usable yards would be $c\left(\frac{2N}{3}\right)$. Therefore, $c\left(\frac{2N}{3}\right) = 0.80\left(\frac{3N}{4}\right)$.

When both sides of the equation are multiplied by 12, the result is c(8N) = 0.80 (9N), 8c = 7.20, and c = $0.90. Thus, the best answer is B. This is a moderately difficult question.

Week	Number of Tickets Sold
1	1,000,000
2	1,000,000
3	750,000
4	250,000

12. The table above shows the number of tickets sold during each of the first 4 weeks after a movie was released. The producer of the movie received 10 percent of the revenue from every ticket sold with a guaranteed minimum of $200,000 each week for the first 4 weeks. If tickets sold for $4 each, how much did the producer receive for the first 4 weeks?

   (A) $800,000
   (B) $900,000
   (C) $1,000,000
   (D) $1,200,000
   (E) $1,300,000

Since the producer received 10 percent of the revenue and each ticket sold for $4, the producer received $0.40 per ticket sold. Therefore, the producer's income each week was:

Week 1 : 1,000,000(0.40) = $400,000
Week 2 : 1,000,000(0.40) = $400,000
Week 3 :   750,000(0.40) = $300,000
Week 4 :   250,000(0.40) = $100,000 + $100,000*

Total = $1,300,000

*There was a guaranteed minimum of $200,000 each week.

Thus, the best answer is E. This is a moderately difficult question.

13. If x, y, and z are single-digit integers and $100(x) + 1,000(y) + 10(z) = N$, what is the units' digit of the number N?

   (A) 0   (B) 1   (C) x   (D) y   (E) z

Since each of the three terms of N is a multiple of 10, N is a multiple of 10. Thus, the units' digit of N must be zero, and the best answer is A. This is a moderately difficult question.

14. Three stacks containing equal numbers of chips are to be made from 9 red chips, 7 blue chips, and 5 green chips. If all of these chips are used and each stack contains at least 1 chip of each color, what is the maximum number of red chips in any one stack?

   (A) 7
   (B) 6
   (C) 5
   (D) 4
   (E) 3

Since there is a total of 21 chips, each of the three stacks must contain 7 chips and at least one chip of each color. If one blue and one green chip are part of the stack, the maximum number of red chips in any one stack is 5. Thus, the best answer is C. This is a difficult question.

15. Three automobiles travel distances that are in the ratios of 1:2:3. If the ratios of the traveling times over these distances for these automobiles are 3:2:1 in the same respective order, what are the ratios of their respective average speeds?

   (A) 1:1:1
   (B) 1:3:3
   (C) 1:3:9
   (D) 3:2:1
   (E) 3:4:3

Since speed $= \dfrac{\text{distance}}{\text{time}}$, the ratios of the speeds for the three automobiles must be $\frac{1}{3} : \frac{2}{2} : \frac{3}{1}$, which is equivalent to $3\left(\frac{1}{3}\right) : 3\left(\frac{2}{2}\right) : 3\left(\frac{3}{1}\right)$ or $1 : 3 : 9$. Thus, the best answer is C. This is a difficult question.

16. Over the last three years a scientist had an average (arithmetic mean) yearly income of $45,000. The scientist earned $1\frac{1}{2}$ times as much the second year as the first year and $2\frac{1}{2}$ times as much the third year as the first year. What was the scientist's income the second year?

   (A) $9,000
   (B) $13,500
   (C) $27,000
   (D) $40,500
   (E) $45,000

The total income for the three years was $(3)(45,000) = \$135,000$. Let x represent the scientist's income the first year. Then the second-year income was $\frac{3}{2}x$ and the third-year income was $\frac{5}{2}x$. Therefore,

$x + \frac{3}{2}x + \frac{5}{2}x = 135,000$, $5x = 135,000$, and $x = 27,000$.

Thus the second-year income was $\frac{3}{2}(27,000) = \$40,500$.

Thus, the best answer is D. This is a difficult question.

17. How many two-digit whole numbers yield a remainder of 1 when divided by 10 and also yield a remainder of 1 when divided by 6?

   (A) None   (B) One   (C) Two
      (D) Three   (E) Four

For a whole number n to have a remainder of 1 when divided by both 10 and 6, n − 1 must be divisible by both 10 and 6, or by the least common multiple of 10 and 6, which is 30. Therefore, the two-digit whole numbers that yield a remainder of 1 when divided by both 6 and 10 are 31, 61, and 91. There are only three such numbers, and the best answer is D. This is a difficult question.

18. If $x \neq 3$ and $\dfrac{x^2 - 9}{2y} = \dfrac{x - 3}{4}$, then, in terms of y, x =

(A) $\dfrac{y - 6}{2}$

(B) $\dfrac{y - 3}{2}$

(C) $y - 3$

(D) $y - 6$

(E) $\dfrac{y + 6}{2}$

First, multiply both sides of the equation by the least common denominator, 4y: $4y\left(\dfrac{x^2 - 9}{2y}\right) = 4y\left(\dfrac{x - 3}{4}\right)$, and $2(x^2 - 9) = y(x - 3)$.

Then, express $x^2 - 9$ as $(x + 3)(x - 3)$ and divide both sides by $x - 3$:

$$\dfrac{2(x + 3)(x - 3)}{x - 3} = \dfrac{y(x - 3)}{x - 3}$$

$$2(x + 3) = y$$

$$2x + 6 = y$$

$$2x = y - 6$$

$$x = \dfrac{y - 6}{2}$$

Thus, the best answer is A. This is a difficult question.

19. The figure above shows the shape of a sign to be placed in front of a flower store. The sign has a semicircle on each side of the square. If the sign is 3 centimeters thick and if each side of the square is 50 centimeters long, what is the volume, in cubic centimeters, of the sign?

(A) $1,250\pi + 2,500$

(B) $3,750\pi$

(C) $3,750\pi + 7,500$

(D) $5,000\pi + 7,500$

(E) $11,250\pi$

The volume of the sign is equal to the surface area times the depth. The surface consists of a square and four semicircles (two whole circles). The area of the square is $(50)^2$ or 2,500. Each of the two circles has diameter 50 and radius 25; therefore, the area of each of the two circles is $\pi(25)^2 = 625\pi$. The total surface area equals $2,500 + (2 \times 625\pi)$, or $2,500 + 1,250\pi$. The volume is $3(2,500 + 1,250\pi)$, or $7,500 + 3,750\pi$. Thus, the best answer is C. This is a difficult question.

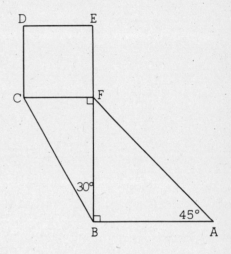

20. In the figure above, square CDEF has area 4. What is the area of $\triangle ABF$?

(A) $2\sqrt{2}$ (B) $2\sqrt{3}$ (C) 4   (D) $3\sqrt{3}$ (E) 6

Since the square has area 4, CF = 2. Triangle BCF is a 30-60-90 right triangle; therefore, CB = 2(CF) = 2(2) = 4. Applying the Pythagorean Theorem to

$$\triangle BCF:\ (BF)^2 = (CB)^2 - (CF)^2 = 4^2 - 2^2 = 12,$$

and BF = $\sqrt{12}$. BF = BA, since they are both opposite 45° angles. Therefore, BA = $\sqrt{12}$ and the area of

$$\triangle ABF = \dfrac{(BA)(BF)}{2} = \dfrac{(\sqrt{12})\sqrt{12}}{2} = 6.$$ Thus, the best answer is E. This is a difficult question.

Answer Sheet: Form B

SECTION 1	SECTION 2	SECTION 3	SECTION 4	SECTION 5	SECTION 6
1 Ⓐ Ⓑ Ⓒ Ⓓ Ⓔ	1 Ⓐ Ⓑ Ⓒ Ⓓ Ⓔ	1 Ⓐ Ⓑ Ⓒ Ⓓ Ⓔ	1 Ⓐ Ⓑ Ⓒ Ⓓ Ⓔ	1 Ⓐ Ⓑ Ⓒ Ⓓ Ⓔ	1 Ⓐ Ⓑ Ⓒ Ⓓ Ⓔ
2 Ⓐ Ⓑ Ⓒ Ⓓ Ⓔ	2 Ⓐ Ⓑ Ⓒ Ⓓ Ⓔ	2 Ⓐ Ⓑ Ⓒ Ⓓ Ⓔ	2 Ⓐ Ⓑ Ⓒ Ⓓ Ⓔ	2 Ⓐ Ⓑ Ⓒ Ⓓ Ⓔ	2 Ⓐ Ⓑ Ⓒ Ⓓ Ⓔ
3 Ⓐ Ⓑ Ⓒ Ⓓ Ⓔ	3 Ⓐ Ⓑ Ⓒ Ⓓ Ⓔ	3 Ⓐ Ⓑ Ⓒ Ⓓ Ⓔ	3 Ⓐ Ⓑ Ⓒ Ⓓ Ⓔ	3 Ⓐ Ⓑ Ⓒ Ⓓ Ⓔ	3 Ⓐ Ⓑ Ⓒ Ⓓ Ⓔ
4 Ⓐ Ⓑ Ⓒ Ⓓ Ⓔ	4 Ⓐ Ⓑ Ⓒ Ⓓ Ⓔ	4 Ⓐ Ⓑ Ⓒ Ⓓ Ⓔ	4 Ⓐ Ⓑ Ⓒ Ⓓ Ⓔ	4 Ⓐ Ⓑ Ⓒ Ⓓ Ⓔ	4 Ⓐ Ⓑ Ⓒ Ⓓ Ⓔ
5 Ⓐ Ⓑ Ⓒ Ⓓ Ⓔ	5 Ⓐ Ⓑ Ⓒ Ⓓ Ⓔ	5 Ⓐ Ⓑ Ⓒ Ⓓ Ⓔ	5 Ⓐ Ⓑ Ⓒ Ⓓ Ⓔ	5 Ⓐ Ⓑ Ⓒ Ⓓ Ⓔ	5 Ⓐ Ⓑ Ⓒ Ⓓ Ⓔ
6 Ⓐ Ⓑ Ⓒ Ⓓ Ⓔ	6 Ⓐ Ⓑ Ⓒ Ⓓ Ⓔ	6 Ⓐ Ⓑ Ⓒ Ⓓ Ⓔ	6 Ⓐ Ⓑ Ⓒ Ⓓ Ⓔ	6 Ⓐ Ⓑ Ⓒ Ⓓ Ⓔ	6 Ⓐ Ⓑ Ⓒ Ⓓ Ⓔ
7 Ⓐ Ⓑ Ⓒ Ⓓ Ⓔ	7 Ⓐ Ⓑ Ⓒ Ⓓ Ⓔ	7 Ⓐ Ⓑ Ⓒ Ⓓ Ⓔ	7 Ⓐ Ⓑ Ⓒ Ⓓ Ⓔ	7 Ⓐ Ⓑ Ⓒ Ⓓ Ⓔ	7 Ⓐ Ⓑ Ⓒ Ⓓ Ⓔ
8 Ⓐ Ⓑ Ⓒ Ⓓ Ⓔ	8 Ⓐ Ⓑ Ⓒ Ⓓ Ⓔ	8 Ⓐ Ⓑ Ⓒ Ⓓ Ⓔ	8 Ⓐ Ⓑ Ⓒ Ⓓ Ⓔ	8 Ⓐ Ⓑ Ⓒ Ⓓ Ⓔ	8 Ⓐ Ⓑ Ⓒ Ⓓ Ⓔ
9 Ⓐ Ⓑ Ⓒ Ⓓ Ⓔ	9 Ⓐ Ⓑ Ⓒ Ⓓ Ⓔ	9 Ⓐ Ⓑ Ⓒ Ⓓ Ⓔ	9 Ⓐ Ⓑ Ⓒ Ⓓ Ⓔ	9 Ⓐ Ⓑ Ⓒ Ⓓ Ⓔ	9 Ⓐ Ⓑ Ⓒ Ⓓ Ⓔ
10 Ⓐ Ⓑ Ⓒ Ⓓ Ⓔ	10 Ⓐ Ⓑ Ⓒ Ⓓ Ⓔ	10 Ⓐ Ⓑ Ⓒ Ⓓ Ⓔ	10 Ⓐ Ⓑ Ⓒ Ⓓ Ⓔ	10 Ⓐ Ⓑ Ⓒ Ⓓ Ⓔ	10 Ⓐ Ⓑ Ⓒ Ⓓ Ⓔ
11 Ⓐ Ⓑ Ⓒ Ⓓ Ⓔ	11 Ⓐ Ⓑ Ⓒ Ⓓ Ⓔ	11 Ⓐ Ⓑ Ⓒ Ⓓ Ⓔ	11 Ⓐ Ⓑ Ⓒ Ⓓ Ⓔ	11 Ⓐ Ⓑ Ⓒ Ⓓ Ⓔ	11 Ⓐ Ⓑ Ⓒ Ⓓ Ⓔ
12 Ⓐ Ⓑ Ⓒ Ⓓ Ⓔ	12 Ⓐ Ⓑ Ⓒ Ⓓ Ⓔ	12 Ⓐ Ⓑ Ⓒ Ⓓ Ⓔ	12 Ⓐ Ⓑ Ⓒ Ⓓ Ⓔ	12 Ⓐ Ⓑ Ⓒ Ⓓ Ⓔ	12 Ⓐ Ⓑ Ⓒ Ⓓ Ⓔ
13 Ⓐ Ⓑ Ⓒ Ⓓ Ⓔ	13 Ⓐ Ⓑ Ⓒ Ⓓ Ⓔ	13 Ⓐ Ⓑ Ⓒ Ⓓ Ⓔ	13 Ⓐ Ⓑ Ⓒ Ⓓ Ⓔ	13 Ⓐ Ⓑ Ⓒ Ⓓ Ⓔ	13 Ⓐ Ⓑ Ⓒ Ⓓ Ⓔ
14 Ⓐ Ⓑ Ⓒ Ⓓ Ⓔ	14 Ⓐ Ⓑ Ⓒ Ⓓ Ⓔ	14 Ⓐ Ⓑ Ⓒ Ⓓ Ⓔ	14 Ⓐ Ⓑ Ⓒ Ⓓ Ⓔ	14 Ⓐ Ⓑ Ⓒ Ⓓ Ⓔ	14 Ⓐ Ⓑ Ⓒ Ⓓ Ⓔ
15 Ⓐ Ⓑ Ⓒ Ⓓ Ⓔ	15 Ⓐ Ⓑ Ⓒ Ⓓ Ⓔ	15 Ⓐ Ⓑ Ⓒ Ⓓ Ⓔ	15 Ⓐ Ⓑ Ⓒ Ⓓ Ⓔ	15 Ⓐ Ⓑ Ⓒ Ⓓ Ⓔ	15 Ⓐ Ⓑ Ⓒ Ⓓ Ⓔ
16 Ⓐ Ⓑ Ⓒ Ⓓ Ⓔ	16 Ⓐ Ⓑ Ⓒ Ⓓ Ⓔ	16 Ⓐ Ⓑ Ⓒ Ⓓ Ⓔ	16 Ⓐ Ⓑ Ⓒ Ⓓ Ⓔ	16 Ⓐ Ⓑ Ⓒ Ⓓ Ⓔ	16 Ⓐ Ⓑ Ⓒ Ⓓ Ⓔ
17 Ⓐ Ⓑ Ⓒ Ⓓ Ⓔ	17 Ⓐ Ⓑ Ⓒ Ⓓ Ⓔ	17 Ⓐ Ⓑ Ⓒ Ⓓ Ⓔ	17 Ⓐ Ⓑ Ⓒ Ⓓ Ⓔ	17 Ⓐ Ⓑ Ⓒ Ⓓ Ⓔ	17 Ⓐ Ⓑ Ⓒ Ⓓ Ⓔ
18 Ⓐ Ⓑ Ⓒ Ⓓ Ⓔ	18 Ⓐ Ⓑ Ⓒ Ⓓ Ⓔ	18 Ⓐ Ⓑ Ⓒ Ⓓ Ⓔ	18 Ⓐ Ⓑ Ⓒ Ⓓ Ⓔ	18 Ⓐ Ⓑ Ⓒ Ⓓ Ⓔ	18 Ⓐ Ⓑ Ⓒ Ⓓ Ⓔ
19 Ⓐ Ⓑ Ⓒ Ⓓ Ⓔ	19 Ⓐ Ⓑ Ⓒ Ⓓ Ⓔ	19 Ⓐ Ⓑ Ⓒ Ⓓ Ⓔ	19 Ⓐ Ⓑ Ⓒ Ⓓ Ⓔ	19 Ⓐ Ⓑ Ⓒ Ⓓ Ⓔ	19 Ⓐ Ⓑ Ⓒ Ⓓ Ⓔ
20 Ⓐ Ⓑ Ⓒ Ⓓ Ⓔ	20 Ⓐ Ⓑ Ⓒ Ⓓ Ⓔ	20 Ⓐ Ⓑ Ⓒ Ⓓ Ⓔ	20 Ⓐ Ⓑ Ⓒ Ⓓ Ⓔ	20 Ⓐ Ⓑ Ⓒ Ⓓ Ⓔ	20 Ⓐ Ⓑ Ⓒ Ⓓ Ⓔ
21 Ⓐ Ⓑ Ⓒ Ⓓ Ⓔ	21 Ⓐ Ⓑ Ⓒ Ⓓ Ⓔ	21 Ⓐ Ⓑ Ⓒ Ⓓ Ⓔ	21 Ⓐ Ⓑ Ⓒ Ⓓ Ⓔ	21 Ⓐ Ⓑ Ⓒ Ⓓ Ⓔ	21 Ⓐ Ⓑ Ⓒ Ⓓ Ⓔ
22 Ⓐ Ⓑ Ⓒ Ⓓ Ⓔ	22 Ⓐ Ⓑ Ⓒ Ⓓ Ⓔ	22 Ⓐ Ⓑ Ⓒ Ⓓ Ⓔ	22 Ⓐ Ⓑ Ⓒ Ⓓ Ⓔ	22 Ⓐ Ⓑ Ⓒ Ⓓ Ⓔ	22 Ⓐ Ⓑ Ⓒ Ⓓ Ⓔ
23 Ⓐ Ⓑ Ⓒ Ⓓ Ⓔ	23 Ⓐ Ⓑ Ⓒ Ⓓ Ⓔ	23 Ⓐ Ⓑ Ⓒ Ⓓ Ⓔ	23 Ⓐ Ⓑ Ⓒ Ⓓ Ⓔ	23 Ⓐ Ⓑ Ⓒ Ⓓ Ⓔ	23 Ⓐ Ⓑ Ⓒ Ⓓ Ⓔ
24 Ⓐ Ⓑ Ⓒ Ⓓ Ⓔ	24 Ⓐ Ⓑ Ⓒ Ⓓ Ⓔ	24 Ⓐ Ⓑ Ⓒ Ⓓ Ⓔ	24 Ⓐ Ⓑ Ⓒ Ⓓ Ⓔ	24 Ⓐ Ⓑ Ⓒ Ⓓ Ⓔ	24 Ⓐ Ⓑ Ⓒ Ⓓ Ⓔ
25 Ⓐ Ⓑ Ⓒ Ⓓ Ⓔ	25 Ⓐ Ⓑ Ⓒ Ⓓ Ⓔ	25 Ⓐ Ⓑ Ⓒ Ⓓ Ⓔ	25 Ⓐ Ⓑ Ⓒ Ⓓ Ⓔ	25 Ⓐ Ⓑ Ⓒ Ⓓ Ⓔ	25 Ⓐ Ⓑ Ⓒ Ⓓ Ⓔ
26 Ⓐ Ⓑ Ⓒ Ⓓ Ⓔ	26 Ⓐ Ⓑ Ⓒ Ⓓ Ⓔ	26 Ⓐ Ⓑ Ⓒ Ⓓ Ⓔ	26 Ⓐ Ⓑ Ⓒ Ⓓ Ⓔ	26 Ⓐ Ⓑ Ⓒ Ⓓ Ⓔ	26 Ⓐ Ⓑ Ⓒ Ⓓ Ⓔ
27 Ⓐ Ⓑ Ⓒ Ⓓ Ⓔ	27 Ⓐ Ⓑ Ⓒ Ⓓ Ⓔ	27 Ⓐ Ⓑ Ⓒ Ⓓ Ⓔ	27 Ⓐ Ⓑ Ⓒ Ⓓ Ⓔ	27 Ⓐ Ⓑ Ⓒ Ⓓ Ⓔ	27 Ⓐ Ⓑ Ⓒ Ⓓ Ⓔ
28 Ⓐ Ⓑ Ⓒ Ⓓ Ⓔ	28 Ⓐ Ⓑ Ⓒ Ⓓ Ⓔ	28 Ⓐ Ⓑ Ⓒ Ⓓ Ⓔ	28 Ⓐ Ⓑ Ⓒ Ⓓ Ⓔ	28 Ⓐ Ⓑ Ⓒ Ⓓ Ⓔ	28 Ⓐ Ⓑ Ⓒ Ⓓ Ⓔ
29 Ⓐ Ⓑ Ⓒ Ⓓ Ⓔ	29 Ⓐ Ⓑ Ⓒ Ⓓ Ⓔ	29 Ⓐ Ⓑ Ⓒ Ⓓ Ⓔ	29 Ⓐ Ⓑ Ⓒ Ⓓ Ⓔ	29 Ⓐ Ⓑ Ⓒ Ⓓ Ⓔ	29 Ⓐ Ⓑ Ⓒ Ⓓ Ⓔ
30 Ⓐ Ⓑ Ⓒ Ⓓ Ⓔ	30 Ⓐ Ⓑ Ⓒ Ⓓ Ⓔ	30 Ⓐ Ⓑ Ⓒ Ⓓ Ⓔ	30 Ⓐ Ⓑ Ⓒ Ⓓ Ⓔ	30 Ⓐ Ⓑ Ⓒ Ⓓ Ⓔ	30 Ⓐ Ⓑ Ⓒ Ⓓ Ⓔ
31 Ⓐ Ⓑ Ⓒ Ⓓ Ⓔ	31 Ⓐ Ⓑ Ⓒ Ⓓ Ⓔ	31 Ⓐ Ⓑ Ⓒ Ⓓ Ⓔ	31 Ⓐ Ⓑ Ⓒ Ⓓ Ⓔ	31 Ⓐ Ⓑ Ⓒ Ⓓ Ⓔ	31 Ⓐ Ⓑ Ⓒ Ⓓ Ⓔ
32 Ⓐ Ⓑ Ⓒ Ⓓ Ⓔ	32 Ⓐ Ⓑ Ⓒ Ⓓ Ⓔ	32 Ⓐ Ⓑ Ⓒ Ⓓ Ⓔ	32 Ⓐ Ⓑ Ⓒ Ⓓ Ⓔ	32 Ⓐ Ⓑ Ⓒ Ⓓ Ⓔ	32 Ⓐ Ⓑ Ⓒ Ⓓ Ⓔ
33 Ⓐ Ⓑ Ⓒ Ⓓ Ⓔ	33 Ⓐ Ⓑ Ⓒ Ⓓ Ⓔ	33 Ⓐ Ⓑ Ⓒ Ⓓ Ⓔ	33 Ⓐ Ⓑ Ⓒ Ⓓ Ⓔ	33 Ⓐ Ⓑ Ⓒ Ⓓ Ⓔ	33 Ⓐ Ⓑ Ⓒ Ⓓ Ⓔ
34 Ⓐ Ⓑ Ⓒ Ⓓ Ⓔ	34 Ⓐ Ⓑ Ⓒ Ⓓ Ⓔ	34 Ⓐ Ⓑ Ⓒ Ⓓ Ⓔ	34 Ⓐ Ⓑ Ⓒ Ⓓ Ⓔ	34 Ⓐ Ⓑ Ⓒ Ⓓ Ⓔ	34 Ⓐ Ⓑ Ⓒ Ⓓ Ⓔ
35 Ⓐ Ⓑ Ⓒ Ⓓ Ⓔ	35 Ⓐ Ⓑ Ⓒ Ⓓ Ⓔ	35 Ⓐ Ⓑ Ⓒ Ⓓ Ⓔ	35 Ⓐ Ⓑ Ⓒ Ⓓ Ⓔ	35 Ⓐ Ⓑ Ⓒ Ⓓ Ⓔ	35 Ⓐ Ⓑ Ⓒ Ⓓ Ⓔ

Print your full name here:_____
                 (last)   (first)   (middle)

Graduate Management Admission Test

SECTION I
Time—30 minutes
35 Questions

<u>Directions:</u> Each passage in this section is followed by numbered considerations that require classification, as illustrated by the following example:

> John Atkins, the owner of a service station in Leeway, wanted to open a station in Eastown. A computer company had plans to set up operations in Eastown, and Atkins, foreseeing an increase in traffic near the plant, was eager to acquire land in Eastown so that he could expand his business to serve commuting workers. Ideally, Atkins wanted a piece of land large enough to permit him to build a tire store as part of the new station; he also wanted to keep the cost of purchasing the land as well as the cost of clearing it for construction as low as possible. Atkins identified three possible properties: one on Moore Road, another on Route 5, and a third on Snow Lane. The purchase prices of the properties were $42,000, $36,000, and $34,000, respectively. The properties required different expenditures for clearing. In the case of the Snow Lane site, a diner would have to be demolished and pavement removed. Atkins knew that his decision required deliberation.

The following numbered considerations are related to the passage above. Evaluate each consideration separately in terms of the passage and on the answer sheet blacken space

A if the consideration is an <u>Objective</u> in making the decision; that is, one of the outcomes, results, or goals that the decision-maker seeks;

B if the consideration is a <u>Major Factor</u> in making the decision; that is, a consideration, explicitly mentioned in the passage, that is basic to reaching the decision;

C if the consideration is a <u>Minor Factor</u> in making the decision; that is, a consideration that is of secondary importance to reaching the decision and that bears on a Major Factor;

D if the consideration is an <u>Assumption</u> in making the decision; that is, a relevant supposition or projection made by the decision-maker before reaching the decision;

E if the consideration is an <u>Unimportant Issue</u> in making the decision; that is, a consideration that is insignificant or not immediately relevant to reaching the decision.

1. Increase in traffic near the new computer plant — Ⓐ Ⓑ Ⓒ ● Ⓔ

2. Acquisition of a sufficiently large piece of land — ● Ⓑ Ⓒ Ⓓ Ⓔ

3. Cost of clearing a piece of land — Ⓐ ● Ⓒ Ⓓ Ⓔ

4. Cost of demolishing the diner on the Snow Lane site — Ⓐ Ⓑ ● Ⓓ Ⓔ

5. Cost of starting up the new computer plant — Ⓐ Ⓑ Ⓒ Ⓓ ●

GO ON TO THE NEXT PAGE.

The best classification for number 1 is (D), an <u>Assumption</u>, since Atkins supposes that automobile traffic will increase near the new computer plant. The best classification for number 2 is (A), an <u>Objective</u>, since one of Atkins' goals is to obtain a piece of land large enough to permit him to include a tire store as part of his new station. (B), a <u>Major Factor</u>, is the best classification for number 3. The cost of clearing a property is a basic consideration to Atkins since he wants to prepare a property for construction at the lowest possible cost. The best classification for number 4 is (C), a <u>Minor Factor</u>. The cost of demolishing the diner on the Snow Lane site contributes to the total cost of clearing that site. That is, the cost of demolition is a secondary consideration that bears on a major factor. Finally, the best classification for number 5 is (E), an <u>Unimportant Issue</u>, since there is no logical connection between the cost of starting up the computer plant and Atkins' decision about which property to choose.

NOW READ THE PASSAGES AND CLASSIFY THE CONSIDERATIONS FOLLOWING THEM.

GO ON TO THE NEXT PAGE.

The Sparkle Springs Corporation, producer of Sparkle, a soft drink, was founded in 1946 in Springs Valley, New Jersey. Over the years, the family-owned company enjoyed a steady growth in the tri-state area of New York, New Jersey, and Connecticut. By 1976, although the market for Sparkle seemed capable of expansion, the production capacity of the company's Springs Valley plant was at its limit, while production costs, especially local labor costs, had soared. In order to cut costs and increase production, company president Mary Spark considered three alternatives for expansion: modernize the company's existing facility, build a new plant near the old site, or choose an entirely new site for the plant outside New Jersey.

Spark believed that Springs Valley would be the most appropriate location for a new plant since the area had become closely associated with Sparkle through thirty years of advertising the purity of the local spring water from which Sparkle was made. In 1971, Spark had expanded Sparkle's advertising to all states east of the Mississippi. Although five years later, in 1976, 75 percent of Sparkle's sales were still accounted for by the tri-state area, Spark intended to build on the marketing spearheads established in the East and win additional markets in the West by extending advertising beyond the Mississippi.

In March of 1977, Spark had located a suitable 107-acre Springs Valley building site for a new plant and had opened negotiations with the owner for a two-year option. But, before a contract could be signed, two manufacturing concerns announced plans to open new plants in Springs Valley, and immediately the owner of the site raised the price to $3,000 an acre. Barely a week later, the workers at the Sparkle Springs plant went on strike. The resulting month-long shutdown caused a temporary loss of sales and resulted in an expensive negotiated settlement calling for a 7.5 percent increase in wages at the beginning of each year of the three-year contract.

In January 1978, Spark started to consider alternative sites for a new plant outside Springs Valley to be run in addition to the company's original plant. In October 1978, she became particularly interested in Martindale County, a region of dairy farms in Colorado within thirty miles of a city with a population of 85,000, all potential Sparkle customers. In addition to its location, which would give Sparkle Springs easier access to western markets, Martindale County boasted an abundance of open farmland, a plentiful supply of high-quality groundwater, and lower regional wages than those in Springs Valley. In March 1979, Spark's representatives found a site suitable for a new plant and recommended the purchase of a thousand acres at $3,000 per acre to protect the company's water rights.

Before committing herself to a course of action, Spark considered the following points. She could increase the production capacity and efficiency of Sparkle Springs' original facility and reduce its labor needs by installing new machinery. However, conversion of the plant to the latest manufacturing processes would require structural changes costing $1,500,000, over and above the million dollars needed for new machinery, without significantly cutting the maintenance costs of the aging building. Alternatively, she could build an entirely new plant in Springs Valley and reduce production in the older facility by ten percent to a level that would maximize the margin between production costs and gross income. A new plant on the proposed site in New Jersey would cost, exclusive of the price of the site, approximately $7,000,000 and increase Sparkle Springs' production capacity by 150 percent, 90 percent more than the increase anticipated from modernization of the original facility. Either of these alternatives, a new plant or a modernized facility, would, when run at full capacity, result in a 30 percent reduction in Sparkle Springs' work force. However, operational costs, exclusive of labor, would be reduced by a third in a new plant, whereas those in a renovated plant would represent a savings of only 20 percent. Because of its New Jersey location, neither plant in itself would give Sparkle Springs easy access to western markets. Lastly, if Spark decided to build in Colorado, construction costs for a Martindale County plant identical to the one proposed for the Springs Valley site would also be approximately $7,000,000, exclusive of the price of the site.

Before Spark reached a decision, news of Sparkle Springs' interest in Martindale County leaked out, and agricultural and environmental opponents of Sparkle Springs mounted a campaign against the company's proposed location in the county. Their slogan, playing on the company's advertising, was "Sparkle Sparks Industrialization—Save Our Farmland."

Wishing to appease its critics, Sparkle Springs Corporation let it be known that the site had the strong endorsement of state and county industrial development agencies. The company also stated that its plant would occupy only 100 acres of its proposed site, the remaining 900 acres being leased back to farmers for continued agricultural use.

As had been the case since 1976, the company continued to operate at full production capacity with orders and sales indicating that larger markets could be served. It was clear that Spark must make firm decisions about her alternatives.

GO ON TO THE NEXT PAGE.

1 1 1 1 1 1 1 1 1 B

Directions: The following questions consist of items related to the passage above. You may refer back to the passage and the directions. Consider each item separately in terms of the passage and on the answer sheet blacken space

A if the item is a Major Objective in making the decision; that is, one of the outcomes or results sought by the decision-maker;

B if the item is a Major Factor in making the decision; that is, a consideration, explicitly mentioned in the passage, that is basic in determining the decision;

C if the item is a Minor Factor in making the decision; that is, a secondary consideration that affects the criteria tangentially, relating to a Major Factor rather than to an Objective;

D if the item is a Major Assumption in making the decision; that is, a supposition or projection made by the decision-maker before weighing the variables;

E if the item is an Unimportant Issue in making the decision; that is, a factor that is insignificant or not immediately relevant to the situation.

1. Family ownership of Sparkle Springs

2. A decrease in the cost of manufacturing Sparkle

3. Future increase in Sparkle Springs' sales outside of the eastern United States

4. Effect on real estate prices of the announcement of two new Springs Valley industries

5. Likelihood that increasing the production of Sparkle will increase the company's profit

6. Net economic advantage of each of the proposed alternatives

7. Proximity of Martindale County to a city

8. Effect of the Martindale opposition on Sparkle Springs' eastern market objectives

9. Exceptionally high quality of the groundwater in Martindale County

10. Relative percentage of Sparkle's sales accounted for by each of the states in the tri-state area

11. Procurement of major markets west of the Mississippi

12. Temporary loss of sales caused by the month-long shutdown of Sparkle's plant in Springs Valley

13. Martindale County's relatively lower wage structure

14. Continued market demand for Sparkle over and above the production capacity of Sparkle Springs' original facility before modernization

15. An increase in Sparkle Springs' production capacity

16. Importance of expanding Sparkle's advertising to all states east of the Mississippi

17. Cost of land at the Martindale County site

GO ON TO THE NEXT PAGE.

Eurocircuits, a French company, manufactures, sells, and services electronics equipment. In the late 1970's, with the aid of the French government, Eurocircuits obtained a substantial share of the market for medium-sized computers in France and West Germany. Pierre Manet, president of Eurocircuits, was impressed with the rapid growth of the personal computer market in the United States. He planned to have Eurocircuits capture a predominant share of the personal computer market in France by becoming the first French company to produce small computers for the mass market. French trade barriers would prevent the Americans and Japanese from dominating the French market, and Manet felt that he would obtain a substantial advantage over his French competitors by being the first to bring out a line of low-cost, personal computers.

In 1981, Western Europe produced less than one-third of the integrated circuits that it used in manufacturing electronic products. Therefore, Manet was forced to look to the United States and Japan for the parts needed to bring out a line of small, low-cost computers. In January 1982, Manet placed an order for three million integrated circuits with Virginia Electronics. These integrated circuits were to be used in the manufacture of the small computers Eurocircuits needed to enter the personal computer market. The circuits were to be delivered in four quarterly shipments beginning in January 1983. Eurocircuits planned to launch its advertising campaign for the French personal computer market in October 1983.

In April 1982, it became apparent that the market for personal computers in the United States was far larger than had been estimated. When Pierre Manet realized how great the demand was for personal computers in the United States, he decided to try to bring out Eurocircuits' line of personal computers for the French market earlier than planned. He feared that the popularity of personal computers in the United States would encourage one of his European competitors to bring out a line of personal computers before Eurocircuits' plans could be realized. However, he faced the prospect of having to wait until January 1983 before he would have the integrated circuits necessary to begin manufacturing the computers. Since manufacturing could begin as soon as the integrated circuits could be obtained, Manet searched for a supplier that could begin shipping integrated circuits immediately. Manet reasoned that an earlier entry into the French market would probably increase the share of the market that Eurocircuits would obtain, and he believed that it might enable his company to obtain a predominant share of the market. Thus, both a substantially improved competitive position and an increase in profits seemed to be possible if an alternative integrated circuits supplier could be found.

Manet realized that there were three crucial elements in choosing an alternative supplier. First, the circuits needed to be highly reliable and trouble-free, or the entire venture might fail. Second, the circuits were needed as soon as possible in order to facilitate early entry into the market. Finally, the circuits must be obtained at the lowest possible price in order to preserve Eurocircuits' profit margin.

After efforts to negotiate an earlier delivery date with Virginia Electronics had failed, Eurocircuits narrowed its list of possible alternative suppliers to three: Boston Electronics, Houston Electronics, and Osaka Electronics. In the past, Eurocircuits had dealt successfully with Osaka Electronics, which had an excellent reputation for highly reliable integrated circuits. Osaka offered to begin shipment of the needed circuits within six months at eight percent above the prevailing market price. Boston Electronics, which produced integrated circuits of satisfactory reliability, was able to promise to begin shipping within three months, but its price was high, twelve percent above the prevailing market price. Houston Electronics had a good reputation for prompt delivery and had promised to begin shipping at once. Houston's price was only six percent above the prevailing market price plus a one percent surcharge for immediate shipping. In the past, the reliability of Houston's integrated circuits had not been good, but the company had recently undergone several changes in its top management.

Had it not been for the emergence of a major competitor for the French personal computer market, the differences in shipping dates would not have been so important. However, Eurocircuits' largest competitor in France had just announced plans to bring out a line of personal computers in early 1983.

A meeting of Eurocircuits' board was held to discuss the situation. The following comments were made at the meeting:

"If our line of personal computers comes out first, our reputation in the industry will be greatly enhanced."

"There is little doubt that early entry into the market will result in an increase in our eventual share of the market."

"Houston offers immediate shipment at a reasonable price, but the reliability of its circuits may be too low. Also, I'm a little concerned by the recent changes in its management."

"We must get our line of personal computers on the market first."

GO ON TO THE NEXT PAGE.

Directions: The following questions consist of items related to the passage above. You may refer back to the passage and the directions. Consider each item separately in terms of the passage and on the answer sheet blacken space

- A if the item is a <u>Major Objective</u> in making the decision; that is, one of the outcomes or results sought by the decision-maker;
- B if the item is a <u>Major Factor</u> in making the decision; that is, a consideration, explicitly mentioned in the passage, that is basic in determining the decision;
- C if the item is a <u>Minor Factor</u> in making the decision; that is, a secondary consideration that affects the criteria tangentially, relating to a Major Factor rather than to an Objective;
- D if the item is a <u>Major Assumption</u> in making the decision; that is, a supposition or projection made by the decision-maker before weighing the variables;
- E if the item is an <u>Unimportant Issue</u> in making the decision; that is, a factor that is insignificant or not immediately relevant to the situation.

18. Western European production of integrated circuits

19. Recent changes in the higher managerial positions of Houston Electronics

20. Dates by which Eurocircuits can obtain delivery of the integrated circuits it needs to enter the French personal computer market

21. Cost of the advertising campaign necessary to enter the French market

22. Likelihood that early entry into the French personal computer market will have an important effect on the share of the market captured by Eurocircuits

23. Purchase of the integrated circuits needed by Eurocircuits at a reasonable cost

24. Capitalizing on the expected demand for personal computers in France

25. Good reputation of Houston Electronics for meeting its shipping dates

26. Reliability of the integrated circuits offered by Boston Electronics, Houston Electronics, or Osaka Electronics

27. Early delivery of the integrated circuits needed by Eurocircuits

28. Eurocircuits' history of successful dealings with Osaka Electronics

29. Eurocircuits' share of the market for medium-sized computers in France and West Germany

30. Cost of additional one percent surcharge for immediate delivery of circuits by Houston Electronics

31. Possibility that Eurocircuits can in fact obtain the parts it needs in order to bring out its line of personal computers before any of its French competitors

32. Effect of early entry into the French personal computer market on Eurocircuits' competitive position in the medium-sized computer market

33. Danger that the Americans and Japanese would dominate the French personal computer market

34. Positive effect on Eurocircuits' profits of timely entry into the French personal computer market

35. Cost of obtaining the integrated circuits needed to enter the French personal computer market

S T O P

**IF YOU FINISH BEFORE TIME IS CALLED, YOU MAY CHECK YOUR WORK ON THIS SECTION ONLY.
DO NOT WORK ON ANY OTHER SECTION IN THE TEST.**

SECTION II

Time—30 minutes

20 Questions

Directions: In this section solve each problem, using any available space on the page for scratchwork. Then indicate the best of the answer choices given.

Numbers: All numbers used are real numbers.

Figures: Figures that accompany problems in this test are intended to provide information useful in solving the problems. They are drawn as accurately as possible EXCEPT when it is stated in a specific problem that its figure is not drawn to scale. All figures lie in a plane unless otherwise indicated.

1. $6.09 - 4.693 =$

(A) 1.397 (B) 1.403 (C) 1.407
(D) 1.497 (E) 2.603

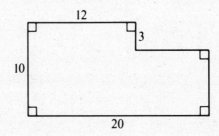

2. What is the area of the region enclosed by the figure above?

(A) 116 (B) 144 (C) 176
(D) 179 (E) 284

3. If $p = 0.2$ and $n = 100$, then $\sqrt{\dfrac{p(1-p)}{n}} =$

(A) $-\sqrt{0.002}$
(B) $\sqrt{0.02} - 0.02$
(C) 0
(D) 0.04
(E) 0.4

4. If each of 4 subsidiaries of Corporation R has been granted a line of credit of $700,000 and each of the other 3 subsidiaries of Corporation R has been granted a line of credit of $112,000, what is the average (arithmetic mean) line of credit granted to a subsidiary of Corporation R?

(A) $1,568,000
(B) $448,000
(C) $406,000
(D) $313,600
(E) $116,000

GO ON TO THE NEXT PAGE.

5. If x is a number such that $x^2 - 3x + 2 = 0$ and $x^2 - x - 2 = 0$, what is the value of x?

(A) -2
(B) -1
(C) 0
(D) 1
(E) 2

6. In traveling from a dormitory to a certain city, a student went $\frac{1}{5}$ of the way by foot, $\frac{2}{3}$ of the way by bus, and the remaining 8 kilometers by car. What is the distance, in kilometers, from the dormitory to the city?

(A) 30   (B) 45   (C) 60   (D) 90   (E) 120

7. A certain elevator has a safe weight limit of 2,000 pounds. What is the greatest possible number of people who can safely ride on the elevator at one time with the average (arithmetic mean) weight of half the riders being 180 pounds and the average weight of the others being 215 pounds?

(A) 7
(B) 8
(C) 9
(D) 10
(E) 11

8. After paying a 10 percent tax on all income over $3,000, a person had a net income of $12,000. What was the income before taxes?

(A) $13,300
(B) $13,000
(C) $12,900
(D) $10,000
(E) 9,000

GO ON TO THE NEXT PAGE.

9. $1 - [2 - (3 - [4 - 5] + 6) + 7] =$

   (A) -2 (B) 0 (C) 1 (D) 2 (E) 16

10. The price of a model M camera is $209 and the price of a special lens is $69. When the camera and lens are purchased together, the price is $239. The amount saved by purchasing the camera and lens together is approximately what percent of the total price of the camera and lens when purchased separately?

   (A) 14%
   (B) 16%
   (C) 29%
   (D) 33%
   (E) 86%

11. If 0.497 mark has the value of one dollar, what is the value to the nearest dollar of 350 marks?

   (A) $174 (B) $176 (C) $524
   (D) $696 (E) $704

12. A right cylindrical container with radius 2 meters and height 1 meter is filled to capacity with oil. How many empty right cylindrical cans, each with radius $\frac{1}{2}$ meter and height 4 meters, can be filled to capacity with the oil in this container?

   (A) 1
   (B) 2
   (C) 4
   (D) 8
   (E) 16

13. If a sequence of 8 consecutive odd integers with increasing values has 9 as its 7th term, what is the sum of the terms of the sequence?

   (A) 22
   (B) 32
   (C) 36
   (D) 40
   (E) 44

GO ON TO THE NEXT PAGE.

14. A rectangular floor is covered by a rug except for a strip p meters wide along each of the four edges. If the floor is m meters by n meters, what is the area of the rug, in square meters?

    (A) $mn - p(m + n)$
    (B) $mn - 2p(m + n)$
    (C) $mn - p^2$
    (D) $(m - p)(n - p)$
    (E) $(m - 2p)(n - 2p)$

15. Working alone, R can complete a certain kind of job in 9 hours. R and S, working together at their respective rates, can complete one of these jobs in 6 hours. In how many hours can S, working alone, complete one of these jobs?

    (A) 18
    (B) 12
    (C) 9
    (D) 6
    (E) 3

16. A family made a down payment of $75 and borrowed the balance on a set of encyclopedias that cost $400. The balance with interest was paid in 23 monthly payments of $16 each and a final payment of $9. The amount of interest paid was what percent of the amount borrowed?

    (A) 6%
    (B) 12%
    (C) 14%
    (D) 16%
    (E) 20%

17. If $x \neq 0$ and $x = \sqrt{4xy - 4y^2}$, then, in terms of y, $x =$

    (A) $2y$
    (B) y
    (C) $\dfrac{y}{2}$
    (D) $\dfrac{-4y^2}{1 - 4y}$
    (E) $-2y$

GO ON TO THE NEXT PAGE.

18. Solution Y is 30 percent liquid X and 70 percent water. If 2 kilograms of water evaporate from 8 kilograms of solution Y and 2 kilograms of solution Y are added to the remaining 6 kilograms of liquid, what percent of this new solution is liquid X?

(A) 30%

(B) $33\frac{1}{3}$%

(C) $37\frac{1}{2}$%

(D) 40%

(E) 50%

19. $\dfrac{1}{\dfrac{1}{0.03} + \dfrac{1}{0.37}} =$

(A) 0.004
(B) 0.02775
(C) 2.775
(D) 3.6036
(E) 36.036

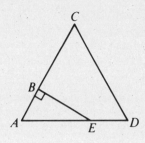

20. If each side of $\triangle ACD$ above has length 3 and if AB has length 1, what is the area of region $BCDE$?

(A) $\dfrac{9}{4}$ (B) $\dfrac{7}{4}\sqrt{3}$ (C) $\dfrac{9}{4}\sqrt{3}$

(D) $\dfrac{7}{2}\sqrt{3}$ (E) $6 + \sqrt{3}$

S T O P

IF YOU FINISH BEFORE TIME IS CALLED, YOU MAY CHECK YOUR WORK ON THIS SECTION ONLY.
DO NOT WORK ON ANY OTHER SECTION IN THE TEST.

SECTION III
Time—30 minutes
25 Questions

Directions: Each passage in this group is followed by questions based on its content. After reading a passage, choose the best answer to each question and blacken the corresponding space on the answer sheet. Answer all questions following a passage on the basis of what is stated or implied in that passage.

In the eighteenth century, Japan's feudal overlords, from the shogun to the humblest samurai, found themselves under financial stress. In part, this stress can be attributed to
(5) the overlords' failure to adjust to a rapidly expanding economy, but the stress was also due to factors beyond the overlords' control. Concentration of the samurai in castle-towns had acted as a stimulus to trade. Commercial efficiency, in
(10) turn, had put temptations in the way of buyers. Since most samurai had been reduced to idleness by years of peace, encouraged to engage in scholarship and martial exercises or to perform administrative tasks that took little time, it is
(15) not surprising that their tastes and habits grew expensive. Overlords' income, despite the increase in rice production among their tenant farmers, failed to keep pace with their expenses. Although shortfalls in overlords' income re-
(20) sulted almost as much from laxity among their tax collectors (the nearly inevitable outcome of hereditary officeholding) as from their higher standards of living, a misfortune like a fire or flood, bringing an increase in expenses or a drop
(25) in revenue, could put a domain in debt to the city rice-brokers who handled its finances. Once in debt, neither the individual samurai nor the shogun himself found it easy to recover.
It was difficult for individual samurai over-
(30) lords to increase their income because the amount of rice that farmers could be made to pay in taxes was not unlimited, and since the income of Japan's central government consisted in part of taxes collected by the shogun from his
(35) huge domain, the government too was constrained. Therefore, the Tokugawa shoguns began to look to other sources for revenue. Cash profits from government-owned mines were already on the decline because the most
(40) easily worked deposits of silver and gold had been exhausted, although debasement of the coinage had compensated for the loss. Opening up new farmland was a possibility, but most of what was suitable had already been exploited
(45) and further reclamation was technically unfeasible. Direct taxation of the samurai themselves would be politically dangerous. This left the shoguns only commerce as a potential source of government income.
(50)   Most of the country's wealth, or so it seemed, was finding its way into the hands of city mer-

chants. It appeared reasonable that they should contribute part of that revenue to ease the shogun's burden of financing the state. A means
(55) of obtaining such revenue was soon found by levying forced loans, known as *goyo-kin;* although these were not taxes in the strict sense, since they were irregular in timing and arbitrary in amount, they were high in yield. Unfortunate-
(60) ly, they pushed up prices. Thus, regrettably, the Tokugawa shoguns' search for solvency for the government made it increasingly difficult for individual Japanese who lived on fixed stipends to make ends meet.

1. The passage is most probably an excerpt from

   (A) an economic history of Japan
   (B) the memoirs of a samurai warrior
   (C) a modern novel about eighteenth-century Japan
   (D) an essay contrasting Japanese feudalism with its Western counterpart
   (E) an introduction to a collection of Japanese folktales

2. Which of the following financial situations is most analogous to the financial situation in which Japan's Tokugawa shoguns found themselves in the eighteenth century?

   (A) A small business borrows heavily to invest in new equipment, but is able to pay off its debt early when it is awarded a lucrative government contract.
   (B) Fire destroys a small business, but insurance covers the cost of rebuilding.
   (C) A small business is turned down for a loan at a local bank because the owners have no credit history.
   (D) A small business has to struggle to meet operating expenses when its profits decrease.
   (E) A small business is able to cut back sharply on spending through greater commercial efficiency and thereby compensate for a loss of revenue.

GO ON TO THE NEXT PAGE.

-236-

3. Which of the following best describes the attitude of the author toward the samurai discussed in lines 11-16?

   (A) Warmly approving
   (B) Mildly sympathetic
   (C) Bitterly disappointed
   (D) Harshly disdainful
   (E) Profoundly shocked

4. According to the passage, the major reason for the financial problems experienced by Japan's feudal overlords in the eighteenth century was that

   (A) spending had outdistanced income
   (B) trade had fallen off
   (C) profits from mining had declined
   (D) the coinage had been sharply debased
   (E) the samurai had concentrated in castle-towns

5. The passage implies that individual samurai did not find it easy to recover from debt for which of the following reasons?

   (A) Agricultural production had increased.
   (B) Taxes were irregular in timing and arbitrary in amount.
   (C) The Japanese government had failed to adjust to the needs of a changing economy.
   (D) The domains of samurai overlords were becoming smaller and poorer as government revenues increased.
   (E) There was a limit to the amount in taxes that farmers could be made to pay.

6. The passage suggests that, in eighteenth-century Japan, the office of tax collector

   (A) was a source of personal profit to the officeholder
   (B) was regarded with derision by many Japanese
   (C) remained within families
   (D) existed only in castle-towns
   (E) took up most of the officeholder's time

7. Which of the following could best be substituted for the word "This" in line 47 without changing the meaning of the passage?

   (A) The search of Japan's Tokugawa shoguns for solvency
   (B) The importance of commerce in feudal Japan
   (C) The unfairness of the tax structure in eighteenth-century Japan
   (D) The difficulty of increasing government income by other means
   (E) The difficulty experienced by both individual samurai and the shogun himself in extricating themselves from debt

8. The passage implies that which of the following was the primary reason why the Tokugawa shoguns turned to city merchants for help in financing the state?

   (A) A series of costly wars had depleted the national treasury.
   (B) Most of the country's wealth appeared to be in city merchants' hands.
   (C) Japan had suffered a series of economic reversals due to natural disasters such as floods.
   (D) The merchants were already heavily indebted to the shoguns.
   (E) Further reclamation of land would not have been economically advantageous.

9. According to the passage, the actions of the Tokugawa shoguns in their search for solvency for the government were regrettable because those actions

   (A) raised the cost of living by pushing up prices
   (B) resulted in the exhaustion of the most easily worked deposits of silver and gold
   (C) were far lower in yield than had originally been anticipated
   (D) did not succeed in reducing government spending
   (E) acted as a deterrent to trade

GO ON TO THE NEXT PAGE.

This history of responses to the work of the artist Sandro Botticelli (1444?-1510) suggests that widespread appreciation by critics is a relatively recent phenomenon. Writing in 1550,
(5) Vasari expressed an unease with Botticelli's work, admitting that the artist fitted awkwardly into his (Vasari's) evolutionary scheme of the history of art. Over the next two centuries, academic art historians denigrated Botticelli in
(10) favor of his fellow Florentine, Michelangelo. Even when antiacademic art historians of the early nineteenth century rejected many of the standards of evaluation espoused by their predecessors, Botticelli's work remained outside of ac-
(15) cepted taste, pleasing neither amateur observers nor connoisseurs. (Many of his best paintings, however, remained hidden away in obscure churches and private homes.)

The primary reason for Botticelli's unpopu-
(20) larity is not difficult to understand: most observers, up until the mid-nineteenth century, did not consider him to be noteworthy because his work, for the most part, did not seem to these observers to exhibit the traditional characteris-
(25) tics of fifteenth-century Florentine art. For example, Botticelli rarely employed the technique of strict perspective and, unlike Michelangelo, never used chiaroscuro. Another reason for Botticelli's unpopularity may have been that his at-
(30) titude toward the style of classical art was very different from that of his contemporaries. Although he was thoroughly exposed to classical art, he showed little interest in borrowing from the classical style. Indeed, it is paradoxical that
(35) a painter of large-scale classical subjects adopted a style that was only slightly similar to that of classical art.

In any case, when viewers began to examine more closely the relationship of Botticelli's work
(40) to the tradition of fifteenth-century Florentine art, his reputation began to grow. Analyses and assessments of Botticelli made between 1850 and 1870 by the artists of the Pre-Raphaelite movement, as well as by the writer Pater (although
(45) he, unfortunately, based his assessment on an incorrect analysis of Botticelli's personality), inspired a new appreciation of Botticelli throughout the English-speaking world. Yet Botticelli's work, especially the Sistine frescoes, did not
(50) generate worldwide attention until it was finally subjected to a comprehensive and scrupulous analysis by Horne in 1908. Horne rightly demonstrated that the frescoes shared important features with paintings by other fifteenth-century
(55) Florentines—features such as skillful representation of anatomical proportions, and of the human figure in motion. However, Horne argued that Botticelli did not treat these qualities as ends in themselves—rather, that he empha-
(60) sized clear depiction of a story, a unique achievement and one that made the traditional Florentine qualities less central. Because of Horne's emphasis on the way a talented artist reflects a tradition yet moves beyond that tradi-
(65) tion, an emphasis crucial to any study of art, the twentieth century has come to appreciate Botticelli's achievements.

10. Which of the following would be the most appropriate title for the passage?

(A) Botticelli's Contribution to Florentine Art
(B) Botticelli and the Traditions of Classical Art
(C) Sandro Botticelli: From Denigration to Appreciation
(D) Botticelli and Michelangelo: A Study in Contrasts
(E) Standards of Taste: Botticelli's Critical Reputation up to the Nineteenth Century

11. It can be inferred that the author of the passage would be likely to find most beneficial a study of an artist that

(A) avoided placing the artist in an evolutionary scheme of the history of art
(B) analyzed the artist's work in relation to the artist's personality
(C) analyzed the artist's relationship to the style and subject matter of classical art
(D) analyzed the artist's work in terms of both traditional characteristics and unique achievement
(E) sanctioned and extended the evaluation of the artist's work made by the artist's contemporaries

12. The passage suggests that Vasari would most probably have been more enthusiastic about Botticelli's work if that artist's work

(A) had not revealed Botticelli's inability to depict a story clearly
(B) had not evolved so straightforwardly from the Florentine art of the fourteenth century
(C) had not seemed to Vasari to be so similar to classical art
(D) could have been appreciated by amateur viewers as well as by connoisseurs
(E) could have been included more easily in Vasari's discussion of art history

GO ON TO THE NEXT PAGE.

13. The author most likely mentions the fact that many of Botticelli's best paintings were "hidden away in obscure churches and private homes" (lines 17-18) in order to

    (A) indicate the difficulty of trying to determine what an artist's best work is
    (B) persuade the reader that an artist's work should be available for general public viewing
    (C) prove that academic art historians had succeeded in keeping Botticelli's work from general public view
    (D) call into question the assertion that antiacademic art historians disagreed with their predecessors
    (E) suggest a reason why, for a period of time, Botticelli's work was not generally appreciated

14. The passage suggests that most seventeenth- and eighteenth-century academic art historians and most early-nineteenth-century antiacademic art historians would have disagreed significantly about which of the following?

    I. The artistic value of Botticelli's work
    II. The criteria by which art should be judged
    III. The features that characterized fifteenth-century Florentine art

    (A) I only
    (B) II only
    (C) III only
    (D) II and III only
    (E) I, II, and III

15. According to the passage, which of the following is an accurate statement about Botticelli's relation to classical art?

    (A) Botticelli more often made use of classical subject matter than classical style.
    (B) Botticelli's interest in perspective led him to study classical art.
    (C) Botticelli's style does not share any similarities with the style of classical art.
    (D) Because he saw little classical art, Botticelli did not exhibit much interest in imitating such art.
    (E) Although Botticelli sometimes borrowed his subject matter from classical art, he did not create large-scale paintings of these subjects.

16. According to the passage, Horne believed which of the following about the relation of the Sistine frescoes to the tradition of fifteenth-century Florentine art?

    (A) The frescoes do not exhibit characteristics of such art.
    (B) The frescoes exhibit more characteristics of such art than do the paintings of Michelangelo.
    (C) The frescoes exhibit some characteristics of such art, but these qualities are not the dominant features of the frescoes.
    (D) Some of the frescoes exhibit characteristics of such art, but most do not.
    (E) More of the frescoes exhibit skillful representation of anatomical proportions than skillful representation of the human figure in motion.

17. The passage suggests that, before Horne began to study Botticelli's work in 1908, there had been

    (A) little appreciation of Botticelli in the English-speaking world
    (B) an overemphasis on Botticelli's transformation, in the Sistine frescoes, of the principles of classical art
    (C) no attempt to compare Botticelli's work to that of Michelangelo
    (D) no thorough investigation of Botticelli's Sistine frescoes
    (E) little agreement among connoisseurs and amateurs about the merits of Botticelli's work

GO ON TO THE NEXT PAGE.

-239-

The antigen-antibody immunological reaction used to be regarded as typical of immunological responses. Antibodies are proteins synthesized by specialized cells called plasma cells, which are
(5) formed by lymphocytes (cells from the lymph system) when an antigen, a substance foreign to the organism's body, comes in contact with lymphocytes. Two important manifestations of antigen-antibody immunity are lysis, the rapid
(10) physical rupture of antigenic cells and the liberation of their contents into the surrounding medium, and phagocytosis, a process in which antigenic particles are engulfed by and very often digested by macrophages and polymorphs.
(15) The process of lysis is executed by a complex and unstable blood constituent known as *complement,* which will not work unless it is activated by a specific antibody; the process of phagocytosis is greatly facilitated when the par-
(20) ticles to be engulfed are coated by a specific antibody directed against them.

The reluctance to abandon this hypothesis, however well it explains specific processes, impeded new research, and for many years anti-
(25) gens and antibodies dominated the thoughts of immunologists so completely that those immunologists overlooked certain difficulties. Perhaps the primary difficulty with the antigen-antibody explanation is the informational problem of how
(30) an antigen is recognized and how a structure exactly complementary to it is then synthesized. When molecular biologists discovered, moreover, that such information cannot flow from protein to protein, but only from nucleic acid to
(35) protein, the theory that an antigen itself provided the mold that directed the synthesis of an antibody had to be seriously qualified. The attempts at qualification and the information provided by research in molecular biology led
(40) scientists to realize that a second immunological reaction is mediated through the lymphocytes that are hostile to and bring about the destruction of the antigen. This type of immunological response is called cell-mediated immunity.
(45) Recent research in cell-mediated immunity has been concerned not only with the development of new and better vaccines, but also with the problem of transplanting tissues and organs from one organism to another, for although cir-
(50) culating antibodies play a part in the rejection of transplanted tissues, the primary role is played by cell-mediated reactions. During cell-mediated responses, receptor sites on specific lymphocytes and surface antigens on the foreign
(55) tissue cells form a complex that binds the lymphocytes to the tissue. Such lymphocytes do not give rise to antibody-producing plasma cells but themselves bring about the death of the foreign-tissue cells, probably by secreting a variety of

(60) substances, some of which are toxic to the tissue cells and some of which stimulate increased phagocytic activity by white blood cells of the macrophage type. Cell-mediated immunity also accounts for the destruction of intracellular parasites.

18. The author is primarily concerned with

    (A) proving that immunological reactions do not involve antibodies
    (B) establishing that most immunological reactions involve antigens
    (C) criticizing scientists who will not change their theories regarding immunology
    (D) analyzing the importance of cells in fighting disease
    (E) explaining two different kinds of immunological reactions

19. The author argues that the antigen-antibody explanation of immunity "had to be seriously qualified" (line 37) because

    (A) antibodies were found to activate unstable components in the blood
    (B) antigens are not exactly complementary to antibodies
    (C) lymphocytes have the ability to bind to the surface of antigens
    (D) antibodies are synthesized from protein whereas antigens are made from nucleic acid
    (E) antigens have no apparent mechanism to direct the formation of an antibody

20. The author most probably believes that the antigen-antibody theory of immunological reaction

    (A) is wrong
    (B) was accepted without evidence
    (C) is unverifiable
    (D) is a partial explanation
    (E) has been a divisive issue among scientists

21. The author mentions all of the following as being involved in antigen-antibody immunological reactions EXCEPT the

    (A) synthesis of a protein
    (B) activation of *complement* in the bloodstream
    (C) destruction of antibodies
    (D) entrapment of antigens by macrophages
    (E) formation of a substance with a structure complementary to that of an antigen

GO ON TO THE NEXT PAGE.

22. The passage contains information that would answer which of the following questions about cell-mediated immunological reactions?

    I. Do lymphocytes form antibodies during cell-mediated immunological reactions?
    II. Why are lymphocytes more hostile to antigens during cell-mediated immunological reactions than are other cell groups?
    III. Are cell-mediated reactions more pronounced after transplants than they are after parasites have invaded the organism?

(A) I only
(B) I and II only
(C) I and III only
(D) II and III only
(E) I, II, and III

23. The passage suggests that scientists might not have developed the theory of cell-mediated immunological reactions if

(A) proteins existed in specific group types
(B) proteins could have been shown to direct the synthesis of other proteins
(C) antigens were always destroyed by proteins
(D) antibodies were composed only of protein
(E) antibodies were the body's primary means of resisting disease

24. According to the passage, antibody-antigen and cell-mediated immunological reactions both involve which of the following processes?

    I. The destruction of antigens
    II. The creation of antibodies
    III. The destruction of intracellular parasites

(A) I only
(B) II only
(C) III only
(D) I and II only
(E) II and III only

25. The author supports the theory of cell-mediated reactions primarily by

(A) pointing out a contradiction in the assumption leading to the antigen-antibody theory
(B) explaining how cell mediation accounts for phenomena that the antigen-antibody theory cannot account for
(C) revealing new data that scientists arguing for the antigen-antibody theory have continued to ignore
(D) showing that the antigen-antibody theory fails to account for the breakup of antigens
(E) demonstrating that cell mediation explains lysis and phagocytosis more fully than the antigen-antibody theory does

S T O P

IF YOU FINISH BEFORE TIME IS CALLED, YOU MAY CHECK YOUR WORK ON THIS SECTION ONLY.
DO NOT WORK ON ANY OTHER SECTION IN THE TEST.

SECTION IV

Time—30 minutes

25 Questions

Directions: Each of the data sufficiency problems below consists of a question and two statements, labeled (1) and (2), in which certain data are given. You have to decide whether the data given in the statements are sufficient for answering the question. Using the data given in the statements plus your knowledge of mathematics and everyday facts (such as the number of days in July or the meaning of counterclockwise), you are to blacken space

A   if statement (1) ALONE is sufficient, but statement (2) alone is not sufficient to answer the question asked;

B   if statement (2) ALONE is sufficient, but statement (1) alone is not sufficient to answer the question asked;

C   if BOTH statements (1) and (2) TOGETHER are sufficient to answer the question asked, but NEITHER statement ALONE is sufficient;

D   if EACH statement ALONE is sufficient to answer the question asked;

E   if statements (1) and (2) TOGETHER are NOT sufficient to answer the question asked, and additional data specific to the problem are needed.

Numbers: All numbers used are real numbers.

Figures: A figure in a data sufficiency problem will conform to the information given in the question, but will not necessarily conform to the additional information given in statements (1) and (2).

You may assume that lines shown as straight are straight and that angle measures are greater than zero.

You may assume that the position of points, angles, regions, etc., exist in the order shown.

All figures lie in a plane unless otherwise indicated.

Example:

In $\triangle PQR$, what is the value of x?

(1) $PQ = PR$
(2) $y = 40$

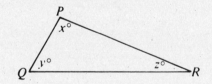

Explanation: According to statement (1), $PQ = PR$; therefore, $\triangle PQR$ is isosceles and $y = z$. Since $x + y + z = 180$, $x + 2y = 180$. Since statement (1) does not give a value for y, you cannot answer the question using statement (1) by itself. According to statement (2), $y = 40$; therefore, $x + z = 140$. Since statement (2) does not give a value for z, you cannot answer the question using statement (2) by itself. Using both statements together, you can find y and z; therefore, you can find x, and the answer to the problem is C.

1. If today the price of an item is $3,600, what was the price of the item exactly 2 years ago?

   (1)   The price of the item increased by 10 percent per year during this 2-year period.

   (2)   Today the price of the item is 1.21 times its price exactly 2 years ago.

2. By what percent has the price of an overcoat been reduced?

   (1)   The original price was $380.

   (2)   The original price was $50 more than the reduced price.

GO ON TO THE NEXT PAGE.

A   Statement (1) ALONE is sufficient, but statement (2) alone is not sufficient.
B   Statement (2) ALONE is sufficient, but statement (1) alone is not sufficient.
C   BOTH statements TOGETHER are sufficient, but NEITHER statement ALONE is sufficient.
D   EACH statement ALONE is sufficient.
E   Statements (1) and (2) TOGETHER are NOT sufficient.

3. If the Longfellow Playground is rectangular, what is its width?

   (1)   The ratio of its length to its width is 7 to 2.

   (2)   The perimeter of the playground is 396 meters.

4. What is the value of $x - 1$?

   (1) $x + 1 = 3$

   (2) $x - 1 < 3$

5. Is William taller than Jane?

   (1)   William is taller than Anna.

   (2)   Anna is not as tall as Jane.

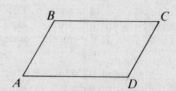

6. In parallelogram $ABCD$ above, what is the measure of $\angle ADC$?

   (1)   The measure of $\angle ABC$ is greater than 90°.

   (2)   The measure of $\angle BCD$ is 70°.

7. Is x^2 equal to xy?

   (1) $x^2 - y^2 = (x + 5)(y - 5)$

   (2) $x = y$

8. Was 70 the average (arithmetic mean) grade on a class test?

   (1)   On the test, half of the class had grades below 70 and half of the class had grades above 70.

   (2)   The lowest grade on the test was 45 and the highest grade on the test was 95.

GO ON TO THE NEXT PAGE.

A Statement (1) ALONE is sufficient, but statement (2) alone is not sufficient.
B Statement (2) ALONE is sufficient, but statement (1) alone is not sufficient.
C BOTH statements TOGETHER are sufficient, but NEITHER statement ALONE is sufficient.
D EACH statement ALONE is sufficient.
E Statements (1) and (2) TOGETHER are NOT sufficient.

9. What was John's average driving speed in miles per hour during a 15-minute interval?

(1) He drove 10 miles during this interval.

(2) His maximum speed was 50 miles per hour and his minimum speed was 35 miles per hour during this interval.

10. Is $\triangle MNP$ isosceles?

(1) Exactly two of the angles, $\angle M$ and $\angle N$, have the same measure.

(2) $\angle N$ and $\angle P$ do not have the same measure.

11. Is n an integer greater than 4?

(1) $3n$ is a positive integer.

(2) $\dfrac{n}{3}$ is a positive integer.

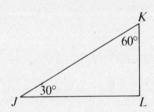

12. In $\triangle JKL$ shown above, what is the length of segment JL?

(1) $JK = 10$
(2) $KL = 5$

13. A coal company can choose to transport coal to one of its customers by railroad or by truck. If the railroad charges by the mile and the trucking company charges by the ton, which means of transporting the coal would cost less than the other?

(1) The railroad charges \$5,000 plus \$0.01 per mile per railroad car used, and the trucking company charges \$3,000 plus \$85 per ton.

(2) The customer to whom the coal is to be sent is 195 miles away from the coal company.

14. Is $x - y > r - s$?

(1) $x > r$ and $y < s$.
(2) $y = 2$, $s = 3$, $r = 5$, and $x = 6$.

15. On a certain day it took Bill three times as long to drive from home to work as it took Sue to drive from home to work. How many kilometers did Bill drive from home to work?

(1) Sue drove 10 kilometers from home to work, and the ratio of

$$\dfrac{\text{distance driven from home to work}}{\text{time to drive from home to work}}$$

was the same for Bill and Sue that day.

(2) The ratio of

$$\dfrac{\text{distance driven from home to work}}{\text{time to drive from home to work}}$$

for Sue that day was 64 kilometers per hour.

GO ON TO THE NEXT PAGE.

A Statement (1) ALONE is sufficient, but statement (2) alone is not sufficient.
B Statement (2) ALONE is sufficient, but statement (1) alone is not sufficient.
C BOTH statements TOGETHER are sufficient, but NEITHER statement ALONE is sufficient.
D EACH statement ALONE is sufficient.
E Statements (1) and (2) TOGETHER are NOT sufficient.

16. The figure above represents the floor of a square foyer with a circular rug partially covering the floor and extending to the outer edges of the floor as shown. What is the area of the foyer that is not covered by the rug?

(1) The area of the foyer is 9 square meters.
(2) The area of the rug is 2.25π square meters.

17. At a certain university, if 50 percent of the people who inquire about admission policies actually submit applications for admission, what percent of those who submit applications for admission enroll in classes at the university?

(1) Fifteen percent of those who submit applications for admission are accepted at the university.
(2) Eighty percent of those who are accepted send a deposit to the university.

18. If x and y are nonzero integers, is $\frac{x}{y}$ an integer?

(1) x is the product of 2 and some other integer.
(2) There is only one pair of positive integers whose product equals y.

19. If x is an integer, what is the value of x?

(1) $\frac{1}{5} < \frac{1}{x+1} < \frac{1}{2}$
(2) $(x-3)(x-4) = 0$

20. Is quadrilateral Q a square?

(1) The sides of Q have the same length.
(2) The diagonals of Q have the same length.

21. If K is a positive integer less than 10 and $N = 4,321 + K$, what is the value of K?

(1) N is divisible by 3.
(2) N is divisible by 7.

GO ON TO THE NEXT PAGE.

A   Statement (1) ALONE is sufficient, but statement (2) alone is not sufficient.
B   Statement (2) ALONE is sufficient, but statement (1) alone is not sufficient.
C   BOTH statements TOGETHER are sufficient, but NEITHER statement ALONE is sufficient.
D   EACH statement ALONE is sufficient.
E   Statements (1) and (2) TOGETHER are NOT sufficient.

22. A jewelry dealer initially offered a bracelet for sale at an asking price that would give a profit to the dealer of 40 percent of the original cost. What was the original cost of the bracelet?

   (1) After reducing this asking price by 10 percent, the jewelry dealer sold the bracelet at a profit of $403.

   (2) The jewelry dealer sold the bracelet for $1,953.

23. If n is an integer between 2 and 100 and if n is also the square of an integer, what is the value of n?

   (1) n is the cube of an integer.

   (2) n is even.

24. Is $x^2 - y^2$ a positive number?

   (1) $x - y$ is a positive number.

   (2) $x + y$ is a positive number.

25. The surface area of a square tabletop was changed so that one of the dimensions was reduced by 1 inch and the other dimension was increased by 2 inches. What was the surface area before these changes were made?

   (1) After the changes were made, the surface area was 70 square inches.

   (2) There was a 25 percent increase in one of the dimensions.

S T O P

IF YOU FINISH BEFORE TIME IS CALLED, YOU MAY CHECK YOUR WORK ON THIS SECTION ONLY.
DO NOT WORK ON ANY OTHER SECTION IN THE TEST.

SECTION V
Time—30 minutes

20 Questions

Directions: In this section solve each problem, using any available space on the page for scratchwork. Then indicate the best of the answer choices given.

Numbers: All numbers used are real numbers.

Figures: Figures that accompany problems in this test are intended to provide information useful in solving the problems. They are drawn as accurately as possible EXCEPT when it is stated in a specific problem that its figure is not drawn to scale. All figures lie in a plane unless otherwise indicated.

1. Which of the following is equal to 85 percent of 160?

    (A) 1.88   (B) 13.6   (C) 136
    (D) 188   (E) 13,600

2. The regular hourly wage for an employee of a certain factory is $5.60. If the employee worked 8 hours overtime and earned $1\frac{1}{2}$ times this regular hourly wage for overtime, how much overtime money was earned?

    (A) $67.20
    (B) $55.40
    (C) $50.00
    (D) $44.80
    (E) $12.00

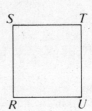

3. Square RSTU shown above is rotated in a plane about its center in a clockwise direction the minimum number of degrees necessary for T to be in the position where S is now shown. The number of degrees through which RSTU is rotated is

    (A) 135°   (B) 180°   (C) 225°
    (D) 270°   (E) 315°

GO ON TO THE NEXT PAGE.

Questions 4-5 refer to the following graphs.

BREAKDOWN OF COST TO CONSUMER FOR THE PRODUCTION
OF 6 OUNCES OF FROZEN ORANGE JUICE

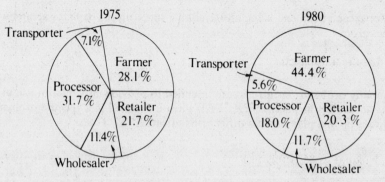

Cost to Consumer: $0.30   Cost to Consumer: $0.70

4. Of the following, which is closest to the increase from 1975 to 1980 in the amount received by the processor in producing 6 ounces of frozen orange juice?

   (A) $0.03   (B) $0.05   (C) $0.06
   (D) $0.08   (E) $0.13

5. In 1980, approximately what fraction of the cost to the consumer for the production of 6 ounces of frozen orange juice went to the farmer?

   (A) $\frac{3}{11}$ (B) $\frac{1}{3}$ (C) $\frac{4}{9}$ (D) $\frac{5}{9}$ (E) $\frac{3}{5}$

GO ON TO THE NEXT PAGE.

6. $\sqrt[4]{496}$ is between

   (A) 3 and 4
   (B) 4 and 5
   (C) 5 and 6
   (D) 6 and 7
   (E) 7 and 8

7. If $x \neq 0$, $2x = 5y$, and $3z = 7x$, what is the ratio of z to y?

   (A) 2 to 21   (B) 3 to 5   (C) 14 to 15
   (D) 6 to 5   (E) 35 to 6

8. A grocer purchased a quantity of bananas at 3 pounds for $0.50 and sold the entire quantity at 4 pounds for $1.00. How many pounds did the grocer purchase if the profit from selling the bananas was $10.00?

   (A)   40
   (B)   60
   (C)   90
   (D) 120
   (E) 240

9. There are between 100 and 110 cards in a collection of cards. If they are counted out 3 at a time, there are 2 left over, but if they are counted out 4 at a time, there is 1 left over. How many cards are in the collection?

   (A) 101   (B) 103   (C) 106   (D) 107   (E) 109

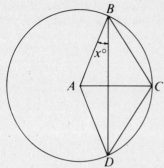

Note: Figure not drawn to scale.

10. If A is the center of the circle shown above and $AB = BC = CD$, what is the value of x?

    (A) 15   (B) 30   (C) 45   (D) 60   (E) 75

11. Out of a total of 1,000 employees at a certain corporation, 52 percent are female and 40 percent of these females work in research. If 60 percent of the total number of employees work in research, how many male employees do NOT work in research?

    (A) 520
    (B) 480
    (C) 392
    (D) 208
    (E)   88

GO ON TO THE NEXT PAGE.

12. An instructor scored a student's test of 50 questions by subtracting 2 times the number of incorrect answers from the number of correct answers. If the student answered all of the questions and received a score of 38, how many questions did that student answer correctly?

(A) 19
(B) 38
(C) 41
(D) 44
(E) 46

13. Which of the following integers does NOT have a divisor greater than 1 that is the square of an integer?

(A) 75
(B) 42
(C) 32
(D) 25
(E) 12

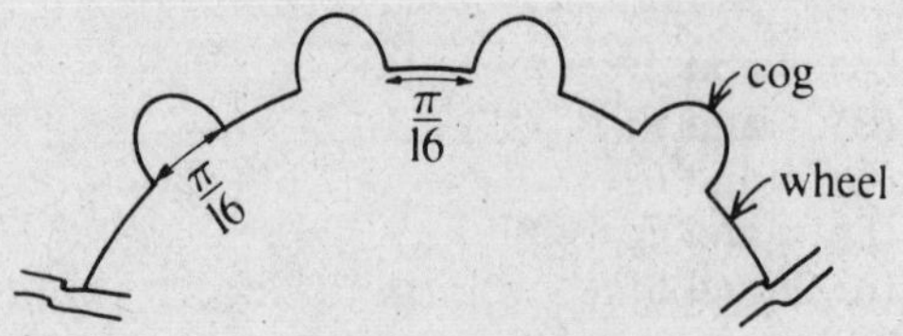

14. There are cogs around the circumference of a wheel and each cog is $\frac{\pi}{16}$ centimeter wide with a space of $\frac{\pi}{16}$ centimeter between consecutive cogs, as shown above. How many cogs of this size, with the same space between any two consecutive cogs, fit on a wheel with diameter 6 centimeters?

(A) 96
(B) 64
(C) 48
(D) 32
(E) 24

GO ON TO THE NEXT PAGE.

15. If $r \odot s = rs + r + s$, then for what value of s is $r \odot s$ equal to r for all values of r?

    (A) -1 (B) 0 (C) 1 (D) $\dfrac{1}{r+1}$ (E) r

16. In each production lot for a certain toy, 25 percent of the toys are red and 75 percent of the toys are blue. Half the toys are size A and half are size B. If 10 out of a lot of 100 toys are red and size A, how many of the toys are blue and size B?

    (A) 15
    (B) 25
    (C) 30
    (D) 35
    (E) 40

17. If $2x + 5y = 8$ and $3x = 2y$, what is the value of $2x + y$?

    (A) 4

    (B) $\dfrac{70}{19}$

    (C) $\dfrac{64}{19}$

    (D) $\dfrac{56}{19}$

    (E) $\dfrac{40}{19}$

18. A ladder 25 feet long is leaning against a wall that is perpendicular to level ground. The bottom of the ladder is 7 feet from the base of the wall. If the top of the ladder slips down 4 feet, how many feet will the bottom of the ladder slip?

    (A) 4
    (B) 5
    (C) 8
    (D) 9
    (E) 15

19. What is the least possible product of 4 different integers, each of which has a value between -5 and 10, inclusive?

    (A) -5040 (B) -3600 (C) -720
    (D) -600 (E) -120

20. If a motorist had driven 1 hour longer on a certain day and at an average rate of 5 miles per hour faster, he would have covered 70 more miles than he actually did. How many more miles would he have covered than he actually did if he had driven 2 hours longer and at an average rate of 10 miles per hour faster on that day?

    (A) 100
    (B) 120
    (C) 140
    (D) 150
    (E) 160

S T O P

IF YOU FINISH BEFORE TIME IS CALLED, YOU MAY CHECK YOUR WORK ON THIS SECTION ONLY.
DO NOT WORK ON ANY OTHER SECTION IN THE TEST.

SECTION VI

Time—30 minutes

25 Questions

<u>Directions:</u> In each of the following sentences, some part of the sentence or the entire sentence is underlined. Beneath each sentence you will find five ways of phrasing the underlined part. The first of these repeats the original; the other four are different. If you think the original is better than any of the alternatives, choose answer A; otherwise choose one of the others. Select the best version and blacken the corresponding space on your answer sheet.

This is a test of correctness and effectiveness of expression. In choosing answers, follow the requirements of standard written English; that is, pay attention to grammar, choice of words, and sentence construction. Choose the answer that expresses most effectively what is presented in the original sentence; this answer should be clear and exact, without awkwardness, ambiguity, or redundancy.

1. Researchers at Cornell University have demonstrated that homing pigeons can sense changes in the earth's magnetic field, see light waves that people cannot see, detect low-frequency sounds from miles away, <u>sense changes in air pressure, and can identify familiar odors</u>.

   (A) sense changes in air pressure, and can identify familiar odors
   (B) can sense changes in air pressure, and can identify familiar odors
   (C) sense changes in air pressure, and identify familiar odors
   (D) air pressure changes can be sensed, and familiar odors identified
   (E) air pressure changes are sensed, and familiar odors identified

2. In ancient times, Nubia was the principal corridor <u>where there were cultural influences transmitted</u> between Black Africa and the Mediterranean basin.

   (A) where there were cultural influences transmitted
   (B) through which cultural influences were transmitted
   (C) where there was a transmission of cultural influences
   (D) for the transmitting of cultural influences
   (E) which was transmitting cultural influences

3. It is a special feature of cell aggregation in the developing nervous system that in most regions of the brain the cells not only adhere <u>to one another and also adopt</u> some preferential orientation.

   (A) to one another and also adopt
   (B) one to the other, and also they adopt
   (C) one to the other, but also adopting
   (D) to one another but also adopt
   (E) to each other, also adopting

4. Among the reasons for the decline of New England agriculture in the last three decades were the high cost of land, the pressure of housing and commercial development, and <u>basing a marketing and distribution system on importing produce from Florida and California</u>.

   (A) basing a marketing and distribution system on importing produce from Florida and California
   (B) basing a marketing and distribution system on the imported produce of Florida and California
   (C) basing a system of marketing and distribution on the import of produce from Florida and California
   (D) a marketing and distribution system based on importing produce from Florida and California
   (E) a marketing and distribution system importing produce from Florida and California as its base

GO ON TO THE NEXT PAGE.

5. Like Byron at Missolonghi, Jack London was slowly killed by the mistakes of the medical men who treated him.

   (A) Like Byron
   (B) Like Byron's death
   (C) Just as Byron died
   (D) Similar to Byron
   (E) As did Byron

6. One of every two new businesses fail within two years.

   (A) fail
   (B) fails
   (C) should fail
   (D) may have failed
   (E) has failed

7. Even today, a century after Pasteur developed the first vaccine, rabies almost always kills its victims unless inoculated in the earliest stages of the disease.

   (A) its victims unless inoculated
   (B) its victims unless they are inoculated
   (C) its victims unless inoculation is done
   (D) the victims unless there is an inoculation
   (E) the victims unless inoculated

8. In a period of time when women typically have had a narrow range of choices, Mary Baker Eddy became a distinguished writer and the founder, architect, and builder of a growing church.

   (A) In a period of time when women typically have
   (B) During a time in which typically women have
   (C) Typically, during a time when women
   (D) At a time when women typically
   (E) Typically in a time in which women

9. As the price of gasoline rises, which makes substituting alcohol distilled from cereal grain attractive, the prices of bread and livestock feed are sure to increase.

   (A) which makes substituting alcohol distilled from cereal grain attractive
   (B) which makes substituting the distillation of alcohol from cereal grain attractive
   (C) which makes distilling alcohol from cereal grain an attractive substitute
   (D) making an attractive substitution of alcohol distilled from cereal grain
   (E) making alcohol distilled from cereal grain an attractive substitute

10. Climatic shifts are so gradual as to be indistinguishable at first from ordinary fluctuations in the weather.

    (A) so gradual as to be indistinguishable
    (B) so gradual they can be indistinguishable
    (C) so gradual that they are unable to be distinguished
    (D) gradual enough not to be distinguishable
    (E) gradual enough so that one cannot distinguish them

11. Although the lesser cornstalk borer is widely distributed, control of them is necessary only in the South.

    (A) the lesser cornstalk borer is widely distributed, control of them is
    (B) widely distributed, measures to control the lesser cornstalk borer are
    (C) widely distributed, lesser cornstalk borer control is
    (D) the lesser cornstalk borer is widely distributed, measures to control it are
    (E) it is widely distributed, control of the lesser cornstalk borer is

GO ON TO THE NEXT PAGE.

12. Traveling the back roads of Hungary, in 1905 Béla Bartók and Zoltán Kodály began their pioneering work in ethnomusicology, and they were armed only with an Edison phonograph and insatiable curiosity.

(A) Traveling the back roads of Hungary, in 1905 Béla Bartók and Zoltán Kodály began their pioneering work in ethnomusicology, and they were armed only
(B) In 1905, Béla Bartók and Zoltán Kodály, traveling the back roads of Hungary, began their pioneering work in ethnomusicology, and they were only armed
(C) In 1905 Béla Bartók and Zoltán Kodály began their pioneering work in ethnomusicology, traveling the back roads of Hungary armed only
(D) Having traveled the back roads of Hungary, in 1905 Béla Bartók and Zoltán Kodály began their pioneering work in ethnomusicology; they were only armed
(E) Béla Bartók and Zoltán Kodály, in 1905 began their pioneering work in ethnomusicology, traveling the back roads of Hungary, arming themselves only

13. It is as difficult to prevent crimes against property as those that are against a person.

(A) those that are against a
(B) those against a
(C) it is against a
(D) preventing those against a
(E) it is to prevent those against a

14. Unlike the acid smoke of cigarettes, pipe tobacco, cured by age-old methods, yields an alkaline smoke too irritating to be drawn into the lungs.

(A) Unlike the acid smoke of cigarettes, pipe tobacco, cured by age-old methods, yields an alkaline smoke
(B) Unlike the acid smoke of cigarettes, pipe tobacco is cured by age-old methods, yielding an alkaline smoke
(C) Unlike cigarette tobacco, which yields an acid smoke, pipe tobacco, cured by age-old methods, yields an alkaline smoke
(D) Differing from cigarettes' acid smoke, pipe tobacco's alkaline smoke, cured by age-old methods, is
(E) The alkaline smoke of pipe tobacco differs from cigarettes' acid smoke in that it is cured by age-old methods and is

15. Joplin's faith in his opera ''Tremonisha'' was unshakeable; in 1911 he published the score at his own expense and decided on staging it himself.

(A) on staging it himself
(B) that he himself would do the staging
(C) to do the staging of the work by himself
(D) that he himself would stage it
(E) to stage the work himself

16. Los Angeles has a higher number of family dwellings per capita than any large city.

(A) a higher number of family dwellings per capita than any large city
(B) higher numbers of family dwellings per capita than any other large city
(C) a higher number of family dwellings per capita than does any other large city
(D) higher numbers of family dwellings per capita than do other large cities
(E) a high per capita number of family dwellings, more than does any other large city

GO ON TO THE NEXT PAGE.

17. During the nineteenth century Emily Eden and Fanny Parks journeyed throughout India, sketching and keeping journals <u>forming the basis of news reports about the princely states where they had</u> visited.

(A) forming the basis of news reports about the princely states where they had
(B) that were forming the basis of news reports about the princely states
(C) to form the basis of news reports about the princely states which they have
(D) which had formed the basis of news reports about the princely states where they had
(E) that formed the basis of news reports about the princely states they

18. School integration plans that involve busing between suburban and central-city areas have contributed, according to a recent study, to <u>significant increases in housing integration, which, in turn, reduces</u> any future need for busing.

(A) significant increases in housing integration, which, in turn, reduces
(B) significant integration increases in housing, which, in turn, reduces
(C) increase housing integration significantly, which, in turn, reduces
(D) increase housing integration significantly, in turn reducing
(E) significantly increase housing integration, which, in turn, reduce

19. The commission acknowledged that <u>no amount of money or staff members</u> can ensure the safety of people who live in the vicinity of a nuclear plant, but it approved the installation because it believed that all reasonable precautions had been taken.

(A) no amount of money or staff members
(B) neither vast amounts of money nor staff members
(C) neither vast amounts of money nor numbers of staff members
(D) neither vast amounts of money nor a large staff
(E) no matter how large the staff or how vast the amount of money

20. Sartre believed <u>each individual is responsible to choose one course of action over another one,</u> that it is the choice that gives value to the act, and that nothing that is not acted upon has value.

(A) each individual is responsible to choose one course of action over another one
(B) that each individual is responsible for choosing one course of action over another
(C) that each individual is responsible, choosing one course of action over another
(D) that each individual is responsible to choose one course of action over the other
(E) each individual is responsible for choosing one course of action over other ones

21. <u>While the owner of a condominium apartment has free and clear title to the dwelling,</u> owners of cooperative apartments have shares in a corporation that owns a building and leases apartments to them.

(A) While the owner of a condominium apartment has free and clear title to the dwelling,
(B) The owner of a condominium apartment has free and clear title to the dwelling, but
(C) Whereas owners of condominium apartments have free and clear title to their dwellings,
(D) An owner of a condominium apartment has free and clear title to the dwelling, whereas
(E) Condominium apartment owners have a title to their dwelling that is free and clear, while

GO ON TO THE NEXT PAGE.

22. Although <u>films about the American West depict coyotes as solitary animals howling mournfully on the tops of distant hills</u>, in reality these gregarious creatures live in stable groups that occupy the same territory for long periods.

    (A) films about the American West depict coyotes as solitary animals howling mournfully on the tops of distant hills
    (B) in films about the American West coyotes are depicted to be solitary animals that howl mournfully on the tops of distant hills
    (C) coyotes are depicted as solitary animals howling mournfully on the tops of distant hills in films about the American West
    (D) films about the American West depict coyotes as if they were solitary, mournfully howling animals on the tops of distant hills
    (E) films about the American West depict coyotes to be solitary and mournfully howling animals on the tops of distant hills

23. In 1980 the United States exported <u>twice as much of its national output of goods as they had</u> in 1970.

    (A) twice as much of its national output of goods as they had
    (B) double the amount of their national output of goods as they did
    (C) twice as much of its national output of goods as it did
    (D) double the amount of its national output of goods as it has
    (E) twice as much of their national output of goods as they had

24. <u>Even though its per capita food supply hardly increased during</u> two decades, stringent rationing and planned distribution have allowed the People's Republic of China to ensure nutritional levels of 2,000 calories per person per day for its population.

    (A) Even though its per capita food supply hardly increased during
    (B) Even though its per capita food supply has hardly increased in
    (C) Despite its per capita food supply hardly increasing over
    (D) Despite there being hardly any increase in its per capita food supply during
    (E) Although there is hardly any increase in per capita food supply for

25. Few people realize that the chance of accidental injury or death <u>may be as great or greater in the "safety" of their own homes than</u> in a plane or on the road.

    (A) may be as great or greater in the "safety" of their own homes than
    (B) is at least as great or greater in the "safety" of their own homes than
    (C) might be so great or greater in the "safety" of their own home as
    (D) may be at least as great in the "safety" of their own homes as
    (E) can be at least so great in the "safety" of their own home as

S T O P

IF YOU FINISH BEFORE TIME IS CALLED, YOU MAY CHECK YOUR WORK ON THIS SECTION ONLY.
DO NOT WORK ON ANY OTHER SECTION IN THE TEST.

Answer Key
And Explanatory Material

ANSWER KEY: FORM B

	SECTION 1	SECTION 2	SECTION 3	SECTION 4	SECTION 5	SECTION 6
1	E	A	A	D	C	C
2	A	C	D	C	A	B
3	A	D	B	C	D	E
4	C	B	A	A	A	E
5	D	D	E	D	B	A
6	B	D	C	B	B	B
7	C	C	D	B	E	D
8	E	B	C	E	E	E
9	C	D	A	A	A	E
10	E	A	C	A	B	C
11	A	E	D	E	E	D
12	D	C	D	D	E	D
13	C	B	B	D	B	D
14	C	E	D	C	C	C
15	A	A	A	A	B	D
16	E	D	C	E	D	C
17	C	A	D	E	D	D
18	E	C	D	E	C	A
19	C	B	C	C	B	D
20	B	B	D	B	D	B
21	E		C	C		C
22	D		A	A		A
23	A		B	A		C
24	A		A	C		B
25	C		B	D		D
26	B					
27	A					
28	C					
29	E					
30	C					
31	D					
32	E					
33	E					
34	D					
35	B					

Explanatory Material: Analysis of Situations

1. Family ownership of Sparkle Springs

The correct classification for this consideration is E, an unimportant issue, because the fact that Sparkle Springs Corporation is family-owned has no bearing on the decision to be made regarding the three alternatives for expansion, and therefore it is not relevant to the decision. That is, it is not a goal of the decision-maker, it is not an assumption she makes, and it is not something she takes into consideration when weighing the alternatives. This classification is very easy.

2. A decrease in the cost of manufacturing Sparkle

The correct classification for this consideration is A, an objective. The passage explicitly states in the second paragraph that "Spark intended to build on the marketing spearheads . . . and win additional markets in the West by extending advertising beyond the Mississippi." Therefore, a "Future increase in Sparkle Springs' sales outside of the eastern United States" is one of the outcomes or results sought by the decision-maker. This classification is relatively difficult.

3. Future increase in Sparkle Springs' sales outside of the eastern United States

The correct classification for this consideration is A, an objective. The passage explicitly states in the second paragraph that "Spark intended to build on the marketing spearheads . . . and win additional markets in the West by extending advertising beyond the Mississippi." Therefore, a "Future increase in Sparkle Springs' sales outside of the eastern United States" is one of the outcomes or results sought by the decision-maker. This classification is relatively difficult.

4. Effect on real estate prices of the announcement of two new Springs Valley industries

The correct classification for this consideration is C, a minor factor. The passage indicates that Spark wants to cut costs and increase production. It follows that the net economic advantage of each of the proposed alternatives is a major factor. The "Effect on real estate prices of the announcement of two new Springs Valley industries" is a minor factor because it bears on and contributes to this major factor by reducing the net economic advantage of Springs Valley. Note that this major factor is influenced by other considerations, such as the cost of building or remodeling a plant and the cost of labor. Because the real estate price only contributes to, is only one influence on, the net economic advantage, this consideration is a minor factor. This classification is difficult.

5. Likelihood that increasing the production of Sparkle will increase the company's profit

The correct classification for this consideration is D, an assumption. According to the statement in the first paragraph, "In order to cut costs . . . company president Mary Spark considered three alternatives. . . ." One of Spark's goals is to increase production. It is unlikely that Spark would want to increase production if she did not already suppose or project that the increased production would lead to an increase in profit. Note that this assumption provides a framework for the decision. Because Spark assumes that increasing production will increase profit, she examines the increased production that the alternatives will produce. This classification is relatively easy.

6. Net economic advantage of each of the proposed alternatives

The correct classification for this consideration is B, a major factor. The first paragraph notes that two of Spark's goals are to cut costs and increase production. Given these objectives, it is logical that the "Net economic advantage of each of the proposed alternatives" will be a major factor because this advantage is basic in determining how well a location will meet the objectives of lowering costs and increasing production. Notice that in the fourth and fifth paragraphs the alternatives are analyzed from the point of view of the extent to which they will meet the goals of lower costs and increased production, this extent being, in effect, their net economic advantage. This classification is relatively easy.

7. Proximity of Martindale County to a city

The correct classification for this consideration is C, a minor factor. The passage indicates that Spark wants to cut costs and increase production. It follows that the net economic advantage of each of the proposed alternatives, including the Martindale County alternative, is a major factor. The fact that the Martindale County site is "within thirty miles of a city with a population of 85,000, all potential Sparkle customers" (paragraph four) is a secondary consideration that bears on the major factor, "net economic advantage of each of the proposed alternatives." That is, whereas the "Proximity of Martindale County to a city" is not a factor that is basic in determining the decision, it does bear on the major factor and is, therefore, a minor factor. This classification is relatively difficult.

8. Effect of the Martindale opposition on Sparkle Springs' eastern market objectives

The correct classification for this consideration is E, an unimportant issue. There is nothing in the passage to suggest that the Martindale opposition will have any effect on Sparkle Springs' eastern market objectives. In other words, the decision-maker does not seek the "Effect of the Martindale opposition on Sparkle Springs' eastern market objectives" as a goal, project it as an assumption, or use it to evaluate alternatives, and therefore the issue is irrelevant to the decision. This classification is relatively difficult.

9. Exceptionally high quality of the groundwater in Martindale County

The correct classification for this consideration is C, a minor factor. The passage indicates that Spark wants to cut costs and increase production. It follows that the net economic advantage of each of the proposed alternatives, including the Martindale County alternative, is a major factor. The "Exceptionally high quality of the groundwater in Martindale County" is a secondary consideration because it bears tangentially on this major factor. Note that this major factor is influenced by other considerations, such as the cost of building or remodeling a plant and labor costs. Because the availability of high-quality ground water is only one influence on the net economic advantage, this consideration is a minor factor. This classification is relatively difficult.

10. **Relative percentage of Sparkle's sales accounted for by each of the states in the tri-state area**

The correct classification for this consideration is E, an unimportant issue, since how Sparkle's sales in the tri-state area are divided among the three states is irrelevant to the decision. That is, Spark does not seek the "Relative percentage of Sparkle's sales accounted for by each of the states in the tri-state area," project it as an assumption, or use it to evaluate the alternatives. This classification is relatively difficult.

11. **Procurement of major markets west of the Mississippi**

The correct classification for this consideration is A, an objective. The passage explicitly states in the second paragraph that "Spark intended to . . . win additional markets in the West by extending advertising beyond the Mississippi," so "Procurement of major markets west of the Mississippi" is an outcome sought by the decision-maker. This classification is of medium difficulty.

12. **Temporary loss of sales caused by the month-long shutdown of Sparkle's plant in Springs Valley**

The correct classification for this consideration is E, an unimportant issue. Although the negotiated settlement referred to in paragraph three has an impact on the production costs because it raised the cost of local labor, the "Temporary loss of sales caused by the month-long shutdown of Sparkle's plant in Springs Valley," while it may have hurt the company financially, has no bearing on the ultimate choice of one of the three alternatives. That is, the temporary loss of sales is not an objective sought by Spark, an assumption she makes, or a consideration she uses to evaluate the alternatives. This classification is difficult.

13. **Martindale County's relatively lower wage structure**

The correct classification for this consideration is C, a minor factor. The passage indicates that Spark wants to cut costs and increase production. It follows that the net economic advantage of each of the proposed alternatives, including the Martindale County alternative, is a major factor. "Martindale County's relatively lower wage structure" is a secondary consideration because it bears tangentially on this major factor. Note that this major factor is influenced by other considerations, such as the cost of building or remodeling a plant. Because the availability of low-cost labor is only one influence of the net economic advantage, this consideration is a minor factor. This classification is relatively difficult.

14. **Continued market demand for Sparkle over and above the production capacity of Sparkle Springs' original facility before modernization**

The correct classification for this consideration is D, an assumption. Since one of Spark's goals is to increase production, it is logical to infer that Spark supposes or has projected that there will be a continued market demand for the increased production, that is, the production over and above the production capacity of Sparkle Springs' original facility before modernization. It is unlikely that Spark would want to increase production if she did not already suppose or project that there would be a continued market demand for Sparkle. This classification is relatively difficult.

15. **An increase in Sparkle Springs' production capacity**

The correct classification for this consideration is A, an objective. The first paragraph of the passage explicitly states that one reason Spark is considering the three alternatives for expansion is "to . . . increase production." Thus, "An increase in Sparkle Springs' production capacity" is one of the outcomes or results sought by the decision-maker. This classification is very easy.

16. **Importance of expanding Sparkle's advertising to all states east of the Mississippi**

The correct classification for this consideration is E, an unimportant issue. Since Spark had expanded Sparkle's advertising to all states east of the Mississippi in 1971, several years before the proposed expansion, the "Importance of expanding Sparkle's advertising to all states east of the Mississippi" has no immediate relevance to the decision as to which plan for expansion should now be chosen. This classification is difficult.

17. **Cost of land at the Martindale County site**

The correct classification for this consideration is C, a minor factor. The passage indicates that Spark wants to cut costs and increase production. It follows that the net economic advantage of each of the proposed alternatives, including the Martindale County alternative, is a major factor. The cost of land at the Martindale County site is a secondary consideration because it bears tangentially on this major factor. Note that this major factor is influenced by other considerations, such as the cost of building or remodeling a plant and labor costs. Because the cost of land is only one influence on the net economic advantage, this consideration is a minor factor. This classification is relatively difficult.

18. **Western European production of integrated circuits**

The correct classification for this consideration is E, an unimportant issue, because "Western European production of integrated circuits" is irrelevant to the decision. The second and fifth paragraphs of the passage indicate that all of Eurocircuits' possible suppliers of integrated circuits will be American or Japanese. Therefore, Western European production of integrated circuits is irrelevant to the decision of which supplier to choose. This classification is very difficult.

19. **Recent changes in the higher managerial positions of Houston Electronics**

The correct classification for this consideration is C, a minor factor. The fourth paragraph of the passage states that the reliability of the integrated circuits is one of the crucial elements in choosing a supplier and is thus a major factor. The fifth paragraph indicates that "In the past, the reliability of Houston's integrated circuits had not been good, but the company had recently undergone several changes in its top management." The changes in management at Houston Electronics is one of the considerations that has potential impact on the reliability of the integrated circuits Eurocircuits wishes to purchase. Therefore, since circuit reliability is a major factor and since changes in Houston's management potentially affect, or bear on, the reliability of the circuits, this consideration is a minor factor. This classification is of medium difficulty.

20. **Dates by which Eurocircuits can obtain delivery of the integrated circuits it needs to enter the French personal computer market**

The correct classification for this consideration is B, a major factor. The fourth paragraph of the passage states that "the circuits were needed as soon as possible" and that this is one of the three crucial elements in choosing a supplier. Thus, the "Dates by which Eurocircuits can obtain delivery of the integrated circuits it needs to enter the French personal computer market" is a major factor; it is basic in determining how well a given supplier will meet the goal of obtaining the circuits as soon as possible. This classification is very easy.

21. **Cost of the advertising campaign necessary to enter the French market**

The correct classification for this consideration is E, an unimportant issue, because this cost is irrelevant to the decision Eurocircuits faces, a choice of a supplier of integrated circuits. The cost of a subsequent advertising campaign necessary to enter the French market is unrelated to the decision concerning the choice of a supplier. This classification is relatively easy.

22. **Likelihood that early entry into the French personal computer market will have an important effect on the share of the market captured by Eurocircuits**

The correct classification for this consideration is D, an assumption. The third paragraph of the passage states that "Manet reasoned that an earlier entry into the French market would probably increase the share of the market that Eurocircuits would obtain. . . ." Thus, Manet is clearly projecting or assuming that it is likely that an early entry into the market would have an important positive effect on the share of the market captured by Eurocircuits. This classification is relatively easy.

23. **Purchase of the integrated circuits needed by Eurocircuits at a reasonable cost**

The correct classification for this consideration is A, an objective. In the fourth paragraph, the passage states that "the circuits must be obtained at the lowest possible price. . . ." In other words, one of Manet's objectives is to purchase the integrated circuits needed by Eurocircuits at a reasonable cost. This classification is very difficult.

24. **Capitalizing on the expected demand for personal computers in France**

The correct classification for this consideration is A, an objective. The third paragraph of the passage states that "in April 1982, it became apparent that the market for personal computers in the United States was far larger than had been estimated. When Pierre Manet realized how great the demand was for personal computers in the United States, he decided to try to bring out Eurocircuits' line of personal computers for the French market earlier than planned." These statements suggest both that Manet believes that a demand for personal computers, similar to the one in the United States, exists in France and that he should take advantage of that demand by bringing out a line of personal computers earlier than planned. In other words, one of Manet's objectives is "Capitalizing on the expected demand for personal computers in France." This classification is relatively easy.

25. **Good reputation of Houston Electronics for meeting its shipping dates**

The correct classification for this consideration is C, a minor factor. In the third paragraph the passage states that one of the crucial elements to be considered in choosing a supplier is that the circuits are needed as soon as possible. Therefore, the dates by which Eurocircuits can obtain delivery of the circuits is a major factor in choosing a supplier. Houston Electronics' good reputation for meeting its shipping dates is a minor factor because it bears on this major factor. Note that this major factor is impacted by other considerations besides Houston's reputation — for example, Houston's promise to begin immediate shipping. Therefore, since the dates by which Eurocircuits can obtain delivery are a major factor, and since Houston's good reputation for meeting its shipping dates is only one influence on this major factor, Houston's reputation is a minor factor. This classification is relatively difficult.

26. **Reliability of the integrated circuits offered by Boston Electronics, Houston Electronics, or Osaka Electronics**

The correct classification for this consideration is B, a major factor. This determination can be made from information in the fourth paragraph, where you are told that one of the three crucial elements in choosing a supplier is that the circuits be highly reliable. Therefore, the reliability of the circuits offered by the three possible suppliers is a major factor in the decision; it is basic in determining how well the suppliers will meet the goal of having highly reliable circuits. This classification is of medium difficulty.

27. Early delivery of the integrated circuits needed by Eurocircuits

The correct classification of this consideration is A, an objective, because the fourth paragraph of the passage indicates that "the circuits were needed as soon as possible." Given this statement, it is clear that Manet wants to have the circuits delivered quickly. In other words, one of Manet's objectives is "Early delivery of the integrated circuits needed by Eurocircuits." This classification is difficult.

28. Eurocircuits' history of successful dealings with Osaka Electronics

The correct classification for this consideration is C, a minor factor. The fourth paragraph of the passage indicates that the circuits are needed as soon as possible, and, therefore, that the dates by which Eurocircuits can obtain the circuits from each of the suppliers, including Osaka, is a major factor. Eurocircuits' history of successful dealings with Osaka indicates that it would be reasonable to give credence to Osaka's promised shipping dates. Therefore, since the dates by which the circuits can be obtained is a major factor, Eurocircuits' history of dealings with Osaka is a minor factor. This classification is of medium difficulty.

29. Eurocircuits' share of the market for medium-sized computers in France and West Germany

The correct classification for this consideration is E, an unimportant issue, because it is irrelevant to the decision being made. Eurocircuits' choice of a supplier of integrated circuits for its personal computers has no effect on, and is not affected by, Eurocircuits' share of the market for medium-sized computers. This classification is difficult.

30. Cost of additional one percent surcharge for immediate delivery of circuits by Houston Electronics

The correct classification for this consideration is C, a minor factor. Paragraph four of the passage indicates that the cost of the circuits is a major factor in choosing a supplier. Since Houston Electronics' additional one percent charge for immediate delivery is one of a number of subparts of the total cost of obtaining the circuits, this consideration is a minor factor. This classification is of medium difficulty.

31. Possibility that Eurocircuits can in fact obtain the parts it needs in order to bring out its line of personal computers before any of its French competitors

The correct classification for this consideration is D, an assumption. The last lines of the passage make it clear that Eurocircuits wants to bring out a line of personal computers before its competitors do. The larger part of the passage addresses different possible ways of obtaining the parts Eurocircuits needs. This makes it clear that Manet is assuming, or projecting, the "Possibility that Eurocircuits can in fact obtain the parts it needs in order to bring out its line of personal computers before any of its French competitors." This classification is difficult.

32. Effect of early entry into the French personal computer market on Eurocircuits' competitive position in the medium-sized computer market

The correct classification for this consideration is E, an unimportant issue, because this effect is irrelevant to the decision being made—choosing a supplier of integrated circuits. Furthermore, nothing in the passage indicates that early entry into the French personal computer market will have any direct effect on Eurocircuits' competitive position in the medium-sized computer market. This classification is difficult.

33. Danger that the Americans and Japanese would dominate the French personal computer market

The correct classification for this consideration is E, an unimportant issue, because the alleged danger is irrelevant to the decision, choosing a supplier of integrated circuits. Furthermore, the first paragraph of the passage states that "French trade barriers would prevent the Americans and Japanese from dominating the French market. . . ." Thus, no such danger exists, and this consideration is an unimportant issue. This classification is of medium difficulty.

34. Positive effect on Eurocircuits' profits of timely entry into the French personal computer market

The correct classification of this consideration is D, an assumption. You are told in the third paragraph that "Manet reasoned that an earlier entry into the French market would probably increase the share of the market that Eurocircuits would obtain. . . ." and that "both a substantially improved competitive position and an increase in profits seemed to be possible. . . ." In other words, Manet reasons, or projects, that a timely entry into the market could have a positive effect on Eurocircuits' profits. This classification is relatively difficult.

35. Cost of obtaining the integrated circuits needed to enter the French personal computer market

The correct classification of this consideration is B, a major factor. The fourth paragraph states that obtaining the circuits at the lowest possible price is one of the three crucial elements in choosing a supplier. Thus, the cost of obtaining the circuits is a major factor in making the decision among suppliers since it is basic in determining how well a supplier will meet the goal of obtaining the circuits at the lowest possible price. This classification is of medium difficulty.

Explanatory Material:
Problem Solving I

1. $6.09 - 4.693 =$

    (A) 1.397   (B) 1.403   (C) 1.407
    (D) 1.497   (E) 2.603

$$\begin{array}{r} 6.090 \\ -4.693 \\ \hline 1.397 \end{array}$$

Thus, the best answer is A. This is a very easy question.

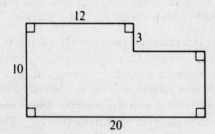

2. What is the area of the region enclosed by the figure above?

    (A) 116   (B) 144   (C) 176
    (D) 179   (E) 284

If a line is drawn dividing the figure into two rectangles, the length of the horizontal segment is $20 - 12 = 8$ and the length of the vertical segment of the smaller rectangle is $10 - 3 = 7$. (See below.)

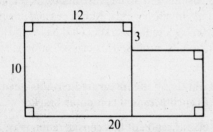

Thus, the area of the region is $(10 \times 12) + (8 \times 7) = 176$. Therefore, the best answer is C. This is an easy question.

3. If $p = 0.2$ and $n = 100$, then $\sqrt{\dfrac{p(1-p)}{n}} =$

    (A) $-\sqrt{0.002}$
    (B) $\sqrt{0.0002} - 0.02$
    (C) 0
    (D) 0.04
    (E) 0.4

Substituting for p and n in the radical expression yields:

$$\sqrt{\frac{(0.2)(1 - 0.2)}{100}} = \sqrt{\frac{(0.2)(0.8)}{100}} = \sqrt{\frac{0.16}{100}} = \frac{0.4}{10} = 0.04$$

4. If each of 4 subsidiaries of Corporation R has been granted a line of credit of $700,000 and each of the other 3 subsidiaries of Corporation R has been granted a line of credit of $112,000, what is the average (arithmetic mean) line of credit granted to a subsidiary of Corporation R?

    (A) $1,568,000
    (B) $ 448,000
    (C) $ 406,000
    (D) $ 313,600
    (C) $ 116,000

The total amount of credit for the 7 subsidiaries is:

$4(\$700,000) + 3(\$112,000) = \$3,136,000$.

Therefore, the average per subsidiary is $\dfrac{\$3,136,000}{7} =$ $448,000, and the best answer is B. This is an easy question.

5. If x is a number such that $x^2 - 3x + 2 = 0$ and $x^2 - x - 2 = 0$, what is the value of x?

    (A) -2
    (B) -1
    (C)   0
    (D)   1
    (E)   2

Since both polynomials are equal to 0, they are equal to each other. Thus, $x^2 - 3x + 2 = x^2 - x - 2$, $-2x = -4$ and $x = 2$. Therefore the best answer is E. This is an easy question.

6. In traveling from a dormitory to a certain city, a student went $\frac{1}{5}$ of the way by foot, $\frac{2}{3}$ of the way by bus, and the remaining 8 kilometers by car. What is the distance, in kilometers, from the dormitory to the city?

    (A) 30   (B) 45   (C) 60   (D) 90   (E) 120

The student went on foot and by bus $\frac{1}{5} + \frac{2}{3}$ of the way, which is $\frac{3}{15} + \frac{10}{15} = \frac{13}{15}$. Therefore, the student went $1 - \frac{13}{15}$ of the way by car. Since $\frac{2}{15}$ of the distance from the dormitory to the city equals 8 kilometers, the distance equals $\frac{15}{2} \cdot 8 = 60$ kilometers. Thus, the best answer is C. This is an easy question.

7. A certain elevator has a safe weight limit of 2,000 pounds. What is the greatest possible number of people who can safely ride on the elevator at one time with the average (arithmetic mean) weight of half the riders being 180 pounds and the average weight of the others being 215 pounds?

(A) 7
(B) 8
(C) 9
(D) 10
(E) 11

If n is the greatest number of people who safely ride on the elevator at one time,

$\frac{n}{2}(180)$ is the total weight of half the group

and $\frac{n}{2}(215)$ is the total weight of the other half.

Therefore, $\frac{n}{2}(180) + \frac{n}{2}(215) \le 2,000$

$$180n + 215n \le 4,000$$
$$395n \le 4,000$$
$$n \le 10.2$$

Since n must be an integer, n = 10. Therefore, the best answer is D. This is a moderately difficult question.

8. After paying a 10 percent tax on all income over $3,000, a person had a net income of $12,000. What was the income before taxes?

(A) $13,300
(B) $13,000
(C) $12,900
(D) $10,000
(C) $ 9,000

If x dollars is the income before taxes, then the net income of $12,000 is equal to $3,000 plus the amount left over after the remaining (x − 3,000) dollars is taxed 10 percent, or (0.9)(x − 3,000) dollars. Therefore,

$$3,000 + (0.9)(x - 3,000) = 12,000$$
$$(0.9)(x - 3,000) = 9,000$$
$$0.9x - 2,700 = 9,000$$
$$0.9x = 11,700$$
$$x = \frac{11,700}{0.9} = 13,000$$

Thus, the best answer is B. This is a moderately difficult question.

9. $1 - [2 - (3 - [4 - 5] + 6) + 7]$

(A) −2 (B) 0 (C) 1 (D) 2 (E) 16

When removing parentheses and brackets, always remove the innermost parentheses first.

$1 - [2 - (3 - [4 - 5] + 6) + 7] =$
$1 - [2 - (3 - [- 1] + 6) + 7] =$
$1 - [2 - (3 + 1 + 6) + 7] =$
$1 - [2 - 10 + 7] =$
$1 - [- 1] = 1 + 1 = 2$

10. The price of a model M camera is $209 and the price of a special lens is $69. When the camera and lens are purchased together, the price is $239. The amount saved by purchasing the camera and lens together is approximately what percent of the total price of the camera and lens when purchased separately?

(A) 14%
(B) 16%
(C) 29%
(D) 33%
(E) 86%

The total price of the camera and lens purchased separately is $209 + $69 = $278. The amount saved by purchasing the two together is $278 − $239 = $39. Therefore, the percent saving is $\frac{\$39}{\$278}$ or approximately 14%. Thus, the best answer is A. This is an easy question.

11. If 0.497 mark has the value of one dollar, what is the value to the nearest dollar of 350 marks?

(A) $174 (B) $176 (C) $524
   (D) $696 (E) $704

Since 0.497 mark equals one dollar, 350 marks equal $\frac{350}{0.497}$ dollars, or $704, to the nearest dollar. Thus, the best answer is E. This is a moderately difficult question.

12. A right cylindrical container with radius 2 meters and height 1 meter is filled to capacity with oil. How many empty right cylindrical cans, each with radius $\frac{1}{2}$ meter and height 4 meters, can be filled to capacity with the oil in this container?

(A) 1
(B) 2
(C) 4
(D) 8
(C) 16

The total capacity of the right cylindrical container is $\pi r^2 h = \pi(2)^2(1) = 4\pi$ cubic meters. Each right cylindrical can has a total capacity of $\pi\left(\frac{1}{2}\right)^2(4) = \pi$ cubic meters. Therefore, the container can fill up $\frac{4\pi}{\pi}$, or 4, cans. Thus, the best answer is C. This is a difficult question.

13. If a sequence of 8 consecutive odd integers with increasing values has 9 as its 7th term, what is the sum of the terms of the sequence?

(A) 22
(B) 32
(C) 36
(D) 40
(E) 44

To derive the terms in the sequences, it is only necessary to write 9 and the six consecutive odd integers less than 9 and the next one greater than 9.

The sequence is: $-3, -1, 1, 3, 5, 7, 9, 11$, and the sum of the terms in the sequence is 32. Thus, the best answer is B. This is a moderately difficult question.

14. A rectangular floor is covered by a rug except for a strip p meters wide along each of the four edges. If the floor is m meters by n meters, what is the area of the rug, in square meters?

(A) $mn - p(m + n)$
(B) $mn - 2p(m + n)$
(C) $mn - p^2$
(D) $(m - p)(n - p)$
(E) $(m - 2p)(n - 2p)$

It may be helpful to draw a diagram:

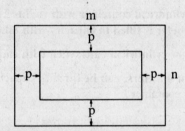

The rug is represented by the inside rectangle with dimensions $m - 2p$ and $n - 2p$. Therefore, its area is $(m - 2p)(n - 2p)$. Thus, the best answer is E. This is a difficult question.

15. Working alone, R can complete a certain kind of job in 9 hours. R and S, working together at their respective rates, can complete one of these jobs in 6 hours. In how many hours can S, working alone, complete one of these jobs?

(A) 18
(B) 12
(C) 9
(D) 6
(C) 3

If x is the number of hours S needs to complete the job alone, then S can do $\frac{1}{x}$ of the job in one hour. Similarly, R can do $\frac{1}{9}$

of the job in one hour, and R and S, working together, can do $\frac{1}{6}$ of the job in one hour. Therefore, $\frac{1}{x} + \frac{1}{9} = \frac{1}{6}$, and $x = 18$ hours. Thus, the best answer is A. This is a difficult question.

16. A family made a down payment of $75 and borrowed the balance on a set of encyclopedias that cost $400. The balance with interest was paid in 23 monthly payments of $16 each and a final payment of $9. The amount of interest paid was what percent of the amount borrowed?

(A) 6%
(B) 12%
(C) 14%
(D) 16%
(E) 20%

The family had to borrow $400 - $75 = $325. They paid back 23(16) + $9 = $377. Therefore, they paid

$377 - $325 = $52 in interest, which was $\frac{52}{325} = 16\%$

of the amount borrowed. Thus, the best answer is D. This is a moderately difficult question.

17. If $x \neq 0$ and $x = \sqrt{4xy - 4y^2}$, then in terms of y, $x =$

(A) $2y$
(B) y
(C) $\frac{y}{2}$
(D) $\frac{-4y^2}{1 - 4y}$
(E) $-2y$

The value of x can be expressed in terms of y as follows:

$$x = \sqrt{4xy - 4y^2}$$
$$x^2 = 4xy - 4y^2$$
$$x^2 - 4xy + 4y^2 = 0$$
$$(x - 2y)^2 = 0$$
$$x - 2y = 0$$
$$x = 2y$$

Therefore, the best answer is A. This is a very difficult question.

-268-

18. Solution Y is 30 percent liquid X and 70 percent water. If 2 kilograms of water evaporate from 8 kilograms of solution Y and 2 kilograms of solution Y are added to the remaining 6 kilograms of liquid, what percent of this new solution is liquid X?

(A) 30%

(B) $33\frac{1}{3}\%$

(C) $37\frac{1}{2}\%$

(D) 40%

(E) 50%

The original 8 kilograms (kg) of solution Y contains 30%, or 2.4 kg, of liquid X. If 2 kg of water evaporate from the 8 kg, that would leave 6 kg, of which 2.4 kg is liquid X. If 2 kg of solution Y is added to the remaining 6 kg of solution, the resulting 8 kg-solution would contain $2.4 + 0.3(2)$ kg of liquid X. Therefore, the percent of liquid X in the new solution would be

$$\frac{2.4 + 0.6}{8} = \frac{3}{8} = 37\frac{1}{2}\%.$$

Thus, the best answer is C. This is a difficult question.

19. $\dfrac{1}{\dfrac{1}{0.03} + \dfrac{1}{0.37}} =$

(A) 0.004

(B) 0.02775

(C) 2.775

(D) 3.6036

(C) 36.036

The value of the expression can be found as follows:

$$\frac{1}{\frac{1}{0.03} + \frac{1}{0.37}} = \frac{1}{\frac{0.37 + 0.03}{(0.03)(0.37)}} = \frac{(0.03)(0.37)}{0.37 + 0.03} = \frac{0.0111}{0.4} = 0.02775$$

Therefore, the best answer is B. This is a moderately difficult question.

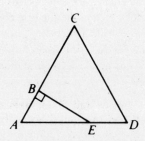

20. If each side of $\triangle ACD$ above has length 3 and if AB has length 1, what is the area of region $BCDE$?

(A) $\frac{9}{4}$ (B) $\frac{7}{4}\sqrt{3}$ (C) $\frac{9}{4}\sqrt{3}$

(D) $\frac{7}{2}\sqrt{3}$ (E) $6 + \sqrt{3}$

The area of region BCDE can be found by subtracting the area of $\triangle ABE$ from the area of $\triangle ACD$. Since ACD is equilateral, an altitude to its base divides the triangle into two identical right triangles with acute angles of 30 and 60 degrees. Since the hypotenuse of each right triangle is 3 and the base is $\frac{3}{2}$, the altitude must be $\sqrt{3^2 - \left(\frac{3}{2}\right)^2}$ or $\frac{3\sqrt{3}}{2}$ which is also the altitude of $\triangle ACD$. Therefore, the area of $\triangle ACD$ is $\frac{1}{2}(3)\left(\frac{3\sqrt{3}}{2}\right) = \frac{9}{4}\sqrt{3}$. Since right $\triangle ABE$ also has acute angles of 30 and 60 degrees and AB = 1, then AE = 2(1) and BE = $\sqrt{2^2 - 1^2} = \sqrt{3}$. The area of $\triangle ABE$ is $\frac{1}{2}(1)(\sqrt{3}) = \frac{\sqrt{3}}{2}$. Therefore, the area of region BCDE is $\frac{9}{4}\sqrt{3} - \frac{1}{2}(\sqrt{3}) = \frac{7}{4}\sqrt{3}$, and the best answer is B. This is a difficult question.

Explanatory Material: Reading Comprehension

1. The passage is most probably an excerpt from

(A) an economic history of Japan
(B) the memoirs of a samurai warrior
(C) a modern novel about eighteenth-century Japan
(D) an essay contrasting Japanese feudalism with its Western counterpart
(E) an introduction to a collection of Japanese folktales

The best answer is A. This question requires you to make two judgments: what is the general nature of the style and content of the passage and in what kind of publication would a passage of that nature appear? The passage is a somewhat technical discussion of the economic situation of a certain class of eighteenth-century Japanese, focusing on an analysis of then prevalent economic practices and trends. Thus, an economic history of Japan (choice A) is certainly a probable source for such material. Although any of the works in the other choices could conceivably contain such material, it is not probable, and there is no internal evidence to suggest that this excerpt could be appropriately placed in the types of works listed in choices B, C, D, or E. This is a very easy question.

2. Which of the following financial situations is most analogous to the financial situation in which Japan's Tokugawa shoguns found themselves in the eighteenth century?

    (A) A small business borrows heavily to invest in new equipment, but is able to pay off its debt early when it is awarded a lucrative government contract.
    (B) Fire destroys a small business, but insurance covers the cost of rebuilding.
    (C) A small business is turned down for a loan at a local bank because the owners have no credit history.
    (D) A small business has to struggle to meet operating expenses when its profits decrease.
    (E) A small business is able to cut back sharply on spending through greater commercial efficiency and thereby compensate for a loss of revenue.

The best answer is D. In order to answer this question you must first determine what were the essential elements of the shoguns' financial situation and then decide which of the choices presents a situation with the same basic elements. Lines 16-18 indicate that the overlords' income failed to keep pace with their expenses. Lines 19-26 describe some of the reasons expenses rose while income declined. Choice D is the only choice that contains these two critical elements. With the exception of E, the other choices describe situations in which one of the elements is analogous to critical elements in the shoguns' situation, but the other is not. Choice E is not analogous in either of its elements. This is a relatively easy question.

3. Which of the following best describes the attitude of the author toward the samurai discussed in lines 11-16?

    (A) Warmly approving
    (B) Mildly sympathetic
    (C) Bitterly disappointed
    (D) Harshly disdainful
    (E) Profoundly shocked

The best answer is B. This question asks about the attitude of the author toward a particular group as that attitude is revealed in the language of the passage. To answer this question, you should first re-examine the lines cited. The samurai are described as idle and given to expensive pursuits. The author, however, does not dismiss them; rather, it is implied that their idleness is not totally a matter of choice: they were "reduced to idleness," (line 11) and their response seems to the author "not surprising." Thus, the author's attitude can be described as "mildly sympathetic." This is a relatively easy question.

4. According to the passage, the major reason for the financial problems experienced by Japan's feudal overlords in the eighteenth century was that

    (A) spending had outdistanced income
    (B) trade had fallen off
    (C) profits from mining had declined
    (D) the coinage had been sharply debased
    (E) the samurai had concentrated in castle-towns

The best answer is A. This question requires you to identify the major reason stated in the passage for the problems of the feudal overlords. To answer the question, it is necessary to distinguish between the major reason and the factors that contributed to, but alone do not completely account for, the problem. Lines 16-18 state that the overlords' income "failed to keep pace with their expenses." The rest of the paragraph goes on to explain the various factors that contributed to the problem. Notice that choices C, D, and E are discussed in the passage as factors influencing the economic situation; they are not, however, the major reason for the problems of the overlords. This is a very easy question.

5. The passage implies that individual samurai did not find it easy to recover from debt for which of the following reasons?

    (A) Agricultural production had increased.
    (B) Taxes were irregular in timing and arbitrary in amount.
    (C) The Japanese government had failed to adjust to the needs of a changing economy.
    (D) The domains of samurai overlords were becoming smaller and poorer as government revenues increased.
    (E) There was a limit to the amount in taxes that farmers could be made to pay.

The best answer is E. This question asks you to identify the reason that individual samurai, once they had become indebted, could not extricate themselves from debt. Lines 16-18 suggest that individual samurai drew their income from rice production among tenant farmers, and lines 30-32 indicate that this income could not be increased indefinitely. Thus, it can be concluded that the samurai could not raise enough money to recover from debt because they could not increase the income derived from tenant farms. Choice E is a statement of this idea. This is a question of medium difficulty.

6. The passage suggests that, in eighteenth-century Japan, the office of tax collector

    (A) was a source of personal profit to the officeholder
    (B) was regarded with derision by many Japanese
    (C) remained within families
    (D) existed only in castle-towns
    (E) took up most of the officeholder's time

The best answer is C. This question asks for a specific supporting detail presented in the passage. To answer the question, it is necessary to locate the reference in the passage to the office of tax collector. Lines 21-22 contain a parenthetical reference to the office of tax collector. It is indicated there that the office of tax collector is hereditary. Choice C presents a paraphrase of this idea: the office "remained within families." There is no evidence to support any of the statements made in the other choices. This is a question of medium difficulty.

7. Which of the following could best be substituted for the word "This" in line 47 without changing the meaning of the passage?

    (A) The search of Japan's Tokugawa shoguns for solvency
    (B) The importance of commerce in feudal Japan
    (C) The unfairness of the tax structure in eighteenth-century Japan
    (D) The difficulty of increasing government income by other means
    (E) The difficulty experienced by both individual samurai and the shogun himself in extricating themselves from debt

The best answer is D. This question requires you to determine the referent of the pronoun "This" in line 47. You should first reread the paragraph containing the sentence, and decide what "This" refers to. The paragraph discusses ways in which the Tokugawa shogun and the government attempted to increase revenues and explains why each of the attempts fell short of solving the problem. The pronoun "This" in line 47 introduces a sentence that draws a conclusion based on the fact that most means of increasing government revenue had been exhausted; "This" can only refer to the difficulty they experienced. Choice D contains a phrase that conveys this idea and that can be substituted for the pronoun "This" without altering the meaning of the sentence. This is a question of medium difficulty.

8. The passage implies that which of the following was the primary reason why the Tokugawa shoguns turned to city merchants for help in financing the state?

    (A) A series of costly wars had depleted the national treasury.
    (B) Most of the country's wealth appeared to be in city merchants' hands.
    (C) Japan had suffered a series of economic reversals due to natural disasters such as floods.
    (D) The merchants were already heavily indebted to the shoguns.
    (E) Further reclamation of land would not have been economically advantageous.

The best answer is B. This question requires you to identify the major reason why the Tokugawa shoguns began to require city merchants to contribute to the state revenues. The second paragraph indicates that the shoguns had exhausted most sources of revenue for the government. Lines 50-54 indicate that the shoguns believed that city merchants had acquired

most of the country's wealth. Because of that belief, they deemed it "reasonable" to turn to the city merchants. Thus, choice B is the best answer. This is a very easy question.

9. According to the passage, the actions of the Tokugawa shoguns in their search for solvency for the government were regrettable because those actions

    (A) raised the cost of living by pushing up prices
    (B) resulted in the exhaustion of the most easily worked deposits of silver and gold
    (C) were far lower in yield than had originally been anticipated
    (D) did not succeed in reducing government spending
    (E) acted as a deterrent to trade

The best answer is A. To answer this question, you must determine why the author of the passage judges the actions of the shoguns as "regrettable," a judgment rendered in the conclusion of the passage. The passage indicates that the forced loans demanded of city merchants by the shoguns (lines 54-60) had the ultimate effect of driving up prices. The next sentence discusses the effects of the rise in prices on the cost of living, an effect that the author finds unfortunate ("Thus, regrettably," line 60). Therefore, choice A is the best answer. This is a very easy question.

10. Which of the following would be the most appropriate title for the passage?

    (A) Botticelli's Contribution to Florentine Art
    (B) Botticelli and the Traditions of Classical Art
    (C) Sandro Botticelli: From Denigration to Appreciation
    (D) Botticelli and Michelangelo: A Study in Contrasts
    (E) Standards of Taste: Botticelli's Critical Reputation up to the Nineteenth Century

The best answer is C because it is the only title that states the central theme of the passage, which is the history of the change in the response to the work of Botticelli, from unpopularity to approbation. This theme is made particularly clear in lines 1-4, 8-10, and 66-67. There are also repeated references to this theme throughout the body of the passage. This is a relatively easy question.

11. It can be inferred that the author of the passage would be likely to find most beneficial a study of an artist that

    (A) avoided placing the artist in an evolutionary scheme of the history of art
    (B) analyzed the artist's work in relation to the artist's personality
    (C) analyzed the artist's relationship to the style and subject matter of classical art
    (D) analyzed the artist's work in terms of both traditional characteristics and unique achievement
    (E) sanctioned and extended the evaluation of the artist's work made by the artist's contemporaries

The best answer is D. In lines 63-65 the author states that "Horne's emphasis on the way a talented artist reflects a tradition yet moves beyond that tradition" is "an emphasis crucial to any study of art." The word "crucial" indicates that the author would be likely to find a study that "analyzed the artist's work in terms of both traditional characteristics and unique achievement" (choice D) to be most beneficial. This is a question of medium difficulty.

12. The passage suggests that Vasari would most probably have been more enthusiastic about Botticelli's work if that artist's work

    (A) had not revealed Botticelli's inability to depict a story clearly
    (B) had not evolved so straightforwardly from the Florentine art of the fourteenth century
    (C) had not seemed to Vasari to be so similar to classical art
    (D) could have been appreciated by amateur viewers as well as by connoisseurs
    (E) could have been included more easily in Vasari's discussion of art history

The best answer is E. Vasari's views are described in lines 4-8, which imply that Vasari was uneasy about Botticelli's work because it did not fit Vasari's evolutionary scheme of the history of art. Thus, it can be inferred that, had Botticelli's work been easier to include in Vasari's discussion of art history, Vasari would probably have been more enthusiastic about Botticelli's work. This is a question of medium difficulty.

13. The author most likely mentions the fact that many of Botticelli's best paintings were "hidden away in obscure churches and private homes" (lines 17-18) in order to

    (A) indicate the difficulty of trying to determine what an artist's best work is
    (B) persuade the reader that an artist's work should be available for general public viewing
    (C) prove that academic art historians had succeeded in keeping Botticelli's work from general public view
    (D) call into question the assertion that antiacademic art historians disagreed with their predecessors
    (E) suggest a reason why, for a period of time, Botticelli's work was not generally appreciated

The best answer is E. The sentence in lines 16-18 appears in parentheses, suggesting that the author is commenting on or qualifying what immediately precedes this sentence. Thus, the purpose of the parenthetical statement is determined by the sentence preceding it. In lines 11-15, the author asserts that Botticelli's work remained "outside of accepted taste." The author then offers the comment in parentheses: in lines 16-18, using "however" as a qualifier, the author mentions the obscure location of many of Botticelli's best paintings, implying that much of the best of Botticelli's work was not

available for viewing. Thus, the author suggests "a reason why, for a period of time, Botticelli's work was not generally appreciated." This is a question of medium difficulty.

14. The passage suggests that most seventeenth- and eighteenth-century academic art historians and most early-nineteenth-century antiacademic art historians would have disagreed significantly about which of the following?

    I. The artistic value of Botticelli's work
    II. The criteria by which art should be judged
    III. The features that characterized fifteenth-century Florentine art

    (A) I only
    (B) II only
    (C) III only
    (D) II and III only
    (E) I, II, and III

The best answer is B (II only). I is incorrect because lines 8-16 indicate that most seventeenth-, eighteenth-, and early-nineteenth-century art historians agreed on the artistic value of Botticelli's work — they all denigrated it. Choice III is wrong because the lines that discuss the features that characterized fifteenth-century Florentine art (lines 20-28) do not suggest that most seventeenth- and eighteenth-century academic art historians would have disagreed with most early-nineteenth-century antiacademic art historians about these features. Choice II is correct because lines 11-14 state that "antiacademic art historians of the early nineteenth century rejected many of the standards of evaluation espoused by their predecessors." This is a very difficult question.

15. According to the passage, which of the following is an accurate statement about Botticelli's relation to classical art?

    (A) Botticelli more often made use of classical subject matter than classical style.
    (B) Botticelli's interest in perspective led him to study classical art.
    (C) Botticelli's style does not share any similarities with the style of classical art.
    (D) Because he saw little classical art, Botticelli did not exhibit much interest in imitating such art.
    (E) Although Botticelli sometimes borrowed his subject matter from classical art, he did not create large-scale paintings of these subjects.

The best answer is A. Lines 32-37 describe Botticelli's use of classical style and subject matter. They state that large-scale classical subjects were the focus of Botticelli's painting and that he borrowed little from the classical style. Thus it can be inferred that Botticelli used classical subject matter more often than he used classical style. This is a question of medium difficulty.

16. According to the passage, Horne believed which of the following about the relation of the Sistine frescoes to the tradition of fifteenth-century Florentine art?

(A) The frescoes do not exhibit characteristics of such art.
(B) The frescoes exhibit more characteristics of such art than do the paintings of Michelangelo.
(C) The frescoes exhibit some characteristics of such art, but these qualities are not the dominant features of the frescoes.
(D) Some of the frescoes exhibit characteristics of such art, but most do not.
(E) More of the frescoes exhibit skillful representation of anatomical proportions than skillful representation of the human figure in motion.

The best answer is C. Lines 53-62 describe Horne's views about Botticelli's Sistine frescoes. According to lines 53-55, "the frescoes shared important features with paintings by other fifteenth-century Florentines"; thus, the frescoes exhibit some characteristics of fifteenth-century Florentine art. Lines 57-62 point out that "Botticelli did not treat these qualities as ends in themselves" and that, in his work, "the traditional Florentine qualities [were] less central"; thus, these qualities are not the dominant features of the frescoes. This is a question of medium difficulty.

17. The passage suggests that, before Horne began to study Botticelli's work in 1908, there had been

(A) little appreciation of Botticelli in the English-speaking world
(B) an overemphasis on Botticelli's transformation, in the Sistine frescoes, of the principles of classical art
(C) no attempt to compare Botticelli's work to that of Michelangelo
(D) no thorough investigation of Botticelli's Sistine frescoes
(E) little agreement among connoisseurs and amateurs about the merits of Botticelli's work.

The best answer is D. According to lines 48-52, "Botticelli's work, specially the Sistine frescoes, did not generate worldwide attention until it was finally subjected to a comprehensive and scrupulous analysis by Horne in 1908." The word "finally" suggests that Horne's study of the frescoes was the first thorough investigation of them. This is a relatively difficult question.

18. The author is primarily concerned with

(A) proving that immunological reactions do not involve antibodies
(B) establishing that most immunological reactions involve antigens
(C) criticizing scientists who will not change their theories regarding immunology
(D) analyzing the importance of cells in fighting disease
(E) explaining two different kinds of immunological reactions

The best answer is E. This question asks for the author's primary interest or concern in writing this passage, or the central idea of the passage as a whole. To answer this question, carefully evaluate the first words in the five choices. Choice A begins with "proving"; choice B begins with "establishing." Both of these words may fit the procedure of the passage, but the statements are false. Choice C can be rejected because, although the author states that reluctance to abandon a hypothesis made new research difficult (lines 22-27), the author does not directly criticize scientists. Paragraphs one and three are almost entirely descriptive; therefore, the author's purpose must not be to analyze immunological reactions (choice D), but to explain them (choice E). This is a relatively difficult question.

19. The author argues that the antigen-antibody explanation of immunity "had to be seriously qualified" (line 37) because

(A) antibodies were found to activate unstable components in the blood
(B) antigens are not exactly complementary to antibodies
(C) lymphocytes have the ability to bind to the surface of antigens
(D) antibodies are synthesized from protein whereas antigens are made from nucleic acid
(E) antigens have no apparent mechanism to direct the formation of an antibody

The best answer is E. First, examine each of the choices to determine which makes an accurate statement, based on evidence in the passage, about the reasons that scientists had to qualify the antigen-antibody theory. The question refers to line 37, which is part of a sentence that says, in combination with the preceding sentence, that scientists qualified the antigen-antibody theory when they could not explain "how an antigen is recognized" (lines 29-30) and "how a structure exactly complementary to it is then synthesized" (lines 30-31). From this, scientists realized that the mechanism for directing the synthesis of the antibody did not operate in the way they had thought. The other choices are plausible statements, but they are not relevant to the cause-and-effect relationship asked about in the question. This is a very difficult question.

20. The author most probably believes that the antigen-antibody theory of immunological reaction

   (A) is wrong
   (B) was accepted without evidence
   (C) is unverifiable
   (D) is a partial explanation
   (E) has been a divisive issue among scientists

The best answer is D. The author mentions "difficulties" with the theory but does not call it "wrong." Therefore, A is incorrect. The author refers to two important manifestations of the antigen-antibody reactions in the first paragraph, and so does not believe, as B states, that the theory "was accepted without evidence," or, as C states, "is unverifiable." Nowhere does the author suggest, as E states, that the theory "has been a divisive issue among scientists." Lines 37-43 do state that research "led scientists to realize that a second immunological reaction" also takes place in the body. Thus, scientists realized that the antigen-antibody theory was, as choice D states, "a partial explanation." This is a question of medium difficulty.

21. The author mentions all of the following as being involved in an antigen-antibody immunological reactions EXCEPT the

   (A) synthesis of a protein
   (B) activation of *complement* in the bloodstream
   (C) destruction of antibodies
   (D) entrapment of antigens by macrophages
   (E) formation of a substance with a structure complementary to that of an antigen

The best answer is C. This question asks you to gather from the first two paragraphs the processes the author attributes to antigen-antibody reactions, and then to recognize which of the choices is not mentioned in the passage. Choice A, synthesis of a protein, is mentioned in lines 3-6. Choice B, activation of *complement* in the bloodstream, is mentioned in lines 15-18. Choice D, entrapment of antigens by macrophages, is explained as phagocytosis in lines 12-14. Choice E, formation of a substance with a structure complementary to that of an antigen, is discussed in paragraph two, lines 28-31, as part of the "primary difficulty" of the antigen-antibody theory. The only choice not mentioned in the passage is the destruction of antibodies. Therefore, the best answer is choice C. This is a very difficult question.

22. The passage contains information that would answer which of the following questions about cell-mediated immunological reactions?

   I. Do lymphocytes form antibodies during cell-mediated immunological reactions?
   II. Why are lymphocytes more hostile to antigens during cell-mediated immunological reactions than are other cell groups?
   III. Are cell-mediated reactions more pronounced after transplants than they are after parasites have invaded the organism?

   (A) I only
   (B) I and II only
   (C) I and III only
   (D) II and III only
   (E) I, II, and III

The best answer is A. The format of this question requires you to evaluate each of the questions designated with Roman numerals separately and carefully. Question I is answered by paragraph three, which indicates that, in cell-mediated immunological reactions, lymphocytes do not produce antibodies but destroy foreign tissue cells by themselves. Nowhere does the passage answer question II; it does not discuss why lymphocytes are more hostile to antigens during cell-mediated reactions than are other cell groups. Nor does the passage answer question III; it does not compare the cell-mediated reaction involved in transplants to the cell-mediated reaction involved in parasite invasion; instead, the passage simply states that the reaction occurs in both cases. Therefore, the passage answers question I only. This is a very difficult question.

23. The passage suggests that scientists might not have developed the theory of cell-mediated immunological reactions if

   (A) proteins existed in specific group types
   (B) proteins could have been shown to direct the synthesis of other proteins
   (C) antigens were always destroyed by proteins
   (D) antibodies were composed only of protein
   (E) antibodies were the body's primary means of resisting disease

The best answer is B. According to the passage, scientists arrived at the theory of cell-mediated immunological reactions because the theory of antigen-antibody immunological reaction could not explain how an antibody, which is made of protein, could recognize and synthesize another protein (lines 27-37). It can be inferred that scientists might *not* have developed the theory of cell-mediated immunological reactions if they had discovered the reverse — that proteins could direct the synthesis of other proteins. This is a relatively difficult question.

24. According to the passage, antibody-antigen and cell-mediated immunological reactions both involve which of the following processes?

    I. The destruction of antigens
   II. The creation of antibodies
  III. The destruction of intracellular parasites

(A) I only
(B) II only
(C) III only
(D) I and II only
(E) II and III only

The best answer is A. The question requires you to compare the information given in the passage about antigen-antibody responses to the information given in the passage about cell-mediated responses, and to decide which of the Roman numeral choices the two reactions have in common. Choice I, the destruction of antigens, is discussed in paragraph one and paragraph two in connection with both types of immunological reaction. Choice II, the creation of antibodies, is discussed in paragraph one in connection with antigen-antibody reactions only. Choice III, the destruction of intracellular parasites, is discussed in paragraph three in connection with cell-mediated reactions only. Therefore, the answer is A: the two reactions have in common choice I only. This is a very difficult question.

25. The author supports the theory of cell-mediated reactions primarily by

(A) pointing out a contradiction in the assumption leading to the antigen-antibody theory
(B) explaining how cell mediation accounts for phenomena that the antigen-antibody theory cannot account for
(C) revealing new data that scientists arguing for the antigen-antibody theory have continued to ignore
(D) showing that the antigen-antibody theory fails to account for the breakup of antigens
(E) demonstrating that cell mediation explains lysis and phagocytosis more fully than the antigen-antibody theory does

The best answer is B. This question requires you to recognize the structure of the passage as a whole. Paragraph one describes the way the antigen-antibody reaction works. Paragraph two discusses the difficulties with the antigen-antibody theory, which are, in this case, that the antigen-antibody theory cannot account for certain phenomena. Paragraph two also claims that accounting for these phenomena led scientists to the theory of cell-mediated reactions. Paragraph three describes the way the cell-mediated reaction works. The discussion is thus structured to support the theory of cell-mediated reactions by explaining how cell mediation accounts for phenomena not explained by the antigen-antibody theory. This is a very difficult question.

Explanatory Material: Data Sufficiency

1. If today the price of an item is $3,600, what was the price of the item exactly 2 years ago?

(1) The price of the item increased by 10 percent per year during this 2-year period.

(2) Today the price of the item is 1.21 times its price exactly 2 years ago.

From (1) it can be determined that if x was the price two years ago, then 110 percent of x, or $1.1x$, was the price one year ago, and $1.1(1.1x) = 1.21x$ is the price today. By solving the equation $1.21x = \$3,600$, it is possible to find x, the price 2 years ago. Therefore, (1) alone is sufficient to answer the question and the answer must be either A or D. Since (2) gives the same information derived in (1), it also is sufficient by itself to answer the question. Therefore, each statement alone is sufficient to answer the question and the best answer is D. This is an easy question.

2. By what percent has the price of an overcoat been reduced?

(1) The original price was $380.

(2) The original price was $50 more than the reduced price.

The percent reduction is the ratio of the amount of reduction to the original price. Since (1) gives no information about the amount of reduction, (1) alone is not sufficient to answer the question, and the answer must be B, C, or E. Statement (2) alone gives $50 as the amount of the reduction but gives no information about the original price. Therefore, (2) alone is not sufficient and the answer must be either C or E. Since (1) and (2) together give both pieces of information needed, the percent reduction can be computed. Therefore, the best answer is C. This is an easy question.

3. If the Longfellow Playground is rectangular, what is its width?

(1) The ratio of its length to its width is 7 to 2.

(2) The perimeter of the playground is 396 meters.

From (1) it can be determined that for some positive number x, the length L of the playground is 7x and the width W is 2x. Since only the ratio $\frac{L}{W} = \frac{7}{2}$ is given, (1) is not sufficient to answer the question and the answer must be B, C, or E. Statement (2) provides the information that the perimeter, or 2L + 2W, is equal to 396, but (2) gives no information about the relationship between L and W. Therefore, (2) alone is not sufficient and the answer must be C or E. From (1) and (2) together, it can be determined that L + W = 7x + 2x = 198. The width can be determined by solving the equation for x. Therefore, the best answer is C. This is an easy question.

4. What is the value of $x - 1$?

   (1) $x + 1 = 3$

   (2) $x - 1 < 3$

From (1) the value of x, and thus x − 1, can be determined, and the answer must be A or D. Since (2) gives a range rather than a specific value of x, the question cannot be answered from (2); therefore, the best answer is A. This is an easy question.

5. Is William taller than Jane?

   (1) William is taller than Anna.

   (2) Anna is not as tall as Jane.

Statement (1) relates William's height to Anna's and (2) relates Jane's height to Anna's. Neither statement relates William's height to Jane's. Therefore, the answer must be either C or E. When (1) and (2) are taken together, it is possible to determine that Anna is the shortest of the three; however, Jane could be either shorter or taller than William. Since the question cannot be answered, the best answer is E. This is an easy question.

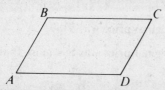

6. In parallelogram ABCD above, what is the measure of ∠ADC?

   (1) The measure of ∠ABC is greater than 90°.

   (2) The measure of ∠BCD is 70°.

From (1) it can only be determined that the measure of ∠ADC is greater than 90° since ∠ABC = ∠ADC. Since this information is not sufficient to answer the question, the answer must be B, C, or E. From (2) alone, it can be determined that the measure of ∠ADC is 110° since ∠ADC is a supplement of ∠BCD. Therefore, the best answer is B. This is an easy question.

7. Is x^2 equal to xy?

   (1) $x^2 - y^2 = (x + 5)(y - 5)$

   (2) $x = y$

If x^2 is equal to xy, then either x = 0 or x = y. From (1), if x = −5 or y = 5, then (x + 5)(y − 5) = 0, so $x^2 - y^2 = 0$, and it follows that x = y or x = −y. Thus, (1) would be true whether x = y = 5 or x = −5 and y = 5. Since there are several possibilities, the question cannot be answered from (1) alone, and the answer must be B, C, or E. From (2) alone, it can be determined that $x^2 = xy$ and the best answer is B. This is an easy question.

8. Was 70 the average (arithmetic mean) grade on a class test?

   (1) On the test, half of the class had grades below 70 and half of the class had grades above 70.

   (2) The lowest grade on the test was 45 and the highest grade on the test was 95.

Note that the average (arithmetic mean) grade depends on the distribution of the grades. Statement (1) alone is not sufficient since it does not specify how the grades are distributed with respect to 70. Therefore, the answer must be B, C, or E. Obviously (2) is also not sufficient since it only indicates the range of the grades but not their distribution. From (1) and (2) together, the distribution of the grades is not known and so the average cannot be determined. Thus, the best answer is E. This is an easy question.

9. What was John's average driving speed in miles per hour during a 15-minute interval?

   (1) He drove 10 miles during this interval.

   (2) His maximum speed was 50 miles per hour and his minimum speed was 35 miles per hour during this interval.

From (1) alone it can be determined that John's average driving speed was 10 miles/0.25 hr = 40 miles per hour. Therefore, the answer is either A or D. Since (2) does not give enough information to determine the total distance driven from which the average driving speed could be derived, the best answer is A. This is an easy question.

10. Is △MNP isosceles?

   (1) Exactly two of the angles, ∠M and ∠N, have the same measure.

   (2) ∠N and ∠P do not have the same measure.

If △MNP has two equal sides, then it is isosceles. If any triangle has two equal angles, the sides opposite the equal angles are also equal. From (1) alone it can be determined that △MNP is isosceles; therefore, the answer must be A or D. From (2) alone, it cannot be determined that △MNP has two equal angles. Therefore, the best answer is A. This is an easy question.

11. Is n an integer greater than 4?

   (1) 3n is a positive integer.

   (2) $\frac{n}{3}$ is a positive integer.

From (1), n could be any positive integer, or even a fraction such as $\frac{1}{3}$. Since the question cannot be answered from (1) alone, the answer must be B, C, or E. From (2) it can be determined that n is a positive multiple of 3, but it cannot be determined whether it is greater or less than 4. Therefore, the answer must be C or E. Since (1) and (2) together do not give any information that precludes n from being 3, it cannot be determined whether n is greater or less than 4 and the best answer is E. This is an easy question.

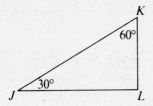

12. In △*JKL* shown above, what is the length of segment *JL*?

(1) *JK* = 10

(2) *KL* = 5

From the angle measures given in the figure, JKL is a right triangle and KL = $\frac{1}{2}$JK. From (1) it can be determined that KL = 5 and, by the Pythagorean relationship, that JL = $\sqrt{100 - 25}$. Therefore, the answer is A or D. Similarly, from (2) alone, all sides of the triangle can be found. Therefore, the best answer is D. This is a moderately difficult question.

13. A coal company can choose to transport coal to one of its customers by railroad or by truck. If the railroad charges by the mile and the trucking company charges by the ton, which means of transporting the coal would cost less than the other?

(1) The railroad charges $5,000 plus $0.01 per mile per railroad car used, and the trucking company charges $3,000 plus $85 per ton.

(2) The customer to whom the coal is to be sent is 195 miles away from the coal company.

Although (1) gives detailed information about the rail and truck rates, it gives no information about the weights and distances to which these rates are to be applied. Therefore, the question cannot be answered and the answer must be B, C, or E. Since (2) only gives information about the distance, and (1) and (2) together do not provide information about the tonnage and the number of railroad cars needed, the best answer is E. This is an easy question.

14. Is *x* − *y* > *r* − *s*?

(1) *x* > *r* and *y* < *s*.

(2) *y* = 2, *s* = 3, *r* = 5, and *x* = 6.

From (1), if x > r and y < s, then −y > −s and x − y > r − s. Since the answer can be determined from (1) alone, the answer must be A or D. From (2), the values of x, y, r, and s can be substituted into the inequality to answer the question. Therefore, the best answer is D. This is a moderately difficult question.

15. On a certain day it took Bill three times as long to drive from home to work as it took Sue to drive from home to work. How many kilometers did Bill drive from home to work?

(1) Sue drove 10 kilometers from home to work, and the ratio of

$$\frac{\text{distance driven from home to work}}{\text{time to drive from home to work}}$$

was the same for Bill and Sue that day.

(2) The ratio of

$$\frac{\text{distance driven from home to work}}{\text{time to drive from home to work}}$$

for Sue that day was 64 kilometers per hour.

From (1) and the information given in the problem, it can be determined that $\frac{\text{Sue's distance}}{\text{Sue's time}} = \frac{\text{Bill's distance d}}{3t}$ or $\frac{10}{t} = \frac{d}{3t}$ and d = 30 kilometers. Therefore, the answer must be A or D. Since (2) gives no information about Sue's time (from which we could compute Bill's time) and Bill's speed, the question cannot be answered from (2) alone and the best answer is A. This is a moderately difficult question.

16. The figure above represents the floor of a square foyer with a circular rug partially covering the floor and extending to the outer edges of the floor as shown. What is the area of the foyer floor that is not covered by the rug?

(1) The area of the foyer is 9 square meters.

(2) The area of the rug is 2.25π square meters.

From (1), the diameter of the circle is equal to the side of the square, or 3 meters, and the area of the uncovered region is $9 - \pi\left(\frac{3}{2}\right)^2$. Therefore, the answer must be A or D. From (2), the radius of the circle is $\sqrt{2.25} = 1.5$ and the side of the square is 2(1.5) = 3. Therefore, the area of the uncovered region is $3^2 - 2.25\pi$, and the best answer is D. This is a difficult question.

17. At a certain university, if 50 percent of the people who inquire about admission policies actually submit applications for admission, what percent of those who submit applications for admission enroll in classes at the university?

(1) Fifteen percent of those who submit applications for admission are accepted at the university.

(2) Eighty percent of those who are accepted send a deposit to the university.

From (1) and (2) taken together, it can only be determined that $(0.15)(0.8) = 12$ percent of the applicants are accepted and make a deposit. Since neither (1) nor (2) gives information as to what portion of this 12 percent actually enrolls in classes, the best answer is E. This is a moderately difficult question.

18. If x and y are nonzero integers, is $\frac{x}{y}$ an integer?

    (1) x is the product of 2 and some other integer.

    (2) There is only one pair of positive integers whose product equals y.

From (1), it can be determined that x is an even integer. Since y may, or may not, be a divisor of x, the question cannot be answered from (1) alone and the answer must be B, C, or E. Statement (2) implies that y is a prime number but gives no information about x. Therefore, the answer must be C or E. From (1) and (2) together, x is an even number and y is a prime number. Since y could be the even number 2, in which case $\frac{x}{y}$ would be an integer, or y could be an odd integer, in which case $\frac{x}{y}$ might not be an integer, the best answer is E. This is a moderately difficult question.

19. If x is an integer, what is the value of x?

    (1) $\frac{1}{5} < \frac{1}{x+1} < \frac{1}{2}$

    (2) $(x - 3)(x - 4) = 0$

From (1) it can be determined that $x + 1 = 3$ or $x + 1 = 4$; thus $x = 2$ or $x = 3$. From (2) it can be determined that $x = 3$ or $x = 4$. Since the precise value of x cannot be determined from either (1) or (2) taken alone, the answer must be C or E. If (1) and (2) are considered together, the only value of x that satisfies both conditions is $x = 3$. Therefore, the best answer is C. This is a difficult question.

20. Is quadrilateral Q a square?

    (1) The sides of Q have the same length.

    (2) The diagonals of Q have the same length.

Statement (1) implies that Q is a rhombus that may, or may not, be a square. Therefore, the answer is B, C, or E. Statement (2) alone does not imply that Q is a square since any rectangle or isosceles trapezoid has diagonals of equal length. Therefore, the answer must be C or E. If (1) and (2) are considered together, Q is a rhombus that has diagonals of equal length. Since only a square has both properties, Q is a square and the best answer is C. This is a difficult question.

21. If K is a positive integer less than 10 and $N = 4{,}321 + K$, what is the value of K?

Statement (1) implies that K is one of the integers 2, 5, or 8, since only these values of K will make N divisible by 3. Since the precise value of K cannot be determined from (1), the answer must be B, C, or E. Statement (2) implies that $K = 5$, since that is the only positive value of K that will make N divisible by 7. Therefore, the answer is B. This is a difficult question.

22. A jewelry dealer initially offered a bracelet for sale at an asking price that would give a profit to the dealer of 40 percent of the original cost. What was the original cost of the bracelet?

    (1) After reducing this asking price by 10 percent, the jewelry dealer sold the bracelet at a profit of $403.

    (2) The jewelry dealer sold the bracelet for $1,953.

The problem states that the initial asking price p was equal to 140 percent of the cost c, or $p = 1.4c$. From (1), the equation $0.9p = c + 403$ can be derived. Substituting 1.4c for p and then solving the equation $0.9(1.4c) = c + 403$ will yield the cost ($1,550). Therefore, the answer must be A or D. From (2) alone, the cost cannot be related to the selling price. The use of "initially offered" suggests that there was at least one subsequent offer about which (2) gives little useful information. Therefore, the best answer is A. This is a very difficult question.

23. If n is an integer between 2 and 100 and if n is also the square of an integer, what is the value of n?

    (1) n is the cube of an integer.

    (2) n is even.

The problem is to find which of the integers 4, 9, 16, 25, 36, 49, 64, or 81 is n. Statement (1) implies that $n = 64$ since 64 is the only one of these squares that is also the cube of an integer. Therefore, the answer must be A or D. From (2) alone, the integer n could be any of the integers 4, 16, 36, or 64. Therefore, the best answer is A. This is a difficult question.

24. Is $x^2 - y^2$ a positive number?

    (1) $x - y$ is a positive number.

    (2) $x + y$ is a positive number.

The expression $x^2 - y^2$ is a positive number if, and only if, both of its factors $x + y$ and $x - y$ are positive or both are negative. From (1) alone it cannot be determined whether $x + y$ is positive. For example, if $x = -2$ and $y = -3$, then $x + y$ is negative, whereas if $x = 3$ and $y = 2$, then $x + y$ is positive. Thus the answer is B, C, or E. Similarly, from (2) it cannot be determined whether $x - y$ is positive, and the answer is C or E. Since both (1) and (2) are needed to establish that the two factors have the same sign, the best answer is C. This is a difficult question.

25. The surface area of a square tabletop was changed so that one of the dimensions was reduced by 1 inch and the other dimension was increased by 2 inches. What was the surface area before these changes were made?

(1) After the changes were made, the surface area was 70 square inches.

(2) There was a 25 percent increase in one of the dimensions.

From the information in the problem and (1), if s is the length of a side of the square tabletop, then $(s - 1)(s + 2) = 70$ or $s^2 + s - 72 = 0$. There are two values of s that satisfy this question, 8 and $- 9$; however, since s cannot be negative in the context of this problem, $s = 8$. Therefore, the answer must be A or D. From (2) it can be determined that $0.25s = 2$ and $s = 8$. Therefore, the best answer is D. This is a very difficult question.

Explanatory Material: Problem Solving II

1. Which of the following is equal to 85 percent of 160?

(A) 1.88   (B) 13.6   (C) 136
(D) 188   (E) 13,600

The number equal to 85 percent of 160 can be found by multiplying $160 \times .85 = 136$. Therefore, the best answer is C. This is a very easy question.

2. The regular hourly wage for an employee of a certain factory is $5.60. If the employee worked 8 hours over-time and earned $1\frac{1}{2}$ times this regular hourly wage for overtime, how much overtime money was earned?

(A) $67.20
(B) $55.40
(C) $50.00
(D) $44.80
(E) $12.00

The employee would have earned $8 \times \$5.60 = \$44.80$ at the regular rate. For overtime he receives an additional amount equal to half the regular rate, or $22.40. The total overtime earnings are therefore $\$44.80 + \$22.40 = \$67.20$, so the best answer is A. This is a very easy question.

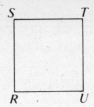

3. Square *RSTU* shown above is rotated in a plane about its center in a clockwise direction the minimum number of degrees necessary for *T* to be in the position where *S* is now shown. The number of degrees through which *RSTU* is rotated is

(A) 135°   (B) 180°   (C) 225°
(D) 270°   (E) 315°

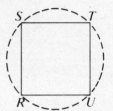

The figure above shows the circle traced by point T as square RSTU rotates about its center. If the square made one complete rotation so that T returned to its original position, the square would have rotated 360 degrees. Since the square rotates clockwise only until point T moves to position S, which is $\frac{3}{4}$ of the way around the circle, the square rotates $\frac{3}{4}$ of 360 or 270 degrees. Thus, the best answer is D. This is an easy question.

BREAKDOWN OF COST TO CONSUMER
FOR THE PRODUCTION OF
6 OUNCES OF FROZEN ORANGE JUICE

1975

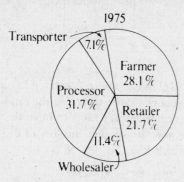

Cost to Consumer: $0.30

1980

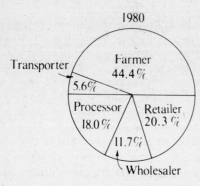

Cost to Consumer: $0.70

4. Of the following, which is closest to the increase from 1975 to 1980 in the amount received by the processor in producing 6 ounces of frozen orange juice?

(A) $0.03 (B) $0.05 (C) $0.06
 (D) $0.08 (E) $0.13

In 1975 the processor received 31.7% of the total $0.30 cost, or approximately $0.10. In 1980 the processor received 18% of the total $0.70 cost, or approximately $0.13. The increase is therefore approximately $0.03. The best answer is therefore A. This is a moderately difficult question.

5. In 1980, approximately what fraction of the cost to the consumer for the production of 6 ounces of frozen orange juice went to the farmer?

(A) $\frac{3}{11}$ (B) $\frac{1}{3}$ (C) $\frac{4}{9}$ (D) $\frac{5}{9}$ (E) $\frac{3}{5}$

The farmer received 44.4% of the total, which is somewhat less than half. Answers D and E can be eliminated because each exceeds $\frac{1}{2}$. A and B can be eliminated because they are too small: $\frac{3}{11}$ is less than 30% and $\frac{1}{3}$ is about 33%. That C is the best answer can be confirmed by finding the decimal equivalent of $\frac{4}{9}$, which is approximately 0.44. This is an easy question.

6. $\sqrt[4]{496}$ is between

(A) 3 and 4
(B) 4 and 5
(C) 5 and 6
(D) 6 and 7
(E) 7 and 8

If $x = \sqrt[4]{496}$, then $x^4 = 496$. Since $4^4 = 256$ and $5^4 = 625$, x must be between 4 and 5. Thus, the best answer is B. This is an easy question.

7. If $x \neq 0$, $2x = 5y$, and $3z = 7x$, what is the ratio of z to y?

(A) 2 to 21   (B) 3 to 5   (C) 14 to 15
 (D) 6 to 5   (E) 35 to 6

To find the ratio of z to y, it is convenient to express both z and y in terms of x. Thus $z = \frac{7}{3}x$ and $y = \frac{2}{5}x$. Then the ratio of z to y is $\frac{7}{3}x : \frac{2}{5}x = \left(\frac{7}{3}\right)\left(\frac{5}{2}\right) = \frac{35}{6}$. Thus, the best answer is E. This is a difficult question.

8. A grocer purchased a quantity of bananas at 3 pounds for $0.50 and sold the entire quantity at 4 pounds for $1.00. How many pounds did the grocer purchase if the profit from selling the bananas was $10.00?

(A) 40
(B) 60
(C) 90
(D) 120
(E) 240

Let P represent the number of pounds purchased. Then the grocer's cost is $\left(\frac{0.50}{3}\right)P$ and his revenue is $\left(\frac{1.00}{4}\right)P$. Profit is revenue minus cost, so

$$10 = \left(\frac{1.00}{4}\right)P - \left(\frac{0.50}{3}\right)P$$

$$120 = 3P - 2P = P$$

Thus, the best answer is D. This is a moderately difficult question.

9. There are between 100 and 110 cards in a collection of cards. If they are counted out 3 at a time, there are 2 left over, but if they are counted out 4 at a time, there is 1 left over. How many cards are in the collection?

(A) 101 (B) 103 (C) 106 (D) 107 (E)109

If the cards are counted three at a time with two left over, the possible totals are 101, 104, or 107. If they are counted four at a time with one left over, the total must be 101, 105, or 109. The only answer that satisfied both conditions is 101, so the best answer is A. This is a moderately difficult question.

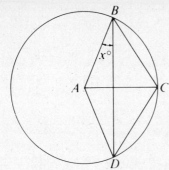

Note: Figure not drawn to scale.

10. If *A* is the center of the circle shown above and *AB* = *BC* = *CD*, what is the value of *x*?

(A) 15 (B) 30 (C) 45 (D) 60 (E) 75

AC = AB = AD, since all are radii of the same circle. Therefore, AB = BC = CD = AC = AD, and the triangles ABC and ACD are both equilateral and their angles are all equal to 60°. Because AB = AD, △ ABD is an isosceles triangle and its base angles are therefore equal. Thus, the measure of ∠ADB is x°. The sum of the degree measures of the angles of triangle ABD is 2x + 60 + 60 = 180, so x = 30. The best answer is therefore B. This is a moderately difficult question.

11. Out of a total of 1,000 employees at a certain corporation, 52 percent are female and 40 percent of these females work in research. If 60 percent of the total number of employees work in research, how many male employees do NOT work in research?

(A) 520
(B) 480
(C) 392
(D) 208
(E) 88

	Total Employees	Research Workers
Female	520	208
Male	480	392
TOTAL	1,000	600

The information presented in the problem is summarized in the table above. Of the 520 females (.52 × 1,000), 208 work in research (.40 × 520 = 208). The number of research workers who are male is 392, since 208 of the 600 (.60 × 1,000) research workers are female. Thus, there are 480 − 392 = 88 males who do not work in research. Therefore, the best answer is E. This is a moderately difficult question.

12. An instructor scored a student's test of 50 questions by subtracting 2 times the number of incorrect answers from the number of correct answers. If the student answered all of the questions and received a score of 38, how many questions did that student answer correctly?

(A) 19
(B) 38
(C) 41
(D) 44
(E) 46

If N is the number of correct answers, 50 − N is the number of incorrect answers. Therefore,

$$N - 2(50 - N) = 38$$
$$3N - 100 = 38$$
$$N = \frac{100 + 38}{3} = 46$$

Thus, the best answer is E. This is a difficult question.

13. Which of the following integers does NOT have a divisor greater than 1 that is the square of an integer?

(A) 75
(B) 42
(C) 32
(D) 25
(E) 12

Note that $75 = 3 \times 5^2$, $32 = 2 \times 4^2$, $25 = 1 \times 5^2$ and $12 = 3 \times 2^2$. Since $42 = 2 \times 3 \times 7$ and so does not have a divisor greater than 1 that is the square of an integer, the best answer is B. This is a difficult question.

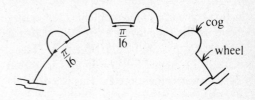

14. There are cogs around the circumference of a wheel and each cog is $\frac{\pi}{16}$ centimeter wide with a space of $\frac{\pi}{16}$ centimeter between consecutive cogs, as shown above. How many cogs of this size, with the same space between any two consecutive cogs, fit on a wheel with diameter 6 centimeters?

(A) 96
(B) 64
(C) 48
(D) 32
(E) 24

The circumference of a circle equals π times the diameter. If the diameter is 6 cm, the circumference is 6π. Each cog, together with a space separating it from the next one, uses

$2 \times \frac{\pi}{16} = \frac{\pi}{8}$ cm. The total number of cogs that would fit is therefore $6\pi \div \left(\frac{\pi}{8}\right) = 6\pi \times \frac{8}{\pi} = 48$. Thus, the best answer is C. This is a difficult question.

15. If $r \odot s = rs + r + s$, then for what value of s is $r \odot s$ equal to r for all values of r?

   (A) -1 (B) 0   (C) 1   (D) $\frac{1}{r+1}$ (E) r

For $r \odot s$ to equal r,
$$rs + r + s = r$$
$$rs + s = 0$$
$$s(r + 1) = 0$$

If s = 0, than s(r + 1) = 0 is true for all values of r. If $s \neq 0$, than s(r + 1) = 0 is true only if r = -1. Thus, the best answer is B. This is a difficult question.

16. In each production lot for a certain toy, 25 percent of the toys are red and 75 percent of the toys are blue. Half the toys are size *A* and half are size *B*. If 10 out of a lot of 100 toys are red and size *A*, how many of the toys are blue and size *B*?

   (A) 15
   (B) 25
   (C) 30
   (D) 35
   (E) 40

	Total	Size A	Size B
Red	25	10	
Blue	75		
Total	100	50	50

The information presented in the problem is summarized in the table above. If 50 of the toys are size A, and 10 are red, then 40 of the size A toys are blue. If 75 toys are blue, and 40 of these are size A, then 75 − 40 = 35 toys are size B and blue. The best answer is therefore D. This is a difficult question.

17. If $2x + 5y = 8$ and $3x = 2y$, what is the value of $2x + y$?

   (A) 4
   (B) $\frac{70}{19}$
   (C) $\frac{64}{19}$
   (D) $\frac{56}{19}$
   (E) $\frac{40}{19}$

Since 3x = 2y, x = $\frac{2y}{3}$. Substituting into the other equation for x yields

$$2\left(\frac{2y}{3}\right) + 5y = 8$$
$$4y + 15y = 24$$
$$19y = 24$$
$$y = \frac{24}{19}$$

Then
$$x = \left(\frac{2}{3}\right)\left(\frac{24}{19}\right) = \frac{16}{19}, \text{ and } 2x + y = 2\left(\frac{16}{19}\right) + \frac{24}{19} = \frac{56}{19}.$$

Thus, the best answer is D. This is a difficult question.

18. A ladder 25 feet long is leaning against a wall that is perpendicular to level ground. The bottom of the ladder is 7 feet from the base of the wall. If the top of the ladder slips down 4 feet, how many feet will the bottom of the ladder slip?

   (A) 4
   (B) 5
   (C) 8
   (D) 9
   (E) 15

It may be helpful to draw a figure showing the information given:

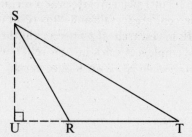

The original height of the top of the ladder can be obtained by the equation $a^2 + b^2 = c^2$ from the Pythagorean theorem. In this case, $7^2 + b^2 = 25^2$, so $b^2 = 625 - 49 = 576$, or b = 24.

After the ladder slips, the hypotenuse of the new triangle is still 25, but the vertical side is now 4 feet shorter, or 20 feet. The new base, x, can be obtained using the same procedure: $20^2 + x^2 = 25^2$, so x = $\sqrt{625 - 400}$ = 15.

Since the bottom of the ladder was originally 7 feet from the wall and is now 15 feet from the wall, it has slipped 8 feet. Therefore, the best answer is C. This is a difficult question.

19. What is the least possible product of 4 different integers, each of which has a value between -5 and 10, inclusive?

   (A) -5040 (B) -3600 (C) -720
   (D) -600 (E) -120

The least possible product in this case is the negative product having greatest absolute value, which can be obtained by multiplying $(-5) \times 10 \times 9 \times 8 = -3,600$. Thus, the best answer is B. This is a difficult question.

20. If a motorist had driven 1 hour longer on a certain day and at an average rate of 5 miles per hour faster, he would have covered 70 more miles than he actually did. How many more miles would he have covered than he actually did if he had driven 2 hours longer and at an average rate of 10 miles per hour faster on that day?

   (A) 100
   (B) 120
   (C) 140
   (D) 150
   (E) 160

Since distance equals rate times time, $D = rt$, where D, r, and t are the actual distance, rate, and time traveled. If the motorist drives 1 hour longer and at a rate 5 mph faster, the new distance

$$D^I = (r + 5)(t + 1) = rt + 70; \text{ thus, } 5t + r = 65.$$
$$rt + 5t + r + 5 = rt + 70$$
$$5t + r = 65$$

If instead he drives 2 hours longer, and at a rate 10 mph faster, the new distance

$$D^{II} = (r + 10)(t + 2) = rt + 10t + 2r + 20$$
$$= rt + 2(5t + r) + 20.$$

Then

$$D^{II} - D = rt + 2(5t + r) + 20 - rt$$
$$= 2(65) + 20 = 150.$$

The best answer is therefore D. This is a difficult question.

Explanatory Material: Sentence Correction

1. **Researchers at Cornell University have demonstrated that homing pigeons can sense changes in the earth's magnetic field, see light waves that people cannot see, detect low-frequency sounds from miles away, _sense changes in air pressure, and can identify familiar odors._**

   (A) sense changes in air pressure, and can identify familiar odors
   (B) can sense changes in air pressure, and can identify familiar odors
   (C) sense changes in air pressure, and identify familiar odors
   (D) air pressure changes can be sensed, and familiar odors identified
   (E) air pressure changes are sensed, and familiar odors identified

This question requires you to choose an answer that completes a series of parallel verbs. Choice A is incorrect because the *can* before *identify* breaks a parallel sequence of verbs that complete the *can* in line 2: A states, *homing pigeons can sense, . . . see, . . . detect, . . . sense, . . . and can identify.* Choice B makes the problem worse by adding *can* before two verbs so that both are nonparallel. Choice C is correct. Choices D and E wrongly substitute independent clauses for the verb phrases in C that continue the parallel construction. This is an easy question.

2. **In ancient times, Nubia was the principal corridor _where there were cultural influences transmitted_ between Black Africa and the Mediterranean basin.**

   (A) where there were cultural influences transmitted
   (B) through which cultural influences were transmitted
   (C) where there was a transmission of cultural influences
   (D) for the transmitting of cultural influences
   (E) which was transmitting cultural influences

Choice A is imprecise and unidiomatic. In choice B, the best answer, *through which* suggests the movement or passage of cultural influences between the ends of the corridor and so provides a clearer description of Nubia's role in the ancient world. Choices C and D, like A, are unidiomatic and needlessly indirect. In choice E, *which* refers to *corridor,* thereby suggesting somewhat imprecisely that the corridor itself, not the civilizations it connected, *was transmitting cultural influences.* Also, *transmitted* is preferable to *transmitting* in a description of past events. This is an easy question.

3. It is a special feature of cell aggregation in the developing nervous system that in most regions of the brain the cells not only adhere to one another and also adopt some preferential orientation.

    (A) to one another and also adopt
    (B) one to the other, and also they adopt
    (C) one to the other, but also adopting
    (D) to one another but also adopt
    (E) to each other, also adopting

Choices A and B are incorrect because *and* should be *but* to conform to the idiomatic construction *not only but also.* Choice B can be faulted for including *they* where there should be only *adopt* to form a parallel with *adhere.* Moreover, *the other* in B is inappropriate because many more than two brain cells are being discussed. Choice C contains *the other* and has *adopting* in place of *adopt,* the verb form parallel to *adhere.* Choice D is correct. In choice E, *adopting* is again wrong and *each other* is less appropriate than *one another* for referring to a multitude of cells. This is a very easy question.

4. Among the reasons for the decline of New England agriculture in the last three decades were the high cost of land, the pressure of housing and commercial development, and basing a marketing and distribution system on importing produce from Florida and California.

    (A) basing a marketing and distribution system on importing produce from Florida and California
    (B) basing a marketing and distribution system on the imported produce of Florida and California
    (C) basing a system of marketing and distribution on the import of produce from Florida and California
    (D) a marketing and distribution system based on importing produce from Florida and California
    (E) a marketing and distribution system importing produce from Florida and California as its base

Choices A, B, and C can be faulted for putting a verb phrase, *basing . . . ,* where a noun phrase is needed to continue the list of parallel elements that begins with *the high cost of land, the pressure of housing. . . .* Also, *the imported produce* in B suggests that the system is based on the produce itself rather than on the practice of importing produce. In C, *the import of produce* is unidiomatic. D, the best choice, presents a noun phrase (. . . *a marketing and distribution system*) that completes the list of parallel elements and refers to the act of *importing produce.* E also supplies the noun phrase but states illogically that the system imports produce *as its base.* The question is moderately easy.

5. Like Byron at Missolonghi, Jack London was slowly killed by the mistakes of the medical men who treated him.

    (A) Like Byron
    (B) Like Byron's death
    (C) Just as Byron died
    (D) Similar to Byron
    (E) As did Byron

Choice A correctly compares two persons, Byron and Jack London. Choice B illogically compares Byron's death to London. Choice C does not compare one person to another and could be read as saying *Just at the time that Byron died.* Choice D misstates the idea: the point is not that London was *similar to Byron* but that he was like Byron in the manner of his death. In choice E, *did* cannot grammatically be substituted for *was* in the phrase *was slowly killed.* This question is a little more difficult than the average.

6. One of every two new businesses fail within two years.

    (A) fail
    (B) fails
    (C) should fail
    (D) may have failed
    (E) has failed

Choice A is wrong because the verb *fail* does not agree in number with *One,* the subject of the sentence; *businesses* is not the subject of the sentence but the object of a prepositional phrase. Choice B is correct. In choice C, *should fail* is inappropriate for a statement of fact and carries the unintended suggestion of *ought to fail.* In choices D and E, *may have failed* and *has failed* wrongly refer to a completed action rather than an ongoing condition. This question is of middle difficulty.

7. Even today, a century after Pasteur developed the first vaccine, rabies almost always kills its victims unless inoculated in the earliest stages of the disease.

    (A) its victims unless inoculated
    (B) its victims unless they are inoculated
    (C) its victims unless inoculation is done
    (D) the victims unless there is an inoculation
    (E) the victims unless inoculated

Choices A and E illogically suggest that rabies rather than the victims of rabies should be inoculated in the earliest stages of the disease. Choice B is best: it is logical, clear, and more precise than C and D, which do not specify who or what is being inoculated. The question is a little easier than the average.

8. In a period of time when women typically <u>have</u> had a narrow range of choices, Mary Baker Eddy became a distinguished writer and the founder, architect, and builder of a growing church.

    (A) In a period of time when women typically have
    (B) During a time in which typically women have
    (C) Typically, during a time when women
    (D) At a time when women typically
    (E) Typically in a time in which women

Choices A and B are wrong because *have had* in the resulting sentence does not correspond to *became;* a simple *had* is needed to match *became* in referring to past events. Choice C drops the erroneous *have,* but *Typically* is misplaced so that it modifies the main clause; in other words, C says that it was typical for Mary Baker Eddy to become distinguished, not that it was typical for women to have a narrow range of choices. Choice E suffers from the same confusion. D is the best answer for this moderately easy question.

9. As the price of gasoline rises, <u>which makes substituting alcohol distilled from cereal grain attractive,</u> the prices of bread and livestock feed are sure to increase.

    (A) which makes substituting alcohol distilled from cereal grain attractive
    (B) which makes substituting the distillation of alcohol from cereal grain attractive
    (C) which makes distilling alcohol from cereal grain an attractive substitute
    (D) making an attractive substitution of alcohol distilled from cereal grain
    (E) making alcohol distilled from cereal grain an attractive substitute

Choices A, B, and C are faulty because the pronoun *which* refers loosely to the whole clause rather than to some noun. The original sentence is intended to say that alcohol is an attractive substitute for gasoline, but the understood phrase *for gasoline* cannot be inserted anywhere in A without producing an awkward construction. Both B and C are illogically worded: the *distillation of alcohol,* not the alcohol itself, is substituted for gasoline in B, as the act of *distilling alcohol* is in C. Choice D is unidiomatic and suggests that the rising price of gasoline is what makes the substitution. Choice E is the best for this question of middle difficulty.

10. Climatic shifts are <u>so gradual as to be indistinguishable</u> at first from ordinary fluctuations in the weather.

    (A) so gradual as to be indistinguishable
    (B) so gradual they can be indistinguishable
    (C) so gradual that they are unable to be distinguished
    (D) gradual enough not to be distinguishable
    (E) gradual enough so that one cannot distinguish them

Choice A, the best answer, presents the idiomatic form (*some things) are so X as to be Y.* Choices B, C, D, and E can be faulted for not following this form. In addition, C confusedly refers to the climatic shifts themselves as being *unable* when it is really people who are unable at first to distinguish climatic shifts. This is a very difficult question.

11. Although <u>the lesser cornstalk borer is widely distributed, control of them is</u> necessary only in the South.

    (A) the lesser cornstalk borer is widely distributed, control of them is
    (B) widely distributed, measures to control the lesser cornstalk borer are
    (C) widely distributed, lesser cornstalk borer control is
    (D) the lesser cornstalk borer is widely distributed, measures to control it are
    (E) it is widely distributed, control of the lesser cornstalk borer is

Choice A is incorrect because the plural pronoun *them* does not agree in number with its singular noun referent, *the lesser cornstalk borer.* Choice B wrongly states that *measures* are widely distributed, not that *the cornstalk borer* is. Similarly, C and E assert that *control* is widely distributed. Choice D is correct for this moderately difficult question.

12. <u>Traveling the back roads of Hungary, in 1905 Béla Bartók and Zoltán Kodály began their pioneering work in ethnomusicology, and they were armed only</u> with an Edison phonograph and insatiable curiosity.

    (A) Traveling the back roads of Hungary, in 1905 Béla Bartók and Zoltán Kodály began their pioneering work in ethnomusicology, and they were armed only
    (B) In 1905, Béla Bartók and Zoltán Kodály, traveling the back roads of Hungary, began their pioneering work in ethnomusicology, and they were only armed
    (C) In 1905 Béla Bartók and Zoltán Kodály began their pioneering work in ethnomusicology, traveling the back roads of Hungary armed only
    (D) Having traveled the back roads of Hungary, in 1905 Béla Bartók and Zoltán Kodály began their pioneering work in ethnomusicology; they were only armed
    (E) Béla Bartók and Zoltán Kodály, in 1905 began their pioneering work in ethnomusicology, traveling the back roads of Hungary, arming themselves only

Choices A and B are wordy and imprecise: the phrasing suggests that Bartók and Kodály were already *traveling the back roads of Hungary* when they began their pioneering work, not that they traveled the back roads in order to conduct such work. Moreover, *and* suggests in both cases that they were armed with a phonograph *in addition* to being on the road, rather than *while* they were on the road, and *only* in B is misplaced before the verb *armed*. Choice C is correct. In choice D, *Having traveled*. . . suggests that the two had finished traveling before they began their work in ethnomusicology, and *only* is again misplaced. Choice E is wordy and awkwardly constructed. The question is a little easier than the average.

13. It is as difficult to prevent crimes against property as <u>those that are against a</u> person.

    (A) those that are against a
    (B) those against a
    (C) it is against a
    (D) preventing those against a
    (E) it is to prevent those against a

This sentence compares two actions, preventing *crimes against property* and preventing *crimes against a person,* in terms of difficulty. These actions should be described in grammatically parallel structures. Consequently, choices A, B, and D are faulty because they fail to parallel the first clause, which has *it* as a subject and *is* as a verb. Choice C contains *it is* but lacks *to prevent those,* words needed to complete the required clause and identify the other action in the comparison. Choice E is best: all of the elements necessary to describe the second action are presented in a form that is both idiomatic and grammatically parallel to the description of the first action. The question is moderately difficult.

14. Unlike the acid smoke of cigarettes, pipe tobacco, <u>cured by age-old methods, yields an alkaline smoke</u> too irritating to be drawn into the lungs.

    (A) Unlike the acid smoke of cigarettes, pipe tobacco, cured by age-old methods, yields an alkaline smoke
    (B) Unlike the acid smoke of cigarettes, pipe tobacco is cured by age-old methods, yielding an alkaline smoke
    (C) Unlike cigarette tobacco, which yields an acid smoke, pipe tobacco, cured by age-old methods, yields an alkaline smoke
    (D) Differing from cigarettes' acid smoke, pipe tobacco's alkaline smoke, cured by age-old methods, is
    (E) The alkaline smoke of pipe tobacco differs from cigarettes' acid smoke in that it is cured by age-old methods and is

Choices A and B illogically compare *the acid smoke of cigarettes* with *pipe tobacco,* not with the *smoke* from pipe tobacco. B is also faulty for making the curing methods rather than the nature of the smoke the basis of comparison. Choice C is best, for it compares cigarette tobacco with pipe tobacco in terms of the type of smoke each produces. Choices D and E garble the intended meaning by saying that the *smoke* of pipe tobacco is *cured by age-old methods.* Moreover, the phrasing is less compact and idiomatic than *Unlike* is for expressing a contrast. This is a difficult question.

15. Joplin's faith in his opera "Tremonisha" was unshakeable; in 1911 he published the score at his own expense and decided <u>on staging it himself.</u>

    (A) on staging it himself
    (B) that he himself would do the staging
    (C) to do the staging of the work by himself
    (D) that he himself would stage it
    (E) to stage the work himself

Choice A is poorly worded: *it* refers to *the score,* not to the opera itself, and *decided on staging it* is unidiomatic. Choice B does not specify what it was that Joplin decided to stage. Choice C is unidiomatic and needlessly wordy. Because the pronoun reference of *it* is faulty, choice D, like choice A, confuses staging the score with staging the work. Choice E is best for this easy question.

16. Los Angeles has <u>a higher number of family dwellings per capita than any large city.</u>

    (A) a higher number of family dwellings per capita than any large city
    (B) higher numbers of family dwellings per capita than any other large city
    (C) a higher number of family dwellings per capita than does any other large city
    (D) higher numbers of family dwellings per capita than do other large cities
    (E) a high per capita number of family dwellings, more than does any other large city

Choice A is illogical because it implies that Los Angeles is not a large city. Choice B emends this problem by specifying *any other large city,* but the plural *numbers* is incorrect in that there is only a single number of such dwellings. Choice C is best. The plural *numbers* is again wrong in choice D, which in addition fails to establish that Los Angeles exceeds *all* other large cities in family dwellings per capita. Choice E is wordy and very awkward. This question is of middle difficulty.

17. During the nineteenth century Emily Eden and Fanny Parks journeyed throughout India, sketching and keeping journals <u>forming the basis of news reports about the princely states where they had</u> visited.

    (A) forming the basis of news reports about the princely states where they had
    (B) that were forming the basis of news reports about the princely states
    (C) to form the basis of news reports about the princely states which they have
    (D) which had formed the basis of news reports about the princely states where they had
    (E) that formed the basis of news reports about the princely states they

In choice A it is not immediately clear whether *forming* modifies *journals* or parallels *sketching and keeping.* Also, *where they had visited* is wordy and inappropriate for a simple reference to past events. Choice B does not establish who visited the *princely states,* and *that were forming* should be *that formed.* Choice C is unclear because *to form* could be read as either *in order to form* or *so as to form,* and the present perfect *have visited* does not agree with the past tense *journeyed.* In choice D, as in choice A, *where they had* is faulty, and *had formed* suggests that the journals and news reports existed before the journey. E is best for this question of average difficulty.

18. School integration plans that involve busing between suburban and central-city areas have contributed, according to a recent study, to <u>significant increases in housing integration, which, in turn, reduces</u> any future need for busing.

    (A) significant increases in housing integration, which, in turn, reduces
    (B) significant integration increases in housing, which, in turn, reduces
    (C) increase housing integration significantly, which, in turn, reduces
    (D) increase housing integration significantly, in turn reducing
    (E) significantly increase housing integration, which, in turn, reduce

Choice A is best. In choice B, the phrase *integration increases in housing* is unidiomatic and imprecise: *integration* cannot modify *increases,* and the increases are not in *housing* but rather in *housing integration.* Choices C, D, and E entail the ungrammatical construction *have contributed. . .to increase.* Moreover, it is not clear whether *which* in C and *reducing* in D refer to *housing integration* or the *increase* in housing integration. In choice E, *which* clearly refers to *housing integration,* making the plural verb *reduce* incorrect. This question is of middle difficulty.

19. The commission acknowledged that <u>no amount of money or staff members</u> can ensure the safety of people who live in the vicinity of a nuclear plant, but it approved the installation because it believed that all reasonable precautions had been taken.

    (A) no amount of money or staff members
    (B) neither vast amounts of money nor staff members
    (C) neither vast amounts of money nor numbers of staff members
    (D) neither vast amounts of money nor a large staff
    (E) no matter how large the staff or how vast the amount of money

In choice A, *amount of. . .staff members* is incorrect; *amount* properly refers to an undifferentiated mass, as in the case of *money.* Choice B does not make clear whether *vast amounts* is supposed to describe *money* only or *money* and *staff members,* and in choice C it is not certain whether *vast* modifies

amounts only or *amounts* and *numbers.* Choice D is best. Choice E cannot fit grammatically into the original sentence because it supplies no noun that can function as a subject for the verb *can.* This question is a little more difficult than the average.

20. Sartre believed <u>each individual is responsible to choose one course of action over another one</u>, that it is the choice that gives value to the act, and that nothing that is not acted upon has value.

    (A) each individual is responsible to choose one course of action over another one
    (B) that each individual is responsible for choosing one course of action over another
    (C) that each individual is responsible, choosing one course of action over another
    (D) that each individual is responsible to choose one course of action over the other
    (E) each individual is responsible for choosing one course of action over other ones

Choice A is faulty because *that* is needed after *believed* to make the clause parallel with the two *that. . .* clauses following it. Also, the idiomatic expression is *responsible for choosing* rather than *responsible to choose,* and *one* is superfluous. Choice B is best. Choice C distorts the intended meaning because it says, in effect, only that individuals are responsible and that they choose a course of action, not that they are *responsible for choosing* such a course. In choice D, *responsible to choose* is unidiomatic and *the other* wrongly suggests that there is some particular alternative under discussion. Choice E lacks the necessary *that,* and *other ones* is less precise than *another.* This question is moderately easy.

21. <u>While the owner of a condominium apartment has free and clear title to the dwelling,</u> owners of cooperative apartments have shares in a corporation that owns a building and leases apartments to them.

    (A) While the owner of a condominium apartment has free and clear title to the dwelling,
    (B) The owner of a condominium apartment has free and clear title to the dwelling, but
    (C) Whereas owners of condominium apartments have free and clear title to their dwellings,
    (D) An owner of a condominium apartment has free and clear title to the dwelling, whereas
    (E) Condominium apartment owners have a title to their dwelling that is free and clear, while

Choices A, B, and D can be faulted for comparing a single *owner of a condominium* with *owners of cooperative apartments.* In choice C, the best answer, the nouns agree in number. Nouns also agree in choice E, but one cannot tell whether the *title* or the *dwelling* is said to be *free and clear.* This question is more difficult than the average.

22. Although <u>films about the American West depict coyotes as solitary animals howling mournfully on the tops of distant hills,</u> in reality these gregarious creatures live in stable groups that occupy the same territory for long periods.

(A) films about the American West depict coyotes as solitary animals howling mournfully on the tops of distant hills

(B) in films about the American West coyotes are depicted to be solitary animals that howl mournfully on the tops of distant hills

(C) coyotes are depicted as solitary animals howling mournfully on the tops of distant hills in films about the American West

(D) films about the American West depict coyotes as if they were solitary, mournfully howling animals on the tops of distant hills

(E) films about the American West depict coyotes to be solitary and mournfully howling animals on the tops of distant hills

Choice A is best. In choice B, *depicted to be* is unidiomatic. The phrase *in films about the American West* is misplaced in choice C so that one cannot tell whether it indicates where the distant hills are, where the animals howl, or where coyotes are depicted as solitary creatures; the phrase should appear next to the word it is meant to modify. Choice D is wordy and awkward, and choice E contains the faulty *depict. . .to be*. This question is a little more difficult than the average.

23. In 1980 the United States exported <u>twice as much of its national output of goods as they had</u> in 1970.

(A) twice as much of its national output of goods as they had

(B) double the amount of their national output of goods as they did

(C) twice as much of its national output of goods as it did

(D) double the amount of its national output of goods as it has

(E) twice as much of their national output of goods as they had

Choice A is incorrect because the plural pronoun *they* does not agree with its singular noun referent, *the United States,* and because *had* cannot substitute for *exported.* In choice B, *double the amount* is a less idiomatic form of comparison than *twice as much;* also, the plural pronouns *their* and *they* are incorrect. Choice C is best: the form of the comparison is idiomatic, the pronouns agree with the noun referent, and *did* — the simple past tense of *do* — can substitute for *exported.* Choice D contains *double the amount* as well as *has* for *exported,* and choice E is faulty because of *their* and *they had.* This question is moderately easy.

24. <u>Even though its per capita food supply hardly increased during</u> two decades, stringent rationing and planned distribution have allowed the People's Republic of China to ensure nutritional levels of 2,000 calories per person per day for its population.

(A) Even though its per capita food supply hardly increased during

(B) Even though its per capita food supply has hardly increased in

(C) Despite its per capita food supply hardly increasing over

(D) Despite there being hardly any increase in its per capita food supply during

(E) Although there is hardly any increase in per capita food supply for

In choice A, the simple past tense *hardly increased* does not match the present perfect *have allowed;* consequently, it seems that two different time periods are being discussed. In B, the best choice, *has hardly increased* parallels *have allowed* to indicate that the events described took place at the same time. Also *in* is the best word here for making a comparison between the beginning and the end of the twenty-year period. Choices C and D are awkward and unidiomatic, and choice E fails to specify *where* there was no increase in per capita food supply. The question is a little more difficult than the average.

25. Few people realize that the chance of accidental injury or death <u>may be as great or greater in the "safety" of their own homes than</u> in a plane or on the road.

(A) may be as great or greater in the "safety" of their own homes than

(B) is at least as great or greater in the "safety" of their own homes than

(C) might be so great or greater in the "safety" of their own home as

(D) may be at least as great in the "safety" of their own homes as

(E) can be at least so great in the "safety" of their own home as

In choices A and B, *as great or greater. . .than* is incorrect: *greater* takes *than,* but *as great* must be completed by *as.* The statement in B is also redundant in that the notion of *greater* is contained in *at least as great,* and *may be* would be better than *is* for expressing a distinct possibility. In choice C, *might* expresses too much doubt, *so* in place of *as* is unidiomatic, *home* should be *homes* to agree with *people,* and *greater. . .as* is erroneous. Choice D is best. In choice E, *so* and *home* are faulty. This is a difficult question.

Answer Sheet: Form C

SECTION 1	SECTION 2	SECTION 3	SECTION 4	SECTION 5	SECTION 6
1 A B C D E	1 A B C D E	1 A B C D E	1 A B C D E	1 A B C D E	1 A B C D E
2 A B C D E	2 A B C D E	2 A B C D E	2 A B C D E	2 A B C D E	2 A B C D E
3 A B C D E	3 A B C D E	3 A B C D E	3 A B C D E	3 A B C D E	3 A B C D E
4 A B C D E	4 A B C D E	4 A B C D E	4 A B C D E	4 A B C D E	4 A B C D E
5 A B C D E	5 A B C D E	5 A B C D E	5 A B C D E	5 A B C D E	5 A B C D E
6 A B C D E	6 A B C D E	6 A B C D E	6 A B C D E	6 A B C D E	6 A B C D E
7 A B C D E	7 A B C D E	7 A B C D E	7 A B C D E	7 A B C D E	7 A B C D E
8 A B C D E	8 A B C D E	8 A B C D E	8 A B C D E	8 A B C D E	8 A B C D E
9 A B C D E	9 A B C D E	9 A B C D E	9 A B C D E	9 A B C D E	9 A B C D E
10 A B C D E	10 A B C D E	10 A B C D E	10 A B C D E	10 A B C D E	10 A B C D E
11 A B C D E	11 A B C D E	11 A B C D E	11 A B C D E	11 A B C D E	11 A B C D E
12 A B C D E	12 A B C D E	12 A B C D E	12 A B C D E	12 A B C D E	12 A B C D E
13 A B C D E	13 A B C D E	13 A B C D E	13 A B C D E	13 A B C D E	13 A B C D E
14 A B C D E	14 A B C D E	14 A B C D E	14 A B C D E	14 A B C D E	14 A B C D E
15 A B C D E	15 A B C D E	15 A B C D E	15 A B C D E	15 A B C D E	15 A B C D E
16 A B C D E	16 A B C D E	16 A B C D E	16 A B C D E	16 A B C D E	16 A B C D E
17 A B C D E	17 A B C D E	17 A B C D E	17 A B C D E	17 A B C D E	17 A B C D E
18 A B C D E	18 A B C D E	18 A B C D E	18 A B C D E	18 A B C D E	18 A B C D E
19 A B C D E	19 A B C D E	19 A B C D E	19 A B C D E	19 A B C D E	19 A B C D E
20 A B C D E	20 A B C D E	20 A B C D E	20 A B C D E	20 A B C D E	20 A B C D E
21 A B C D E	21 A B C D E	21 A B C D E	21 A B C D E	21 A B C D E	21 A B C D E
22 A B C D E	22 A B C D E	22 A B C D E	22 A B C D E	22 A B C D E	22 A B C D E
23 A B C D E	23 A B C D E	23 A B C D E	23 A B C D E	23 A B C D E	23 A B C D E
24 A B C D E	24 A B C D E	24 A B C D E	24 A B C D E	24 A B C D E	24 A B C D E
25 A B C D E	25 A B C D E	25 A B C D E	25 A B C D E	25 A B C D E	25 A B C D E
26 A B C D E	26 A B C D E	26 A B C D E	26 A B C D E	26 A B C D E	26 A B C D E
27 A B C D E	27 A B C D E	27 A B C D E	27 A B C D E	27 A B C D E	27 A B C D E
28 A B C D E	28 A B C D E	28 A B C D E	28 A B C D E	28 A B C D E	28 A B C D E
29 A B C D E	29 A B C D E	29 A B C D E	29 A B C D E	29 A B C D E	29 A B C D E
30 A B C D E	30 A B C D E	30 A B C D E	30 A B C D E	30 A B C D E	30 A B C D E
31 A B C D E	31 A B C D E	31 A B C D E	31 A B C D E	31 A B C D E	31 A B C D E
32 A B C D E	32 A B C D E	32 A B C D E	32 A B C D E	32 A B C D E	32 A B C D E
33 A B C D E	33 A B C D E	33 A B C D E	33 A B C D E	33 A B C D E	33 A B C D E
34 A B C D E	34 A B C D E	34 A B C D E	34 A B C D E	34 A B C D E	34 A B C D E
35 A B C D E	35 A B C D E	35 A B C D E	35 A B C D E	35 A B C D E	35 A B C D E

Print your full name here:_____
(last)   (first)   (middle)

Graduate Management Admission Test

SECTION I

Time—30 minutes

20 Questions

Directions: In this section solve each problem, using any available space on the page for scratchwork. Then indicate the best of the answer choices given.

Numbers: All numbers used are real numbers.

Figures: Figures that accompany problems in this test are intended to provide information useful in solving the problems. They are drawn as accurately as possible EXCEPT when it is stated in a specific problem that its figure is not drawn to scale. All figures lie in a plane unless otherwise indicated.

1. What is the average (arithmetic mean) of the numbers 15, 16, 17, 17, 18, and 19?

   (A) 14.2 (B) 16.5 (C) 17 (D) 17.5 (E) 18

2. Kathy bought 4 times as many shares in Company X as Carl, and Carl bought 3 times as many shares in the same company as Tom. Which of the following is the ratio of the number of shares bought by Kathy to the number of shares bought by Tom?

   (A) $\dfrac{3}{4}$

   (B) $\dfrac{4}{3}$

   (C) $\dfrac{3}{1}$

   (D) $\dfrac{4}{1}$

   (E) $\dfrac{12}{1}$

3. Of the following, which is closest to $\dfrac{0.15 \times 495}{9.97}$?

   (A) 7.5 (B) 15 (C) 75 (D) 150 (E) 750

4. A manager has $6,000 budgeted for raises for 4 full-time and 2 part-time employees. Each of the full-time employees receives the same raise, which is twice the raise that each of the part-time employees receives. What is the amount of the raise that each full-time employee receives?

   (A) $750
   (B) $1,000
   (C) $1,200
   (D) $1,500
   (E) $3,000

GO ON TO THE NEXT PAGE.

5. $x^2 - \left(\frac{x}{2}\right)^2 =$

(A) $x^2 - x$

(B) $\frac{x^2}{4}$

(C) $\frac{x^2}{2}$

(D) $\frac{3x^2}{4}$

(E) $\frac{3x^2}{2}$

6. A hospital pharmacy charges $0.40 per fluidram of a certain medicine but allows a discount of 15 percent to Medicare patients. How much should the pharmacy charge a Medicare patient for 3 fluidounces of the medicine? (128 fluidrams = 16 fluidounces)

(A) $9.60
(B) $8.16
(C) $3.20
(D) $2.72
(E) $1.02

7. $(-1)^2 - (-1)^3 =$

(A) -2 (B) -1 (C) 0 (D) 1 (E) 2

8. At a certain bowling alley, it costs $0.50 to rent bowling shoes for the day and $1.25 to bowl 1 game. If a person has $12.80 and must rent shoes, what is the greatest number of complete games that person can bowl in one day?

(A) 7
(B) 8
(C) 9
(D) 10
(E) 11

GO ON TO THE NEXT PAGE.

9. If $\frac{x}{y} = 2$, then $\frac{x - y}{x} =$

(A) -1

(B) $-\frac{1}{2}$

(C) $\frac{1}{2}$

(D) 1

(E) 2

10. If each photocopy of a manuscript costs 4 cents per page, what is the cost, in cents, to reproduce x copies of an x-page manuscript?

(A) $4x$ (B) $16x$ (C) x^2

(D) $4x^2$ (E) $16x^2$

11. Ken left a job paying $75,000 per year to accept a sales job paying $45,000 per year plus 15 percent commission. If each of his sales is for $750, what is the least number of sales he must make per year if he is not to lose money because of the change?

(A)   40
(B) 200
(C) 266
(D) 267
(E) 600

GO ON TO THE NEXT PAGE.

MONTHLY KILOWATT-HOURS

	500	1,000	1,500	2,000
Present	$24.00	$41.00	$57.00	$73.00
Proposed	$26.00	$45.00	$62.00	$79.00

12. The table above shows present rates and proposed rates for electricity for residential customers. For which of the monthly kilowatt-hours shown would the proposed rate be the greatest percent increase over the present rate?

(A)   500
(B) 1,000
(C) 1,500
(D) 2,000
(E) Each of the percent increases is the same.

13. If a, b, and c are three consecutive odd integers such that $10 < a < b < c < 20$ and if b and c are prime numbers, what is the value of $a + b$?

(A) 24
(B) 28
(C) 30
(D) 32
(E) 36

14. Of a group of people surveyed in a political poll, 60 percent said that they would vote for candidate R. Of those who said they would vote for R, 90 percent actually voted for R, and of those who did not say that they would vote for R, 5 percent actually voted for R. What percent of the group voted for R?

(A) 56%
(B) 59%
(C) 62%
(D) 65%
(E) 74%

15. If $r = 1 + \frac{1}{3} + \frac{1}{9} + \frac{1}{27}$ and $s = 1 + \frac{1}{3}r$, then s exceeds r by

(A) $\frac{1}{3}$ (B) $\frac{1}{6}$ (C) $\frac{1}{9}$ (D) $\frac{1}{27}$ (E) $\frac{1}{81}$

GO ON TO THE NEXT PAGE.

16. $\dfrac{0.025 \times \dfrac{15}{2} \times 48}{5 \times 0.0024 \times \dfrac{3}{4}} =$

(A)   0.1
(B)   0.2
(C)   100
(D)   200
(E)   1,000

17. A student responded to all of the 22 questions on a test and received a score of 63.5. If the scores were derived by adding 3.5 points for each correct answer and deducting 1 point for each incorrect answer, how many questions did the student answer underline{incorrectly}?

(A) 3   (B) 4   (C) 15   (D) 18   (E) 20

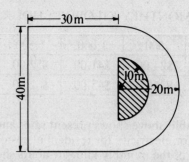

18. The figure above represents a rectangular parking lot that is 30 meters by 40 meters and an attached semicircular driveway that has an outer radius of 20 meters and an inner radius of 10 meters. If the shaded region is not included, what is the area, in square meters, of the lot and driveway?

(A) 1,350π
(B) 1,200 + 400π
(C) 1,200 + 300π
(D) 1,200 + 200π
(E) 1,200 + 150π

GO ON TO THE NEXT PAGE.

-296-

19. One-fifth of the light switches produced by a certain factory are defective. Four-fifths of the defective switches are rejected and $\frac{1}{20}$ of the nondefective switches are rejected by mistake. If all the switches not rejected are sold, what percent of the switches sold by the factory are defective?

   (A) 4%
   (B) 5%
   (C) 6.25%
   (D) 11%
   (E) 16%

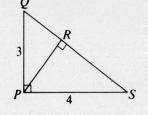

20. In $\triangle PQS$ above, if $PQ = 3$ and $PS = 4$, then $PR =$

   (A) $\frac{9}{4}$ (B) $\frac{12}{5}$ (C) $\frac{16}{5}$ (D) $\frac{15}{4}$ (E) $\frac{20}{3}$

S T O P

**IF YOU FINISH BEFORE TIME IS CALLED, YOU MAY CHECK YOUR WORK ON THIS SECTION ONLY.
DO NOT WORK ON ANY OTHER SECTION IN THE TEST.**

SECTION II

Time—30 minutes

25 Questions

<u>Directions:</u> In each of the following sentences, some part of the sentence or the entire sentence is underlined. Beneath each sentence you will find five ways of phrasing the underlined part. The first of these repeats the original; the other four are different. If you think the original is better than any of the alternatives, choose answer A; otherwise choose one of the others. Select the best version and blacken the corresponding space on your answer sheet.

This is a test of correctness and effectiveness of expression. In choosing answers, follow the requirements of standard written English; that is, pay attention to grammar, choice of words, and sentence construction. Choose the answer that expresses most effectively what is presented in the original sentence; this answer should be clear and exact, without awkwardness, ambiguity, or redundancy.

1. A fire in an enclosed space burns with the aid of reflected radiation that preheats the fuel, making ignition much easier and <u>flames spreading</u> more quickly.

    (A) flames spreading
    (B) flame spreads
    (C) flames are caused to spread
    (D) causing flames to spread
    (E) causing spreading of the flames

2. Roy Wilkins was among the last of a generation of civil rights activists who led the nation through decades of change <u>so profound many young Americans are not able to imagine, even less to remember</u>, what segregation was like.

    (A) so profound many young Americans are not able to imagine, even less to remember
    (B) so profound that many young Americans cannot imagine, much less remember
    (C) so profound many young Americans cannot imagine nor even less remember
    (D) of such profundity many young Americans cannot imagine, even less can they remember
    (E) of such profundity that many young Americans are not able to imagine, much less to remember

3. The residents' opposition to the spraying program has rekindled an old debate <u>among those who oppose the use of pesticides and</u> those who feel that the pesticides are necessary to save the trees.

    (A) among those who oppose the use of pesticides and
    (B) between those who oppose the use of pesticides and
    (C) among those opposing the use of pesticides with
    (D) between those who oppose the use of pesticides with
    (E) among those opposing the use of pesticides and

4. In cold-water habitats, certain invertebrates and fish convert starches into complex carbohydrates called glycerols, <u>in effect manufacturing its own antifreeze</u>.

    (A) in effect manufacturing its own antifreeze
    (B) effectively manufacturing antifreeze of its own
    (C) in effect manufacturing their own antifreeze
    (D) so that they manufacture their own antifreeze
    (E) thus the manufacture of its own antifreeze

5. Slips of the tongue do not necessarily reveal concealed beliefs or intentions <u>but rather are the result from</u> the competition between various processing mechanisms in the brain.

    (A) but rather are the result from
    (B) and instead are the result from
    (C) being rather the result of
    (D) and rather result from
    (E) but rather result from

6. The new contract <u>forbids a strike by the transportation union</u>.

    (A) forbids a strike by the transportation union
    (B) forbids the transportation union from striking
    (C) forbids that there be a strike by the transportation union
    (D) will forbid the transportation union from striking
    (E) will forbid that the transportation union strikes

GO ON TO THE NEXT PAGE.

7. <u>Monitoring heart patients' exercise, as well as athletes exercising, is now done by small transmitters broadcasting physiological measurements to nearby recording machines.</u>

(A) Monitoring heart patients' exercise, as well as athletes exercising, is now done by small transmitters broadcasting physiological measurements to nearby recording machines.

(B) Monitoring the exercise of heart patients, as well as athletes exercising, is now done by small transmitters broadcasting physiological measurements to nearby recording machines.

(C) Small transmitters broadcasting physiological measurements to nearby recording machines are now used to monitor the exercise of both heart patients and athletes.

(D) Broadcasting physiological measurements to nearby recording machines, small transmitters are now used to monitor heart patients' exercise, as well as athletes exercising.

(E) Both athletes exercising and heart patients' exercise are now monitored by small transmitters broadcasting physiological measurements to nearby recording machines.

8. The commission has directed advertisers to restrict the use of the word "natural" to foods that do not contain color or flavor additives, chemical preservatives, <u>or nothing that has been</u> synthesized.

(A) or nothing that has been
(B) nor anything that was
(C) and nothing that is
(D) or anything that has been
(E) and anything

9. <u>Bringing the Ford Motor Company back from the verge of bankruptcy shortly after the Second World War was a special governmentally sanctioned price increase during a period of wage and price controls.</u>

(A) Bringing the Ford Motor Company back from the verge of bankruptcy shortly after the Second World War was a special governmentally sanctioned price increase during a period of wage and price controls.

(B) What brought the Ford Motor Company back from the verge of bankruptcy shortly after the Second World War was a special price increase that the government sanctioned during a period of wage and price controls.

(C) That which brought the Ford Motor Company back from the verge of bankruptcy shortly after the Second World War was a special governmentally sanctioned price increase during a period of wage and price controls.

(D) What has brought the Ford Motor Company back from the verge of bankruptcy shortly after the Second World War was a special price increase that the government sanctioned during a period of wages and price controls.

(E) To bring the Ford Motor Company back from the verge of bankruptcy shortly after the Second World War, there was a special price increase during a period of wages and price controls that government sanctioned.

10. <u>Like Haydn, Schubert</u> wrote a great deal for the stage, but he is remembered principally for his chamber and concert-hall music.

(A) Like Haydn, Schubert
(B) Like Haydn, Schubert also
(C) As has Haydn, Schubert
(D) As did Haydn, Schubert also
(E) As Haydn did, Schubert also

GO ON TO THE NEXT PAGE.

11. Charlotte Perkins Gilman, a late nineteenth-century feminist, called for urban apartment houses including child-care facilities and clustered suburban houses including communal eating and social facilities.

(A) including child-care facilities and clustered suburban houses including communal eating and social facilities

(B) that included child-care facilities, and for clustered suburban houses to include communal eating and social facilities

(C) with child-care facilities included and for clustered suburban houses to include communal eating and social facilities

(D) that included child-care facilities and for clustered suburban houses with communal eating and social facilities

(E) to include child-care facilities and for clustered suburban houses with communal eating and social facilities included

12. The odds are about 4 to 1 against surviving a takeover offer, and many business consultants therefore advise that a company's first line of defense in eluding offers like these be to even refuse to take calls from likely corporate raiders.

(A) that a company's first line of defense in eluding offers like these be to even refuse

(B) that a company's first line of defense in eluding such offers be to refuse even

(C) a company defending itself against offers of this kind that, as a first line of defense, they should even refuse

(D) companies which are defending themselves against such an offer that, as a first line of defense, they should even refuse

(E) that the first line of defense for a company who is eluding offers like these is the refusal even

13. Japan received huge sums of capital from the United States after the Second World War, using it to help build a modern industrial system.

(A) Japan received huge sums of capital from the United States after the Second World War, using it to help build

(B) Japan received huge sums of capital from the United States after the Second World War and used it to help in building

(C) Japan used the huge sums of capital it received from the United States after the Second World War to help build

(D) Japan's huge sums of capital received from the United States after the Second World War were used to help it in building

(E) Receiving huge sums of capital from the United States after the Second World War, Japan used it to help build

14. Although one link in the chain was demonstrated to be weak, but not sufficiently so to require the recall of the automobile.

(A) demonstrated to be weak, but not sufficiently so to require

(B) demonstrated as weak, but it was not sufficiently so that it required

(C) demonstrably weak, but not sufficiently so to require

(D) demonstrably weak, it was not so weak as to require

(E) demonstrably weak, it was not weak enough that it required

15. Although the Supreme Court ruled as long ago as 1880 that Blacks could not be excluded outright from jury service, nearly a century of case-by-case adjudication has been necessary to develop and enforce the principle that all juries must be drawn from "a fair cross section of the community."

(A) has been necessary to develop and enforce the principle that all juries must be

(B) was necessary for developing and enforcing the principle of all juries being

(C) was to be necessary in developing and enforcing the principle of all juries to be

(D) is necessary to develop and enforce the principle that all juries must be

(E) will be necessary for developing and enforcing the principle of all juries being

16. The modernization program for the steel mill will cost approximately 51 million dollars, which it is hoped can be completed in the late 1980's.

(A) The modernization program for the steel mill will cost approximately 51 million dollars, which it is hoped can be completed in the late 1980's.

(B) The modernization program for the steel mill, hopefully completed in the late 1980's, will cost approximately 51 million dollars.

(C) Modernizing the steel mill, hopefully to be completed in the late 1980's, will cost approximately 51 million dollars.

(D) The program for modernizing the steel mill, which can, it is hoped, be completed in the late 1980's and cost approximately 51 million dollars.

(E) Modernizing the steel mill, a program that can, it is hoped, be completed in the late 1980's, will cost approximately 51 million dollars.

GO ON TO THE NEXT PAGE.

17. Camus broke with Sartre <u>in a bitter dispute over</u> the nature of Stalinism.

    (A) in a bitter dispute over
    (B) over bitterly disputing
    (C) after there was a bitter dispute over
    (D) after having bitterly disputed about
    (E) over a bitter dispute about

18. Nowhere in Prakta is the influence of modern European architecture <u>more apparent than their</u> government buildings.

    (A) more apparent than their
    (B) so apparent as their
    (C) more apparent than in its
    (D) so apparent than in their
    (E) as apparent as it is in its

19. Federal legislation establishing a fund for the cleanup of sites damaged by toxic chemicals permits <u>compensating state governments for damage to</u> their natural resources but does not allow claims for injury to people.

    (A) compensating state governments for damage to
    (B) compensating state governments for the damaging of
    (C) giving state governments compensation for damaging
    (D) giving compensation to state governments for the damage of
    (E) the giving of compensation to state governments for damaging

20. The lawyer for the defense charged that she suspected the police of having illegally taped her confidential conversations with her client and then <u>used the information obtained to find evidence supporting</u> their murder charges.

    (A) used the information obtained to find evidence supporting
    (B) used such information as they obtained to find evidence supporting
    (C) used the information they had obtained to find evidence that would support
    (D) of using the information they had obtained to find evidence that would support
    (E) of using such information as they obtained to find evidence that would be supportive of

21. According to surveys by the National Institute on Drug Abuse, about 20 percent of young adults used cocaine in 1979, <u>doubling those reported in the 1977 survey</u>.

    (A) doubling those reported in the 1977 survey
    (B) to double the number the 1977 survey reported
    (C) twice those the 1977 survey reported
    (D) twice as much as those reported in the 1977 survey
    (E) twice the number reported in the 1977 survey

GO ON TO THE NEXT PAGE.

22. Inflation has made many Americans reevaluate their assumptions about the future; they still expect to live better than their parents have, but not so well as they once thought they could.

    (A) they still expect to live better than their parents have
    (B) they still expect to live better than their parents did
    (C) they still expect to live better than their parents had
    (D) still expecting to live better than their parents had
    (E) still expecting to live better than did their parents

23. Europeans have long known that eating quail sometimes makes the eater ill, but only recently has it been established that the illness is caused by a toxin present in the quail's body only under certain conditions.

    (A) Europeans have long known that eating quail sometimes makes
    (B) Europeans have long known quail eating is sometimes able to make
    (C) Eating quail has long been known to Europeans to sometimes make
    (D) It has long been known to Europeans that quail eating will sometimes make
    (E) It has long been known to Europeans that quail, when it is eaten, has sometimes made

24. The caterpillar of the geometrid moth strikes when special tactile hairs on its body are disturbed, after capturing its prey, holds the victim so that it cannot escape.

    (A) strikes when special tactile hairs on its body are disturbed,
    (B) striking when special tactile hairs on its body are disturbed, but
    (C) which strikes when special tactile hairs on its body are disturbed,
    (D) which, striking when special tactile hairs on its body are disturbed,
    (E) strikes when special tactile hairs on its body are disturbed and,

25. In assessing the problems faced by rural migrant workers, the question of whether they are better off materially than the urban working poor is irrelevant.

    (A) In assessing the problems faced by rural migrant workers, the question of whether they are better off materially than the urban working poor is irrelevant.
    (B) The question of whether the rural migrant worker is better off materially than the urban working poor is irrelevant in assessing the problems that they face.
    (C) A question that is irrelevant in assessing the problems that rural migrant workers face is whether they are better off materially than the urban working poor.
    (D) In an assessment of the problems faced by rural migrant workers, the question of whether they are better off materially than the urban working poor is irrelevant.
    (E) The question of whether the rural migrant worker is better off materially than the urban working poor is irrelevant in an assessment of the problems that they face.

S T O P

IF YOU FINISH BEFORE TIME IS CALLED, YOU MAY CHECK YOUR WORK ON THIS SECTION ONLY. DO NOT WORK ON ANY OTHER SECTION IN THE TEST.

SECTION III

Time—30 minutes

25 Questions

Directions: Each passage in this group is followed by questions based on its content. After reading a passage, choose the best answer to each question and blacken the corresponding space on the answer sheet. Answer all questions following a passage on the basis of what is stated or implied in that passage.

Those examples of poetic justice that occur in medieval and Elizabethan literature, and that seem so satisfying, have encouraged a whole school of twentieth-century scholars to "find"
(5) further examples. In fact, these scholars have merely forced victimized characters into a moral framework by which the injustices inflicted on them are, somehow or other, justified. Such scholars deny that the sufferers in a tragedy are
(10) innocent; they blame the victims themselves for their tragic fates. Any misdoing is enough to subject a character to critical whips. Thus, there are long essays about the misdemeanors of Webster's Duchess of Malfi, who defied her brothers, and
(15) the behavior of Shakespeare's Desdemona, who disobeyed her father.
Yet it should be remembered that the Renaissance writer Matteo Bandello strongly protests the injustice of the severe penalties issued to
(20) women for acts of disobedience that men could, and did, commit with virtual impunity. And Shakespeare, Chaucer, and Webster often enlist their readers on the side of their tragic heroines by describing injustices so cruel that readers
(25) cannot but join in protest. By portraying Griselda, in The Clerk's Tale, as a meek, gentle victim who does not criticize, much less rebel against the persecutor, her husband Walter, Chaucer incites readers to espouse Griselda's
(30) cause against Walter's oppression. Thus, efforts to supply historical and theological rationalizations for Walter's persecutions tend to turn Chaucer's fable upside down, to deny its most obvious effect on readers' sympathies. Similarly,
(35) to assert that Webster's Duchess deserved torture and death because she chose to marry the man she loved and to bear their children is, in effect, to join forces with her tyrannical brothers, and so to confound the operation of poetic
(40) justice, of which readers should approve, with precisely those examples of social injustice that Webster does everything in his power to make readers condemn. Indeed, Webster has his heroine so heroically lead the resistance to tyranny
(45) that she may well inspire members of the audience to imaginatively join forces with her against the cruelty and hypocritical morality of her brothers.
Thus Chaucer and Webster, in their different

(50) ways, attack injustice, argue on behalf of the victims, and prosecute the persecutors. Their readers serve them as a court of appeal that remains free to rule, as the evidence requires, and as common humanity requires, in favor of
(55) the innocent and injured parties. For, to paraphrase the noted eighteenth-century scholar, Samuel Johnson, despite all the refinements of subtlety and the dogmatism of learning, it is by the common sense and compassion of readers
(60) who are uncorrupted by the prejudices of some opinionated scholars that the characters and situations in medieval and Elizabethan literature, as in any other literature, can best be judged.

1. According to the passage, some twentieth-century scholars have written at length about

(A) Walter's persecution of his wife in Chaucer's *The Clerk's Tale*
(B) the Duchess of Malfi's love for her husband
(C) the tyrannical behavior of the Duchess of Malfi's brothers
(D) the actions taken by Shakespeare's Desdemona
(E) the injustices suffered by Chaucer's Griselda

2. The primary purpose of the passage is to

(A) describe the role of the tragic heroine in medieval and Elizabethan literature
(B) resolve a controversy over the meaning of "poetic justice" as it is discussed in certain medieval and Elizabethan literary treatises
(C) present evidence to support the view that characters in medieval and Elizabethan tragedies are to blame for their fates
(D) assert that it is impossible for twentieth-century readers to fully comprehend the characters and situations in medieval and Elizabethan literary works
(E) argue that some twentieth-century scholars have misapplied the concept of "poetic justice" in analyzing certain medieval and Elizabethan literary works

GO ON TO THE NEXT PAGE.

3. It can be inferred from the passage that the author considers Chaucer's Griselda to be

(A) an innocent victim
(B) a sympathetic judge
(C) an imprudent person
(D) a strong individual
(E) a rebellious daughter

4. The author's tone in her discussion of the conclusions reached by the "school of twentieth-century scholars" (line 4) is best described as

(A) plaintive
(B) philosophical
(C) disparaging
(D) apologetic
(E) enthusiastic

5. It can be inferred from the passage that the author believes that most people respond to intended instances of poetic justice in medieval and Elizabethan literature with

(A) annoyance
(B) disapproval
(C) indifference
(D) amusement
(E) gratification

6. As described in the passage, the process by which some twentieth-century scholars have reached their conclusions about the blameworthiness of victims in medieval and Elizabethan literary works is most similar to which of the following?

(A) Derivation of logically sound conclusions from well-founded premises
(B) Accurate observation of data, inaccurate calculation of statistics, and drawing of incorrect conclusions from the faulty statistics
(C) Establishment of a theory, application of the theory to ill-fitting data, and drawing of unwarranted conclusions from the data
(D) Development of two schools of thought about a factual situation, debate between the two schools, and rendering of a balanced judgment by an objective observer
(E) Consideration of a factual situation by a group, discussion of various possible explanatory hypotheses, and agreement by consensus on the most plausible explanation

7. The author's paraphrase of a statement by Samuel Johnson (lines 55-63) serves which of the following functions in the passage?

(A) It furnishes a specific example.
(B) It articulates a general conclusion.
(C) It introduces a new topic.
(D) It provides a contrasting perspective.
(E) It clarifies an ambiguous assertion.

8. The author of the passage is primarily concerned with

(A) reconciling opposing viewpoints
(B) encouraging innovative approaches
(C) defending an accepted explanation
(D) advocating an alternative interpretation
(E) analyzing an unresolved question

GO ON TO THE NEXT PAGE.

Woodrow Wilson was referring to the liberal
idea of the economic market when he said that
the free enterprise system is the most efficient
economic system. Maximum freedom means
(5) maximum productiveness; our "openness" is to
be the measure of our stability. Fascination with
this ideal has made Americans defy the "Old
World" categories of settled possessiveness *versus*
unsettling deprivation, the cupidity of retention
(10) *versus* the cupidity of seizure, a "status quo"
defended or attacked. The United States, it was
believed, had no *status quo ante*. Our only "station" was the turning of a stationary wheel, spinning faster and faster. We did not base our
(15) system on property but opportunity—which
meant we based it not on stability but on mobil-
ity. The more things changed, that is, the more
rapidly the wheel turned, the steadier we would
be. The conventional picture of class politics is
(20) composed of the Haves, who want a stability to
keep what they have, and the Have-Nots, who
want a touch of instability and change in which
to scramble for the things they have not. But
Americans imagined a condition in which spec-
(25) ulators, self-makers, runners are always using the
new opportunities given by our land. These economic leaders (front-runners) would thus be
mainly agents of change. The nonstarters were
considered the ones who wanted stability, a
(30) strong referee to give them some position in the
race, a regulative hand to calm manic speculation; an authority that can call things to a halt,
begin things again from compensatorily staggered "starting lines."
(35)   "Reform" in America has been sterile because
it can imagine no change except through the
extension of this metaphor of a race, wider inclusion of competitors, "a piece of the action," as it
were, for the disenfranchised. There is no
(40) attempt to call off the race. Since our only stability is change, America seems not to honor the
quiet work that achieves social interdependence
and stability. There is, in our legends, no hero-
ism of the office clerk, no stable industrial work
(45) force of the people who actually make the system
work. There is no pride in being an employee
(Wilson asked for a return to the time when
everyone was an employer). There has been no
boasting about our social workers—they are
(50) merely signs of the system's failure, of opportunity denied or not taken, of things to be eliminated. We have no pride in our growing
interdependence, in the fact that our system can
serve others, that we are able to help those in
(55) need; empty boasts from the past make us
ashamed of our present achievements, make us

try to forget or deny them, move away from
them. There is no honor but in the Wonderland
race we must all run, all trying to win, none
(60) winning in the end (for there is no end).

9. The primary purpose of the passage is to

(A) criticize the inflexibility of American
economic mythology
(B) contrast "Old World" and "New World"
economic ideologies
(C) challenge the integrity of traditional political
leaders
(D) champion those Americans whom the author
deems to be neglected
(E) suggest a substitute for the traditional metaphor of a race

10. According to the passage, "Old World" values
were based on

(A) ability
(B) property
(C) family connections
(D) guild hierarchies
(E) education

11. In the context of the author's discussion of regulating change, which of the following could be most
probably regarded as a "strong referee" (line 30)
in the United States?

(A) A school principal
(B) A political theorist
(C) A federal court judge
(D) A social worker
(E) A government inspector

12. The author sets off the word " 'Reform' " (line 35)
with quotation marks in order to

(A) emphasize its departure from the concept of
settled possessiveness
(B) show his support for a systematic program of
change
(C) underscore the flexibility and even amor-
phousness of United States society
(D) indicate that the term was one of Wilson's
favorites
(E) assert that reform in the United States has
not been fundamental

GO ON TO THE NEXT PAGE.

13. It can be inferred from the passage that the author most probably thinks that giving the disenfranchised " 'a piece of the action' " (line 38) is

(A) a compassionate, if misdirected, legislative measure
(B) an example of Americans' resistance to profound social change
(C) an innovative program for genuine social reform
(D) a monument to the efforts of industrial reformers
(E) a surprisingly "Old World" remedy for social ills

14. Which of the following metaphors could the author most appropriately use to summarize his own assessment of the American economic system (lines 35-60)?

(A) A windmill
(B) A waterfall
(C) A treadmill
(D) A gyroscope
(E) A bellows

15. It can be inferred from the passage that Woodrow Wilson's ideas about the economic market

(A) encouraged those who "make the system work" (lines 45-46)
(B) perpetuated traditional legends about America
(C) revealed the prejudices of a man born wealthy
(D) foreshadowed the stock market crash of 1929
(E) began a tradition of presidential proclamations on economics

16. The passage contains information that would answer which of the following questions?

I. What techniques have industrialists used to manipulate a free market?
II. In what ways are "New World" and "Old World" economic policies similar?
III. Has economic policy in the United States tended to reward independent action?

(A) I only
(B) II only
(C) III only
(D) I and II only
(E) II and III only

17. Which of the following best expresses the author's main point?

(A) Americans' pride in their jobs continues to give them stamina today.
(B) The absence of a *status quo ante* has undermined United States economic structure.
(C) The free enterprise system has been only a useless concept in the United States.
(D) The myth of the American free enterprise system is seriously flawed.
(E) Fascination with the ideal of "openness" has made Americans a progressive people.

GO ON TO THE NEXT PAGE.

No very satisfactory account of the mechanism that caused the formation of the ocean basins has yet been given. The traditional view supposes that the upper mantle of the earth behaves as a
(5) liquid when it is subjected to small forces for long periods and that differences in temperature under oceans and continents are sufficient to produce convection in the mantle of the earth with rising convection currents under the mid-
(10) ocean ridges and sinking currents under the continents. Theoretically, this convection would carry the continental plates along as though they were on a conveyor belt and would provide the forces needed to produce the split that occurs
(15) along the ridge. This view may be correct; it has the advantage that the currents are driven by temperature differences that themselves depend on the position of the continents. Such a back-coupling, in which the position of the moving
(20) plate has an impact on the forces that move it, could produce complicated and varying motions.

On the other hand, the theory is implausible because convection does not normally occur along lines, and it certainly does not occur along
(25) lines broken by frequent offsets or changes in direction, as the ridge is. Also it is difficult to see how the theory applies to the plate between the Mid-Atlantic Ridge and the ridge in the Indian Ocean. This plate is growing on both sides, and
(30) since there is no intermediate trench, the two ridges must be moving apart. It would be odd if the rising convection currents kept exact pace with them. An alternative theory is that the sinking part of the plate, which is denser than the
(35) hotter surrounding mantle, pulls the rest of the plate after it. Again it is difficult to see how this applies to the ridge in the South Atlantic, where neither the African nor the American plate has a sinking part.
(40) Another possibility is that the sinking plate cools the neighboring mantle and produces convection currents that move the plates. This last theory is attractive because it gives some hope of explaining the enclosed seas, such as the Sea of
(45) Japan. These seas have a typical oceanic floor, except that the floor is overlaid by several kilometers of sediment. Their floors have probably been sinking for long periods. It seems possible that a sinking current of cooled mantle material
(50) on the upper side of the plate might be the cause of such deep basins. The enclosed seas are an important feature of the earth's surface and seriously require explanation because, in addition to the enclosed seas that are developing at
(55) present behind island arcs, there are a number of older ones of possibly similar origin, such as the Gulf of Mexico, the Black Sea, and perhaps the North Sea.

18. According to the traditional view of the origin of the ocean basins, which of the following is sufficient to move the continental plates?

(A) Increases in sedimentation on ocean floors
(B) Spreading of ocean trenches
(C) Movement of mid-ocean ridges
(D) Sinking of ocean basins
(E) Differences in temperature under oceans and continents

19. It can be inferred from the passage that, of the following, the deepest sediments would be found in the

(A) Indian Ocean
(B) Black Sea
(C) Mid-Atlantic
(D) South Atlantic
(E) Pacific

20. The author refers to a "conveyor belt" in line 13 in order to

(A) illustrate the effects of convection in the mantle
(B) show how temperature differences depend on the positions of the continents
(C) demonstrate the linear nature of the Mid-Atlantic Ridge
(D) describe the complicated motions made possible by back-coupling
(E) account for the rising currents under certain mid-ocean ridges

21. The author regards the traditional view of the origin of the oceans with

(A) slight apprehension
(B) absolute indifference
(C) indignant anger
(D) complete disbelief
(E) guarded skepticism

GO ON TO THE NEXT PAGE.

3 3 3 3 3 3 3 3 3 C

22. According to the passage, which of the following are separated by a plate that is growing on both sides?

(A) The Pacific Ocean and the Sea of Japan
(B) The South Atlantic Ridge and the North Sea Ridge
(C) The Gulf of Mexico and the South Atlantic Ridge
(D) The Mid-Atlantic Ridge and the Indian Ocean Ridge
(E) The Black Sea and the Sea of Japan

23. Which of the following, if it could be demonstrated, would most support the traditional view of ocean formation?

(A) Convection usually occurs along lines.
(B) The upper mantle behaves as a dense solid.
(C) Sedimentation occurs at a constant rate.
(D) Sinking plates cool the mantle.
(E) Island arcs surround enclosed seas.

24. According to the passage, the floor of the Black Sea can best be compared to a

(A) rapidly moving conveyor belt
(B) slowly settling foundation
(C) rapidly expanding balloon
(D) violently erupting volcano
(E) slowly eroding mountain

25. Which of the following titles would best describe the content of the passage?

(A) A Description of the Oceans of the World
(B) Several Theories of Ocean Basin Formation
(C) The Traditional View of the Oceans
(D) Convection and Ocean Currents
(E) Temperature Differences Among the Oceans of the World

S T O P

IF YOU FINISH BEFORE TIME IS CALLED, YOU MAY CHECK YOUR WORK ON THIS SECTION ONLY.
DO NOT WORK ON ANY OTHER SECTION IN THE TEST.

SECTION IV

Time—30 minutes

25 Questions

Directions: Each of the data sufficiency problems below consists of a question and two statements, labeled (1) and (2), in which certain data are given. You have to decide whether the data given in the statements are sufficient for answering the question. Using the data given in the statements plus your knowledge of mathematics and everyday facts (such as the number of days in July or the meaning of counterclockwise), you are to blacken space

A   if statement (1) ALONE is sufficient, but statement (2) alone is not sufficient to answer the question asked;

B   if statement (2) ALONE is sufficient, but statement (1) alone is not sufficient to answer the question asked;

C   if BOTH statements (1) and (2) TOGETHER are sufficient to answer the question asked, but NEITHER statement ALONE is sufficient;

D   if EACH statement ALONE is sufficient to answer the question asked;

E   if statements (1) and (2) TOGETHER are NOT sufficient to answer the question asked, and additional data specific to the problem are needed.

Numbers: All numbers used are real numbers.

Figures: A figure in a data sufficiency problem will conform to the information given in the question, but will not necessarily conform to the additional information given in statements (1) and (2).

You may assume that lines shown as straight are straight and that angle measures are greater than zero.

You may assume that the position of points, angles, regions, etc., exist in the order shown.

All figures lie in a plane unless otherwise indicated.

Example:

In $\triangle PQR$, what is the value of x ?

(1) $PQ = PR$

(2) $y = 40$

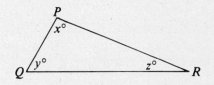

Explanation: According to statement (1), $PQ = PR$; therefore, $\triangle PQR$ is isosceles and $y = z$. Since $x + y + z = 180$, $x + 2y = 180$. Since statement (1) does not give a value for y, you cannot answer the question using statement (1) by itself. According to statement (2), $y = 40$; therefore, $x + z = 140$. Since statement (2) does not give a value for z, you cannot answer the question using statement (2) by itself. Using both statements together, you can find y and z; therefore, you can find x, and the answer to the problem is C.

GO ON TO THE NEXT PAGE.

A   Statement (1) ALONE is sufficient, but statement (2) alone is not sufficient.
B   Statement (2) ALONE is sufficient, but statement (1) alone is not sufficient.
C   BOTH statements TOGETHER are sufficient, but NEITHER statement ALONE is sufficient.
D   EACH statement ALONE is sufficient.
E   Statements (1) and (2) TOGETHER are NOT sufficient.

1. Who types at a faster rate, John or Bob?

   (1) The difference between their typing rates is 10 words per minute.

   (2) Bob types at a constant rate of 80 words per minute.

2. What is the average distance that automobile D travels on one full tank of gasoline?

   (1) Automobile D averages 8.5 kilometers per liter of gasoline.

   (2) The gasoline tank of automobile D holds exactly 40 liters of gasoline.

3. If l_1, l_2 and l_3 are lines in a plane, is l_1 perpendicular to l_3?

   (1) l_1 is perpendicular to l_2.

   (2) l_2 is perpendicular to l_3.

4. In a certain packinghouse, grapefruit are packed in bags and the bags are packed in cases. How many grapefruit are in each case that is packed?

   (1) The grapefruit are always packed 5 to a bag and the bags are always packed 8 to a case.

   (2) Each case is always 80 percent full.

5. What is the value of x?

   (1) $x + y = 7$

   (2) $x - y = 3 - y$

6. A rectangular floor that is 4 meters wide is to be completely covered with nonoverlapping square tiles, each with side of length 0.25 meter, with no portion of any tile remaining. What is the least number of such tiles that will be required?

   (1) The length of the floor is three times the width.

   (2) The area of the floor is 48 square meters.

GO ON TO THE NEXT PAGE.

A   Statement (1) ALONE is sufficient, but statement (2) alone is not sufficient.
B   Statement (2) ALONE is sufficient, but statement (1) alone is not sufficient.
C   BOTH statements TOGETHER are sufficient, but NEITHER statement ALONE is sufficient.
D   EACH statement ALONE is sufficient.
E   Statements (1) and (2) TOGETHER are NOT sufficient.

7. If a rope is cut into three pieces of unequal length, what is the length of the shortest of these pieces of rope?

(1) The combined length of the longer two pieces of rope is 12 meters.

(2) The combined length of the shorter two pieces of rope is 11 meters.

8. A certain company paid bonuses of $125 to each of its executive employees and $75 to each of its nonexecutive employees. If 100 of the employees were nonexecutives, how many were executives?

(1) The company has a total of 120 employees.

(2) The total amount that the company paid in bonuses to its employees was $10,000.

9. What fraction of his salary did Mr. Johnson put into savings last week?

(1) Last week Mr. Johnson put $17 into savings.

(2) Last week Mr. Johnson put 5% of his salary into savings.

10. For integers a, b, and c, $\frac{a}{b-c} = 1$. What is the value of $\frac{b-c}{b}$?

(1) $\frac{a}{b} = \frac{3}{5}$

(2) a and b have no common factors greater than 1.

11. If the price of a magazine is to be doubled, by what percent will the number of magazines sold decrease?

(1) The current price of the magazine is $1.00.

(2) For every $0.25 of increase in price, the number of magazines sold will decrease by 10 percent of the number sold at the current price.

12. If J, K, L, M, and N are positive integers in ascending order, what is the value of L?

(1) The value of K is 3.

(2) The value of M is 7.

GO ON TO THE NEXT PAGE.

A   Statement (1) ALONE is sufficient, but statement (2) alone is not sufficient.
B   Statement (2) ALONE is sufficient, but statement (1) alone is not sufficient.
C   BOTH statements TOGETHER are sufficient, but NEITHER statement ALONE is sufficient.
D   EACH statement ALONE is sufficient.
E   Statements (1) and (2) TOGETHER are NOT sufficient.

13. If a, b, and c are integers, is the number $3(a + b) + c$ divisible by 3?

(1) $a + b$ is divisible by 3.

(2) c is divisible by 3.

14. Each M-type memory unit will increase the base memory capacity of a certain computer by 3 megabytes. What is the base memory capacity, in megabytes, of the computer?

(1) 2 M-type memory units will increase the computer's base memory capacity by 300 percent.

(2) The memory capacity of the computer after 2 M-type memory units are added to the base memory capacity is 1.6 times the memory capacity of the computer after 1 M-type memory unit is added to the base memory capacity.

15. If $xyz \neq 0$, what is the value of $\dfrac{x^5 y^4 z^2}{z^2 y^4 x^2}$?

(1) $x = 1$

(2) $y = 3$

16. What fractional part of the total surface area of cube C is red?

(1) Each of 3 faces of C is exactly $\dfrac{1}{2}$ red.

(2) Each of 3 faces of C is entirely white.

17. If positive integer x is divided by 2, the remainder is 1. What is the remainder when x is divided by 4?

(1) $31 < x < 35$

(2) x is a multiple of 3.

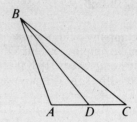

18. In the figure above, D is a point on side AC of $\triangle ABC$. Is $\triangle ABC$ isosceles?

(1) The area of triangular region ABD is equal to the area of triangular region DBC.

(2) $BD \perp AC$ and $AD = DC$

19. If x is an integer, what is the value of x?

(1) $-2(x + 5) < -1$

(2) $-3x > 9$

GO ON TO THE NEXT PAGE.

A   Statement (1) ALONE is sufficient, but statement (2) alone is not sufficient.
B   Statement (2) ALONE is sufficient, but statement (1) alone is not sufficient.
C   BOTH statements TOGETHER are sufficient, but NEITHER statement ALONE is sufficient.
D   EACH statement ALONE is sufficient.
E   Statements (1) and (2) TOGETHER are NOT sufficient.

Food	Number of Calories per Kilogram	Number of Grams of Protein per Kilogram
S	2,000	150
T	1,500	90

20. The table above gives the number of calories and grams of protein per kilogram of foods S and T. If a total of 7 kilograms of S and T are combined to make a certain food mixture, how many kilograms of food S are in the mixture?

(1) The mixture has a total of 12,000 calories.

(2) The mixture has a total of 810 grams of protein.

21. If $y \neq 0$ and $y \neq -1$, which is greater,

$\frac{x}{y}$ or $\frac{x}{y+1}$?

(1) $x \neq 0$

(2) $x > y$

22. Each person on a committee with 40 members voted for exactly one of 3 candidates, F, G, or H. Did Candidate F receive the most votes from the 40 votes cast?

(1) Candidate F received 11 of the votes.

(2) Candidate H received 14 of the votes.

23. S is a set of integers such that

i) if a is in S, then −a is in S, and
ii) if each of a and b is in S, then ab is in S.

Is −4 in S?

(1) 1 is in S.

(2) 2 is in S.

24. If the area of triangular region RST is 25, what is the perimeter of RST?

(1) The length of one side of RST is $5\sqrt{2}$.

(2) RST is a right isosceles triangle.

25. If x and y are consecutive odd integers, what is the sum of x and y?

(1) The product of x and y is negative.

(2) One of the integers is equal to −1.

S T O P

IF YOU FINISH BEFORE TIME IS CALLED, YOU MAY CHECK YOUR WORK ON THIS SECTION ONLY.
DO NOT WORK ON ANY OTHER SECTION IN THE TEST.

SECTION V

Time—30 minutes

35 Questions

Directions: Each passage in this section is followed by numbered considerations that require classification, as illustrated by the following example:

> John Atkins, the owner of a service station in Leeway, wanted to open a station in Eastown. A computer company had plans to set up operations in Eastown, and Atkins, foreseeing an increase in traffic near the plant, was eager to acquire land in Eastown so that he could expand his business to serve commuting workers. Ideally, Atkins wanted a piece of land large enough to permit him to build a tire store as part of the new station; he also wanted to keep the cost of purchasing the land as well as the cost of clearing it for construction as low as possible. Atkins identified three possible properties: one on Moore Road, another on Route 5, and a third on Snow Lane. The purchase prices of the properties were $42,000, $36,000, and $34,000, respectively. The properties required different expenditures for clearing. In the case of the Snow Lane site, a diner would have to be demolished and pavement removed. Atkins knew that his decision required deliberation.

The following numbered considerations are related to the passage above. Evaluate each consideration separately in terms of the passage and on the answer sheet blacken space

A if the consideration is an Objective in making the decision; that is, one of the outcomes, results, or goals that the decision-maker seeks;

B if the consideration is a Major Factor in making the decision; that is, a consideration, explicitly mentioned in the passage, that is basic to reaching the decision;

C if the consideration is a Minor Factor in making the decision; that is, a consideration that is of secondary importance to reaching the decision and that bears on a Major Factor;

D if the consideration is an Assumption in making the decision; that is, a relevant supposition or projection made by the decision-maker before reaching the decision;

E if the consideration is an Unimportant Issue in making the decision; that is, a consideration that is insignificant or not immediately relevant to reaching the decision.

1. Increase in traffic near the new computer plant   Ⓐ Ⓑ Ⓒ ● Ⓔ

2. Acquisition of a sufficiently large piece of land   ● Ⓑ Ⓒ Ⓓ Ⓔ

3. Cost of clearing a piece of land   Ⓐ ● Ⓒ Ⓓ Ⓔ

4. Cost of demolishing the diner on the Snow Lane site   Ⓐ Ⓑ ● Ⓓ Ⓔ

5. Cost of starting up the new computer plant   Ⓐ Ⓑ Ⓒ Ⓓ ●

GO ON TO THE NEXT PAGE.

The best classification for number 1 is (D), an <u>Assumption</u>, since Atkins supposes that automobile traffic will increase near the new computer plant. The best classification for number 2 is (A), an <u>Objective</u>, since one of Atkins' goals is to obtain a piece of land large enough to permit him to include a tire store as part of his new station. (B), a <u>Major Factor</u>, is the best classification for number 3. The cost of clearing a property is a basic consideration to Atkins since he wants to prepare a property for construction at the lowest possible cost. The best classification for number 4 is (C), a <u>Minor Factor</u>. The cost of demolishing the diner on the Snow Lane site contributes to the total cost of clearing that site. That is, the cost of demolition is a secondary consideration that bears on a major factor. Finally, the best classification for number 5 is (E), an <u>Unimportant Issue</u>, since there is no logical connection between the cost of starting up the computer plant and Atkins' decision about which property to choose.

NOW READ THE PASSAGES AND CLASSIFY THE CONSIDERATIONS FOLLOWING THEM.

GO ON TO THE NEXT PAGE.

In June 1981 the World Camera Corporation asked its advertising agency, Young, Lyons, and Metz, to select three cities to be test markets for World Camera's new product, a "high-quality color-resolution" camera to be called the World Camera. The agency selected two of the test markets, areas in or near Huntsville and Phoenix, quite readily, but had difficulty selecting the third. In order to make that decision, Frank Jardin, the vice-president of marketing, called a meeting; attending that meeting were Martin Miranda, the manager of the World Camera account, and Dave Goltz, a research director.

Jardin: "As I see it, we can choose Pomona, Corpus Christi, or Tampa Bay as our third test market. Obviously, none of them is ideal, but we'll have to make the best choice we can. As you know, we're looking for a test market that contains at least a million people but no more than six million. Equally important, we would like at least 20 percent of the population of the test market to be between the ages of 35 and 44."

Miranda: "That's important. Our research indicates that the 35 to 44 year olds are the most likely customers for the new camera."

Jardin: "Also important, of course, are both the index of media spill-out, that is, the number of people outside the test market who will see advertisements for the camera on television, and the index of media spill-in, that is, the number of people included in the test market who watch programs carried on television stations that are outside the test market."

Miranda: "We need to consider the percentage of two-income families in each test market as well, since two-income families are likely to have the discretionary income to spend on a luxury item like the World Camera."

Goltz: "Let me just say that I think we ought to use Pomona as our third test market. Both the spill-out and spill-in indexes for Pomona are below 0.2, which is excellent. Pomona also has the largest percentage of 35 to 44 year olds."

Miranda: "That's certainly true, but we have to remember that Pomona has an unusually high percentage of 18 to 25 year olds because of the colleges in the area. In addition to everything else, we would like the general age-group pattern of the test market to be as close to the patterns of the other two test markets, Huntsville and Phoenix, as possible."

Goltz: "Pomona has a high percentage of two-income families, Martin."

Miranda: "True, but a significant number of those two-income families are academicians. Research has shown that, in general, academicians are less willing to try new products than are members of other professions."

Jardin: "What about Corpus Christi?"

Miranda: "Corpus Christi has very nearly the same percentage of 35 to 44 year olds as Pomona, so it is a strong candidate for that reason. But the percentage of two-income families in Corpus Christi is not as large as it is in Pomona."

Goltz: "I did notice, though, that the 35- to 44-year-old group in Corpus Christi has a higher level of income per capita than that group has in any of the other test markets. The higher level of income might offset the lower percentage of two-income families."

Miranda: "Good point."

Jardin: "Both Pomona and Corpus Christi meet the general market size, as does Tampa Bay. What else do we have on Corpus Christi?"

Goltz: "Spill-out is acceptable—the index is 0.5—but spill-in is a little high, around 0.7. Moreover, another local station is scheduled to begin broadcasting near the proposed test market area in about four months, so spill-in could go even higher. For either spill-out or spill-in, an index higher than 0.8 is unacceptable."

Miranda: "Tampa Bay has a spill-in index of 0.4."

Goltz: "Let's see—Tampa Bay has a spill-out index of 0.5. The percentage of 35 to 44 year olds is a little bit low, but the percentage of two-income families is right on target."

Jardin: "How does Tampa Bay compare in terms of the 55- to 64-year-old group? As I remember, the percentage is a little larger than the percentage in Huntsville or Phoenix."

Goltz: "Yes, it is. Also, the general population in Tampa Bay doesn't spend as many hours watching television as do the general populations of our other test markets."

Jardin: "Something else that we need to consider is the ability of the World Camera Corporation to distribute the new product in each of these proposed test markets. It's vital that a distribution network already be in place."

Goltz: "I have the information on that. The World Camera Corporation now distributes at least one of its products in 53 percent of the camera outlets in Pomona, 47 percent in Corpus Christi, and 44 percent in Tampa Bay. None of those figures is very encouraging."

Jardin: "But are those figures reliable?"

Miranda: "I think so. But there has been a recent change in camera suppliers in the Tampa Bay area, so the distribution percentage there may actually be lower than 44."

Jardin: "What about the past performances of each of these test markets? How closely have sales of new products in these test markets conformed to sales when the new products went on the market nationally?"

Goltz: "Tampa Bay has an enviable record in that respect and Corpus Christi's record is acceptable. We have not used Pomona as a test market enough to determine how well sales patterns there conform to national sales patterns."

Jardin: "What I would now like each of you to do is to make your recommendation to me in a memorandum. Then we can meet next Monday and select the test market."

GO ON TO THE NEXT PAGE.

GO ON TO THE NEXT PAGE.

Directions: The following numbered considerations are related to the passage above. You may refer back to the passage and to the directions at the beginning of this section. Evaluate each consideration separately in terms of the passage and on the answer sheet blacken space

A if the consideration is an Objective in making the decision; that is, one of the outcomes, results, or goals that the decision-maker seeks;

B if the consideration is a Major Factor in making the decision; that is, a consideration, explicitly mentioned in the passage, that is basic to reaching the decision;

C if the consideration is a Minor Factor in making the decision; that is, a consideration that is of secondary importance to reaching the decision and that bears on a Major Factor;

D if the consideration is an Assumption in making the decision; that is, a relevant supposition or projection made by the decision-maker before reaching the decision;

E if the consideration is an Unimportant Issue in making the decision; that is, a consideration that is insignificant or not immediately relevant to reaching the decision.

1. A way to improve the quality of the World Camera

2. General age-group pattern of Pomona, Corpus Christi, or Tampa Bay

3. Unacceptability of any test market in which the total population exceeds 6 million

4. The number of people outside a proposed test market site who would see advertisements for the new camera

5. A test market in which sales of new products have conformed to sales of the new products when those products were marketed nationally

6. Determining the age-group that is most likely to purchase the World Camera

7. Percentage of 55-64 year olds in Tampa Bay

8. Selecting a test market in which at least 20 percent of the people are between 35 and 44 years old

9. Recent change of camera suppliers in Tampa Bay

10. A way to reduce the development costs of the World Camera

11. Importance of the 35- to 44-year-old age-group to sales of the World Camera

12. Percentage of two-income families in a proposed test market

13. Number of cameras currently being sold in each of the test markets under consideration

14. A test market with a total population of at least 1 million

15. Number of 18-25-year-old college students in Pomona

16. Unlikelihood of finding a test market more suitable than the three under consideration

17. The number of people within each test market under consideration who watch television programs carried on stations outside the test market area

Meddevco is the division of the Lauberg Corporation that produces medical equipment. Anthony Cuomo, Meddevco's president, and Louise Rothstein, Meddevco's director of personnel, are discussing Charles Ryan, Meddevco's current vice-president for research.

Cuomo: "Charles just told me that he's leaving us for Syntrex because he'll head a larger research division there and earn a better salary. I'm not sorry to lose him; he didn't have much managerial ability. But he's leaving soon, and it would be unwise to have the vice-presidency vacant for long. What are our options for filling it?"

Rothstein: "I assume you want to conduct a search for a replacement in accordance with corporate personnel policy. If not, we'll have to get a special exemption."

Cuomo: "I definitely want to comply with corporate policy."

Rothstein: "Then we have three alternatives, Tony—fill the position with an internal search by promoting one of the two research directors, hire an executive search firm to recruit and screen external candidates for us, or mount our own external recruitment campaign through advertisements, personal contacts, and professional meetings."

Cuomo: "I want to complete the search quickly and hire someone who can take the job right away. Once the current recession hits us, we'll probably have to cut our personnel office budget, so we'd better make the search as economical as possible in cash outlay. We should also keep to a minimum the hours that the vice-presidents and I spend on the search. And I'd like you to try not to spend much time on it. How do the three recruiting methods stack up against these considerations, Louise?"

Rothstein: "Well, an internal search is certainly quick. Only Ted McClellan and Alan Blake would be considered, and either of them could take the job immediately. It is also extremely inexpensive."

Cuomo: "True, but I see some serious disadvantages. I consider the vice-presidency for research to be a central position in a company like ours; I think we need the best qualified person we can get. We've always known that in order to succeed, a vice-president for research has to have both managerial ability and imagination. Alan has managerial ability, and Ted has imagination, but neither has both. The corporate senior vice-president for research has suggested Ted for the job but, luckily, I don't have to listen to him; this is my decision. On the other hand, experience in medical equipment research is also essential for success as vice-president for research."

Rothstein: "And Alan and Ted both have that, whereas many external candidates don't."

Cuomo: "Right. But another disadvantage of restricting the choice to the research directors is that they're both White males. I am under the impression that corporate officers are concerned about any laxness in implementing the corporation's affirmative action plan. I myself take our division's affirmative action plan very seriously—I want to fulfill not only the letter of the plan, by recruiting a variety of candidates, but also its spirit, by giving full and serious consideration to women and minority candidates. Another disadvantage is that Ted and Alan are in their fifties . . ."

Rothstein: "Tony, surely you know by now that we can't discriminate on the basis of age."

Cuomo: "Of course. We can't consider age."

Rothstein: "Our second alternative is to use an executive search firm. I recommend Execuco. Based on our past experience with them, I think they'd probably find candidates with the qualifications we want. Execuco also has a large computer bank of minority and women candidates and has been highly effective in the past in affirmative action recruiting."

Cuomo: "They sound excellent. What are the disadvantages of using Execuco?"

Rothstein: "For one thing, cost—we'd have to pay Execuco's fee and all travel expenses for candidates we interview. Also, hours—I'd have to spend a substantial amount of time working with Execuco, as well as do things like review the best twenty resumés. You and the vice-presidents would also have to review the best resumés and would need to interview the top five candidates. Then there's speed—the search would probably take three months, and the person we choose might not be able to start until several months after that."

Cuomo: "How would an external search that we handle ourselves be different?"

Rothstein: "It would be somewhat less expensive, even with the costs of advertisements, long distance phone calls, and travel to professional meetings. But it would take more of my time, since I would have to screen the large number of applications we would receive. But the deluge of applications will make our chances of getting qualified candidates, including a large number of minority and women candidates, even better than with Execuco, since the recession has caused so many layoffs in other companies that even top-notch managers are job hunting, and since our ads reach hundreds of people that Execuco doesn't have on file. But doing it ourselves would take a long time—we'd need at least six months for that kind of search."

Cuomo: "Thanks, Louise; this discussion has given me a lot to consider. Let me think it over and get back to you tomorrow."

GO ON TO THE NEXT PAGE.

Directions: The following numbered considerations are related to the passage above. You may refer back to the passage and to the directions at the beginning of this section. Evaluate each consideration separately in terms of the passage and on the answer sheet blacken space

A if the consideration is an Objective in making the decision; that is, one of the outcomes, results, or goals that the decision-maker seeks;

B if the consideration is a Major Factor in making the decision; that is, a consideration, explicitly mentioned in the passage, that is basic to reaching the decision;

C if the consideration is a Minor Factor in making the decision; that is, a consideration that is of secondary importance to reaching the decision and that bears on a Major Factor;

D if the consideration is an Assumption in making the decision; that is, a relevant supposition or projection made by the decision-maker before reaching the decision;

E if the consideration is an Unimportant Issue in making the decision; that is, a consideration that is insignificant or not immediately relevant to reaching the decision.

18. Execuco's fee

19. Alan Blake's lack of imagination

20. Economy of cash outlay in the search

21. Low expenditure of time on the search by the director of personnel

22. Need to fill the position of vice-president for research quickly

23. Necessity of obtaining a special exemption if the search is not done in accordance with corporate personnel policy

24. Appointment to the vice-presidency of a person who has experience in medical equipment research

25. Hours that the director of personnel must spend reviewing resumés if Meddevco hires Execuco

26. Ages of candidates who would be considered if Meddevco either promotes internally or hires Execuco or does its own external search

27. Rapidity with which Meddevco can fill the vice-president for research position by either searching internally or employing Execuco or running its own external search

28. Likelihood of poor performance as vice-president for research of any applicant who lacks experience in medical equipment research

29. Effectiveness of the three recruiting methods in providing Meddevco with women and minority candidates

30. Avoidance of excessive use of the president's and the vice-presidents' time for the search

31. Compliance with the suggestion of the corporate senior vice-president for research

32. Number of women and minority candidates in Execuco's computer bank

33. Cost of conducting an internal search, an Execuco search, or a self-run external search

34. Charles Ryan's managerial ability

35. Cost of advertisements for the position of vice-president for research

S T O P

IF YOU FINISH BEFORE TIME IS CALLED, YOU MAY CHECK YOUR WORK ON THIS SECTION ONLY.
DO NOT WORK ON ANY OTHER SECTION IN THE TEST.

SECTION VI
Time—30 minutes
20 Questions

Directions: In this section solve each problem, using any available space on the page for scratchwork. Then indicate the best of the answer choices given.

Numbers: All numbers used are real numbers.

Figures: Figures that accompany problems in this test are intended to provide information useful in solving the problems. They are drawn as accurately as possible EXCEPT when it is stated in a specific problem that its figure is not drawn to scale. All figures lie in a plane unless otherwise indicated.

1. If x is an even integer, which of the following is an odd integer?

   (A) $3x + 2$

   (B) $7x$

   (C) $8x + 5$

   (D) x^2

   (E) x^3

2. On a purchase of $120, a store offered a payment plan consisting of a $20 down payment and 12 monthly payments of $10 each. What percent of the purchase price, to the nearest tenth of a percent, did the customer pay in interest by using this plan?

   (A) 16.7%

   (B) 30%

   (C) 75.8%

   (D) 106.7%

   (E) 107.5%

3. $\dfrac{5}{4}\left(42 \div \dfrac{3}{16}\right) =$

   (A) 6.3   (B) 9.8   (C) 179.2

   (D) 224   (E) 280

4. When magnified 1,000 times by an electron microscope, the image of a certain circular piece of tissue has a diameter of 0.5 centimeter. The actual diameter of the tissue, in centimeters, is

   (A) 0.005

   (B) 0.002

   (C) 0.001

   (D) 0.0005

   (E) 0.0002

GO ON TO THE NEXT PAGE.

-323-

5. In 1970 there were 8,902 women stockbrokers in the United States. By 1978 the number had increased to 19,947. Approximately what was the percent increase?

   (A) 45%

   (B) 125%

   (C) 145%

   (D) 150%

   (E) 225%

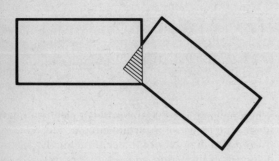

6. In the figure above, two rectangles with the same dimensions overlap to form the shaded region. If each rectangle has perimeter 12 and the shaded region has perimeter 3, what is the total length of the heavy line segments?

   (A) 15 (B) 18 (C) 21 (D) 22 (E) 23

7. If one root of the equation $2x^2 + 3x - k = 0$ is 6, what is the value of k?

   (A) 90

   (B) 42

   (C) 18

   (D) 10

   (E) −10

8. Bottle R contains 250 capsules and costs $6.25. Bottle T contains 130 capsules and costs $2.99. What is the difference between the cost per capsule for bottle R and the cost per capsule for bottle T?

   (A) $0.25

   (B) $0.12

   (C) $0.05

   (D) $0.03

   (E) $0.002

GO ON TO THE NEXT PAGE.

-324-

9. Trucking transportation rates are x dollars per metric ton per kilometer. How much does it cost, in dollars, to transport one dozen cars, which weigh two metric tons each, n kilometers by truck?

(A) $\dfrac{x}{12n}$ (B) $\dfrac{x}{24n}$ (C) $\dfrac{xn}{24}$

(D) $12xn$ (E) $24xn$

10. For a positive integer n, the number $n!$ is defined to be $n(n - 1)(n - 2) \ldots (1)$. For example, $4! = 4(3)(2)(1)$. What is the value of $5! - 3!$?

(A) 120

(B) 114

(C) 20

(D) 15

(E) 2

11. A man who died left an estate valued at $111,000. His will stipulated that his estate was to be distributed so that each of his three children received from the estate and his previous gifts, combined, the same total amount. If he had previously given his oldest child $15,000, his middle child $10,000, and his youngest $2,000, how much did the youngest child receive from the estate?

(A) $50,000

(B) $48,000

(C) $46,000

(D) $44,000

(E) $39,000

GO ON TO THE NEXT PAGE.

12. If $y > 0$, which of the following is equal to $\sqrt{48y^3}$?

(A) $4y\sqrt{3y}$

(B) $3y\sqrt{4y}$

(C) $2\sqrt{12y}$

(D) $3\sqrt{8y}$

(E) $16y\sqrt{3y}$

13. The volume of a box with a square base is 54 cubic centimeters. If the height of the box is twice the width of the base, what is the height, in centimeters?

(A) 2

(B) 3

(C) 4

(D) 6

(E) 9

$$q = 3\sqrt{3}$$
$$r = 1 + 2\sqrt{3}$$
$$s = 3 + \sqrt{3}$$

14. If q, r, and s are the numbers shown above, which of the following shows their order from greatest to least?

(A) q, r, s (B) q, s, r (C) r, q, s

(D) s, q, r (E) s, r, q

15. The sum of the interior angles of any polygon with n sides is $180(n - 2)$ degrees. If the sum of the interior angles of polygon P is three times the sum of the interior angles of quadrilateral Q, how many sides does P have?

(A) 6 (B) 8 (C) 10 (D) 12 (E) 14

16. In Company X, 30 percent of the employees live over ten miles from work and 60 percent of the employees who live over ten miles from work are in car pools. If 40 percent of the employees of Company X are in car pools, what percent of the employees of Company X live ten miles or less from work and are in car pools?

(A) 12%

(B) 20%

(C) 22%

(D) 28%

(E) 32%

GO ON TO THE NEXT PAGE.

-326-

17. If an organization were to sell n tickets for a theater production, the total revenue from ticket sales would be 20 percent greater than the total costs of the production. If the organization actually sold all but 5 percent of the n tickets, the total revenue from ticket sales was what percent greater than the total costs of the production?

(A) 4%

(B) 10%

(C) 14%

(D) 15%

(E) 18%

18. When the integer n is divided by 6, the remainder is 3. Which of the following is NOT a multiple of 6 ?

(A) $n - 3$ (B) $n + 3$ (C) $2n$

(D) $3n$ (E) $4n$

19. How many liters of pure alcohol must be added to a 100-liter solution that is 20 percent alcohol in order to produce a solution that is 25 percent alcohol?

(A) $\frac{7}{2}$

(B) 5

(C) $\frac{20}{3}$

(D) 8

(E) $\frac{39}{4}$

20. If 10 persons meet at a reunion and each person shakes hands exactly once with each of the others, what is the total number of handshakes?

(A) $10 \cdot 9 \cdot 8 \cdot 7 \cdot 6 \cdot 5 \cdot 4 \cdot 3 \cdot 2 \cdot 1$

(B) $10 \cdot 10$

(C) $10 \cdot 9$

(D) 45

(E) 36

S T O P

IF YOU FINISH BEFORE TIME IS CALLED, YOU MAY CHECK YOUR WORK ON THIS SECTION ONLY.
DO NOT WORK ON ANY OTHER SECTION IN THE TEST.

Answer Key
And Explanatory Material

ANSWER KEY: FORM C

#	SECTION 1	SECTION 2	SECTION 3	SECTION 4	SECTION 5	SECTION 6
1	C	D	D	E	E	C
2	E	B	D	C	B	A
3	A	B	A	C	D	E
4	C	C	D	A	B	D
5	D	D	D	B	A	B
6	B	A	C	D	B	B
7	D	D	B	D	C	A
8	C	D	C	D	A	D
9	C	B	A	B	B	B
10	D	A	B	A	D	B
11	D	C	C	C	D	D
12	B	C	D	E	B	B
13	D	C	C	B	E	D
14	A	D	C	D	A	B
15	E	A	B	A	B	B
16	E	E	D	C	D	C
17	A	A	D	A	B	C
18	E	D	B	B	D	D
19	B	A	B	B	D	C
20	B	D	A	D	A	D
21		E	D	E	A	
22		B	D	A	D	
23		A	A	B	E	
24		E	B	B	B	
25		C	B	B	C	
26					D	
27					B	
28					D	
29					B	
30					A	
31					E	
32					C	
33					B	
34					E	
35					C	

Explanatory Material:
Problem Solving I

1. What is the average (arithmetic mean) of the numbers 15, 16, 17, 17, 18, and 19?

   (A) 14.2   (B) 16.5   (C) 17   (D) 17.5   (E) 18

The "brute force" method of solving this problem is to add the six numbers and divide the sum by 6. However, the same answer can be obtained by inspection, by observing that the mean of the first three numbers is 16 and the mean of the last three numbers is 18. The mean of the original six numbers is equal to the mean of 16 and 18, or 17. Thus, the best answer is C. This is an easy question.

2. Kathy bought 4 times as many shares in Company X as Carl, and Carl bought 3 times as many shares in the same company as Tom. Which of the following is the ratio of the number of shares bought by Kathy to the number of shares bought by Tom?

   (A) $\frac{3}{4}$

   (B) $\frac{4}{3}$

   (C) $\frac{3}{1}$

   (D) $\frac{4}{1}$

   (E) $\frac{12}{1}$

Let K = Kathy's shares, C = Carl's shares, and T = Tom's shares. Then

K = 4C
C = 3T
K = 4(3T) = 12T
$\frac{K}{T} = \frac{12}{1}$

Therefore, E is the best answer. This is an easy question.

3. Of the following, which is closest to $\frac{0.15 \times 495}{9.97}$?

The value of the expression can be estimated by calculating
$$\frac{0.15 \times 500}{10} = 7.5.$$

Thus, the best answer is A. This is an easy question.

4. A manager has $6,000 budgeted for raises for 4 full-time and 2 part-time employees. Each of the full-time employees receives the same raise, which is twice the raise that each of the part-time employees receives. What is the amount of the raise that each full-time employee receives?

   (A) $ 750
   (B) $1,000
   (C) $1,200
   (D) $1,500
   (E) $3,000

If P is the raise a part-time employee receives, each full-time employee receives 2P. Then the total for the 2 part-time and 4 full-time employees is 2P + 4(2P) = 6,000; so 10P = 6,000 and P = 600. Then each full-time employee receives $1,200, and C is the best answer. This is an easy question.

5. $x^2 - \left(\frac{x}{2}\right)^2 =$

   (A) $x^2 - x$

   (B) $\frac{x^2}{4}$

   (C) $\frac{x^2}{2}$

   (D) $\frac{3x^2}{4}$

   (E) $\frac{3x^2}{2}$

$$x^2 - \left(\frac{x}{2}\right)^2 = x^2 - \frac{x^2}{4} = \frac{4x^2 - x^2}{4} = \frac{3x^2}{4}.$$

Therefore, D is the best answer. This is an easy question.

6. A hospital pharmacy charges $0.40 per fluidram of a certain medicine but allows a discount of 15 percent to Medicare patients. How much should the pharmacy charge a Medicare patient for 3 fluidounces of the medicine? (128 fluidrams = 16 fluidounces)

   (A) $9.60
   (B) $8.16
   (C) $3.20
   (B) $2.72
   (B) $1.02

One fluidounce equals $\frac{128}{16}$ or 8 fluidrams, so 3 fluidounces equal 24 fluidrams. The regular cost would be $0.40 × 24 = $9.60, and a 15 percent discount ($1.44) would yield a cost to the Medicare patient of $9.60 − $1.44 = $8.16. Thus, the best answer is B. This is an easy question.

7. $(-1)^2 - (-1)^3 =$

   (A) -2 (B) -1 (C) 0   (D) 1   (E) 2

$(-1)^2 - (-1)^3 = (1) - (-1) = 2$. Thus, the best answer is E. This is an easy question.

8. At a certain bowling alley, it costs $0.50 to rent bowling shoes for the day and $1.25 to bowl 1 game. If a person has $12.80 and must rent shoes, what is the greatest number of complete games that person can bowl in one day?

   (A) 7
   (B) 8
   (C) 9
   (B) 10
   (B) 11

The amount the bowler has to spend on games is $12.30 after subtracting the $0.50 to rent shoes. The quotient $\frac{12.30}{1.25}$ is greater than 9 but less than 10, so he can bowl at most 9 games. Thus, the best answer is C. This is an easy question.

9. If $\frac{x}{y} = 2$, then $\frac{x - y}{x} =$

   (A) -1
   (B) $-\frac{1}{2}$
   (C) $\frac{1}{2}$
   (D) 1
   (E) 2

If $\frac{x}{y} = 2$, $x = 2y$. Then $\frac{x - y}{x} = \frac{2y - y}{2y} = \frac{y}{2y} = \frac{1}{2}$. Thus, the best answer is C. This is an easy question.

10. If each photocopy of a manuscript costs 4 cents per page, what is the cost, in cents, to reproduce x copies of an x-page manuscript?

   (A) $4x$ (B) $16x$ (C) x^2
   (D) $4x^2$ (E) $16x^2$

The total cost is the cost per page times the number of pages per copy times the number of copies, or $4 \cdot x \cdot x = 4x^2$. Thus, the best answer is D. This is a moderately difficult question.

11. Ken left a job paying $75,000 per year to accept a sales job paying $45,000 per year plus 15 percent commission. If each of his sales is for $750, what is the least number of sales he must make per year if he is not to lose money because of the change?

   (A) 40
   (B) 200
   (C) 266
   (D) 267
   (E) 600

The difference between Ken's base salary and his previous salary is $30,000. To make up the difference in 15 percent commissions on $750 sales, the number of sales he must make is at least $\frac{30,000}{0.15 \times 750} = 266.67$. Thus, the least

(integer) number of sales he must make to avoid losing money is 267, and the best answer is therefore D. This is a moderately difficult question.

MONTHLY KILOWATT-HOURS

	500	1,000	1,500	2,000
Present	$24.00	$41.00	$57.00	$73.00
Proposed	$26.00	$45.00	$62.00	$79.00

12. The table above shows present rates and proposed rates for electricity for residential customers. For which of the monthly kilowatt-hours shown would the proposed rate be the greatest percent increase over the present rate?

   (A) 500
   (B) 1,000
   (C) 1,500
   (D) 2,000
   (E) Each of the percent increases is the same.

	500	1,000	1,500	2,000
Percent Change	$\frac{2}{24}$ (8.3%)	$\frac{4}{41}$ (9.7%)	$\frac{5}{57}$ (8.8%)	$\frac{6}{73}$ (8.2%)

The table above shows that the highest percent change is for 1,000 kilowatt-hours, so the best answer is B. This is a moderately difficult question.

13. If a, b, and c are three consecutive odd integers such that $10 < a < b < c < 20$ and if b and c are prime numbers, what is the value of $a + b$?

   (A) 24
   (B) 28
   (C) 30
   (D) 32
   (E) 36

The only sets of consecutive odd integers for which $10 < a < b < c < 20$ are $\{11,13,15\}$, $\{13,15,17\}$, and $\{15,17,19\}$. The first two sets are eliminated because b and c must be prime and 15 is not a prime. Therefore, $\{15,17,19\}$ is the only set that meets all the conditions, so $a = 15$ and $b = 17$. Then $a + b = 32$, and the best answer is D. This is a moderately difficult question.

14. Of a group of people surveyed in a political poll, 60 percent said that they would vote for candidate *R*. Of those who said they would vote for *R*, 90 percent actually voted for *R*, and of those who did not say that they would vote for *R*, 5 percent actually voted for *R*. What percent of the group voted for *R*?

(A) 56%
(B) 59%
(C) 62%
(D) 65%
(E) 74%

Of the 60 percent who said they would vote for R, 90 percent (54 percent of the total group) actually did. Of the 40 percent who did not say they would vote for R, 5 percent (2 percent of the total group) actually did. Thus, 54 + 2 = 56 percent of the total group voted for R. The best answer is therefore A. This is a moderately difficult question.

15. If $r = 1 + \frac{1}{3} + \frac{1}{9} + \frac{1}{27}$ and $s = 1 + \frac{1}{3}r$, then *s* exceeds *r* by

(A) $\frac{1}{3}$ (B) $\frac{1}{6}$ (C) $\frac{1}{9}$ (D) $\frac{1}{27}$ (E) $\frac{1}{81}$

One way to solve this problem is first to compute r by adding the four terms. However, note that each successive term of r is $\frac{1}{3}$ the previous term. Thus,

$$s = 1 + \frac{1}{3}r = 1 + \frac{1}{3} + \frac{1}{9} + \frac{1}{27} + \frac{1}{81} = r + \frac{1}{81},$$

and s exceeds r by $\frac{1}{81}$. Therefore, the best answer is E. This is a difficult question.

16. $$\frac{0.025 \times \frac{15}{2} \times 48}{5 \times 0.0024 \times \frac{3}{4}} =$$

(A)   0.1
(B)   0.2
(C)   100
(D)   200
(E)   1,000

Multiplying both the numerator and denominator by 10,000 yields

$$\frac{250 \times \frac{15}{2} \times 48}{5 \times 24 \times \frac{3}{4}}.$$

Simplifying the numerator and denominator further yields

$$\frac{250 \times 15 \times 24}{5 \times 6 \times 3} = 1,000.$$

Thus, the best answer is E. This is a difficult question.

17. A student responded to all of the 22 questions on a test and received a score of 63.5. If the scores were derived by adding 3.5 points for each correct answer and deducting 1 point for each incorrect answer, how many questions did the student answer <u>incorrectly</u>?

(A) 3 (B) 4 (C) 15 (D) 18 (E) 20

If c is the number of correct answers, the number of incorrect answers is (22 − c) and

$$3.5c - 1(22 - c) = 63.5$$
$$3.5c - 22 + c = 63.5$$
$$4.5c = 85.5$$
$$c = 19$$
$$22 - c = 3$$

Thus, the number of incorrect answers is 3 and the best answer is A. This is a difficult question.

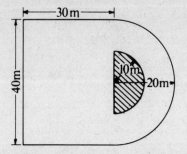

18. The figure above represents a rectangular parking lot that is 30 meters by 40 meters and an attached semicircular driveway that has an outer radius of 20 meters and an inner radius of 10 meters. If the shaded region is <u>not</u> included, what is the area, in square meters, of the lot and driveway?

(A) 1,350π
(B) 1,200 + 400π
(C) 1,200 + 300π
(D) 1,200 + 200π
(E) 1,200 + 150π

The area of the rectangular section is 30 × 40 = 1,200. Since the area of a semicircle is $\frac{1}{2}\pi r^2$, the large semicircular area is $\frac{1}{2} \times \pi \times 20^2 = 200\pi$. The shaded area, also semicircular, is $\frac{1}{2} \times \pi \times 10^2 = 50\pi$. Thus, the total area of the lot, excluding the shaded part, is

$$1,200 + 200\pi - 50\pi = 1,200 + 150\pi.$$

The best answer is therefore E. This is a difficult question.

19. One-fifth of the light switches produced by a certain factory are defective. Four-fifths of the defective switches are rejected and $\frac{1}{20}$ of the nondefective switches are rejected by mistake. If all the switches not rejected are sold, what percent of the switches sold by the factory are defective?

(A) 4%
(B) 5%
(C) 6.25%
(D) 11%
(E) 16%

The following table describes the condition of each hundred switches the firm makes:

	Rejected	Sold	Total
Nondefective	4	76	80
Defective	16	4	20
Total	20	80	100

If $\frac{4}{5}$ of the defective switches are rejected, 16 are rejected and 4 are sold. If $\frac{1}{20}$ of the 80 nondefective switches are rejected, 4 are rejected and 76 are sold. Thus, a total of 80 switches are sold, of which 4 are defective, or $\frac{4}{80} = 5\%$. Therefore, the best answer is B. This is a difficult question.

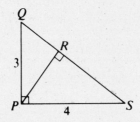

20. In $\triangle PQS$ above, if $PQ = 3$ and $PS = 4$, then $PR =$

(A) $\frac{9}{4}$ (B) $\frac{12}{5}$ (C) $\frac{16}{5}$ (E) $\frac{15}{4}$ (E) $\frac{20}{3}$

By the Pythagorean Theorem,
$QS = \sqrt{3^2 + 4^2} = \sqrt{9 + 16} = 5$. One way to find c, or PR, is by again using the Pythagorean Theorem to express a and b, in the figure above, each in terms of c. However, this method results in a radical equation that is tedious to solve. A quicker way to find c is to note that PR, or c, is the altitude from P to side QS. Since the area of a triangle is equal to $\frac{1}{2}$ the product of the length of any side and the length of the altitude to that side, $\frac{1}{2}(5c) = \frac{1}{2}(3 \cdot 4)$, or $c = \frac{12}{5}$. Therefore, the best answer is B. This is a difficult question.

Explanatory Material: Sentence Correction

1. A fire in an enclosed space burns with the aid of reflected radiation that preheats the fuel, making ignition much easier and <u>flames spreading</u> more quickly.

(A) flames spreading
(B) flame spreads
(C) flames caused to spread
(D) causing flames to spread
(E) causing spreading of the flames

Choices A, B, and C are incorrect because a present participial (or "—ing") verb must precede *flames* to form a structure parallel to the phrase *making ignition much easier.* . . . Choice D is correct. Choice E is wordy, unidiomatic, and also awkward in that *spreading,* although used here as a noun, appears at first to be another present participle that could be modified by *more quickly.* This is an easy question.

2. Roy Wilkins was among the last of a generation of civil rights activists who led the nation through decades of change <u>so profound many young Americans are not able to imagine, even less to remember</u>, what segregation was like.

(A) so profound many young Americans are not able to imagine, even less to remember
(B) so profound that many young Americans cannot imagine, much less remember
(C) so profound many young Americans cannot imagine nor even less remember
(D) of such profundity many young Americans cannot imagine, even less can they remember
(E) of such profundity that many young Americans are not able to imagine, much less to remember

Choice A can be faulted for omitting *that* after *profound;* the idiomatic form of the expression is *"so X that Y."* Also, *much less remember* is more idiomatic than *even less to remember,* and *cannot imagine* is more concise than *are not able to imagine.* Choice B is best. Choice C lacks *that* after *profound,* and *nor* is incorrectly used to join verbs modified by *cannot.* In choice D, *of such profundity* is wordy, *that* is missing, and *even less can they remember* is not an idiomatic way to complete *cannot imagine.* In choice E, *of such profundity* and *are not able to imagine* are wordy, and the *to* in *to remember* is unnecessary. This is a fairly easy question.

3. The residents' opposition to the spraying program has rekindled an old debate <u>among those who oppose the use of pesticides and</u> those who feel that the pesticides are necessary to save the trees.

(A) among those who oppose the use of pesticides and
(B) between those who oppose the use of pesticides and
(C) among those opposing the use of pesticides with
(D) between those who oppose the use of pesticides with
(E) among those opposing the use of pesticides and

Choices A, C, and E can be faulted for using *among* in place of *between* to refer to two factions. Choice B is correct. Choices C and D incorrectly use *with* in place of *and*. Finally, *those opposing* in choices C and E is not parallel with *those who feel*. This question is a little easier than the average.

4. In cold-water habitats, certain invertebrates and fish convert starches into complex carbohydrates called glycerols, in effect manufacturing its own antifreeze.

   (A) in effect manufacturing its own antifreeze
   (B) effectively manufacturing antifreeze of its own
   (C) in effect manufacturing their own antifreeze
   (D) so that they manufacture their own antifreeze
   (E) thus the manufacture of its own antifreeze

Choices A and B are incorrect because the pronoun *its* does not agree in number with *invertebrates and fish,* the noun referents. B also distorts the intended meaning of the sentence by making a statement about how effectively the invertebrates and fish manufacture their own antifreeze. Choice C is correct. In D and E, *so that they manufacture* and *thus the manufacture* do not form logical connections with the rest of the sentence, and *its* in E is incorrect. This is an easy question.

5. Slips of the tongue do not necessarily reveal concealed beliefs or intentions but rather are the result from the competition between various processing mechanisms in the brain.

   (A) but rather are the result from
   (B) and instead are the result from
   (C) being rather the result of
   (D) and rather result from
   (E) but rather result from

Choices A and B are incorrect because *are the result from* is unidiomatic; *result from* or *are the result of* are the idiomatic forms. Choices B, C, and D are faulty because *but* is needed to complete the construction *do not reveal but (verb)*. E is correct for this moderately easy question.

6. The new contract forbids a strike by the transportation union.

   (A) forbids a strike by the transportation union
   (B) forbids the transportation union from striking
   (C) forbids that there be a strike by the transportation union
   (D) will forbid the transportation union from striking
   (E) will forbid that the transportation union strikes

Choice A is best. B, C, D, and E are unidiomatic: a form of the verb *forbid* may be completed by a noun, as in *forbids a strike,* or by a noun and an infinitive, as in *forbids the union to strike.* This question is of middle difficulty.

7. Monitoring heart patients' exercise, as well as athletes exercising, is now done by small transmitters broadcasting physiological measurements to nearby recording machines.

   (A) Monitoring heart patients' exercise, as well as athletes exercising, is now done by small transmitters broadcasting physiological measurements to nearby recording machines.
   (B) Monitoring the exercise of heart patients, as well as athletes exercising, is now done by small transmitters broadcasting physiological measurements to nearby recording machines.
   (C) Small transmitters broadcasting physiological measurements to nearby recording machines are now used to monitor the exercise of both heart patients and athletes.
   (D) Broadcasting physiological measurements to nearby recording machines, small transmitters are now used to monitor heart patients' exercise, as well as athletes exercising.
   (E) Both athletes exercising and heart patients' exercise are now monitored by small transmitters broadcasting physiological measurements to nearby recording machines.

Choices A and B incorrectly juxtapose *heart patients' exercise* and *athletes* who are *exercising,* not *patient's exercise* and *athletes' exercise,* as is more logical. Choice C, which clarifies the comparison, is best. D and E, like A and B, imply a comparison between *athletes* who are exercising and the *exercise* of heart patients. The question is moderately easy.

8. The commission has directed advertisers to restrict the use of the word "natural" to foods that do not contain color or flavor additives, chemical preservatives, or nothing that has been synthesized.

   (A) or nothing that has been
   (B) nor anything that was
   (C) and nothing that is
   (D) or anything that has been
   (E) and anything

Choices A, B, and C are faulty because the *not* in *do not contain* makes the negatives *nothing* and *nor* unidiomatic. Choice D is best. In E, *and* fails to indicate that *anything. . .* is an all-inclusive term, not another separate item in the list *additives, . . . preservatives. . . .* This question is fairly easy.

9. Bringing the Ford Motor Company back from the verge of bankruptcy shortly after the Second World War was a special governmentally sanctioned price increase during a period of wage and price controls.

(A) Bringing the Ford Motor Company back from the verge of bankruptcy shortly after the Second World War was a special governmentally sanctioned price increase during a period of wage and price controls.
(B) What brought the Ford Motor Company back from the verge of bankruptcy shortly after the Second World War was a special price increase that the government sanctioned during a period of wage and price controls.
(C) That which brought the Ford Motor Company back from the verge of bankruptcy shortly after the Second World War was a special governmentally sanctioned price increase during a period of wage and price controls.
(D) What has brought the Ford Motor Company back from the verge of bankruptcy shortly after the Second World War was a special price increase that the government sanctioned during a period of wages and price controls.
(E) To bring the Ford Motor Company back from the verge of bankruptcy shortly after the Second World War, there was a special price increase during a period of wages and price controls that government sanctioned.

Choice A, awkward and imprecise, leaves one confused about what it was that happened *during a period of wage and price controls* — the revitalization of the Ford Motor Company or the sanctioning of a price increase. B, the best answer, clarifies the matter by making *during. . .* modify *the government sanctioned.* Choice C, wordy and awkward, suffers from the same imprecision as choice A. The present perfect *has brought* in D is inappropriate for action completed well in the past, and *wages,* which should modify *control,* is not idiomatic. In choice E, *wages* is again wrong, and E, contrary to intent, suggests that the government sanctioned a *period of . . . controls* rather than *a special price increase.* The question is of middle difficulty.

10. Like Haydn, Schubert wrote a great deal for the stage, but he is remembered principally for his chamber and concert-hall music.

(A) Like Haydn, Schubert
(B) Like Haydn, Schubert also
(C) As has Haydn, Schubert
(D) As did Haydn, Schubert also
(E) As Haydn did, Schubert also

Choice A is correct. In B, *also* is redundant after *Like,* which establishes the similarity between Haydn and Schubert. *As* in choices C, D, and E is not idiomatic in a comparison of persons; *has* in C wrongly suggests that the action was recently completed; and *also* in D and E is superfluous. This question is a little more difficult than the average.

11. Charlotte Perkins Gilman, a late nineteenth-century feminist, called for urban apartment houses including child-care facilities and clustered suburban houses including communal eating and social facilities.

(A) including child-care facilities and clustered suburban houses including communal eating and social facilities
(B) that included child-care facilities, and for clustered suburban houses to include communal eating and social facilities
(C) with child-care facilities included and for clustered suburban houses to include communal eating and social facilities
(D) that included child-care facilities and for clustered suburban houses with communal eating and social facilities
(E) to include child-care facilities and for clustered suburban houses with communal eating and social facilities included

The function and meaning of the *including . . .* phrases are unclear in choice A: for example, it is hard to tell whether Gilman called for urban apartment houses that included child-care facilities or whether such facilities represent one variety of the urban apartment houses she wanted built. Choice B resolves the ambiguity concerning *child-care facilities,* but *called for . . . houses to include . . . facilities* is unidiomatic in B and C. Choice D is best. In E, *to include* is again faulty. This question is more difficult than the average.

12. The odds are about 4 to 1 against surviving a takeover offer, and many business consultants therefore advise that a company's first line of defense in eluding offers like these be to even refuse to take calls from likely corporate raiders.

(A) that a company's first line of defense in eluding offers like these be to even refuse
(B) that a company's first line of defense in eluding such offers be to refuse even
(C) a company defending itself against offers of this kind that, as a first line of defense, they should even refuse
(D) companies which are defending themselves against such an offer that, as a first line of defense, they should even refuse
(E) that the first line of defense for a company who is eluding offers like these is the refusal even

Choice A is awkward and poorly phrased: *these* has no plural noun to which it can refer, and *even* should be placed immediately before *to take calls,* the phrase it modifies. Choice B is best. In C, the plural *they* does not agree with the singular *company, even* is misplaced, and *advise . . . that . . . they should* is unidiomatic. D has the plural *companies* but retains the other flaws of C. In E, *who* in place of *that* is an inappropriate pronoun for *company, these* does not agree with the singular *offer,* and *is the refusal* should be *be to refuse.* This question is difficult.

13. Japan received huge sums of capital from the United States after the Second World War, using it to help build a modern industrial system.

    (A) Japan received huge sums of capital from the United States after the Second World War, using it to help build
    (B) Japan received huge sums of capital from the United States after the Second World War and used it to help in building
    (C) Japan used the huge sums of capital it received from the United States after the Second World War to help build
    (D) Japan's huge sums of capital received from the United States after the Second World War were used to help it in building
    (E) Receiving huge sums of capital from the United States after the Second World War, Japan used it to help build

Choice A can be faulted because *it*, a singular pronoun, does not agree with *sums of capital*; also, *using* does not establish a logical time sequence in which Japan first received and then used the capital from the United States. In B, *it* is again wrong, and *to help in building* is less compact and idiomatic than *to help build*. Choice C is best. In D, *to help it in building* is flawed, and *it* has no free noun as its referent since *Japan's* is a possessive modifier of *sums*. In E, *it* is again without a singular noun referent, and *Receiving huge sums . . ., Japan used . . .* does not make clear the sequence of events. This question is of middle difficulty.

14. Although one link in the chain was demonstrated to be weak, but not sufficiently so to require the recall of the automobile.

    (A) demonstrated to be weak, but not sufficiently so to require
    (B) demonstrated as weak, but it was not sufficiently so that it required
    (C) demonstrably weak, but not sufficiently so to require
    (D) demonstrably weak, it was not so weak as to require
    (E) demonstrably weak, it was not weak enough that it required

Choices A and C entail ungrammatical constructions because they do not produce a sentence that has a main clause with a subject and a verb. In choice B, *demonstrated as weak* is unidiomatic; also in choices B and C *Although* and *but* should not be used together because only one is needed to express the relationship between the ideas. Choice D is best. Choice E is less concise and idiomatic than D; moreover, it is imprecise to say that *one link in the chain* (the referent of *it*) actually *required the recall*. The question is of middle difficulty.

15. Although the Supreme Court ruled as long ago as 1880 that Blacks could not be excluded outright from jury service, nearly a century of case-by-case adjudication has been necessary to develop and enforce the principle that all juries must be drawn from "a fair cross section of the community."

    (A) has been necessary to develop and enforce the principle that all juries must be
    (B) was necessary for developing and enforcing the principle of all juries being
    (C) was to be necessary in developing and enforcing the principle of all juries to be
    (D) is necessary to develop and enforce the principle that juries must be
    (E) will be necessary for developing and enforcing the principle of all juries being

Choice A is best: *has been* appropriately refers to recently completed action. In B, *was* does not indicate that the action is recent. Also, *necessary for developing . . .* is less idiomatic than *necessary to develop . . .*, and *principle of all juries being* is less direct than *principle that all juries must be*. The *to be* infinitives make choice C incorrect. The present tense *is* in D and the future tense *will be* in E make these choices faulty. This question is of middle difficulty.

16. The modernization program for the steel mill will cost approximately 51 million dollars, which it is hoped can be completed in the late 1980's.

    (A) The modernization program for the steel mill will cost approximately 51 million dollars, which it is hoped can be completed in the late 1980's.
    (B) The modernization program for the steel mill, hopefully completed in the late 1980's will cost approximately 51 million dollars.
    (C) Modernizing the steel mill, hopefully to be completed in the late 1980's will cost approximately 51 million dollars.
    (D) The program for modernizing the steel mill, which can, it is hoped, be completed in the late 1980's and cost approximately 51 million dollars.
    (E) Modernizing the steel mill, a program that can, it is hoped, be completed in the late 1980's, will cost approximately 51 million dollars.

Choice A can be faulted because *which* grammatically refers to *51 million dollars*, the nearest noun phrase. At any rate, it is not clear in choices A, B, C, or D whether the modernization program or the steel mill is supposed to be completed in the late 1980's. In B and C, the use of *hopefully* for *it is hoped* still meets with strong and widespread objection from many editors, lexicographers, and authors of usage handbooks. Aside from having an ambiguous *which*, D contains no independent clause and so cannot stand as a sentence. Choice E is the correct answer for this very difficult question.

17. Camus broke with Sartre in a bitter dispute over the nature of Stalinism.

   (A) in a bitter dispute over
   (B) over bitterly disputing
   (C) after there was a bitter dispute over
   (D) after having bitterly disputed about
   (E) over a bitter dispute about

Choice A is correct. In B, *over* is misused: the idiomatic form of expression is *broke . . . in,* not *broke . . . over,* and *over* should appear immediately before the issue in dispute (i.e., *the nature of Stalinism*). Choice C, wordy and imprecise, does not specify who was involved in the dispute. In D and E, *dispute(d) about* is less direct and idiomatic than *dispute(d) over.* Also, D is needlessly wordy and *over* is misused in E. This is a difficult question.

18. Nowhere in Prakta is the influence of modern European architecture more apparent than their government buildings.

   (A) more apparent than their
   (B) so apparent as their
   (C) more apparent than in its
   (D) so apparent than in their
   (E) as apparent as it is in its

Choice A is incorrect because *in* must appear after *than* and because the plural pronoun *their* does not agree in number with the singular noun *Prakta.* B also lacks *in* and misuses *their.* Choice C is correct. In D, *so . . . than* in place of *more . . . than* is unidiomatic, and *their* is again wrong. Choice E is confusing because *it* refers to *architecture* whereas *its* refers to *Prakta.* This question is a little easier than the average.

19. Federal legislation establishing a fund for the cleanup of sites damaged by toxic chemicals permits compensating state governments for damage to their natural resources but does not allow claims for injury to people.

   (A) compensating state governments for damage to
   (B) compensating state governments for the damaging of
   (C) giving state governments compensation for damaging
   (D) giving compensation to state governments for the damage of
   (E) the giving of compensation to state governments for damaging

Choice A is correct. Choices B, C, and E could be read as saying that state governments can be compensated for damaging their own natural resources. The phrasing in C, D, and E is needlessly wordy, and *for the damage of* in D is unidiomatic. This question is difficult.

20. The lawyer for the defense charged that she suspected the police of having illegally taped her confidential conversations with her client and then used the information obtained to find evidence supporting their murder charges.

   (A) used the information obtained to find evidence supporting
   (B) used such information as they obtained to find evidence supporting
   (C) used the information they had obtained to find evidence that would support
   (D) of using the information they had obtained to find evidence that would support
   (E) of using such information as they obtained to find evidence that would be supportive of

Choices A, B, and C are incorrect because *then* must be followed by a construction that parallels *of having* in line 2 — that is, by *of* and a present participial, or ''-ing,'' verb form. Choice D is best. Choice E is very wordy, awkward, and indirect. The question is of middle difficulty.

21. According to surveys by the National Institute on Drug Abuse, about 20 percent of young adults used cocaine in 1979, doubling those reported in the 1977 survey.

   (A) doubling those reported in the 1977 survey
   (B) to double the number the 1977 survey reported
   (C) twice those the 1977 survey reported
   (D) twice as much as those reported in the 1977 survey
   (E) twice the number reported in the 1977 survey

Choice A is phrased illogically in that it says the young adults in the 1979 survey somehow doubled the people in the 1977 survey, not that the *number* of young adults using cocaine doubled. The infinitive *to double,* used unidiomatically in B, carries the sense of *in order to double.* Again in choice C, *twice the number* would be preferable to *twice those (people).* It is not clear in choice D whether *twice as much . . .* refers to the number of young adults using cocaine in 1979 or the amount of cocaine they used. Choice E is best for this moderately easy question.

22. Inflation has made many Americans reevaluate their assumptions about the future; they still expect to live better than their parents have, but not so well as they once thought they could.

   (A) they still expect to live better than their parents have
   (B) they still expect to live better than their parents did
   (C) they still expect to live better than their parents had
   (D) still expecting to live better than their parents had
   (E) still expecting to live better than did their parents

Choice A is incorrect because *have* cannot function as the auxiliary of *live*; i.e., *have live* is ungrammatical. Choice B, which substitutes *did* for *have,* is correct and logically places the parents' action in the past. In C and D, *had* places the parents' action in the past but is wrong as an auxiliary, just as *have* is in A. Choices D and E are faulty because neither is the independent clause that is needed to complete a grammatical sentence. The question is a little more difficult than the average.

23. Europeans have long known that eating quail sometimes makes the eater ill, but only recently has it been established that the illness is caused by a toxin present in the quail's body only under certain conditions.

    (A) Europeans have long known that eating quail sometimes makes
    (B) Europeans have long known quail eating is sometimes able to make
    (C) Eating quail has long been known to Europeans to sometimes make
    (D) It has long been known to Europeans that quail eating will sometimes make
    (E) It has long been known to Europeans that quail, when it is eaten, has sometimes made

Choice A is correct. Choice B is awkward: *that* is preferable after *known* to introduce the clause describing what *Europeans have long known,* and *quail eating is . . . able* is unidiomatic. Choices C, D, and E are also awkward; moreover, *will . . . make* in D and *has . . . made* in E are inappropriate to describe a condition that holds true in the present as well as in the future or the past. This is a question of middle difficulty.

24. The caterpillar of the geometrid moth strikes when special tactile hairs on its body are disturbed, after capturing its prey, holds the victim so that it cannot escape.

    (A) strikes when special tactile hairs on its body are disturbed,
    (B) striking when special tactile hairs on its body are disturbed, but
    (C) which strikes when special tactile hairs on its body are disturbed,
    (D) which, striking when special tactile hairs on its body are disturbed,
    (E) strikes when special tactile hairs on its body are disturbed and,

Choice A is incorrect because it provides no word or construction that can form a grammatical link with the remainder of the sentence. By substituting *striking* for *strikes,* choice B removes the verb form that functions with *caterpillar,* the grammatical subject, to make a complete sentence. C is awkward and also ambiguous because it is not immediately clear whether *which* is meant to refer to *caterpillar* or *moth.* In D, *which* is again ambiguous, and with *striking* in place of *strikes, which* takes *holds* as its verb, leaving no verb for the subject of the sentence. Choice E is correct: *and* links the verbs *strikes* and *holds* to form a compound verb for the subject, caterpillar. This question is of middle difficulty.

25. In assessing the problems faced by rural migrant workers, the question of whether they are better off materially than the urban working poor is irrelevant.

    (A) In assessing the problems faced by rural migrant workers, the question of whether they are better off materially than the urban working poor is irrelevant.
    (B) The question of whether the rural migrant worker is better off materially than the urban working poor is irrelevant in assessing the problems that they face.
    (C) A question that is irrelevant in assessing the problems that rural migrant workers face is whether they are better off materially than the urban working poor.
    (D) In an assessment of the problems faced by rural migrant workers, the question of whether they are better off materially than the urban working poor is irrelevant.
    (E) The question of whether the rural migrant worker is better off materially than the urban working poor is irrelevant in an assessment of the problems that they face.

Choice A presents a dangling modifier because nothing mentioned in the sentence can perform the action of *assessing the problems faced by rural migrant workers.* Choice A states illogically that *the question* is assessing these problems. In B, the plural pronoun *they* cannot refer as intended to the singular *rural migrant worker.* C is awkward and ambiguous: again, *the question* is not *assessing the problems,* and *irrelevant in assessing* could be taken to mean either that the act of assessing the problems is irrelevant or that the question described is irrelevant in an assessment of the problems. Choice D is best. Lack of agreement between *worker* and *they* makes E wrong. This question is difficult.

Explanatory Material:
Reading Comprehension

1. According to the passage, some twentieth-century scholars have written at length about

   (A) Walter's persecution of his wife in Chaucer's *The Clerk's Tale*
   (B) the Duchess of Malfi's love for her husband
   (C) the tyrannical behavior of the Duchess of Malfi's brothers
   (D) the actions taken by Shakespeare's Desdemona
   (E) the injustices suffered by Chaucer's Griselda

The best answer is D because lines 12-16 state that "long essays" have been written by scholars about the "behavior of Shakespeare's Desdemona." This is a question of medium difficulty.

2. The primary purpose of the passage is to

   (A) describe the role of the tragic heroine in medieval and Elizabethan literature
   (B) resolve a controversy over the meaning of "poetic justice" as it is discussed in certain medieval and Elizabethan literary treatises
   (C) present evidence to support the view that characters in medieval and Elizabethan tragedies are to blame for their fates
   (D) assert that it is impossible for twentieth-century readers to fully comprehend the characters and situations in medieval and Elizabethan literary works
   (E) argue that some twentieth-century scholars have misapplied the concept of "poetic justice" in analyzing certain medieval and Elizabethan literary works

The best answer is E. The author argues in the passage that a school of twentieth-century scholars has inappropriately applied the concept of poetic justice to a number of medieval and Elizabethan literary figures, including the Duchess of Malfi, Desdemona, and Griselda. Thus the first paragraph describes these scholars as having "merely forced victimized characters" (line 6) into the framework of poetic justice, the second paragraph presents specific examples of the misapplication of poetic justice, and the third paragraph argues that it is readers "uncorrupted by the prejudices of some opinionated scholars" (lines 60-61) who can best judge medieval and Elizabethan literature. This is a question of medium difficulty.

3. It can be inferred from the passage that the author considers Chaucer's Griselda to be

   (A) an innocent victim
   (B) a sympathetic judge
   (C) an imprudent person
   (D) a strong individual
   (E) a rebellious daughter

The best answer is A, because lines 25-30 indicate that the author considers Griselda to be "a meek, gentle victim" who does not even criticize her husband, and thus is an innocent victim of his "oppression." This is a relatively easy question.

4. The author's tone in her discussion of the conclusions reached by the "school of twentieth-century scholars" (line 4) is best described as

   (A) plaintive
   (B) philosophical
   (C) disparaging
   (D) apologetic
   (E) enthusiastic

The best answer is C. The whole thrust of the author's argument is that the "school of twentieth-century scholars" referred to in line 4 has come to the wrong conclusions about a number of medieval and Elizabethan works. Thus she describes these scholars as having "merely forced victimized characters" into a framework (lines 6-7), "somehow or other" justified injustices (lines 7-8), subjected characters to "critical whips" (line 12), confounded poetic justice with social injustice (lines 39-41), and been corrupted by prejudices (line 60). In all these ways the author establishes a tone of disparagement toward these scholars and their work. This is a relatively difficult question.

5. It can be inferred from the passage that the author believes that most people respond to intended instances of poetic justice in medieval and Elizabethan literature with

   (A) annoyance
   (B) disapproval
   (C) indifference
   (D) amusement
   (E) gratification

The best answer is E, because lines 1-3 indicate that the examples of poetic justice that do occur in medieval and Elizabethan literature are very "satisfying" to the readers of that literature. This is a relatively difficult question.

6. As described in the passage, the process by which some twentieth-century scholars have reached their conclusions about the blameworthiness of victims in medieval and Elizabethan literary works is most similar to which of the following?

   (A) Derivation of logically sound conclusions from well-founded premises
   (B) Accurate observation of data, inaccurate calculation of statistics, and drawing of incorrect conclusions from the faulty statistics
   (C) Establishment of a theory, application of the theory to ill-fitting data, and drawing of unwarranted conclusions from the data
   (D) Development of two schools of thought about a factual situation, debate between the two schools, and rendering of a balanced judgment by an objective observer
   (E) Consideration of a factual situation by a group, discussion of various possible explanatory hypotheses, and agreement by consensus on the most plausible explanation

The best answer is C. The author describes the twentieth-century scholars as using a few clear examples of poetic justice as models for analyzing other literary works (lines 1-5). Their ''discoveries,'' the author implies, were cases that fit the model poorly, for she describes the scholars as having ''to 'find' further examples'' (lines 4-5), and as forcing characters into a moral framework (lines 6-7). The results of these activities, the author points out, are that these scholars deny obvious effects (lines 33-34), and ''confound the cooperation of poetic justice'' (lines 39-40). Thus the author portrays these twentieth-century scholars as establishing a theory, applying it to ill-fitting data, and then drawing from this data unwarranted conclusions. This is a relatively difficult question.

7. The author's paraphrase of a statement by Samuel Johnson (lines 55-63) serves which of the following functions in the passage?

   (A) It furnishes a specific example.
   (B) It articulates a general conclusion.
   (C) It introduces a new topic.
   (D) It provides a contrasting perspective.
   (E) It clarifies an ambiguous assertion.

The best answer is B. The author's point is that a group of scholars has misjudged a body of literature by holding too tenaciously to their preconceived theory about the prevalence of poetic justice in medieval and Elizabethan literature. In so doing they are unable to act as the authors of this literature intended their readers to act, and it is left to the average reader to serve ''as a court of appeal that remains free to rule, as the evidence requires, in favor of the innocent and injured parties'' (lines 52-55). The quote from Samuel Johnson serves to articulate this conclusion with precision, for it contrasts ''opinionated scholars'' (line 61) with ''the common sense and compassion'' (line 59) of average readers. This is a question of medium difficulty.

8. The author of the passage is primarily concerned with

   (A) reconciling opposing viewpoints
   (B) encouraging innovative approaches
   (C) defending an accepted explanation
   (D) advocating an alternative interpretation
   (E) analyzing an unresolved question

The best answer is D. The author begins by criticizing the use of the theory of ''poetic justice'' by a group of twentieth-century scholars, in particular condemning them for having to ''blame the victims themselves for their tragic fates'' (lines 10-11). In contrast, the author offers an alternative explanation, best expressed in lines 49-51: ''Thus, Chaucer and Webster, in their different ways, attack injustice, argue on behalf of the victims, and prosecute the persecutors.'' She analyzes two specific cases, Chaucer's Griselda and Webster's Duchess of Malfi, to substantiate this claim. She concludes with a paraphrase of Samuel Johnson that she uses to chastise the twentieth-century scholars and to reiterate her own alternative interpretation. This is a question of medium difficulty.

9. The primary purpose of the passage is to

   (A) criticize the inflexibility of American economic mythology
   (B) contrast ''Old World'' and ''New World'' economic ideologies
   (C) challenge the integrity of traditional political leaders
   (D) champion those Americans whom the author deems to be neglected
   (E) suggest a substitute for the traditional metaphor of a race

The best answer is A. The passage is structured so that the first paragraph sets out the basic issue to be explored—the nature of the dominant economic mythology in America—and the second paragraph provides the actual purpose of the passage—the presentation of a sharp critique of this mythology. In particular, lines 35-60 describe this mythology as resulting in sterile reform, not permitting change in the race metaphor, not honoring quiet work or social work or interdependence, and not valuing present achievements. Choice B is incorrect because the passage focuses mainly on the ''New World'' ideologies; C is incorrect because no one's integrity is challenged; D is only a supporting point; and E does not appear in the passage. This is a relatively difficult question.

10. According to the passage, ''Old World'' values were based on

    (A) ability
    (B) property
    (C) family connections
    (D) guild hierarchies
    (E) education

The best answer is B. In lines 6-11, ''the 'Old World' categories of settled possessiveness'' and ''the cupidity of retention'' are contrasted with the American categories of ''unsettling deprivation'' and ''the cupidity of seizure.'' This contrast is continued in lines 14-17: "We did not base our system on property but opportunity." All of these references state or imply that property was the basis for "Old World" values. This is a relatively easy question.

11. In the context of the author's discussion of regulating change, which of the following could be most probably regarded as a "strong referee" (line 30) in the United States?

    (A) A school principal
    (B) A political theorist
    (C) A federal court judge
    (D) A social worker
    (E) A government inspector

The best answer is C. Lines 31-34 describe the "strong referee" mentioned in the question as "a regulative hand to calm manic speculation; an authority that can call things to a halt, begin things again from compensatorily staggered 'starting lines.'" Of the choices, only C has sufficient and appropriate authority to satisfy this description. This is a relatively difficult question.

12. The author sets off the word " 'Reform' " (line 35) with quotation marks in order to

    (A) emphasize its departure from the concept of settled possessiveness
    (B) show his support for a systematic program of change
    (C) underscore the flexibility and even amorphousness of United States society
    (D) indicate that the term was one of Wilson's favorites
    (E) assert that reform in the United States has not been fundamental

The best answer is E. Lines 35-39 assert that "reform" has been "sterile because it can imagine no change" except in the terms already described by the passage. Since it is the entire thrust of the second paragraph that the race metaphor is the problem, "reform" that accepts this metaphor can in no way solve the underlying problem. The author signals this point by setting the word "reform" off with quotation marks. This is a question of medium difficulty.

13. It can be inferred from the passage that the author most probably thinks that giving the disenfranchised " 'a piece of the action' " (line 38) is

    (A) a compassionate, if misdirected, legislative measure
    (B) an example of Americans' resistance to profound social change
    (C) an innovative program for genuine social reform
    (D) a monument to the efforts of industrial reformers
    (E) a surprisingly "Old World" remedy for social ills

The best answer is B. The author implies, in lines 35-39, that Americans will not permit fundamental reform (i.e., social change); they will permit only sterile "reform," such as giving the disenfranchised "a piece of the action." Thus, giving

the disenfranchised "a piece of the action" is, for the author, an example of Americans' resistance to profound social change. This is a relatively difficult question.

14. Which of the following metaphors could the author most appropriately use to summarize his own assessment of the American economic system (lines 35-60)?

    (A) A windmill
    (B) A waterfall
    (C) A treadmill
    (D) A gyroscope
    (E) A bellows

The best answer is C. The author states in lines 58-60 that "There is no honor but in the Wonderland race we must all run, all trying to win, none winning in the end (for there is no end)." Of the choices given, only a treadmill fits this description of people running without end. This is a question of medium difficulty.

15. It can be inferred from the passage that Woodrow Wilson's ideas about the economic market

    (A) encouraged those who "make the system work" (lines 45-46)
    (B) perpetuated traditional legends about America
    (C) revealed the prejudices of a man born wealthy
    (D) foreshadowed the stock market crash of 1929
    (E) began a tradition of presidential proclamations on economics

The best answer is B. Woodrow Wilson's ideas about the economic market are mentioned in lines 1-4 and lines 47-48. Both appear in contexts that imply that Wilson's ideas are consistent with the "legends" (line 43) that Americans have traditionally held about their economic system. This is especially evident in lines 46-48, where it is noted that Wilson called specifically for "a return to the time when everyone was an employer," which corresponds to the legend that "There is no pride in being an employee." In articulating ideas such as these, Wilson was perpetuating traditional legends about America. This is a relatively difficult question.

16. The passage contains information that would answer which of the following questions?

    I. What techniques have industrialists used to manipulate a free market?
    II. In what ways are "New World" and "Old World" economic policies similar?
    III. Has economic policy in the United States tended to reward independent action?

    (A) I only
    (B) II only
    (C) III only
    (D) I and II only
    (E) II and III only

-341-

The best answer is C. Question I can be eliminated because the passage never mentions specific techniques of manipulation. Question II can be eliminated because the passage discusses only differences between the "Old World" and the American economic systems, not similarities. Question III can be answered on the basis of information contained in the passage. Lines 40-43 indicate that America is a land of change where "work that achieves social interdependence and stability" is not honored. What is honored is that which promotes constant change, the work of speculators, self-makers, and runners who consistently respond to new opportunities (lines 24-28). Thus those who are rewarded by the American economic system, according to the passage, are those who act independently. This is a very difficult question.

17. Which of the following best expresses the author's main point?

    (A) Americans' pride in their jobs continues to give them stamina today.
    (B) The absence of a *status quo ante* has undermined United States economic structure.
    (C) The free enterprise system has been only a useless concept in the United States.
    (D) The myth of the American free enterprise system is seriously flawed.
    (E) Fascination with the ideal of "openness" has made Americans a progressive people.

The best answer is D. The first paragraph compares Americans' ideas concerning their own economic system with "Old World" beliefs and provides a basis for criticism of the American view in the second paragraph. Thus, the main point of the passage is that the "myth" described in the first paragraph is "seriously flawed," as shown in the second paragraph. Choice A does not describe a point made in the passage. Choice B inaccurately states a point made in the passage. Choice C is an overstatement and does not articulate the idea of "myth" as it is developed in the first paragraph. Choice E does not convey the criticism that is the concern of the second paragraph. This is a question of medium difficulty.

18. According to the traditional view of the origin of the ocean basins, which of the following is sufficient to move the continental plates?

    (A) Increases in sedimentation on ocean floors
    (B) Spreading of ocean trenches
    (C) Movement of mid-ocean ridges
    (D) Sinking of ocean basins
    (E) Differences in temperature under oceans and continents

The best answer is E. The traditional view of the origin of the ocean basins is described in lines 3-21. Lines 6-7 state that, according to the traditional view, "differences in temperature under oceans and continents are sufficient to produce convection in the mantle of the earth." Lines 11-13 state that, according to the traditional view, "this convection would carry the continental plates along as though they were

on a conveyor belt." Thus, it can be inferred that the temperature differences are sufficient to move the continental plates, according to the traditional view. This is a relatively easy question.

19. It can be inferred from the passage that, of the following, the deepest sediments would be found in the

    (A) Indian Ocean
    (B) Black Sea
    (C) Mid-Atlantic
    (D) South Atlantic
    (E) Pacific

The best answer is B. Lines 42-58 discuss the enclosed seas, describing them in lines 45-47 as having "a typical oceanic floor, except that the floor is overlaid by several kilometers of sediment." From this it can be inferred that seas that are not enclosed do not have deep sediments on their floors. Of the choices, only the Black Sea is mentioned in the passage as an enclosed sea (lines 51-57). Therefore, it can be inferred that, of the five choices, the Black Sea has the deepest sediments. This is a question of medium difficulty.

20. The author refers to a "conveyor belt" in line 13 in order to

    (A) illustrate the effects of convection in the mantle
    (B) show how temperature differences depend on the positions of the continents
    (C) demonstrate the linear nature of the Mid-Atlantic Ridge
    (D) describe the complicated motions made possible by back-coupling
    (E) account for the rising currents under certain mid-ocean ridges

The best answer is A because "as though they were on a conveyor belt" in lines 12-13 refers to the manner in which convection in the mantle carries the continental plates along. The "conveyor belt" image enables the author to illustrate the effects of convection. This is a question of medium difficulty.

21. The author regards the traditional view of the origin of the oceans with

    (A) slight apprehension
    (B) absolute indifference
    (C) indignant anger
    (D) complete disbelief
    (E) guarded skepticism

The best answer is E. Throughout the passage, the author refers to the traditional view of the origin of the oceans in terms that indicate a cautious and doubtful but not totally disbelieving attitude. Lines 1-3 state, "No very satisfactory account of the mechanism that caused the formation of the ocean basins has yet been given." Line 15 says, "This view may be correct." Lines 22-23 say, "On the other hand, the theory is implausible because. . . ." Lines 26-27 add, "Also it is difficult to see how. . . ." Line 31 says, "It would be odd if. . . ." Taken together, these references convey an attitude of guarded skepticism, though not complete disbelief, toward the traditional view. This is a question of medium difficulty.

22. According to the passage, which of the following are separated by a plate that is growing on both sides?

    (A) The Pacific Ocean and the Sea of Japan
    (B) The South Atlantic Ridge and the North Sea Ridge
    (C) The Gulf of Mexico and the South Atlantic Ridge
    (D) The Mid-Atlantic Ridge and the Indian Ocean Ridge
    (E) The Black Sea and the Sea of Japan

The best answer is D because lines 27-29 mention "the plate between the Mid-Atlantic Ridge and the ridge in the Indian Ocean," and line 29 then refers to it, stating, "This plate is growing on both sides." This is a very easy question.

23. Which of the following, if it could be demonstrated, would most support the traditional view of ocean formation?

    (A) Convection usually occurs along lines.
    (B) The upper mantle behaves as a dense solid.
    (C) Sedimentation occurs at a constant rate.
    (D) Sinking plates cool the mantle.
    (E) Island arcs surround enclosed seas.

The best answer is A. If it could be demonstrated that convection usually occurs along lines, the objection to the traditional view that is stated in lines 22-24 would be removed, and the traditional view's assumptions about the way in which convection occurs would be supported. The other choices either contradict the traditional view (and thus would weaken it) or are irrelevant to it. This is a relatively difficult question.

24. According to the passage, the floor of the Black Sea can best be compared to a

    (A) rapidly moving conveyor belt
    (B) slowly settling foundation
    (C) rapidly expanding balloon
    (D) violently erupting volcano
    (E) slowly eroding mountain

The best answer is B. Lines 53-57 indicate that the Black Sea is an enclosed sea, and lines 47-48 state that the floors of enclosed seas "have probably been sinking for long periods." Thus it can be inferred that the floor of the Black Sea has been slowly settling. Since the floor of an ocean supports water in the same general way that the foundation of a building supports a building, the floor of the Black Sea can be compared to a slowly settling foundation. The passage provides no support for the comparisons in the other choices. This is a relatively easy question.

25. Which of the following titles would best describe the content of the passage?

    (A) A Description of the Oceans of the World
    (B) Several Theories of Ocean Basin Formation
    (C) The Traditional View of the Oceans
    (D) Convection and Ocean Currents
    (E) Temperature Differences Among the Oceans of the World

The best answer is B. The passage discusses three theories of ocean basin formation—the "traditional view" in lines 1-33, an "alternative theory" in lines 33-39, and a third theory in lines 42-58. These theories are the focus of the passage and constitute its entire content. Therefore, B is an excellent description of the content of the passage. Choice A is incorrect because the passage describes only a few oceans of the world and then only peripherally. Choice C is too narrow, leaving out two of the theories. Choices D and E refer to only small portions of the passage's content. This is a very easy question.

Explanatory Material: Data Sufficiency

1. Who types at a faster rate, John or Bob?

   (1) The difference between their typing rates is 10 words per minute.
   (2) Bob types at a constant rate of 80 words per minute.

Statement (1) alone is not sufficient to answer the question since it does not identify who types at the faster rate. Thus, the answer must be B, C, or E. Clearly (2) alone is not sufficient since it provides no information about John's rate. Thus, the answer must be C or E. From (1) and (2) together it can be determined only that John's rate is 70 or 90 words per minute; therefore, the best answer is E. This is an easy question.

2. What is the average distance that automobile D travels on one full tank of gasoline?

   (1) Automobile D averages 8.5 kilometers per liter of gasoline.
   (2) The gasoline tank of automobile D holds exactly 40 liters of gasoline.

Statement (1) alone is not sufficient because the capacity of the automobile's gasoline tank is not given. Thus, the answer must be B, C, or E. Statement (2) alone is not sufficient because the average mileage of the automobile is not given. Since (1) and (2) together supply both of these pieces of information, the average distance traveled per tank of gasoline can be determined; thus the best answer is C. This is an easy question.

3. If ℓ_1, ℓ_2 and ℓ_3 are lines in a plane, is ℓ_1 perpendicular to ℓ_3?

(1) ℓ_1 is perpendicular to ℓ_2.
(2) ℓ_2 is perpendicular to ℓ_3.

Clearly (1) alone and (2) alone are not sufficient to answer the question since neither statement alone gives any information concerning the pair ℓ_1 and ℓ_3. Thus, the answer must be C or E. From (1) and (2) together it can be determined that ℓ_1 and ℓ_3 are parallel rather than perpendicular, since two coplanar lines perpendicular to the same line are parallel. Therefore, the best answer is C. This is an easy question.

4. In a certain packinghouse, grapefruit are packed in bags and the bags are packed in cases. How many grapefruit are in each case that is packed?

(1) The grapefruit are always packed 5 to a bag and the bags are always packed 8 to a case.
(2) Each case is always 80 percent full.

Statement (1) alone is sufficient since it can be determined from (1) that the grapefruit are packed 40 to a case. Therefore, the answer must be A or D. Clearly (2) alone is not sufficient since it provides no information about how many grapefruit are packed in a case that is 80 percent full. Thus, the best answer is A. This is an easy question.

5. What is the value of x?

(1) $x + y = 7$
(2) $x - y = 3 - y$

Statement (1) alone is not sufficient since the value of y is not known. Thus, the answer must be B, C, or E. From (2) it can be determined that $x = 3$ after y is added to both sides of the equation. Therefore, the best answer is B. This is an easy question.

6. A rectangular floor that is 4 meters wide is to be completely covered with nonoverlapping square tiles, each with side of length 0.25 meter, with no portion of any tile remaining. What is the least number of such tiles that will be required?

(1) The length of the floor is three times the width.
(2) The area of the floor is 48 square meters.

From (1) it can be determined that the number of tiles required is $\dfrac{4(3 \cdot 4)}{(0.25)^2}$. Thus, the answer must be A or D.
From (2) it can be determined that the number of tiles required is $\dfrac{48}{(0.25)^2}$. Therefore, the best answer is D. This is an easy question.

7. If a rope is cut into three pieces of unequal length, what is the length of the shortest of these pieces of rope?

(1) The combined length of the longer two pieces of rope is 12 meters.
(2) The combined length of the shorter two pieces of rope is 11 meters.

Let x, y, and z be the lengths of the pieces, $x < y < z$. Statement (1) indicates that $y + z = 12$, and therefore $y < 6$ and $z > 6$. Since (1) alone provides no information about the value of x, the answer must be B, C, or E. Statement (2) indicates that $x + y = 11$, and therefore, $x < 5\frac{1}{2}$ and $y > 5\frac{1}{2}$. Thus, the answer must be C or E. From (1) and (2) together, it can only be determined that $5 < x < 5\frac{1}{2}$, which is a range of values and not a particular value. Therefore, the best answer is E. This is an easy question.

8. A certain company paid bonuses of $125 to each of its executive employees and $75 to each of its nonexecutive employees. If 100 of the employees were nonexecutives, how many were executives?

(1) The company has a total of 120 employees.
(2) The total amount that the company paid in bonuses to its employees was $10,000.

Let e be the number of executives and n the number of nonexecutives. From (1) alone it can be determined that $120 = 100 + e$, or $e = 20$. Thus, the answer must be A or D. The information in (2) can be expressed by the equation $10,000 = 75 \cdot 100 + 125e$, which can also be solved for e. Therefore, the best answer is D. This is an easy question.

9. What fraction of his salary did Mr. Johnson put into savings last week?

(1) Last week Mr. Johnson put $17 into savings.
(2) Last week Mr. Johnson put 5% of his salary into savings.

Clearly (1) alone is not sufficient since Mr. Johnson's salary is not given. Thus, the answer must be B, C, or E. But (2) alone is sufficient since $5\% = \dfrac{5}{100} = \dfrac{1}{20}$. Therefore, the best answer is B. This is an easy question.

10. For integers a, b, and c, $\dfrac{a}{b - c} = 1$. What is the value of $\dfrac{b - c}{b}$?

(1) $\dfrac{a}{b} = \dfrac{3}{5}$
(2) a and b have no common factors greater than 1.

Note that $a = b - c$, since $\frac{a}{b - c} = 1$; and so $\frac{b - c}{b} = \frac{a}{b}$.
Since (1) gives the value of $\frac{a}{b}$, (1) alone is sufficient. Therefore, the answer must be A or D. However, (2) alone is clearly not sufficient since the value of $\frac{a}{b}$ cannot be determined. Thus, the best answer is A. This is a moderately difficult question.

11. **If the price of a magazine is to be doubled, by what percent will the number of magazines sold decrease?**

    (1) **The current price of the magazine is $1.00.**

    (2) **For every $0.25 of increase in price, the number of magazines sold will decrease by 10 percent of the number sold at the current price.**

From (1) it can be determined that the price of the magazine is to be increased by $1.00, but no information is given as to what effect this price increase will have on sales. Thus, (1) alone is not sufficient, and the answer must be B, C, or E. Statement (2) indicates how sales are affected by price increases of $0.25 increments, but it does not indicate the number of such increments equal to the total increase. Thus, (2) alone is not sufficient, and so the answer must be C or E. From (1) and (2) together, it can be determined that sales will decrease by 40 percent of current sales. Therefore, the best answer is C. This is a moderately difficult question.

12. **If J, K, L, M, and N are positive integers in ascending order, what is the value of L?**

    (1) **The value of K is 3.**
    (2) **The value of M is 7.**

Note that $J < K < L < M < N$. From (1) it can only be determined that $L \geq 4$. Therefore, (1) alone is not sufficient, and so the answer must be B, C, or E. From (2) it can only be determined that $L \leq 6$; thus (2) alone is also not sufficient. From (1) and (2) together, $4 \leq L \leq 6$, that is $L = 4$, 5, or 6. But since the precise value of L cannot be determined, the best answer is E. This is a moderately difficult question.

13. **If a, b, and c are integers, is the number $3(a + b) + c$ divisible by 3?**

    (1) **$a + b$ is divisible by 3.**
    (2) **c is divisible by 3.**

Note that $3(a + b)$ is a multiple of 3 and so is divisible by 3 for any integers a and b. Thus $3(a + b) + c$ will be divisible by 3 if and only if c is divisible by 3. Statement (1) is not sufficient since it gives no information about c. Thus, the answer must be B, C, or E. However, (2) alone is sufficient, in view of the information given above. Therefore, the best answer is B. This is a moderately difficult question.

14. **Each M-type memory unit will increase the base memory capacity of a certain computer by 3 megabytes. What is the base memory capacity, in megabytes, of the computer?**

    (1) **2 M-type memory units will increase the computer's base memory capacity by 300 percent.**

    (2) **The memory capacity of the computer after 2 M-type memory units are added to the base memory capacity is 1.6 times the memory capacity of the computer after 1 M-type memory unit is added to the base memory capacity.**

Let c be the base memory capacity of the computer in megabytes. The information given in (1) can be expressed by the equation $6 = 3c$. Therefore (1) alone is sufficient, and the answer must be A or D. The information in (2) can be expressed by the equation $c + 6 = (1.6)(c + 3)$, from which the value of c can again be determined. Thus, (2) alone is also sufficient, and the best answer is D. This is a moderately difficult question.

15. **If $xyz \neq 0$, what is the value of $\frac{x^5 y^4 z^2}{z^2 y^4 x^2}$?**

    (1) **$x = 1$**
    (2) **$y = 3$**

Since $xyz \neq 0$, the expression $\frac{x^5 y^4 z^2}{z^2 y^4 x^2}$ is equal to x^3. Now it is easy to see that (1) alone gives the needed information and that (2) is irrelevant. Therefore, the best answer is A. This is a moderately difficult question.

16. **What fractional part of the total surface area of cube C is red?**

    (1) **Each of 3 faces of C is exactly $\frac{1}{2}$ red.**
    (2) **Each of 3 faces of C is entirely white.**

Neither (1) nor (2), considered separately, gives sufficient information to answer the question since each provides information about only three of the six faces. Therefore, the answer must be C or E. From (1) and (2) together, it can be determined that $\frac{1}{4}$ of the surface area of the cube is red. The best answer is C. This is a moderately difficult question.

17. **If positive integer x is divided by 2, the remainder is 1. What is the remainder when x is divided by 4?**

    (1) **$31 < x < 35$**
    (2) **x is a multiple of 3.**

Since x has a remainder of 1 when divided by 2, x is an odd integer. From (1), it can be determined that $x = 33$, since 32 and 34 are not odd integers. Therefore, (1) alone is sufficient, and the answer must be A or D. However, (2) alone is not sufficient, since an odd multiple of 3 may have a remainder of either 1 or 3 when divided by 4. For example, $21 = 4(5) + 1$ and $27 = 4(6) + 3$. Thus, the best answer is A. This is a difficult question.

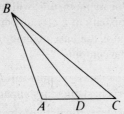

18. In the figure above, D is a point on side AC of △ABC. Is △ABC isosceles?

(1) The area of triangular region ABD is equal to the area of triangular region DBC.

(2) BD ⊥ AC and AD = DC

From the fact in (1) that the area of region ABD is equal to the area of region DBC, and the fact that the two triangles have the same altitude from B, it can be determined that AD = DC, but not that △ABC is isosceles. Thus, (1) alone is not sufficient, and the answer must be B, C, or E. From (2) it follows that △ABD and △DBC are right triangles. Since AD = DC and BD is a common side, it follows, by the Pythagorean theorem, that AB = BC, and so △ABC is isosceles. Thus (2) alone is sufficient, and the best answer is B. This is a difficult question.

19. If x is an integer, what is the value of x?

(1) $-2(x + 5) < -1$

(2) $-3x > 9$

Clearly (1) alone and (2) alone are insufficient since there is a range of integers for which (1) is true and a range of integers for which (2) is true. Thus, the answer must be C or E. To determine whether the two inequalities, taken together, limit the range sufficiently to determine the value of x, one must solve each inequality. Inequality (1) is equivalent to $x > -4\frac{1}{2}$, and inequality (2) is equivalent to $x < -3$. If x is an integer and $-4\frac{1}{2} < x < -3$, then $x = -4$, and the best answer is C. This is a difficult question.

Food	Number of Calories per Kilogram	Number of Grams of Protein per Kilogram
S	2,000	150
T	1,500	90

20. The table above gives the number of calories and grams of protein per kilogram of foods S and T. If a total of 7 kilograms of S and T are combined to make a certain food mixture, how many kilograms of food S are in the mixture?

(1) The mixture has a total of 12,000 calories.

(2) The mixture has a total of 810 grams of protein.

Let s equal the number of kilograms of food S in the mixture, and (7-s) the number of kilograms of food T in the mixture. Then (1) yields the equation

$$2{,}000s + 1{,}500(7 - s) = 12{,}000.$$

Since this equation may be solved for s, (1) alone is sufficient, and the answer must be A or D. Since (2) yields the equation $150s + 90(7 - s) = 810$, which can also be solved for s, the best answer is D. This is a difficult question.

21. If $y \neq 0$ and $y \neq -1$, which is greater, $\frac{x}{y}$ or $\frac{x}{y + 1}$?

(1) $x \neq 0$

(2) $x > y$

In approaching a question such as this, you should remember to consider the possibility of negative values of x and y. Note that $y < y + 1$ for all values of y, so that $\frac{1}{y} > \frac{1}{y + 1}$ for $y > 0$ or for $y < -1$, whereas $\frac{1}{y} < \frac{1}{y + 1}$ for $-1 < y < 0$. Thus, if $x > y > 0$, then $\frac{x}{y} > \frac{x}{y + 1}$, but if $y < x < -1$, then $\frac{x}{y} < \frac{x}{y + 1}$. Therefore, the order relation between $\frac{x}{y}$ and $\frac{x}{y + 1}$ cannot be determined from (1) and (2) together, and the best answer is E. This is a difficult question.

22. Each person on a committee with 40 members voted for exactly one of 3 candidates, F, G, or H. Did Candidate F receive the most votes from the 40 votes cast?

(1) Candidate F received 11 of the votes.

(2) Candidate H received 14 of the votes.

From (1), it can be determined that F did not receive the most votes since G and H received the remaining 29 votes, and G and H could not both have received less than 11 votes. Thus, from (1) alone it can be determined whether or not F received the most votes, and the answer must be A or D. From (2), it can only be determined that F and G received 26 votes combined; however, F may or may not have received more than 14 votes. Therefore, the best answer is A. This is a difficult question.

23. S is a set of integers such that

  i) if a is in S, then −a is in S, and
  ii) if each of a and b is in S, then ab is in S.
  Is −4 in S?

(1) 1 is in S.

(2) 2 is in S.

From (1) and the definition of S, it can only be determined that 1 and −1 are in S. Thus, (1) alone is not sufficient, and the answer must be B, C, or E. From (2) and part (i) of the definition of S, it can be determined that −2 is in S. Thus, (2) alone is sufficient, and the best answer is B. This is a difficult question.

24. If the area of triangular region *RST* is 25, what is the perimeter of *RST*?

(1) The length of one side of *RST* is $5\sqrt{2}$.

(2) *RST* is a right isosceles triangle.

It may be helpful to draw a figure:

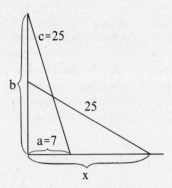

If the length of RT is $5\sqrt{2}$, then it can be determined that the altitude SU from S to side RT has length $5\sqrt{2}$, since $\frac{1}{2}(5\sqrt{2})h = 25$. If this altitude coincides with side SR, then $\triangle$RST is a right triangle and, by the Pythagorean theorem, the length of the hypotenuse ST may be computed and the perimeter determined. However, as the figure shows, side SR need not be perpendicular to side RT, in which case the perimeter cannot be determined. Therefore, (1) alone is not sufficient and the answer must be B, C, or E. From (2) alone, two sides of the triangle are equal and are perpendicular to each other. If these two sides have length x, then $\frac{1}{2}x^2 = 25$ and $x = 5\sqrt{2}$. Now that the lengths of the legs are known, the hypotenuse can be determined using the Pythagorean theorem, and then the perimeter of the triangle can be computed. Therefore, (2) alone is sufficient, and the best answer is B. This is a difficult question.

25. If *x* and *y* are consecutive odd integers, what is the sum of *x* and *y*?

(1) The product of *x* and *y* is negative.

(2) One of the integers is equal to -1.

If $x < y$, it can be determined from (1) that x is negative and y is positive, since the product of two negative numbers or two positive numbers is positive, whereas the product of a negative number and a positive number is negative. Since x and y are consecutive odd integers, $y - x = 2$, so x cannot be less than -1. Hence $x = -1$ and $y = 1$, and the answer must be A or D. However, (2) alone is not sufficient since it cannot be determined whether $x = -3$ and $y = -1$ or whether $x = -1$ and $y = 1$. Therefore, the best answer is A. This is a difficult question.

Explanatory Material: Analysis of Situations

1. A way to improve the quality of the World Camera

The correct classification for this consideration is E, an unimportant issue, because it is irrelevant to the decision being made. The decision-makers do not seek ''A way to improve the quality of the World Camera'' as an objective, consider it when evaluating the alternatives, or project it as an assumption. The first paragraph of the passage specifically states that World Camera Corporation is seeking to market the World Camera; there is no mention in the passage of improving the camera's quality. This classification is very easy.

2. General age-group pattern of Pomona, Corpus Christi, or Tampa Bay

The correct classification for this consideration is B, a major factor. Martin Miranda states in his third comment that ''we would like the general age-group pattern of the test market to be as close to the patterns of the other two test markets, Huntsville and Phoenix, as possible.'' Given this objective, the ''General age-group pattern of Pomona, Corpus Christi, or Tampa Bay'' is a major consideration because it is basic in determining which test market best meets the decision-makers' objective. This classification is very easy.

3. Unacceptability of any test market in which the total population exceeds 6 million

The correct classification for this consideration is D, an assumption. In his first comment, Frank Jardin states that ''we're looking for a test market that contains at least a million people but no more than six million.'' In other words, Jardin supposes or projects that cities with populations of less than one million or more than six million will not be appropriate test market areas for the World Camera. Notice that this consideration provides a framework for the decision: because Jardin believes a test market with a total population that exceeds six million is unacceptable, he sets as an objective the selection of a test market with a population of more than one but less than six million. This classification is difficult.

4. The number of people outside a proposed test market site who would see advertisements for the new camera

The correct classification for this consideration is B, a major factor, because it is explicitly identified in the passage as basic to reaching the decision. ''Also important,'' states Jardin in his second comment, ''[is] the index of media spill-out, that is, the number of people outside the test market who will see advertisements for the camera on television. . . .'' Media spill-out is among the primary criteria used by the decision-makers when evaluating alternatives. This classification is relatively difficult.

5. A test market in which sales of new products have conformed to sales of the new products when those products were marketed nationally

The correct classification for this consideration is A, an objective, because it is an outcome explicitly sought by the decision-makers. In his eighth comment, Jardin asks, "How closely have sales of new products in these test markets conformed to sales when the new products went on the market nationally?" The decision-makers then examine the past performances of the proposed test markets in this respect, weighing each performance in light of the objective of selecting "A test market in which sales of new products have conformed to sales of the new products when those products were marketed nationally." This classification is relatively difficult.

6. Determining the age-group that is most likely to purchase the World Camera

The correct classification for this consideration is E, an unimportant issue, because it is not relevant to the decision. "Determining the age-group that is most likely to purchase the World Camera" is not among the decision-makers' objectives, or among the factors they use when evaluating alternatives, or among their assumptions. In fact, the decision-makers already believe they know what age-group is most likely to purchase the World Camera. In his first comment, Martin Miranda tells Jardin: "Our research indicates that the 35- to 44-year-olds are the most likely customers for the new camera." This classification is very difficult.

7. Percentage of 55-64-year-olds in Tampa Bay

The correct classification for this consideration is C, a minor factor. According to the passage, the general age-group pattern of Pomona, Corpus Christi, or Tampa Bay is a major factor in the decision. Therefore, any single age-group segment in the pattern is a minor factor, bearing on this major factor. According to Jardin, the percentage of 55-64-year-olds in Tampa Bay is slightly higher than in Huntsville or Phoenix. This disproportion in the test population is a secondary consideration in reaching the decision and is therefore a minor factor. This classification is relatively easy.

8. Selecting a test market in which at least 20 percent of the people are between 35 and 44 years old

The correct classification for this consideration is A, an objective. As Frank Jardin states in his first comment, "we would like at least 20 percent of the population of the test market to be between the ages of 35 and 44." In other words, "Selecting a test market area in which at least 20 percent of the people are between 35 and 44 years old" is one of the goals sought by the decision-makers. This classification is of medium difficulty.

9. Recent change of camera suppliers in Tampa Bay

The correct classification for this consideration is C, a minor factor, because it is of secondary importance in reaching the decision. According to Jardin, one consideration that is basic to reaching the decision is "the ability of the World Camera Corporation to distribute the new product in each of these proposed test markets." He goes on to say, "It's vital that a distribution network already be in place." Goltz cites the distribution percentage in Tampa Bay as 44 percent, but Miranda adds that the actual percentage may be lower because of a change in camera suppliers. The "recent change of camera suppliers in Tampa Bay" is thus a minor factor, bearing on the size of the existing distribution network, a major factor in the decision. This classification is of medium difficulty.

10. A way to reduce the development costs of the World Camera

The correct classification for this consideration is E, an unimportant issue, because "A way to reduce the development costs of the World Camera" is not one of the objectives sought by the decision-makers, or a factor in their decision, or a supposition or projection they make. The World Camera has already been developed; its development costs are fixed and cannot now be altered. They do not bear in any way on the decision as to where the newly developed camera should now be test-marketed. This classification is very easy.

11. Importance of the 35- to 44-year-old age-group to sales of the World Camera

The correct classification for this consideration is D, an assumption. Among the decision-makers' stated objectives is to select a test market whose population is at least 20 percent 35- to 44-year-olds. According to Martin Miranda, "That's important. Our research indicates that the 35- to 44-year-olds are the most likely customers for the new camera." In other words, Miranda and the other decision-makers are supposing or projecting that the 35- to 44-year-old age-group is important or crucial to sales of the World Camera. They project that this group represents the largest pool of prospective customers. This supposition or projection, made on the basis of market research, provides a framework for the decision. It leads the decision-makers to set the objective of "Selecting a test market in which at least 20 percent of the people are between 35 and 44 years old." This classification is relatively difficult.

12. Percentage of two-income families in a proposed test market

The correct classification for this consideration is B, a major factor. In his second comment, Martin Miranda specifically cites this consideration as fundamental to the decision at hand: "We need to consider the percentage of two-income families in each test market as well, since two-income families are likely to have the discretionary income to spend on a luxury item like the World Camera." The "Percentage of two-income families in a proposed test market'' is thus a major factor, one that is basic to reaching the decision. This classification is of medium difficulty.

13. Number of cameras currently being sold in each of the test markets under consideration

The correct classification for this consideration is E, an unimportant issue, because it is not directly relevant to the decision. Jardin, Miranda, and Goltz are not interested in the total number of cameras being sold in Pomona, Corpus Christi, and Tampa Bay. They are interested solely in the percentage of camera outlets that sell World Camera products and would therefore be available to distribute the new camera. The "Number of cameras currently being sold in each of the test markets under consideration" is not one of the decision-makers' objectives, or a factor used to evaluate alternatives, or a supposition or projection made by the decision-makers. Therefore, it is an unimportant issue. This classification is relatively difficult.

14. A test market with a total population of at least 1 million

The correct classification for this consideration is A, an objective. Jardin explicitly states in his first comment that he and the other decision-makers are "looking for a test market that contains at least a million people. . . ." This classification is relatively difficult.

15. Number of 18-25-year-old college students in Pomona

The correct classification for this consideration is C, a minor factor. The "Number of 18-25-year-old college students in Pomona" is only one component bearing on Pomona's general age-group pattern and is therefore a minor factor bearing on the major factor "General age-group pattern of Pomona, Corpus Christi, or Tampa Bay." Like the percentage of 55- to 64-year-olds in Tampa Bay, the number of 18-25-year-old college students in Pomona is a secondary consideration in reaching the decision, and thus a minor factor. This classification is relatively easy.

16. Unlikelihood of finding a test market more suitable than the three under consideration

The correct classification for this consideration is D, an assumption. According to Jardin, the decision-makers have only three choices available for a third test market. He states in his first comment that "none of them is ideal, but we'll have to make the best choice we can." In this statement, he is assuming the "Unlikelihood of finding a test market more suitable than the three under consideration." In other words, he supposes that no prospective test market exists that would be more suitable than the three already under consideration. Note that this assumption provides a framework for the decision in that it forces the decision-makers to weigh only the three alternatives under consideration. This classification is of medium difficulty.

17. The number of people within each test market under consideration who watch television programs carried on stations outside the test market area

The correct classification for this consideration is B, a major factor. Jardin, in his second comment, states that "the number of people included in the test market who watch programs carried on television stations that are outside the test market," known technically as the index of media spill-in, is an important consideration. As part of the evaluation process, the decision-makers weigh the spill-in indexes of all three cities under consideration, measuring each against a standard of 0.8 or less. The spill-in indexes are thus a basic consideration, or major factor, in reaching the decision. This classification is relatively difficult.

18. Execuco's fee

The correct classification for this consideration is C, a minor factor. The passage indicates in several places that one of Cuomo's major requirements is that the search process be an economical one that minimizes cash outlay. Thus the cost of the search alternatives, including an Execuco search, is a major factor. Therefore, "Execuco's fee" is a minor factor because it contributes to or bears on this major factor. Note that this major factor is influenced by other minor factors, such as travel costs for all candidates who are interviewed. This classification is relatively difficult.

19. Alan Blake's lack of imagination

The correct classification for this consideration is C, a minor factor. Cuomo states explicitly in his fourth comment that Meddevco "need[s] the best qualified person" and that the relevant qualifications include "both managerial ability and imagination." The qualifications of the prospective candidates who would be found by means of each search method is logically a major factor in making the decision about which search plan to use. Alan Blake is one of the two prospective candidates if Meddevco chooses to promote from within, and therefore Alan Blake's lack of imagination would be a secondary consideration that would bear on that major factor. Note that several other considerations, such as Ted McClellan's lack of managerial ability, also bear on the major factor. This classification is relatively difficult.

20. Economy of cash outlay in the search

The correct classification for this consideration is A, an objective, because Cuomo states explicitly in his third comment that "we'd better make the search as economical as possible in cash outlay." That is, one of Meddevco's goals is "Economy of cash outlay in the search." This classification is difficult.

21. Low expenditure of time on the search by the director of personnel

The correct classification for this consideration is A, an objective. Cuomo, in his third comment, explicitly tells Rothstein, the director of personnel, that "I'd like you to try not to spend much time on [the search]." Therefore a "Low expenditure of time on the search by the director of personnel" is one of the goals sought by the decision-maker. This classification is difficult.

22. Need to fill the position of vice-president for research quickly

The correct classification for this consideration is D, an assumption. Cuomo, in his first comment, says that "it would be unwise to have the vice-presidency vacant for long"; he also says, in his third comment, "I want to complete the search quickly and hire someone who can take the job right away." In other words, Cuomo supposes or projects that there is a "Need to fill the position of vice-president for research quickly." This classification is very difficult.

23. Necessity of obtaining a special exemption if the search is not done in accordance with corporate personnel policy

The correct classification for this consideration is E, an unimportant issue. Since Cuomo states explicitly in his second comment that "I definitely want to comply with corporate policy," the issue of the "Necessity of obtaining a special exemption if the search is not done in accordance with corporate personnel policy" is irrelevant to the decsion being made. This classification is relatively difficult.

24. Appointment to the vice-presidency of a person who has experience in medical equipment research

The correct classification for this consideration is A, an objective. Cuomo, in his fourth comment, explicitly states that "experience in medical equipment research is also essential for success as vice-president for research." Since Cuomo obviously wants the new vice-president to be successful, it is clear that one of his goals is "Appointment to the vice-presidency of a person who has experience in medical equipment research." This classification is relatively difficult.

25. Hours that the director of personnel must spend reviewing resumés if Meddevco hires Execuco

The correct classification for this consideration is C, a minor factor. Cuomo states explicitly that he wants Rothstein, the director of personnel, not to spend much time on the search. It follows that the amount of Rothstein's time required by the search methods, including an Execuco search, is a major factor. Therefore, the "Hours that the director of personnel must spend reviewing resumés if Meddevco hires Execuco" is a minor factor because it contributes to or bears on this major factor. Note that this major factor is influenced by other minor factors, such as the time Rothstein would have to spend working with Execuco. This classification is relatively difficult.

26. Ages of candidates who would be considered if Meddevco either promotes internally or hires Execuco or does its own external search

The correct classification for this consideration is E, an unimportant issue. Since Cuomo explicitly states in his sixth comment, "We can't consider age," the "Ages of candidates who would be considered if Meddevco either promotes internally or hires Execuco or does its own external search" is irrelevant to the decision. That is, Cuomo does not seek this as an objective, use it to evaluate the three alternatives, or project it as an assumption. This classification is of medium difficulty.

27. Rapidity with which Meddevco can fill the vice-president for research position by either searching internally or employing Execuco or running its own external search

The correct classification for this consideration is B, a major factor. This can be determined from Cuomo's comment that "it would be unwise to have the vice-presidency vacant for long," and from his comment that he wants "to complete the search quickly and hire someone who can take the job right away." Therefore, it is logical that the "Rapidity with which Meddevco can fill the vice-president for research position by either searching internally or employing Execuco or running its own external search" will be a major factor because it is basic in determining how well a search plan will meet the objective of filling the vacancy as quickly as possible. This classification is relatively difficult.

28. Likelihood of poor performance as vice-president for research of any applicant who lacks experience in medical equipment research

The correct classification for this consideration is D, an assumption. Cuomo, in his fourth comment, says that "experience in medical equipment research is. . . essential for success as vice-president for research." In other words, Cuomo believes or supposes the "Likelihood of poor performance as vice-president for research of any applicant who lacks experience in medical equipment research." Note that this assumption provides a framework for the establishment of an objective: Cuomo's assumption that any applicant who lacks experience will perform poorly leads him to set the objective "Appointment to the vice-presidency of a person who has experience in medical equipment research." This classification is relatively easy.

29. Effectiveness of the three recruiting methods in providing Meddevco with women and minority candidates

The correct classification for this consideration is B, a major factor. One of Cuomo's objectives is to fulfill the spirit of the division's affirmative action plan "by giving full and serious consideration to women and minority candidates" (Cuomo's fifth comment). Given this objective, it is logical that the "Effectiveness of the three recruiting methods in providing

Meddevco with women and minority candidates'' will be a major factor because it will be basic in determining how well a recruiting method will meet the objective of fulfilling the affirmative action plan. This classification is relatively difficult.

30. Avoidance of excessive use of the president's and the vice-presidents' time for the search

The correct classification for this consideration is A, an objective. Cuomo, in his third comment, says, "We should also keep to a minimum the hours that the vice-presidents and I spend on the search." In other words, one of Cuomo's goals is "Avoidance of excessive use of the president's and the vice-presidents' time for the search." This classification is relatively difficult.

31. Compliance with the suggestion of the corporate senior vice-president for research

The correct classification for this consideration is E, an unimportant issue. Since Cuomo, in his fourth comment, explicitly states that, although the corporate vice-president for research has suggested promoting Ted McClellan, Cuomo doesn't "have to listen to him; this is my decision." Thus, "Compliance with the suggestion of the corporate senior vice-president for research" is irrelevant to the decision. This classification is of medium difficulty.

32. Number of women and minority candidates in Execuco's computer bank

The correct classification for this consideration is C, a minor factor. The passage indicates that Cuomo wants to give full and serious consideration to women and minority candidates. It follows that the number of minorities and women who would be considered under the search alternatives, including the Execuco alternative, is a major factor. The "Number of women and minority candidates in Execuco's computer bank" is a minor factor because it bears on and contributes to this major factor. Note that this major factor is influenced by other minor factors, such as Execuco's record of effectiveness in affirmative action recruiting. This classification is of medium difficulty.

33. Cost of conducting an internal search, an Execuco search, or a self-run external search

The correct classification for this consideration is B, a major factor. Cuomo stresses the need for an economical search process. He sets objectives of both "Economy of cash outlay in the search" and a "Low expenditure of time on the search by the director of personnel." Given these objectives, it is logical that the "Cost of conducting an internal search, an Execuco search, or a self-run external search" will be a major factor because this cost will be basic in determining how well a search plan will meet these objectives. This classification is relatively easy.

34. Charles Ryan's managerial ability

The correct classification for this consideration is E, an unimportant issue. Since Charles Ryan is leaving Meddevco, his managerial ability is irrelevant to the decision. This classification is of medium difficulty.

35. Cost of advertisements for the position of vice-president for research

The correct classification for this consideration is C, a minor factor. The passage indicates in several places that Cuomo wants an economical search process, one that minimizes cash outlay. It follows that the cost of the search alternatives is a major factor. Therefore "Cost of advertisements for the position of vice-president for research" is a minor factor because it contributes to or bears on this major factor. Note that this major factor is influenced by other minor factors, such as long-distance phone calls and travel. This classification is of medium difficulty.

Explanatory Material: Problem Solving II

1. **If x is an even integer, which of the following is an odd integer?**

   (A) $3x + 2$
   (B) $7x$
   (C) $8x + 5$
   (D) x^2
   (E) x^3

Since x is an even integer, it contains the factor 2 and any multiple (or power) of x contains the factor 2. Therefore, choices B, D, and E list expressions that must be even. The expression $3x + 2$ is even because it is the sum of two even integers. Since $8x + 5$ is the sum of an even integer and an odd integer, it must be odd, so the best answer is C. This is an easy question.

2. **On a purchase of $120, a store offered a payment plan consisting of a $20 down payment and 12 monthly payments of $10 each. What percent of the purchase price, to the nearest tenth of a percent, did the customer pay in interest by using this plan?**

   (A) 16.7%
   (B) 30%
   (C) 75.8%
   (D) 106.7%
   (E) 107.5%

The purchase price was $120, but the customer actually paid a total of $20 + 12($10) = $140. Thus, the interest is equal to the difference $140 − $120 = $20, and the interest as a percent of the purchase price is $\frac{20}{120} = \frac{1}{6} = 16\frac{2}{3}\%$. The best answer is therefore A. This is an easy question.

3. $\frac{5}{4}\left(42 \div \frac{3}{16}\right) =$

   (A) 6.3   (B) 9.8   (C) 179.2
   (D) 224   (E) 280

This computation can be done in a number of ways. Perhaps the easiest is: $\frac{5}{4}\left(42 \div \frac{3}{16}\right) = \frac{5}{4}\left(42 \times \frac{16}{3}\right) = \frac{5}{4}(14 \times 16) =$
$5 \times 14 \times 4 = 20(14) = 280$.
Thus, the best answer is E. This is an easy question.

4. When magnified 1,000 times by an electron microscope, the image of a certain circular piece of tissue has a diameter of 0.5 centimeter. The actual diameter of the tissue, in centimeters, is

   (A) 0.005
   (B) 0.002
   (C) 0.001
   (D) 0.0005
   (E) 0.0002

Let d be the diameter, in centimeters, of the piece of tissue. Then $1,000d = 0.5$, and $d = \frac{0.5}{1000} = \frac{5}{10,000} = 0.0005$ cm.
Thus, the best answer is D. This is an easy question.

5. In 1970 there were 8,902 women stockbrokers in the United States. By 1978 the number had increased to 19,947. Approximately what was the percent increase?

   (A) 45%
   (B) 125%
   (C) 145%
   (D) 150%
   (E) 225%

From 1970 to 1978, the number of women stockbrokers increased from approximately 8,900 to 19,900, an increase of a little more than 11,000. Thus, the percent increase is a little more than $\frac{11,000}{8,900}$, which is approximately $\frac{11}{9}$ or 122.2%.
The best answer therefore is B. This is an easy question.

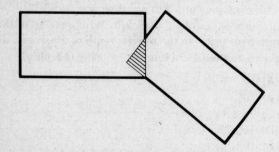

6. In the figure above, two rectangles with the same dimensions overlap to form the shaded region. If each rectangle has perimeter 12 and the shaded region has perimeter 3, what is the total length of the heavy line segments?

   (A) 15   (B) 18   (C) 21   (D) 22   (E) 23

The total length of the heavy line segments is equal to the sum of the perimeters of the two rectangles (24) minus the total length of the light line segments forming the shaded region. Since the total length of the light line segments is equal to the perimeter of the shaded region, the heavy line segments have total length $24 - 3 = 21$. The best answer is C. This is an easy question.

7. If one root of the equation $2x^2 + 3x - k = 0$ is 6, what is the value of k?

   (A)   90
   (B)   42
   (C)   18
   (D)   10
   (E) −10

If 6 is a root of the equation, then $x = 6$ must satisfy the equation. Thus, $2(6)^2 + 3(6) - k = 0$, and $k = 2(36) + 18 = 90$. The best answer is A. This is an easy question.

8. Bottle R contains 250 capsules and costs \$6.25. Bottle T contains 130 capsules and costs \$2.99. What is the difference between the cost per capsule for bottle R and the cost per capsule for bottle T?

   (A) \$0.25
   (B) \$0.12
   (C) \$0.05
   (D) \$0.03
   (E) \$0.002

The cost per capsule in bottle R is $\frac{625}{250} = 2.5$ cents. The cost per capsule in bottle T is $\frac{299}{130} = 2.3$ cents. The difference is $2.5 - 2.3 = 0.2$ cents, or \$0.002, so the best answer is E. This is an easy question.

9. Trucking transportation rates are x dollars per metric ton per kilometer. How much does it cost, in dollars, to transport one dozen cars, which weigh two metric tons each, n kilometers by truck?

   (A) $\frac{x}{12n}$ (B) $\frac{x}{24n}$ (C) $\frac{xn}{24}$

   (D) $12xn$ (E) $24xn$

The total weight of the 12 cars to be transported is $12(2) = 24$ metric tons. Since the cost per kilometer for 1 meter ton is x dollars, the cost per kilometer for 24 metric tons is 24x dollars. If the cost to transport the entire shipment is 24x dollars per kilometer, the cost is 24xn dollars for a distance of n kilometers. The best answer is E. This is an easy question.

10. For a positive integer n, the number $n!$ is defined to be $n(n - 1)(n - 2) \ldots (1)$. For example, $4! = 4(3)(2)(1)$. What is the value of $5! - 3!$?

   (A) 120   (B) 114   (C) 20
   (D) 15   (E) 2

$5! - 3! = 5(4)(3)(2)(1) - (3)(2)(1) = 120 - 6 = 114.$
Thus, the best answer is B. This is a moderately difficult question.

11. A man who died left an estate valued at $111,000. His will stipulated that his estate was to be distributed so that each of his three children received from the estate and his previous gifts, combined, the same total amount. If he had previously given his oldest child $15,000, his middle child $10,000, and his youngest $2,000, how much did the youngest child receive from the estate?

    (A) $50,000
    (B) $48,000
    (C) $46,000
    (D) $44,000
    (E) $39,000

The total value of the estate and the three previous gifts was $111,000 + $15,000 + $10,000 + $2,000 = $138,000. Since each child was to receive an equal share of this total, each was to receive $\frac{\$138,000}{3}$, or a total of $46,000. Therefore, the youngest child, who had previously received only $2,000 of the $46,000 share, received $46,000 − $2,000 = $44,000 from the estate, and the best answer is D. This is a moderately difficult question.

12. If $y > 0$, which of the following is equal to $\sqrt{48y^3}$?

    (A) $4y\sqrt{3y}$
    (B) $3y\sqrt{4y}$
    (C) $2\sqrt{12y}$
    (D) $3\sqrt{8y}$
    (E) $16y\sqrt{3y}$

To simplify, $\sqrt{48y^3} = (\sqrt{16y^2})(\sqrt{3y}) = 4y\sqrt{3y}$. Thus, the best answer is A. This is a moderately difficult question.

13. The volume of a box with a square base is 54 cubic centimeters. If the height of the box is twice the width of the base, what is the height, in centimeters?

    (A) 2
    (B) 3
    (C) 4
    (D) 6
    (E) 9

The volume of the box is $x^2y = 54$, where x is the length of a side of the square base and y is the height of the box. Since $y = 2x$, it follows that $x^2(2x) = 54$, or $x = 3$. Therefore, $y = 2x = 2(3) = 6$ centimeters, and the best answer is D. This is a moderately difficult question.

$$q = 3\sqrt{3}$$
$$r = 1 + 2\sqrt{3}$$
$$s = 3 + \sqrt{3}$$

14. If q, r, and s are the numbers shown above, which of the following shows their order from greatest to least?

    (A) q, r, s (B) q, s, r (C) r, q, s
    (D) s, q, r (E) s, r, q

In comparing q, r, and s, it is convenient to subtract $\sqrt{3}$ from each of the numbers and then to compare only the residues Q, R, and S; the order of q, r, and s will be the same as the order of Q, R, and S. Now $Q = 2\sqrt{3}$, $R = 1 + \sqrt{3}$, and $S = 3$. Clearly $Q > R$ since $\sqrt{3} > 1$. Also note that $Q^2 = 12$ and $S^2 = 9$; therefore, $Q > S$. Since Q is greater than either R or S, the answer must be A or B. If 1 is subtracted from both R and S, it can be seen that $S > R$ since $2 > \sqrt{3}$. Therefore $Q > S > R$, and the best answer is B. This is a moderately difficult question.

15. The sum of the interior angles of any polygon with n sides is $180(n - 2)$ degrees. If the sum of the interior angles of polygon P is three times the sum of the interior angles of quadrilateral Q, how many sides does P have?

    (A) 6   (B) 8   (C) 10   (D) 12   (E) 14

The sum of the interior angles of quadrilateral Q is 360 degrees, since Q has 4 sides and $180(4 - 2) = 360$. The sum of the interior angles of polygon P is $3(360) = 1,080$ degrees. Now $1,080 = 180(n - 2)$ where n is the number of sides polygon P has. When each side of the equation is divided by 180, $6 = n - 2$ and $n = 8$. Thus, the best answer is B. This is a difficult question.

16. In Company X, 30 percent of the employees live over ten miles from work and 60 percent of the employees who live over ten miles from work are in car pools. If 40 percent of the employees of Company X are in car pools, what percent of the employees of Company X live ten miles or less from work and are in car pools?

    (A) 12%
    (B) 20%
    (C) 22%
    (D) 28%
    (E) 32%

To solve problems of this type, where the categories are mutually exclusive, it is most convenient to organize the information in a two-dimensional table as shown below:

	10 Miles or Less from Work	More Than 10 Miles from Work	Total
Car Pool		18% (60% of 30%)	40%
No Car Pool			
Total		30%	100%

-353-

It is very easy to complete the table by finding the necessary percents to make the totals in each row or column. In this case, since a total of 40 percent of the employees are in car pools and 18 percent live more than 10 miles from work, 40 − 18 = 22% live 10 miles or less from work and are in car pools. Thus, the best answer is C. This is a difficult question.

17. If an organization were to sell n tickets for a theater production, the total revenue from ticket sales would be 20 percent greater than the total costs of the production. If the organization actually sold all but 5 percent of the n tickets, the total revenue from ticket sales was what percent greater than the total costs of the production?

  (A) 4%
  (B) 10%
  (C) 14%
  (D) 15%
  (E) 18%

Let p be the price per ticket. Then if n tickets were sold, total revenues would be np. Let c be the total cost of the production. Then, if np is 20 percent greater than c, np = 1.2c. Since only 95 percent of the n tickets were sold, 0.95(np) = 0.95 (1.2c) = 1.14c. Therefore, the total revenue from ticket sales was 14 percent greater than the total cost of production. Therefore, the best answer is C. This is a difficult question.

18. When the integer n is divided by 6, the remainder is 3. Which of the following is NOT a multiple of 6?

  (A) $n - 3$ (B) $n + 3$ (C) $2n$
  (D) $3n$ (E) $4n$

If the integer n has a remainder of 3 when it is divided by 6, then n is a number of the form 6q + 3, where q is an integer. Therefore, 6q + 3 can be substituted for n in each of the expressions listed until an expression is found that is not a multiple of 6 (does not have 6 as a factor). For example:
n − 3 = (6q + 3) − 3 = 6q;
n + 3 = (6q + 3) + 3 = 6q + 6 = 6(q + 1);
2n = 2(6q + 3) = 12q + 6 = 6(2q + 1);
3n = 3(6q + 3) = 18q + 9 = 6(3q + 1) + 3. Since the expression given for choice D has a remainder of 3 when divided by 6, it is not a multiple of 6. Therefore, the best answer is D. This is a difficult question.

19. How many liters of pure alcohol must be added to a 100-liter solution that is 20 percent alcohol in order to produce a solution that is 25 percent alcohol?

  (A) $\frac{7}{2}$

  (B) 5

  (C) $\frac{20}{3}$

  (D) 8

  (E) $\frac{39}{4}$

If x is the number of liters of alcohol that must be added to a solution that already contains 20 liters of alcohol (20% of 100 liters), then 20 + x liters must be 25 percent of the total number of liters in the new solution, which will consist of 100 + x liters. Therefore, the equation to be solved is 20 + x = 0.25(100 + x). This reduces to 20 + x = 25 + 0.25x, and 0.75x = 5. The value of $x = \frac{5}{0.75} = \frac{20}{3}$, and the best answer is C. This is a difficult question.

20. If 10 persons meet at a reunion and each person shakes hands exactly once with each of the others, what is the total number of handshakes?

  (A) $10 \cdot 9 \cdot 8 \cdot 7 \cdot 6 \cdot 5 \cdot 4 \cdot 3 \cdot 2 \cdot 1$
  (B) $10 \cdot 10$
  (C) $10 \cdot 9$
  (D) 45
  (E) 36

Each of the 10 persons shakes hands 9 times, once with each of the other 9 people at the reunion. Since there are 10 people, each of whom shakes hands with the other 9 people, it would seem at first that there are 10(9) or 90 handshakes. However, since each handshake was counted twice, once for each of the two people involved, the correct number of handshakes is $\frac{90}{2}$, or 45. Thus, the best answer is D. This is a difficult question.

Scoring Information

How to Calculate Your Scores: Form A

Your Verbal Raw Score

Step 1:	Using the answer key, mark your answer sheet as follows: put a C next to each question that you answered correctly; put an I next to each question that you answered incorrectly. Cross out any questions that you did not answer or for which you marked more than one answer; these will not be counted in the scoring.
Step 2:	Sections 2, 4, and 5 are used to determine your verbal score. In these sections only, count the number of correct answers (marked C) and enter this number here . . . . _____
Step 3:	In these same sections 2, 4, and 5, count the number of questions that you answered incorrectly (marked I). Enter the number here . . . . _____
Step 4:	Count the number of questions in sections 2, 4, and 5 that you crossed out because you didn't answer them or marked more than one answer. Enter this number here . . . . _____
Step 5:	Add the numbers in Steps 2, 3, and 4. Enter the number here . . . . _____ (This number should be 85, the total number of verbal questions. If it is not, check your work for Steps 2, 3, and 4.)
Step 6:	Enter the number from Step 2 here . . . . _____
Step 7:	Enter the number from Step 3 here $\dfrac{_____}{4}$; divide it by 4. (This is the correction for guessing.) Write the resulting number here . . . . − _____
Step 8:	Subtract the number in Step 7 from the number in Step 6; enter the result here . . . . _____
	+ _____.5_____
Step 9:	Add .5 to the number in Step 8. Enter the result here . . . . _____
Step 10:	Drop all the digits to the right of the decimal point and write the result here . . . . _____
	This is your verbal raw score corrected for guessing. Instructions for converting this score to a scaled score are on page 364.

Your Quantitative Raw Score

Step 1:	Sections 1, 3, and 6 are used to determine your quantitative score. In these sections only, count the number of correct answers (marked C) and enter this number here	_____
Step 2:	In these same sections (1, 3, and 6), count the number of questions that you answered incorrectly (marked I). Enter the number here	_____
Step 3:	Count the number of questions in sections 1, 3, and 6 that you crossed out because you didn't answer them or marked more than one answer. Enter this number here	_____
Step 4:	Add the numbers in Steps 1, 2, and 3. Enter the total here . . . . (This number should be 65, the total number of quantitative questions. If it is not, check your work for Steps 1, 2, and 3.)	_____
Step 5:	Enter the number from Step 1 here	_____
Step 6:	Enter the number from Step 2 here _____; divide it by 4. (This is the correction for guessing.) Write the resulting number here	− _____
Step 7:	Subtract the number in Step 6 from the number in Step 5; enter the result here	_____
Step 8:	Add .5 to the number in Step 7. Enter the result here	+ _____.5_____ _____
Step 9:	Drop all the digits to the right of the decimal point and write the result here	_____

This is your quantitative raw score corrected for guessing. Instructions for converting this score to a scaled score are on page 364.

Your Total Raw Score

Step 1:	Using all the sections of the test, count the number of correct answers (marked C) and enter this number here	_____
Step 2:	Count the number of questions in all the sections that you answered incorrectly (marked I). Enter the number here	_____
Step 3:	Count the number of questions in all sections that you crossed out because you didn't answer them or marked more than one answer. Enter this number here	_____
Step 4:	Add the numbers in Steps 1, 2, and 3. Enter the total here .... (This number should be 150, the total number of questions in the test. If it is not, check your work for Steps 1, 2, and 3.)	_____
Step 5:	Enter the number from Step 1 here	_____
Step 6:	Enter the number from Step 2 here _____; divide it by 4. (This is the correction for guessing.) Write the resulting number here .... $\dfrac{}{4}$	− _____
Step 7:	Subtract the number in Step 6 from the number in Step 5; enter the result here	_____
		+ _____.5_____
Step 8:	Add .5 to the number in Step 7. Enter the result here	_____
Step 9:	Drop all the digits to the right of the decimal point and write the result here	_____

This is your total raw score corrected for guessing. It is possible that the sum of your verbal and quantitative raw scores may be one point higher or lower than the total raw score due to the rounding procedures for each score. Instructions for converting this score — along with your verbal and quantitative raw scores corrected for guessing — to scaled scores are on page 364.

How to Calculate Your Scores: Form B

Your Verbal Raw Score

Step 1:	Using the answer key, mark your answer sheet as follows: put a C next to each question that you answered correctly; put an I next to each question that you answered incorrectly. Cross out any questions that you did not answer or for which you marked more than one answer; these will not be counted in the scoring.
Step 2:	Sections 1, 3, and 6 are used to determine your verbal score. In these sections only, count the number of correct answers (marked C) and enter this number here .... _____
Step 3:	In these same sections 1, 3, and 6 count the number of questions that you answered incorrectly (marked I). Enter the number here .... _____
Step 4:	Count the number of questions in sections 1, 3, and 6 that you crossed out because you didn't answer them or marked more than one answer. Enter this number here .... _____
Step 5:	Add the numbers in Steps 2, 3, and 4. Enter the number here .... _____ (This number should be 85, the total number of verbal questions. If it is not, check your work for Steps 2, 3, and 4.)
Step 6:	Enter the number from Step 2 here .... _____
Step 7:	Enter the number from Step 3 here $\dfrac{_____}{4}$; divide it by 4. (This is the correction for guessing.) Write the resulting number here .... − _____
Step 8:	Subtract the number in Step 7 from the number in Step 6; enter the result here .... _____
Step 9:	+ _____.5_____ Add .5 to the number in Step 8. Enter the result here .... _____
Step 10:	Drop all the digits to the right of the decimal point and write the result here .... _____
	This is your verbal raw score corrected for guessing. Instructions for converting this score to a scaled score are on page 364.

Your Quantitative Raw Score

Step 1:	Sections 2, 4, and 5 are used to determine your quantitative score. In these sections only, count the number of correct answers (marked C) and enter this number here	_____
Step 2:	In these same sections (2, 4, and 5), count the number of questions that you answered incorrectly (marked I). Enter the number here	_____
Step 3:	Count the number of questions in sections 2, 4, and 5 that you crossed out because you didn't answer them or marked more than one answer. Enter this number here	_____
Step 4:	Add the numbers in Steps 1, 2, and 3. Enter the total here . . . . (This number should be 65, the total number of quantitative questions. If it is not, check your work for Steps 1, 2, and 3.)	_____
Step 5:	Enter the number from Step 1 here	_____
Step 6:	Enter the number from Step 2 here $\dfrac{}{4}$; divide it by 4. (This is the correction for guessing.) Write the resulting number here	− _____
Step 7:	Subtract the number in Step 6 from the number in Step 5; enter the result here	_____
		+ ___.5___
Step 8:	Add .5 to the number in Step 7. Enter the result here	_____
Step 9:	Drop all the digits to the right of the decimal point and write the result here	_____
This is your quantitative raw score corrected for guessing. Instructions for converting this score to a scaled score are on page 364.		

Your Total Raw Score

Step 1:	Using all the sections of the test, count the number of correct answers (marked C) and enter this number here	_____
Step 2:	Count the number of questions in all the sections that you answered incorrectly (marked I). Enter the number here	_____
Step 3:	Count the number of questions in all sections that you crossed out because you didn't answer them or marked more than one answer. Enter this number here	_____
Step 4:	Add the numbers in Steps 1, 2, and 3. Enter the total here .... (This number should be 150, the total number of questions in the test. If it is not, check your work for Steps 1, 2, and 3.)	_____
Step 5:	Enter the number from Step 1 here	_____
Step 6:	Enter the number from Step 2 here _____; divide it by 4. (This is the correction for guessing.) Write the resulting number here	− _____
Step 7:	Subtract the number in Step 6 from the number in Step 5; enter the result here	_____
		+ _____.5
Step 8:	Add .5 to the number in Step 7. Enter the result here	_____
Step 9:	Drop all the digits to the right of the decimal point and write the result here	_____

This is your total raw score corrected for guessing. It is possible that the sum of your verbal and quantitative raw scores may be one point higher or lower than the total raw score due to the rounding procedures for each score. Instructions for converting this score — along with your verbal and quantitative raw scores corrected for guessing — to scaled scores are on page 364.

How to Calculate Your Scores: Form C

Your Verbal Raw Score

Step 1:	Using the answer key, mark your answer sheet as follows: put a C next to each question that you answered correctly; put an I next to each question that you answered incorrectly. Cross out any questions that you did not answer or for which you marked more than one answer; these will not be counted in the scoring.
Step 2:	Sections 2, 3, and 5 are used to determine your verbal score. In these sections only, count the number of correct answers (marked C) and enter this number here . . . . _____
Step 3:	In these same sections (2, 3, and 5), count the number of questions that you answered incorrectly (marked I). Enter the number here . . . . _____
Step 4:	Count the number of questions in sections 2, 3, and 5 that you crossed out because you didn't answer them or marked more than one answer. Enter this number here . . . . _____
Step 5:	Add the numbers in Steps 2, 3, and 4. Enter the number here . . . . _____ (This number should be 85, the total number of verbal questions. If it is not, check your work for Steps 2, 3, and 4.)
Step 6:	Enter the number from Step 2 here . . . . _____
Step 7:	Enter the number from Step 3 here $\dfrac{_____}{4}$; divide it by 4. (This is the correction for guessing.) Write the resulting number here . . . . $-$ _____
Step 8:	Subtract the number in Step 7 from the number in Step 6; enter the result here . . . . _____
Step 9:	$+$ ____.5____ Add .5 to the number in Step 8. Enter the result here . . . . _____
Step 10:	Drop all the digits to the right of the decimal point and write the result here . . . . _____
This is your verbal raw score corrected for guessing. Instructions for converting this score to a scaled score are on page 364.	

Your Quantitative Raw Score

Step 1:	Sections 1, 4, and 6 are used to determine your quantitative score. In these sections only, count the number of correct answers (marked C) and enter this number here	_____
Step 2:	In these same sections (1, 4, and 6), count the number of questions that you answered incorrectly (marked I). Enter the number here	_____
Step 3:	Count the number of questions in sections 1, 4, and 6 that you crossed out because you didn't answer them or marked more than one answer. Enter this number here	_____
Step 4:	Add the numbers in Steps 1, 2, and 3. Enter the total here .... (This number should be 65, the total number of quantitative questions. If it is not, check your work for Steps 1, 2, and 3.)	_____
Step 5:	Enter the number from Step 1 here	_____
Step 6:	Enter the number from Step 2 here _____ ; divide it by 4. (This is the correction for guessing.) Write the resulting number here	$-$ _____
Step 7:	Subtract the number in Step 6 from the number in Step 5; enter the result here	_____
Step 8:	Add .5 to the number in Step 7. Enter the result here	$+$ _____.5_____ _____
Step 9:	Drop all the digits to the right of the decimal point and write the result here	_____
This is your quantitative raw score corrected for guessing. Instructions for converting this score to a scaled score are on page 364.		

Your Total Raw Score

Step 1:	Using all the sections of the test, count the number of correct answers (marked C) and enter this number here	_____
Step 2:	Count the number of questions in all the sections that you answered incorrectly (marked I). Enter the number here	_____
Step 3:	Count the number of questions in all sections that you crossed out because you didn't answer them or marked more than one answer. Enter this number here	_____
Step 4:	Add the numbers in Steps 1, 2, and 3. Enter the total here . . . . (This number should be 150, the total number of questions in the test. If it is not, check your work for Steps 1, 2, and 3.)	_____
Step 5:	Enter the number from Step 1 here	_____
Step 6:	Enter the number from Step 2 here $\dfrac{\_\_\_\_\_}{4}$; divide it by 4. (This is the correction for guessing.) Write the resulting number here	$-$ _____
Step 7:	Subtract the number in Step 6 from the number in Step 5; enter the result here	_____
		$+$ ___.5___
Step 8:	Add .5 to the number in Step 7. Enter the result here	_____
Step 9:	Drop all the digits to the right of the decimal point and write the result here	_____

This is your total raw score corrected for guessing. It is possible that the sum of your verbal and quantitative raw scores may be one point higher or lower than the total raw score due to the rounding procedures for each score. Instructions for converting this score—along with your verbal and quantitative raw scores corrected for guessing—to scaled scores follow.

Converting Your Raw Scores to Scaled Scores

The raw scores corrected for guessing that you have obtained (last step in each worksheet) may be converted to scaled scores using the conversion tables on the following pages. Raw scores are converted to scaled scores to ensure that a score earned on any one form of the GMAT is directly comparable to the same scaled score earned (within a five-year period) on any other form of the test. Scaled scores are "standard scores" with understood and accepted meanings. The scores reported to schools when you take the actual GMAT will be scaled scores.

Using the conversion tables, for each form of the test that you took (A, B, C), find the GMAT scaled scores that correspond to your three raw scores (verbal, quantitative, total), corrected for guessing. For example, a verbal raw score of 44 on Form A would correspond to a scaled score of 31; a quantitative raw score of 44 on Form A would correspond to a scaled score of 37. A total raw score of 88 on Form A would correspond to a scaled score of 570.

When you take the GMAT at an actual administration, one or more of your scores will probably differ from the scaled scores you obtained on these representative GMAT tests. Even the same student performs at different levels at different times—for a variety of reasons unrelated to the test itself. In addition, your test scores may differ because the conditions under which you took these tests could not be exactly the same as those at an actual test administration.

After you have scored your test(s), analyze the results with a view to improving your performance when you take the actual GMAT.

- Did the time you spent reading directions make serious inroads on the time you had available for answering questions? If you become thoroughly familiar with the directions given in this book (in Chapter 1, Chapters 3-7, and the representative tests), you may need to spend less time reading directions in the actual test.

- Did you run out of time before you reached the end of a section? If so, could you pace yourself better in the actual test? Remember, not everyone finishes all sections; accuracy is also important.

- Look at the specific questions you missed. In which ones did you suffer from lack of knowledge? Faulty reasoning? Faulty reading of the questions? Being aware of the causes of your errors may enable you to avoid some errors when you actually take the GMAT.

What Your Scaled Scores Mean

The tables on page 368 contain information that will be of help in understanding your scaled scores. Each table consists of a column marked "Scaled Scores" and a column indicating the percentage of test takers in the time period specified who scored below the scores listed. For example, if you earned a total scaled score of about 600 on a representative test and you are able to achieve the same score on an actual GMAT, the 87 opposite 600 tells you that 87 percent of the 569,607 people taking the test in the 1982 to 1985 period earned scores lower than that; the remainder earned the same or a higher score. Also given in each table is the average score of the group tested in the 1982–1985 time period.

Graduate school admissions officers understand the statistical meaning of GMAT scores, but each institution uses and interprets the scores according to the needs of its own programs. You should, therefore, consult the schools to which you are applying to learn how they will interpret and use your scores.

Some Cautions about Score Interpretation

1. The GMAT is designed to yield only the reported verbal, quantitative, and total scaled scores. One should not calculate raw scores for individual test sections and infer specific strengths or weaknesses from a comparison of the raw score results by section. There are two reasons for this.

   First, different sections have different numbers of questions and, even if the numbers were the same or if percentages were used to make the numbers comparable, the sections might not be equally difficult. For illustrative purposes only, suppose that one section had 20 items and another had 25. Furthermore, suppose you received a corrected raw score of 10 on the first and 10 on the second. It would be inappropriate to conclude that you had equal ability in the two sections because the corrected raw scores were equal, as you really obtained 50 percent on the first section and only 40 percent on the second. It could be equally inappropriate, however, to conclude from the percentages that you were better on the first section than on the second. Suppose the first section was relatively easy for most candidates (say, an average corrected raw score percentage across candidates of 55 percent) and the second was relatively difficult (an average corrected raw score percentage of 35 percent). Now you might conclude that you were worse than average on the first section and better than average on the second.

   Differences in difficulty level between editions are accounted for in the procedure for converting the verbal, quantitative, and total corrected raw scores to scaled scores. Since the raw scores for individual sections are not converted to produce scaled scores by section, performance on individual sections of the test cannot be compared.

   Second, corrected raw scores by section are not converted to scaled scores by section because the GMAT is not designed to reliably measure specific strengths and weaknesses beyond the general verbal and quantitative abilities for which separate scaled scores are reported. Reliability is dependent, in part, on the number of questions in the test—the more questions, the higher the reliability. The relatively few questions in each section, taken alone, are not sufficient to produce a reliable result for each section. Only the reported verbal, quantitative, and total scaled scores (which include questions across several sections) have sufficient reliability to permit their use in counseling and predicting graduate school performance.

2. It is possible, if you repeat the test, that your second raw scores corrected for guessing could be higher than on the first test, but your scaled scores could be lower and vice versa. This is a result of the slight differences in difficulty level between editions of the test, which are taken into account when corrected raw scores are converted to the GMAT scaled scores. That is, for a given scaled score, a more difficult edition requires a lower corrected raw score and an easier edition requires a higher corrected raw score.

Verbal Converted (Scaled) Scores Corresponding to Corrected Raw Scores for Three Forms of the GMAT

Corrected Raw Scores	Scaled Scores			Corrected Raw Scores	Scaled Scores			Corrected Raw Scores	Scaled Scores		
	Form A	Form B	Form C		Form A	Form B	Form C		Form A	Form B	Form C
85	56	—	53	56	38	36	37	27	21	19	20
84	55	53	52					26	20	19	20
83	55	52	52	55	38	36	36				
82	54	52	51	54	37	35	35	25	19	18	19
81	54	51	50	53	37	35	35	24	19	17	19
				52	36	34	34	23	18	17	18
80	53	51	50	51	35	33	34	22	18	16	18
79	52	50	49					21	17	16	17
78	52	49	49	50	35	33	33				
77	51	49	48	49	34	32	33	20	16	15	17
76	51	48	48	48	34	32	32	19	16	15	16
				47	33	31	32	18	15	14	15
75	50	48	47	46	32	30	31	17	15	13	15
74	49	47	47					16	14	13	14
73	49	46	46	45	32	30	30				
72	48	46	45	44	31	29	30	15	13	12	14
71	48	45	45	43	30	29	29	14	13	12	13
				42	30	28	29	13	12	11	13
70	47	45	44	41	29	28	28	12	12	10	12
69	46	44	44					11	11	10	12
68	46	43	43	40	29	27	28				
67	45	43	43	39	28	26	27	10	10	9	11
66	44	42	42	38	27	26	27	9	10	9	10
				37	27	25	26	8	9	8	10
65	44	42	42	36	26	25	25	7	9	7	9
64	43	41	41					6	8	7	9
63	43	40	40	35	26	24	25				
62	42	40	40	34	25	23	24	5	7	6	8
61	41	39	39	33	24	23	24	4	7	6	8
				32	24	22	23	3	6	5	7
60	41	39	39	31	23	22	23	2	5	5	7
59	40	38	38					1	5	4	6
58	40	38	38	30	23	21	22	0	4	3	5
57	39	37	37	29	22	20	22				
				28	21	20	21				

Quantitative Converted (Scaled) Scores Corresponding to Corrected Raw Scores for Three Forms of the GMAT

Corrected Raw Scores	Form A	Form B	Form C	Corrected Raw Scores	Form A	Form B	Form C	Corrected Raw Scores	Form A	Form B	Form C
65	51	53	51	43	37	38	37	21	23	24	22
64	50	52	51	42	36	38	36				
63	49	52	50	41	36	37	36	20	22	23	22
62	49	51	49					19	22	23	21
61	48	50	49	40	35	36	35	18	21	22	20
				39	34	36	34	17	20	21	20
60	47	50	48	38	34	35	34	16	20	21	19
59	47	49	47	37	33	34	33				
58	46	48	47	36	32	34	32	15	19	20	18
57	46	48	46					14	19	19	18
56	45	47	45	35	32	33	32	13	18	19	17
				34	31	32	31	12	17	18	16
55	44	46	45	33	30	32	30	11	17	17	16
54	44	46	44	32	30	31	30				
53	43	45	43	31	29	30	29	10	16	17	15
52	42	44	43					9	15	16	14
51	42	44	42	30	29	30	28	8	15	15	14
				29	28	29	28	7	14	15	13
50	41	43	41	28	27	28	27	6	14	14	12
49	41	42	41	27	27	28	26				
48	40	42	40	26	26	27	26	5	13	13	12
47	39	41	40					4	12	13	11
46	39	40	39	25	25	26	25	3	12	12	10
				24	25	26	24	2	11	11	10
45	38	40	38	23	24	25	24	1	10	11	9
44	37	39	38	22	24	25	23	0	10	10	8

Total Converted (Scaled) Scores Corresponding to Corrected Raw Scores for Three Forms of the GMAT

Corrected Raw Scores	Scaled Scores			Corrected Raw Scores	Scaled Scores			Corrected Raw Scores	Scaled Scores		
	Form A	Form B	Form C		Form A	Form B	Form C		Form A	Form B	Form C
150	800	—	800	100	620	610	610	50	410	400	400
149	800	800	800	99	610	610	600	49	400	400	390
148	800	800	800	98	610	610	600	48	400	390	390
147	800	800	800	97	610	600	600	47	390	390	390
146	800	800	800	96	600	600	590	46	390	380	380
145	800	800	800	95	600	590	590	45	390	380	380
144	800	800	790	94	590	590	580	44	380	380	370
143	800	800	790	93	590	590	580	43	380	370	370
142	800	790	790	92	580	580	580	42	370	370	360
141	790	790	780	91	580	580	570	41	370	360	360
140	790	790	780	90	580	570	570	40	360	360	360
139	780	780	770	89	570	570	560	39	360	350	350
138	780	780	770	88	570	560	560	38	360	350	350
137	780	770	770	87	560	560	550	37	350	350	340
136	770	770	760	86	560	560	550	36	350	340	340
135	770	760	760	85	560	550	550	35	340	340	330
134	760	760	750	84	550	550	540	34	340	330	330
133	760	760	750	83	550	540	540	33	330	330	330
132	750	750	740	82	540	540	530	32	330	320	320
131	750	750	740	81	540	530	530	31	330	320	320
130	750	740	740	80	530	530	520	30	320	320	310
129	740	740	730	79	530	530	520	29	320	310	310
128	740	730	730	78	530	520	520	28	310	310	310
127	730	730	720	77	520	520	510	27	310	300	300
126	730	730	720	76	520	510	510	26	300	300	300
125	720	720	710	75	510	510	500	25	300	290	290
124	720	720	710	74	510	500	500	24	300	290	290
123	720	710	710	73	500	500	490	23	290	290	280
122	710	710	700	72	500	500	490	22	290	280	280
121	710	700	700	71	500	490	490	21	280	280	280
120	700	700	690	70	490	490	480	20	280	270	270
119	700	700	690	69	490	480	480	19	270	270	270
118	700	690	680	68	480	480	470	18	270	260	260
117	690	690	680	67	480	470	470	17	270	260	260
116	690	680	680	66	470	470	470	16	260	260	250
115	680	680	670	65	470	470	460	15	260	250	250
114	680	670	670	64	470	460	460	14	250	250	250
113	670	670	660	63	460	460	450	13	250	240	240
112	670	670	660	62	460	450	450	12	250	240	240
111	670	660	660	61	450	450	440	11	240	230	230
110	660	660	650	60	450	440	440	10	240	230	230
109	660	650	650	59	440	440	440	9	230	230	220
108	650	650	640	58	440	440	430	8	230	220	220
107	650	640	640	57	440	430	430	7	220	220	220
106	640	640	630	56	430	430	420	6	220	210	210
105	640	640	630	55	430	420	420	5	220	210	210
104	640	630	630	54	420	420	410	4	210	200	200
103	630	630	620	53	420	410	410	3	210	200	200
102	630	620	620	52	410	410	410	2	200	200	200
101	620	620	610	51	410	410	400	1	200	200	200
								0	200	200	200

Test Content

If you have questions about specific items in the representative tests or in any of the sample tests included in Chapters 3–7, please write to School and Higher Education Test Development, Educational Testing Service, CN 6656, Princeton, NJ 08541-6656. Please include in your letter the page number on which the item appears and the number of the question, along with specifics of your inquiry or comment. If you have a question about a particular item or items in an actual GMAT, please write to the same address and include in your letter your name, address, sex, date of birth, the date on which you took the test, the test center name, the section number(s) and number(s) of the questions involved. This information is necessary for ETS to retrieve your answer sheet and determine the particular form of the GMAT you took.

Percentages of Examinees Tested from June 1982 through March 1985 (including Repeaters) Who Scored below Selected Total Test Scores

Scaled Scores	Percentages below
720-800	99 +
700	99
680	97
660	96
640	94
620	91
600	87
580	82
560	76
540	70
520	63
500	56
480	48
460	41
440	34
420	27
400	21
380	16
360	12
340	9
320	6
300	4
280	3
260	2
240	1
220	1 –
Number of Examinees	569,607*
Average Score	478

*Self-selected sample

Percentages of Examinees Tested from June 1982 through March 1985 (including Repeaters) Who Scored below Selected Verbal and Quantitative Test Scores

Scaled Scores	Percentages below	
	Verbal	Quantitative
48-60	99 +	99
46	99	98
44	98	96
42	95	93
40	92	89
38	88	84
36	82	79
34	75	71
32	68	64
30	60	55
28	50	47
26	42	38
24	34	29
22	27	22
20	21	15
18	15	10
16	11	6
14	8	3
12	5	1
10	3	1 –
8	2	—
6	1 –	—
Number of Candidates	569,607*	569,607*
Average Score	27	29

*Self-selected sample

Guidelines for Use of Graduate Management Admission Test Scores

Introduction

These guidelines have been prepared to provide information about appropriate score use for those who interpret scores and set criteria for admission and to protect students from unfair decisions based on inappropriate use of scores.

The guidelines are based on several policy and psychometric considerations.

- The Graduate Management Admission Council has an obligation to inform users of the scores' strengths and limitations and the users have a concomitant obligation to use the scores in an appropriate, rather than the most convenient, manner.

- The purpose of any testing instrument, including the Graduate Management Admission Test, is to provide information to *assist* in making decisions; the test alone should not be presumed to be a decision maker.

- GMAT test scores are but one of a number of sources of information and should be used, whenever possible, in combination with other information and, in every case, with full recognition of what the test can and cannot do.

The primary asset of the GMAT is that it provides a common measure, administered under standard conditions, with known reliability, validity, and other psychometric qualities, for evaluating the academic skills of many individuals. The GMAT has two primary limitations: (1) it cannot and does not measure all the qualities important for graduate study in management and other pursuits, whether in education, career, or other areas of experience; (2) there are psychometric limitations to the test —for example, only score differences of certain magnitudes are reliable indicators of real differences in performance. Such limits should be taken into consideration as GMAT scores are used.

These guidelines consist of general standards and recommended appropriate uses of GMAT scores as well as a listing of inappropriate uses.

Specific Guidelines

1. **In recognition of the test's limitations, use multiple criteria.** Multiple sources of information should be used when evaluating an applicant for graduate management study. The GMAT itself does not measure every discipline-related skill necessary for academic work, nor does it measure subjective factors important to academic and career success, such as motivation, creativity, and interpersonal skills. Therefore, all available pertinent information about an applicant must be considered before a selection decision is made, with GMAT scores being *only* one of these several criteria. The test's limitations are discussed clearly in the GMAT *Bulletin of Information* and in the *GMAT Technical Report.*

2. **Establish the relationship between GMAT scores and performance in your graduate management school.** is incumbent on any institution using GMAT scores in the admissions process that it demonstrate empirically the relationship between test scores and measures of performance in its academic program. Data should be collected and analyzed to provide information about the predictive validity of GMAT scores and their appropriateness for the particular use and in the particular circumstances at the score-using school. In addition, any formula used in the admissions process that combines test scores with other criteria should be validated to determine whether the weights attached to the particular measures are appropriate for optimizing the prediction of performance in the program. Once set, these weights should be reviewed regularly through the considered deliberation of qualified experts.

3. **Avoid the use of cutoff scores.** The use of arbitrary cutoff scores (below which no applicant will be considered for admission) is strongly discouraged, primarily for the reasons cited in the introduction to these guidelines. Distinctions based on score differences not substantial enough to be reliable should be avoided. (For information about reliability, see the GMAT *Bulletin of Information*.) Cutoff scores should be used only if there is clear empirical evidence that a large proportion of the applicants scoring below the cutoff scores have substantial difficulty doing satisfactory graduate work. In addition, it is incumbent on the school to demonstrate that the use of cutoff scores does not result in the systematic exclusion of members of either sex, of any age or ethnic groups, or of any other relevant groups in the face of other evidence that would indicate their competence or predict their success.

4. **Do not compare GMAT scores with those on other tests.** GMAT scores cannot be derived from scores on other tests. While minor differences among different editions of the GMAT that have been constructed to be parallel can be compensated for by the statistical process of score equating, the GMAT is not intended to be parallel to graduate admission tests offered by other testing programs.

5. **Handicapped persons.** The GMAT is offered with special arrangements to accommodate the needs of candidates with visual, physical, and learning disabilities. However, no studies have been performed to validate GMAT scores earned under nonstandard conditions. Therefore, test scores earned under nonstandard conditions are reported with a special notice that handicapped persons may be at a disadvantage when taking standardized tests such as the GMAT, even when the test is administered in a manner chosen by the candidate to minimize any adverse effect of his or her disability on test performance. In using these scores, admissions officers should note the usual caution that GMAT scores be considered as only one part of an applicant's record.

Normally Appropriate Uses of GMAT Scores

1. **For selection of applicants for graduate study in management.** A person's GMAT scores tell how the person performed on a test designed to measure general verbal and quantitative abilities that are associated with success in the first year of study at graduate schools of management and that have been developed over a long period of time. The scores can be used in conjunction with other information to help estimate performance in a graduate management program.

2. **For selection of applicants for financial aid based on academic potential.**

3. **For counseling and guidance.** Undergraduate counselors, if they maintain appropriate records, such as the test scores and undergraduate grade-point averages of their students accepted by various graduate management programs, may be able to help students estimate their chances of acceptance at given graduate management schools.

Normally Inappropriate Uses of GMAT Scores

1. **As a requisite for awarding a degree.** The GMAT is designed to measure broadly defined verbal and quantitative skills and is primarily useful for predicting success in graduate management schools. The use of the test for anything other than selection for graduate management study, financial aid awards, or counseling and guidance is to be avoided.

2. **As a requirement for employment, for licensing or certification to perform a job, or for job-related rewards (raises, promotions, etc.).** For the reasons listed in #1 above, the use of the GMAT for these purposes is inappropriate. Further, approved score-receiving institutions are not permitted to make score reports available for any of these purposes.

3. **As an achievement test.** The GMAT is not designed to assess an applicant's achievement or knowledge in specific subject areas.

4. **As a diagnostic test.** Beyond general statements about verbal and quantitative ability, the GMAT does not provide diagnostic information about relative strengths of a person's academic abilities.

Public Interest Principles for the Design and Use of Admissions Testing Programs

The Graduate Management Admission Council has formally adopted as policy these Public Interest Principles for the Design and Use of Admissions Testing Programs. The principles were originally proposed for public discussion on December 30, 1979, by the leaders of the GMAC, Educational Testing Service, and three other organizations responsible for major admissions testing programs. They address concerns that have been raised about the design and use of standardized tests in admission to higher education, e.g., public access to test questions and answers, verification of scoring procedures, and appropriate use of the information derived from the testing programs. The GMAC strongly supports the principles and is committed to implementing them within the Graduate Management Admission Test program.

Principles

A number of the principles enumerated below have been cornerstones of most testing programs for some years. We believe it is important, however, to reaffirm them here to provide a fuller view of our beliefs and our expectations for the future.

1. We recognize the legitimate interest of the public in knowing what the tests contain and their efficacy in performing their intended functions. Therefore, we will implement the principle of publication of test content to a degree limited only by reasonable safeguards of efficiency, cost, quality, and the educational impact of the programs.

2. We fully support the principle of equity, and we will continue to maintain and strengthen credible procedures for detecting bias and eliminating it from the content of the tests, while making such procedures visible to the public.

3. We recognize the need for routine procedures that allow the test taker to arrange for verification of the accuracy of the procedures determining the score attributed to him or her.

4. We believe that tests should be readily available to all individuals, regardless of conditions such as physical handicap or religious beliefs that may prevent the taking of exams under circumstances that meet the convenience of the majority.

5. We recognize that tests, together with the procedures for scoring them and reporting the results, should be designed to provide test takers with as much useful information as may be feasible about the specifics of their performance on the tests.

6. We affirm the right of individuals and institutions to privacy with regard to information by and about them, which should be safeguarded from unauthorized disclosure.

7. We recognize the need to formulate, maintain, and publish widely principles of appropriate use of scores and other test information derived from testing programs and to be alert to and actively discourage misuse.

8. We recognize that both the institutions making use of test scores and the test takers themselves should have mechanisms through which to express their legitimate interests concerning the design and operation of testing programs and the use of the information derived from them.

Operational Elements

The separately constituted and governed groups sponsoring testing programs may choose to implement these principles in different ways. This probable diversity stems from differences in the nature and purposes of the tests in the several programs and from the specifics of their structure and operation. Examples of possible approaches include the following:

1. Each prospective examinee should be able to receive a full-length sample of each test, similar to the one he or she will take, with the intended answers and with instructions for self-administration and self-scoring.

2. For tests given to a sufficient number of students annually to support the cost, at least one operational form of the test should be published periodically, in addition to the regular sample. A specific schedule of publication should be designated for each program.

3. Nontechnical information about the testing program should be furnished routinely to test takers, users, and the general public. It should include a description of what each test measures, the error of measurement, how the scores are intended to be used, and a summary of the validity of the scores for the intended uses.

4. A technical publication should provide information on the same topics in sufficient depth to permit professionals in the field to assess the evidence and the accuracy of the nontechnical summary.

5. Studies of the use of the test by professionals other than those in the sponsoring or administering agency should be actively encouraged and facilitated byd provision of the necessary data with safeguards for individual privacy. The results of those studies should be published in regular journals and also incorporated in the technical and non-technical publications.

6. The test sponsor should ensure that operational forms of the test are independently reviewed before they are given. The review should include the appropriateness of the content of the test and in particular should seek to detect and remove potential racial, cultural, or sex bias or other influences extrinsic to the characteristics, skills, or knowledge to be measured. The review should also determine that the operational form is fairly represented by the sample test already distributed.

7. Test takers should have the right to question the accuracy of scoring, administrative procedures, specific questions in a test, or allegations of irregularities in test administrations. Current procedures to deal with this right should be reviewed and modified if necessary to ensure a fair and prompt response.

We hope communication of these principles and operational guidelines leads to greater understanding and constructive dialogue about the important issues surrounding testing. We stand ready to work with all interested groups in discussion of the policies and improvement of the procedures under which testing programs are conducted.

Order Forms for the Official Guides

Both *The Official Guide for GMAT Review* and *The Official Guide to MBA Programs* are sold in many bookstores at the list price of $9.95 each. They (and *The Official Software for GMAT Review*) may also be ordered directly from ETS. Fill out the order form and mailing label below and send it with the appropriate payment to ETS, either with your GMAT registration form or in a separate envelope addressed to Graduate Management Admission Test, Educational Testing Service, CN 6108, Princeton, NJ 08541-6108.

All orders to be sent to addresses in the United States or U.S. territories will be shipped by priority mail (first class) at no additional charge. Please allow two weeks for delivery to U.S. addresses.

For delivery outside the United States and its territories, allow about four weeks. Be sure to check the appropriate box on the order form.

– – – – – – – – – – – – – – CUT HERE TO DETACH – – – – – – – – – – – – – –

> Complete the address label at the right and enclose both this order form and the address label with a check or money order made payable to Graduate Management Admission Test. **Do not send cash.** Orders received without payment cannot be processed.

My payment is enclosed for:

	U.S. Priority delivery*	Foreign Airmail**
Both books	☐ $17.00	☐ $ 33.00
The Official Guide for GMAT Review	☐ $ 9.95	☐ $ 21.95
The Official Guide to MBA Programs	☐ $ 9.95	☐ $ 21.95
The Official Software for GMAT Review (including *The Official Guide for GMAT Review*)		
Apple II version	☐ $79.95	☐ $ 95.00
IBM PC version	☐ $79.95	☐ $ 95.00
The Official Software for GMAT Review (with *The Official Guide for GMAT Review* and *The Official Guide to MBA Programs*)		
Apple II version	☐ $85.00	☐ $110.00
IBM PC version	☐ $85.00	☐ $110.00

* Airmail delivery to United States, Guam, Puerto Rico, U.S. Virgin Islands, and U.S. territories
**Airmail delivery to countries and areas other than those named above

(address label, right side:)

Graduate Management Admission Test
Educational Testing Service
CN 6108
Princeton, NJ 08541-6108

(Please print.)

Name
Number and
Street

City

Country

State or
Province

Zip or
Postal Code

DO NOT DETACH

692-82

– – – – – – – – – – – – – – CUT HERE TO DETACH – – – – – – – – – – – – – –

> Complete the address label at the right and enclose both this order form and the address label with a check or money order made payable to Graduate Management Admission Test. **Do not send cash.** Orders received without payment cannot be processed.

My payment is enclosed for:

	U.S. Priority delivery*	Foreign Airmail**
Both books	☐ $17.00	☐ $ 33.00
The Official Guide for GMAT Review	☐ $ 9.95	☐ $ 21.95
The Official Guide to MBA Programs	☐ $ 9.95	☐ $ 21.95
The Official Software for GMAT Review (including *The Official Guide for GMAT Review*)		
Apple II version	☐ $79.95	☐ $ 95.00
IBM PC version	☐ $79.95	☐ $ 95.00
The Official Software for GMAT Review (with *The Official Guide for GMAT Review* and *The Official Guide to MBA Programs*)		
Apple II version	☐ $85.00	☐ $110.00
IBM PC version	☐ $85.00	☐ $110.00

* Airmail delivery to United States, Guam, Puerto Rico, U.S. Virgin Islands, and U.S. territories
**Airmail delivery to countries and areas other than those named above

(address label, right side:)

Graduate Management Admission Test
Educational Testing Service
CN 6108
Princeton, NJ 08541-6108

(Please print.)

Name
Number and
Street

City

Country

State or
Province

Zip or
Postal Code

DO NOT DETACH

692-82

GRADUATE MANAGEMENT ADMISSION TEST   666-17
EDUCATIONAL TESTING SERVICE   GMAT
CN 6101   BULLETIN
PRINCETON, NJ 08541-6101

TO

This is your mailing label. Type or print clearly.

Order Form for GMAT Bulletin of Information

Applicants to schools requiring the Graduate Management Admission Test (GMAT) may arrange with Educational Testing Service to take the test on one of four dates. If you wish to receive a **Bulletin of Information** describing arrangements for taking the test, the nature of the exam, and scoring procedures, complete the address label at the right and mail it to:

**Graduate Management Admission Test
Educational Testing Service
CN 6101
Princeton, NJ 08541-6101**

*Please note that, although you may receive this notice from several schools, you need only one **Bulletin** and registration form.*

A registration form and return envelope accompany each **Bulletin of Information.** Depending on where and when you want to take the test, your completed registration form and fee must be postmarked between five and eight weeks before the test date you select (requests for supplementary and Monday centers and special arrangements for the handicapped have even earlier deadlines). See the calendar on the reverse side for test dates and deadlines. It is to your advantage to send for your **Bulletin** and to complete your registration form as early as possible.

GRADUATE MANAGEMENT ADMISSION TEST   666-17
EDUCATIONAL TESTING SERVICE   GMAT
CN 6101   BULLETIN
PRINCETON, NJ 08541-6101

TO

This is your mailing label. Type or print clearly.

Order Form for GMAT Bulletin of Information

Applicants to schools requiring the Graduate Management Admission Test (GMAT) may arrange with Educational Testing Service to take the test on one of four dates. If you wish to receive a **Bulletin of Information** describing arrangements for taking the test, the nature of the exam, and scoring procedures, complete the address label at the right and mail it to:

**Graduate Management Admission Test
Educational Testing Service
CN 6101
Princeton, NJ 08541-6101**

*Please note that, although you may receive this notice from several schools, you need only one **Bulletin** and registration form.*

A registration form and return envelope accompany each **Bulletin of Information.** Depending on where and when you want to take the test, your completed registration form and fee must be postmarked between five and eight weeks before the test date you select (requests for supplementary and Monday centers and special arrangements for the handicapped have even earlier deadlines). See the calendar on the reverse side for test dates and deadlines. It is to your advantage to send for your **Bulletin** and to complete your registration form as early as possible.

GRADUATE MANAGEMENT ADMISSION TEST   666-17
EDUCATIONAL TESTING SERVICE   GMAT
CN 6101   BULLETIN
PRINCETON, NJ 08541-6101

TO

This is your mailing label. Type or print clearly.

Order Form for GMAT Bulletin of Information

Applicants to schools requiring the Graduate Management Admission Test (GMAT) may arrange with Educational Testing Service to take the test on one of four dates. If you wish to receive a **Bulletin of Information** describing arrangements for taking the test, the nature of the exam, and scoring procedures, complete the address label at the right and mail it to:

**Graduate Management Admission Test
Educational Testing Service
CN 6101
Princeton, NJ 08541-6101**

*Please note that, although you may receive this notice from several schools, you need only one **Bulletin** and registration form.*

A registration form and return envelope accompany each **Bulletin of Information.** Depending on where and when you want to take the test, your completed registration form and fee must be postmarked between five and eight weeks before the test date you select (requests for supplementary and Monday centers and special arrangements for the handicapped have even earlier deadlines). See the calendar on the reverse side for test dates and deadlines. It is to your advantage to send for your **Bulletin** and to complete your registration form as early as possible.

Registration Calendar

Test Dates	DOMESTIC REGISTRATION GMAT administrations in the U.S., Guam, Puerto Rico, U.S. Virgin Islands, and U.S. Territories			FOREIGN REGISTRATION GMAT administrations in all other countries (including Canada)	
	REGULAR REGISTRATION	LATE REGISTRATION & CENTER CHANGE	SPECIAL REQUESTS	FINAL REGISTRATION & CENTER CHANGE	SPECIAL REQUESTS
	Registration forms post-marked after this date must be accompanied by a $10 late registration fee.	Add $10 late registration fee. Registration forms post-marked after this period will be returned.	Last postmark date for supplementary centers, Monday administrations,* and arrangements for the handicapped.	Registration forms post-marked after this date or received too late for processing will be returned.	Last postmark date for requests for supplementary centers,† Monday administrations,* and arrangements for the handicapped.
	Postmark Dates			Airmail Postmark Dates	
Oct. 18, 1986*†	Sept. 15	Sept. 16-22	Aug. 27	Aug. 27	Aug. 11
Jan. 24, 1987*	Dec. 22	Dec. 23-31	Dec. 3	Dec. 3	Nov. 17
March 21, 1987*	Feb. 17	Feb. 18-24	Jan. 28	Jan. 28	Jan. 12
June 20, 1987*	May 18	May 19-26	April 29	April 29	April 13

*Monday administration dates will be October 20, 1986, January 26, 1987, March 23, 1987, and June 22, 1987.
†No supplementary centers will be established for foreign registration for the October 1986 test date.

Registration Calendar

Test Dates	DOMESTIC REGISTRATION GMAT administrations in the U.S., Guam, Puerto Rico, U.S. Virgin Islands, and U.S. Territories			FOREIGN REGISTRATION GMAT administrations in all other countries (including Canada)	
	REGULAR REGISTRATION	LATE REGISTRATION & CENTER CHANGE	SPECIAL REQUESTS	FINAL REGISTRATION & CENTER CHANGE	SPECIAL REQUESTS
	Registration forms post-marked after this date must be accompanied by a $10 late registration fee.	Add $10 late registration fee. Registration forms post-marked after this period will be returned.	Last postmark date for supplementary centers, Monday administrations,* and arrangements for the handicapped.	Registration forms post-marked after this date or received too late for processing will be returned.	Last postmark date for requests for supplementary centers,† Monday administrations,* and arrangements for the handicapped.
	Postmark Dates			Airmail Postmark Dates	
Oct. 18, 1986*†	Sept. 15	Sept. 16-22	Aug. 27	Aug. 27	Aug. 11
Jan. 24, 1987*	Dec. 22	Dec. 23-31	Dec. 3	Dec. 3	Nov. 17
March 21, 1987*	Feb. 17	Feb. 18-24	Jan. 28	Jan. 28	Jan. 12
June 20, 1987*	May 18	May 19-26	April 29	April 29	April 13

*Monday administration dates will be October 20, 1986, January 26, 1987, March 23, 1987, and June 22, 1987.
†No supplementary centers will be established for foreign registration for the October 1986 test date.

Registration Calendar

Test Dates	DOMESTIC REGISTRATION GMAT administrations in the U.S., Guam, Puerto Rico, U.S. Virgin Islands, and U.S. Territories			FOREIGN REGISTRATION GMAT administrations in all other countries (including Canada)	
	REGULAR REGISTRATION	LATE REGISTRATION & CENTER CHANGE	SPECIAL REQUESTS	FINAL REGISTRATION & CENTER CHANGE	SPECIAL REQUESTS
	Registration forms post-marked after this date must be accompanied by a $10 late registration fee.	Add $10 late registration fee. Registration forms post-marked after this period will be returned.	Last postmark date for supplementary centers, Monday administrations,* and arrangements for the handicapped.	Registration forms post-marked after this date or received too late for processing will be returned.	Last postmark date for requests for supplementary centers,† Monday administrations,* and arrangements for the handicapped.
	Postmark Dates			Airmail Postmark Dates	
Oct. 18, 1986*†	Sept. 15	Sept. 16-22	Aug. 27	Aug. 27	Aug. 11
Jan. 24, 1987*	Dec. 22	Dec. 23-31	Dec. 3	Dec. 3	Nov. 17
March 21, 1987*	Feb. 17	Feb. 18-24	Jan. 28	Jan. 28	Jan. 12
June 20, 1987*	May 18	May 19-26	April 29	April 29	April 13

*Monday administration dates will be October 20, 1986, January 26, 1987, March 23, 1987, and June 22, 1987.
†No supplementary centers will be established for foreign registration for the October 1986 test date.